A Teacher's Tale

A Memoir

JOE GILLILAND

TRUE DIRECTIONS
AN AFFILIATE OF TARCHER BOOKS

iUniverse®

A TEACHER'S TALE
A MEMOIR

iUniverse books may be ordered through booksellers or by contacting:

iUniverse
1663 Liberty Drive
Bloomington, IN 47403
www.iuniverse.com
1-800-Authors (1-800-288-4677)

Because of the dynamic nature of the Internet, any web addresses or links contained in this book may have changed since publication and may no longer be valid. The views expressed in this work are solely those of the author and do not necessarily reflect the views of the publisher, and the publisher hereby disclaims any responsibility for them.

Any people depicted in stock imagery provided by Thinkstock are models, and such images are being used for illustrative purposes only.
Certain stock imagery © Thinkstock.

ISBN: 978-1-4917-4583-0 (sc)
ISBN: 978-1-4917-4585-4 (hc)
ISBN: 978-1-4917-4584-7 (e)

Library of Congress Control Number: 2014915682

Print information available on the last page.

iUniverse rev. date: 03/15/2017

Dedicated to the memory of

Professor J. Gilbert McAllister,
University of Texas, Austin

Soji Inoue sensei,
Wakayama University, Japan

Dean Walter Rundell,
Lee College, Texas

Contents

Preface

I couldn't wait to get to college, and I couldn't stand to leave at graduation, so I became a professor.
　　　　　　　　　　　　　　　　　　　—James Axtell, PhD.

When I enrolled as a freshman at The University of Texas in the autumn of 1943 I had no intention of becoming a teacher, certainly not an English teacher and even more certainly not a college teacher. *A Teacher's Tale* covers events from my earliest days as a student through the apprenticeship, first as an instructor in conversational English in Japan and then as a teaching assistant at UT in Austin, and the apprenticeship that led me to a life of teaching, a life of great satisfaction and greater joy. I have borrowed the opening sentence of Professor James Axtell's Preface to his memoir *The Pleasures of Academe* (1998) for the epigraph to my Preface because it expresses my own feelings and desires, but there the similarities between his excellent memoir of teaching and mine end, for Professor Axtell, apparently knew what he would teach; I did not.

I have dedicated my memoir to three men who inspired me and showed me the way as a student and a teacher: Professor J. Gilbert McAllister, Inoue Soji sensei, and Dean Walter Rundell. Dr. McAllister, in his freshman Introduction to Physical Anthropology introduced us to the concept of "education by irritation," instantly implanting in me the idea of becoming a teacher. Three years later after returning to Austin and enrolling in a second class with "Dr. Mac" I left more determined than ever that I would become a professor.

Two years after graduating from UT in Austin, still determined on becoming a teacher, yet still undecided as to what academic field I would choose, I met Inoue sensei, chairman of English at Wakayama University. I had accepted a position as short-term teaching missionary with Board of Foreign Missions of the Methodist Church, but I was still undecided what I would teach one day as a college professor. When Inoue sensei asked if I would, in addition to my classes in conversational English, assist him in his translation of the plays of Eugene O'Neill, I agreed. In doing so I discovered my teaching field; three years later I returned to Austin and began working on a master's degree in English that would prepare me for a life in teaching.

Two years later Dean Walter Rundell of Lee College in Baytown, Texas, hired me to teach English and I began life as a college instructor of English and humanities. Today, at this writing I consider all three men to be the most important persons in my life as a student and a teacher. *A Teacher's Tale* is only the first part of the journey. The second part of the journey, which I call *The Pleasures and Perils of Academe*—still indebted to Dr. Axtell—takes the tale from my apprenticeship through almost sixty years as a community college instructor.

Neither this volume nor the one that follows would have been possible but for the inspiration and the guidance of the men I have mentioned as well as a host of students, colleagues, family, and friends. But finally, were it not for a close friend and colleague, one Howard Dewitt, PhD, I would not have come this far; his prodding and pressure kept me aware of a story I wanted to tell and made me finish my early, overly long and seriously prolix first draft. It was then the people at **iUniverse,** in particular, my editorial consultant, Krista Hall, took over and encouraged me to get through the tortuous editing stages. To all I owe a huge debt of gratitude.

Chapter 1

Beginnings

September 1932, Beaumont, Texas

My earliest memory of school was taking an entrance exam for first grade at Averill Elementary School. Because my sixth birthday was more than a month past the deadline for early enrollment, school authorities in Beaumont agreed to admit me only if I passed a "readiness exam." It was not that my mother or anyone in the family believed me to be precocious or that I had demonstrated an unusual urge to learn. It was because my mother, recently widowed, had been forced to find a job and needed a babysitter; therefore, with public schools in Beaumont being free, she considered enrolling me a clear possibility.

My father died in December of 1931, in the depth of the Great Depression, leaving Mama, a young widow with four children, all under the age of ten— the youngest, Donnie, only eighteen months. I was a middle child barely five when he passed away. So in the fall of 1932, long before there was any kind of public preschool or day care for working mothers with small children, it was imperative that I begin school. To ensure I was ready for the readiness exam, my sisters Dorothy and Jane, using a *Dick and Jane* primer, taught me to read, made sure I could count to twenty, that I could name all my colors, and could print my name. For me it was a lark. I loved the attention. Dorothy and Jane had been reading to me as long as they themselves could read. Listening attentively to every word, I had memorized stories and poems from *Grimm's Fairy Tales* and *A Child's Garden of Verses*. Memorizing the comings and goings of Dick, Jane, and Spot was a simple if boring task, far easier than Stevenson's verses, and even less interesting.

When I walked into the testing room that fall, I could "read," could print my name, and count to twenty. Jane and Dorothy had coached me well. But the so-called entrance exam required none of the skills I had studied so assiduously. It consisted of nothing more than drawing circles or squares around appropriate figures, of answering a series of routine questions, or coloring, more or less, within the lines of a figure. In other words, I was ready to listen and follow simple directions. It was a great disappointment, not being allowed to demonstrate my vast skills. The questions were laughingly easy and

1

certainly no challenge, but the final and most interesting question, I still recall in detail. Handing us each a paper with various object pictured, the lady told us to draw a circle around a picture of everything that could fly. I saw pictures of a biplane, a car, a dog, a Zeppelin, an eagle, a horse, a kite, a bee, a butterfly, a bicycle, and several other objects. How easy, I thought. She hovered over us, checking on how long it took us to complete the task, I suppose. I quickly circled all the obvious choices, and then after studying the sheet carefully, I circled a horse. The horse had given me something of a problem at first, but I remember making the circle just as the testing lady passed my chair. She stopped, bent down, and asked softly why I had circled the horse.

Joe with Dorothy and Jane, ca 1930

With just a touch of sarcasm I'd heard so often at home when anyone would ask a question having an obvious answer, I replied, "Haven't you ever heard of a *horsefly*?"

Truth was, I had only *heard* of horseflies, but I couldn't recall ever having seen one. In fact, I'd often wondered what one actually looked like.

She laughed softly and said she had certainly *heard* of horseflies, but horsefly was "really not the same as a 'flying horse' because horses don't fly."

Those were her exact words. I came back immediately with a question in the same sarcastic tone, "Haven't you seen the flying red horse at the filling station across the street?"

It was true. A Mobil Oil station was just across the street, and rising above its canopy was Mobil's logo, the ubiquitous bright red Pegasus. I had seen those Mobil Oil signs for as long as I could remember and had always wondered what kind of horse it could be, but no one had ever explained it to me. She smiled and shook her head, called the other tester to her side, and repeated my remarks. They chuckled and admitted I was probably right. Whatever. I passed the "entrance exam" with "flying colors," for they placed me in 1-A, the advanced track of Averill School's first grade, and while I remained in the A-track class, all my years at Averill, I was generally on the right side of the bell curve, except in reading classes. If my performance on that test did not portend a highly successful academic career at Averill or any school I attended in Beaumont, it placed me with the more elite members of the academic community as well as Beaumont's socially elite, and that, for Mama, was the most important thing of all.

In addition to being the youngest child in class, I was also the smallest, as small as even the smallest girl. To make up for physical size, I did what many children who regard themselves as outsiders do: I drew attention to myself in any way I could. And very early, I became the most disruptive member of Miss Connors's 1-A class, not by misbehaving but by constantly jabbering. When the word reached Mama that I was disrupting the class with my constant talking, she shrugged, smiled, and claimed I had always been the most talkative and disruptive of all her children. I had learned to speak earlier than any of my sisters or cousins. Once I learned to talk, I never stopped, she would add. But it was not just my constant jangling that disturbed my teachers; it was my interrupting the class and "correcting" grammatical errors of my classmates.

Though Mama had never graduated from high school, nor had Daddy ever attended university (only a small business college in San Antonio), they both insisted we speak only the best grammar because being "well-spoken" was a mark of good breeding. After graduating from high school, Daddy had attended business college in San Antonio, and as many young men around the turn of the century, he had learned to type, take shorthand, write proper business letters, and do bookkeeping. He had also been raised in a milieu of schooling where "correct English" was not only a given, but it was also a road to success. In class, I followed the pattern I learned at the table and corrected my classmates when they misspoke, just as I or anyone would at home. But I also would make unseemly remarks, often ridiculing the one who made the error, not unlike the way we did at home.

At first, my interruptions were considered "smart." On the first day of class, not realizing that she was releasing upon the 1-A class an uncontrollably loquacious force, Miss Connors complimented me on my knowledge of good English. But constant interruptions soon resulted in her sending me to the cloakroom for short periods. I don't believe I ever felt that the punishment was unjust or that I felt shame in doing what I firmly believed was the only proper thing to do.

In spite of being the smallest and the youngest in my class, I felt that school was fundamentally egalitarian. Punishment for disrupting class was mild and never done with rancor, and to me, it was proof of my exceptionalism, for each time I would interrupt to correct another's error, heads would turn, and some would smile, while others scowled, but they were all focused on me.

From the third grade through fifth, we had different teachers for arithmetic, art, geography, nature, reading, and music. When the bell sounded at the end of each period, our teacher would lead us out into the hall where we lined up and were admonished not to speak or play around. The teacher, or a class monitor, would lead us to the next classroom. When we arrived at our destination, we went directly to our desks and waited for the teacher. Total silence never prevailed, nor did anyone attempt to achieve it. "Good citizenship," however, did prevail, more or less. I noticed quite early that the larger boys did not cause trouble with other large boys, nor smaller boys with other small boys. It was always a larger boy beating up on the smallest. Since I was the smallest, I was frequently the target of one or two out to prove their manhood. The tallest and strongest boys never seemed to need to prove themselves. It was always those the next size down or one size up who were so insecure as to need a constant proof of manhood. Harvey G. was my nemesis. The system encouraged bullyboys. When we lined up to move, the tallest boys and girls were at the head of the line, so when entering the next class, the tallest would move smoothly to the back rows, while the smallest entering last took the front rows. The end of the line was the least well monitored, and thus, the smaller were the most conveniently placed for the bullyboys to pester.

My favorite classes, those that most shaped my mind and values, were geography and library or reading class. Mrs. Hilliard, a dour, always serious woman, created for us a world of wonder, whether we were studying Mesopotamia or the geography of Texas. Mrs. Neal's class, library, with its walls of books and large tables, held for me a fascination as great as Mrs. Hilliard's. Like the geography room with its many maps, the library, with all its books, was magic. The two walls of books from the floor to a height I could not reach without the special stepladder held me in thrall, for at home we had few books— only a small, glass front case with a *Compton's Pictured Encyclopedia* and a *Lincoln Library*, a single volume quick-search universal encyclopedia. Mrs. Neal allowed us to read above our "level" and taught us how to talk about the books we were reading. Most of her classes began with our taking turns reading aloud from a text we were using at the time, followed by short questions about what we had just read. Mrs. Neal called these "discussion periods." She encouraged us to raise hands and offer answers or raise questions about words or ideas. We also made oral book reports on the books we checked out of the library. I was thrilled when she asked us to read from the book of our choice, especially if I was reporting on a book above grade level. She never failed to praise our choice, and when she corrected us, she always began with mild praise of what had gone before. Mrs. Neal never embarrassed us but always made a suggestion "how to improve" our remarks or delivery.

Today I lay my love of reading almost entirely at the door to her class. Much of the appeal came directly from Mrs. Neal herself, who we all thought was the prettiest and most elegant teacher in school. I can't recall either Mrs. Hilliard or Mrs. Neal ever scolding me or asking me to be silent. It may have been I made fewer outbursts and spoke out of turn less in their classes because those were the classes that most held my attention and where comments were encouraged. Even my occasionally obstreperous behavior could not shake their equanimity.

Mrs. Hilliard's class was nothing like the relaxed and easy atmosphere of Mrs. Neal's across the hall. In geography, you always sat up straight at your desk, always looked to the front of the room, and spoke only when she called your name. My sisters, Dorothy and Jane, had warned me to behave in her class, and I tried. We were all frightened of Mrs. Hilliard, though I never believed that she was as mean as everyone said. As in Mrs. Neal's class, she had us read aloud from the texts and would ask us to explain what we had just read and to tell the class what parts we thought the most interesting and why we thought so. Sometimes she would stop and ask us the meaning of a word or a phrase, tell us to write the word down in our notebooks.

I loved it when she called on me to read. I knew all the geographical terms, like "hemisphere", "latitude", and "longitude"— terms I picked up from Jane and Dorothy. I shone at first because having elder sisters helped, though terms like "Tropic of Cancer" and "Tropic of Capricorn" puzzled me. Once, I asked her why it was called "Tropic of *Cancer.*" She explained patiently that they were only marks upon the map and the globe and that the words came from ancient myths and stories and from astrology. She never treated any question as an intrusion. Even as early as the third grade, Mrs. Hilliard required short reports and encouraged us to raise our hands and speak up in the "discussion periods." Having traveled to many of the places described in the text, she could tell fascinating stories of her personal experiences along the Tigris and Euphrates, in the Fertile Crescent where the Hanging Gardens were.

Boys rarely made Mrs. Hilliard smile, and we accepted that, but I recall a time when I made her smile. Mary Keen, one of the two, or three, "top girls" in the class, had just made an oral report on something she had read, and Mrs. Hilliard remarked, "I want to compliment you, Mary, on a fine report."

Mary had taken her seat with the proper nod of humility and thanks while the rest of the class looked on in awe and envy. I liked Mary, considered her beautiful, but she was the tallest girl in class and never noticed me. Ordinarily, I would silently scorn such praise from teachers, perhaps because I was envious or even skeptical that the praise was overstated, but I knew such could not be the case with Mrs. Hilliard, and besides, I admired Mary too much to doubt the praise was deserved.

When Mrs. Hilliard asked if we had any questions about the report, I raised my hand. She turned and said, "What is it, Joe?"

"Mrs. Hilliard," I began with trepidation, "when are you going to compliment Mary for her report?"

"What do you mean, Joe?" she asked sternly. I was sure I had stepped in it then.

"When are you going to compliment Mary?" I repeated then added, "You said you *wanted to* compliment her, but you never did. When are you going to do it?" I truly wanted to hear what her compliment sounded like.

She paused and looked around the class, her glance silencing their murmurs, and then with uncommon gentleness, she said, "That's just a way of speaking, Joe. Saying I *want to* is another way of complimenting her." Then she turned away smiling. Since she rarely smiled, I felt I had truly accomplished something good.

In the fifth grade, my education took its first important turn, one that would inspire and shape all my interests until the end of my freshman year at the University of Texas. For Christmas, I got the Gilbert Chemistry Set for Beginners, the first of three such sets over the next three years, each one larger and more sophisticated than the one before. Its test tubes, spirit lamp, and vials of chemicals were unlike anything I had ever seen before, and from the moment I opened the box, I was captivated. Nothing else I received that Christmas held any interest for me. Before the end of the holidays, I had performed all the "experiments" in the instruction book: a mini-chemistry text for beginners. I read the little book from cover to cover several times, struggling with the pronunciation of an entirely new vocabulary of reagents, chemical elements, and basic principles of chemistry.

What made it so important to me, at the time, was that neither Jane nor Dorothy or my mother could pronounce the new words any better than I.

What's more, none of my cousins had ever gotten such a present. All the time, I wondered why I had never heard of such marvels before. It was a brave new world of ideas and facts that I never knew existed, and as far as I was concerned, I was the only one in my family who knew or understood these new ideas. I would look around the room from where I was sitting and focus on one item after another and tell myself each was made of elements. Nothing seemed ever the same again; now everything was a mixture of elements and compounds. As far as I knew, no one in my class at school had heard of any of this either.

Henceforth, the usual toys would hold little interest for me. When I returned to school after the holidays, I told no one about my chemistry set, except our nature teacher, Miss Touchstone. Although she had never talked about elements or compounds as the "building blocks of nature," in the words of my mini-text that came with the set, I assumed that nature and science were the same. When I told her about the book of experiments with its story of elements and compounds, she only smiled and said "How nice," then turned away uninterested, even when I told her I was *studying* chemistry and learning the names of elements: chlorine, oxygen, hydrogen, sodium, potassium, carbon, and nitrogen. Because she had rebuffed my attempts to talk about my discoveries and because she never mentioned chemistry in her nature class, not even the word, I assumed that anything I wanted to know would have to come from my own "research," which I began to call all my reading in that area. Dorothy had once said that Ms. Touchstone was more interested in how pretty she was than in nature or her pupils. *Maybe she was right, but she did have awfully pretty red hair,* I thought.

My first source of discovery was the new *World Book* encyclopedia Mama bought the year before. I had leafed past "The Story of Chemistry" many times and had wondered what it was all about; now, I read and reread it, struggling with the small print and opaque style that was far more difficult than the instruction booklet that came with the chemistry set. I began making trips with Dorothy to the public library every Saturday. But the public library's section for grade school children was not much better for science and chemistry than the library at Averill School. The librarian, seeing me browsing the science section in the intermediate stacks, shooed me back upstairs where she located several introductory books with labels like *Adventures in Chemistry for Boys* and *A Boy's First Book of Chemistry,* (presumably chemistry was not a proper subject for girls) I checked out these books repeatedly, copying out experiments I could perform at my "lab" in the corner of the big back room, but mostly, I checked them out to learn all I could about chemistry. I neglected my classes that spring because of my "research" into the new world of chemistry.

In just over a year, with the librarian's permission, I was reading books from the main section. When she stopped me once and suggested I read books in my section, I explained, as politely as I knew how, avoiding the tone of sarcasm I had developed when challenged by authority figures, that I was interested in chemistry and couldn't find the books I needed in the children's section upstairs. Opening a chemistry text off the shelf, I read it aloud to prove I was serious and knew what I was talking about. She was so impressed that she let me stay on the main floor, but even then, she allowed me to check out only one book at a time. She was right, of course: the text I carried home that day was beyond my abilities. I could read the words, say them aloud, but what they meant was beyond me. The mystery only added to the excitement I felt every time I opened the book. At the time, I was the only one in my class who expressed an interest in chemistry or science. From that, I got a tremendous satisfaction in thinking I was all alone in my new endeavors.

A year later, while browsing through the Christmas toy display at the White House, Beaumont's largest department store, lingering over the Chemcraft and Gilbert chemistry sets, hoping Mama would get me one of the larger, better-equipped versions, a voice behind me asked, "Do you like chemistry too, Joe?"

It was Mary Alice Clark, the tall, dark-haired girl who sat across the aisle from me in class. I said that I did and asked her if she was interested too. I could hardly believe there was another person, a girl, who was as interested in chemistry as I was. She asked if I was getting a chemistry set for Christmas, and I told her I was hoping to get the large Chemcraft set I was looking at. She turned and told her father that the one I had chosen was the one she was hoping to get too. Then she introduced me to her father as the boy who sat across from her in class. I was too young at the time to have a real girlfriend but decided then if I were to have one, Mary Alice would be the one to have, even though she was a full head taller than I. Later that year, we would often exchange thoughts about our experiments. That she was also a *zinger* in the looks department made those conversations about science and chemistry even more important, at least for me.

As it turned out, I didn't get that particular Chemcraft that Christmas. Instead, I got an even larger Gilbert set, the one that came in a wooden cabinet with doors that folded out with test tube racks, making it a perfect little lab that I could set on the card table in a corner of the big back room. And marvel of marvels, along with it, there was another present, a microscope set. It was a complete surprise. The large Gilbert set had a small balance, a beaker, and

Erlenmeyer and Florence flasks, all complete with fitted rubber stoppers. They were not large, almost miniatures, but it was equipment I had only seen in books but never touched. My cup indeed was filled to overflowing that Christmas. How Mama had been able to afford such a grand outfit plus the microscope—a gift I had not dared to hope for—puzzled me.

When I told her how surprised I was to get the larger set, the one in the wooden cabinet with more glassware than I had ever seen before, she admitted that she had planned to get the one I had asked for then explained that when she finally got to the store after work on Christmas Eve, all toys had gone on sale. A slow item that year, the larger Gilbert set was on sale for half price, and on top of that, the clerk had thrown in the microscope set for just a dollar more. *Thank God for depressions,* I thought. The most important boon was a large and more detailed book about chemistry.

Next to chemistry, the most important aspect of my life in grade school was music, which, unlike science, was a subject highly integrated into the world of Averill Elementary School. Mrs. Shaddocks conducted a lively and interesting class that introduced us to scales and clefs and to the classics with accompanying stories about the composers, whose portraits adorned the walls of her class.

Averill School had a symphony orchestra, with strings, horns, woodwinds, tympani and, of course, a grand piano. Most of my friends played an instrument. The boys played horns, woodwinds, and a few strings, while the girls played piano and strings, though one girl played a soprano saxophone. Almost everyone in the fourth grade, except me, played an instrument of some kind, so in the second week of fourth grade, I announced to Mama that I wanted to take violin lessons and play in the Averill School orchestra. Jane and Dorothy had taken piano lessons when we lived in Dallas, and we had an upright piano in the living room, but I explained to Mama that only the girls played piano. I knew the horns and woodwinds were much too expensive so I settled on a violin because I had heard Aunt Ethel still had her old violin.

Averill School Orchestra; Joe, sixth from center

At first, Mama looked doubtful and asked me who would give violin lessons. I had done my homework and had learned that Mrs. Anita van Meter taught a beginners class and charged only a dollar a lesson and, moreover, lived only two blocks from our house. Without hesitating a second, she agreed, and that afternoon she came home from work with a half-sized violin, Aunt Ethel's violin being a full-sized instrument and much too large for me. After only two months of lessons from Mrs. Van Meter, I joined the orchestra and became "umpteenth" chair second violin. It was a joyous moment, just sitting there with my music resting on my own music stand.

When Mama allowed me the use of the living room to practice my violin, or rather insisted, I used the room to avoid disturbing others. I felt I had grown a whole step in importance, if not in size, for the living room was always kept neat and clean in case company came. There was the upright piano which allowed me an A key to tune my violin. Without question, the once off-limits living room became my own sanctuary, or what I thought of as my own. I had acquired rights to Jane and Dorothy's piano and began to teach myself to pick out melodies by ear and by reading notes, but even more important, I claimed rights to the tall Truetone radio simply because of my love of music. In the past, when I misbehaved or pestered Donnie, Mama sent me to sit alone in the living room, away from the troubles, and at those times, usually on Saturday or Sunday, when she was home from work, I was able to tune the radio into the Metropolitan Opera or the NBC Symphony. By the time I was in junior high school, I knew the stories of nearly all the major operas by Puccini, Verdi, Donizetti, and Mozart. I could not only recognize the major arias, but I also knew what the words meant. I also knew the names of major composers and recognized the main themes of the symphonies and concerti.

For me, the major musical event those years in Beaumont was a production of Gounod's *Faust* put on by the San Carlo Opera Company. For two weeks before the performance, in Mrs. Shaddocks' class, we studied the story of Faust and his pact with Mephistopheles and listened to recordings of major arias and choral numbers. Mrs. Shaddocks played the melody of the "Soldier's Chorus" on the piano, and we sang the words, in English, she had mimeographed for us. When Mama bought the half-priced student tickets for Dorothy, Jane, and me, I was overjoyed. Our student tickets were for seats so far back in the huge city auditorium that I could hardly see the stage, but when the curtain rose, Dorothy boldly moved us down to unsold vacant seats on the first and second row left. It was magnificent. From the first notes of the overture to the incredible final trio, I was frozen to my seat. Only a few yards from the stage, I could see every gesture, could feel the notes right down to my toes.

Mrs. Shaddocks had prepared us so well that not an aria was lost on me. The strains of the "Soldier's Chorus" soared through my brain all the way home. I was so moved by the spectacle and the singing, especially the trio in the last act when Marguerite is lifted to heaven by a host of angels, that I came close to abandoning chemistry forever. In Mrs. Shaddocks' class on Monday, she asked who had seen the opera and what did we think of it, what parts we liked best, and I told about the last act and the great trio.

I was amazed that so few in my class had seen it, but because it was about a man who sells his soul to the Devil, several of the parents had forbidden their children to go. I said it was about angels too and explained that Mephistopheles wasn't really a devil but just the Devil's helper.

From fifth grade through seventh, my world was divided into two areas: science and music. My schoolwork, especially arithmetic, was not outstanding. Except for reading and social studies, I was considered a barely average pupil. I had a secret pleasure that offset my poor grades in arithmetic: I was the only one who knew anything about chemistry. I didn't know that for sure, but no one I knew ever talked about experiments or the nature of chemical reactions. I also loved the stories of discovery and movies like *The Story of Louis Pasteur*. The heroic figures in books by Paul de Kruif like *Microbe Hunters*, *Men against Hunger*, and *Men Against Death* were as exciting, to me, as the stories of Magellan and Sir Francis Drake. The same librarian who had steered me away from the adult section had given me the books by De Kruif, though they too were classified as adult reading. In books and movies, scientists were always outsiders, men—rarely women—dedicated to a higher calling, to the service to mankind, yet in the end, they always got the top girl. In *Magnificent Obsession*, Robert Taylor won the love and devotion of Irene Dunne, and in *Green Light*, Errol Flynn won Loretta Young. *The Citadel* with Robert Donat and Rosalind Russell a few years later convinced me that there was only one true path for me to follow. Romantic themes carried me ever deeper into science and a realm of understanding that far exceeded what I had encountered in the classroom. What did it matter that my grades in arithmetic were weak? What I was learning through reading on my own was far more interesting, far more important.

From about the fifth grade on, my "royal road" to everything came through reading. Movies, rather than being a substitute for reading, were a stimulant and led me to read far above my "level." After seeing movies like *The Citadel* and *Lost Horizon* I talked the librarian into letting me check out the books they were based on. Reading a sample page for her and not mispronouncing any of the words, as I had done earlier with a chemistry text, got me past my level. Later, because she remembered my reading to her, she allowed me to check out any book I wished. It was a matter of great pride that I could browse the adult sections on the main floor to the Terrell Library. Like most children, I would read a book two or three times if I liked it; what I didn't get in the first reading, I knew I would get in subsequent attempts. Classics always demanded rereading. It was Dorothy, my "big sister," who actually introduced me to the library— taking me with her the summers between fourth and fifth grade and later fifth and sixth. We were lucky that the streetcar had its final stop just around the corner from our house and connected us directly without transfer to the library stop in town, all for a nickel. In those days, I hadn't even a vague idea of what a classic was. Perhaps it was Dorothy's fault that I never read any of the famous Hardy Boys or Tom Swift books. The friendly and well-meaning librarian had urged both series on me before, but I recall Dorothy picking out a book and handing me it. "Here's something good you can read, and you'll like it." She believed I could "handle" anything. It was later, after discovering chemistry, that the library became a focus of my life, and Mrs. Neal's class became a lesser source than the Terrell Library downtown across from the city auditorium. I was a good reader, though not a fast reader; that is, I retained a lot of what I read. I read slowly in order to savor passages of prose, and I even moved my lips while I was reading, if I had become totally immersed in the book and if the prose was sufficiently purple. We were scolded and told that moving lips was taboo, second only to reading aloud, which I often did for the sheer pleasure of hearing the wonderful sounds of the words. Some books I thought sounded better than others, and I couldn't resist the temptation to hear my voice sound the words; I would even adopt accents or tones I thought best fit the subjects.

My political education grew out of two sources: Ms. Watson's history class in junior high and seeing practical applications of New Deal economics at home. Mama had always regarded the old garage beside the house an eyesore, which it was. There was nothing quite like it in the entire neighborhood. Two years after we moved in, she had it torn down, less for aesthetic reasons than for sound economics. With the removal of the old outhouses from the back of the lot—servants quarters, wash house, stable, and carriage house, all falling to pieces—Mama had built in their place a handsome garage apartment with spaces for two cars and a servant's quarters on the ground floor. I could not understand where she found the money for such a venture, and it worried me that she was going to spend us into the same "poor house" my aunts and uncles and mother talked about so often. The new garage apartment, the wide concrete driveway, as handsome as the Millers' drive next door, and the elegant sliding doors on the double garage greatly enhanced the appearance of our house, I thought. But Mama insisted she had not made the change for more income, not for appearances.

Roosevelt made it all possible, she said. A low-interest FHA loan provided the capital. The garage apartment and the small servant's quarters were an extra source of income that almost doubled Mama's salary at Pure Oil Company. Two years later, she added a second story to the house and began renting rooms, again almost doubling her income as switchboard operator. It was possible, she explained, because of Franklin Roosevelt, whom she regarded all her life was a man sent by God to help widows like her. Unlike my Uncle Walter, who, in his more generous moods, always referred to FDR as "that damn man in the White House," my mother swore that Roosevelt was a godsend for most Americans. While the new source of income did not make us wealthy or even "well-off," it provided extras we otherwise might not have had. Most important, for Jane and Dorothy, adding the second story gave them their own room and some privacy. The large back room now became "the back living room" or the "big back room."

Upstairs now were five good-sized bedrooms and three bath. Mama, it turned out, was a good businesswoman and ran a very tight rooming house, several times asking a roomer to vacate the premises when she thought he was behaving badly. One night, I heard her prevent a tenant from inviting a friend to his room. From my bed on the sleeping porch, I could hear an altercation in the living room where Mama blocked a young woman, who had apparently had too much to drink, from following the "indiscreet" tenant to his room. By the way, "indiscreet" or "indiscretion" was my mother's favorite term, indicating unspeakable behavior, so often used in fact that, for years, it carried an almost erotic connotation. The next morning at breakfast, Mama told how the man had given Mama no argument and had let his girlfriend go without any trouble.

"The problem was *her*," Mama said. "She was just white trash."

I was amazed at how well she handled people. Once, she rented the large front upstairs room to a pair of young men, recent grads of The University of Texas, who worked for the Magnolia Petroleum Company. She boasted to everyone about how nice it was to have college men in the house, one a petroleum engineer, the other a geologist specializing in *paleontology*, both "clean-cut young men," she said. One Saturday, the paleontologist asked her if his friend, also a paleontologist, could come upstairs and spend the afternoon, studying fossil specimens under his microscope. Mama insisted it was perfectly all right because his friend, a nice-looking young woman, was also a paleontologist and a graduate of the University of Texas. Noticing, I suppose, my interest in their work, the young woman invited me into the room and let me view some of the samples through a low-powered binocular microscope. I had never seen such an instrument. I wrote down the scientific names of all the specimens, and when I went back downstairs, I asked Mama why she had allowed this young woman upstairs but had refused the other. She answered sharply that the other woman was "just trash," but this young woman was a college graduate. "Don't you see, they're scientists. You might even learn something from them," she said.

I did, indeed, many things, for when Mama left for town later, I went back up hoping to see more specimens, but the door was closed and sounds from the room suggested that paleontology was a far more rigorous science than I had supposed. However, I didn't pass on my discovery, and paleontology would for many years have for me titillating connotations.

When we left Dallas and moved to Beaumont, Mama had not only chosen well the house, but she also chose well the neighborhood and the neighbors. Only Mrs. Boles, two houses down, proved to be an early problem for us children. She never spoke to any of us unless we walked across her well-cut lawn, and then she would scold vociferously. Once, she screamed at me for taking a shortcut through her lovely backyard. The yard wasn't fenced; she had no pets to disturb or taunt. I could never understand why it was so serious an offense. Mr. Boles was another matter. He was the kindest and gentlest person in the neighborhood who made up for his lack of children by supplying all the neighborhood boys with kites and toy guns that he had made in his elaborate wood shop off the garage. The sturdy six-cornered, brown, paper kite he made for me, I will never forget. I'd never seen such a large, heavy kite before, had never had one of those *hexagonal* (a word he taught me on the spot) kites. It was almost my height and had a strong, well-made harness to keep it balanced perfectly against the wind. But from the first, I doubted it would fly. We had no wide-open spaces on our block from which to launch or even fly a kite that large, what with the telephone lines crisscrossing overhead and only the street to run it to get it aloft. On good windy days, we had learned to launch our flimsy store-bought kites from the flat roof of the Latsons' garage. Clifford, Bobby, and Dimples Latson lived next door to Mr. and Mrs. Boles.

Mr. Boles assured me I would not need a long runway to get his kite aloft; all it would take was a good windy day, he said, and it would be aloft in seconds--and I with it, if I weren't careful. My pride knew no bounds when the kite lifted and immediately soared over the telephone lines, high above the neighboring houses. Mr. Boles watched the kite pull out almost to the end of the ball of heavy cord I was struggling to hold. He left, returned immediately to his wood shop, and, in no time, fashioned a boxed reel that I could hook on to my belt, like the large reels deep-sea fishermen use. It was ingenious. I could let it out or reel it in or stop it with a little toggle he made. I became the center of attention for all the boys and girls in the neighborhood who came from blocks away, following the string on my high-flying kite, to watch me sending up and reeling in or letting out my priceless kite.

Then on a Saturday, I got up early just as a steady breeze began to blow, ran to the Latson garage and flew the kite, this time using three balls of kite string. It went out so far that we couldn't see it; I knew it was there only by the inexorable tug of the string. Only Clifford Latson and Jane had permission to strap the reel to their waists and fly the marvelous kite and then only when I needed a bathroom break. Boys came from blocks around to see whose kite was out there so far and begged for the privilege of sharing my glorious adventure. It was indeed glorious. Mr. Boles, from time to time, would check on me, sharing my joy. I admired the man greatly, for I knew he was as happy about that kite as we all were. Kites have had deep archetypal and Jungian significance for me ever since. Tethered to the flyer by a long umbilicus, they reached to the sky gods and carried with them our loftiest aspirations, though always with that inevitable risk of final and tragic separation.

In the end, I lost it. It was my kite's second trip aloft. As darkness began to fall, I had begun to reel it in ever so slowly, when tragedy struck. I had watched and worried how the length of the three balls of string sagged when the wind lessened its pull, and now, slowly reeling it in, I saw the string sagging low and catching on a roof tile of an apartment house two blocks away. I stopped reeling, fearing it would break if it chaffed along the rough edge of the tile. Break it did just as I tried to tease it free. When it happened, I was alone on the roof; Jane and the others had all gone in as the sun began to drop. It was clear to them that I would lose it; they knew it was doomed and couldn't stand seeing me lose the wonderful kite. Suddenly, I felt the string go slack, and I knew it was down, lost and so far out I couldn't see. When we got on our bikes early the next morning, we found not a sign of it, only a length of string blocks away hanging from a telephone line.

Mr. Boles had hung around all day, going in and out of his house, checking the progress of the great kite and its flyer. I can see him now standing below, smiling encouragement. He told me and the gathering I was the best kite flyer he had ever seen, but I knew it was the kite, not me. Today, I still honor and appreciate the man who gave me my day of fame, a good deal more than the requisite fifteen minutes Andy Warhol would allot each of us.

He shared our pleasure, never interfering or offering advice, only soft praise and the encouragement of his presence. I have loved the sight of soaring kites ever since. The memory of the flight, the steady tug at my waist, the curious onlookers, all that went to assuage any sense of loss that I realized then was no loss at all, only a gain.

The Christmas I got my first chemistry set, I also got my first bicycle, a twenty-four-inch hand-me-down Western Flyer with wide handlebars and a wide saddle. It had belonged to my cousin Herndon who graduated to a twenty-six-inch balloon-tired bike with chromium fenders. Aunt Ethel, rather than trading Hernie's old bike, had given it to me, and Mama had thrown in new tires, a new paint job, and new chrome fenders. I honestly believed that my secondhand bike, with its red and black color scheme and the shiny chromed fenders, was much handsomer than Herndon's brand new balloon-tired bike, but it lacked one important feature that I begged Mama to get for me—a basket to fit on the handlebars. I needed it to carry my books when I rode it to school and to carry the bag of *Saturday Evening Post* magazines that I had started selling door to door over our end of town. The bike allowed me to sell more by ranging farther from our immediate neighborhood. Riding my bike into distant territory and parking it at the end of a block, I could walk from house to house, making a loop up one side of the street and down the other back to my bike. I would ring the doorbell, politely ask for the lady or the man of the house, and would ask, "Would you like to buy this week's *Saturday Evening Post*? It has a new story by . . . and an article about the . . .."

Aunt Ethel coached me on how to make my pitch. "Always mention an article or an author," she explained.

I tried it, though, in the beginning, I often mispronounced an author's name. Nevertheless, it would impress the "man of the house" who, caught off guard, would buy a magazine. But once, in the beginning, one of my more or less regulars looked at me and frowned when I made my spiel and said, "Oh, yeah, what's the story about?"

I told him I didn't know, that I hadn't read it yet. He looked skeptical, obviously doubting I would have understood the story had I read it, and said, "OK, you read it and come back and tell me if it's any good," then turned and closed the door.

Aunt Ethel hadn't explained what I should say in the circumstance, so I went home and read the article, surprised that an adult article was a much easier read than I thought it would be. Well, there were parts I couldn't grasp completely, but I could at least tell what it was about, and I went to the dictionary fewer times than I thought I would. The next day, when I returned with a summary of what I had understood, he stuck to his promise, gave me a nickel, and became a regular customer. But from then on I always read the story I was going to tout. My career as a magazine salesman lasted almost a year and a half, and in that time, I grew from a ten- to a twenty-a-week magazine salesman. In the end, when the agent forced me to take twenty-five magazines, I was never able to sell them all and would have to return all the unsold copies, and then when he failed to show up for two or three weeks to collect his money and pay me my commission, Mama was concerned at first that he might expect me to sell them all or pay for the unsold copies, but he never asked me to pay for the leftover magazines. We talked it over and decided I should return all the magazines the next time he stopped by and formally resign as a door-to-door salesman. The few dollars I would have to turn over now seem like nothing, but it was a time when Mama was making a salary of twenty-five dollars a week. My totals never came to ten dollars, but that seemed an enormous amount for a small boy to be custodian of.

Two things occurred that made it easier to terminate: First, they changed agents without informing me, the new agent being an older man and, unlike my original agent, "not at all clean," according to Mama's estimate. Second, I wrecked my bike beyond repair. The day of the wreck, I had ranged far from my regular route, looking for new territories. The market in the immediate neighbor being saturated, I had begun to range into other neighborhoods, perhaps more for the adventure of being on my own in a new territory than for true entrepreneurial interests. I hadn't been too successful that morning and was pedaling as fast as I could to get back home for lunch and the Saturday opera broadcast. As I hurried, face down, across an intersection, I slammed head on into the side of a car coming from my right. I can still recall the thud, the terrible jolt, and my flight across the hood of the car. He had not seen me or I him. He stopped immediately. Only slightly dazed, I picked myself up quickly to see what damage the bike had suffered. I had a scrape on my chin and nothing more, but the bike—my lovely bike—was finished, at least the front wheel that was now a very flat oval.

He was out of the Buick in a flash and was stooping over to help me up, asking if I was hurt. I told him I was fine, that it was my bicycle I was worried about. I was relieved that I didn't recognize him. I didn't want Mama to know I had ridden so far outside the boundary she had set for my territory. He was equally relieved, I think, for he didn't say a word about the large scratch I had left on his fender. When he offered to take me home and I said I could manage, he looked even more relieved, got back into his car, and hurried away. It was only later I realized he was as concerned as I that no one knew about it.

It wasn't easy toting the bicycle and carrying the remaining magazines. When I got home and saw that, along with the mangled wheel, the front fork on my bike was also bent and could probably never be straightened properly, I was crushed. To be wheelless after being so mobile was a disaster. I lied and told Mama I had run into a wall. She thought no more of it, apparently having other things to worry about. I wasn't injured, which was really all that mattered, she said. Considering myself lucky that she neither probed nor scolded me, I let the business of a repair die and, along with it, my short happy life as an adventurer on wheels.

Week after week, I had approached strangers in their homes and had spoken directly and clearly and found that they, not all, but enough, had listened. I had not enjoyed it but had done it because it was a means, I thought, to a greater end. For a period, I had a few coins of my own to spend as I pleased. Perhaps more important, when I found that I could read an adult magazine, I became hooked, stopping by newsstands and thumbing through *Life* and *Time*, even picking up the forbidden *Police Gazette* or *True Detective* in the barbershop, and reading lurid tales of murder and detection while I waited my turn. Only once did one of the barbers warn me that my mother might not like it if she knew I was reading "barbershop trash." That made the reading all the more engrossing.

Averill School, as I said earlier, was in its day an exceptional school with a dedicated and enlightened faculty, the best of whom would be exceptional today and the worst, like Ms. Touchstone (great name for a nature teacher, a charactonym right out of Dickens or Fielding), only occupied classroom space. I believe I benefited immensely from my experiences there and do not believe my early years in school would have had nearly as positive an influence on my future had I gone to any other elementary school in the Beaumont of the time. In Beaumont, there was a pervasive and often wounding atmosphere of snobbery and class distinction, overlaid with a thin veneer of gentility and good manners constantly reinforced by the teachers and by the parents and children themselves. Deeply conscious of the socioeconomic differences, Mama urged us to always make friends with the "right people," insisting that who we knew would make a difference in the future. I was never sure I understood what she meant or even who the right people actually were. I did discover that several boys I had made friends with were not welcome in our house, and I never understood why, but as I grew older, I learned that their names, Italian or Greek usually, separated them from the "right people" in Mama's mind. Apparently, my classmates' parents agreed, for cliques formed from the beginning, and rarely did friendships established in the classroom with a member of the clique ever extend beyond the school grounds. In the end, I had few friends at Averill and none I could call a close friend. Clifford Latson, a year ahead of me in school, was a good chap, amiable, but his family were rigid churchgoers, and I never felt really welcome, though I made myself "at home" on the roof of the old garage. While I had few even casual friends, I was never lonely or envious of those who did have friends.

Dick Dowling Junior High School, named after the hero of "Sabine Pass," the only Civil War battle fought on Texas soil, was quite a change from Averill, mostly to the good, I found, though my grades did not improve and my report cards continued to show mediocre to poor marks for conduct. I showed improvement in social studies and in a class called forum and even won certificates of achievement in sixth and seventh grade history; in forum class, Ms. Fife praised my speechifying and my performance in a one-act play we performed for the school, in which I had the lead.

Forum was unlike any class I've ever heard of, before or since. It was twice the size of a normal class and was taught by two teachers. Using a simplified form of *Robert's Rules of Order*, they taught parliamentary procedure and emphasized "public speaking" and drama. Every quarter, or report card period, the class was reorganized and elected a new president, vice president, and secretary-treasurer. Everyone in class was a member of a committee that held regular meetings and made reports. No one was allowed to remain unassigned; everyone had a job to perform in the "organization." Each class began with a call to order by the president or vice president of the class, followed by a roll call by the secretary who then reads the "minutes" of the previous week's activities. Committees reported once a week. It was the most orderly and democratically run class in school. We learned to write outlines and present speeches in class, students with the best speeches presenting theirs over the school's public address system. In my first year, I read my "Reasons for a Red Cross" to the entire student body.

The two teachers in Forum class had the responsibility for conducting school elections, which were the major events during each school year. Each year, Dowling's students elected a mayor, a governor, or a president, following the same general procedures those elections followed in the world outside of school. We were following John Dewey's theory of learning by doing, and it succeeded in teaching basic lessons in government, all about the methods of nominating, filing, campaigning, and voting. In the spring, we held primaries and runoff elections after a week of rallies and stump speaking. For about two weeks, all classes would integrate the campaigns and the elections into the regular lesson plans. Even the boys' shop classes and the girls' sewing classes contributed by making the placards and banners and bunting that decorated the auditorium. The "national" presidential elections, understandably, were the most exciting and most colorful of all the elections. For several weeks, before the nominating convention, our forum class studied the United States Constitution and the electoral system, and in library class, we read short essays based on the *Federalist Papers*. Each homeroom became a state or a territory and chose delegates to the nominating convention. In the seventh grade, my homeroom was Delaware, and I was chosen to chair our delegation of three to the "national" convention. Since all homerooms had approximately equal populations, there were no giant delegations, though as I recall, I believe the eighth grade or senior class homerooms had larger voter representation.

All day on convention day, we met in the school auditorium, the delegates occupying the main floor close to the stage. Banners flew and placards waved on poles. The morning began with a roll call of the states, Principal Morgan presiding until a permanent chairman of the convention was elected. When we had elected a new chairman, Mr. Morgan stepped down, and from then on, the students ran the convention. Ms. Fife and her partner had taught us well; everyone knew the scenario and followed it step by step, first the nomination speeches then the seconding speeches then the voting of the states. I was chosen as chairman of our Delaware delegation because I could shout the votes from the floor and could be heard. The only microphones were on the stage, one for the public address system and one for Beaumont's KFDM radio. Dick Dowling's presidential convention went out on the local airwaves, and people all over town listened in. In 1938, when we elected a student president, nationwide broadcasting of national conventions was still a novelty. Dowling's broadcasting of its convention was an original. It took three ballots each to choose the two candidates for the election of a president and a vice president to be held a week away. Several times "spontaneous demonstrations" of marching bands interrupted the orderly but noisy proceedings from time to time, and caucuses of states caused delays in the voting. We had all the trappings of a true political convention of the period. There was even a bit of political skullduggery in the Delaware delegation. Our homeroom had voted to support Mary Jane Barnes for the vice presidential nomination, but on the second ballot, I rose and declared, "Delaware votes two votes for Mary Jane Barnes, and one vote for Gloria Bowers."

Gloria was not the favorite of Mr. Urquhart's homeroom, but she was the favorite of delegate Joe Gilliland. I immediately got a note from Mary Jane's manager in the balcony, demanding I change the vote, but Mr. Urquhart had told us that the delegates were bound to our state's choice only on the first ballot, and the chairman or a caucus of the delegation could change the vote. I knew Gloria was going to win anyway and thought Mary Jane's decision not to concede—she was a distant third—after the first ballot was a mistake. Mary Jane was an old friend, but Gloria, well, that is another story. Mary Jane did not speak to me for the rest of the term, but I did get smiles from Gloria that I might not have gotten. That year, at Dick Dowling Junior High School, I learned a lot more than the method of choosing a presidential candidate.

When final votes were tallied at the end of the week, everyone in Dick Dowling understood the election process. Each homeroom, rather each state, chose electors as members of the Electoral College where the final selection was made. In the spirit of the age, there were rumors, no doubt, manufactured for the sake of realism that this "state" or that was going to cast its electoral votes independently of the popular vote, but it didn't occur. Just to make sure Delaware would go the way of the popular vote, my homeroom's elector was not me. The teachers in forum class made sure the election went off as close to a real election as they could. It seemed odd at first, but I realize now how appropriate it was that those responsible for teaching us about the political system were also those who produced plays and school's entertainment programs.

At Dick Dowling, world history with Mrs. Graham and American history with Ms. Watson were my favorite classes and the ones where I did my best work. It was strange. My two teachers were as unlike in teaching style, in personality, in appearance, and in every conceivable way, as two people could be. Mrs. Graham was calm, nondirective, gentle, and permissive, yet she got us through ancient and medieval history and up to the age of exploration and colonization with remarkable ease. We had uniform exams at the end of the year, and all through the year, we made oral reports, map reports, and had weekly classroom "debates." I really can't recall her actively "teaching" a class. She would make reading assignments and then begin class by asking the same question: "Now who wants to tell us what the chapter was about?"

The reports and debates were dovetailed into the activities we practiced in the forum class. By contrast, Ms. Watson was directive, demanding, and sometimes frightening. No one ever risked coming to her class unprepared or underprepared. Her reputation as a strict disciplinarian was deserved, but if she scolded and berated the laggards, she also rewarded and praised them when they came through. Receiving an accolade from Ms. Watson was worth all the fear and trembling. All of Dowling's history classes required weekly reports on "outside" readings. That meant we had to crowd into the main library room as soon as the bell rang for the last class and check out supplemental readings. Multiple copies of the history books were arranged under the individual teacher's name. In addition to the pages assigned in the class text, the outside readings ranged from ten to fifteen pages. One of the things we had learned to do in forum was to take notes so that when we reported in class on our readings, we had notes before us. Mrs. Graham had never required us to cite according to any specific design. But Ms. Watson would not allow us to deviate from the directions she had given. I never failed to receive a compliment for my reports either in Graham's or Watson's class.

Perhaps the most profound lesson in social justice came not from the teachers in school but from what may appear to have been a most unlikely source. However, given the structure of East Texas society and most of the South in those days, it really wasn't all that unusual. The day-to-day governance of many white, middle-class children in those days was overseen by people of color, most often women like Ida, our washwoman and general factotum, who came to our house early every morning and left for her house in the Negro quarters after supper or late afternoon. Because my mother worked and was rarely home when we got home from school, Ida was our most frequent contact with the adult world, aside from school, and in our part of town, the same was true for most of my classmates. I have no idea what level of schooling Ida reached; she read the newspaper every morning, and I often found her reading magazines when she wasn't cleaning, washing, or washing the dishes. She joked a lot, laughed at our stories, and joined in conversation with all of us, though her place was more often the kitchen than the large family room. She never scolded or complained, but she did express displeasure when we, usually I, did or said something wrong, and I recall that I tried to avoid her disapproval. One afternoon, when she was preparing to leave the house, wrapping some "leftovers" from the table for her own evening meal, I saw her put a bottle of Falstaff Beer in her poke with the other things. I knew that Mama often bought Ida a bottle of Falstaff, which she preferred to Mama's Shiner or Grand Prize, and I wondered why Ida didn't like Mama's brand.

"Ida," I began, "is Falstaff a nigger beer? Is that why you don't drink Mama's beer?"

Just the two of us were there in the kitchen, and I was enjoying the pleasure of being alone with her. She looked at me and said very emphatically, "There ain't no such thing as nigger." Her voice was soft but stern.

I said, "Yes, there is. You're a nigger."

"No, I ain't. I am not a nigger. I'm a Negro. I'm a colored. And don't you ever say that word nigger again. It's bad."

I could see she was serious and that I had earned her displeasure. She almost always corrected my misstatements or my misdeeds with a smile and a laugh, but this was clearly different. I said I was sorry and that I would remember. Words had always fascinated me, and this was a lesson I told myself I would never forget, for it ran counter to all I had heard before. "Nigger" was one of the most common epithets of East Texas American English, and Ida's instruction went counter to everything I had heard from my elders and boys in the playground.

That evening, after Ida had left and we were all sitting down to eat, I chimed up, hoping to surprise everyone with the bit of wisdom I had learned from Ida.

"Mama," I began, "did you know that Ida isn't a nigger?" I was sure that I had learned something no one else was aware of.

Mama looked at me sharply and said, "Of course not, she's a 'negra.' Ida's 'colored,' and don't use that word. It's impolite."

How had I missed that? No one had ever told me that "nigger" was taboo. All the men I knew used it freely without concern. Social justice was not a discussed or recognized topic; certainly, the concept of civil rights was virtually unknown, particularly when it came to race, and equality was an abstraction not clearly understood or even professed, except in the abstract. But I was aware at a very early age of the conflicted attitudes that underlay the concept. I was aware that colored people, the most socially acceptable term in those days, always rode in the back of the street cars, that they always addressed white people as "sir" or "ma'am," that they always "knew their place," and were never "uppity" if they wanted to keep their jobs. When Ida was at the house, we always tried to please her and mind when she told us to do something, but she was different from our aunts or adult friends. Negro men were different too. They generally ignored us little ones, or when they did not, they always spoke to us politely if indifferently, though occasionally, one would stoop and ask what we were playing and then go on about his yard work or whatever chore he had been hired to perform.

Ida had a friend who tended the yard regularly and received a steady stipend of seventy-five cents every Saturday for mowing the lawn, but I recall one week he missed us and let the yard go. The next time he came by, Mama stopped him and asked him why he had neglected to mow. It was a terrible scene as I recall. I was standing next to Mama on the little back porch, and Nathan was below us, speaking softly, head down in an attitude of shame or something like it. He was huge and black and one of the friendliest of men, always letting me help rake leaves when he was working the yard, but now he was diminished to begging Mama's pardon. It seemed so strange, and I felt Mama had gone too far for 75¢, even though I had never held that much change in my hand myself.

When she said with cold finality, "Well, Nathan, what are you going to do about it? You owe me seventy-five cents," he reached into the small watch pocket of his trousers and pulled out a tightly folded dollar bill and handed it up, saying that was all he had.

Mama said she'd get his change. I stood there embarrassed and deeply ashamed to have witnessed his humiliation, my friend's utter degradation. When Mama handed him a quarter, she added, "From now on, Nathan, I don't think I'll pay you until *after* the work is done." He nodded and apologized again then left. Mama looked at me and told me we had to watch "them." I mumbled that it was only seventy-five cents. Mama replied, "That's the same as three school lunches." I could not understand it; Mama had been so adamant about "nigger," yet she had been ruthless in making sure that Nathan be kept in his place—besides *my* lunch was always fifteen cents.

A few years later, I saw another contradiction in the pattern when on Halloween, Aunt Elma, Uncle Walter's wife, whom we all loved dearly, and Aunt Millie, Mama's elder sister, whom we loved but sometimes were shocked by her rude and often frank remarks about friends and neighbors, came to the front door, trick-or-treating and dressed in white robes and peaked hoods.

Holding their hands over what appeared to be a heavily embroidered shield or badge, they laughed and shouted, "Trick or treat!" and made booing sounds.

Mama stood behind me and said in a low, angry tone, "Mildred! Elma! Get away from here in those robes! You ought to be ashamed!"

They seemed as shocked by her tone and anger as I was. "Why, Dot? It's just Halloween, you know that!"

"It's not *just*, and those aren't Halloween costumes. They're Klan robes, and I don't ever want to see them in my house. Go home and take them off, right now. There are children all about the neighborhood." She slammed the door in their faces and pulled Donnie and me back into the room.

At first, when I asked what was wrong, she wouldn't answer, but when I insisted, she spoke in whispered tones about how Uncle Walter and Uncle Waukee, Aunt Millie's husband, had been members of the Klan. "Everybody was back in the twenties," she said, "but it was a bad thing, and you should never mention it to friends or to anyone."

When I asked if Daddy had been a member, she said vehemently, "NO! He hated them."

That was the end of it at our house, but I did ask Ms. Watson once what the KKK was all about, and she told the class about how the Klan burned and lynched and frightened Negroes, Jews, and Catholics and were a bad bunch, then added, "Now don't ask any more about it."

Mama would insist all her life that she had no prejudice against colored people or Jews, and as she grew older, she gradually lived up to her denial, even refused membership in the United Daughters of the Confederacy when she was invited. Mama's grandfather McKessen had fought with Lee all through Virginia and, later after the war, as a guerilla and outlaw with Cantrell in Arkansas. She was a product of the age and social class, and as she passed into another age and began to associate with Northern immigrants, her attitudes would change. My stepfather, whom she married in 1939, had the quaint habit of referring to colored women as "Negro ladies," which Mama attributed to his being a Yankee from Wisconsin. At the time, I was twelve or thirteen and told her he was right, for I said I believed in the sacred truth that all men were created equal. She only glowered and told me I didn't know what I was talking about. She was indeed a product of East Texas.

Dowling, like Averill, was located in the white-collar section of town, the part of town where professional men and successful businessmen and their families lived. It was the part of town where there were several old mansions built in the times of an oil-boom shortly after the gushers of Spindletop came in. One would assume that there were parents in that part of town who, like my Uncle Walter, heartily disapproved of "that man in the White House." I cannot recall Ms. Watson ever tempering her remarks about Harding, Coolidge, or Hoover or the causes of the Depression or tempering her praise of "Franklin Delano Roosevelt and his wife, Eleanor." One day, while we were reading and writing out the answers to questions she had written on the blackboard, she suddenly interrupted, telling us all to stop writing and to come to the window where she was standing. Her back was to the room. Our ground-floor room looked directly to the street that ran along the side of the building. The first thing we saw as we looked out the window was an elderly man, dirty and unshaven, in ragged clothes, dragging a large, partly filled gunnysack. He was picking through a garbage can at the curb, pulling out bits of food, bones, bread, leaves of vegetables and putting them in the sack.

She told us all to look at the old man and tell her what we saw. "He's just a dirty old man, Ms. Watson. I've seen him lots," one girl said.

"Yes, he's poor and hungry, and he's out of work. We should never allow people to be that poor and hungry in this great country. It is wrong when people have to eat garbage, don't you forget it." She returned us to our seats and said very quietly with quiver in her voice, almost as if she were about to cry, "Don't you *ever* let that happen to you or anyone in your family. Learn all you can so you will *never* let that happen."

We always believed Ms. Watson, for we knew she had no reason to lie to us. That day, there was a quiver in her voice and a tremor in her face; she was close to crying, and we sensed it. We knew she meant what she said. When I got home that evening, I told Mama what Ms. Watson had said, and she agreed but added that there were a lot of people who didn't really care, who believed the government had no business interfering with things like that, people who criticized Roosevelt's WPA, CCC, NRA, and the new labor laws.

"Mr. Hoover was one who believed government had no business helping those people," she said. I said something about how much Grandmother liked Hoover, and Mama replied that her mother was not a widow with four mouths to feed in the Depression either.

"You listen to Ms. Watson. She's a good teacher," and then she repeated her favorite remark about Roosevelt being a "godsend."

All through junior high school, arithmetic was my worse subject, and I came close to failing it in the seventh grade and even closer to not qualifying for algebra when I entered the eighth grade. Mr. Urquhart was generous, not with grades but with the time that he took helping several others and me. Science was still not a subject taught or even eluded to in grades 6 and 7, and once, Mr. Urquhart helped me balance a chemical equation and patiently explained how *valences* worked. His encouragement meant a lot and partly convinced me I could handle freshman algebra.

Although I was not a star member of Dowling's orchestra and was stuck back in second violin, it became an important part of my life as a seventh grader. In the first week of my seventh grade at Dowling, Dr. Milam, the Superintendent of Music, came to orchestra class and asked if anyone wished to change from violin to cello. She held up a full-sized instrument and told us we were free to use it for as long as we played in the orchestra. Stuck in umpteenth chair second violin scratching away, never playing the melodic line of a main theme, I immediately volunteered and accepted the large instrument and took my place beside Martha Nees, the orchestra's only cellist. I had always admired Martha, though we had never been friends. She smiled and welcomed me as I sat down next to her and pointed to the cello part on the music stand then demonstrated how I was to hold the instrument. Everyone watched, and I felt quite proud at the moment. Dr. Milam looked down, also smiling, apparently pleased with herself and me. I felt good sitting there next to Martha with the full-sized cello between my knees.

After three weeks' instruction from Ivan Streichoff, Beaumont's only cello teacher, I was allowed to bow my instrument with the orchestra. Mrs. Van Meter said she was sorry she was losing me as a student, but she was glad

I had found an instrument I liked and assured me Mr. Streichoff was a fine teacher. I found him patient and free with compliments and mild praise that encouraged me to practice. When Martha also complimented me for being able to read the bass cleft so well and so soon, I was even more inspired, for Martha was one of the "top girls," right up there with Gloria and Mary Kyle. By spring that year, Dr. Milam "auditioned" me and invited me to play third-chair cello in the Beaumont's Junior Symphony that was made up of players from three junior highs in the district. All through the seventh grade at Dowling my main passions were music and chemistry.

In the late spring of 1939, Mr. Urquhart passed out information sheets that described the two routes toward graduation from high school. Like many cities in Texas, Beaumont was still operating on the eleven-year system, thus making eighth grade the first year of high school. It was time now to decide whether we would take the vocational route or the college-entrance route to graduation. He explained the options and told us to take the sheets home and to discuss with our parents. I had looked forward to the time when I would finally be allowed to select the classes I would take that would prepare me for college, although I had no clear idea what college was about. No one in our family in Beaumont had ever gone to college. My father had gone to a business college in San Antonio and had studied bookkeeping and other business courses, and his sister Kate had attended the state normal school San Marcos, Texas, later Southwest State Teacher's College, where Lyndon Johnson had earned his bachelor's degree. Her son, my cousin Ted, was just finishing his electrical engineering degree at Texas A&M. Jane and Dorothy before me had taken the college-entrance route, and both were hoping to enroll in Lamar Junior College in Beaumont. I was no blooming genius like Ted, but ever since the fifth grade, with Dorothy's encouragement and, to some degree, Mama's, I had talked about becoming a chemist or a doctor some day.

The college-entrance diploma in Texas required four years of English, two years of algebra, two years of a foreign language, a year of American history, and a semester of civics. American history and civics were state requirements for all graduates, regardless of the route they chose. If you were planning to major in science or engineering, you were also required to take solid geometry and trigonometry and four years of science. I can't recall having any formal advising, only a brief chat with Mr. Urquhart, who put me down for English, algebra, general science, Latin, orchestra, and physical education. That year, only four of us chose to take Latin, and it appeared that Dick Dowling might not offer it if more did not sign up. As I was filling out the form, Mr. Urquhart questioned the wisdom of my choice, suggesting I take world history instead of Latin and wait until I went on to Beaumont High to take my foreign language. I respected his suggestion, but I was intent on following in the path set down by Jane and Dorothy.

As it turned out, the Latin question was moot, for I did not return to Dick Dowling in the fall of 1939. Shortly after school let out that spring, my mother married Albert Delsman and informed us that before school began in the fall, we would be moving from Beaumont to Corpus Christi. I was overjoyed. For more than two years, Mama had been "going out" with Mr. Delsman, who was an auditor at the Pure Oil Co. He was tall, rather good-looking, and a few years younger than Mama. Everyone said he was a sort of cross between Franchot Tone and Humphrey Bogart. But more important, he had an important job: district auditor for the Pure Oil Company. Mama whispered to me once he made almost five thousand dollars a year! Though raised on a farm in Wisconsin, he had studied accounting at Northwestern University in Chicago, though had not finished "because of the Depression." In the winter of 1939, he left Pure Oil, taking a position as an auditor and chief accountant with the American Mineral Spirits Company (AMSCO), a small refinery and pipeline company in Corpus Christi, and now he was making "more than five thousand dollars a year"—according to another whispered report.

I liked Mr. Delsman, though we had never spoken more than a few words, and it came as no surprise, really, when Mama called us long distance from Corpus Christi and told us the news. I was twelve at the time and understood nothing about "affairs of the heart," except what I had seen in the movies. I could hardly believe that older people like my mother ever fell in love or ran off and got married. But apparently, at thirty-six, Mama was not old. Jane said that she had thought they might get married sometime but didn't think they would do it that soon. I was overjoyed because I believed there would be great changes ahead when we left Beaumont, which I had grown to dislike intensely.

As I look back now on the years at Dick Dowling, I recall that I was in trouble at home as well at school much of the time. I had no one to talk to or confide in at a time when boys as well as girls need someone to whom they can go to with questions not only about sex but also about that whole system of values and meanings that rule our lives. Don was too young, and Jane too busy with her many friends. My only close ally, Dorothy, left the family late one night in the early fall, not long after her seventeenth birthday, when she announced that she and Lewis Dahlsheimer were married and that she was expecting a baby. It was a terrifying night as I recall; I could hear it all, Dorothy's crying and begging Mama not to be angry. I could not understand what was happening, but I did gather that Mama was beyond anger, was in crisis actually. At thirty-five, she was facing the prospect of becoming a grandmother and was telling both Dorothy and Lewis in a coldly intolerant tone that if Dorothy left they would not be welcome, that Dorothy could not come back. It was unbelievable and incomprehensible.

While I was eating my bowl of cereal the next morning, Mama told me that Dorothy was married and had gone to live with Lewis and his parents, the Dahlsheimers. It had not been a dream after all. She said nothing more then, though later, we would hear her condemn Dorothy and Lewis and his mother often enough. I could not understand it: they were married, had been married since the summer, and even had the marriage license to prove it. *Where's the shame*, I wondered. The shame was that she had eloped and had lied about her age; according to Mama and the mores of the time that was shame enough. Mama would explain how people like us who had so little money or position did have those things which no one could deny: their reputation, their good name, their respectability. "Running off" to get married washed all that away, she claimed. There was nothing romantic about a teenage girl eloping, Mama insisted. Though she had gotten married to our father at sixteen, it was entirely different: she had not "run off."

I looked up to and admired Jane, often held her in awe for the way she could pitch a hard ball, but we rarely talked as Dorothy and I had. Though she was closer to me in age, she seemed light-years away in her interests and friends at the time. She and Hernie, Cousin Herndon, were closer than she and I, and I resented his special status in the family, much as I resented Donnie's special status. Only Dorothy had understood where I stood, and while she was living at home, I never felt isolated or forgotten. With her departure and the manner in which she left, I felt bereft of any real support.

The popular psychology of the time would have attributed my status as an *isolato* to the absence of a father or a "father figure." The stories that revolved around the memory of my father never died. Later, Dorothy spoke of him frequently when we were alone, always recalling the happy times before his illness or telling stories about his sense of humor, which Mama, in her last months, denied, according to Jane. I was able then, finally, to tell her how important she had been those years that followed, how her insisting that I finish *Emil and the Detectives* had left a mark so that even today I feel pangs of guilt if I fail to finish reading a book once I start.

Chapter 2

A New World To Conquer

The year 1939 was a year of many changes, and I loved it. I could hardly wait for school to begin; I'd be taking "real" classes: science, algebra, *real* English with literature, Latin, and, of course, orchestra. I was eager to get the summer vacation behind me. Mama had OK'd my lab bench in the garage back in the corner under the stairs. All I needed was some lumber. But I really needed some help and someone who really knew how to build it. So far, that was the only problem I was facing. Nothing would happen until Mama got back from her vacation.

In the past, she had always enjoyed her two-week vacations in the company of women from her office. She would leave us in the charge of Grandma or on old family friend like Mrs. Rogers, or Dorothy would be here. But this year, she had embarked alone, taking the train to Corpus Christi to visit Mr. Delsman, Mama's steady gentleman friend now for several years. She'd been gone less than a week when the call came, and Jane answered. I watched her nod and say OK and that she understood. Then she turned and looked at Don and me.

"Mama and Mr. Delsman— *Albert*— are married," she said, smiling.

How strange it sounded. No one was shocked or surprised, least of all Grandma, who was standing behind Donnie and me. But it still sounded strange.

Mr. Delsman, Albert, and Mama had been "seeing each other," dating, going together, whatever, for several years; I had seen them "billing and cooing" late at night on the screened-in front porch. Betrothed at fifteen and married to Daddy at seventeen, Mama had skipped life as a young girl. When Gilly, my father, enlisted in the army immediately after war was declared in 1917, Mama was only fourteen, and it was then Grandmother promised that Dot would be waiting for him when he returned. She and Daddy were married immediately after he got back from Germany, not even waiting for her to graduate from high school. When Daddy died on December 5, 1931, she was two weeks from her twenty-ninth birthday; in months she went to work at the Pure Oil Company where her brother Walter was office manager.

We all knew Mama liked Albert a lot. She was happy and talked about him constantly, always repeating things he said, sometimes making fun of the way he pronounced words. He was a Yankee from Wisconsin, and he "talked different." But ever since New Year's, she had clearly not been happy. He had quit his job with Pure Oil, and taken a much better position in Corpus Christi as head auditor and accountant at a small independent oil company, American Mineral Spirits Company.

All in all, it was a happy phone call. We all had a chance to speak to both Mama and Albert. Even Donnie said a few words. Grandma, who was staying at the house in Mama's absence, spoke the longest. A few days after the phone call, Mama was back. She was so happy, so full of excitement, telling us how nice Corpus Christi was and how different it was from Beaumont. I couldn't recall seeing her so happy. Albert Delsman, I thought, must be a fine man. She said they were looking for a house and making sure we'd be close to good schools and not far from the bay.

I told Mama, first thing, that I would be glad to leave Beaumont and live in a new place, but Jane was miserable. Leaving Beaumont and missing her senior year in high school with all her friends, the people she had known since her days at Averill wouldn't be easy. The important thing, however, was that Mama was happy. I had the feeling that everything would be different now, whether we liked it or not. But when I expressed my joy to Grandma, she seemed annoyed that I would be so happy, and when I told Dorothy about Grandma's reaction, she explained that Grandma had worshipped Daddy and probably disapproved of Albert, for he was certainly no Gilly. Albert, Dorothy explained, was not only a "damn Yankee," he was also a Roman Catholic, and Grandma didn't like either.

Once when we were alone, I asked Grandma, "What's so wrong about being Catholic? The Pivitos next door are all Catholics. They're not bad. Aunt Lizzy is a Catholic, isn't she?"

Something rare happened then; Grandma began to talk to me like one person to another. Sitting by the radio, she reached over and switched it off and told me to sit and listen. In hard matter-of-fact terms she began to speak.

"I was born and raised Catholic. All my children—yes, your mother too—were baptized Catholic, but I left that church and took them with me. Dot, your mama, was just a baby. We didn't just stop going to church. I stood right up in the middle of mass one Sunday and spoke right out loud and told the priest and everybody why I was leaving the church." She paused, looked hard at me, and said, "He had just begun saying mass. I told him and everyone in the church that I was leaving and taking my family with me."

"Why, Grandma?" I asked. "Why in the middle of mass?" I couldn't imagine anyone doing such a thing.

"I told them all. I said, 'I'm leaving the Roman Catholic Church because the priests and the bishop have abandoned my sister, a widow with two small children. This church has abandoned them in Mexico during a revolution!' I said that, just like that! They refused to help her. Her husband, Plumley, had died of TB down there."

I'd never heard such things before. "A revolution? In Mexico? Gosh! Grandma, when? Aunt Lizzy was in a revolution? Was she living in Mexico then?" I was confused. I'd never heard of such a thing before. What a family, I thought.

"It was a long time ago," she said and then told me the story.

"Let's talk about something else, honey," she said. "Albert Delsman is a good man. He'll be a good father, and he'll make your mama happy."

Her voice had completely changed, but now I was really curious. Mama always talked about how Grandma loved Aunt Lizzy and about how she loved her cousins. I liked talking to Grandma, just the two of us, and made up my mind that very moment that if we were ever alone like that again, we'd talk some more.

I recalled another time, three years earlier, when we talked, rather she talked, and I listened. We were alone in the house on Broadway. I had just walked through the back door into the kitchen. Grandma had cooked us a pot of her "chili con carne from scratch," and I had smelled it as soon as I turned the corner at the end of the block; the rich chili odor had filled the air. A big black pot would be simmering, and I knew it! I'd get a bowl of rice and chili as soon as I came through the door. But to my surprise, there was a stranger sitting at the kitchen table, a young man in high lace-up boots and a strange-looking jacket, just finishing a bowl of chili and rice.

"Drink your milk," Grandma told him. He didn't say a word but did as she said.

She was sitting there watching him, then looked up and told me to have a seat. Without a word, she rose, went to the stove, and filled a bowl for me. Just then, he rose to leave. You couldn't help noticing the fine lace-up boots he was wearing.

As she put the bowl, along with a glass of milk, in front of me, she said to him, "Young man, I've been wondering since I first saw you. How is it you have such an expensive pair of books and you're going from house to house asking for work and something to eat?"

"The last man I worked far couldn't pay me and my pal both, so he give me these boots," he replied softly.

Grandma said, "I see. I wish I could give you a dollar, son, but we just can't." He said he understood and thanked her for the bowls and told her it was "sure good," then left.

All the while, I was spooning the delicious stuff into my mouth, happy to know I'd have some more later at supper. When he left, Donnie came in and sat beside me on the bench against the wall.

Then, looking straight at us, Grandma said, "You should never turn away anyone who comes to the house and asks to work for food. It's hard times out there, you know, honey." I nodded. I'd been hearing about "hard times" a lot, and I honestly could see that it must be really hard. When I asked her what kind of work he did, she said he raked some leaves out back. There weren't any leaves to speak of, hadn't been since we shook the last pecans from the tree, but I just put another spoonful of rice and chili in my mouth.

She said again, "I bet the house here is marked some way, maybe the bark in one of the camphor trees out front has a mark on it. I bet we'll never really be able to tell."

"Chili sure is good, Grandma," I said and was about to ask for more when she said, "Remember what I said, honey, you too, Donnie, sweetheart, never turn a man away who asks to work for food. It doesn't have to be real work. Remember." I nodded. And that evening, when Mama came home from work, I told the story just as I'd heard it from Grandma. You never forget things like that, or I never do.

I began this chapter about changes that lay ahead, about that long-distance call from Corpus that had triggered a change I had not expected, although, as I said earlier, it had not come as a shock or as a total surprise. The truth was I never thought about things like that; I had only one dominant interest, my chemistry lab, rather my chemistry lab of the imagination.

The day before Mama was to return to Corpus Christi, I got the first really exciting news I'd had in a long time, and it came as a real surprise. I learned I would be going to San Antonio to stay with Aunt Kate for the rest of the summer, would not even be in Beaumont when they made the move to Corpus Christi. Gosh! San Antonio! Every kid in Texas loved "San Antone." Jane had suggested it to Mama to get me away from the constant conflicts and, more than likely, to get me out of her hair. She had enough to manage. Mama told me that she and Jane thought I would be happier with Aunt Kate and that I would enjoy meeting the Gilliland clan, Daddy's people whom I barely knew. The happy prospect of living all summer with Aunt Kate in San Antonio, being able to spend a summer there near the Gilliland clan, had capped the sense of change.

Aunt Kate, an elementary school teacher, was not at all "well-off." Her son Ted, our only first cousin on that side of the family, was studying electrical engineering and was finishing college at Texas A&M. I liked Ted a lot. People said he was a genius. Jane and Dorothy found him quite wonderful, but he wouldn't be in San Antonio, Mama said, because he had a job that summer. Then she told me that Aunt Kate was living with Catherine Gunn, who was Aunt Ada Smith's daughter, and Aunt Ada, who really wasn't an aunt, was a favorite of us all and was quite wealthy.

The summer passed swiftly, and when the time came for me to join everyone in Corpus, it almost came as a surprise. I was more than ready to go, and when I finally saw our new house with its detached garage, where Albert and I would build my chemistry lab, my spirits really soared. On top of it all, Don and I would share a room with our own desk, our own chest of drawers, and our own closet; there would be no more sleeping porch, thus ending what I felt had been my period of isolation.

I arrived in Corpus on a Saturday, and the next Monday, I enrolled in the eighth grade at Wynne Seale Jr. High School. The school was within walking distance of our house on Clifford Street. It seemed strange that Mama went with me the first day. Before, she had always had to be at work and had never gone with me to school, but because she had read that parents should accompany new students, she made a point of going with me. We were both concerned about the orchestra class and whether Corpus schools system would provide a cello. Right off, the assistant principal handed Mama and me two schedules of recommended classes: one schedule was for the college-entrance diploma and the other was for the vocational diploma. As it was in Beaumont, the eighth grade was the first year of high school. Returning the vocational schedule, Mama told him I was planning to go to college and asked about orchestra class. He told us that Wynne Seale had no orchestra and added there was no Latin, only Spanish. Everything else was the same. So in place of orchestra, Mama signed me up for boys' glee so I could continue with music.

That was that. The idea of glee club sounded crazy to me. I could still hear Mrs. Shaddocks telling everyone that I "couldn't carry a tune in a basket." But it was a music class after all, and as it turned out, I would meet Luther Terry who became my best friend all through high school. Most of all, I looked forward to my class in general science and to be taking a *real* English class where we would read *real* literature, works by Shakespeare and Dickens, maybe even Walter Scott. But best of all, we would read Shakespeare's *Julius Caesar* and stories by Irving, Poe, and Dickens. *"Language arts" classes, where everything seemed so watered down, were behind me,* I thought.

The enrollment in all the classes at Wynne Seale was overflowing that fall, some classes having standing room only on the first day. Thirty-five of us were so crammed into algebra class that a few had to sit in the windows. When I got to the class, all seats near the front were taken, so I had to find a place in the very back. We in the back were new kids in town; those up front were native sons and daughters who already knew Miss Liggon. I could have taken a lower level math, and probably should have, but because I planned to go to college and major in science, I had to take four years of "real" math if I wanted a college-entrance diploma.

Most of the kids at Wynne Seale enrolled in general science, unlike Dick Dowling that had only one laboratory class with benches; Wynne Seale, on the other hand had three modern well-equipped classroom science labs with sinks, gas jets, and hoods. From the beginning, general science was my favorite class. Mr. Griffin, who was witty and always interesting, became my favorite teacher that first semester. His class was relaxed and full of activity. During the lab sessions, that we usually had twice a week, Mr. Griffin passed through the room, making sure we were focusing on the experiment, and allowed us to discuss the experiment with one another. I did so well on all my lab reports that fall that he moved me into Mr. Humphrey's class that was for the brighter students, like my new friend Luther Terry. It was the first time I could recall being advanced or promoted to the top group.

However, one thing did not change when we moved to Corpus: my poor performance in math. I never caught on in Miss Liggon's algebra 1a, barely making a C in the first quarter, making a D in all but the last quarter when I made an F, which meant I would have to repeat the semester, making me ineligible for graduation. I did well enough when I repeated it in the spring term, earning a B-, which was high indeed for me. One compensation, for me, that offset my sad performance in algebra was Mr. Humphrey's surprise when he learned that I had not passed algebra 1a but was earning an "A" in his science class. He said that my work in his class was going so well that he assumed I was also a good math student. While it did not remove the stigma of not graduating with my class in the spring, his surprise at my not having passed algebra made me feel better about myself.

My greatest disappointment at Wynne Seale was Miss Burrus' English class. Ever since I had first heard Jane and Dorothy talking about Shakespeare's *Julius Caesar*, I had looked forward to taking freshman English. When Dorothy then Jane would recite Antony's famous funeral oration, I was compelled to memorize it too. I went on to memorize speeches by Cassius and Casca and, finally, Brutus' speech after the death of Caesar. It was either Dorothy or

Jane who told me that Brutus made a far better speech than Antony's famous funeral speech, and I felt the line, "Not that I lov'd Caesar less, but that I lov'd Rome the more," just made more sense than Anthony's.

I had looked forward to meeting the class all that first day, and now, when I walked into the bright corner room and found a place at one of the large tables I felt I was ready. Each table had six places, two chairs on either side and one at each end. I took one of the places on the side facing the teacher's desk. Sitting opposite me was Bobby Curry, who lived across from us on Clifford Street. He said hello and asked how my classes were going. Next to him was a quiet, short, redheaded boy not much taller than I.

When I asked if they knew the teacher, Bobby said, "You've seen her. She's tall and skinny. Her name's Miss Burrus." Then added, "Don't worry, she's real easy. I had her last year."

So far, I had only one teacher I thought would be hard, Miss Liggon in algebra, though, actually, I knew it was not her; it was the subject. Just at the ringing of the bell, Ms. Burrus came in, stood before her desk, and announced in a dry sarcastic tone that, for some reason, the class was overfilled, that someone would have to go next door and drag in a couple of tablet arm desks, and after class, they would have to take them back. She seemed tired and out of sorts even before the class began. Then she called the roll and told any new student who had never been in her class to raise his or her hand when she called the names. When she got to Joe Gilliland, she pronounced it "Gilland" as people often did.

I raised my hand as she had asked and corrected her, emphasizing the second *i*. "It's Gill-i-land, Ms. Burrus," I said. It was my first mistake.

"What? What did you say?" she shouted.

"I said my name's pronounced Gill-i-land," I repeated.

"Oh! All right, Joe *Gill-i-land*," she said sarcastically, exaggerating each syllable, making the class laugh. She obviously intended to have fun embarrassing me, getting even for my correcting her.

Thinking only those at my table could hear, I mumbled, "What's funny about that?"

"What did you say, *little* boy?" she asked, moving toward the table where we were.

The others at the table were looking at me strangely, all except Bobby Curry who was shaking his head as if to warn me. He knew how she hated for anyone to talk back to her or to say anything. When she reached our table, staring down at me, she repeated, "What did you say, *little boy*?" emphasizing the last part.

I said, "I didn't see anything to laugh at."

"Don't ever talk back or speak unless you're spoken to in my class, Joe *Gill-i-land*."

They snickered again. The redhead smiled, more of a smirk than a smile. *Why?* I wondered. He didn't know me, and I didn't know him. What satisfaction was there in seeing me humiliated the first day, I wondered.

She announced some of the things we would be doing, such as dictionary assignments, reading short stories, giving oral book reports, reading *Julius Caesar*, and a "major project," which she would announce later. When the bell rang, I resisted jumping to my feet, trying to avoid any further confrontation.

The next day, I arrived just after Bobby and Peggy Ruth Howard, one of the girls who had sat at the table the day before, a pretty dark-haired girl, made even more attractive by the fact that she wasn't much taller than I. She had spoken to me after class, commiserating for Miss Burrus' sarcasm. She was sitting where Bobby had been sitting, and Bobby had my chair the first day, so I sat where the redheaded guy, Don Vaughn, had been. Ms. Burrus made a point the first day that she would *not* assign places until the new tables had been moved into the room. Just before the bell rang, I felt a book strike me lightly on the head and heard someone say I was in his place. Without looking up, I said that we had no assigned seats and told him to find another place.

"You're in my seat!" he said again, and this time the book struck harder.

I turned and saw the redhead. "Go find your own." I said. "We don't have assigned seats," I said about as loudly as he had.

Peggy Ruth and Bobby agreed that there were no assigned seats, but just then, Ms. Burrus said, "Joe Gill-i-land, give him his seat."

"You said there weren't any—"

I hadn't finished when she said, "Give . . . him . . . his . . . seat! And don't you talk back to me! Go sit in the window with your books. Maybe you'll fall out into the mud where you belong."

I was stunned. Peggy Ruth and Bobby Curry seemed as surprised as I, but redheaded Vaughn just smirked.

How did she know about me? I wondered. How had my reputation preceded me? I'd only been there two days. Had someone in Beaumont written a letter and told all about my being a bigmouth? I took my books and sat on the wide window ledge as she ordered and looked down into the hedges checking for mud. It was dry. A cool breeze made the window seat quite comfortable, though difficult for writing. For most of the period, we did exercises, correcting the sentences she had written on the board, followed by some grammar drill.

When the bell rang, I waited, dangling my legs over the windowsill into the room. Then I had an inspiration and turned quickly, leaping to the ground, holding my books close.

A voice shouted, "What do you think you're doing?"

I turned, shouted back, "Jumping down into the mud where I belong!"

The roar of laughter coming from the room told me I had made the right decision. Dashing off across the wide lawn toward our house, I felt triumphant. I looked back once. There stood the tall, spare figure of Ms. Burrus, staring after me.

It was like that all year. I did well in the writing and grammar exercises but was always graded down for conduct, mostly for talking when I should've held my peace, for answering without raising my hand, for getting laughs for smart-ass quips. It was Dowling all over again. The only difference between my behavior in her class and Miss House's Spanish was that Dorothy House often found my remarks amusing and never said I was rude, but then I learned early that she had a sense of humor. She was much younger, not yet jaded, and she was a real beauty; she did, several times, put me out in the hall for laughing too loudly and, once, made me scrunch down into the well of her desk so I would *not* to miss conjugation exercises. Later, Weller, a tall guy who liked to make me laugh, and some others, even asked me to make them laugh and get into trouble, saying they'd die for the chance to be that close to her knees. When a few days later, at Weller's suggestion, I moved to take my place below the desk, Dorothy House took me by the ear and, laughing all the way, led me to my seat. Burrus was different. She only laughed to ridicule, and that inspired me to more talking and "rude behavior."

Dorothy House wasn't just good-looking; she was beautiful. They said she that she was the daughter of that same Colonel House who was an aide to President Wilson and that she had been a "Blue Bonnet Belle" or a "Longhorn Sweetheart" at the University of Texas. Reading *Julius Caesar* turned into a great disappointment. First off, I had read it already, not once but twice, and was eager to hear the teacher's explanations the way Jane and Dorothy said their English teacher had don. The play still held many questions for me. Also, I had read about or heard how Orson Welles had produced the play as a modern drama about dictators, and since 1939 was the first year of the war, I wanted to talk about Caesar as an example of a dictator. But Miss Burrus had no class discussions and gave no explanations. We took turns reading aloud, each one taking so many lines until we reached Octavius' final line: "To part the glories of this happy day."

For me, there had been no glories, no happy day. In the final ten minutes of each class, we had dictionary exercises consisting of lists of words that we would look up and write down in our notebooks. That was all we did in the way of "studying Shakespeare." We discussed neither key passages nor speeches nor talked about the background history, the poetry, or the characters or even why the conspirators assassinated Caesar or any mention that Caesar could be compared to Mussolini or Hitler.

Just weeks before school started, Hitler had marched through Poland and started the Second World War. In our class was a girl from England, Jean Sommes, whom her parents had sent to stay with relatives in Corpus when the war started. Newsreels, magazines, especially *Life* and *Reader's Digest*, were filled with stories of dictatorships. And of course, Hitler stories had occupied us for years, but Miss Burrus never mentioned the parallels between Il Duce and Caesar, never even suggested that Brutus was a tragic defender of the Roman republic. Jane and I had listened to a discussion about *Julius Caesar* on the radio program *Invitation to Learning*. When I asked Miss Burrus if it were true that Shakespeare's play was about dictators, she replied, "Of course not. The play is about Roman history. It's a history play."

It was never clear to several others and me; if the play were a tragedy, why was the title *Julius Caesar*, who died so early in the play? Why wasn't it named after Brutus, who was actually a tragic figure? But Ms. Burrus ignored the question. Instead of talking about the ideas in the play or the play's great poetry, each of us read aloud at our desk followed by another and another until the act was finished or the bell rang. I don't recall the word tragedy being mentioned, except when she read the title the first day. I asked Bobby and Peggy Ruth to ask Ms. Burrus, why the play was called *Julius Caesar*, but they didn't want to. I had asked Bubba Roddy, the smartest guy in the room, to ask, but he shook his head. He wondered too.

When we came to the murder of Caesar and the scene where Brutus offers Antony a place at the capital to speak of Caesar, I wanted Ms. Burrus to talk about the differences between Antony's and Brutus' speeches. I had read the Brutus speech over and over, and I said it seemed really honorable to me. I had heard some men on the radio talk about the "rational" speech by Brutus, and I asked her to explain why everyone thought Antony's speech, which I said was dishonest, was so much better. True, most of the class thought I was strange for interrupting the smooth but boring method she had established. But all she said in reply was that "everyone" thought Antony's was a much better speech and let it go at that. I wasn't convinced but said no more.

For two days, we listened while everyone recited Antony's speech from memory. Several made brave attempts to "perform" the speech, but she never seemed to care how fast or how expressionless they spoke the lines. When it came time for me to recite, I began by reciting Brutus's prose explanation of what they had done and why and followed it with a performance of Antony's oration, emphasizing each of his ironies. She did not stop me or say anything and rarely even looked in my direction. I had half expected her to interrupt me and tell me to speak only Antony's lines, but it was as if I had recited only the speech of Antony. I concluded she had heard no one and that no one had heard anyone recite. But for me, it was a triumph, while her silence was her triumph.

That spring, while browsing the shelves in the school library, I ran across the novel Sinclair Lewis' novel *Arrowsmith*, a title I had seen or heard about somewhere. The title intrigued me. When I opened it and read on the title page that Paul de Kruif had assisted Lewis in writing the novel, I immediately decided to check it out. I *knew* de Kruif! From the opening paragraphs, I could tell it was not like any novel was meant for grown-up readers. A few words here and there stumped me, but it wasn't difficult, and as soon as I got home, I began reading and became totally engrossed in the story of a young man on his way to becoming a doctor. In fact, it was quite easy to read; I found the language and the sentences not nearly as literary as the stories I had read by Kipling. The scenes of medical school transported me in a world I ached to join, and later, when young Dr. Martin Arrowsmith goes to work as a researcher at the institute and discovers the "bacteriophage phenomenon," I pictured myself bent over a microscope, gazing at microorganisms. De Kruif's *Microbe Hunters* had prepared me. *Arrowsmith*: the title itself sounded magical. When I looked up Lewis in the *World Book* and read that he had won the Nobel Prize for literature, the first American to do so, I told myself it was because of *Arrowsmith*, probably his finest book. The romance between the young Arrowsmith and the girl who becomes his wife I found more affecting than any love story I had seen at the movies.

Neglecting my other homework, I read it straight through, hardly putting it down. Never had I become so absorbed by a book, not even *Lost Horizon* or Cronin's *The Citadel* had occupied me so. I was so immersed in it that I decided to use it as my project for English class and was sure. Burrus would approve my selection, but she did not on grounds it was not appropriate; it was too adult.

If Miss Burrus' class was a disappointment, Mr. Humphrey's science class was everything I had hoped for and more. His class was free and open to discussion so long as we dealt in observation and "empirical" evidence. He disallowed any argument that began with "they say that . . ." And he insisted that any opinion we held had to have evidence to support it. This got him into trouble with some parents, especially when we began studying astronomy. I liked Humphrey, liked the way he called the boys and girls by their last names and even the way he ignored my offhand remarks in class, the remarks that sent Burrus up the wall and made poor Dorothy House so distraught that one day she left the class rather than shout back at me.

In spite of my failure in the first semester of algebra and the disappointment in English class, at the end of the school year, I felt I had made a great strides toward my goal. My summer plans were simple: First, I would improve my laboratory in the garage. Albert had excellent tools, proper saws and hammers, and boxes of nails of all sizes. He had helped me with the wide "lab bench" and deep shelves suspended on braces from the wall studs, but we agreed my shelves for reagents and glassware were inadequate. He approved my plans and oversaw the changes, but this time he was an adviser only. My *pièce de résistance* was the new water supply I made from a large five-gallon bottle he had brought me from the refinery's laboratory. I could now siphon the water I needed as I performed experiments, refilling the bottle with a garden hose by using a stepladder.

Second, I planned to perform all the experiments described in the old chemistry text I had bought at the used books stall at Six Points. And third, I would go swimming every day off the Cole Park pier. I was allowed to go to the park alone, allowed to dive off the long pier. But I rarely had to go alone; someone from a small circle of friends in the neighborhood was always available.

I got a job that summer as a "carhop" at the Alameda Pharmacy in Six Points, working from six until ten every evening, six days a week. That summer, with the job, I was able to expand my lab, buy more reagents and several beakers and flasks. Bob Gerdes and I sat on a bench outside the pharmacy and waited on customers who drove up in their cars, fetching everything from lime sodas and hamburgers to prescription drugs and prophylactics—the latter we were told to get from the pharmacist and never from his female assistant. That he would explain to us the functions of such items we thought was a high compliment so we took his advice with great seriousness. At thirteen and fourteen, we had grown up. After three weeks, we got a raise to fifteen cents an hour, from $2.40 a week to $3.60, a sixty percent increase, not counting tips which almost always came to a dollar or a dollar and a half a shift. If we got really good, there was the promise of working behind the fountain at twenty cents an hour, and that meant we might get an earlier shift from noon to six, longer hours and more pay. I never got the chance to move up that summer, except as a substitute when one of the soda jerks took off for dinner; I was still too small to work behind the fountain, but there was always the next summer. The money was good, we thought. The twelve to thirteen dollars a week, including tips, were enough to replenish my chemicals and even buy better test tubes and glassware. More important, it gave me a feeling of independence, freedom from constantly being checked on. Because Albert did not believe in allowances or in paying Don and me to do the yard work, the carhop job was a necessity.

I had been happy when Mama and Albert were married because she would be at home more, but that had its drawbacks. In Beaumont, most of the day, I was on my own. Now, I felt I was under constant surveillance. The job liberated me and made me solvent at the same time. It gave me status. Always the youngest in my class, I never got over the feeling I was somehow inferior to the others, but now I had a job and my own source of income. Bob Gerdes and I were the only ones actually working that summer. Don Vaughn, the redhead from English class, worked for his father's shoe repair shop, delivering shoes on his motorized bike, and T. M. Gannaway drove a delivery service in an old coupe for his father's laundry, one of several enterprises Mr. Gannaway owned. Only fifteen, TM somehow was given a special permit to drive. The condition I believe was that he could carry no passengers, only the bundles of laundry. But these summers, our "Tom Sawyer" summers, he managed to get around the restrictions laid down by civic and family law, and almost every afternoon, before I went to work, he would stop by the house and pick me up to accompany him on his deliveries, and then we would speed across the bascule bridge to North Beach and go for a quick swim from the only decent beach on the bay. He always carried his bathing trunks in the car and would change quickly in the car. North Beach was safe territory, far from the neighborhood around Six Points where a friend of the family would more likely see us and report us. These illicit trips to the beach, where we did nothing more than swim out to the buoy and back, were great adventures. When my mother found out that TM was driving without a full license, that we were sneaking off to *North Beach*, she threatened to tell TM's mom. After that, I agreed to meet him a block away from our house.

Senior high school was a complete change from the eight years that had just gone before. I was still one of the smaller boys in my class but not the smallest. Corpus Christi, its *boomtown* population hovering at a hundred thousand, had only one public senior high, though the city could have easily supported two, perhaps three. In the large high school, I was only one of many and practically anonymous. I still had only a few friends, the small knot I had met at Wynne Seale, and still no really close friends, but they would come. There was, of course, the science clique: Luther, Harvey, and me. They were strong students and interested in science and didn't seem to care that I had not graduated with them. I already knew them better than anyone I had known in Beaumont, but they were natives of Corpus and had grown up with a strong circle of old friends, so in a sense, I was still an outsider, though I would learn from Luther that it was not important, not at all like Beaumont with its "old family" mentality. My neighbors, Harold and Carroll Nelson, a year older, went to the Jesuit school, and their closest friends were all students at the Catholic College Academy. At first, I had mixed feelings about moving from junior high school to the large and crowded high school, but that would all change in the second term after Christmas. High school would be my liberation.

It wasn't announced, but the high school in those days used a system of ranking, placing students in fast, medium, or slow sections, depending on the recommendations of their teachers. Having failed algebra, I believe I was tracked into the slow biology class and into Ms. Cobb's English class and, understandably, in algebra 1b. Everyone in the class, having failed either 1a or 1b, felt himself or herself to be a loser. It was a struggle, and right up to the end of the first semester, I felt I wasn't going to make it. Mr. Perkins, who was the worst teacher I had in eleven years of school, had assumed we were losers and had, therefore, not bothered to teach. Assuming we were never going to take algebra 2, he let us float. This was no act of kindness, only an act of conscious neglect built on laziness or his own refusal to accept the challenge every good teacher accepts. Only in the last two weeks did he cram some algebra into us so our scores on the uniform final exam would not suggest his failure (or refusal?). I figured he must have experienced a moment of charity in giving me a passing grade, albeit the lowest passing grade he could give. By all rights, I should not have been passed on to algebra 2a, nor should have anyone else in his class. Though he often regaled us with stories of his days in graduate school, telling us he had a master's degree in math, we learned that it was not in math at all but in some spurious major. I honestly believed he was aware of his shortcomings. So many of us had failed so many of the tests that semester that he began holding special tutoring sessions so we could pass the state exam for all algebra 1b students. That year, I did all of my homework assignments but never got them back. Jane helped me from time to time, always explaining the problems more clearly than either Mr. Perkins or Ms. Liggon had, and in the end, it was her tutoring that got me through 1b.

In my English class that year, I had been placed in a class with low achievers, probably because of Miss Burrus' recommendation and my having failed algebra. In retrospect, it was probably a good thing. No one labeled these sections or identified them as fast or slow, but all you had to do was listen and watch and see that most of your classmates were not getting anything or were not interested in getting anything. I didn't realize it at first, but when I looked around Miss Cobb's and failed to recognize anyone from any of my previous classes and then found myself in biology, sharing a lab table with two of the most notorious losers in school, I realized what my failing algebra 1a had done. This was not a class of college prep students; I had been, without knowing it, placed in a class of pupils tracked for vocational classes. It wasn't the stigma so much as having to work with people who neither understood nor cared to understand anything about the subject they were studying.

I liked my biology teacher, Mr. Shannon; he was a good teacher and could explain anything to anyone, but he was simply not demanding enough. Knowing he had students who would not likely ever take a higher science, he gave the class only what he believed them, believed us, to be capable of. Once I asked, when no one else was listening, why we didn't do as many dissections as Mr. Babb's class was doing. I had made perfect scores on all the tests he gave and was on the way to making an A in the class. He smiled and said if I wanted to do those things, I could go ahead and do them, that he would grade them for me, and since it was the last period of the day, he would let me stay and finish a dissection. I did as he suggested, and he did as he agreed. Near the end of the winter term one day, he asked me what I was doing in the slower class. I took it as recognition that I was doing good work, but I told him I didn't know unless failing algebra 1a had brought my average down. He told me he would see that I got transferred into Mr. Babb's section after we finished the first term. Tracking students, except for high honors or advanced placement, goes counter to conventional educational policy today, and many parents today would probably sue the school system that did so, but it has its virtues; however, doing so and not informing the student or his parents was and is wrong.

Transferring from one section of a class to another wasn't easy. The schedules were fixed, and any change upset the system or changed the balance in the classes; it meant that someone was getting special treatment, which was taboo unless you were the child of an important person. Mr. Shannon had to go to some trouble to ensure I was transferred out of his section and into Babb's. His resigning at the end of the term to take a job with the post office because of better pay freed him from possible repercussions, and so he went out on a limb and got me transferred. When I found out my transfer was approved, I asked my adviser about another English class as well, but she simply said there was no reason; I was doing "well enough" with Ms. Cobb. When I tried to explain that we weren't doing anything in the class, she said since I was making a B she saw no reason for a change. I tried telling her making a B didn't mean anything; Cobb gave everybody in the class B, except two really slow students who couldn't read at all and they were getting Cs. I tried to tell her how Miss Cobb had announced the first day of class that she disliked teaching English unless it was business English, that Shakespeare and Dickens and the other writers were just a waste of our time and would never help anyone get a job, but she ignored me and said it would mean readjusting my entire schedule. I could hardly believe my ears.

I had no run-ins with La Cobb, as we called her, since she sat at her desk quietly grading papers from her business classes while we read the stories in our book aloud or to ourselves. As in Ms. Burrus' class, no one raised a question or ever talked about a story, but in Cobb's class, it was different, no one wanted to. Every week, we had a true-false test over whatever stories we were reading. That was the way we got through a shortened version of *A Tale of Two Cities*.

Once, when I asked if we were going to talk about a passage we'd just read, she asked, "What is there to talk about?" The expressions on the faces of my classmates told me I should shut up, so I did. If we weren't reading, we were doing exercises in correcting faulty grammar she had mimeographed, but I don't ever recall her explaining the correct grammatical forms. She did mark our papers and return them, which is more than what Perkins did in algebra.

In Mr. Babb's biology, I was once again paired with T. M. Gannaway. When I looked around and saw Bob Wood, Jean Brock, Peggy Gilliam, and a host of friends I had made at Wynne Seale, people like Luther Terry and Harvey Dunn, I knew, for once, I had done something right. Babb was a taskmaster; I had no need to ask him if I could do extra work. To my great pride, I made mostly As in his class. But it wasn't the grades I made in the class that made it better; it was the way he made us work, made us talk and ask and answer questions. The class was never silent, especially during the lab sessions, but there was a sense of order to the noise.

The most heartening thing that spring occurred in my algebra 2a class. I had not learned anything from Perkins, except to despise and fear math more than ever. At the end of the term, when he was passing out the report cards, he handed me mine, and there, before everyone, he said out loud so everyone could hear that he passed me because he was sure I would never go to college. I was stunned and hurt and, for a brief moment, was deeply ashamed that everyone had heard his remark, but when I looked up and saw the faces of those who had heard him, they were as stunned as I was. He had written on my card a D with four minuses after it. Since minuses were not recorded on our permanent record, I told myself to ignore it. I knew I was poor in math but also knew I had not done any worse than most of the others.

When I signed up for my spring classes during the registration period before Christmas, I was afraid Perkins would be teaching algebra again, but the counselor, Dr. Love, told me we would have a new teacher, Mrs. Burns, the young wife of an assistant coach and physical education teacher. I had mentioned, while he looked over my schedule, that if Perkins was teaching it, I would prefer not to sign up for it but would take it in summer school. I felt he understood when he told me not to worry and explained about the new Mrs. Burns. It was a small class with a few survivors of 1b and three or four I'd never seen. We were the school dummies in math, but I made up my mind that this time I was going to learn algebra; Mr. Shannon had shown me that I was not stupid, and I would prove to Mrs. Burns I could learn algebra. She apparently never thought otherwise. We could tell she was no Perkins from the minute she walked into class and began talking to each one of us. Since she was the wife of the coach and a brand new college graduate, at first, we expected her to be an athletic type. But when she began by asking each of us what else we were taking and what we wanted to do after high school, it was obvious that we were all college prep.

From the first day of class, there was a difference; she not only explained the problems and answered every question, often asking if anyone in the class wished to answer, but she also made sure each of us understood. When we would be working at our desks, she passed around the room, stopping to see if we were making progress, often drawing up a chair and sitting beside us to see how we were working. If we made an error, she would stop and ask why we had done it and then would talk us through the steps, or she would turn to a page in the textbook that explained the problem. She would ask us to read it and repeat it. I never felt threatened or belittled in anyway. If several of us were making the same mistake, she would move us together and have us work it out together. I never had the feeling of isolation I had had before, and I'd never had a math teacher who could always find a way to explain things. That she would actually teach us and that we would enjoy her class was the last thing anyone had expected. One day, she sat in the desk next to mine and asked me what classes I was interested in. I told her about Babb's biology class and that I hoped to go to medical school. I told her I had my own chemistry lab in my garage at home and was looking forward to taking Mr. Schultz's chemistry class. Then I told her what Mr. Perkins had said when he handed me my report card. At first, she didn't say anything, but then I could see she was angry. She suddenly stood and told us she had to leave the room, which was rare, and told us to get on with our work. When she came back, Ms. Heatley, the head of the math department, was with her, and the two walked to my desk.

"Tell Miss Heatley what you just told me, Joe," she said softly.

When I repeated Perkins's comment about my never going to college, she did not act as if I were making it up.

"What is your name?" she asked.

When I told her, she asked if I was Jane's brother. I said I was. Then I thought she was going to burst. All the time this was happening, the others in the class, heads down, were straining to hear what was transpiring, thinking I had done something wrong. After class, I told my friend John what had happened. He said nobody ever did anything about bad teachers like Perkins, but at the end of the school year, we learned that Perkins had resigned in the middle of term and had returned to the police force.

I couldn't remember a semester that had been so productive; I made not a single C, not even in Spanish. Inspired by Mr. Shannon's offer to grade my extra work, I made Miss Cobb's class more enjoyable by reading everything in the large text: *Prose and Poetry for Enjoyment*. That I began to do so well in all my classes was largely because of teachers like Mr. Shannon, Mrs. Burns, and Mr. Babb, who clearly enjoyed what they were doing and always took time to answer questions or sometimes just talk and listen. I had always liked school, but now it was more than just matter of liking. I no longer looked forward to the last bell of the last class of the day, and I actually hated it when school was out that spring. The friendships I had formed with just a handful of boys like Luther, Tot, Harvey, and Bob Gerdes meant more to me than any I had ever had.

Corpus Christi was a good place to grow up in the 1940s, a much better place to spend summer vacations than Beaumont had been. When school was out, there were far more things to do than in Beaumont. I could go swimming every day in the bay, just blocks from the house, and since it was free and I never had to ask Mama for money. I spent many hours at Cole Park, diving off the end of the long pier, and Luther invited me many times to go out in his little sailing dinghy, and several times, Tot Westervelt, Luther, and I took off across the bay in Tot's skiff powered by a little two-horse outboard motor.

I put off asking for my old job at the Alameda Pharmacy for as long as I could, even though they had gone up to fifteen cents an hour; there was a wave of prosperity hitting Corpus that summer, what with the construction of the naval air station. That meant more tips. Bill Reiss's brother, Pat, had a job with Brown and Root, the construction company building the air station, and anyone over sixteen or seventeen who wanted a job paying more than fifty cents an hour, some as much as a dollar an hour, could get it. War news filled the air, but no one thought we'd be getting into it anytime soon. Twice, there had been a "brownout" or a dimming of lights in town because of sightings of German submarines in the Gulf of Mexico, and they even said that if the sightings continued, we would have no more night football games. We half hoped there would be a sighting in our sector of the Gulf. Once, a flight of twenty twin-engine Beechcraft planes passed low over the Six Points area—I counted and identified them, something all the guys could do back then—and the story followed they had come to patrol the coast. But the truth was they were twin-engine navigation and bombardier trainers. But we were convinced the war had come to South Texas.

Just as I was about to relent and ask for my job, Kenneth Weller called and asked if I wanted to work for the city at a dollar a night, keeping score for the softball league. A dollar a night! I took it, learned to keep proper score, and became rich making a minimum of five dollars a week. Then Bob Gerdes told me about a new pharmacy, Drugs Incorporated, that needed carhops and potential soda jerks, and I applied and found I could work afternoons on Tuesday, Thursdays, and Saturdays at fifteen cents an hour with a promise of moving inside and work at the counter at twenty cents. At the beginning of the summer, I was barely tall enough to "jerk" sodas, but it was my growth summer, and by the end of the season, I'd grown tall enough to wait at the counter, so the head counter-man let me work an hour every afternoon, mixing sodas and scooping ice cream.

Early one afternoon that summer as I was coming out of the Alameda Pharmacy I met one of the most unusual boys I'd ever known, Henry Owens. I had bought a small vial of phenolphthalein solution for my lab, and overhearing me order it, assumed that I had a chemistry lab at home. Until I met Henry, the only person I knew who fooled around with chemistry was Harvey Dunne, but he did not have a permanent lab space like I did. Right off Henry asked me if I was interested in chemistry and then what was I planning to do with the phenolphthalein. I told him yes and explained how I used it to do tricks, changing clear water to red and back again. It was an acid and base indicator, I explained. He said he knew all about that. Pulling two vials from his pants pocket, asked if I would like to see some dyes he had synthesized in his lab. One was a deep violet and the other a dark blue.

"Gentian violet and methyl blue," he said, adding, "I synthesized these myself in my lab."

"Wow! You must be pretty far into organic," I told him. "I've just started reading organic, but haven't done anything yet."

We introduced ourselves and walked the half block to my lab where I proudly displayed my shelves of chemicals and the sturdy lab table that Albert and I had built into one wall of the garage. I showed him the five-gallon water jug with a siphon attached that I used for "running water." He told me his garage lab was cramped into a smaller space but had running water and even a gas jet so he could use a Bunsen burner. He described how he was able to make aniline dyes and even gun cotton. I'd never met anyone like Henry. He was smaller than I was and talked more because he had something to say. He mentioned how glad he was he stopped me, that he never had anyone to talk to about chemistry or science. I told him about my friend Luther Terry and said that Luther would talk science all day if he had a chance but that he wasn't as interested in chemistry as I was; electricity and radio were his fields, I said. Whatever he lacked in size—he was even skinnier than I was—he made up for in enthusiasm. After he looked over my lab, he insisted I follow him to his house and see his lab, telling me he had a jar of pure sodium and a piece of phosphorous. I was astounded; pure sodium had to be kept in kerosene because it oxidized explosively when it came in contact with water. And phosphorus was even more dangerous since it combusted spontaneously in air. He smiled the smile of triumphant satisfaction. Henry may have loved science with passion, but he was also about the most naturally theatrical boy I had ever met.

The next day we met at my lab and I took him by to meet Luther who was as amazed as I when he met Henry. Luther's mother invited us in and supplied us with Cokes and cookies while we talked and talked about science up in Luther's fine room filled with electrical paraphernalia and stacks of classical records. Henry was asking most of the questions and providing most of the answers. I never knew anyone with such a range of interest in science, not just chemistry but also physics, electricity, botany, geology—everything.

The next day was my afternoon off at Drugs, Inc. Henry, Luther, and I conceived the idea of forming a science club at the high school, one that would find and draw in other "men" like us. Luther and I ticked off the names of people who would probably join. To start with Luther and I told Henry about our cohorts in science who had gassed the conservatory with hydrogen sulfide and said knew there were others. Henry mentioned Bill Reiss who had read a lot about science and whom I had met through a neighbor, Carroll Nelson. They had attended the Catholic College Academy together.

"I didn't know Reiss was interested in science," I said.

Henry assured me he was. He too lived within a three-block radius. Henry and Bill were a school year behind Luther, Tot, Harvey, and me, "but we're moving up fast," Henry said with a smile.

I said I was leery of high school clubs. There were always people who joined clubs, I explained, just to have their names on the rolls, I said. "They're always taking over anything they join," I said and added I'd never been a joiner, partly for that very reason.

"None of us is a joiner, we just get together and talk," Luther came back and explained that we were satisfied with a close-knit group of friends. "Perhaps we could have entrance requirements that would weed out those who aren't really interested in science like we are," he suggested.

It had begun. Somebody suggested we have an entrance test over general science and a test in a special area like chemistry, physics, botany, and physiology—I'd been reading *Gray's Anatomy* and a used physiology text I'd bought at the Six Points bookstore. We agreed each of us would be responsible for a couple of tests: Luther for physics and electricity, Henry for geology and chemistry, and I for biology and part of Henry's chemistry. All three would contribute to the general exam.

When we met next, Luther offered us a name for the club: the Texas Order of Science or TOS for short. At one point, we thought we'd call it Tau Omega Sigma to give it a cachet no other school club or society had. But the high school had a strict policy against Greek fraternities or sororities, so we backed off. We had even designed pins and keys to elevate the club. But all this passed in the early days when we settled on the idea of the least organization, the better—no president or vice president, only a secretary-treasurer to keep the twenty-five cent dues at every meeting and the *W. H. Curtin* catalog, the large bound volume of scientific and technical equipment sold out of a company in Houston, a wish-book-to-end-all-wish-books.

At our second meeting we decided that passing the entrance exam was not enough; initiates would have to present a lecture/demonstration to the assembled membership who would vote by secret ballot as to whether it was acceptable or not. We also decided that "passing" he lecture/demonstration wasn't as crucial as simply having one, anything. Our first initiate was Harvey who passed the chemistry test in a breeze, though neither Harvey nor any of us had yet taken high school chemistry. He surprised us by "qualifying" in geology by giving a lecture on seismology.

By the time school started, we added two more, Tot Westervelt and David Fraser and, soon after, Bill Reiss, making nine of us. Every fortnight, we met in the home of one of the members who also acted as chairman of the business meeting and presented a lecture on a topic of his interest. The membership was never large and consisted of only males; no girls we knew of were interested in science, though had there been, they would have been welcome. In 1941 and 1942, it was still unseemly for girls to flaunt brains, particularly in such male-dominated fields of study as ours. The truth was that until the fall of 1941, none of the membership had gone so far as to go out on a date with a member of the opposite sex; we were a pretty nerdy group in today's parlance. But we didn't know it. Luther and Tot broke the bachelor barrier and were the first ones to go out. Harvey and I followed, not reluctantly, though with some fear and trepidation. The summer of 1941 was the summer of growth for me, so by the end of the spring term of 1942, I had gained enough height to be able to ask a girl who was not taller than I. There were indeed now "newer worlds to conquer."

Chapter 3

Triumphs

When the spring semester of 1941 ended, I knew that 1941–1942 was going to be the best school year ever. Simply the thought that I'd be taking chemistry from Benjamin Shultz made that clear. At CCHS, the word was that Benjamin Schultz—everyone called him "Uncle Benny"—was the greatest science teacher ever. Along with that, for the first time in memory, I was no longer afraid of math. Mrs. Barnes had seen to that. Incredibly, I had not only passed the first semester of algebra 2, but I had also actually made, emphasis on "made," a B. I'll never forget her telling us, "You *made* your grades. I don't *give* grades. I'm proud of each of you." Well, I never forgot those words, and all through my years as a teacher, I preached the same sermon, tried always never to "give" grades.

Almost everything I had hoped for was coming to pass. Each of us— Luther, Henry, and I—had been his own science teacher for most of his school life; each had found his own way in discovering his "field," and each was eager to share it all with anyone who would listen. None of the others who joined the Texas Order of Science later was ever as eager to share his "discoveries" or any piece of knowledge or understanding he might have come across while dickering in his lab or "radio shop." Now Luther, Henry, and I, motivated by the same desire to share with others, had put together a high school science club where we could do just that.

When the principal, Mr. Miller, approved of our club and Mr. Schultz agreed to be our sponsor, the word went out. Not even geometry could threaten my serenity. I was confident I could do whatever the redoubtable Miss Heatley required. The core of the Texas Order of Science—Luther, Harvey, Tot, and I—would be in her morning geometry class and in Mr. Schultz's afternoon chemistry class. The last two years of high school would be the happiest, most successful years of all my years before college. At the time I couldn't know what had brought about this protean change, but I was aware that something alchemical had occurred. Two things happened in the summer of 1941: First, the natural process of aging had finally taken me through a window of learning closed to me before—I had caught up, had joined a parade of peers. Second, I had the amazing good fortune to have teachers like Mr. Steakley in U.S. history, Mr. Schulze in chemistry, and Mary Hoyle Heatley in geometry. It was obvious: they found pleasure in the challenge of teaching. All three had reputations that spread beyond the school, even beyond Corpus Christi, and in a few years, two of them, Schultz and Heatley, would join the faculty at Del Mar College. Steakley resigned from teaching in 1942 to accept a position with the Office of War Information, in Washington DC.

It was a new "intellectual landscape." Though Jacques Barzun was referring to college or university when he wrote those words, the change that occurred in my landscape was real. I was always happier in school than at home, and when classes began, my junior year, I believe I was happier than I had ever been in my life. Along with my friends in science, I began to think seriously about where I would be going to college and what I would be studying. I knew I would major in chemistry and minor in biology and would enroll in the University of Texas in Austin, would forego junior college. We talked about it constantly.

Although age had much to do with my step forward, another factor played a significant part, although it was something I had nothing to do with: I grew several important inches that summer, outgrew all my clothes, so when I returned to class that fall, I was no longer the smallest boy. Indeed, I was taller than average and taller than all but one girl, the uncommonly good-looking Virginia Rankin. But the real change that year had nothing to do with age or inches; it was a handful of teachers who had begun to speak to us and approach us as though we were partners in learning. They could allude to ideas or events outside the subject we were discussing as if they assumed we knew what they were talking about. It was as if they were sharing ideas with us rather than "teaching" us. Steakley never talked down to the class, never acted like we were kids in high school. If we weren't sure what an allusion meant, someone might ask, and he would smile and ask, "Peggy, could you tell Carl what I'm talking about," or "Joe, I'm sure you can explain." If we couldn't, he'd say something like "I know that's hard but . . .," and then he'd explain. But there was no hint he thought the question out of line. I caught on almost immediately; they weren't speaking to us as if we were children anymore. Once in a while, Schultz would just remark, "Look it up," and we usually did. I found it fun to see how many allusions I could follow without having to "look it up."

While CCHS was not an earthly paradise of learning, not yet, I did believe, and many agreed, it was close. Mr. Steakley, for instance, in American history assigned readings in "real" books, not just the textbook for the class but books that might be read by anyone, by adults outside the walls of the classroom. He recommended magazine articles, pointed to editorials, and suggested titles of major sources. No more *Reader's Digest* pieces either. He'd say, "Why read a digest? Read the original and digest it for yourself." If he overheard someone remark about one of the suggested readings, he would ask her to speak up and report to the class what she thought of it. Twice, he asked me to "expand" on what I was saying. He was not "testing" us but seemed genuinely interested and made us feel as if our ideas had importance. Somehow he was able to direct whatever interests we had outside his class into a relevant path that led us always back to American history. He taught us to want to share what we had learned.

One thing stood out clearly in Steakley's class: he wasn't biased in favor of "top" students or those who talked a lot or raised questions. The range in his class was wide and noticeable. When a tall, skinny kid named Skrobarszyk from one of the outlying farms brought in a large model of an antebellum Southern plantation house resembling the movie version of Tara in *Gone With the Wind*, Steakley moved all his stuff to a small table in the corner and had it placed on his desk at the front of the room. The next day, he asked Skrobarszyk to tell us about how he made it and how the plantation house figured into the Southern way of life. "Skro" was probably the slowest guy in class, but for Steakley, he acted like it was no big deal and explained it all clearly.

After that first class, with Tara before us, I asked Mr. Steakley if someone shouldn't build a model of the "quarters," the ramshackle cabins where the slaves were forced to live. I remarked how the movie *Gone with the Wind* never showed the real living conditions of Mammy and the slaves. Agreeing, he asked me to bring him a sample cabin. When I got home that afternoon, I dug through my model airplane materials and found enough balsa "planks" to construct a small cabin, rubbing the sides with charcoal, etching shapes of old shingles, even making broken-down front stairs leading up to the small porch. I really got carried away, even checked the library for more information about Harriet Beecher Stowe and her novel *Uncle Tom's Cabin* that had become a play. At the bookstore in Six Points, I was able to get a large piece of poster board and fashioned a show bill for the play. At the bottom of the poster, I printed in what I thought was Victorian-style font: "By Harriet Beecher Stowe, 'The Little Lady Who Started the Civil War.'" Lincoln's famous comment was in our text. When Steakley saw it, he placed my creation behind and to one side of Skrobarszyk's Tara.

Miss Heatley was always connecting math with the world outside the classroom. I recall how she introduced geometry to us that first day, drawing a diagram of how geometric problems were "argued," using "geometric logic," as she called it.

"There's no difference between geometric proofs and the proofs you use in any other logical argument. Remember," she said, "geometry is a language of reasoning."

Perhaps not her exact words, but that was the gist. One day, when she was passing back our homework papers, she noticed I was reading Lewis's novel *Arrowsmith* and stopped, took the book from my desk, glanced over the page I was reading, then asked me if I liked Lewis's novels and why.

I told her I was rereading it and said *Arrowsmith* was the only book of his I had ever read, and I asked her if she had read it. She said she had but that she didn't like it nearly as much as she did *Main Street* or *Babbitt*. It was weird, I thought to myself, a geometry teacher talking about a novel.

"I hated the way he had the hero solved his problems in the end by getting drunk.," she said, "Arrowsmith, the man I mean. I thought, was a better man than that."

Recalling the episode from my first reading, I told her I hadn't thought of it like that but I'd would "look into it."

"You do that, Joe, look into it and let me know what you think," she said then moved on.

I'd never had a teacher speak to me like that. She spoke of the character Arrowsmith as though he were a real person, not a fictional character in a story. Also, the way she spoke to me was different, as if we were just two people talking about a book, not a teacher and a student. A math teacher, I thought, who reads novels and talks about them as if they were real, as thought they were important. The same kind of thing happened with Miss Cole when I took Texas history later in my senior year. She also stopped by my desk and asked what I thought about a novel I was reading: George Sessions Perry's *Hold Autumn in Your Hand*. I told her I liked it, especially since it was about the rural area in East Texas during the Depression. Then very seriously, she remarked how important it was because it was so truthful. Sadly, at CCHS, none of my English teachers even wanted to talk about anything but the dull assignments, not even the literature.

However, my English class that year was an improvement over the two previous years, though again it failed to live up to my expectations. Recalling how Dorothy, Jane, Cousin Ted, and I had acted out stories from Edgar Allen Poe, I had looked forward to reading stories like "The Pit and the Pendulum," "The Purloined Letter," and "The Cask of Amontillado," all three of which Ted had made us read that summer when he and Aunt Kate had visited us.

In Miss Kelly's class, we read one story, "The Pit and the Pendulum," took a short test on it, mostly true-false questions, but we barely discussed it. The real experience of literature was left to those who were interested enough to find an experience on their own. Jan Kelly—a really attractive, tall, handsomely built redheaded woman in her mid-forties—was probably the *nicest* teacher in the school, perhaps even the prettiest teacher I had all the time I was in CCHS; no one disliked her. She had the brightest copper red hair I had ever seen, and she always wore the brightest colors that highlighted her hair and her luminous complexion. I was sure she was aware of the boys' admiration, especially when she had a chance to lean forward and offer one of us a forbidden glance into the valley, but she was lazy beyond compare, which was probably explained why she was so well-liked.

But one day, before the bell rang for class to begin, I simply couldn't resist reading aloud to classmates around me—reluctant listeners, I must admit—a poem in our text by Elinor Wylie, the one about a child's drowning near a seaside village. I hadn't discovered it on my own, but I knew it was in the text, for Jane had recited the poem to me when she was using the same text in Miss Percy's class in Beaumont. This one had moved Jane obviously, and it moved me too. Its haunting meter and dark imagery suggested the rhythms of the sea and the slow, last heartbeats of a dying child. I read,

> *The sea creeps to pillage,*
> > *She leaps on her prey.*
> *A child of the village*
> > *Was murdered today.*

Wylie was a dramatic departure from those poets Miss Kelly assigned, like James Whitcomb Riley or John Greenleaf Whittier. Reading the poem aloud was fun. I wanted those around me to see or feel what Wylie was doing. But other than a few poems by Poe or Lindsay, "The Congo," and poems from Kipling's *Barracks Room Ballads*, I had seriously never had much to do with poetry. Jane had jerked me awake with Wylie's poem, neither explaining nor dwelling on the morbidity. By urging me to listen to the sounds and the beat, she had caught my attention. I recall her reading aloud pieces of Shelley from "Adonaïs": "Life like a dome of many colored glass stains the white radiance of eternity," lines that ring and sing and say more than words can ever completely encompass on the page. Most boys considered poetry girls' stuff, and only a few teachers were knowledgeable or brave enough to tackle the problems of poetry's ambiguities, which finally were what I loved most about the poems.

Several around me in the class were listening silently to my reading the eerily morbid imagery when Jan Kelly walked in and listened with them. She let me continue and complimented my reading, and then, unaware that she was opening a door into dangerous territory, my territory, she asked me if I would like to read other poems aloud to the class. The last time anyone had handed me that opportunity was Miss Fife in the seventh grade, but unlike Miss Kelly, Fife had known what she was doing.

Always eager to show off, I said I would and asked her which poems I should read. I was nothing if not confident. She told me to choose three or four of my favorites while she was checking the roll.

"When I finish calling the roll, Joe, you read them and tell us why you like them," she said in that sweet tone of voice edged with an implied, *That'll teach you to show off.*

I had, the night before, for the first time, read Edna Millay's "Euclid Alone Has Looked on Beauty Bare" and had seen a connection between poetry and the geometric logic Miss Heatley had preached to us so carefully, so I read the sonnet aloud and explained what I thought Millay was writing about and how she was defining beauty as a form of pure geometry and vice versa. When I read Millay's sonnet for the first time the night before, the last lines from "Ode on a Grecian Urn" had come to mind. Beauty and truth and Euclidean harmony had come together for me, and I was amazed how a poet like Millay, clearly no mathematician, would make the connection, and I tried to explain it. My audience was attentive, if puzzled, and I realized their attention was as much an appreciation of Miss Kelley's releasing us once again from class work than from any desire to hear me jabber away. To me, it was ecstasy, pure enjoyment. Nothing like that would have ever occurred in Ms. Cobb's class.

The serious reading I had begun to do that fall, entirely unrelated to class, my "un-required reading," was another reason junior year was such a pleasure. This reading had nothing to do with Schultz or chemistry and was completely unplanned. When I learned that we would get extra credit for making oral book reports, I was elated. The books I loved to read had often come at the expense of my other school work, but now I could read a book of my own choosing and earn points, rather than lose points, and since the reports were oral, I would not have to agonize over writing them out. It worked for her as well since it meant she wouldn't have to grade or mark the papers, and too, our oral reports would take up class time that she would otherwise have had to prepare for.

Until that year, my "serious" reading had been a hodgepodge, a collection of trash and treasure, rich in stories about medicine and adventure, novels by men like A. J. Cronin and James Hilton stimulated by films like *The Citadel*, *Lost Horizon*, and *Good-bye, Mr. Chips*. In the years before high school, I had read the travel adventures of Richard Halliburton, *Royal Road to Romance*, *The Glorious Adventure*, and an illustrated edition of *Typee* that had caught my eye early. The author, I would later use as my dissertation topic. I recalled mostly its strange exoticism that more than lived up to the travel books of Halliburton.

I checked out *Arrowsmith* and read it again for my first report, and I was surprised how much I had missed the first time through (such as Martin Arrowsmith's "solving his problems with alcohol" when his wife died). It was still my favorite work of fiction and would continue to be until I read Scott Fitzgerald's short story, "Babylon Revisited," a few months later.

Miracle of miracles, I thought when I found "Babylon Revisited." There it was at home in a BOMC anthology. Reading Fitzgerald was like being overwhelmed by an avalanche, and within a period of a few weeks, I read two other stories in the same anthology that had a similar impact: Hemingway's "The Short Happy Life of Francis Macomber" and Faulkner's "That Evening Sun Go Down." Of those three writers, the only one I had heard of was Hemingway. I had heard people mention *A Farewell to Arms* and *For Whom the Bell Tolls* in connection with the World War and the Spanish Civil War, but I knew little about either author other than that he was famous. Faulkner was quite unknown to me. It was the title that caught my eye and rattled my imagination, that line from "St. Louis Blues." All three stories had an impact on me; unlike any stories I had read before, they were "real," not stories taught in school but stories about "real" people, none had a "happy ending." Indeed, all three were adult stories, I felt. They held my attention and made me want to read more, further proof, as I see it now, that a window of learning was opening for me. Each of the stories ended on a heavily ironic note, or one we often referred to as an "unhappy ending," an ending many would say was not satisfying. None of the stories ended with that surprise twist I had come to expect in short stories, especially in the highly popular stories of O. Henry, stories that had become too predictable to hold my interest. There was, I felt, nothing predictable in any of the three, yet in all three, the real irony was that the endings, though disappointing in a way, were totally consistent with everything that had gone before.

I had to tell someone about Fitzgerald, had to talk about the story, but there was no one to tell. Like Henry Owens, with his vials of dye, I had no one to talk to about my discoveries. Jane was too busy with her classes at Del Mar College, and none of the guys in TOS read fiction. I knew no one who read fiction, certainly no one who would want to talk about a short story in which "nothing happens." "Babylon Revisited" seemed to end back where it started with nothing resolved, which was proof that "nothing happens." In that short space of eighteen or twenty pages, I felt that Fitzgerald had delved deeply into his hero's character without actually telling us anything, but I had never been so moved by a story or felt such sympathy for a character, yet nowhere in the story did the author tell me what I should or should not be thinking. The extra credit report for Miss Kelly, I thought, would give me not only an opportunity to tell someone why it was such a great short story but it would give me the grade I needed.

I asked Miss Kelly if I could make a report on "Babylon Revisited" and the two other stories; she said no and suggested I report on one of the stories from our text that we had not read for class. She said she was not familiar with the story or with the author, and she said so in way that suggested she didn't consider either story or author "serious" enough for a report. She admitted she had read some of Hemingway's stories but regarded them as "inappropriate for high school students," and then she asked if my parents approved of my reading Hemingway. I sort of lied and said yes because I didn't want to say they neither knew nor cared what I read. I don't recall the stories I finally settled on. I doubted then, as I do now, that it would have made any difference what I reported on. She was very nice about it and gave me a B for the two reports, but in the end, I felt she was barely a notch up from Burrus or Cobb.

If literature was exciting, chemistry was my *raison d'être*. Of all the teachers in high school, the most respected was Mr. Schultz, Uncle Benny as we called him. As is often the case, he was also, along with Mary Hoyle Heatley, reputed to be the hardest teacher in school. An A or a B from Uncle Benny was always a cause for celebration, not because he gave them so rarely but because he made you work so hard to get one. While he set the highest standards, he taught us how to reach those standards. I assumed, when I first walked into his class, that I was going to do well. Probably, for the first time since Miss Connors's first grade class, I was confident I would succeed, possibly excel, and I did, but it was far from a breeze; I feared handing in a homework assignment or a lab report that was not as close to perfect as I could make it.

Even though Mr. Schultz was the sponsor of the science club and often met with us to discuss club projects, we never presumed, never crossed the line, and as long as we were in class, he never gave any of us special recognition. Only once in front of the class did he do so and it had nothing to do with TOS. It came the last day of the semester after the final exam.

He complimented me for a job well done, for making the highest score on the state chemistry exam. Every year, Mr. Schulze administered to one of his chemistry classes a state exam, more to test himself than to evaluate us; this final exam did that. I made 98, but only because I chose to answer an optional question on organic chemistry, a subject we had only touched on briefly in class. I substituted it for a question involving mathematics. He announced my grade to the class, adding I had answered the organic section that, he said, astonished him. After class, I thanked him for his remarks and told him that if it had been Henry Owens, he would have made 125, answering both the organic and the quantitative problems. Then I told him the math had frightened me, that Henry and I had been studying organic on our own for over a year. He agreed with me about Henry's probability of success but insisted I not apologize for skipping the quantitative section. He said only a very few had answered it correctly, Harvey and Luther being the only two who did.

In the summer of 1942, the war was not going well: everywhere in the Pacific, the Japanese were on the move. We knew there was a strong possibility some if not all of us would be a part of it before it was over. Although we were devoted to our science, most silently regretted we weren't a year or two older. Already, friends or brothers of friends were dropping out of school or college to join up. I was constantly torn between envy of their "great adventure" and relief that I was only fifteen.

Aside from the science club, my main sources of entertainment, even more than any time in the past, were La Retama Public Library and the swimming pier at Cole Park. That summer, I was reading *Gray's Anatomy*, physiological chemistry, and introductory texts in bacteriology, but more and more, I had begun to lean toward literature and historical works dealing with World War I. I long ago had graduated from the *Reader's Digest* to *Time* and devoured each month's *Popular Science* while nibbling through copies of *Scientific American* I found in the library. I had tried *Science*, the publication of the American Association for the Advancement of Science, but found most of the articles beyond me. I read stories by Stephen Crane as well as his *The Red Badge of Courage* and George Sessions Perry's *Hold Autumn in Your Hand*—a gritty, realistic, rural novel in the tradition of Steinbeck's *Grapes of Wrath*. Perry's novel had been a bestseller as well as an important critical success and was one of the novels that opened my eyes to the importance of fiction—first, Fitzgerald and Faulkner, now Perry. I also read some Steinbeck that summer for the first time, first a short story, "The Leader of the People," then *Tortilla Flat*, of which my mother roundly disapproved (without having read it) when she found me reading it one afternoon. One of the ladies who gave "readings," that is reviews of bestsellers and readings from the books, had told my mother and her ladies that she could not review *Grapes of Wrath* for them because reading it had made her feel that she needed a bath. I'd checked it out of the library and read it when no one was around, disappointed that it was far from dirty or even very *racy*, was almost religious in places. In fact, I mentioned that point to Mr. Shannon who was still my Sunday school teacher at the South Bluff Methodist Church, and he agreed that *Grapes of Wrath* was an important book and encouraged me to read more Steinbeck.

It was about then I realized that I had begun to lose touch with Mama; she rarely spoke to me about school, about my classes or teachers. When she saw me reading books, for pleasure and not for school, she realized, too, that we were losing touch with each other. Jane's and Dorothy's reading had been a puzzle to her, perhaps because they were girls, but my reading was different. I was a boy and was going to be to be a scientist, possibly a doctor; she must have wondered why I was reading novels by dirty authors.

As I said earlier, in Beaumont we had not had many books in the house, only a set of encyclopedias and a few books Jane, Dorothy, and I had received as presents. When we moved to Corpus Christi, however, two tall bookcases filled with books suddenly appeared from somewhere. In addition to the encyclopedias, the two tall bookcases were filled with recent editions of novels, biographies, anthologies, and histories—all from the Book of the Month Club, all belonging to Albert. While he was not an avid reader, he did hold that one should always be reading "something of value." He had attended Northwestern University, but the Depression had forced him to drop out before finishing his accounting degree. Admitting that he had read few of the books in the little library, he insisted that joining the BOMC was his way of making up for lost years in college. It didn't make sense at the time, but years later, he explained to me that while he was studying for his degree in business, he was working full time as a bookkeeper and was taking accounting courses that would help him in his job. He had to pass up the liberal arts classes required for the degree. One day his boss, the head accountant, told him he was missing valuable experiences by not taking a course in literature and advised him to read more literature, thus the books in the book cases..

Soon after we arrived in Corpus, Jane joined the BOMC and began adding more works to the library, collections of short stories, along with a marvelous anthology of modern drama with plays by G. B. Shaw, Maxwell Anderson, Eugene O'Neill, and Sidney Kingsley. Interestingly, she rarely ordered the month's selection, concentrating on the alternates or back selections. In effect,

I was following Albert's plan for getting a liberal education while Jane was laying a foundation for her college major.

In my senior year, I had the same high quality of instruction I had in my junior year. In English paticularly the class experience was a great improvement over everything that had gone before. In math, Vina Craddock replaced Miss Heatley. While her classroom style was not at all like Heatley's, she had the same high standards and taught with the same seriousness. She got to know each of us early in the term, knew our main interests, knew why we had chosen to take trig and what and where we intended to study after graduation. Surprisingly, I did as well as I had in geometry. If geometry had been like "beauty bared," trigonometry was magic revealed to my nonmathematical mind and seemed to transcend all the rules. While she urged us to learn the conventional "textbook" routes to the identities, she encouraged us to find our own routes to proofs, urging us to use anything we knew to find our own routes, even if ours took longer to balance it all out.

"Learning to think is what you're here for," she would say and then look at you with a stare. Vina Craddock rarely smiled, but she had a dry sense of humor and often dropped outrageous puns that I believed she used just to check if we were listening. I thought it was interesting how trigonometry and physics really identified us as seniors.

The idea of "finding your own way" went in the very face of what I once believed was a fundamental tenet of all mathematics, that there was only one way to balance an equation. Like geometry, trig was an exercise in thought. It was largely because of the support I had in TOS that I did as well as I did that year in physics. Every time I became stumped trying work through a problem in electricity or magnetism, I would rely on Luther to rescue me and re-teach me what Mr. Schultz had tried to teach in class. However, Mr. Schultz showed us, as Luther had tried to in TOS meetings, that physics was really the core of all science. Even chemistry, I learned, was ruled by fundamentals of physics. Later, in a freshman-level college physics class, I leaned heavily on what I had with Luther's tutoring in Schultz's class to get through.

I hoped I would be going to Austin after graduation but assumed that I would probably go to Del Mar College as Jane had. Tuition at Del Mar was less than either the university or A&M. It was almost nothing, and of course, the cost of living at home was nothing, I thought. After graduating from Del Mar, Jane worked over a year for the FCC in Kingsville, Texas, to get the money to finish her BA in Austin. The civil service job paid well enough for her to live away from home and to save enough for her tuition and room and board in Austin. But Albert urged her to continue working for the FCC or to get a job in Corpus. He said with the diploma from Del Mar, she would have no trouble getting a job as a secretary. But even though the oil and chemical industries were booming more than ever, salaries for young women in Corpus could not compete with the civil service salaries in Kingsville. Jane had no intention of being a secretary, but she told me nothing of her plans or what she would major in at the university.

In the spring of 1943, Jane enrolled at UT with plans to major in English. Mama's stories of Austin and the university campus fueled my determination more than ever. I spent half of one TOS meeting relating Mama's description of the buildings and the campus, enthralling even those heading to "aggie land." Against Mama's advice and the advice of counselors, I also chose the school in Austin, and before graduation that spring, I told the secretary in Mr. Miller's office to forward my transcripts to the UT registrar. I knew from the beginning that I would have to find work after graduation from high school and would have to work part time when I began classes wherever I enrolled. It was simply a given. The main argument for my staying on in Corpus Christi and enrolling at Del Mar was the savings in room and board, *I thought,* but then I learned I was expected to pay my "share" were I to remain at home. I was then even more determined to leave home as soon as possible. I was neither angry nor bitter, though I was ashamed and never told my friends, certainly not Luther or Harvey, that my parents were charging me for living at home. I knew they would not have understood, would have thought it weird because from all outward appearances we were as well-off as they, seeing that Albert drove a Buick and was able to maintain memberships in both the Oso Golf and Country Club and the more exclusive Corpus Christi Country Club. In addition, Mama and Albert enjoyed a circle of close, very well-to-do friends.

I was more encouraged when I heard Jane had found a typing job at the university and a second job answering the switch board in the large Scottish Rite Dormitory for women, the only dormitory not taken over by the navy for its V-12 and V-5 students. I studied the UT catalog eagerly that winter and spring and wrote the dean of men's office for lists of rooming and boarding houses. The rent for rooms was surprisingly so reasonable and so plentiful, even with all the men's dorms occupied by navy students, that I decided I could do it. I would have to go to work immediately on graduation and work all through the summer, saving my money.

One Saturday during my senior year, Albert took me to the AMSCO refinery for a visit to the lab and to meet the chemist, Bob Allison, who showed me the kinds of tests he routinely ran in the lab. When I told him I was hoping to major in chemistry as a premed student, he encouraged me to apply for lab jobs, saying that with my grades in chemistry and my interest in science, I would have no trouble. I mentioned to Albert Allison's suggestions, and he agreed it was a good plan. A few days later, he told me he had spoken to Allison and Mr. Manly, one of the owners, about a job for me and they had agreed. I had a job at AMSCO as Bob's assistant if I wanted it. It was the finest graduation gift anyone could have given me. The pay was magnificent, thirty dollars a week for a forty-hour week with time and a half for overtime and double time on Sundays—real adult wages in those days. Though AMSCO was not union, the pay was regular union level. It was a half again as much as my mother had been making at the Pure Oil Company when she remarried. With monthly college expenses roughly in the range of my weekly wages at the lab, I assumed there would be no problem financing at least three semesters in Austin before I was eighteen and eligible for the draft. It meant even more, were I able to get a really good job at the university.

A few weeks before graduation, I visited the lab again and spoke to Bobby Allison about the job. He took me into the stillman's room and introduced then set me to running distillations tests.

"You won't be mixing chemicals or doing experiments, just running tests. I hardly ever *do chemistry* like I did in college," he said and smiled then added "or like Albert says you do in your own lab at home."

All during my senior year, I had wondered how any year could have been better than my junior year. From the beginning, it was obvious I would have a good year, although the really good bits began in the spring of 1942 when I met a special person and discovered I really enjoyed the company of girls, rather one girl in particular. Eve was the daughter of Reverend Doctor Munds, rector of the Church of the Good Shepherd, and right away, I wished I could lop off Methodist from my Methodist Episcopal affiliation. Luther, an Episcopalian, arranged my first date, set it up but left it up to me to make a confirming telephone call. Three couples crammed into his parents' Buick quite literally, forcing Eve and me to become "close" friends from the start. But after a second date, our dating ended for the summer when she and her family took off for their summer cottage in Chautauqua, New York, spending the summer going to lectures, attending concerts, and sailing on the lake.

I'd honestly never met anyone like that—very pretty to look at, easy to talk to, and eager to listen and talk about *something*. After the movie triple date, I dropped by to see her several times, just to talk, and she always seemed glad to see me. I'd never thought I'd do such a thing. When I asked if she minded if I wrote a letter now and then while she was in Chautauqua, she said yes and gave me the address. It worked. We exchanged half a dozen letters, maybe more. It was another thing I'd never done. The letters weren't *that* special, just letters about what I was doing—swimming, sailing with Luther, going to summer school, reading—and her letters were about the same, except she wrote about the concerts, which she said she thought I'd be interested because Luther had told her I liked listening to classical recordings. At first, I was surprised that she would answer so soon or even at all. More important for me and what came out of it all was how much I enjoyed writing "about something." My letters got longer and longer.

When she returned, we became even better friends and had several dates, usually double dates because I still had no driver's license, though, twice, we were alone, and because the parsonage was on the edge of downtown, we walked to the movie theater and back. The way to town was through a scenic old neighborhood with well-kept lawns and large trees, a good place to walk with a girl I thought. Sadly, she had only a few months left in Corpus, her father having answered a call to preside over a congregation at church in Wilmington, Delaware, the family church of the Delaware DuPonts—yep, those DuPonts.

Although I had met girls whom I found interesting, attractive, and pleasant to be with as far back as Beaumont, I had not dated or even thought about taking anyone out. I was too small and always broke, but now I was taller than all the girls in our group and had pocket money from carrying golf bags on weekends. After Eve left, I continued to "see" others, friends of Eve, most of whom were a grade behind me. One of the girls, Cack, rather Caroline, had elder sisters dating navy men, usually officers or cadets. Fact was that most girls in Corpus Christi dated sailors, officers, or cadets, and that was always a problem for most of the guys I knew. One evening, while I was waiting for Cack, a young ensign was there, waiting for her sister. She had introduced us once and had told me that, according to her sister, he was quite intelligent, "almost brilliant," and a university graduate. While we waited and made the usual small talk, I asked where he had graduated and what he had taken as a major. He said he had graduated from Marquette University in Wisconsin with a BA in philosophy. Although I noticed he wasn't much interested in chatting with a high school boy, I forged ahead and asked why he'd chosen philosophy. He said philosophy was the easiest way to get a degree at Marquette then dropped the discussion, clearly uninterested in answering more questions.

I was shocked and thought, *How could anyone waste his time in such a way?* That an institution like Marquette would grant such degrees seemed odd indeed. Later, when we met Harvey and his date and were driving to the movie, I told Cack what I thought.

"Silly," she said, laughing, "Stan was studying to be a priest but joined the navy. He's really brilliant. Ray said that most pre-theologs majored in philosophy."

When I got home, I browsed Albert's bookcase, looking for a title I had passed over many times: *The Story of Philosophy* by Will Durant. I found it and pulled it down and scanned the table of contents, and the next day, I asked Albert if he had read it. He had never had the time, he said, but assured me it had been strongly recommended. Now I opened it and began reading, hoping I'd discover why anyone would choose to major in the subject. I'd doubted philosophy was as easy as he claimed it was and was convinced he had said it only to end the conversation. I sat there in our living room reading until Mama came in and asked what I was doing up so late, remarking that it was past eleven. I assured her I would be turning in shortly, that I wanted to finish the chapter. When she asked what I was reading that was so interesting, I told her. "Why are you reading that?" she asked. When I explained it was just a curiosity, she said good night and left. I took the book off to my room and never returned it to its place in the bookcase.

Durant's *The Story of Philosophy* made a big difference in my life, opened up a whole new world. Later, friends who were actually majoring in philosophy would scoff at Durant's book, comparing it to *Cliff Notes*, and would tell me I should read the primary sources. Because of Durant's introductory chapters, I read *The Apology* before the year was out and discovered that it was indeed a lot like reading a *story*. The only guy in TOS who read outside his "field" was Bill Reiss, who had also read "a little" philosophy.

The job at AMSCO lay like a bird nest on the ground, a marvelous unexpected gift arranged entirely by Albert. AMSCO was much smaller than the other refineries around Corpus and would have closed had it not been for the war, did in fact close and sell out within two years after the war ended.

My first morning on the job, Bobby gave me a tour of the refinery and its storage facilities, showing me how to grab samples of gasoline, gas oil, fuel oil, and sometimes crude from storage tanks, tank cars, and even occasionally an oceangoing tanker. Most of the crude that came into the refinery passed through the AMSCO pipelines. Although Allison claimed it would eventually become a dull routine, it was a giant leap from my earlier jobs: carhopping, score keeping, and clerking in a jewelry store. I had never driven through a giant tank farm with rows on rows of steel storage tanks shaped like giant pillboxes and holding from ten-thousand-barrel tanks to the giant hundred-thousand-barrel tanks.

As we climbed the long steel ladder of the first hundred-thousand-barrel tank, Allison began my instruction in safety procedures. First of all, he explained,

I should never wear shoes with nails exposed, should never smoke, and must never carry anything that might strike a spark. Because the tanks built such great pressure during the day, I must open the small hatch and stand back and avoid breathing any of the hot fumes before lowering the sample bottle.

"Never be in a hurry," he said and showed me how to secure the end of the heavy cord to make sure I didn't let it slip through my fingers and let it disappear into the tank, bottle and all.

After the second tank, I began grabbing the samples while Allison watched, and we trudged up and down a half dozen tanks then drove back to the lab and ran distillation tests on the entire collection. He was a good teacher, and I caught on so well that the next day, I collected all the samples and ran most of the tests alone.

By noon, we had run all our samples and had done corrosion and viscosity tests on a dirty batch of fuel oil samples collected the day before. He said it was too bad we didn't have a batch of crude to run, patting a large black drum-like object in one corner of the lab.

"This little still is just like the one out the door, only smaller," he said then added, "Everything you see here is about twenty years out of date, like everything else is at AMSCO, but it all works. But there *is* a war on, and they want every drop of aviation gas we produce, and our aviation is the best there is." I could see he wasn't bragging. "It's easier to control small batches."

We talked organic chemistry a little, mostly about octane numbers of the fuel we had been testing earlier, and he drew chains of hydrocarbons, illustrating the molecular structure of the product, a bit surprised I was already familiar with the fundamentals of saturated hydrocarbons.

I started at AMSCO the Monday after graduation, and after that first day, I grabbed all the samples alone then drove back to the lab and ran all the distillation tests. There was very little chemistry involved in anything I did. Anyone could have learned to do the job in the same time I learned it which was roughly a half hour or an hour at the most. Even though I realized this too would become routine and boring, I liked it and enjoyed the ambience, the sound of the roaring still, the maze of pipes and steel scaffolding; and most of all, I enjoyed having the responsibility of driving alone out to the tank farm in the old pickup and taking samples off the giant tanks. From the first day, when Allison gave me the numbers of the tanks and tank cars to be sampled and pointed me to the pick-up—I had only just gotten my driver's license the week before graduation—I knew I had passed over into a new world.

Over the weeks, I came to know the men who worked in the other half, testing and checking the large production still, a kind of ongoing "quality control," and we became friends. Though Bob Allison was a chemist holding a college degree, most of the older stillmen had not even graduated from high school and had worked most of their lives in one refinery or another. In 1943, the petroleum industry, as we knew it then, was less than half a century old and considered "high tech." There appeared to be no hierarchy, no pecking order in the crew, and no one seemed particularly impressed that I was working in order to go to college. I would learn that their indifference was a high compliment. On those days, when there was a large load of testing and sampling because we were trying to meet a heavy demand for one or more fuels, Bob and I would bring our brown bag lunches and work right through lunch and on into the evening, taking brief rest breaks in the stillmen's rooms. There, in the company of workingmen, I found I always felt most at ease. Their talk followed a set plan or pattern: first, they would talk about the latest war news coming over their small radio, and then about the company, usually Mr. Bartlett's latest foray down into the still area and some stupid remark he might have made, and then the talk drifted to the weekend and where they each planned to go fishing. Since they were all shift workers, there was rarely any overtime for them unless a still broke down and was shut down for repairs and service. Bob said he was envious that they could usually depend on having a weekend free, while he and I, when there was a heavy run, would spend Saturday or even a Sunday morning in the lab, testing samples. A topic they all loved most was fishing; everything else was just prologue to fishing stories, obligatory topics to be dispensed with.

Rarely did anyone mention the work unless it had to do with the navy's inspection team or some new scheme thought up by Mr. Bartlett, whom they only tolerated, as they did anyone in the office up the hill. Over the weeks, I came to realize that none of them really liked their work. It was just a job one had to do in order to buy food and pay rent and pay for their cherished fishing trips. I assumed that because Bob had gone to college and had his BS in chemistry, he felt differently; after all, he was a chemist. But one day near the end of my stay, I remarked that I was surprised that none of the stillmen seemed to like their jobs and wondered why. Bobby shook his head and said that if he had a choice, he wouldn't work there either; he wished he could have stayed on his mother's farm instead of "going off to become a damned chemist." On the farm, he said he could have gone fishing whenever he wanted. I said nothing, but I thought how miserable it must be to *have* to work at a job you dislike, even hate, all your life. Then he said wistfully that after the war, he would probably quit this kind of work and go back to farming and fishing. For now, the job exempted him from military service, and the wages were too good to pass up.

I listened to his story about his mother and the farm and the fact that he'd grown tired of college soon after arriving, and I wondered how it would be to work at a job all one's life, wishing you were somewhere else doing something different. That first day on the job after I'd left the lab and AMSCO behind and had gotten back home, Mama met me at the door to congratulate me, her elder son, on his first day on the job, a man's job. I was dirty, smeared with oil that had dripped from the sample bottles or from the grimy tank cars on the railroad siding.

She smiled with pride and asked, "Well, how did you like your first day?"

I knew I shouldn't say it, but the temptation to shock and dismay was too great. "Well," I began, pretending I was in deep serious thought, "if I had my choice, I'd simply rather not work at all."

Her face froze into a stare of disbelief then thawed into an angry scowl. "Well! You'd better learn and learn it quick. This world doesn't offer free rides!"

I was tempted to respond to the contrary, but instead, I placated, "I'm only saying what I *prefer.*" I paused. "I'm teasing, Mama." It was only a half lie, teasing with a bit of truth. To me, "doing science" or "practicing medicine," I could not regard as a job or as work in the way this job in the lab was defined. It was later, shortly before I ended my tenure at the AMSCO lab and headed for Austin, when Bobby told me of his dream to return to the farm and fishing that my joke took on a more prescient meaning.

The wartime paycheck I earned that summer was indeed remarkable for a boy my age. When I got my first pay envelope and saw that my wages for the first week, before ordinary deductions, came to just under forty dollars, I was stunned. It was almost twice the salary Mama had received when she began working at the Pure Oil Company just over ten years ago. I was only sixteen, barely a week out of high school, and was already making more than many men who were heads of families made before the war. *My base pay of thirty dollars a week, supplemented by overtime, would be enough to finance my entire year in Austin,* I thought.

The reality, however, turned out to be quite different from what I had expected. Two days before I was to leave for Austin, I asked Mama how we should deposit my money for the year, the money that she had been holding for me. Should we get a cashier's check to deposit in a checking account in Austin, or should I open a checking account here in Corpus?

"What money?" she asked.

"The money I gave you every payday to hold for me," I answered and suddenly felt weak all over. Her comment was completely unexpected.

She had been withholding the cost of room and board she said. "Since you held a full-time job and were being paid the same as the adult men at the refinery, neither Albert nor I could see why you shouldn't pay for you room and meals," she said calmly.

I was stunned, but ironically, not incredulous. I asked why she hadn't made it clear.

"I thought you and Albert understood, that you knew I was working for my college expenses."

If I had complained it was unfair, I knew she would unload with that earlier argument how we all had to pull our weight in this world. I also knew any counter remarks about my summer in the AMSCO lab being just that, pulling my own weight, would just make matters worse. Jane had said nothing about this when she had gone to work in Kingsville. Years later, when he graduated from high school, Don would discover the same rules, only he had shown more guts than I had; all the time he was living at home in Corpus before going to New York, he took his meals at a boarding house several blocks away, rather than pay for meals at home *and* be expected to wash the dishes. No one had told me or had even hinted at the possibility. Moreover, I had never understood the true conditions we lived under or the marital agreement between my mother and my stepfather, who now seemed even less a father than I had realized. Mama had never explained or discussed the rules we were to live under after she married Albert, though we were often reminded that we should be grateful to Albert for "giving" us a home. It would be many years before I would see Albert's refusal to tell us of our obligations as a flaw in character. I could understand and even forgive Mama's not telling us the facts of our new lives in Corpus Christi, but Albert's, I could not accept. He had told me once, years later, that when he left home for college, his mother had given him all of her "egg and butter money," that is, the money she had saved that his father had said was hers. Instead, I had given Mama *my* money.

At that moment I was sure of only one thing: I would be leaving Corpus Christi on the MKT for Austin in two days and would be enrolling as a freshman premed student, regardless of what financial arrangements my mother had agreed to when she married Albert Delsman. I felt the deep chill of disappointment along with a burning anxiety over the likelihood of finding a job that would pay me enough to live on once I got to Austin.

When I asked if she had any money at all, she told me there was some.

"You can have it all," she said trying to sound like the soul of generosity, then turned and retrieved it from her vanity's drawer.

When I counted it, I found I had enough money for books and tuition and two months' room and board. She promised to pay for the second semester's books and tuition. In 1943 -1944 tuition and fees came to less than fifty dollars a semester, books slightly less.

All summer, Albert and she had tried to convince me to stay at home and enroll in Del Mar and continue working part-time at AMSCO. I would have been able to keep the job at the lab, take a light load of courses, yet still complete my premed requirements before being drafted. It would gradually become clear like a veil slowly lifting: they had planned it all along but had never openly explained any of it. At sixteen, I believed I had arrived at my majority. What with a well-paying job and all, I believed I had actually reached a point where I was no longer obligated to trim the hedges, to *"coup de grace"* or to carry Albert's golf bag. Now, I was in a kind of haze for the next two days, a haze of the alienated, cut off, disowned, for Mama showed no regret, showed no sign she had deceived me. I waited now only for the trip to the station and a wave good-bye.

That I blocked out my disappointment and turned all my thoughts to the possibilities that lay ahead was less an act of courage than an overwhelming desire to leave home and get on with college. I had one more idea to propose, though I had no real feeling that it would work. That next day I reminded Mama of the Veteran's Administration check Jane, Don, and I, received each month as dependents of M.Sgt. Joe D. Gilliland. It wasn't much, eighteen dollars each, but it would help. She said she had been planning to send Jane thirty dollars a month that we could divide it evenly between us. That was something, I thought. When I added that the Veteran's checks were now eighteen dollars a month, a considerable sum in all, she replied that she had to have something for herself. I never really understood how important money had become to Mama. I said it would help, but I wanted to say we had to have it all, and I wanted to ask what Helen Stewart, Olive McCauley, Mrs. Geiger, or her any of her well-to-do rich friends would think about her need "to have something for herself," six dollars. But I didn't.

Instead of a nest egg of almost nine hundred dollars, what I had was closer to a goose egg, just enough to pay for two semesters' books and tuition and enough to get me through my first month. I still had money left over from my "spending money," a bit over a hundred dollars, money I was considering a buffer, no small amount in 1943. I had no way of knowing Mama's thoughts when she told me I had been paying her room and board, for she, or any of us, rarely spoke frankly about unpleasant realities or the depths of our personal feeling. After our father died she had saved us from the mythical "poor farm" and had kept us all together by pinching pennies "until Old Abe squealed," she used to say. Somehow, to bring in more money, she had managed to build a garage apartment and to put a second story on the house at 2346 Broadway. We'd never missed a meal, nor had we ever gone to school in rags. We had always lived in a nice house in a good neighborhood, which made it possible for us to attend the "better schools" and were thus able to enjoy the company of "nicer people." It was never required that we understand her reasons for doing what she did, but this was different I felt. She had taken pride in my job, my success in science, and my decision to study premed. I had heard her brag about me and my achievements, about my "grown man's" job, and I had heard her tell friends that I, "still just sixteen," was refusing Del Mar College and planning to enroll at The University of Texas. I had no way of disputing her boasts or charging her with misrepresenting things; at sixteen, I just wasn't equipped to do that. Instead, I let it out that all my glassware, the retorts, beakers, flasks, condensing coils, and distillation flasks, along with ring stands and clamps and a half liter of CP nitric acid and a dozen or so recently purchased reagents, were all for sale, along with two microscopes—one with a revolving turret and three lenses, purchased with Christmas money saved over the years—and all the old chemistry texts lined up on the shelves above my lab bench in the garage. I felt a pang of remorse selling off pieces I recalled buying with such pride, but only for a moment, and when I took my last look at the empty shelves, the sadness faded to joy when I thought of what lay ahead.

Chapter 4

University Days

As I settled in at Mrs. Carter's house at 2212 Pearl Street, I could only think how good it was to be in Austin and finally be "on my way." As soon as I put my clothes away and stashed my father's old Gladstone bags beneath my bed, I hurried down the hall to get Hollis Porcher and drag him off with me to the campus. I had not known Hollis well in high school or his roommate Bill Talbert, who had enrolled in the short fall term and had made arrangements at Mrs. Carter's for Hollis and now me. Hollis said Bill was planning to join the navy in the spring, possibly the V-12 college program, when it opened for new applicants. When I asked him what Bill and he were majoring in, he blithely said he didn't know but that he hoped to find a major that might get him deferred. Talbert was majoring in business, but since he was a brain, he could probably switch to something vital for the "war effort" if he didn't get into V-12. I had set my goal early and found it absurd that a person could be so undecided as Hollis. I was definitely a premed, I said, but whether I would emphasize chemistry or zoology, I wasn't sure, but I would decide by the time I finished my sophomore year, adding, "If I get that far before I have to go in."

We spent the day exploring the Forty Acres, which was actually more like eighty acres, the university having long ago outgrown its old boundaries. In spite of his less than enthusiastic interest in the buildings and the wide expanses, he was as impressed as I by the size and number of buildings. The newer buildings had a touch of the Mediterranean style, heavy Spanish tile roofs, white limestone walls, wide overhanging eaves, and arched window frames on the ground floor. A few of the drab monsters, like Old B Hall and MLB (Modern Languages Building), still occupied prominent positions, but it was the twenty-seven-story tower with its quasi-Greek outhouse on top that was, still is, the campus's dominant feature. The solid white limestone tower rose twenty-seven stories atop the quasi-classical eclecticism of the Main Library. While it impressed most people, I heard, to my surprise, that it was not generally loved. Seen from the south end of the mall through the Littlefield Fountain's spray and fish-finned hooves of the horses, it is a unique monstrosity. The famous Texas folklorist and U.T. professor, J. Frank Dobie, suggested they lay it on its side so it would more fittingly represent a gigantic ranch house. The silliness of that Greek temple with its Baroque decorations surrounding the Tower clock above the observation deck sets it off from any other building in the country; however, I loved it then and do even today.

When we first approached the arches of the Main Library, we both read aloud the words incised into Austin limestone above the portal: "YE SHALL KNOW THE TRUTH AND THE TRUTH SHALL SET YOU FREE."

"That's really appropriate for a library, don't you think?" I said.

He replied, "Yeah. Who said it—Sam Houston, Stephen F. Austin, or Mirabeau Lamar?"

"I'm sure they all said it at least once," I replied and laughed, "but I think Jesus said it first."

"Are you sure?" he said, looking up with reverence and awe.

"Pretty sure."

This was Sunday morning. Jane was not due back in Austin until Monday. There were a few people from Corpus that I was sure to meet, but none of the TOS were here, except me. Bill Reiss would arrive in January when he finished, and Henry Owens would make it the first summer session. Harvey, who was 4-F because of a broken arm that had not healed properly, had enrolled in Del Mar and was planning to transfer to U.T. when he graduated.

Now I was in Austin and confident I would do well in zoology and chemistry and that I had made the right choice not choosing to stay in Corpus. But the truth was, I knew very little about what I should expect from the professors. English, I was sure, would be the drag it always had been, and algebra, which they said was mostly a review of algebra 2b, should go OK. My question was, what should I take as a fifth class: history, German, philosophy? Everyone said it would depend on what was open. Registering late as I was, it might be difficult to get all the classes I wanted at the best hours.

On Monday morning, when I showed up at Gregory Gymnasium for registration, I was an hour early for the *G* through *J* call. When they finally called for *G* through *J*, I picked up registration materials and went directly to the table with a sign reading SCIENCE, MATH, PREMED and handed over my packet of materials. A distinguished-looking gentleman took my packet, gave it a cursory glance, handed it back, and asked me my major. When I told him, he handed me a small mimeographed slip with the words PREMED across the top and a list of courses: English, algebra, chemistry, physics, zoology. He pointed to another much larger collection of tables with a sign reading SECTIONIZING and told me to proceed and have someone "sectionize" me with those courses. After reading the list of classes, I recalled reading in the university catalog a warning that entering freshmen should avoid taking more than two laboratory classes. There, on the list, were the lab classes, one of which was physics. I didn't need to be warned about physics: I knew I should not take it until I had finished all my required math courses. I turned and said I believed it better that I take one of the recommended electives, perhaps German or history. He took back the slip and asked which of the lab courses I wanted to drop. When I told him physics, he scratched off, initialed it, and then told me to tell the "sectionizer" what I'd like in its place.

When I asked him what he recommended, he said, "I recommend what's there in your hand, son."

Turning to the others at the table who were looking on with what seemed to me stares of disapproval, he said so I could hear, "He probably wants to take a Bible or philosophy class."

They all smiled and nodded, and that was the extent my freshman advising and would be the last academic advising I would ever receive at the university; however, at the time, it seemed perfectly reasonable. I simply assumed that was the way it was supposed to be and thought that a philosophy class or a Bible class might *not* be a bad idea.

When the sectionizer asked what I would like in the place of physics, I suggested Introduction to Philosophy to which he promptly announce, "Prerequisite for philosophy is sophomore standing," so I selected Introduction to the New Testament.

"Where do you want to take it?" he asked. "All Bible classes are taught off campus: Wesley Bible Chair, St. Austin's, Baptist Bible Chair, Westminster Bible Chair, and there are others."

I chose the Wesley chair, and in less than half an hour, my *sectionizer* had *sectionized* me, and I had paid my fees, and was a bona fide freshman at The University of Texas. Lab fees, student activity fee, and tuition came to the grand total of fifty-five dollars. I was euphoric. What struck me most at the time was the five-day-a-week schedule with classes beginning at eight o'clock some mornings. My sectionizer had given me two eight-o-clock zoology labs on Monday and Wednesday mornings, two chemistry labs from two o'clock to four o'clock on Tuesday and Thursday, and two TTS morning classes, algebra and English at nine o'clock and eleven o'clock, with the rest of my classes spaced through the day on MWF. That was they way everyone talked about schedules: *TTS* and *MWF*. If Saturday classes seemed strange, stranger still seemed all that "free" time between classes; I'd soon learn there was no such thing as free time.

After I'd bought my books, all used, except my chemistry text, I dropped by Jane's rooming house to show her my schedule and the names of my instructors. Immediately recognizing the name of my English instructor, Helen James, she told me how she had met *Dr.* James in the commons one evening at supper. I recall her telling me how odd it felt having dinner and chatting there in the commons with a college instructor who was also a Ph.D..

"She just recently finished her PhD at the University of Wisconsin, and she's been at UT for two years," she said. "I'm sure you'll like her."

Though this was Dr. James's first university job, Jane said she had taught several years in high school in Wisconsin. When Jane told me she, herself, was majoring in English, I wondered, aloud, what a person with a BA in English would do other than teach.

"It would be nice, really interesting, I said, to read all that good stuff, but what does anyone really do with it?"

She answered curtly, "They can do whatever they *want* to do, I suppose."

When I mentioned it was strange having so much time off between classes, she warned me that there was no such thing as "time off": "You have to watch out, especially with two lab courses. You'll be surprised how far it is between classes, between Main Building and Waggoner Hall or Waggoner and MLB."

I told her my money was holding out pretty well, and that I thought I could make it through November if I stuck to two meals a day. She advised I get to the employment center and make out my job application now; with the influx of new students, there just might be a job shortage. Then she added another note of reality, "Don't depend on your money lasting. It won't."

Those autumn mornings in Austin were magic: red, yellow, and russet leaves; clear air; long oak and hackberry branches spanning the streets—scenes of college I'd always dreamed of. The walk from the house on Pearl Street to the Drag was magic indeed those first few days of class. After Pearl Street, it was Rio Grande then Nueces then San Antonio and, finally, Guadalupe; the streets were named after the rivers of Texas flowing west to east. *I'm actually going to college, There's no place like Austin,* I would tell myself. I was floating in a wonderland of dreams.

Then my first real shock: I walked into my Algebra 101 class and discovered I was the only male in a class of twenty. Everything they'd said about the male-female ratio was true. I moved to the back of the class, took a seat, and reminded myself it was the same position where I'd had flunked algebra 1a at Wynne Seale. But chemistry lecture was a greater shock: the lecture hall, an amphitheater, held three hundred and sixty; and the zoology lecture's two hundred was only slightly less a shock. But in the New Testament class, we were only seven and met in Dr. Hall's own book-lined office at the Wesley Bible Chair at the University Methodist Church. Texas adhered strictly to the separation doctrine teaching all Bible classes off campus in various "bible chairs." Most people who took Bible took it at the chair of their own denomination, though several of the professors like Dr. Hall attracted students from across the spectrum.

I had chosen Hall's class because it was scheduled at the most convenient time, not because it was held in the Wesley Bible Chair. I'd heard Hall was a great teacher, holder of three doctorates, only one of which was honorary. He was brilliant, not because he was a sparkling or charismatic lecturer but because of the ideas he threw out and the knowledge of Biblical history he poured forth and the way he spoke to each of us personally. We met every Monday, Wednesday, and Friday at one o'clock in his office, sitting or lounging in well-padded chairs or at the large library table where dozing off was more easily avoided. Dr. Hall became one of my favorite professors that first year. Quizzes and exams were rare. One of the students said he followed the "seminar" method": oral reports, class discussion and short essays.

After talking to Jane, I was curious what Dr. James would be like. I'd never met a woman with a doctorate before, but then I'd never *met* anyone with a doctorate before. Helen James was small, straight-backed, and rather plump. At first, I had the impression she was overly serious, almost humorless, but I was wrong. The first day in class, she had us write a one-page paper about ourselves and what we hoped to accomplish while we were at the university. Aside from short essay answers for Mr. Steakley's and Ms. Cole's history classes, I had not written more than a half dozen papers of any kind in all four years of high school, but I was sure I could write clearly, concretely, and concisely, which she emphasized was what she looked for in our writing. But when she returned our papers the next class meeting, I learned I had been neither concise nor concrete, that my language, while not ungrammatical, was "vague, ambiguous, and shallow"—her words—and not at all "clear." She had marked the paper with a C- and had written "careless" beneath the letter grade. Besides the lack of clarity and the shallowness, she'd made several other comments about "parallelism" and "unity" and three places where she had made a large K, meaning the passage was too "awkward" to suggest a mending.

It was not an auspicious beginning. Nevertheless, I liked Helen James and her class from the beginning. Unlike any English teacher I had had before, she was always talking, questioning, explaining, urging us to talk, and challenging us to think and disagree, especially when we were discussing one of the essays in our anthology. She was also constantly surprising us with her fund of knowledge that ranged over a wide area outside of English or rhetoric, subjects such as art history, philosophy, psychology, political science, even science. I had never learned how to approach a teacher directly, how to speak informally and casually, but she made it possible without ever becoming familiar or personal. I was always Mr. Gilliland, never Joe, and I loved it. Unlike all my past English teachers, Helen James made every class seem important.

The class responded well to her. I never heard anyone complain about her teaching or her grading, though many of us were disappointed that we weren't making better grades on our papers. She gave few As that first semester and only a few more Bs, many Cs along with Ds, and even several Fs. I was not content with a C or even C+ but was relieved that my papers never slid into the D category. When I showed a paper now and then to Jane, she would always agree with Dr. James and said my chief fault was careless proofreading and revising.

In my first conference period, we talked about my interest in chemistry and science. When she asked how I was doing, I admitted I was not doing as well as I hoped, except in the lab sections in both zoology and chemistry. She seemed genuinely interested and pressed me to think about what I was doing wrong and asked if I had developed good study habits. I said frankly that I didn't know what she meant by "study habits" and explained that I studied whenever I could and tried not to be interrupted. When she focused on my faulty proofreading and the gaps that appeared in my logic or the ordering of paragraphs, I told her I had only the vaguest notion of what she was talking about.

She looked at me long then asked, "Where did you go to high school?"

When I told her I had graduated from Corpus Christi High School, she replied that I shouldn't have any problems then and asked me what my grades were. I had made mostly Bs, rarely an A, but hardly ever a C, I said; and then I told her we had never written themes like the ones she assigned, that I had already learned more about writing in just a few weeks in her class than I had learned in all four years of high school English. She shook her head in disbelief. I repeated what I said about having learned more in the past few weeks and added as convincingly as I could that I wasn't just saying that to make her feel good—I really had.

"If you want to improve your writing, you must read as much good writing as you can as often as you can." Then she said something I would remember and use many times as a teacher, especially with my better students who would agonize as I would go over their errors in style, their wooden banalities. "Read everything you can—good magazines, newspapers, essays, and stories in the anthology that I don't assign," she said. "Avoid things like the *Reader's Digest*. I know from your first paper that you like to read, but you have to focus on what you're reading."

My recollection of that meeting, the first conference I had ever had with a teacher, is clear even today. What impressed me most was she seemed honestly concerned that I understand.

English took off for me that fall when she assigned *The Autobiography of Lincoln Steffens* and *Ethan Frome*. I came to the university with what I thought was a strong background in a variety of genre: fiction, history, political science, biography, and science. From my earliest days, I had always read more than anyone I knew but had believed novels and biographies were purely recreational. Books about science or history were different, were serious, and deserved my attention; though the years just prior to reaching UT, fiction began to take on new importance. I made no effort to examine a novel or ask myself questions why or how unless the writer posed the questions himself.

After our first class discussion over the Steffens autobiography, I saw how superficially I had been reading all these years. That something so "factual" as a biography could suggest levels of meaning, could suggest ideas that may not be stated directly was new to me. "*Nuances*," she would say, "look for the nuances when you read. Ask yourself if he's saying something more than appears on the page." *Nuance* wasn't a new word. I had heard it before, and I believed I understood it, but I had never really used it, and Dr. James had said we probably would truly not know a word unless we actually used it in a context.

When I first picked up my copy of the Lincoln Steffens book at the co-op, I was dismayed. It was huge, for one thing, and was expensive, even for a well-used copy. That we would have to read it *all* in addition to all the other required reading, I thought it was unreasonable. Others in the class voiced the same concern, but Dr. James offered no sympathy, though she did abridge the assignment by omitting some of the chapters about his muckraking, which she said were repetitious. However, all of the chapters dealing with Steffens's boyhood and education and his New York experience, she retained. I found the book engrossing, especially the sections describing his education after high school. It set a tone, expressed what I thought a real college or university education should be, even though I had always thought college was intended to prepare a person for a job or a profession. I began to understand why that young ensign dating Cack's sister had majored in philosophy, and the autobiography may have set me to thinking more seriously beyond my own plans. As a supplementary text it accomplished one of its tasks by forcing me to think outside the parameters I had set for myself. I didn't change my mind about the importance of my major, but I did begin to see the importance of studying subjects beyond science or in addition to chemistry.

Both the autobiography and *Ethan Frome* had a lasting effect on me, and I wrote my best themes about the two works. Because of Wharton's novel, I began to read fiction with greater attention to ironies or contradictions or, as Dr. James put it, to "indirect meanings." When Steffens, in his chapter "I Go to College," wrote of his interest in courses others called useless "highbrow" or "cultural" courses, I began to take notice. When he wrote, "I think now that I had as a boy an exhausting experience of *being* something great [his italics]. I did not want now to be but rather to *know things* [my italics]," I knew exactly what he meant. Although I understood what he was saying and sympathized entirely with his feelings, I believed I had no time to indulge this desire. There was a war going on; we only had time to pursue facts, fundamentals, and things we needed to know in order to do "what needed to be done."

Dr. James had asked us to find a passage or a section of the book that we felt had a personal meaning for us and to write about it as specifically as we could, avoiding vague, general platitudes. I wrote my paper expressing my sympathy for and understanding of the passage just quoted, and I explained my frustration, writing rather grandiosely of the importance of the broader approach over the narrower, stating that this kind of education provided him with a value system that allowed him to uncover corruption and deceit in public life. I thought it a significant insight. Dr. James pointed out I had made a great "leap in logic" and suggested I show a more direct relation between cause and effect. On the whole, she praised the paper and gave me the best mark I would ever receive in her class. Frankly, now as I recall the incident, I must admit that her advice became one of the lessons most preached in my own freshman comp classes.

When we began discussing Wharton's novel, everyone had an opinion about the setting, characters, and events. Some blamed everything on Ethan's hypochondriac wife, Zena, but no one would explain why. Others said Ethan was justified in falling in love with Mattie, but they were unable to supply a justification, only a strongly *felt* opinion. Few blamed the sweetly attractive Mattie for her part in the tragedy. "Feelings are not enough," Dr. James would tell us, "and opinions without reasons are nothing more than feelings. You must convince me with arguments, not your *feelings*." Then other times, she would tell us that emotions were a kind of knowledge we should not ignore. It was confusing, but it was also exciting, a complete departure from my high school classes. Several in the class countered with the argument that none of it really made a difference since it was *only a novel*. But when she challenged them to explain why "it made no difference" when serious works of fiction actually did deal with fundamental moral truths, they had to admit it was "just an opinion."

It was clear that if any novel revolved around a moral issue, *Ethan Frome* certainly did. When it came to writing our essay about the novel, I backed away from the moral ambiguities and told her after class that I felt they were too complex for me to handle. I chose not to write on the moral dilemma but on the way Wharton's descriptive language influences my attitudes toward the actions of Zena, Ethan, and Mattie. I felt an aura throughout the novel made them all seem real; that aura was an emotion conditioned by "a grey New England Puritanism." It was my most difficult paper to write that semester, though I wrote it at one sitting and made only minor changes before proofreading the final draft. I took it to Jane and asked her to read it over and tell me if it made sense or if it was completely off base. She warned me that she would not point out errors in form or style but only inconsistencies in the logic or argument. When she finished, she said it was good and left it at that and told me not to change anything. When I turned in my paper the next day, it was unrevised or unchanged, the same paper I had shown to Jane.

"Why don't you write this well all the time, Mr. Gilliland?" she said when she finished reading it. Sitting there in her office, basking in the warmth of her approval, I answered that I tried to, but the fact was I wrote this paper more easily than all the others. It was practically a one-draft paper, I explained. "It was the hardest paper for me to begin, but once I started, it just wrote itself," I said. She said it was probably because I really believed I understood the novel. I agreed and then told her it had hit me almost as hard as Fitzgerald's "Babylon Revisited." She looked straight me and asked why. I knew better than to leave what I said as just an opinion, so I spoke of how both stories were about people, good and bad, who struggle with moral obligations and justice and that neither had an easy solution to the problem. I ended saying that both authors left the moral question there for the reader to answer.

Then she asked, "Why do you like stories that end unresolved?"

I told her that I really wasn't sure until now, that I hadn't thought about "Babylon Revisited" in connection with *Ethan Frome* until I just said what I did. I said I guessed that life, as most people live it, is full of unresolved situations. It was strange how easy it was to talk to her. She thanked me for coming in then mentioned that she looked forward to my taking the English 2 class from her in the spring semester. It was a high compliment I felt. As expected, I made a C in English 101, but I was far from disappointed.

Barely two weeks into the term, Jane's warning that my money would *not* last came true; economic realities sent me to the student employment services. At the rate I was spending, I would have to dip into my nest egg for second semester just to pay next month's rent. The employment clerk told me right off they had plenty of jobs and almost no one to fill them because of the war. I could have my pick, she said, but when I said I preferred a job on or near campus that wouldn't take me out of the area, she apologized and said *that* was the one area she couldn't promise. My first interview was at a pharmacy downtown, but it paid too little and was miles off campus. The second one sounded interesting, if macabre. The job was driving an ambulance and a *hearse* with a *morgue assistant* thrown in, and it offered me a place to live at "no cost." I called from the pharmacy and asked to speak to Mr. Hyltin, the owner and director of Hyltin's Funeral Home. When I told him I heard he had a job opening and that I wished to apply, he said I should come right away and asked if I could start immediately. I told him it was highly possible and almost leaped from the booth.

Both father and son interviewed me. Mr. Hyltin, a short stout man in his late fifties or early sixties with the bright ruddy complexion of a Swede, and his son, a younger image of the father, asked how old I was, and I said I was just a few weeks past seventeen, and they both made the usual remark that I looked much younger. We talked about the job requirements, one of which was that I had to live at the funeral home and would be on emergency call every evening after five. I would have every other weekend off and would be expected to assist in the morgue when one of the regular morticians was off.

"Will that disturb you?" Mr. Hyltin asked.

I told him I was a premed and would not be at all disturbed. The job would require me to drive an emergency as well as a transfer ambulance that carried patients to and from the hospital. In addition to assisting in the morgue, I would drive the hearse or family car at funerals. The important thing was to be on call after five every evening and every other weekend. When I explained my class schedule and the Saturday morning classes, both agreed there would be no problem. It sounded, at least, as if I would have plenty of time to study.

"We'd like for you to begin tonight. Although it's Wednesday, we'll count this as your first full week." *They are desperate,* I thought, *but so am I.*

They were so anxious that I begin immediately that Harley drove me to Mrs. Carter's and helped load my stuff in the back of the small "hot shot" emergency ambulance. It felt weird moving into the large roomy efficiency apartment behind the morgue and just off the garage with its row of somber funeral vehicles. The room had three single beds, two chests of drawers, a large closet, and a large bath with shower and tub. It looked comfortable enough. In a small anteroom were two study desks and a small bookcase I assumed for the student driver. Mr. Edmiston, one of the morticians, was stretched out on one of the beds, reading a heavy book. On the other was a young man I guessed to be my age; any older and he would have been in the service. They greeted me, introduced themselves, and told me where to stow the stuff. The young man, Monk, offered to show me around and explain the job as he saw it.

Hyltin Funeral Home was a long way from the university, more than ten blocks. Monk agreed and said it would be a long walk every morning and sometimes a long wait for the bus. The bus stop was almost at the front door and was cheap, five cents. To me, the most important thing was that it was a job, a "free" room, and enough money to live on, I thought—a dollar a day for meals plus fifteen dollars from the Veterans Administration.

Before I finished stowing my shirts in the chest, a loud claxon sounded, and Monk answered the phone, wrote down an address, and turned to me. "We're on. Follow me and do what I tell you."

That first call was a minor emergency as it turned out: Down in the very old section of town, an elderly man, having a mild heart attack, was lying on the living room floor surrounded by concerned and nervous family members. As Monk and I entered, rolling the cot, a bright-looking woman in her early thirties approached and told us the doctor had been there and gone and had said it was OK to move him to the ER at Breckinridge Hospital, Austin's only ER facility. He was slight, easy to lift, couldn't have weighed as much as I did, probably only a hundred pounds at most. Assuming the position as number one driver, Monk told me to ride in the back with the patient and to make room for the young woman who wanted to ride along. On the way to the pick-up, we had driven through the streets of Austin with lights flashing and siren screaming as if we were headed for a major accident, but when we pulled away, Monk switched off the siren, leaving roof lights flashing.

"Sirens advertise Hyltin. That's really what they're for," Monk told me, "but they scare shit out of the patient and disturb the neighbors. But Hyltin wants the siren every time out." The last comment he added with a tone of mild disgust.

Most of the time, it was that simple and routine. In all the months while I was driving or assisting, we had only three major accidents and one fatality. The most disturbing was an elderly woman who had committed suicide. I never, fortunately for the patients, had to perform a single act of first aid. My first weeks were mostly an education in human relations that carried me far beyond anything I had ever done before. Some of it was pleasant, even exciting, such as the night I helped deliver two babies. One delivery came in the ambulance before we could reach the ER; the other waited until we delivered her and her child to the ER. The first call had come shortly after I had turned in for the night, around midnight. Howard Edmiston was on call with me and drove to and from the pick-up, telling me that since I was a premed, I should ride in the back and learn something. The first new mother delayed delivering just long enough for us to make it to the hospital. I sat in the back beside the cot, holding her hand, talking to her, and allowing her to squeeze my arm when the contractions came. She looked as if she were about seventeen, or eighteen at the oldest, and was quite pretty even under the circumstances. She told me her husband was overseas in the Pacific. Between contractions, she would laugh and apologize for "messing up the cot." I tried to assure her that's what the cots were for.

When we arrived and wheeled her into the emergency room, the head nurse glanced down at the cot, took one look at me, and said, "Get him some ammonia. She's fine. It's him I'm worried about." The ER attendants laughed and led me to a chair. To tell the truth, I was woozy, but I felt fine otherwise, elated really that I had been there. On the way back to the home, Howard smiled, congratulated me, and said I had done fine, but I told him I'd really done nothing.

"That's what I meant," he said, smiling. "When you got in the back with the mama, her mother came to me and said you looked too young to be there with all that going on." Laughing, he said, "I told her it was OK, that you're a medical student and y'did this all the time. But, honestly? You were as pale as those sheets when we wheeled her into the emergency." He paused in thought. "I bet that kid still won't get born for a couple of hours."

"I thought it was ready to be born when she got on the cot," I said.

"Hell, no. First one is always later and longer. I've seen too many. Three of my own."

Edmiston always made a good partner in emergencies—so experienced, he was never nervous or excited, and he had extensive emergency first-aid training.

I was back in bed by one o'clock, but then at two o'clock, the second call came. This time it was the doctor on the phone, telling us he was at the house and that the birth was imminent. He said he would ride along with the mother to the hospital.

As we wheeled the cot out, he said to Howard, "Put the boy in the back with us, Howard. I prefer for you to drive." I was impressed how calm he and Howard were, how politely he told me to sit and help if needed.

This time I did learn, for the doctor described it all, every step, as Howard drove carefully along on the way to the hospital. Once again, I was the squeezing post, but now there was no laughter, no apologies, and no talk, and this time, as we wheeled the patient directly to the delivery room, no one joked about the assistant driver. It was all business. Howard and I waited briefly in the hall outside the ER until the head nurse returned to tell us the mother and the baby were fine. She looked at me, patted me on the arm, and smiled then asked if I was sure that this was what I wanted to do for a living. I don't recall my answer, but god, I felt good. At the moment, I couldn't answer her, could only think it had been a night to remember.

The next morning in Zoo 1 lab, my lab partner and I were dissecting a *prenatal sus,* pig. Looking at the pink creature in the black dissecting pan brought back the last minutes of the ride in the back of the ambulance. I turned to my partner and said, "You know I helped deliver two babies early this morning. This pig has a remarkable resemblance to the second one."

"Are you kidding?" she asked then begged for a description of it all, insisting I tell her what it was like when it "came out." I told her it was exciting and pretty marvelous and explained that everything was so busy back there that there wasn't really much time to contemplate it.

"I was only a bystander, a hand holder," I explained, but in spite of downplaying my part in parturition, she said I was a very unusual guy. Well, that made the day.

All in all, Hyltin's was not a pleasant place to work, nor was Mr. Hyltin a pleasant man to be around, though Harley was more than just pleasant; he was actually pretty nice. My hours were erratic, the pay low, and the people, except for Harley and Howard, often unpleasant. Monk, especially, got to be a bore. The worst part was the long distance to campus and waiting for the bus, sometimes walking the ten or so blocks, saving the nickel for a cup of coffee for breakfast. After chem. lab I always spent some time in the library before heading back to the funeral home because noise off the garage at Hyltin's made it impossible to concentrate until late at night. Some nights, I would find a quiet place in an unused "visitation" room to read or do the algebra homework, but most nights, I became involved with the chatter in the room and neglected required readings. Howard Edmiston was a good man— intelligent, thoughtful, and helpful. Monk, even more erratic about studying than I, resigned just before Christmas, and when I returned to Austin the day after Christmas, Pinky, Monk's replacement, was in place and turned out to be a good driver and good a man. I found it odd that he was over draft age, twenty-two or twenty-three, but not in the army. I didn't ask.

Because most funerals were held in the mornings or early afternoons, I assisted at few for the time I worked at Hyltin's. On Saturdays, days when I assisted either as a driver of the family car or as the driver of the "hot shot" that delivered flowers to the graveside, I always felt uncomfortable about the old man's method of getting the "most" out of the services. His cold-hearted commercialism and sheer hypocrisy was creepy. When he was with the members of the family grieving for the "loved one," his tears would flow with theirs, but one step into another room, he would laugh and joke or rub his hands in glee over having sold an expensive "half couch *and* concrete vault." As the year wore on, he and his son Harley made more and more demands on my time by asking me to come in earlier in the afternoon, which meant I had even less time to study or to grab my supper at the worst dirty spoon dive in town. However, I could not deny there were advantages. I was able to observe two autopsies performed by a pathologist who loved to lecture as he cut and probed. He and the patients' physicians always welcomed me and answered any question I raised. These were the times I was convinced I had the greatest job in the world.

Truth was, autopsies or no, the job seriously affected my performance as a student, and quite early, I realized my remaining in Corpus Christi and attending Del Mar, even working with Bobby Allison in the lab, would have been better. A different job near the campus, one that would have allowed me to remain at the house on Pearl Street, would have made a great difference. I learned later that had I been working at one of the other funeral homes that hired students, it would have been different. All others offered better schedules and higher pay; one offered almost twice the pay.

Chemistry, except for the laboratory sections, began to unravel for me early in the first semester. I couldn't understand why at first, but I began to realize that, at best, I had only a superficial grasp of those important fundamental concepts Dr. Andersen was trying to teach in the boring lectures. Why did they have to be boring, I wondered? Chemistry had never been boring before. Over three hundred students scribbled notes, hardly lifting their heads even to see what he was writing on the huge chalkboards behind the lectern. Everything I had carried over from high school chemistry seemed superficial, but I soon realized that my interest in chemistry was not what it had been. Nothing seemed important enough to make me cram and "regurgitate" the correct answers on the exams or the weekly quizzes in study sessions taught by graduate assistants. Studying seemed all rote memorization. In the beginning, I credited the graduate students with my failure to rise to the material, but after discussing methods and content with others in the class, I realized it was not the graduate assistants. I was encouraged for a time when I got a B on the midterm exam, but on the rest of the tests that semester and the critical final, the best I could do was a C, never a D, however. I simply could not do the work. No matter how I figured it, even with the excellent results in the qualitative analysis, my average always came out a C+.

Passing college algebra came as a pleasant surprise. All through the semester, I never had any idea of where I stood in the class. It was not until I saw the C posted beside my initials on the door of our classroom that I knew. Being the only male in a class of twenty seemed a freshman's dream come true, though I don't recall that I ever spoke to more than two or three of the girls, young women, all semester. The instructor posted no As on the roster and only a few Bs and same number of Cs with the same number of Ds and two Fs. I knew I had no reason to feel joy, but I did. It was the last time I'd ever crack an algebra text or have to think about quadratic equations.

The most glaring incongruity of my freshman year was my joining Lambda Chi Alpha. My limited finances should have made it impossible, and it went counter to all wisdom. When I first arrived on campus, I received several invitations to have lunch or dinner at various frat houses, all of which I readily accepted because of the free meals. One week, I had invitations for every lunch that week. A few invitations came from total strangers, though in almost every case, I met an old acquaintance, someone I had known in grade school in Beaumont or high school in Corpus. After Christmas break, I accepted a Lambda Chi Alpha pledge pin from Bob Woods, whom I had known well at Corpus Christi High School. None of the other houses interested me, and one or two were downright offensive, either because of the outright snobbery that no one even attempted to disguise or because of the rancid anti-Semitism. From the first visit, Lambda Chi was different in every way.

I joined, I told myself, to have some place to land after classes, someplace to hang out before I had to show up for work at the funeral home. For almost the entire first term, the only person I saw socially on anything like a regular basis was Jane. We always met for supper when the check arrived from home or other times when we were able to arrange a lunch together or just meet to talk. Until Christmas break, I had rarely seen anyone I knew from Corpus, rarely spoken to anyone, except the people I worked with at Hyltin's. I once asked my zoology lab partner to have coffee after lab, but our conversation came slowly, and I could see she was anxious to be off. Dating a classmate or a friend from home was impossible. More important than social contacts, however, was having at least one good meal a day. I had found that of all the lunches and dinners I had taken as a "rushee," the meals at the Lambda Chi Alpha house were the best, far better than any of the meals I could afford at the boarding houses. Food in the commons, though cheap, became inedible after a week. When Bob Woods explained that I could take noon meals every day at a cost that truly amazed me, I told Jane how reasonable they were and how I had often missed noon meals entirely either by accident or by not having money for lunch *and* dinner, and when I reported the Lambda Chi's meals cost even less than her meals in SRD (Scottish Rite Dormitory), she told me to go for it.

I was sure Mama would disapprove because of the initiation cost. Bob had assured me that the fraternity was so hard up for new members—the war, you know—that the treasurer and house manager would gladly make a time payment arrangement if I needed it. The seven full meals a week were of overriding importance; moreover having lunch in the company of agreeable guys only enhanced the quality of the meals. So when I returned after Christmas break, which ended on December 28, I pledged to a fraternity and no longer felt like an alien.

When the new semester began at the end of January, I had the same class and lab schedule I had had in the fall. The only difference, a major difference as it turned out, was physical anthropology in place of math. Anthropology and Bible meant I was two courses separated from a normal premed path. The difference would reverberate down through the years, and I could almost say it changed my life, that it set me on a path to a life in teaching. When I signed up for it in preregistration, I was not even sure what Introduction to Physical Anthropology actually encompassed; what I knew about the subject was rudimentary at best and rested on one book I had read in my sophomore year in high school, *To Lhasa in Disguise* by the anthropologist William Montgomery McGovern. My motivation for choosing Anthropology 105 had little to do, at the time, with any real desire to learn about the physical characteristics of *Homo sapiens* but had much to do with filling out my schedule and of finding a class at the right time on the right days and, most important, a class that was not mathematics. William McGovern's book had introduced me to cultural anthropology, not physical, but the course description and my normal powers of deduction told me all I needed to know.

More important than the subject was the professor who taught the course. I've always found it difficult—no, impossible—to avoid hyperbole when speaking or writing about Dr. J. Gilbert McAllister. Hundreds—nay, thousands—have had the same difficulty. Whether loved or hated, whether admired and worshiped or reviled and vilified, he was one whom no one could take for granted. After the first week of class, after the first class actually, I fell into the camp of those who "loved the man this side idolatry." He put us on notice that first class that he would do everything he could to make us reexamine all the assumptions about humankind we had carried with us to his class; all "old baggage," all our "most cherished assumptions" about human beings, physically and culturally, would come under scrutiny. The tiered classroom, filled to capacity, held slightly more than a hundred bodies, but unlike the larger lectures I had in chemistry and zoology, we were all quite literally engaged and as wide-awake and as attentive as we would have been in any smaller class. He stood on a raised dais behind a lectern that held a large black binder, though he rarely glanced at it or opened it, and he read from it only when a long quotation was better served when read aloud. McAllister was not very tall, not more than five feet six or seven inches, not as tall as I, and he was uncommonly good-looking with steel gray hair and sharp blue eyes, his face deeply marked from days on archeological digs. He always wore a slight smile. I can't recall him ever frowning, even when he was confronting or debating an angry student, which happened frequently. The subtle smile gave us the impression that he was putting us on in some way which we were unaware, that in the end, the ideas he threw out were all a sham or a hoax. We learned early, however, that he was forcing us to think, throwing us into doubt.

When someone blurted out that first day, "You mean, everything we were told before was wrong? What makes you think you're always right? Why should we believe you?"

He was obviously pleased with the student's question as well as with himself. He had stirred the somnambulant, had gotten exactly the reaction he had planned for, and had gotten it early. He rocked back on heels and smiled the wicked smirk of a devil. It was a marvelous performance; I had never been so involved in a class before.

"The answer to your first question is *yes!*" he said. "The answer to the second is I don't know that I *am* right, I'm still trying to find that out. And finally, you probably *shouldn't* believe me. My job is not to make you believe *me* but to make you learn, to teach you think, and to settle your own doubts. You see, I believe in EDUCATION BY IRRITATION."

His words left his mouth in large block capitals. He paused, waiting for his words to sink in. Some in the class, I suspected, had heard these words before, either in a previous anthropology class with McAllister or from some who already had been irritated by this now famous method. I noticed heads nodding and faces smiling, along with a few heads shaking and faces frowning. I wrote the words down and underlined them.

"Since so many instructors *and professors*"—the last dripping with sarcasm—"at this university believe in examination by regurgitation, I insist on education by irritation."

He was into it now, was power-pumping each new thought, and it explained why the room was filled. This was why an elective, a class not required in any curriculum, with the exception of that rare student majoring in anthropology in 1944, was packed with freshmen, sophomores, juniors, *and* seniors. Then he continued, "If I irritate you enough, you will try to prove me wrong. To do that, you will have to think for yourselves and find the evidence to prove me wrong and yourselves right; and, prove all those precious assumptions you carried here—and if you do that—you will have taught yourself more than you intended to or more than you expected to learn. The result will be real learning, perhaps for the first time, and I won't have to 'teach' you anymore."

"What if we find out you're wrong? Aren't we wasting our time if you are giving us false information?" Another challenger's voice encouraged nods and hums and muttered *yeses*.

"Of course, you *are* wasting your time. You should be out there learning on your own, but you aren't smart enough--*yet*. You don't know how, and like most, you're probably too lazy. It's too easy to carry around all the precious myths that you accept as truths that you were nurtured on. Too easy to remain ignorant and self-satisfied. It takes a brilliant teacher like me to make you think, to irritate you enough to think for yourselves." His smile spread across his face. Hate and love burbled and boiled all through the tiered class. Another pause, another smirk: he was enjoying it.

These words are the closest I can come to describing the essence of that first experience; of course, they are not his remarks verbatim but are as close as I can come now, lo, after all these many years. After the war, when I returned to the university and signed up for a class with Dr. Mac, I heard again this same lecture on education by irritation and found then that the reaction was essentially the same, though not as strong as it was that first time, for you see, the later class was over half filled with ex-GIs who were older and who had lived lives a far cry from those in Anthropology 105 class of 1944. I have no reason to doubt that previous as well as subsequent first days differed very much from the class I just described.

That first day in Introduction to Physical Anthropology in spring of 1944 was, I believe, a typical first day. Rather than irritate him, the challenges from several brave ones brought forth all that was good in his method, for it showed him that the class was engaged, intellectually and morally. His method, we knew, would not leave unmoved any contending bone. We were all to be subjected to mind searches as well as soul searches. At the end came the remark he apparently had been waiting for.

"How can we challenge you, Dr. McAllister? You have a PhD, most of us are only freshmen," the voice entreated.

And now we could all see he was pleased beyond pleasing, proud of the bold student's bold thought and proud of himself, and if my own fifty years of experience in the classroom has taught *me* anything, I am sure he was proud of the class. "You have a library with all the evidence you need to prove me wrong. I never grade you for how well you regurgitate what I say but how well you support what you *think* you've learned. Go to the library," he said calmly and slowly, and then as if he could not resist a note of sarcasm, he added, "Go to the library. It's that large Austin limestone structure with its large phallic erection in the middle of the campus. You can't miss it." Then he added softly, "I do not grade you for giving me 'correct' answers, those things I believe. I grade you on how you think, not what you think, in other words how you make *me think*."

He supplied us with an extensive list of reading assignments in books and periodicals he had placed in the Reserve Reading Room of the Main Library to which he had directed us. Many of the items we discovered contradicted his own statements in class. He expected us to know enough about these other positions to be able to respond to them on the hour quizzes and the final. Until his class, I had never taken such a thought-challenging essay exam; he required us to develop different kinds of study habits in order to prepare for his tests. I continued my plodding pace and ended his class with a perfect 75 in his course, a C, but I learned far more than any grade was capable of indicating, things that would remain part of me for the rest of my life, most of which went far beyond the limits of physical anthropology. From the first day of class, he constantly derided the importance that schools place on grades.

That second semester, coinciding with McAllister's insisting we learn to question and to think critically, Dr. Helen James's assigned S. I. Hayakawa's introductory book on general semantics, *Language in Action*, which the author said was designed to clear "the mind of harmful obstruction." All my earlier learning had been based on the idea that knowledge consisted of accumulating a warehouse of irrefutable fact, and my excursions into chemistry and biology was just that, a studious accumulation of facts and definitions; it would be several years before I learned that science was not a fixed and immutable system of truth but only another system of knowing within the limits of probability or within tolerances. When Mr. Schultz told us that results of our experiments had to fall within the limits of "experimental error," I simply assumed that was a conventional way of speaking and never looked beyond its implication. "Ideal experimental conditions" never suggested to me that the universe was in constant flux or that absolutes exist only in the realm of intellect. "Scientific truth" was an absolute I never questioned, but I would soon learn that such a belief was the chief obstruction to real knowledge. It meant that I would have to reread all I had read in *The Story of Philosophy* if I were to understand what I had already read. But rather than feeling confused, I felt that I was actually on the *way* to becoming enlightened. It meant nothing to cram the notes I had taken in class lectures or to commit to memory the facts stated in a text. It meant reading with insight, for the *nuance* as well as the fact. Words shifted meanings as contexts changed, "cow^1 was not cow^2" and "the map was not the territory." These ideas were not difficult to grasp, though it was difficult not to fall into the pattern of a belief that stated otherwise. Thinking critically was never easy, never meant to be easy. Most of the courses we had been taking earlier never demanded that we approach ideas critically, only that we recite them accurately, in other words, regurgitate in the form and style in which they were administered. Every MWF, Helen James challenged us to think about Hayakawa's "scientific and literary principles," the principles of general semantics. And every TTS morning at eleven, McAllister forced us to rethink dogmas and "received opinions." Nothing was the same as it was before. But I also knew that neither of these classes was helping me reach the goal I had set for myself when I left Corpus Christi. It seemed that indeed all academic occasions did "inform against me" or conspire to derail me from my charted course.

The fraternity did not directly add to that distraction, but it didn't help. Lunch at the house became a source of pleasure, not because the food was healthy and well prepared but because the company, the friendship, and the talk were nourishing in other ways. Our talk ranged widely over subjects I had never heard of nor had ever discussed before. So many academic majors were represented at table that I felt they contributed to my loss of focus on my original idea for coming to school in Austin. Bob Wood did not seem to suffer from these distractions; he was maintaining his B+ or A- average needed to apply for medical school, and while he probably would have to answer the call and go into the service after spring term ended, he would return knowing that there was nothing he had to undo when he got back. My grades stayed in the C category, even though I loved the classes and approved of my instructors. My lab grades in zoo and qualitative analysis hovered around A and A-, but lecture grades never got above C, even in zoology, which had been my strongest class in the fall term. Bob tried to soften the blow of my constant C when he remarked he was amazed and wondered how I carried a full load and spent so much time at Hyltin's on call at all hours. I could only reply that, in effect, I really *did not do it*, not at all.

One February morning, when I met Jane for coffee and the monthly allowance, she noticed a rash on my throat and cheeks and mentioned that a girl in her dorm had come down with German measles and had to go to the hospital. Not to worry her, I told her I'd already had the measles and couldn't possibly be sick since I felt quite well. As we were walking in the vicinity of Old B Hall, where the University Health Service was located, she insisted I pop down to the basement and get it checked out. Sure enough, I had German measles. I called Hyltin's immediately, told them that I was contagious and probably shouldn't come in. They agreed. The doctor reported that health service wards at St. Stephens were full and couldn't accept more students, so I called Walter Varner, the fraternity house manager, and asked if there was a room where I could be quarantined. Walter Varner, the most humane of all the brothers, said of course and insisted I stay where I was, that he would come for me in his car. So far, none of the Lambda Chis had fallen ill, he said.

"There's a war on, remember? We have several empty rooms," he said.

Walter set me up in the empty room, drove to Hyltin's, got a pair of my pajamas, my books, and a change of clothes. They had a house porter in those days who covered the windows with blankets that darkened the room. He and Walter moved a record player and a stack of classical records into the room then left me to listen and "get well."

"I know, with measles you are supposed to save your eyes, but I read when I had German measles, and it didn't hurt me, so here are your books and some of mine. Read this, it's pretty good."

He handed me Charles Jackson's *The Lost Weekend,* a bestseller that I had read about, though hadn't read.

Varner was an interesting guy. Though he was a business administration major, he was always reading something totally outside his field and was frequently making one or more of the brothers angry with witty and ironic remarks about their lack of "cooth and culchure." Varner had been severely burned as a child, leaving one side of his torso covered with a bizarre skin transplant. He appeared quite un-self-conscious about it, although he was conscious it had made him 4-F and for that he was self-conscious. Varner was also one of the most generous men I'd ever known.

I went to work on the record collection that was heavy in Russian composers—Prokofief, Stravinsky, Glinka, Shostakovich, the music of our "heroic ally"—but there was also a sampling of romantics like Berlioz and

Bruch. All were composers whose names I knew but not the works. I'd always heard how men's lives were changed when they fell ill as children and were confined for months or years, and I'd heard how they turned in upon themselves and their books and how these hours of idleness and reading changed their lives. So for five days, I listened to "*Sacre du Printemps*," "*Symphonie Fantastique*," "The Red Poppy," and Bruch's Violin Concerto, music that made me wish for an illness that might stretch from five to ten to fifteen days. I read the rest of Hayakawa and finished *Giants in the Earth*, and then I tackled the Jackson and Wilson books, though the latter disappointed me in not being any more scandalous than it was.

Helen James was the only instructor who'd be concerned, I thought. A medical excuse was all the others needed, so I asked Jane to tell her why I was out. Dr. Hall might be concerned, but I would call him for the reading assignment. I was so far behind reading in the travels and writings of St. Paul that I needed these hours to catch up.

In the end, my German measles were less a hindrance than a boon, and I walked out of the house after five days un-speckled, and to my surprise Varner and the fraternity never sent me a bill. Aside from the brief vacation from class, I came through my week of isolation better off than I was before. Hyltin reduced the number of hours I was expected to be on call, keeping as a third driver the man he used during my absence; from then on, I worked only two nights a week and every other weekend for the same pay. Also, while lying there in the darkened room, I developed a broader understanding of "serious" music, particularly Stravinsky and Shostakovich, which I had always taken to be too modern for my taste. I had used the time to read ahead for English. When I returned to Dr. James's class and told her I had finished reading *Giants in the Earth* and that I had liked it even more than *Ethan Frome*, she seemed pleased and said she would expect an even better paper from me than the one I had written on *Ethan Frome*. That she recalled the earlier paper made me determined to write a better paper, and I began immediately working on a critique of Bret Hansa, calling the paper "Madness on the Prairie." I also checked out Rølvaag's sequel to *Giants*, called *Peder Victorious*, hoping I might pick up something on Bret's madness to give depth to the paper. It wasn't to make points but simply because I'd found *Giants in the Earth* so remarkable; however, I couldn't resist "dropping" a remark about the sequel that impressed her enough to ask in class one day, in a rather informal or off-hand manner, what I thought of the other Rølvaag novel. Couldn't hurt, I thought.

Jackson's *The Lost Weekend* was too disturbing to be called a *joy* to read, but I liked its tone of realism and his alcoholic hero's arguing the merits of

Scott Fitzgerald, saying how one day he would teach a course in college called the "Great American Novel" and would put Fitzgerald right up there on top. Varner explained to me that Jackson's character would better be referred to as an "antihero," not hero. I understood Jackson's reason for choosing Fitzgerald, recalling "Babylon Revisited" whose "hero" was also destroyed by alcohol. I felt serious satisfaction in being able to grasp Jackson's allusion to Fitzgerald and felt satisfied that Jackson corroborated my own original assessment.

For the rest of the spring term, I spent more time preparing for English and anthropology than for all my other classes combined. McAllister's lectures often turned into debates between him and an irate student who refused to accept his views on race or his pronouncements about culture, particularly cultural relativism. "BM," Before McAllister, few of us had ever thought it possible that all human values were not handed to us a priori, like simple Euclidean axioms. It was highly unreasonable that our values evolved within our culture, that others evolved in other cultures, and that one "culture's" set of absolutes were not necessarily another's or, even more disturbing, that our cultural values, the values of white, predominantly Northern European middle-class culture, were not universal or, as we put it, *ought* to be universal. Ruth Benedict's *Patterns of Culture*, which was an imperative read on the reserve-reading list, figured often in the exams. Dr. Mac had told us in our first class that we would cover all the requirements of physical anthro syllabus, but he would be emphasizing the importance of cultural anthro all through the term, chiefly because knowing the importance of cultural theories and observations was far more important than measuring skeletons. In our first class, he had hinted how the physical anthropologists placed so much emphasis on physical characteristics of race it distorted the axis of racist beliefs; he cited, in darkly sarcastic tones, Ernest Albert Hooton on race, probably the most widely read, most popular physical anthropologist, and pronounced Hooton's name with such vitriolic emphasis that many in the class, sufficiently irritated, promptly headed straight to the Tower library.

In 1943 and 1944, such views were anathema to most good white Texans; they bordered on the un-American, even worse the un-Texan. Few of us had ever heard anyone speak openly and critically of ethnic and racial prejudices, such concepts we had never heard spoken of with anything resembling rational objectivity. Dr. Mac began a discussion of comparative cultural values one day by describing his visit to a local butcher where he heard the butcher offer a customer horse meat as a substitute for beef because of the wartime beef shortage. When he described her revulsion at the idea, most of us agreed, not because anyone had ever eaten horse steaks or knew for certain that horse meat was inedible or harmful but because we felt "you just don't eat horse meat." He smiled his usual smile of triumph and asked us why. I had encountered the idea in Ruth Benedict's *Patterns of Culture* that he had placed on reserve and said so. He smiled again, "Well, Gilliland, what do you think?"

I answered simply, "I have no evidence to disagree with Ruth Benedict. Taste is a cultural condition."

He began then, "The Apache and Comanche always preferred horse meat to beef or any other meat." He paused, waited. When no one challenged him, he began again, "They apparently thrived on horse meat, and when I lived with the Mescalero Apache, I often ate horse meat and suffered no ill effects. There is nothing *un-natural*—whatever that means—eating horseflesh or dog or earthworms, for that matter, or anything that isn't poisonous . . . I know people, some otherwise quite intelligent and highly cultivated, who would refuse to eat a raw oyster." He waited.

I could see, glancing around the class, it was sinking in slowly. From there, he related a series of cultural practices which many members of the class found disgusting, nauseating, and finally immoral.

"If I were in China and offered my Chinese guest a glass of milk, it would be practically the same as offering him or her a tall warm glass of urine," he said.

"That's disgusting!" one young woman said as she gathered her coat and books and left.

He smiled as if to thank her for departing; he had made his point. However, only a few diehards in the class continued to be shocked or dismayed after that. He was preparing us for a giant leap: the discussion of race and the meaning of racism. Referring to a recent article in *Life* magazine that quoted Ernest . . . Albert . . . Hooton, whom McAllister had earlier proclaimed an idiot and his article an example of unscientific bigotry, he began to challenge the controversial idea of types in more and more detail. "Bigotry has no place in science, has no place anywhere, but it exists all around us," he said.

The class began to stir uneasily. Most people in Texas of 1944, in that class, believed God had made some men black and some white, some inferior and some superior, for a reason. McAllister had accomplish what he had intended to, but some in class were so enraged that he questioned the unassailable truth, the sanctity of racial distinction, that they could not see he was manipulating the class into thinking about one of the most taboo subjects of the times. Few in class had been raised to look on racial arguments with any degree of objectivity; many even considered themselves to be racially tolerant, even those who abhorred the Jim Crow laws. I had learned and accepted the polite bigotries of the day from Mama. At the dinner table,

I had learned never to use the N word, to use "nirgah" instead, for it was polite. We might avoid ugly racial epithets and refuse to condone their usage by others, but we could not totally abandon feelings of discomfort if required to "mix" socially, to shake hands or sit at a table with "them." I recalled how TM's mother, a genuinely kind and generous woman, had found "them" out of place one Sunday at South Bluff Methodist Church, although Brother Mason had openly welcomed the two boatswains and had "extended to them the hand of Christian fellowship." Arguments for segregating races had grown more sophisticated, more "scientific," and McAllister was about to attack the mythology of racial superiority and about to expose its cultural foundation, its fallacies, and its bad science.

Ironically, at almost exactly the same time, just an hour before our anthropology class, I had the "good luck" to hear the other side propounded vigorously from the lectern in my zoology 1b lecture by Dr. Griffin as he laid out a "statistical proof of the racial inferiority of the Negro race." Taking up the issue of genetics and eugenics, Griffin had begun a series of lectures only a day or so before Dr. Mac sallied forth to expose the mythology of racial superiority and inferiority. Griffin's lecture would have done Rosenberg, Hitler's "anthropologist," proud. While Dr. Griffin avoided overt anti-Semitic statements, he was not loath to using "nigger." His bell-shaped curves and statistical "evidence" preached the arguments of racial purity using for support the logic of "mongrelization." Education by irritation was not his intention; education by indoctrination was. In a way, the conflict of racial theory was spectacular theater; most of us had never encountered an academic battle of any kind.

Dr. McAllister announced that he did not welcome an intramural conflict of this sort, but neither was he unwilling, he said, to deflate Griffin's claims argument by argument. Using physical measurements of bone structure and hard empirical evidence of physical anthropology, he destroyed utterly Griffin's claim that the Negro race had not "evolved" physically and was, therefore, "inferior." Although he did cover, I suppose, the required details of physical anthropology, his telling discussions of human cultural or ethnic characteristics were the most interesting part of his lectures, while Dr. Mack offended all groups by exploding racial myths and exposing them as cultural or ethnic distinctions rather than biological or physical distinctions.

In Helen James's class, Hayakawa's discourses on general semantics challenged all our earlier assumptions about language and the tools of thought. Hayakawa brought the class close to the edge of an abyss, so close in fact that some students could not follow and fled, either physically absenting themselves from the class or by dropping it altogether or, most often, by simply closing their minds. A fraternity brother shut out the class entirely by studiously learning how to regurgitate Dr. Mac's ideas cleverly and convincingly. For some, however, his method was much liberation from mind control as was Helen James's introduction to general semantics *ala* Hayakawa.

To the shock of many, we learned the president of the university, Homer Price Rainey, had recommended ending racial segregation at the university in the early years of his presidency and had come under heavy attack by members of the board of regents and the legislature. Few Texans sided with Rainey on this matter, though a slim majority of the faculty agreed. The campus Greek fraternities could not support Rainey, all having in their charters and initiation rites racial and religious conditions for membership. On this tough issue, however, individual members did agree with the need to desegregate state colleges and universities. No one, however, would risk criticizing the racial slurs directed toward the enemy in the Pacific—no one, that is, except Dr. J. Gilbert McAllister, who attacked even the racist propaganda directed toward the Japanese.

While I had begun to drift away from my commitment to chemistry and science, I neither consciously nor unconsciously ever rejected scientific method as the most reliable means of discovering truth. I continued to believe in the efficacy of inductive and deductive reasoning as well as the virtues of objectivity over subjectivity for establishing broader truths. That spring term, I was beginning to learn how intellectual experiences could overwhelm a person as effectively as physical or religious ones. It was then that I began to realize that I preferred the academic life to all other forms of life. I had experienced nothing like it before. It was indeed a protean change, a change so profound I knew, I believed, I could never return to what or who or where I had been before.

Near the beginning of the semester, I had read in the *Daily Texan* that the navy V-12 and ASTP (Army Specialized Training Program) exams would be administered sometime during the semester and that applications for either program were available in the Dean of Men's office. At the time, I thought seriously about applying for V-12 when the next cycle came around because I was under the impression that ASTP had been discontinued. Late in the winter and early spring and almost every weekend, a half dozen or so men from the 102nd Infantry Division in training at Camp Swift would camp out occupying extra beds and couches at the Lambda Chi house; they came as visiting brothers from colleges all over the country. They told how they had enlisted, not waiting for the draft, had volunteered for ASTP with the understanding that after a period in college, they would be sent to Officers

Candidate School and become second lieutenants to serve in the branch of their specialty. But after two terms, three for a few, the army discontinued the program and sent them all to the infantry, forming new divisions that would become reinforcements, replacements after the D-Day landings. A few went to the signal corps, and a very small number of premeds remained to go to medical school. All of the men visiting the house from Camp Swift, near Bastrop, Texas, were completing their combat infantry training with the 102nd Ozark Division and were part of the build-up for the invasion of Europe. When I mentioned to several that I had taken and passed the exam, they quickly advised me to apply for V-12, insisting it was by far the better program. I have never been sure why I chose the army. When I received my letter of acceptance, there was still a chance for me to change my mind and go navy, but I stayed with my original choice. Had I checked the box that read Navy, I would probably not have left Austin but would have continued on into the summer term as a swabbie college boy.

As the semester wound down and my grades continued to slide or stagnate, it became obvious that I would have to change my major. I also knew that I wanted to stay in college, to continue what I was doing as long as possible, perhaps forever, but I also knew it was impossible. I was broke. There was one way to stay in school. I was still six months from a call from my draft board, six months more of college had I had the money. The age for enlisting in ASTP was seventeen and required a parent's permission, something Mama said she refused to do until I convinced her that ASTP, now ASTRP (the R standing for reserve), was a noncombat branch intended only for college students. I was not entirely honest, for from the beginning I had no intentions of remaining in the program when I reached eighteen. I was caught between two desires, one to remain a student in perpetuity and the other to become part of the Great Crusade. However, were the war to end when I became eighteen, I would remain a student. I hadn't heard it put just so, but I knew it to be a fact: "All wars are boyish." I simply wanted to be there as my father had.

June 17, eleven days after D-Day the week before the final exams, I hitchhiked to San Antonio to take the oath and sign the papers for the ASTRP. Immediately after my swearing in, I returned to Austin and took my finals, and a few days later learned I had passed everything, though some just barely. I hated the idea of returning to Corpus Christi and wished I could have gone into the program immediately, thereby avoiding all explanations. Had I been able to find a full-time job at one of the other funeral homes, I would have. Too many things had happened before my leaving for Austin to ever make me feel homesick for the house on Clifford Street again.

Chapter 5

You'll Never Get Rich

For as long as I could remember, I had thought of becoming a doctor one day, or perhaps a scientist working in a medical field. It had been my *raison d'être* all through school and was *the* reason for leaving Corpus and enrolling in the university. But each passing week throughout the spring semester in Austin, I began to see that it was not to be. Had my interests not shifted from my beloved chemistry, my grades would have convinced me that I simply didn't have the ability or the commitment to continue down that road. Accepting that truth had not been easy. Oh, I could spin out reasons why I had done so poorly: I had been too young and lacked discipline, or I should have gone to Del Mar and continued working at the refinery, or I shouldn't have joined a fraternity, or I shouldn't have taken the job at Hyltin's, or had I put my money in the bank instead of giving it to Mama, I wouldn't have had to work at all. In the end, they all sounded more like excuses than reasons. Whatever the "truth" was, I was no longer "committed" as I had been when I first enrolled. Other interests intruded on the dream of a lifetime, new interests that began to shape new dreams perhaps. I had changed but had not changed my love for the university.

At the time, I barely understood my growing love affair with academe. The idea of being in college and going to lectures, of class discussions like those in English or anthropology transcended chemistry and zoology lectures and labs. Mostly, I loved hearing Dr. McAllister rip apart the "logic" of bigotry. He was the first *provocateur académique* I had ever met. I loved that French one of my classmates used before class one day when referring to the good doctor, and I memorized it immediately. Going to the Biological Sciences Library and digging out bizarre facts about East Texas infestations of *necatur americanus*, American hookworm, and writing the term paper on the subject for English 2 composition had been a kind of joy. As I was leaving Austin, I dreamed of returning to the university after the war, dreamed of walking to class through those overarching oaks or dropping in on lectures that would interest me, perhaps getting a job in the library, the incredible Main Library with its stacks and stacks and stacks that were like nothing I had ever seen or imagined. *There's no place like a great university*, I told myself, and the University of Texas *was* a great university. I would return and take only courses that interested me: anthropology or archaeology, maybe even philosophy or a poetry class. I thought of becoming a "harmless drudge" in pursuit of . . .? Who knows?

Our ability to change, I told myself, is our greatest blessing as human beings. It's why *Homo* is *sapien*, I told myself. So in spite of my disappointment, I was still optimistic about the future, for I knew I could find something I could do and recalled how, when I was in grade school, I *had* found *it*, that "something" in the chemistry sets and in the orchestra, things that allowed me to be where I wanted to be and to be who I wanted. The "protean self"— where did I read that?—saves us from atrophy and stagnation. Finding a new goal is simply an act of survival in a sea of change. I read it years later in R. J. Lifton; the "protean self" makes it possible.[1] At the time, I had no way of understanding what was happening or why, but I had the good fortune to face this change at a time when everything else around me was changing, when everyone was adjusting to the necessity of circumstance. And joining the Army Specialized Training Reserve Program was my tool of change, the lever lifting me out of a trench of despair. (Did *I* say that? Oh my.) ASTRP offered me a way to stay in school while fulfilling my "obligation." Everyone I knew was in or on his way into the navy, army, or air corps.

Orders to report to A&M College of Texas at College Station, Texas, on August 15 arrived the day after I arrived back in Corpus. With orders in hand, everything was coming together after all. Who knew how long Hitler would last in the East *and* the West? In all likelihood, I would be overseas before the war ended. All I had to do was wait a month and I'd be gone. In the meantime, finding a real job for those few weeks, I thought, was out of the question. There was always carrying Albert's golf clubs or mowing the lawn. Did they have "college men" caddying at Oso Golf Club? Probably not—maybe the country club. That sounded right. There was a joke going around: What's the English for the *coup de grace*? Answer: *Mow de lawn*. I would just have to bite the bullet and *coup de grace*.

But once again, as he had a year ago, Albert came to my rescue. I hadn't been home a day when he called from his office to say that Dunne's Funeral Home, needed an ambulance driver. Earlier. Albert had told Pete Dunne that I was driving ambulances for Hyltin's in Austin, so when Pete heard I was home from UT, he called and asked Albert to tell me if I wanted had a job driving for him until I was "called up." It was perfect. Pete's younger brother had joined the army, and all but one of his drivers and assistants had been

---

[1]   *The Protean Self: Human Resilience in an Age of Fragmentation* (1993).

called up. I liked Pete. Of all the men I had caddied for, Pete was the one I most enjoyed being with. He was witty, intelligent, and liberal in his politics, unlike most of Alert's golf buddies that hated Roosevelt and all Democrats. Pete never failed to pay me for the full eighteen holes instead of a rate for bagging double. When I told him I had barely a month and a half before I had to report, he said he would be glad to put me on for that long. It was a windfall in more ways than money. It would keep me occupied. Having a job driving for Pete would solve everything.

When Pete told me the pay was twenty-five dollars a week and that I would be off call every other night and every other Sunday, I almost blurted out that I'd work every night if he wanted. Once more, I was being paid adult wages. When he showed me the room for on duty drivers—a cavernous high-ceilinged attic room cooled by a giant exhaust fan—I asked Pete if I could stay there every night, even though I wasn't on call. I'd go home for meals from time to time, I told him, but I really preferred not staying in the room I shared with Donnie. The attic room was cooler than mine at home, and I liked the isolation and being able to read undisturbed. I had hoped to use Jane's room and leave Don to our old room. Mama was renting Jane's room to Naval officer couples. He agreed without questioning, but he insisted I take the time off when I had it, and I agreed to that.

It was more than I had hoped for; the huge attic was more private than my room at home or at Hyltin's. The bed was set back in a dormer with a little nook where I stacked my books and hung my clothes. I had a quiet cozy private space all to myself; the other driver's bed was across the wide room in the other dormer. The attic had its own inclosed toilet and there was a shower and sink on the floor below. Even the constant low hum of the exhaust fan was no bother, rather served to dampen all other sounds. Rustic unpainted paneling covering the studs of the attic and the steep slope of the ceiling reminded me what Rudolph's and Marcello's garret in *La Bohème* must look like. God! I felt good. For the time, what was behind seemed far behind, and what lay ahead . . . well, it was ahead.

A happy Irish Catholic clan, the Dunne family was fun to be around, as was their circle of friends that now included me. Pete was a good employer, one of the most ethical funeral directors in the business, and Pete's father, no longer a practicing mortician, was always there like the patriarch, sitting at the main desk in the foyer, greeting people, and answering the phone during the days. He didn't speak to the drivers much, but he rarely passed me a weekly pay envelope that did not have a five-dollar bonus in it. Billy, the other full-time driver and assistant, and I rarely made calls together. We'd gone in high school together but hadn't known each other. He and Jenny, also in our class in high school, had gotten married as soon as they'd graduated, and he had gone to work for Pete right off and had gotten a deferment from the draft.

Riding with Pete, whether night or day, was entirely different from my experience in Austin. Pete and his brother had graduated from St. Edwards University in Austin, a Jesuit college, and were both qualified RNs, Pete a qualified ER nurse as well as a mortician. As far as Pete knew, I was still studying premed, so each call we made together was accompanied by a mini-lecture in emergency medical procedures. Peter never allowed anyone to refer to ambulances or hearses as "meat wagons" and never regarded the emergency service as a means of advertising the funeral home, as Mr. Hyltin and other funeral directors did. I enjoyed listening to his advice and watching him deal with clients. He and Virgin, his younger sister, and old Mr. Dunne treated me as an equal, spoke to me not as a callow seventeen-year-old but as an adult. When Pete had something to teach, he did so with clarity and emphasis.

When I left Corpus, there were no sad farewells and no tearful send-off. To keep Mama from worrying, I had explained that, being in ASTRP, I was not likely to ever be in combat, and I convinced her that the college program would probably keep me occupied until the war ended.

August 1944 was the busiest month of the war, according to historian Geoffrey Perrett,[2] and in the Pacific, the movement through the islands and the bombing raids on Japan gave everyone a feeling that it would all soon be over, that it might not last another year. Optimists were even saying that the war in the European Theater of Operations would be over by Christmas, and the likelihood that I would ever be in danger was slight.

When Dorothy asked me to visit her in Beaumont before reporting for duty at A&M, I was happy to accept her invitation. Mama agreed I should make the visit to say good-bye to Grandmother and all the Seiberts whom I hadn't seen since I was a sophomore in high school. As far as I could recall, I had never been made over so much before. Dorothy's two daughters—Dorothy Rose, five, and Jo Dell, three—made me feel "plumb growed-up" by calling me Uncle Joe. Dorothy even had a family gathering of all the Seibert clan she could muster. All in all, it was rather strange being treated so, and I mentioned it to her at the party. Uncle Walter had heard me confide and said, "You *are* grown up, boy. You're in the army now."

That night, as we sat around and picked on the leftovers, Lewis, her husband, served me a beer like it was the normal thing to do. When I told

---

[2]   *There's a War to Be Won* (1991).

Dorothy that, all I knew for sure was that I wanted to return to college as soon as possible after the war, and from the way I felt then, I didn't care if I never finished college. That was the first time I'd said out loud just how I had begun to feel about the university, and it pleased me that she smiled and looked as pleased as I.

When I arrived at A&M, I found a pretty homogenous group, all the same age and in the upper quarter of their graduating class, nearly all from Texas, Oklahoma, Arkansas, or Louisiana. I was the only one who had completed a full year of college. The others were all fresh from high school, though a few had some credits from junior colleges. A few had attended military academies. My roommate, Jerry Hayes, had graduated from a top parochial high school in New Orleans. Arthur Dykes, the son of a doctor from Italy, Texas and I would stay friends until he passed away in 2012. Several members of that class were truly exceptional academically, young men like Carlos Lovejoy, Dave Brown, and Leslie McNair. The testing process had determined the quality of students.

The not-so-young master sergeant that greeted us as we stepped off the bus from the station told us, in a friendly collegiate manner, not to unpack since we would be moving to assigned rooms once everyone had arrived and once our class schedules were posted. In a day or two, he said, we would be assigned to platoons and given platoon leaders, but for the present, we were to relax and get acquainted with our classmates, about half of whom had already moved in. When someone asked if we were to be issued uniforms, he laughed, saying, "Yes, soldier, you're in the army now and not behind a plow." We laughed too when he added, "Things will change, you'll see, when you put on the uniform, but for now, relax and wait."

By mid-afternoon, when the last "Asstraper" arrived, our CO, Major Apple, ordered the first sergeant to assemble us all on the grass in front our dorm, Duncan Hall no. 1. It was all very collegiate or what I thought must have been what college was like before the war—slow, lazy, comfortable, friendly. Major Apple began by telling us right off that he was an Old Army man retired many years ago and called back to oversee this bunch of young scholars. He referred to us as "young lads." He had been, he said, a young lieutenant of cavalry with Pershing in Mexico and later also with Pershing in France. He then introduced First Lieutenant Jors, his middle-aged executive officer.

"Lieutenant Jors, my executive officer, will be your military science instructor and the man you go to when you have questions," he said; then the lieutenant took over.

It would be two days before we would receive our uniforms and equipment, but until then, we would be "falling out" in more or less regular formations and marching to mess in as orderly a manner as we were capable of. Three regular army noncoms were in charge of our training, mostly close-order drill, calisthenics, and indoctrination; like Jors, they were all "over-age-in-rank" reservists or National Guard soldiers called up to train the likes of us. All in all, I found the formations and the parade to the mess hall stimulating. For all three meals, we fell out in formations, followed by strict roll call, and then marched off with cadence counted by one of ours. By the end of the week, our chow formations were as rigid and proper as the Aggies and no longer an embarrassment.

The first time we lined up in platoons, we were still in civilian clothes and on the wide parade ground in front of our dorm. La Rue from New Orleans, a skinny young fellow—we were all skinny in those days--was our acting "battalion commander." His trousers were hiked up so high you could see the tops of his white socks, and he stood stiffly, swayed back at attention, awaiting orders. The entire Aggie corps had also lined up in formation on both sides the great quad that was the length of two football fields. Our ASTRP unit, raggedly conspicuous and obviously out of place, occupied only a small corner of the field. We were laughing, joking, wondering how La Rue and the others had been selected, when the boom of a cannon startled us into silence. Then a booming voice from far in the distance shouted an indecipherable order, and our leader, La Rue, straightened bolt upright and, in his own surprisingly booming voice, shocked us all and called out what sounded like "Tally-ho!"

Somebody behind me laughed and said, "Where's the fox?"

"You're at attention, soldier!" A voice behind us growled.

My god, he's right, I thought, *we're supposed to be soldiers.* "Tally-Ho" was followed by a loud "Commmmpny!" and then from the platoon leaders bellowed, "'Toon!" followed by "'Ten-SHUN!" The Aggie corps came to attention with a loud shuffle of feet on gravel followed by silence. A bugle began to sound tattoo, and we all stood at attention. It was clear, pure, and beautiful, played without a blip or a flaw, and then another blast of cannon. When the lovely tattoo ended, the commands repeated and finally came the command from far down the parade ground: "Pree-SENNNNT ARMS!" None of us, rather few of us, had any idea what was happening until La Rue and our leaders each snapped a perfect about-face and saluted as the bugle began to sound retreat, as stately a call as you would ever hear, one that still brings a catch in my throat and a tear to the eye—well, almost. Some of us raised our hands in salute, but the sergeant behind us shouted, "Put down your hands and stand at attention!" We did.

When the bugle stopped, there were more shouts, and then the mass of cadets on our side of the quad made a sharp left face, and the A&M band began playing "Caissons Go Rolling Along." As we turned and began marching in step, I was stirred, stiffened, and deeply moved as the realization came: I was in the army. We repeated this ritual every evening at chow, and it never bored me.

Our dorm rooms in Duncan Hall were stark but comfortable: a metal double bunk, two metal desks, two closets, hard linoleum floors, and a large window. The chow in Duncan Hall, in quantity and quality, was superior to any mess I would have for the rest of my time in the army. We had few complaints about the service, either in the way we lived or in the manner that the staff treated us. Discipline was light, our real duties being limited to academics. We had no guard duty, no KP, no barracks scrubbing, only one room inspection a week, though rooms were expected to be clean at all times. Surprise inspections were more of a threat than a practice. We had a half hour of close-order drill every morning and another half hour every afternoon before retreat formation. After the morning drill, we marched to class route step—no cadence—in platoon formation, talking allowed. At first, humiliated by the Aggies' derisive laughter, we improved rapidly and, within a week, no longer resembled a battalion of sad sacks or snafus. Only a fool, we believed, would have wished for a different assignment.

The Monday after we arrived, counselors interviewed each of us and gave us our schedule of classes and informed us that everyone was a pre-engineering major. I would be repeating freshman English, chemistry, and college algebra, finding that my previous college experience meant nothing. We had three "choices" of majors: civil engineering, electrical engineering, or mechanical engineering. When I told the counselor that I had indicated on my application that I was majoring in premed and asked why I hadn't been assigned to a premed unit, he looked at me with a blank stare. "The premed students were all sent to Baylor," he said.

I asked, "Then why wasn't I sent to Baylor?"

"Because you were sent here," he answered and smiled.

It was moot anyway. Before leaving Corpus Christi, I had decided my premed career was over. The former ASTP men I'd met from Camp Swift had been right: Navy V-12 was a far better program. I felt at I was caught up in a looking-glass world: the reason I was not there was because I was here, and I was here because I was not there. Only a fool argued with such logic. It didn't matter. I had decided I would apply for transfer to active duty and basic training when I turned eighteen, about the time our first term ended.

If I was correct in thinking, the war would not last longer, and if I was even more determined to get overseas, I knew I would not be able to spend more time than necessary here in Aggie land.

Our ASTRP battalion was divided into two groups: a "college prep" group for those from small rural schools lacking a full math and science program, and one for those from large city schools that had full departments for science and math. I was in the latter and was scheduled for English, U.S. history, physics, chemistry, combined algebra-trigonometry, plus an hour a week of something called military science, which was really not very military and certainly not science. The three hours of physical education every week consisted of intensive calisthenics and a three-mile cross-country run once a week. What we got was a solid core of essential courses taught by some of A&M's best instructors and professors. There was no one like McAllister, to be sure, but all our professors were tenured faculty. Our math instructor, who taught algebra three days and trigonometry two days, was a far better teacher than the retired major I'd had at UT. The physics and chemistry professors were full professors, the latter being chairman of the Chemistry Department. And unlike the science lectures in Austin, our classes were never larger than thirty, the size of a platoon, though once a week we had a physics lecture that combined all the sections. Though he knew his subject and lectured without a note and with great enthusiasm for his subject, our history instructor informed us on the first day that we would not be discussing anything in class, that he was not interested in what we might think about the causes or the results of any historical event. All exams would be "objective," that is, true-false or multiple choice. Dr. Eckfeldt's English class, while totally different in style and content, rivaled Helen James's freshman composition in interest. Without her class and her emphasis on critical thinking, I believe I would have missed much in Eckfeldt's, although he assigned a rich variety of essays, classical and modern, that we discussed in detail. Because the term was shorter, we did not have time to read longer works as we had done in Helen James's class, but Dr. Eckfeldt encouraged us to do outside reading and to choose our own topics for our weekly essays. It was my favorite class; I had never read such a variety of essays: Montaigne, Bacon, Coleridge, as well as Haslett, Huxley, William James, Emerson, Thoreau, and most of the great English essayists and contemporary Americans like Bernard DeVoto and E. B. White. Every week, Eckfeldt read a student's essay aloud in class and we discussed its subject and style. One week he read one of my essays, a totally new experience.

Eckfeldt's suggestion that we read outside the assigned texts gave me a reason to visit the main library and check out works unrelated to any of the assigned topics. After the first few days of class, I had found and checked out works by Steinbeck, Cronin, Hilton, Farrell, Dos Passos, Hervey Allan, Upton Sinclair, and Sinclair Lewis, potboilers and classics, trash and treasure, "classics and commercials." I read with no real sense of discrimination, more interested in quantity than quality. A novel's record as a best seller was, to me, more important than literary merit, of which I knew so little that it made no difference. What mattered was only if there was a "good story" or characters who "stood for something." Novels of ideas, such as Dos Passos' *U.S.A.,* were just beginning to have an influence on me.

About halfway through the term, letters from Jane began to arrive with *Daily Texan* clippings about an academic freedom conflict between the president, H. P. Rainey, and the board of regents. Dos Passos had been the focus of some controversy in Austin during my second semester, large sections of the novel having been assigned by a number of the freshman comp faculty. A new untenured instructor, Helen James, might have chosen a Rølvaag novel, some of us thought, to avoid conflict. I had, nevertheless, borrowed a copy and had read most of *The 42nd Parallel* at the time. When Eckfeldt suggested we write our weekly essay based on an unassigned reading, I took a plunge, and checked out *U.S.A.* with the intention of writing one of my weeklies on the novel and the controversy in Austin. When I appeared at the checkout with the novel, the reading room checker asked with a smile if I was sure I wanted to read it. I told her I had read one of the novels in the trilogy and had been at UT in the spring and then mentioned that the UT board of regents wanted to ban the novel. She laughed and said censorship was the best way to ensure a book's success. I visited the undergraduate reading room so often that we became friends and talked about books and writers when she could find some free time.

At least one in the platoon read as much as I read, Carlos Lovejoy. I noticed that he went to the library even more than I did those first few weeks. One evening at chow time, I asked him about books he had read. When he recommended J. T. Farrell's *Studs Lonigan* and said it had made him think about politics, I put him on to Dos Passos' trilogy and told him that my sister had written me from Austin about its becoming a really controversial book and that some instructors were being fired because of its politics and its "obscenity." I was reading it and told him, from what I had read, it seemed more likely it was the political slant and not the obscenity that caused the trouble. Although I considered myself a Democrat and a "liberal," I really didn't know what either meant, except in the most general sense. Texas having only one party divided between the pro-labor and the anti-labor factions, I claimed to be pro-labor (Mr. Steakley's influence probably). Carlos was a proclaimed liberal and even an admitted socialist (another reason for his nickname, "Russian," as I recall), and he was deeply interested in books like Dos Passos' and Upton Sinclair's that professed radical or liberal views. While *U.S.A.*'s radical social and political elements had a strong appeal, its experimental format interested me the most. When I told Carlos about it, he immediately checked it out and expressed so much enthusiasm for Dos Passos' style and his radical thought that he felt compelled to read the earlier works, particularly *Three Soldiers*.

Before many more weeks, Carlos and I became a kind of two-man seminar-discussion group, attracting others into bull sessions. In spite of a plethora of second-rate novels in the open stacks reading room, our reading list took on the aura of a highbrow. Carlos was the first person I had ever discussed books with seriously. I regretted now that I had not talked to Jane more when we were in Austin. She had already read so much more than I, and now as she was entering her senior year in Austin and *majoring in English*, I was sure she would have given me a lot of good advice about what to read. Carlos and I constantly pumped each other for thoughts, opinions, and criticism.

By early October, reading novels had begun to eat into my study time, just as the novel reading had in Austin, and I saw my grades in physics and algebra/trig begin to deteriorate in direct proportion to my time in the library. My interests ran off in all directions, but I brought them back into line before finals. Since I had never seriously intended to return to the program for the second term, I never felt that the time I spent reading was a waste, but I was concerned that I leave a better transcript at A&M than I left at UT; my grades that term were much better than they had been in Austin, perhaps because of the discipline we were under, perhaps because I was older. Free hours were not unrestricted; even the library time I sneaked into my schedule was regulated to the time between my last afternoon class and retreat. The main reason I made better grades was that I had learned something about "study habits" at UT. There was no comparison between the academic environment at A&M and the one I had grown accustomed to in Austin; order and discipline, though mild compared to the rigors of the "real" army, required truly creative efforts on my part to avoid "homework," which was not necessarily the same as study. In Austin, I had no rules or regulations. Indeed, the university *appeared* to be run entirely by students; whereas, at A&M, no one seemed able to make any decision unless he consulted the appropriate regulation or got official permission. The greatest difference, however, the one that decided my next move, was the lack of conscious intellectual stimulation, the absence of ideas or any concern for ideas. Eckfeldt's class was an exception because of the essays he assigned and the papers he encouraged us to write, but our history lecturer never welcomed questions and brooked few interruptions. Only one or two classmates, dare I say colleagues, like Lovejoy or Brown, were seriously concerned that we discussed nothing in the U.S. history class, and most seemed bored by conversations ranging outside the subjects of sex or sports. Eckfeldt encouraged discussions, tried to stimulate debate or questioning by reading aloud the occasional student essay that dared to deal with controversy or social issues. But his attempts often resulted in ridicule of the "odd ball." When he read a portion of my essay on censorship and *U.S.A.* and a portion of another student's personal essay about the Depression, groans and murmurs arose from the class that Eckfeldt sharply criticized.

By the end of September, I had decided to apply for transfer out of reserves to active duty—in effect, into basic infantry training—which was always in need of fresh recruits. It was not that I was tired of attending class, but having neither talent for nor interest in engineering, I could see no future in what I was taking. I liked A&M, had begun to enjoy the brilliant physics lectures and lab, and in spite of "old school" loyalties to UT, A&M's chief rival, I found the military routine oddly stimulating. In the late summer and fall of 1944, with war still raging in the Pacific and the ETO, I found the campus surreal; the uniforms, the cannon salute and bugle tattoo and retreat, the Aggie upperclassmen sporting anachronistic cavalry boots and sabers seemed more like young boys playing soldier while thousands were still dying on beaches and in foxholes. "Men" holding deferments peopled the campus and waved flags. It made no sense. I enjoyed the friendship and camaraderie of men like Lovejoy, Dykes, McNair, and Brown. Hayes, my roommate, who studied so diligently, could not carry on a three-sentence conversation. I knew the second term would offer little variation, except in math; analytical geometry and beginning calculus would be a disaster, and for what? I could see no future for me. The academics I needed most were simply not there in pre-engineering. I spoke to others whose eighteenth birthdays would fall before term's end to see if any had thought about the war's ending "too soon." I decided that, in any case, I would resign at the end of the term and request a transfer to basic infantry training. Shortly before finals and the week's leave, two others decided to go with me, Leslie McNair and Arthur Dykes. We agreed to request basic infantry training, knowing that requesting any other branch would put us on a waiting list. We admitted it sounded foolish, sounded vainglorious, but there you are. We were eighteen, pathological idealists eager to prove the manhood we had little right to claim. By the end of October, the war in the ETO, by all appearances, was to wind down by year's end. In the Pacific, the story was quite different.

At the end of finals, we received a seven-day leave with travel and per diem allowance. When I told the first sergeant that I had decided to request an active duty assignment, he refused to pass on my request to Lieutenant Jors, saying that I had to get permission from my parent or guardian. I told him I was eighteen and no longer needed her permission, but because the paperwork was probably too much a hassle, I said I would take the pass and report back in when I returned. There was nothing in Corpus Christi for me at the time; all my friends were in the service or away at school. Jerry Jarbeaux, whom I had dated in high school after Eve Munds moved to Wilmington, was still consumed by flying lessons and her airborne friends. I had only one interest at the time: visiting Austin to experience all the strange things that were happening on the campus that fall. If I hitched free rides, travel expenses and per diem, in cash, would pay for several days in Austin before returning to College Station. I could stay free of charge at the fraternity house both as an alumnus and a service man. The main reason for my stopping in Austin was to see Jane and to find out what had been happening at the university that fall.

She had been sending me clippings and whole pages from the *Daily Texan*, stories about faculty firings and threats by the AAUP to blacklist the university for violating tenure rules and principles of academic freedom. The red scare heads in the *Texan* were larger than any I had ever seen in the paper. I didn't know whether the red ink was the inspiration of left-leaning editors or just a tradition of old yellow journalism or both. I shared the clippings with friends and even showed some of the clippings to Dr. Eckfeldt, who admitted having heard about the troubles, though he refused to say more. Controversy stopped at the edge of campus at A&M; it would have been different in Austin. I had no idea what blacklisting meant and only vaguely understood what the AAUP stood for. "Academic freedom" was equally vague when I first began reading the stories, but the more I read, the clearer it became, and I began to recall McAllister's comments about the regents and their threats of firing. Once, during the early lectures on race, he had said he did not think the regents would ever fire him for un-American sentiments because his family was one of the oldest in San Antonio and could boast the first flush toilet in town and probably in the state. He doubted, he said, that they would fire anyone who could make such a claim since their chief interests were with the flushings and all "things flushed." I knew the uproar had its beginnings back in the spring semester.

The university president, Homer Price Rainey, who had endorsed racial desegregation of higher education in Texas, refused to comply with the regents' demands, citing the university's tenure rule and the policy of academic freedom. The Regent's true target was Dr. Rainey, a liberal molded in the metal of New Dealism and the Bill of Rights, both of which were anathema, and still are, to the extreme right of Texas politics. Some months earlier, Rainey had voiced the opinion that it was time for the university system to admit Negroes, to admit all qualified applicants regardless of race. He complicated matters by acting as a "traitor to his class." When he was hired, the regent majority found him well qualified as an educator, holding two doctorates, a PhD and a doctorate of divinity. He was also an ordained minister of the Southern Baptist persuasion, which there was a no more conservative class or one more obedient to the seats of power, although in 1944, the Southern Baptist Conference (pre-Ronald Reagan) was still vigorously opposed to the marriage of church and state. Conservative churches were then particularly obedient and worshipful of economic and social power resting in the precincts of the National Association of Manufacturers, the independent oil producers, the ranching and corporate farming cliques as well as the American Legion, the DAR, the UDC, or Daughters of the Republic. McAllister had excoriated all filial-pietistic organizations as mindlessly reactionary and militantly protective of know-nothing-ism and the rights of the privileged class. He did not call them fascists or crypto-Nazi outright, rather waiting until after the war to label them so.

My concern, as I read through the clippings, was whether McAllister was on the list to be dismissed. On the one hand, the Longhorn football team was being rated as the *numero uno* team in the nation, its team having been stocked with choice beeves from across the nation via the V-12 program (which was another advantage that the navy college program had over the army). But here in the midst of real collegiate glory was this troubling instance of a board of regents run amok, demanding the dismissal of the university president because he wished to adhere to a Bill of Rights and a system of law, because he advocated policies that the president and Congress, as well as the prime minister and Parliament, had endorsed in the famous Four Freedoms. The *Daily Texan* proclaimed Rainey's heroism and denounced the un-American posturing of the regents.

Anxious to be there and to see firsthand how it was working, I left Corpus Christi on Thursday morning so that I could be on campus and witness the announced sit-down strike of students on Friday. My mother thought all strikes were disgusting, even when they supported her interests, as they had all through the Depression, and even though she still regarded Roosevelt as the greatest of presidents, along with Washington, Lincoln, and Wilson. The sit-down strike echoed the troubles of the early days of the New Deal, and that was bad. All demonstrations she felt were ugly and rude and deserved her disapprobation.

Just before going on leave, we had been issued OD uniforms, and I proudly wore the new blue and gold ASTP patch with its sword and flaming lamp of knowledge (often called the flaming piss pot, the lamp of knowledge resembling a hospital urinal). The fact that I was a mere reservist, not even a legitimate private, made no difference. I felt I should lend symbolic authority of the armed forces to the struggle for human rights and intellectual freedom. When I arrived at the fraternity house and asked about the events taking place, the first reaction I met was one of indifference, the second was measured interest but not sympathy, and the third was a warning that I should not go near the demonstrators because the navy had warned all its people to stay away. The service commands traditionally never oppose or support political demonstrations. I was mystified why members of the armed forces were not allowed to express opinions freely until I recalled one of Lieutenant Jors' comments: "You aren't paid to think, soldier. You're paid to do what you're told to do!" Any actions protesting violations of civil rights were clearly products of thinking.

As soon as I arrived in Austin, I called Jane at her dorm, and she told me that a minority of students did not approve of Rainey, mostly those in fraternities and sororities. She said that at seven that evening at Gregory Gymnasium she was attending a rally called by the student body president Mack Wallace, who was going to announce plans for the strike and a parade for Friday. I had come just at the right moment, she said, and then said she was glad I had been able to get to Austin.

When I hung up, I called Adele, a girl I had dated once or twice in the spring and one who I thought would be on the side of the demonstrators, even though she was a Chi Omega. I recalled that Adele, a pre-law student, believed strongly in the cause of civil rights. On the phone, she admitted that, to her, the issues were not all as simple as I thought, but we made plans to attend the rally together. Her reservations about the cause surprised me. To me, they couldn't be clearer. Before I left the fraternity house, I was warned again not to attend any of the rallies or meetings in uniform, so to satisfy the cautious, I left my cap at the house and took off my necktie, making me technically out of uniform. If I were picked up or stopped by an MP or SP, my pass would show I was a mere reservist and not subject to arrest, though they could and probably would tell me to go home.

At the rally, as I predicted, no one took the slightest notice of me or anyone else, except Mack Wallace and the student government officers. The speeches were eloquent, the crowd responsive, and the air crisp with excitement. Wallace, a Navy Cross and Purple Heart hero, was charismatic. His credentials were impeccable, even more impeccable than a handful of Texas oil millionaires. He urged all who wished to go out on strike to treat the events seriously, to avoid any show of frivolity or violence, and because of his leadership, no incidents marred the solemnity. The strike would last three days—Friday, Saturday, and the following Monday. He invited the faculty to participate but did not urge them to do so. Some dismissed classes, some simply failed to show up for class. Others met but didn't lecture. Oddly, I learned later, the faculty was deeply split into several factions: one faction fully supporting Rainey; another, the "lukewarms," supported him in principle; and a third remained loyal to the Board of Regents, the flag of Texas and Dixie. Moreover, they opposed all demonstrators whom they regarded as a "bunch of reds." The strike would demonstrate student support for academic freedom and for Rainey who refused to fire faculty, and the march on the capital would be called the funeral of academic freedom, complete with a flag-draped coffin and the university Longhorn band marching to the music of Mahler and Beethoven.

I met Jane the next morning on the wide grassy area in front of the Main Building, below the engraved inscription, "Ye Shall Know the Truth and the Truth Shall Make You Free," the mighty words I had read the first time I walked across the campus. A crowd of almost a thousand students was quietly sitting around the flagpoles. It was an orderly crowd, though not a somber one. "Sit-down" strikers had assembled in other parts of the campus, but those in front of Main made the largest crowd. Members of the Drama Department, to keep the crowds in place for the morning, were performing an impromptu reader's theater production of James Thurber's *The Male Animal*, the plot of which paralleled the protest for academic freedom there in Austin. In several locations across the campus, the play held the strikers' attention, informing many of them, for the first time, the meaning of academic freedom. It was a totally new concept for many; most had never thought seriously about the significance of a professor's right to teach an idea, one way or another. I was aware of its significance because I had taken McAllister's class in the spring and because Jane had been sending me the editorials and stories out of the *Daily Texan*.

At noon, we moved to the Drag, Guadalupe Street, that bordered the west side of the campus and passed by the student union. The funeral procession was for the "death of academic freedom" and would march from the university roughly to Twenty-First Street, all the way down to Sixth Street, a distance of more than thirteen blocks. There, it would make a U-turn and move up Congress Avenue heading to the capitol. As the crowds assembled, the parade marshals moved up and down and through the gathering throng, urging all those wishing to make light of the procession to leave. It was a funeral, not a joyous occasion, though doubtless many looked on the strike as a kind of holiday. Six young women students, clad all in black, followed by two similarly clad groups, carried a crepe-draped coffin that in turn was followed by the Longhorn band marching with black arm bands and caps reversed, traditionally signifying a loss. Jane and I formed in the third or fourth rank behind the coffin, but when one of the marshals saw me in uniform, or rather "out of uniform," he mistook me for a veteran and asked me to march in the front rank. When I told him I was not a veteran but was merely on leave, he was even more anxious I walk in front. We set off solemnly to a death march played by the band.

When the procession reached Sixth Avenue, we could look back up Guadalupe and see a steady line of marchers, six to eight abreast, reaching as far as the eye could see to Nineteenth Street. The cortege then marched east on Sixth Street and then up wide Congress Avenue through the middle of town to the capitol grounds. We marched in solemn procession accompanied by the band beating out a funeral cadence and playing whatever funeral music they could assemble on short notice, band arrangements of slow movements by Beethoven and Mahler. It was indeed solemn. We were filled with pride, knowing our cause was just and our acts significant. When we reached the capitol, student body president Mack Wallace went in to ask Governor Coke Stevens to meet with the marchers and to assure us that freedom was a worthy cause. Governor Stevens' aid approached the huge crowd, now milling about under the giant trees among statues of Texas heroes, and announced that the governor had left Austin for his ranch where he had gone to "calculate" what he should do. From that point on, he became known as "Calculatin' Coke," an epithet he was unable to shed right through his famous campaign for senator in 1948, which he lost in the famous "landslide" to Lyndon B. Johnson, the election which won Johnson the label "Landslide Lyndon."

We felt that we had made history or had taken part in something far greater than anything we had taken part in before. For me, it was a great historical moment. Justification for Rainey and the others would come many years later when Rainey's chief supporter at the time, and later in his campaign for governor of the state, would serve as chairman of that same Board of

Regents that would name a new building the Homer Price Rainey Building. It is still a campus where issues of academic freedom are fought out with feeling. A recent issue had the regents "erring" on the side of liberal thought, an episode in UT history that gave deeper meaning to another inscription, one carved into the lintel of the old Geology Building just around the corner from the Main Library. It reads, "Oh, Earth, What Changes Hast Thou Seen?"

When I arrived at College Station early Sunday morning, tired and aching from sitting up in a cold and lonely bus station in Giddings, Texas, my mind was clear. I spoke to McNair and Dykes and told them I had decided to resign from the program and request immediate induction into basic training. We three turned eighteen the week before. Leslie and Arthur were also determined to resign. When we appeared before Lieutenant Jors, first thing Monday morning, he tried to dissuade us, assuring us that we could stay in the program probably until the war ended, but we told him our minds were made up.

Speaking for Arthur and me, Leslie spoke in clear and measured tones, "We don't want to miss the war, sir. We figure that we'll finish our basic infantry about the time we'll be landing on the Japan islands."

Lieutenant Jors was silent a moment then said, "OK, men, you are released. Send us your uniforms when you get home. Good luck!"

Almost as we had rehearsed we each took one step back and saluted the lieutenant, did an about turn then stepped out letting McNair lead the way.

We didn't have long to wait. My orders to report on December 4 to the induction center at Fort Sam Houston arrived the morning after Thanksgiving, and the next morning, letters from Dykes and McNair arrived, saying they had also received their letters to report to Fort Sam. Both sounded happy and expressed a wish to get on with it, Leslie saying again he hoped we could stay together. As Mama, Don, and I drove to the station on the morning of the third, I felt almost the same excitement I had felt that late October morning a year ago when I had left for Austin. Just as before, I felt that a new world was opening to me. This time I was better prepared to face the changes I would face than I had been then. I was older for one thing.

It had seemed strange being back home for those three weeks; it was like being in a kind of limbo. When I showed up Monday evening, so soon after being home on leave, Mama was quite shocked. Though I had mentioned it to Don, I think, I had not said anything to her about my plans to resign from ASTRP. It had been hard enough to tell her that I had planned to spend part of my leave in Austin, but telling her I was planning to request a transfer from the safe haven of ASTRP was seriously beyond my powers.

Now I finally would explain it all, and I would admit I had deceived her into signing permission back in June—that all along I had planned to go into active service as soon as I turned eighteen. Never could I have explained to her why I no longer intended to major in premed. She accepted my decision without recriminations but asked what I planned to do while I waited around for my orders. I explained I was moving back into the attic room at Pete's, that he still needed a driver and that I needed the money. The money part, I knew, she would understand. Then I really felt like shit when she asked if I couldn't at least take *some* of my meals at home and asked if I couldn't spend *some* of my nights in my room. So I moved back into the room with Don for four nights a week and took most of my meals at home. Actually, it was more like purgatory than limbo. All the time I was there, I felt as if I were doing penance. Knowing it might be my last one for some time, Pete insisted I spend Thanksgiving Day at home, though they were even more short-handed than before. I thanked him and agreed to have dinner at home but promised I would come back and listen to the UT and A&M "Turkey Day" game in the lobby and be there to answer calls. It was not a happy time; Jane had not come down from Austin because the wartime schedule allowed for only a one-day holiday, and then the imminence of my departure cast a gloom over the table. Mama, as always, had invited two sailors, total strangers from the naval air station to join us. They were first-time guests at Mama's dinner table and seemed quite awkward and terribly shy. Both were just my age, barely eighteen and fresh from boot camp, and were curious why I had volunteered for the army and had resigned from ASTRP. Mama, I recall, listened intently to my explanation, hoping, I assumed, to understand better my reasoning. Neither of them had been to college nor had ever planned to go beyond high school; they had joined the navy to avoid being drafted and being sent to an infantry basic training camp. When the meal was finished and I sensed we had exhausted all topics of conversation, I excused myself and returned to the funeral home to relieve Pete or his old man at the telephone. We received no emergency or death calls all afternoon, and I was able to listen to Kern Tips broadcast the game between UT and A&M in Austin. Texas won again, even more decisively than the year before.

I was elated the next morning when the mail arrived with my orders to report. Mama seemed resigned to the fact and hopeful that the war news would continue to be good, and as she drove me to the bus station a few days later, I tried again to explain why I had decided to apply for active duty. I told her about my friends, Arthur and Leslie, and she seemed to understand, remarking that she could see that I was happy to be going and said she was glad I had no regrets. In the end, we agreed on one thing: regrets were a waste of one's time and energy, that people should live for the possible, not for what should be.

At the induction center at Fort Sam Houston, I met Leslie and Arthur, along with about a hundred draftees. Immediately after the first formation and roll call, we were marched off to a tent city and assigned to a square, pyramidal six-man squad tent that would be our home for the next five days. After we had dumped our blankets, thick comforter, and rough cotton mattress cover, called a fart sack, we fell out and marched off to a huge supply warehouse where we received our uniforms and all equipment for basic training. Contrary to the old cliché that army uniforms came in only two sizes, too large and too small, my uniform fit quite well; even the large heavy boots fit. I would part with them later with deep remorse. As soon as we drew all our equipment, we returned immediately to our squad tent and changed into the OD wool uniform—trousers, boots and socks, wool shirt, necktie, cloth cap, and field jacket.

Now our sergeant told us, "That's the last you're gonna see of civilian clothes for the duration and six months. Uncle Sam owns your ass now, and he don't like nothing but GI issue. Mail 'em home or toss 'em in them GI cans at the end of the street. You're in the fuckin' army now."

Until we received our uniforms, all our noncoms treated us with something like respect and issued orders to us in calm unmilitary tones, but once we were all dressed alike in the olive drab, they metamorphosed into fire-breathing martinets. Leslie, Arthur, and I laughed at the transformation and heaved a sigh of relief at the sound of their angry commands, each of us agreeing that their change of manner was proof that we had indeed arrived. After the trip to the barbers and the loss of all our locks, we lined up for a series of shots. Rumors flew of needles pronged like fishhooks and vaccines that were worse than the diseases, especially the one administered in the left testicle, not the right, but the left. We had gotten the full series—typhoid, tetanus, and smallpox—at A&M and agreed that it was foolish to go through it a second time. I said I wasn't even sure it was a good idea to get a second tetanus so soon after the first. As usual, there was a long wait for the medics to get set up, so I stepped out of the line and told our sergeant we three— Dykes, McNair, and Gilliland—had had all the shots only a few months before. The men around us laughed, saying we'd have to get them again and called us chicken. Already, we had been separated out from the mass because we were "college men." When the sergeant ordered me back in line, I told him we could easily have a negative reaction by getting them again so soon.

He frowned, looked worried, hesitated, then pulled us out and took us to the head medical officer, a major, sitting at a table and filling out printed forms. This time Leslie, who was taller, bigger, and physically more impressive than either Arthur or I, went to the front. Even without chevrons on his sleeve, he always looked as if he were in command of something.

The major casually looked up at Leslie and said with just the right tone of sarcasm, "OK, General, what can I do for you?"

Leslie, braced at attention like a West Point cadet, said loud and clear, "Sir, I wish to report that we three have already had our shots."

"Oh? And when was that and where?" he asked looking up, still using the same sarcastic tone.

"In August, sir. At Texas A&M when we reported for ASTRP, sir." His military manner impressed even Arthur and me, and we congratulated ourselves for putting Leslie up as our spokesman.

"OK, *General*, at ease. Now what is your name?" he asked with "marvelous condescension."

"McNair, sir."

The major looked up straight at Leslie now, raised his eyebrows, and said flatly, "First name and middle initial?"

"Leslie G., sir," he answered. I stifled a laugh as did Arthur, and the sergeant slowly shook his head.

"Are you trying to be funny, soldier?" the major said, no longer condescending, as he began looking down the list of names.

"No, sir. That's my name," Leslie said, now braced more stiffly than ever.

In 1944, Lt. Gen. Leslie McNair was the commanding general of all U.S. ground forces in the U.S. We had joked about McNair's name many times before back at A&M and had wondered what would happen if such an unlikely thing as this would ever take place. The sergeant looked at the three of us smiling, shaking his head, and obviously enjoying the major's perplexity.

"Who are these other men, *Private McNair*?" he asked. Leslie gave him our names. Our service records were all there with our shot records stapled to the proper page. "All right, Private McNair. It's all here. You were right, soldier. It's not a good idea to repeat the shots so soon. Thank you, you're dismissed." Then the doctor laughed and said, "And don't expect me to salute *you, General!*"

McNair saluted and did a perfect about-face. As we walked back to the end of the line, the sergeant congratulated McNair and told us to head back to the tent city to await the next formation. Arthur and I congratulated McNair who laughed repeatedly at the major's questions and his own answers. He said he was more afraid of the sergeant's wrath than the major's who was, after all, just a doctor, but a sergeant was a sergeant.

"I've been wanting to say my name like that ever since we got here," Les said with chuckle. "When he called me "General," I knew I had him." For the next few days, the men in our casual company always referred to Leslie as "the General."

We spent the second day indoors, taking the Army General Classification Test and a battery of aptitude tests to see which specialty we were best suited for. After the noon chow and the usual formation, we returned to be interviewed. Incredibly, I learned I had passed the tests that qualified me for medical corps aid man (not surprising), signal corps (surprising), mechanics school (more surprising), driver's school, and clerk's school, which really was a surprise because I didn't know how to type and had checked "no" where it asked if I had typing skills.

Then we spent a long afternoon waiting to be interviewed by a T-5 clerk to determine what branch of the service we were best suited for, and after another long wait in the overheated room, an officious and prissy T-5 called my name and ordered me to sit and wait while he riffled through a stack of papers, sharpened his pencils, and rearranged his manuals. Then he looked up, mispronounced my name, and read off my serial number, and asked if I was sure everything sounded correct. I said it was and congratulated him for pronouncing Gilliland correctly. He asked why my serial number began with the numeral 1 instead of a 3 like all the others. I was much too young, he said, to have been called in the first draft back in 1940. The second digit always denoted the service command—in my case, the eighth service command—but he couldn't understand that my army serial number began with *1*, which denoted, he said, that I had been in the first draft back in 1940. I told him I would have been only fourteen in 1940 and considered it highly unlikely. All I knew was that it was the number I received back in July when I enlisted.

"You enlisted?" he asked incredulously. "Why did you do that?"

His asking seemed strange, I said, and asked if all this was necessary. I wondered if his T-5 rating required him to cross-examine me. I asked what difference it could possibly make.

"It's all in my service record there, Corporal," I told him. "I was in the ASTRP."

"Oh that. Yes. Well, now which branch would you like to select?" he asked and began to write on the form before him.

"Infantry," I said.

He looked up and said with a straight face, "It's closed."

For a moment, I believed he was joking. I laughed and pushed back from the table. "You mean the war's over?"

"No, I'm reading here that infantry placement centers are all closed," he said indignantly.

"OK, then what about the medics? Combat medics, that is. I was studying premed in college, and they told me I passed the test for the medic school."

He flicked through a packet of papers on a clipboard and said with the same officious finality, "The medics are filled at this time."

"Well, I guess armored or artillery."

"Your physical says here you are too light for armored."

"I can't believe this, Corporal. This is ludicrous! You know every one of us in this room is going to an IRTC, no matter what we request. Too light for the armored? That's absurd. I'd be riding in the tank, not carrying it. I tell you what. You pick one for me, anything that's open, or if you're all full up, I'll call a taxi and wait until next year." I felt for a moment I was lost in an Abbot and Costello movie and was thinking what a story this will make at chow this evening or in the squad tent.

He frowned, marked something on my sheet, and looked up. "You'll be notified in a few days. That's all."

When I walked out, I understood, for the first time, the reasons for the acronyms SNAFU, FUBAR, and TARFU. The army had need for these designations. Leslie and Arthur had experienced the same silliness. Arthur was still inside. The sergeant who had marched us over was smoking off to one side and overheard us. He said, "They do that silly shit all the time in there. I guess they got nothin' else to do. I never seen a T-5 that didn't have shit for brains." Then he said, "You need brains to get that fucked up." We were finished until time for chow, he said, and that we could go to over to the service club but to make sure we were at the four-o-clock formation. I loved it.

Shipping orders for Arthur and me came through two days later. In spite of the prissy T-5's insistence, we found ourselves headed to the Infantry Replacement Training Center (IRTC) at Camp Wolters, Texas, just outside the famous Texas resort of Mineral Wells, better known as "Venereal Wells" our sergeant said. But Leslie's name did not appear on the orders. When I told him we were on shipping orders for IRTC the next morning, he looked disappointed but said little other than that he was sorry we were breaking up and was sorry he'd talked Art and me into requesting out with him, especially now we were no longer going to be together. I was honestly touched by his sentiment. But it was not usual, I learned, to find friends quickly and hold them close like brothers.

Chapter 6

Arms And The Boy

Camp Wolters was one of the basic training camps originally intended for the first wave of draftees and later became an Infantry Replacement Training Center (IRTC). The camp was just outside one of Mineral Wells, the most famous Texas spa that had high recognition as a health center for its Crazy Water Crystals, for the Crazy Water and Baker Hotels, and for its popular live radio broadcasts in the 1930s. I had heard of Mineral Wells, I suppose, all my life, and now I would finally see it. Wolters was an Infantry Replacement Training Center, but *replacement* had begun to have too many negative connotations, so they tried *reinforcement* to disguise the reality of the dead and wounded that left gaps in division rosters. I doubted that *reinforcement center* fooled anyone, though it might soften harsh realities for some, which was as much as anyone could expect After three years of casualties most had become inured to the casualty figures.

Our casual company of new trainees that Sunday filled out the quota for Company A, 57th Battalion, IRTC, the rest having arrived the day before. It took only a few hours for us to be assigned to our barracks and to go through a full orientation that explained to us what we were there for and how long we'd be. Arthur went to the first platoon and I to the second. Although assigned to adjoining barracks, we would see each other rarely after leaving the train. We would meet a few times at the service club, attend a film or two together, even visit Mineral Wells once, but after that, we would meld into our platoons and form new connections.

The cadre NCO in charge of the second platoon, Corporal Ortiz, was nothing like the movie version, the in-your-face growler who shouted and threatened and demeaned his awkward new recruits. After chow that first evening, Ortiz gathered the platoon together on the first floor and laid down his rules, clearly and distinctly without threats of reprisals if we failed in any way to carry out his orders; however we never doubted he was complete charge of our lives. Every platoon had a lead cadre noncom, along with two others. Corporal Ortiz was a slight, well-spoken Mexican-American from Arizona, totally and surprisingly without pretensions of power or authority yet obviously "in charge." Earlier, when we had lined up in front of our cots and had counted off by twos, he explained we were now paired with our new buddy, the man we would share shelter half and pup tent.

"He's your buddy,' he said, "From no on, you watch out for him, he'll watch out for you. This is the army way."

I had met my new "buddy," Gaston, when we got our cot assignments, and we had talked about our army experience up to that moment. I learned then that the army was unlike any other organization I had ever known. Gaston asked me right off how long I had been in, and I told him just that week at the reception center at Fort Sam Houston and three months in ASTRP, which was a special training program. I purposely did *not* say it was a college.

He smiled broadly and said, "Me too, I thought you been in a while when I seen you make your bed the army way. I was in STU for six weeks, Student Training Unit."

When I asked what he did in STU, he said that they taught him how to read and write. "I could already read a little. But they taught me to read better. What was yours?" I said it was a college program and that I'd had enough and had asked to transfer.

He smiled a broad gap-toothed smile and said, "Then you're a college boy?" I laughed and said, "Well, I guess so." We shook hands.

The army had paired us, two boys only weeks apart in age, but with a wide gap in everything else. He told me matter-of-factly, without embarrassment, that his last year in school was the second grade. I realized, from the very first moment we spoke that Gaston was not your run-of-the-mill GI.

"I was sure you'd been in a while too," I told him, "because I watched you make up your cot the army way. Like they say, it is tight enough 'to bounce a quarter off.'"

He smiled and pointed at my bed. "I guess they teach you that in college too."

Gaston was from Greenfields, a small farming town in North Texas, where his father was a sharecropper, never owning a tractor. First thing I noticed was that my new buddy had a sense of humor and liked to joke. He talked about himself and his daddy with pride, complained about nothing, and raved about Company A's good chow. He was, by nature, a stoic and had come straight from a hard scrabble North Texas farm, where he had plowed with a team of mules from the age of twelve right up to the time he was drafted. His daddy, he told me, never had a tractor or a piece of motorized equipment, adding with a broad smile, "I was all the motorized equipment Daddy ever had." There was not an iota of bitterness in his tone, only pride.

His following that mule team had affected his style of walking, especially marching. So tuned to the gait of his mules was his marching gait that anyone following him step for step on a long march would find it a challenge to march behind him. I never mentioned it, but one other guy did, trying to make fun of his gait. Gaston just laughed and admitted he'd done a lot more miles behind "them mules" than he'd ever do in the army.

Once during that first week, when we were all taking a break from the M1 rifle instruction, Ortiz bent close asked me what I thought of my buddy Gaston. Since cadre rarely spoke to any of us for any reason other than about training, his question surprised me at first. We had been indoors all morning, going over the rifle and naming all the parts, when Ortiz called a "piss break." I was sitting cross-legged, reassembling my rifle, when he knelt on one knee and asked point-blank, "Gilliland, what do you think of your buddy Gaston?"

The direct personal question surprised me at first. "Gaston's a good man. He's fine. Why?"

"I just wondered, you being a *college boy*, and Gaston a *plow* boy," he answered with a touch of sarcasm.

"Gaston's a great guy," I shot back, and added, "I heard you're a college man too. Where'd you go to college?"

He straightened up. "University of Arizona, BS in Biochemistry."

"Wow!" I said, "I started out a chem. major, U Texas, but they called my bluff, so here I am." When he smiled, I almost asked why he hadn't gotten a commission but decided it was none of my business, but he must have thought I was thinking it because he explained, "The army had already met its quota for Mexican officers before I came along. " He turned and walked off, then turned back and said, "Army's a funny place, Gill. You'll find some GIs don't to make friends with people who are different. You'll see."

Well, he answered my question.

Seconds later, he blew his whistle. "Back to it, snap some shit in there!" They all filed back in and resumed "the naming of parts."

He had broken some kind of taboo, I felt, had spoken to me, an ordinary private, person-to-person, even called me "Gill." Something had changed, nothing like a revolution, but now, aside from a chat with Arthur and constant chats with Gaston or Gilmore, who had the cot on the other side, it would seem I could maybe just talk to Ortiz, you know, one college man to another. I hadn't exactly made friends with anyone else in the platoon, hadn't really expected to or hadn't even thought about it. The point was Gaston, Gilmore, and I got along so normally; they were unlike any guys I'd met before. What opportunity would I ever have had to meet a Gaston or a Gilmore? Ortiz was right, "Army's a funny place." I was beginning to like it.

Our first morning of training was cold and miserable, real "brass monkey weather," some said. Under my fatigues, I was wearing, for the first time in my life, long johns, long wool underwear, and over my fatigues, I was wearing my field jacket, along with probably the worst rubberized raincoat ever made. I was still cold. Aside from my early years in Dallas, I had never been north of Austin in the winter. I was finding Mineral Wells in the winter an unlikely place for a spa. From the company formation after chow, we march out to a small amphitheater for a formal welcoming by the battalion commander, Major McGruder. You could hear rumblings in the ranks suggesting we could just as easily have met him someday when the sun was shining or indoors at the company theater.

"Quiet! No talking in the ranks!" Ortiz shouted, and on to the open-air theater, we marched.

When the company were all seated, a tall, middle-aged, handsomely clad major in long trench coat came front and center and began to speak, introducing himself in a mellifluously ringing voice tinged with a deep Southern accent.

Apparently oblivious of the cold and rain he shouted, "My name is Major McGruder, and I am the CO of the Fifty-Seventh IRTC Battalion. I'm your commanding officer. I am a book soldier, which means I have not served in combat. They say I am too old, but I know the book, and you'll all see I go by the book." He paused as if to let it all sink in. "I am proud to introduce you to two men who have seen combat, who earned their bars in combat. Your company commander, Lieutenant Banks, earned his bar in North Africa, and Lieutenant Smythe, that's Smythe with a *y*. He earned his gold bar in Sicily. Both men, like you young men, began their army careers as enlisted men. Lieutenant Smythe even went through basic raining. Their training as soldiers of the ranks prepared them for leadership. When the time came, they did their duty, and the army made them officers on the spot. Listen to your officers and learn. Now Lieutenant Smythe has some announcements."

Smythe, taller and leaner than the Major or Lieutenant Banks, stepped forward, pulled a rolled-up *Life* magazine from inside his trench coat, and opened it, showing us the cover picture of an infantry GI "somewhere in France."

"Gentlemen," he began, "*Life* magazine says that the infantry is queen of battles." He paused. "But sometimes the queen's a whore and everyone gets a royal fucking."

The stands roared and cheered, and Lieutenant Banks nodded vigorously, but the book soldier frowned and moved as if to interrupt the Lieutenant who continued, "Camp Wolters will try to teach you what to do and how to do it to prevent rape either by the queen or the enemy. First, we will teach you the army way, and if you work hard and learn, your chances of survival will outweigh your chances of getting killed or wounded. Good luck!"

He dismissed us then, and we filed out. The major and Lieutenant Banks approached him, Banks offering his hand, the major scowling.

After watching films about military discipline and the Articles of War and the M1 rifle, they marched us in alphabetical order to the supply room a supply sergeant issued each one a weapon. I had never held .30-caliber rifle before, never even fired anything larger than a .22 short and that only at a fairgrounds. We immediately moved indoors out of the rain, moved the cots to the wall, and took up places on the floor for our first instruction in the care of our "best friend," the M1 Garand. All through, I heard guys talking about how great it was to soon be firing a real rifle, some boasting how they had "got their deer every year" with their dad's .30-30. Corporal Ortiz calmly explained that they would soon learn the M1 was nothing like their daddy's Winchester. He gathered all of us on the first floor around him and preached the required sermon about the M1's importance as our best friend, and he told us how, in the afternoon after chow and an hour of close-order drill, we would begin the learning of the "nomenclature" of the M1 and the function of parts.

"You *will* learn and be able to repeat tomorrow from memory the nomenclature for all the parts, along with your rifle's serial number. Remember," he ended, "that M1 is your best friend. Remember, it is a *rifle*, not a gun. You piss with your gun," he said, grabbing his crotch, "but you *fire* your rifle." We all laughed on cue as he smiled and left for his office opposite the latrine.

We spent a week learning the nomenclature, or "norman closure," of the M1 parts, and learned to take it apart and reassemble it faster and faster. We learned how to clean the bore and the chamber, and finally, how to aim the rifle, to "lay on target," according to our instructor, an old regular arm noncom with five stripes.

I recall one guy asking almost in a dither, "What the hell is the 'norman closure' he's always talkin' about?" There was silence.

"It's nomenclature," I pronounced slowly, "means the same as names. It's just 'army talk,' that's all," I said.

A voice in the back came back, "Thanks, college boy!"

I answered, "Anytime, soldier."

The week flew by and ended with our giving the barracks a thorough "GI-ing," that is a thorough scrubbing on hands and knees with brushes and GI soap. It became more a game, the British would say, "a lark," with lots of joking and nonsense—I figured a game to let off steam and all the unspoken feelings of first-week tensions. It worked. More men were speaking to others outside the small, three-men circles we'd formed with bunkmates like the Gaston–Gilmore–Gilliland nexus at our end of the barracks. Our names stamped across the front of our helmet liners helped bring us all into a tighter unit, but I found the regular "mail call" before the evening chow call helped even more. That first night, after the rainy day, only two names rang out, but by the second day, mail began to arrive, and that night, after the GI party, there came a flood of mail for almost everyone in the barracks. I got four letters: two from my mother, one from Jane, and one from friend Jerry Jarbeaux. Both Gilmore and Gaston marveled at the miracle of so many letters until I explained, "That's why I write every night. Send one, get one."

By the end of our second week, I had hardly missed getting a letter each mail call but began to notice my buddy was growing somber, even depressed and unfocussed. In all the instruction sessions, I'd watched how he would concentrate on everything coming from the instructor and would ask me to repeat anything that he was not sure about. I had also noticed he'd gotten only one letter the full time we'd been at Wolters.

"What's the problem, Gaston?" I asked.

He mumbled, "My girl at home says she won't write no more unless I write her."

"Did she write you that?" I asked.

"No, I called collect over at the service club. She only wrote me once."

"Then write her, man. I told you, that's why I write a letter or two every night. Hell, postage is free and paper and envelopes free at the service club."

"I cain't write. I can print but cain't write." It hurt to hear him painfully confess. His humor and all his positive take on everything we did suddenly seemed shut down.

"Printing's fine. I know guys in college who print better than they write. Hell, I print. It's easier for people to read my printing than my lousy *writing*," I told him.

"But I don't know what to say." He was listening, but the reality to him lay far too deep for my platitudes.

"Look, Gaston, she wants to hear from you as bad as you want to hear from her. I'll help." We faced each other, sitting on the bunks. "I've got paper here in my foot locker. Look, let's talk about letter writing. You've got lots to write about, I'll help and I'll correct a word or two, but you can get it down."

"Git what down?"

"You can get down on paper things you did today, tell how much you miss her, and how good you felt when you talked to her. Tell her how you think about her when you're not naming the parts." I saw him smile.

"About norman closure?"

"Sure."

He began printing slowly, first telling her he missed her. Then he stopped, and I mentioned the short "forced march" we did over a hill they called the Burma Road and I interjected, "Tell her how your dumb buddy fell down but wasn't hurt." He laughed, returned to the pad, the page almost filled. "Now tell her again that you miss her and say you hope she will write soon. Underline soon, like this." I printed SOON in caps.

When he finished, I watched him print her address on the envelope. He looked up smiling—proud, satisfied, transformed—and handed it to me. I felt as satisfied as he.

"Now read it to yourself and think about what you might tell her *next* time. Just think about things we do and things you like about her," I said.

I picked up the envelope I'd addressed earlier to Jane and suggested we go to the service club for a Coke and mail the letters together. His depressed look had vanished entirely. At mail call on Tuesday, it happened. Her letter arrived. I don't recall her name, but when Gaston reached for and read the return address, he shouted her name loud and clear. Later, telling me she promised to write often, the wide Gaston smile lit the whole first floor of the barracks.

I said, "OK, now remember what I said, 'send one, get one.' Write her right now and start by telling her—"

He stopped me. "I know. I'll tell her how happy I am."

I helped him on his second and his third letters, but after that, I helped only when he had a word to spell like *nomenclature.*

Gaston rarely talked about his home or his parents, except to say he'd worked "every since" he was in the second grade. He never spoke bitterly about how hard it had been for him, the plowing with mules or anything. Mostly, he spoke of how he hoped to get his daddy a tractor after the war.

In that first week, we learned to break down our M1 rifles and reassemble them, repeating the process over and over, naming the parts. Gaston couldn't understand "why anyone had to know the names of all the parts." So I went over it step by step with him, making sure I remembered, and sometimes one or two others would sit, watch, and listen. We had to know the names of parts, I said, in case we needed to replace one. After that, I never went anywhere unless Gaston went too. He followed me like an oversized shadow. Practically every lecture or problem required an explanation, not much, just the major points, and those first weeks right through the trips to the rifle range, we'd go over the lessons. It never embarrassed him to ask. I don't believe that he didn't understand but that he only expected he wouldn't. Frankly, it always gave me a boost. If something passed him by in a field exercise of lecture, it made no difference, he'd ask. He'd grin and say, "It's OK. Gill's gonna explain it."

I found myself enjoying it, but then Gilmore would shake his head and mock him and grumble, "Jus' like a goddam teacher."

In arguments with other men, he would always defer to me and say, "Gill knows," or sometimes "Gilly knows." Being Gaston's friend had its ups and downs, mostly ups, for he was generous, sometimes too generous. On our first long march with full forty-pound-plus field packs, it was Gaston who packed Gilmore's load and his own the last mile, and he did so with pleasure and pride, even when Ortiz told him he shouldn't, in fact urged him not to, but wouldn't insist, and that was a fault other cadre noncoms would never be guilty of.

Gaston was in thrall to his habits. Nothing I could say or do would release him from his bonds, the most demanding being his morning cigarette. No matter where we were or what conditions we were under, before he could do anything, he had to find and light a cigarette, even if it was only the butt of one from the night before. This would drive me crazy; if we woke with orders to strike the tent and get under way, I alone pulled tent pegs, divided and rolled the shelter halves, while he frantically searched for a butt. I got used to it and understood it was his condition for living, and I made sure at night that the cigarettes and matches were always close at hand. Making plans ahead was, for Gaston, a new light in the firmament.

The army was/is, in reality, one giant educational institution; some form of instruction was taking place at all times, regardless of the branch of service. In basic training, a lot more was going on than just training in weapons or military protocols; every minute of the day, we were involved in learning something we didn't know before or improving skills we already had. With the wide range of aptitudes and the great number of pupils combined with the time limits, instructional methods were crucial. Over and over, we heard there were three methods of doing anything: the right way, the wrong way, the army way. We never questioned the army way, teaching "by the numbers," which became, emphatically, the *only* way. Every lesson, they broke into mnemonic steps, from simple to complex, and every step had a number. They taught, and we learned every step in the numbered sequence, and we had to know what each number signified, whether it was in order or not. A popular bawdy barracks room ballad describing the art of seduction, each step in the art having a number, begins,

Oh, this is number one,
and the fun has just begun;
lay me down, roll me over,
do it again . . .

It ends,

Oh, this is number ten,
and we're doin' it again . . .

It was all by the numbers, and I am sure it derived from the mnemonic system the army had in place for teaching everything from firing the M1 to setting up a pup tent to digging for antipersonnel mines. It worked because they based it on the idea that in the beginning, no one knew anything about anything and that if he did, then he must forget it and relearn it all the army way, thus the right way differed from the army way for a reason. This was easy for those who knew nothing, especially if they knew they knew nothing.

In the subtler crafts of military life, such as map reading or platoon tactics, my greatest difficulty was assuming I "knew nothing." Pope's line that a "little learning is a dangerous thing" was truer than I wanted to admit. Drinking deeply from the Hyperion Spring of basic infantry training rectified that, however, especially in learning the arts and skills of firing weapons: the M1, Browning Automatic Rifle, light machine gun, carbine, pistol, .60-mm. mortar, and bazooka. I had to learn how to assume nothing, how to follow numbers of the system without question, as I would a catechism, for the army way led always to a special salvation.

For the first four weeks, we learned to care and maintain our "best friend," our gas-operated, eight-round, semiautomatic .30-caliber M1 Garand rifle. At the beginning of the fourth week, we went to the rifle range and finally began to fire live ammunition at targets. But on the weeks while we were learning how it worked, we also learned by the numbers how to fire it the army way, over and over until each numbered move became second nature, as natural as cutting a steak and lifting a fork. The monotony overwhelmed the boys who had "gotten their deer every year with Daddy's Winchester." For those like me, it worked a miracle.

When we reached the range, the Battle of the Bulge in the ETO was in its wipe-up stages, and the flood of replacements that had left Wolters the weeks before was stemmed. In the first days of the Bulge, just a few days after that dour lieutenant had spoken of the queen of battles, we had seen entire battalions ship out. The first one to ship had its training cut to fourteen weeks, then a day later one still in its thirteenth week, then one in its twelfth, and so on, down to a battalion just finishing its sixth week of training, its week on the BAR, the heavy automatic rifle range. They had received a few hours of instruction with hand grenades and, thus, were "qualified" as rifleman 745 and sent overseas as infantry replacements. History tells us the casualties in this batch were staggering. Rumors reached us that we would be going to the rifle range early and would soon be on our way; Lt. Smythe's dour prophecy was true after all, our queen was a whore or at least a pimp. Oddly, although they wished otherwise, few of the men I knew complained, so unified was the feeling among "men" our age, so readily had we subscribed to Major McGruder's "inspiring" words.

The week before we went to the range, we performed hours and hours of "dry runs," sighting our rifles, pulling, rather *squeezing*, the triggers, as our buddy made a pencil mark at the spot we said was on target. It was an interesting teaching system, I thought, everything by the numbers: (1) Place the leaf sight just below the circle or the "bull." (2) Let out half a breath and hold. (3) Take up the slack in the trigger. (4) Squeeze the trigger evenly and steadily—don't jerk. The click of the firing pin would signal the man at the target to mark the spot we said was on target. He would hold it steady, requiring you to resight each time, and then would mark the pattern. If it was widely scattered, you needed practice; if it made a neat triangle, you were learning. Or if by a miracle all three pencil points hit the same point, you were an expert rifleman. As I testified earlier, I had never fired a rifle larger than a single-shot .22, had never experienced the recoil of a .30-30. Therefore, I took the instructor's words to heart, never thinking or second-guessing the process or assuming otherwise.

"Hold that butt tight to your shoulder, grip the rifle tight and press the butt hard against your cheek, and squeeze, don't jerk. It'll kick, but it won't jump, and you'll hit that Jap sonuvabitch between the eyes!"

I believed it all. Others who had hunted "all their lives" scoffed at the dry runs and asked when we were going to shoot real ammo. They constantly complained that no one had ever killed a Jap or Kraut with a pencil marker. "I been huntin' all my life, and I know how to shoot a .30-30. They ain't nothin' to it," they would say. The cadre sergeants would tell them to shut up and listen and do what they were told and "do it by the fuckin' numbers."

First firings were at one hundred yards to "zero in" our sights, make sure the elevation and the windage were accurate. Firing from a prone position with sandbags to steady our rifle and the slings pulled tight, we did as we had been taught, and it worked amazingly. My first round hit at four o'clock, in the no. 4 circle just outside the bull's eye. I clicked in right windage and one click up elevation then checked the reading on my sight and made a mental note. The second round--we loaded one at a time--hit in the bull at ten o'clock. The sergeant watching said, "That's good enough. Don't touch it, Gillan. Fire three rounds for effect."

I didn't touch windage or elevation but *thought windage and declination* and the next three rounds hit dead center, just like I'd been taught.

Gaston whistled low, "They gonna make you a sniper."

"It's the rifle, Gaston. Just doin' it by the numbers. It sure isn't me," I said, but wow—what a feeling!

Gaston was one who had hunted deer with his father and uncles and usually got some "meat" every year, but in the training, he had followed the army way while laughing at the "silliness." He also scored high.

From the three-hundred-yard range, we fired prone and kneeling, and the results were about the same. Later, we went back to the two-hundred-yard range and fired, "for record," sitting and standing. My sitting record was six 5s ("bulls"), a 3, and a 4. Standing was more difficult, the nine-pound rifle refusing to hold steady, so the first two rounds hit in the 3 circle. After that, I lined up at the center of the bull, took up the slack in the trigger, raised the sight just out of the black bull's eye, and slowly let it fall until the leaf sight bisected the circle just beneath the black bull then squeezed, didn't jerk. My spotter, waited for the pointer to spot my hit, then called out, "Four! Six o'clock! Wow!"

The next five rounds were in the bull, and each time, he said, "wow! Man, you must have been raised huntin' squirrels."

"First time I ever fired a rifle bigger than a .22," I said.

The same sergeant who had watched me zero in said, "That's right, by the numbers, huh, Gillan?"

Something was happening—something *big*, I felt. It was a high moment quite unexpected, one that did more for my self-esteem than passing my chemistry final or bringing in my unknown in qualitative analysis before anyone else. I could have fired all day, but we were finished for the day, and we marched back, route step, talking about the day's firing, jibing how several of the experienced hunters were marching back with black eyes and bruised cheeks, apparently men who ignored the "numbers."

Heavy rain clouds hovering over mesas to the north brought out remarks like: "Hell, we probably won't be out here if it's raining," "Won't be able to even see the five-hundred-yard targets, much less hit the fuckers. Thank

God!" Route step let us boast or bitch aloud, all the way jubilant and angry by turns, and I figured the army's psychology was well tuned to the training schedule. After a day's firing our weapon, our morale was high. The cracks of the rifles, the odor of cordite, the kick of the butt to shoulder, the feel of the stock against your cheek, and the satisfaction of hitting the target left a rich taste and occupied all the senses. Marching back in route step, no cadence counting, talking while we marched, magnified the meaning of life for eighteen-year-old buck-ass privates in basic. Just fifty yards from the battalion quadrangle, Ortiz called, "'Ten-shun!" and began counting cadence. Suddenly, we *were* Company A. It was the first day I felt I was an infantryman, a "subject of the queen" ready to get fucked without the value of intercourse. And I didn't give a damn.

Reading our minds, a sergeant marching alongside shouted about the weather and our expectations, "You wanna bet they won't send you out? This is when they really like to put your asses on range. Cold, windy, sleet, and rain—that's the best time." We laughed. We felt like soldiers. "Or dry hot and windy with the sun in your face!"

Someone shouted, followed by a chorus, "Fuckin' a right!"

Shit, I'm a soldier, I thought.

The next morning, it was raining, ice mixed with rain. Standing there in formation waiting to leave for the range, I heard my named called.

"Gilliland! Fall out for sick call, you go t'the dentist,'" the field first sergeant called.

Why dentist, I thought, as I fell out and joined the others going on sick call. At the moment, I really had mixed feelings, happy not to be marching the four miles in freezing rain but disappointed not to be on the range again, feeling the jolt of my own M1, serial number 447119, and hearing the sharp crack, more a crack than a boom as it is in Hollywood, and smelling the lovely burned powder I had begun to love.

As I leaned back in the dental chair, the captain was explaining I had a molar growing in on top of another and needed to have it pulled to make way for new one. *Good*, I thought. "That's the second one I've had pulled," I told him. *Too many teeth, too small a mouth. Who'd a thought it?*

It was sleeting now, and I was enjoying the warmth of the dental office. I'll qualify another day. I was sure they wouldn't risk my getting an infection in the open socket, I thought, as he shot me full of Novocain and began to pull, cracking the crown and digging for the roots. When a claxon sounded, he dropped his pliers and announced it was lunch break.

I mumbled, "What?"

He replied, "At ease, soldier. It's not your problem," then turned to another dentist and told him to take over, repeating some dental jargon, then left.

The pulling and cracking continued and then a probing, and finally, a piece of root came out. He said to rinse my mouth. "Spit! Now take this down the hall, get an X-ray, then come back here and wait."

"I thought you took X-rays *before* you extracted," I said.

"Before *and* after to see if we left a piece of root in. It could cause infection."

I thanked him but said, "No one took any pictures before."

He frowned and then said, "Well, that was the CO. He knows what he's doing, don't worry."

When I got back, the captain had returned and was looking at the little X-ray squares and frowned. "Marshal! What the hell did you do? You pulled them both?"

"I pulled the one you said. There was only one there," the second dentist replied, but then he was only a lieutenant.

I looked from one to the other, understanding that the last roots pulled were the roots of the replacement. So much for replacements, I thought. "What are you going to do now, *sir*?" I asked.

"Quiet, soldier." The captain turned to the lieutenant. "Well, no matter. We got rid of the bad one."

"Excuse me, sir. Do I get a bridge or something to fill the gap?"

He looked at me as he would a smart ass, "We build bridges only when we pull three, soldier."

"Well, here I am. Pick a tooth and pull it," I said, trying not to sound too pissed off.

The younger man shook his head smiling as the CO said, "Get the hell outta here and back to your unit."

"Do I get a light duty slip, sir?" I asked.

He hesitated then said, "No."

I turned and left, slipping into my raincoat, and walked in the sleet and rain back to the company. It was past noon, and the mess hall was closed, but the cook gave me coffee and a sandwich, same food the men in the field were eating, then a very pissed off corporal marched with me to the range at quick march all the way. I had never walked a quick four miles before in my life, and now I was doing it in freezing rain and actually enjoying the physicality of it all, knowing I would be soon firing the rest of my qualifying rounds.

When I arrived, the first platoon guys were firing prone on the three-hundred-yard range, the positions' shallow dishes filled with rain and ice.

The second platoon men, their firing order completed, stood behind the line, warming themselves around fifty-gallon drums of fire. Private Gold was probably peeing his pants and smelling up the area as he was constantly doing these days trying to get a medical discharge. "I got bad kidneys," he'd whine. "I allus had 'em." Gold really pissed us off when he pissed his pants; we knew he was faking it—son of a bitch had gotten married just before he was drafted, just to avoid the draft, but there he was.

The same sergeant who had watched me yesterday came up, greeted me, and told me to fire with the third platoon. They would rue the day if I caught a secondary infection in the open socket or caught the flu and had to go to the hospital everyone said was a hellhole with the worst food in the world. As I lay there, the rain letting my front sights freeze into a cake of ice, the rear protected by my freezing and gloveless right hand, an order came to fire two rounds high over the targets to melt ice on our sights. We fired as ordered then aimed and fired the six rounds for record, reloaded two more, and fired. I hit five bulls and a three 4s then rose and began the two-hundred-yard walk back to the next line at five hundred yards.

The sergeant said, "Good shootin' in this weather, Gill. You look like you'll at least shoot expert now." I was well within the range of sharpshooter but I figured I'd had fallen out of the expert category with the 4s in the last clip. Still, it was better than merely qualifying, and for me, it was like a miracle.

From five hundred yards out, you could hardly see the bunker where the targets were, but when the targets came up, they were visible and clear, the rain having slacked. The size of the bull's eye was almost five feet in diameter, the size of a small man, but five hundred yards was more than a quarter of a mile, closer to a third. If I hit anywhere in the black bull's eye at this distance without a scope, then I'd be pretty good, I thought.

I lay down prone, resting my left forearm on a sandbag, and felt the icy slush soak through my fatigues and long underwear and could hear a steady patter of rain on my helmet liner. I still wore the leather and wool glove on my left hand but had removed my right glove. It was pretty clear. The black bull's eye rested on the squared leaf of my sight, and I squeezed off the first round and waited.

"Four at six, Gil," the sergeant said.

My first two rounds were 4s at six o'clock. "Perfect windage but in need of a little elevation," I muttered to myself.

The firing sergeant was beside me, bending over. "I come to watch you, Gill. Don't take no elevation. You'll miss the whole fuckin' target, but from here, 4s are damn good."

I looked around. Gaston was my spotter. A cadre corporal was there, and so was the new lieutenant, and then Banks was near with the field first sergeant. I wondered, *why me? Was I the last one qualifying?*

I lay back on the target just as the sergeant said, but this time I *thought* elevation, let out half a breath, took up slack and squeezed, heard the loud slapping sound, and felt the pressure of the butt plate against my shoulder. I thought at the moment, *that's a five dead center.* The target dropped out of sight then rose with a large white circle dead center.

"Five! Dead damn center!" the sergeant said. The lieutenant knelt in the mud close to Gaston's shoulder. I had five more rounds in the clip and fired, waited—another bull exactly as the one before.

"Five! Dead center."

The next three rounds and then, "Five at eleven o'clock. Goddam good shooting, Gill. Goddam good!"

The lieutenant tapped my helmet with his pimp stick and said, "Good shooting, soldier."

When I got up, Banks nodded at me and smiled. God, I loved the moment. I qualified two rounds short of expert rifleman, which Banks later said I didn't want anyway because I didn't want to be a sniper. Gaston shook his head and laughed and said five hundred yards was all the way to hell and gone and asked if I was sure I hadn't ever been deer hunting. But I hadn't shot the best qualifying round in the company or the platoon. Several had shot much better than I had fired in the standing position, but I was satisfied.

After that, I was put in charge of all the live ammo problems and demonstrations for our platoon, and several days later, we ran a problem of squad in combat, using live ammo and pop-up targets. Our scores in the field firing demonstrations weren't all that good, I thought, but the new second john in charge thought so. There were fifteen or so silhouette targets, some standing in bushes, some "lying" flat, others sitting, moving back and forth. We hit three targets with one round each out of all that firing, and we fired a total of 192 rounds, but had only three hits against targets that weren't shooting back. Banks said that looked pretty good. Fully automatic would have not been much better. In a real fire fight with automatic weapons, a light machine gun and a couple of BARs, the enemy would have stayed buttoned up, so the effect would have been the same, the lieutenant explained.

"If they're hunkered down, they're not shooting back," he said But I always felt they were just trying to make recruits feel good. At the Battle of the Rosebud in Montana, three days before Custer died at Little Big Horn, Crook's men fired eighty thousand rounds and killed only six Sioux in a battle that lasted hours. We weren't that bad, but then again, we were not firing at living targets that were firing back.

In the field one day, an NCO instructor ordered me to explain to an Italian-American GI who claimed he spoke no English how the recoil spring in the M1917 LMG operated. The soldier claimed he couldn't understand English well enough to make it work. For some reason, the sergeant demonstrating the mechanism turned to me and said, "Gilliland, you explain it to him while the rest of these men work on their guns."

I couldn't believe he wasn't faking his lack of English. We'd exchanged comments from time to time in my rudimentary Spanish and his Italian. But when I tried to explain the operation of the bolt, my basic Spanish got me nowhere. Sitting beside me was a Mexican-American guy my age from Victoria, Texas; when I glanced toward him, he slid over and began explaining in simple but clear Spanish that even I could understand. The Italian seemed to understand then performed the maneuver simply and quickly. The guy from Victoria smiled and said that Spanish and Italian were practically the same.

I wondered why the sergeant had asked me to instruct him instead of the guy from Victoria, and then I recalled what had happened a week earlier when we were learning to fire and maintain the Browning automatic rifle. The BAR fired automatically or semi-automatically with the flick of a switch marked *F* and *A*: *F* for fire and *A* for automatic. (Our sergeant said, "F for fast and A for awful fast.") The rifle, like the M1, used a gas port and gas expansion system for operating the piston to automatically reject, reload, and fire. A *seer* or catch at the rear of the action would or would not allow a fully automatic sequence; it depended on whether the switch was at *A* or *F*. The *A* switch simply took the seer out of play; it was a simple and ingenious system, I thought. During the demonstration, the first time a few days before, our instructor had used a large wooden cutaway model of the rifle to explain the process. One of the ninety-day wonders, a little longer in the tooth than most second johns fresh out of OCS and one we had come to hate for his strutting pomposity, was lecturing away in a jargon most of the men could not follow, a jargon some believed even he didn't comprehend. My mind wandered off across the fields, and unconsciously, I turned facing away from the platform. It was unusually warm and clear that day in early January, so warm we wore only our fatigue uniform and field jacket. I lay back supported on my elbows, legs stretched out in front. It had happened in classroom a dozen times, several times to me: the lecturer would stop and focus on the daydreamer who continued gathering lazy thoughts from birds, trees, or rocks, more likely from the memory of *the* girl back home, in other words from anything besides the lecturer; then sudden silence would wake the dreamer, and he would realize he was being called to attention. Gaston's whisper woke and brought me back to the lecture.

"Stand up, soldier, and give me your name, rank, and serial number!" the officer shouted.

"Sir! Private Gilliland, Joe D., 18233708, sir!" I shouted back across the field.

"Now tell us how the seer and the seer-releasing mechanism on the BAR works," he said in a voice heavy with sarcasm and ridicule; he was that sure he had a live one for his collection.

I began at the beginning, the way I'd seen it demonstrated by the noncom instructor in our platoon a day before, "Sir! The Browning automatic rifle, model 1917, is a gas-operated, magazine-fed, automatic and semiautomatic, .30-caliber weapon. When the cartridge is fired, the expanding gas from the exploding cartridge passes through the gas port and drives the piston back, forcing the bolt to turn, ejecting the spent cartridge, and releasing the seer, the collision of the mechanism with the recoil absorbing coils and the recoil spring expands, moving the bolt forward—" He stopped me.

"That's enough, Private." I had covered the entire process as well as the seer function.

I stood at attention, waiting for his next orders. Out of the corner of my eye, I saw Corporal Ortiz turn away smiling. I knew it had impressed him, although it was nothing more than the lesson our instructor the day before had demonstrated so well with the cutaway model of a BAR. I had just memorized it the way he'd taught it, by the numbers, the army way. I waited.

Finally, he asked, "Have you had any previous military training?"

"Not with weapons, sir," I replied.

"All right, Private, take your seat and stay alert."

I caught the eye of Banks as I sat down. He was grinning. He knew I was a smart-ass college boy, but I knew he thought the new second john was a bigger smart-ass and a pompous one as well. Banks would have not tried to catch me in an error; he would have just chewed my ass out on the spot the way any good NCO would have. But it was dangerous stuff for an eighteen-year-old arrogant horse's-ass-of-a-buck private to think he'd put a second john in his place.

Our CO was a case study in the fortunes and misfortunes of war. We liked him from the first day in the rain when Major McGruder had introduced him as an officer with a combat commission earned along with a Silver Star and a Purple Heart in North Africa. But we understood that the battlefield commission meant also that he was not originally considered officer material.

His language, carelessness in uniform--he rarely wore the dark officers' greens and never the officers' pinks--and his two female companions at our Christmas and New Year's parties all qualified him as a lower rank in the "old army." He was rude, crude, and slightly unattractive in manner and appearance, and quite lacking in the spit and polish officers as gentlemen were expected to display. Some of the new second johns he obviously considered unfit for the role of leadership in combat. Banks also had an un-officer-like habit of sitting in the midst of EM during breaks on long marches. He liked shooting the breeze informally, joking and gossiping. Moreover, he could call us by name without having to look straight at us in order to read a name printed on our helmet liners. We never saw him mix with the officers in the field unless, like him, they were overseas veterans or were sitting down at a meal in the field. Once he had fallen out beside the road along with us and was eating a box lunch like ours. More often, the officers took hot meals served by enlisted orderlies, but today Banks had ordered the officers and cadre to eat with the men. It is the same in all times and all armies. Men, especially men in training and still not yet members of a unit, feel special pride when a CO condescends to not condescend. We had all about finished, a few lighting cigarettes, and one of the men in my squad was feeding a portion of his sandwich to one of the mongrel dogs that always tagged along, probably from one of the farmhouses of the Palo Pinto.

Banks called out, "Don't feed that dog. You eat that food, you worked for it. That sonabitch ain't worked for anything. I never want to see my men feed stray dogs. You get a company mascot, it's OK. But we don't have mascots in basic training." There was no rancor in his voice, just pieces of useful information told more to men as friends than trainees. "Dogfaces work for their chow, those dogs don't." He paused, smiling. He had our attention. "You know why everybody calls the infantry GI a dogface or dog soldier? Because they finally found something low enough to compare him to." We laughed; we had learned in the weeks that a serious put down always speaks pride. To be the lowest is superlative. At the time, we were far enough into training we had begun to feel like soldiers, though we weren't, not yet. Lieutenant Banks' sharing with us his disregard for the niceties made us feel he had accepted us. At that moment, I loved the army.

I was sitting near him at the time, and he began asking where we were all from. Most answered Texas, Oklahoma, or Kansas.

"Where are you from, sir?" someone asked.

One of the cadre corporals, a Navajo Indian from New Mexico, looked up and called out, "The lieutenant's from Virginia."

Banks nodded and said, "Anyone know who the best soldier in the army is today? Not that asshole MacArthur."

The cadre corporals were smiling but wouldn't answer; they knew the drill. I said, "Gen. George Marshall."

"Right! And you know what school he went to?"

I said, "VMI." It wasn't fair. He had said it all before, I just remembered.

"Right, soldier, V fucking MI. No damned West Point man Marshall."

The corporals stood up, one blew a whistle and called out, "Police the area, assholes and elbows, I don' wanna see no butts of any kind on this here ground."

Banks drifted back to the other platoons that were strung out along the deep ditch. He was telling a noncom the men should learn to scatter out, not bunch up.

He had spoken to us before, once asking where we were the day Pearl Harbor was bombed and told how he had been CQ in a field artillery command post on Hawaii, in one of the famous barracks. I can never forget those conversations with Banks. We liked him. I believe all the enlisted ranks liked him, mainly for his stories, his irreverent humor, and his lack of polish that, in the end, led to his being relieved of command of A Company just two weeks before we left for maneuvers. In our beers at the PX or an out-of-the-way steak house in Mineral Wells, we would tell "Banks stories" and confess how we'd gladly serve with him if we ever got into combat; we knew he would keep the queen of battles honest if anyone could.

But one morning, on the .60-mm. mortar range, he showed up late, wearing a mixed uniform of officer greens and an enlisted men's OD shirt without epaulets, his silver bars pinned crookedly on his collar tabs. Major McGruder, in creased pinks and his short camel's hair coat, was already at the range and obviously unhappy that A Company's CO was not in the field with his men. We all supposed he was still with one of the Mineral Wells "ladies" he had escorted to New Year's dinner, or we hoped he was. When his jeep spun up in a cloud of dust, he stepped out in the odd uniform without leggings, his pants folded and stuffed into the tops of his socks like some rooky. We were embarrassed for him, not ashamed, for he had served beyond the need for shame, we felt. We could see but couldn't hear McGruder chewing him out just before he returned to the jeep and spun off. One of the cadre sergeants nearby sighed and mumbled that we had just seen the last of Banks. In a few days, his replacement, Captain Pulaski, took over in a quick ceremony on the company street. But Banks was around, showing up during our maneuvers in Dry Valley or Hell's Bottom. I'd never spoken to Banks, except when he was shooting the breeze with us during one of our roadside breaks, though he had spoken to me after the incident at the five-hundred-yard range—man, that was a proud moment.

He popped up in odd places. Once on a map-reading problem, I had a squad and thought we were lost, off the map entirely, or so I thought, when we walked right into him sitting all alone as if he was expecting us. We saluted as we approached, and he waved back, asking if we were lost. I didn't want to admit it, but he could tell I was.

"I don't think I have the right map or the right country?" I said.

"You're the third squad to pass through here looking lost," he said and reached for my map, unfolded it, put his finger on a landform and pointed it out to us a few yards from where we were standing.

When I thanked him, he asked "How you men doing?"

We said everything was about normal, *SNAFU.*

"I'm supposed to be refereeing, seeing that you dogfaces don't stay lost."

As he passed us, he tapped me on the helmet liner with his swagger stick, that mini-baton of command they all carried and that we unaccountably called a "pimp stick." That tap was an endorsement and thanks, I felt, for sticking it, just a little, to a swaggering asshole that time I answered the question about the seer mechanism. He also knew that I had befriended the "Three Garcias" when all the others were treating them like shit. The three Garcias, all from some place near Brownsville, were in second platoon, and Banks had said once they were probably the best natural soldiers in the company; they had in fact scored high on the rifle range. I hadn't done much but had helped one of them memorize his general orders one night when we were all on guard duty: "I'll walk my post in a military manner and *take no shit from the comp'ny commaner.*" In doing so, I had become a friend. Knowing Banks knew, I felt great satisfaction.

We called Lieutenant Pulaski the Polish officer. I was the acting platoon leader of the second platoon, and we had arrived at our bivouac area past midnight after a twenty-mile forced hike, and I had pointed out the platoon's areas, had "ordered" the squad leaders to assign tent spots. It was a mock combat zone, so each platoon had men posted to "foxholes," circles scratched in the rocky ground, but in the dark without flashlights—simulating combat security—some of the assignments were jumbled. The cadres passed down the word to observe a "hygiene drill," that all the men were expected to "wash their privates pats." Our sergeant called me over and said that each of the acting platoon leaders was required to witness the "washing of balls." A large tank truck parked on the edge of the company perimeter furnished the water—cold water. When two of the squad leaders told me that the line at the tank truck was so long it'd be morning before anyone in our platoon could get to bed, I said, "Forget it, they can do it tomorrow." We were expected to fall out at 5:00 a.m. A voice behind me said, "Soldier, report to me first thing after breakfast." It was the Polish officer.

He didn't "bust" me the next morning because there was nothing to bust. I was only "acting" as platoon leader. When he asked why I had disobeyed a direct order, I told him just what I told the sergeant, because the line was too long and the men were exhausted. He listened and informed me I was to carry out the order first then discuss it. I had learned that ass-chewing now and then was a small price to guarantee the respect and loyalty of your men. When I got back from the CP, all four squad leaders reported they'd watched everybody scrub his balls.

Something important happened to me in basic training, in fact had begun to happen the day I left for College Station in August. It was more than the classes and excellent instructors at A&M or the challenges that taught me to do things I never thought I would be capable of doing: hitting six bulls dead center on the five-hundred-yard range or being in charge of a platoon all through maneuvers. It was discovering a potential I never knew I had. For all those years, from Averill on through high school, I always felt that I was destined to accept the lesser side of the middle, something down on the right slope of the bell-shaped curve. There were so many others who seemed brighter, better looking, stronger, and faster that I was content to warm myself in their reflected heat. I simply didn't know what I was capable of. I heard teachers say, "Be quiet, Joe," or others simply say, "Shut up and don't be silly," and even heard my mother warn that I talked too much, or "your tongue will be your ruination" and I believed that it was true. The "o'ergrowth of some mole of nature" in me had shaped me to fill the role of a loquacious pest. I found no real friends, except possibly Bill Reiss, to hold with "hoops of steel" or friends who would do likewise with me until now. It changed when I left for College Station. Perhaps the friendship and interest that Dr. James offered was the first glimmer, the first light on an otherwise dim horizon. Then at A&M, my tongue and voice held me in good stead. I discovered that many of my classmates actually listened, and a few, for whom I had great respect, sought my company—Arthur, Carlos, and Leslie, men as unlike one another or me as *Homo Sapiens* can be, and here, I honestly mean *sapiens*—came to me and offered themselves as friends, and I was grateful, for I already admired and respected each in different ways. I found it too in the respect Pete Dunne showed to me in his refusal to patronize or condescend;

how foolish I was not making an effort to return that respect and admiration. Then in basic training, Corporal Ortiz, in the early weeks, let me carry the platoon guerdon then gave me a squad, and later making me acting platoon sergeant. I hadn't asked or made an effort for any of these "promotions." and considered each step simply part of the training program. I took them then as signs that I was doing something right.

Several weeks before our battalion went on maneuvers, our final phase before "graduation," after we had seen all those *Why We Fight* movies, Sergeant Gates, the Navajo noncom who replaced Ortiz, appointed me I & E (Information and Education) noncom, without rank, of course. The I & E leader's job was, more or less, to take over where the *Why We Fight* movies left off, i.e. to lead discussions about the war and the "nature of the enemy," to lead discussions about the meaning of the Four Freedoms, the meaning of topics like "total surrender" and "negotiated peace." The officer who "orientated" us leaders tried to explain how the "new" civilian army was, at least in theory, not just an army of blind followers but one of thinking men who needed to know why they were in the army and what the war was about.

When one of the I & E leaders from another platoon interjected loudly, "Hell, we know what we're doing. We're replacements for those poor fuckers that got shot," we all laughed, and the officer frowned and tried to continue. We understood it was simply part of an indoctrination process. It didn't matter.

I read the pamphlets the night before and, the next day, introduced the topics and tried to get the men to raise questions or just talk about it. Most were content to go along with the charade and enjoy an hour indoors out of the freezing wind. I enjoyed standing there, summarizing what I had read, and then raising questions I thought might lead to discussion. They tolerated the "college boy's" efforts, but the only "heated" discussion arose around the question: "Will Japan accept a negotiated peace, or will we have to fight until Japan is absolutely defeated?"

The fact was clear: no one knew. Only one man in the platoon had ever met any Japanese. He had worked for a Japanese farmer in California and had shocked everyone when he said the "Jap" was one of the nicest bosses he'd ever had, "But I guarantee you they ain't gonna ask for no nee-gosh-ated surrender."

Near the end of the second, and last, session a wave of boredom swept over the crowd, and I had a feeling that I was barely being tolerated. Only a small fistful cared about being informed or educated about the war; most were merely grateful we had the hour indoors and weren't marching off across country to some field problem or doing close-order drill or calisthenics. The clock said we had another half hour, but as far as I could tell, we were finished. Just then a hand shot up from the clique of Swedes we had from Minnesota.

"You want to know the cause of this here war, Gilliland?" one Gunderson asked, "Everybody knows that all wars are caused by big money. It's all tied up with economic exploitation of the working class."

I was startled. I had never heard anyone outside of college debate ever say such a thing or use such words as "economic exploitation." It was the most articulate sentence I'd heard in the platoon since I'd arrived at Camp Wolters.

"OK, Gunderson, le's hear it, explain what—" I never finished. The new ninety-day-wonder in the back rose and spoke, "Time's up, men. We need a break. Take ten, piss call, light up."

No argument. Gunderson smiled, winked, and began to walk up to where I was standing.

I talked to the Swede later, and he told me his father was a member of a socialist farm labor group. Most of the people in his town were also. He announced it with the pride of a man who understood the meaning and importance of solidarity. He could have been a descendant of a Per Hansa or of Peder or Rølvaag himself, I thought, and I asked if he'd ever heard of O. E. Rølvaag. He said, of course, everyone from his part of the country had heard of Rølvaag. He was surprised that I had. I can see his face smiling now, the long jaw, blue eyes like northern ice, "Map of Sweden or Norway?" all over his face.

Six weeks into the program, I learned that I had qualified for mechanics', signal, and clerks' schools, but I declined and told the sergeant major the only school that interested me was the one for combat medics. But as the T-5 told me back at induction, he said the quota had been filled. When I told Gaston and Gilmore I turned down the offers, they acted like I was crazy.

"You dizzy shit!" Gilmore said, using his favorite epithet. "You'd rather get your ass shot off in some rifle squad? You are crazy! I'd a taken it." Gaston understood, but he would have liked the offer for mechanic's school, so I told him to apply, and he said he had applied but was turned down.

Later, a few weeks before we went on maneuvers, the entire battalion marched into the theater to see a recruiting film for airborne infantry. Airborne was the most glamorous, most colorful of all the branches in the army ground forces and offered a monthly pay boost of fifty dollars a month. In addition to four weeks jump training, the paratroops, like the rangers, went through the most rigorous combat training of any troops in ground forces, even rougher than marine boot camp, they said. The rangers and the airborne infantry were the army's elite troops, so elite that most volunteers cared more about serving in an elite branch than they did about the bonus. The film described a far more rigorous training schedule than anything we had seen in our infantry basic. Even though paratroopers and glider troops wore the best looking boots, boasted the most handsome badge and shoulder patch, it figured that they also had the highest casualty rate. The recruiting pitch was so effective, mainly in its appeal to the youngest recruits, that about fifty men stepped out and signed up as we marched out of the theater; I was one. Though I was one of the smaller ones who signed his name, I was at my peak physically. I had never fallen out on a forced march, had always finished first in my platoon in a cross-country, and could do as many push-ups as the most athletic, and at 145 pounds, I weighed twenty pounds more than I did when I arrived at Fort Sam. I was no Leslie McNair, but I was in good shape. So I volunteered, knowing that if I completed the training at Fort Benning, I would be too late for the ETO, but I figured I would be just in time to drop into Honshu or Kyushu.

All my conditioning, however, came to naught, for ten days into maneuvers, they called us back to take our physicals for jump school, and I flunked. Living mostly on skimpy K rations and D bars I had lost almost twenty pounds and was almost down to what I weighed when I arrived at the Dodd Field Induction Center, 127 pounds. I was too light, the doctor told me, and jokingly remarked they needed men who would reach the ground before the fighting stopped. I tried to explain that we had been eating nothing but K rations and D bars, but he replied that anyone who lost that much weight that fast might not be able to handle combat conditions. He did note on my forms that I had just come off ten days of extended field exercises. When we finished the last four days of maneuvers and returned to our barracks, I saw my name was not on the Fort Benning shipping list; it was the first serious blow I would suffer since enlisting.

There was one compensation more important in the long run than being accepted for airborne. Shortly before leaving on the two-week maneuvers, or "removers," our new cadre sergeant, Sergeant Gates, the Navajo I mentioned earlier, announced that I would be the acting platoon leader for the two weeks we'd be on maneuvers. His selecting me was a tremendous boost to my self-confidence. When he called me into his office-bedroom at the end of the barracks and told me, he was quite complimentary, saying that Ortiz told him to keep an eye on me, and he had. He said he knew Ortiz was telling the truth when he found the men trusted me, and told him that they would take orders from me. I caught on quickly to new things, he said, and knew how to explain things to the men in a way they understood. He didn't say it in so many words, but then he didn't have to; truth was, I had no *real* authority as the acting platoon sergeant and the platoon knew it.

"I'll announce it at roll call in the morning, and from then on, you'll be in command," he said, "and I'll back you."

We headed out the next morning under full-field gear and weapons, on our first twenty-mile forced march, a winding route to Pinto Ridge. The direct route that we had often taken was only four or five miles. The other acting platoon leaders and I were marching along out of ranks with the officers and cadre. I had never felt as proud or more self-confident.

Maneuvers were a success; I, the platoon, made no serious blunders, and I learned a lot. We had miserable weather our first five days on Pinto Ridge, where we ran combat problems that stressed squads in combat. That first morning, we learned how to advance, leap-frogging squads through a "field of fire," that is, through a field where high explosives set in strategically placed holes would go off without warning, simulating enemy artillery. All morning, heavy clouds shifted on the horizon, some resembling tornado clouds. Mineral Wells is smack in the middle of the North Texas tornado alley. It was the beginning of storm season. In the afternoon, the second platoon observed from the small open stands as an officer instructed how, after chow, we would practice a retreat through a field of fire, only this time it would be an entire platoon.

"Gilliland," the officer ended, "you'll take the point squad and weave your way, leap-frogging all the way back along this line." His pointer traced a line through pits where they had set explosives. "Put two flanking squads out at the edge of the field," he said, tracing a line from the far edge of the field through the foxholes. "Give the squad leaders orders how to proceed, and make sure you are always in contact."

After supper, I picked for the point my original squad with Gaston and led them out to the far point while two NCOs took charge of the other squads to our right and left. First thing I did was to divide us into fire teams that would retreat leap-frogging and maintaining constant fire (blanks, of course) and roughly instructed the flanking squads to move on my hand signals. Everyone found it quite ludicrous, but the cadre noncoms backed me up.

The clouds now were more ominous than ever, with one large, dark cloud on the horizon threatening to form a funnel. Just as we were expecting a loud claxon to signal the beginning, a huge wind hit, and the black cloud moved over us, turning the late afternoon into dark night. A cadre noncom with the squad out to our left signaled us to come over to a large tree; the other was taking his group back on a run to the elevated stands. I knew the first rule in a storm was to avoid large trees, and the second was to avoid high ground, so I called out for my squad to stay with me. They did. Our route was through a field broken by barbed wire and holes filled with simulated "mortar rounds," quarter-pound blocks of nitro-starch, and was more than the length of a football field.

"Hit the ground and lock arms!" I shouted, giving the order just as the wind hit and sheets of rain crashed down.

The ground was flooded in seconds and soaked us through, but a funnel didn't touch down; instead, it passed over, forming its funnel and touching down, decimating our company's bivouac on the ridge behind us. It left as quickly as it came. When I stood up and saw the squad at the tree breaking up and lifting downed branches, I gave the order to follow me. Only one casualty from another platoon was reported: a man caught when the large map board at the amphitheater blew down.

Day and night, problems filled the next four days in clear weather. All during the Pinto Ridge exercises, we were fed only combat field rations, D bars. I enjoyed the experience. It was the culmination of all that we had learned and a test to see how well we learned it. The so-called hardships and combat conditions were nothing compared to conditions we would really experience one day, and we knew that, but what we accomplished was a revelation. The men in all four platoons really did behave so well under unrelieved combat-*like* conditions that they surprised themselves.

After Pinto Ridge, we moved to Dry Valley, where typically, it rained four days. And we spent our last five days at Hell's Bottom, where all problems involved live ammunition, street fighting, and crawling through barbed wire under a steady stream of live .30-caliber machine-gun fire. Here, the pressure was greatest, but the food much improved, no constipating D bars, but hot meals for the evening meals. The final day took the second platoon through a long problem called platoon in combat, in which we employed every weapon we had fired on range. My job was to select the men who would fire the BAR and the bazooka, as well as the men who throw grenades or fire a rifle grenade at the final target, a small hut supposedly an enemy's command post. An instructing officer outlined our "objective" and described to me how we would approach the enemy's FPL, final protective line, and then I met the platoon and assigned the tasks and repeated what he told me. I had a big, hefty guy who I knew ran easily with the heavy BAR, and I told him about the targets he would be firing on, explaining how we would be scored for the attack's execution. He grinned broadly and thanked me for the job. We were big boys playing war, I thought, but with live ammunition. It went well, the officer-instructor at my side watching and standing out of the way when we all reached the enemy's FPL.

Garcia set up and angled the M1 with its grenade launcher and aimed at the oversized outhouse shack and asked, "OK if I blow it up?"

I said, "Do it!"

The lieutenant laughed. "No one's hit it yet on these maneuvers."

Up and down the line, "my men" were firing at pop-up targets; the big guy was firing the BAR as rapidly as he could slide the bolt, the "seer" mechanism having jammed on semiautomatic fire, but he was, nevertheless, emptying his twenty-round magazines almost as fast as if it were on *automatic.* The lieutenant signaled and gave Garcia the nod. He fired. The grenade arched and landed square on the shack's roof and exploded. The roof and half a wall collapsed. It was over. At the critique, our instructor announced no one failed in the mission and gave praise to the BAR and Garcia. I do not recall which of the "Three Garcias" was the grenadier of the hour, but I do recall wishing at the time that Lieutenant Banks had seen one of his men vindicate him.

That was our last exercise. After the critique, we broke our bivouac and returned to battalion where we got new orders. Nearly everyone in the company had shipping orders for Fort Meade, Maryland, the main replacement depot for troops going to the ETO. Arthur was removed from shipping orders and sent to the hospital for an emergency hernia operation, which meant we would not be shipping out together. I hadn't seen Art much in the last few weeks, and only once on maneuvers. Our platoons rarely came together during those two final weeks.

The news from Europe was all good. The only thing left, we heard, was largely a mopping-up operation, although at the time we "graduated" from infantry basic, Berlin had still not fallen to the Soviet Union. While we knew that the war would very likely be over in Europe by the time we landed as replacements, we also heard that there was possibility that pockets of guerilla resistance would continue in the "Bavarian redoubt." It was not the kind of war we had been training for during the past fifteen weeks, but neither had anyone else. Hovering above it all was a bizarre state of confusion and optimism mixed with the realization that the war in the Pacific might be many months, possibly a year, before it would be finished. They told us that orders can be changed even at the last moment and that it was possible we would be sent to the Pacific. The battle for Okinawa was still to come.

From a purely personal perspective, with no consideration for the political or the strategic questions involved, I wanted my orders to read Meade and the ETO, for at that moment, the East was of no interest to me. I had been reading European history, studying the geography of Germany, the Rhine, all of Southern France. If the war ended after I got there, I would see and learn for myself what was left of European civilization, perhaps know first hand what I had been reading about; and if I hurried, I hoped to hear a shot, a shell, or see something to authenticate my enlistment. I believed the *Why We Fight* films we watched during basic training and fiercely accepted all the symbols of our freedoms, though I realized—after my last visit to Austin—more than ever that the fruit on the vine of liberty was sometimes cankered. Our system was still the best hope of mankind, even with its limits. Trinity was barely a month away and Hiroshima almost three months.

The day after we got off maneuvers Captain Pulaski held a semiformal "graduation exercise" where he handed us each a "diploma" that announced we had successfully completed the fifteen weeks of basic infantry training that prepared us to be "riflemen 745." The war in Europe was winding down; the Ninth Army was on the Elbe and awaiting the Russian, and all this put less pressure on the training command to get us on our way. They even spoke of a glut in the Pacific, a very temporary glut, to be sure, since they had not yet landed in Okinawa. So we had our graduation ceremony; we were breathing, had ten toes and ten fingers, though no one had to swear to the toe count. Pulaski, cold as ever, shook each man's hand and made encouraging noises such as "I hope you're ready," "Keep your head down and watch out for your buddy," "Don't be brave, be smart." When I got there, he remembered my name from the ass-chewing he had given me for not ensuring my men had "washed their privates" during our maneuvers in Hell's Bottom. He smiled as if recalling the incident and said, "Be smart, Gilliland, act dumb and be safe." I wasn't sure what he meant, but it sounded friendly, and I assumed it was one of a dozen pet sayings he used, and that was the one that had come to him when I got up.

We took army buses into Forth Worth and stood in line for tickets to our destination. A Mexican-American boy from Victoria, Contreras, who had stepped in and helped explain to the Italian fellow how to extract the recoil spring in an LMG bolt, and to whom I had spoken to several times about South Texas, came up to me and asked if I knew the bus schedules south. They'd told him the bus for San Antonio had just left and the next one was already sold out. We had a pocket full of money for our travel and per diem plus our month's pay, but we didn't have much time. The crowd of OD-clad GIs, most of whom had just come in from Camp Wolters, looked as dejected as we felt. All through the past fifteen weeks, we had joked about how army life meant hurry and wait, but now here we were, standing in the Fort Worth Greyhound Bus Station, in the civilian world, and waiting with no end of waiting in sight. Then Contreras suggested we check out the private cars. "They're cheaper and faster. Maybe we'll find one going to San Antonio."

I followed him to a line of sedans of all makes and ages and asked when they were leaving. The operator, a wizened little man in his thirties, wearing a cheap, snap brim hat, his shirt cuffs hiked up two turns halfway between wrist and elbow, a cigarette dangling from his mouth, was standing there looking like a kind of spider with the hairs on his scrawny arms standing like quills— self-confidence in every pore but conveying none of it to his prospective riders. He needed two more for a full car and would leave immediately but, pointing to Contreras, said, "Ain't takin' no Meskin."

I backed away and announced loudly, "Then you ain't takin' me or anyone else from Camp Wolters. We just finished infantry basic together, and we're going overseas. You refusing a service man?" I wondered later if I would have barked so loud before my fifteen weeks of basic. I hoped I would, but I wasn't sure.

The driver glanced around, his cigarette and wrists still dangling. "These people don', mind, I don' either."

The other passengers were already seated three in the back, so Contreras and I got in the front. It was a hair-raising ride from Fort Worth to San Antonio, but it cut our travel time significantly, and we were in time for a bus to Corpus and for one to Victoria. We shook hands and said our good-byes and hoped we would meet again at Fort Meade. I suddenly realized I had missed saying farewell to Dykes.

I got home to a warm welcome and felt I was surrounded by much pride. I took pleasure in relating to Albert my experience on the range and saw he was pleased too. But neither Albert nor Mama found my teaching Gaston how to write his girl very interesting. Instead, they were surprised I had such friends. Once, sitting and having a beer together, I told Albert we had no boys from Wisconsin in the platoon, but I had several Swedes from Minnesota who were all solid farm-labor socialists.

"I'd never met a true socialist before," I told him. "It was really interesting," I said. He smiled and said nothing.

When Mama told me she had invited a bunch of her friends for a backyard farewell dinner I wondered who it could be. She apologized that none of my high school crowd was in town so she had to stick with people she knew best and knew were interested in me, which meant they would mostly be officers and wives from the Naval Air Station. The weather had just turned warm in Corpus, so the navy men were wearing whites, while I was still in wool OD. These navy whites were not middy blouses and bell-bottoms but high collars, shoulder boards, and much gold. To show off her "graduate" (basic training), she had invited a few "close friends," the lowest rank being a lieutenant commander. There were two captains and a vice admiral. I was appalled. All but one were graduates of the naval academy. I had earlier met all but the admiral and his wife while I was a college student, so that part was easy. Mama's greatest talent was meeting and entertaining the "right" people. When she saw my undisguised look of dismay at all the braid, she took me aside and explained these were her "best friends" and she was proud of me.

"I think they should see what a infantry private really looks like and acts like," she insisted. I enjoyed it: all that white and navy blue and gold in the backyard *and* a vice admiral deferring to a buck private. How could I complain?

This time, instead of going up to Austin, I stayed my full leave in Corpus, visiting only one close high school friend, Jerry Jarbeaux, who was still in town. She was the only person from high school I had written to regularly while I was at A&M and at Wolters. Bill Reiss was in the air corps somewhere. Harvey Dunn and I had lost touch. But Jerry had stayed in Corpus, refusing to go off to college until she had finished her private pilot's training.

I received a startling letter from her just before leaving on maneuvers. It told in vivid detail about her really serious accident in which she had nose-dived her light plane into the ground when another student pilot, who had tried to land his plane on top of hers, had severed the tail of her light plane with his propeller. She had lost the entire tail section and had nosed straight into the ground, but as she walked away from the crash to check on the other pilot she had collapsed and learned later she had broken several vertebra. The other pilot survived with only minor injuries. I wrote her immediately but received no reply until a late mail call in Hell's Bottom.

I called Jerry as soon as I got home and spoke to her mother who said she was doing well but in a body cast; she asked me to come around anytime. When I got to her house, I found her encased in a body cast from her neck to her hips, but she was laughing and relating it all, detail by detail, with pride and humor. Jerry and I had been close those last two years, so this was a deeply moving visit for me, even though we had less to say and less in common than we once had. I realized then, sitting there talking, that our friendship, the one really great friendship of my youth, would never see its former days. We didn't talk about the war or what was to come or what had been. Our talk was mostly about her flying and my learning how to "lead men," which I tried to talk down and she talked up with humor if not disbelief. She had written that Tom, her brother, was MIA, believed lost over Germany in 1944. Tom, a year older than I, volunteered for the army air corps and was a gunner-crew chief on a B-24. At first, he was listed killed in action, but while I was at Wolters, she wrote that the Swedish Red Cross had sent word he was in a German prison. Tom escaped, was recaptured, and then just a week before I arrived back in Corpus, he escaped again and joined the American forces, thus having the most adventurous service of us all. We talked a long time that afternoon until her mother came in and told me she needed to rest. It was the best afternoon, the best time of my short furlough.

Chapter 7

Wilkommen

From the time the train pulled into the siding at Fort Meade until we shipped out for Camp Kilmer in New Jersey, no one, officers or noncoms, mentioned even a possibility that new orders might suddenly send us to the Pacific. Barely a week had passed from the time I left Corpus until we boarded the HMS *Louis Pasteur* in New York Harbor. One would have thought we were urgently needed as replacements when, actually, all up and down the front in Germany, the guns had grown silent. It was the first time since I joined the army when a long stagnant wait had not followed the "hurry-up." We moved as rapidly as troops heading into a major battle, or so it seemed. The important thing was I was on my way, and at the time, it didn't matter which way we were going, as long as I wasn't stuck stateside. The idea of serving as a stateside "desk jockey" was most odious. We were all sure that the war would be over soon in the Europe, even before we reached our outfit. For that, I was disappointed, although I could never voice such feelings at the time. The possibility that we all would find ourselves in the Pacific was quite real.

The small shipping company I found myself in was easily the most congenial outfit I ever joined. They were men all my age, all brand new graduates of some IRTC, though none of the guys held "diplomas" from Camp Wolters, which seemed odd at the time. It appeared I hade been intentionally cut from my graduating class at Wolters. When we boarded, the first casual company to arrive, we found ourselves separate and distinct from the troops who arrived later. Our troopship, a converted French luxury liner, was operated by the Royal Navy and named the *HMS Louis Pasteur*. Not in the same class as the *Normandy*, now out of it all completely, or the *Queen Mary*; like most converted liners, the *Pasteur* was fast enough to sail without convoy. Its speed, even with evasive steer, made it impossible for a German U-boat to sight and sink, they said. Before we left Camp Kilmer, they assured us that the German U-boat fleet was all but defunct; though "all but" lacked the certitude we silently desired, we were all eager to be heading out, and I doubt anyone in my shipment had serious misgivings.

As I stood there in line in the giant shed of the pier, drinking a half pint of chocolate milk, I recalled seeing the week before that *Life* magazine ran a picture story describing a replacement's journey from New York Harbor to his unit in Germany. Those pictures of the pier with the high gangway and the line of helmeted GIs appeared to be the scene I was witnessing that April morning, even down to the coffee and milk and the pleasant Red Cross lady volunteers serving us. It felt wonderful to be standing there on perhaps the exact spot pictured in *Life*. I recalled that a week before we began our training at Wolters, *Life* had run a story about the "queen of battles," about the life of an infantryman on the line in Europe. Seeing our re-creation of the more recent picture story and recalling the earlier story, there was no way you could tell me I was not swimming in the mainstream of *Time* or *Life*. Like every man, I was a part of it all.

When the *Pasteur* cast off and backed out of its slip beside the pier, I was high in a .20-mm. gun pit all alone watching the tugs nose her into the Hudson River. A few hours earlier, our company had come aboard and dumped our packs in our new quarters just off the main promenade deck. The large space looked more like a troop mess than a sleeping deck. There were no ranks of bunks stacked one on the other to a high overhead as we had seen in training films. The spacious and light-filled compartment had only rows of long mess tables and benches. The low ceiling ("overhead" now) had a series of iron rods running the width of the compartment. No one could figure it out.

A British seaman had counted us off as we filed in, and when we were all there, he asked for quiet and, in a thick Cockney accent, began to explain why there were no bunks. We would be sleeping in hammocks stored in a large locker, which held stacks of canvas hammocks, along with thin straw-filled mattresses, one set for each of us. He grabbed one and showed us how to tie it taut to the steel rods overhead and how to stuff the straw mattress, and then he swung himself up as gracefully as a trapeze artist, finishing his demonstration as he lay swinging above us. We would hang them for sleeping, he said, and take them down when we got up. As he swung down with equal grace, he told how we would take meals here too.

Someone asked if all the troops aboard had quarters like ours, if everyone had meals delivered to sleeping bays.

"Oh no." He smiled. "You Yanks are gunners' mates now, and here are you gun assignments," he said, posting them on the bulletin board behind him. Then he passed out mimeographed sheets of instructions describing the kinds of guns we would be manning and where they were located. I saw "Gilliland" listed with three others under the name of the British gunner manning P-10: port (left) side, gun 10. None of us was trained as antiaircraft gunners or had we fired anything larger than a .30-caliber light machine gun. The man next to me remarked that the war in the ETO really must be about over if they were making *us* gunners on guns we'd never seen, much less fired. Our Brit sailor laughed and said, "Oh! You men ain't gunners, you are loaders."

That we had the best of the troop accommodations was for a reason, and it explained why we had come aboard early and why our company was smaller than the others. Somewhere along the line, probably at Meade, we had been selected and our fate sealed by an IBM card sorter, and it began to explain why some of us had sensed that something different was afoot from the time we first assembled for roll call at Kilmer. I could hear it, hear it in the language and the accents of young guys in the company: I was no longer the only "college boy." The army, with its system of classification and its IBM punch cards, had run us through machines and picked us out as "quick learners" on guns we'd never seen. Asking around, I found quite a few of our small casual outfit had attended a term of ASTRP and a few others had finished a semester of college, and no one had failed to graduate from high school.

In the afternoon, shortly before shoving off, we met our British gunners. No matter that we had no training with the Oerlikon, a 20-mm. Swiss automatic drum-fed cannon, we were there to assist the gunner and to load the large drum magazine if the time came. Out on deck, we found our gun "pits," not pits at all but raised steel platforms enclosed in a shoulder-high circle of heavy, double-walled steel. There were three such pits on the starboard and three on the port. First, we had to learn to talk the talk. Along with our .20-mm. guns, on the lower decks were four pits of automatic .40-mm Bofors cannons, two on each side of the ship. On the fantail was a large three- or four-inch Y-gun.

Our pits, the prime postings, rose high above the ship's superstructure, giving us a view of the ship fore and aft, away from crowded decks. In heavy seas, we swayed in wider arcs, and climbing the ladder required concentration and perseverance for us infantry types, though not for navy types who could virtually fly up the ladders, regardless of the seas. Shifts were four hours on, eight hours off, except when rotations changed; and then for one twelve-hour period, it was four on, four off, and four on. For us, it seemed all a lark. Gun loader-watchman was a good assignment, considering the perks that went with it, so long as we never *had* to fire the guns. I enjoyed my aerie above the deck; day or night my shift was never boring, for in the day, we "stood down" an hour then watched an hour. When down, we could do as we pleased— read a book or gaze off at the Atlantic, even doze, provided we woke in time. Troopship crossings can be boring and unpleasant in the extreme: crowded sleeping bays, crowded decks, long chow lines, and no privacy, not to mention periods when you must contend with heavy seas. We missed out on a lot of that. Our mess deck was light and airy during the day, unlike the dark holds where the troops lived. I always carried my book aloft and read. Unless the day was warm and clear, then I would stand and watch the sea, astounded by the lovely vast expanse of deep blue, almost purple, water.

As soon as I heard we were about to cast off, I hurried to P-10 and shimmied up the ladder to gaze at the New York skyline and watch Lower Manhattan fade and Staten Island appear. On our way into Manhattan from Kilmer, we had passed through a long tunnel under the Hudson and had seen almost nothing from the canopied truck bed of the six-by. But now, as the stern gradually came about and the bow pointed east down into the Hudson, I could see the outline of tall buildings growing taller as we slowly pulled away. God, seeing real skyscrapers for the first time was magnificent. Breathtaking doesn't come close to the feeling. I thought to myself how lucky I had been. In little over a week, I had taken my first airline flight; traveled by troop train through St. Louis and Chicago, all the way to Maryland; had seen the most important icons of our American civilization—the Capitol in Washington, the Lincoln Memorial, and the White House; and now here I was, seeing Manhattan ("and Staten Island too," even hummed the tune as well as talked the talk) and the top of the Empire State Building and, just barely, the incredibly beautiful Chrysler Building and soon the Statue of Liberty. I forgot to mention, Albert's gift of an airline ticket to Fort Worth had extended my stay in Corpus a whole day—thus my first passenger flight in a DC-3.

The trip across to Liverpool was uneventful. The food was bad, coffee weak, and tea strong. But I enjoyed it all from the moment we cast off until we docked in Liverpool. I had never been to sea, had never sailed on anything larger than the ferry from Point Bolivar to Galveston, or Luther's nineteen-foot sailboat, the *Wench*. Lucky to have the first shift where I could stand high in P-10, I watched the tugs push us out into the river and set us on our way past the Statue of Liberty and on through the narrows. Lower Manhattan appeared stuffed and crowded with skyscrapers. For eighteen years, I had lived in a triangle formed by lines connecting Dallas, Beaumont, and Corpus Christi, rarely going outside that area and then only briefly and for only short distances. Now I gazed out at the world's greatest city and looked east across a vast expanse of ocean. It was a high moment indeed. From the day we left Fort Meade and passed through Maryland and a corner of Pennsylvania, I had been on a special high. Now I thought, *I'm a gunner's assistant on a British troopship!* How could all this happen to *me*?

Gradually, as we moved further and further down the river and into the narrows, the sparkle dulled and the skyline became only a shadowy outline. We cut through a light green sea scored by white caps, and behind us, ubiquitous seagulls swooped and soared. As we passed Staten Island, I could see houses and neighborhoods and tree-shaded parks and realized I was finally on my way to somewhere. No one in our company voiced any regrets or even suggested he didn't want to go, though six months earlier, it might have been a different story. None of us believed we would see action in the ETO.

The trip across took just four and a half days; except for one rough night of rain and strong wind, the weather was perfect all the way. When we arrived in Liverpool, the harbor was jammed with shipping, rusting freighters and warships, mostly destroyers, American and British. Four and a half days ago, I was saying good-bye to the U.S., to Manhattan. Now here I was in Liverpool, smoky, dirty, redolent of coal fires, overcast, and dreary in the morning air. We disembarked and marched through town straight to a railway station and loaded into neat little compartmented cars just like the ones I saw in so many movies set in England. Just for effect and to recall later that I had done it, I dropped the glass window in the door opening on to the platform and leaned out to see if Greer Garson or Vivian Leigh was running down the platform to kiss me good-bye. But alas, they had failed to deliver my last-minute message, or, more likely, had written me out of the script, and so I left without the tears.

"Anyway, I hate those long good-byes on the platform," I whispered to myself as I raised back the window, sat back, and pulled an Armed Services paperback from my pocket.

Our train took us through the countryside of green velvet April meadows and plowed fields, passing through storybook villages of thatch-roofed cottages and cobbled streets. "Oh, to be in England," wrote Browning. It was indeed April, and I was here. I had seen it all in the movies and in my mind's eye, but this was real, not the back lot at MGM, not my imagination stirred by Cronin or Hilton. The fields, the deep railroad cuts, the high toy whistle of the train, the crossing guards with paddles to wave road traffic to a stop, which was never there—it was all as I had seen it in the movies. I was *someplace* now for sure. I was in England, and it was April.

We stopped a long hour at a London station. Was it Waterloo? Victoria? I can't remember. At Southampton, we embarked on another troopship with strict orders not to lose our yellow ID tags we had just been handed. "That's your meal ticket," our sergeant told us. "No ticket, no meal." But the ship was jammed "to the gunwales," and no one checked tags in a serpentine chow line through passageways and up and down ladders. Our assigned sleeping bay was already full, so several of the original group of "gunners' mates" found an open spot on the deck and settled down. It seemed odd at first that we had no noncom to escort us, to make sure we didn't stray off and get lost. Then we realized we couldn't get off the ship until it docked, so why did we need a noncom to watch over us? We had to heft our packs all the way, even through the chow lines, since there was no place to stow them. The last aboard, we climbed the steep gangway as hawsers and lines fell away.

This was a different world. The smiling excitement of the *Pasteur* had vanished. No holiday here. Most of the men on board were not replacements like us. Our new uniforms and the absence of identifying unit patches announced us as replacements, the lowest order of humanity next to the enemy. Everyone else looked ages older than we looked, and they were, though maybe not in years. Lounging next to me on the cargo hatch was an "old guy," twenty-five at least, wearing the Screaming Eagle patch of the 101st Airborne Division, and I asked him where they were coming from.

"Hospitals, I guess, some from R & R in London," he said and looked over my new gear. *So many!* I thought.

"You guys replacements?" he asked, and we nodded. "Look, if they ask you to volunteer for airborne, don't do it."

"I did already," I said. "They turned me down."

His eyes opened wide. "No shit, when was that?"

I explained it was in the States while we were in basic.

He said, "No, they'll ask you over here too. They need glider troops. Don't do it. I did. Landed once and I've been in the hospital ever since."

Crossing the channel was smooth, and it was warm enough to sleep on deck. Did you get that? *"Crossing the channel!"* I had heard the words on the radio and in the movies, and I'd read them, and now write it about myself: *Crossing the channel,* wondrous, *"frabjous day!"*

Early the next morning, when we docked at Le Havre, a loudspeaker announced the order of disembarking. Lo, we found our yellow tags bore a unit number indicating when we would leave the ship. What had appeared to be total confusion was in fact highly organized, and we were in a formation with the same sergeant who had greeted us at the Southampton docks. All other troops aboard the ship drifted into their own units. Somehow out of the chaos of Southampton and Le Havre, we were delivered intact to the proper section of a sprawling tent city called Camp Lucky Strike, the ETO's largest *repple depple,* or replacement depot. Once again, there, all stacked in the middle of a company street, were the duffel bags we had not seen since leaving Kilmer. The long squad tents had solid wooden floors and rows of steel army cots with mattresses. I had half expected we would have to sleep on the ground or on rickety canvas cots. We managed somehow, without formations or lines to stand it, to find a mess hall serving hot breakfast, scrambled (powdered) eggs and sausage ("horse cock").

When we found our bags and turned to the tents, our Southampton sergeant shouted one order, "Read the bulletin board for the time you'll be shipping out! Be there with all your gear!"

One simple order—"Be there!"—was all we needed.

That night, I visited the Red Cross Club, wrote three letters home, and went to a movie in a large tent and saw Humphrey Bogart and Lauren Bacall in *To Have and Have Not*. But no one told us where we were going. Plastered across a bulletin board outside the headquarters tent where we were encamped was a map of Europe that had, scrawled across the face of Germany in wide black letters, the words *Deutschland* KAPUT. It was a new word, *kaput*, one I would hear over and over and one that would become part of the common language. *Kaput* would appear everywhere like the cartoon of a helmeted GI, his large nose hanging over a fence, and the caption, "Kilroy was here."

The next day, with no "processing" other than roll call, we marched through the city to a railhead and climbed into the famous *forty-and-eights*, French boxcars so famous in WWI that the American Legion named one of its elite organizations the Forty and Eight Society. One colorful touch I forgot to mention about the march from Liverpool docks to the station was, in Liverpool, where a boy, perhaps twelve or younger, had walked beside me in perfect step, left-right-left-right, then asked, "Cigarette, Yank?"

I replied, "Don't smoke, sorry," and smiled, to which he said, "Fuckin' Yank sonofabitch!" Now here, just steps before we reached our forty-and-eights, a young French boy said, "Please, cigarette, Yank."

"Don't smoke," I replied, and in a thick French accent came the same curse. "Ah well, such are the ways of friendly allies," I muttered.

Theoretically, each of our cars could hold either forty men or eight horses; ours held the "gunners' mates," no more, along with our small field packs and our duffels all stacked neatly against the rear, and we wondered how anyone could have expected forty men with no packs to cram themselves in so tight a space. Two days later, we arrived at Fontoy, a small town near Thionville and Metz on the Maginot Line. Our repple depple was a small, dismal tent city of a couple of dozen long squad tents in the middle of a muddy field. As soon as we left the 40&8 we heard the war in Europe had ended, that in *Deutschland alles* really was *kaput*. There was no shouting, no whistles, and no fanfare. I, everyone, expected it all along, but now I knew that I had missed it, and I strangely had no regrets. In the Pacific, however, the end was nowhere in sight.

It was a dreary early May, overcast and misting, but the countryside was lustrous green with an occasional blasted tree or an unplowed field holding the jagged remains of a tail section or a pile of twisted aluminum and canvas from wrecked gliders. I was in France. My father, Gilly, had been here twenty-eight years ago in the First Great War. I wished I had learned more about his experiences here—where, what, things like that. Mama had said, like all the men she knew who were in the AEF, he was proud of his service and his volunteering the day war was declared, but he would never talk about it. Mama's brother, my uncle Walter, told me stories of his year in France in the first war. He and Daddy, or Gilly, were best friends and met several times when Uncle Walter's sanitary train delivered wounded to the army hospital where Daddy was stationed.

Once we stopped for a half hour to wait for the track ahead to clear. The station name read Tours, and I wondered if it was the Tours of *La Pucelle*, but no one knew, not even the army people on the platform. It probably was, since Joan's Tours was on the circuitous route we took to Thionville.

The camp was three or four kilometers out of the small town of Fontoy and consisted of two long rows of squad tents and a muddy street. We were only the second group of replacements to pass through, they said; the "front" had been so fluid for two months this repple depple unit had been constantly on the move. Here we would await assignment to our division. Since we were all riflemen replacements, we would likely be going to the same outfit, the lieutenant said, but no one could tell us the name or number of the division. Here we would receive new rifles and bayonets and "zero in" the sights. We wondered, *why all the trouble since the war was over?* There was talk we might have to fight the Russians, or that Hitler's SS and the Hitler *Jügend* had formed "wolf packs" to carry on a guerrilla war in the mountains of Bavaria. The rumors persisted too that we would be taking trains to Marseilles to be shipped through the Suez Canal for China-Burma-India, the CBI, or South Pacific. The invasion of Okinawa had begun on April 1, and the battle continued to rage with higher casualties than anywhere in the Pacific. On Okinawa, the so-called island war had become a land war of brutal charge and retreat. Everyone was convinced that the war in Asia was far from over. Even the most optimistic didn't believe that Japan would surrender short of an all-out invasion.

At Fontoy, we stayed in tents without floors and slept on rickety canvas cots that sank into the mire up to where the cot's legs crossed. It was spring in France, and mud was to be expected, and it was still cold enough for us to use the new wool sleeping bags with outer shell. A hard rain flooded the floors of the tent and made a quagmire of the company street. But I heard no complaints. There were "amenities": good food, considering it came from a field kitchen, and electric lights in the tents that allowed me to read the books I had picked up on the *Pasteur,* those neat, free paperbacks called Armed Services Editions.

Oh, that is a story. On board the ship, we had seen our first collection of the Armed Services Editions. The box, a true gift, was sitting there on one of the mess tables, as unannounced as the box in our squad tent at Fontoy, one in every tent along the street. I read or rather reread a Lloyd C. Douglas novel on the ship and a couple of mysteries and Westerns but nothing really remarkable. Here in the new box was Summerset Maugham's latest novel *The Razor's Edge.* I had seen it advertised in a *Harper's* before we left the States. I had read *Of Human Bondage* in Corpus while working at Dunne's and had seen the old movie with Bettie Davis and Leslie Howard but had found both the picture and the novel tiresome. His short stories, especially "Rain" and "The Outstation," I liked but had not been turned on by them as I had by the Faulkner or Fitzgerald stories. I heard that many people considered Maugham a major writer in those days, and he was, as far as sales were concerned.

No one seemed greatly interested in my discovery. I dug through the box finding Westerns and detectives, along with a number of nonfiction and humor titles, and I also found Lillian Smith's *Strange Fruit* that I had heard a good deal about it, not all of it good. Mostly, I heard that it was not acceptable reading in some parts of the country. But I hadn't read serious criticism in those days, only a few sketchy reviews, so I stuffed both novels into my pack. It was perfect weather for reading. The rain fell all day, and there were no formations after morning roll call.

The Razor's Edge was good, different from what I recalled of *Of Human Bondage.* Its upper-class young hero, a returning veteran of the first war, and his sweetheart, a perfect example of the best there was, the "top girl," Fitzgerald would have said, were appealing, and the tone of Maugham's frank, anti-materialistic, often preachy, and half-satiric criticism of twentieth-century American mores grabbed me at first. I enjoyed the characters' sophistication and Maugham' critical barbs aimed at Americanization of morals between the wars. The second half of the novel, all immensely "wise" and even more "sophisticated," explored Eastern philosophy drawn from Maugham's travels in British India and the East.

Having never read serious literary criticism, only a few book reviews like those in *The Saturday Review of Literature,* I wouldn't have understood it if I had, but I could tell that *The Razor's Edge* was not a major work, perhaps a little better than a Lloyd C. Douglas, probably no more important than a best seller potboiler, but I enjoyed it. The two novels we read in Dr. James's class, *Giants in the Earth* and *Ethan Frome*, by comparison, had body (the words of Helen James). *The Razor's Edge* entertained with just an illusion of insight. I congratulated myself, however. Dr. James would say I was learning to think critically. The novel's polite eroticism and its descriptions of Parisian life with the dollops of Eastern mysticism appealed to me at the time. The part that dealt with India echoed Hilton's *Lost Horizon* that I had once thought the "best novel I ever read." When I finished it, I passed it to the man in the cot next to mine, and he liked it too. I could never have done that at Wolters.

Strange Fruit, with its story of racial bigotry and a love story that crossed the racial barrier, was startling. I can't imagine what my reaction to Smith's novel would have been had I read it before taking Dr. Mac's anthropology. I would have been puzzled and disturbed by the injustice I found. But *Strange Fruit* put into context the ideas about racial bigotry that Dr. Mac had laid out for us a year before, and the novel forced me to see its consequences in a way I could not have imagined prior. I was beginning to understand, through Lillian Smith's novel, that fiction could make you see, know things differently. Fiction became far more than a means to escape reality. I had begun to understand this long ago with Fitzgerald, Faulkner, Hemingway, and in writers like Dos Passos, Farrell, Steinbeck, and George Sessions Perry. When I passed Lillian Smith's novel on to the same GI who had taken *The Razor's Edge*, I warned him it would be a different experience from the Maugham book. "It won't be as entertaining, but it's a lot better. It's also the first serious novel I've ever read that uses the word 'fuck.'"

Our company fit an entirely different profile from the men in A Company at Camp Wolters. Here at Fontoy, several like myself had been to college, one or two had been in ASTRP, and all had high school diplomas. Most were readers. Obviously, back at Fort Meade, someone had run us through a sorter and had come up with a more than less homogeneous group. When a few of us went into town we found we were not very welcome, neither by the citizens of Fontoy or the other GIs who were billeted in the area. One of the Americans we met at a bar told us about a dance in town and suggested we see if there were any girls we'd like. When the three of us arrived, we found neither unattached girls nor a cordial welcome. The GI had set us up, knowing we were ignorant replacements and knowing that in this part of France, Alsace, American soldiers were no more welcome than the Krauts, perhaps even less. This part of France had changed sides so many times down through history it apparently considered loyalty a purely local phenomenon. So in the end, it was the books that saved us.

In the tents across the quagmire we called a company street were men returning to their units from hospitals in the UK or France. Most were returning to rifle companies, tank battalions, combat engineering units, artillery batteries, or whatever— more or less fit for duty. They would stay a few days, hardly leaving the tents, except to go to the latrine or into town to drink calvados or cognac and come back drunk. While we waited as a replacement unit, they waited as individuals, and when they left, it was singly or in pairs in a jeep to return directly to their unit.

One of the guys who accompanied me to Fontoy said, "Man, some of those guys really look beat down. Makes me glad I got here late, you know. Could have been me."

Another remarked, "You notice the NCOs here never tell any of those guys what or what not to do. Nobody tells them nothin', they never even look at the officers, much less salute them." Why would they, we thought? If we missed the shooting, we hadn't missed "the war"; there it was across the street.

Most didn't know where their units had gone, some didn't care, and in some ways, they seemed more in limbo than we did. Until they returned to their outfits, they were lost souls. They never spoke to us or acknowledged that we were even there. We, after all, *were* a unit, such as it was, but they were looking for "home," such as it was. No one in basic had ever mentioned this aspect of war. Banks knew about it, so did Pulaski. If McGruder had known, I thought, he might not have sacked Banks. NCOs and officers at the depot were more tolerant and patient with these returning troops than they were with us, and with us, they were pretty tolerant.

Once when the sergeant had blown his whistle and no one stirred, I heard the top sergeant say to the young CO, "It's OK, sir, I'll check later. Let 'em sleep."

A few days later, we put on our packs, marched to the railhead at Thionville and climbed back into more forty-and-eights. My field pack and gas mask carrier were crammed now with Armed Services Edition (ASE) paperbacks. My other "library" was in my large duffel bag that was somewhere ahead or behind us. No one told us where we were going or how long it would take to get there, and it wouldn't have made any difference anyway. We knew only that we were heading for an infantry division and not to Marseilles and the CBI, that is, the China-Burma-India theater. The cases of C rations stacked at the back of each car suggested it might be days before we got there. There would be nothing to do for hours and hours but read and watch the countryside of Luxembourg and pieces of Belgium, Holland, and Germany roll by. That in itself was wonderment most of us appreciated. Everywhere were fields pocked by shell fire, damaged homes, and all along the right of way were rows on rows of forty-and-eight boxcars with sides blown out or burned, but there were also long stretches where we could see no signs of war. It was May, and every day was warmer and brighter than the day before. Sometimes our train would slow to a crawl as it passed through a village station and civilians would run alongside selling loaves of fresh bread, and sometimes they would ask for food or cigarettes.

Once early one morning, while we were parked for what seemed hours, two young girls in tattered dresses, their cheeks crimson from the cold, came to our car with loaves of bread—thick-crusted, dark, and fresh. We thought they were bartering for the usual cigarettes or candy, but when we offered a handful of loose Camels, they shook their heads and handed up the loaves with great big grins. We were in Holland as best as we could figure, but no one in our car spoke Dutch. The fellow from Fredericksburg, Texas, tried his German and found out the loaves were gifts. Until a week ago, Holland had been on the verge of starvation, and now they were thanking *us* for liberating them and delivering flour that they had used to bake the loaves.

Someone said, "Take the bread, and see if they want to come along," doubling his fist and making a suggestive back-and-forth movement. A few laughed, but the rest were silent—stunned, I think, as I was—that they might have thought us to be their liberators. We told our translator to thank them and beg them to take a couple of cans of C rations. They took the cans joyfully and kept the bread then moved on to the next car. Fifty yards from the tracks across a field was a row of houses and trees, and in the doorway of one, we saw a woman watching. We waved. She waved back. I thought she might have been the girls' mother and had baked the loaves and sent them across to us. Gifts! God!

For four days, our train wound through the Low Countries and Northern Germany, moving slowly over tracks in serious need of repair, through towns large and small where aerial bombs or field artillery had obliterated stations and most of the houses. Some towns were completely deserted, others showed signs of returning to normal, except for the complete absence of any cars other than U.S. jeeps and army trucks or an occasional German staff car painted OD and driven by a GI. Every mile we rolled was like turning a page of history. Most of the time, I sat in the open door of the car with my legs dangling over the side and watched the country slide by. It was difficult to read while we were moving because of the swaying and jerking of the car. But I rotated from time to time and leaned back against my pack, trying to study a German language phrase book, wishing I had taken German instead of Bible my first year.

Several times, we had to wait on a siding for trainloads of refugees always waving and cheering us as though we were their liberators. Our cars passed so close we could almost touch hands. One of the men in our car said quietly, "Most of them are Poles. I can actually understand them." There were Poles, Latvians, Lithuanians, and even some French, the first displaced persons, DPs, we met, people from the occupied countries who had been conscripted by the Nazis to work in war plants. They looked ill fed and sickly, but they were joyously cheering us all the way as their train crept by. When we stopped opposite one of their trains, our officer and our noncoms dismounted and stood along the tracks, ordering us not to fraternize, to stay back. The train commander, a middle-aged transportation officer, explained that they might be carrying diseases like TB or typhus. There was already an epidemic of gonorrhea threatening in the ETO, and no one knew what the Germans might have done to sabotage our occupation, or so the story went. When we saw them holding out their arms asking for food, our first reaction was to share our C rations, but the captain explained it would be too cruel since there was not enough for all. He assured us they would be getting full rations at their next stop.

On the morning of our last full day, we woke to find our train halted in a bombed-out station. The engine had disconnected and gone on ahead, the sergeant said. A new engine had been dispatched to pick us up, but there was only one complete track safe enough to carry traffic, so we would have to wait for the priority traffic to pass through. A month earlier, we would have been the priority traffic, the sergeant said. Now the priority was food. Rows of ruined German antiaircraft cars, their twisted and splayed barrels pointed in all directions, stretched up and down the tracks, and belts of unspent cartridges were scattered about the tracks, along with unexploded .88-mm. shells. Our NCOs ran up and down the tracks to warn us to stay off the ammunition train, warning of booby traps. We had strict orders not to even approach the ack-ack (anti-aircraft) cars. Army engineers had obviously not gotten around to clearing the area. None of us had ever been this close to so much destruction.

We saw a bombed-out station earlier and a famous example of American "daylight precision bombing," the Gothic Cologne Cathedral that stood only yards from what was once a large station and rail yards.

"Daylight precision bombing, they call it," I said as we stared up at the fine Gothic spires and carvings that were now pocked and split by shrapnel and gunfire, but the cathedral and its spires and arches was still intact. I wished out loud that I knew more about architecture and understood more about how they built those peaked arches that could withstand so much destruction.

Our train stopped at the area where the station once stood, and my first inclination was to jump down and run across the twenty yards or so that separated us from the famous building. I remembered reading about the bombing, seeing first aerial shots of the results of Norden bombsight precision, and then later, after Cologne had been taken by American troops, I'd seen in *Life* or *Look*, perhaps a newsreel, the ground picture. Now here I was. But the word was out, "Don't leave your cars!"

But we stayed and stayed. I thought, *if I really want to see it I can make it across and be back before the train picks up speed.* The way was clear along the tracks. I found no one willing to risk the wrath of our sergeant in charge or of being left behind, so I dashed the few yards, stepped inside—no doors hung in the main portal. Inside, it was just a shell, no statuary or stained glass, of course, the altar too far for me to see clearly. Someone had swept the long nave and the apse, but damage was everywhere. Great walls of sandbags on the exterior covered the high Gothic windows from which all the glass had been removed. Still, it was a real Gothic cathedral with soaring arches and vaulted ceiling. The fact that it had remained standing through the bombardment that had leveled the station and had obliterated so many other buildings was as awe-inspiring as the cathedral must have been before. When I heard the sergeant calling, I walked double time back to the cars and waited for the train to get under way, which didn't happen for another hour or more.

The next morning, after our stop in Münster, our cars were still again and all alone at a siding far out into the countryside. We were deserted, even the engine gone, but during the night we had made good time, and by early morning, we were far to the east near a place called Gotha. We all wondered if it was another delay. But then we heard the orders, "Everybody out! Saddle up and fall out in front of your cars! This is it. Hubba-hubba!"

Another morning without hot water to make Nescafé or heat water for oatmeal, I mixed the battery acid they called lemonade and chewed a cold dry oatmeal cake. In the back of our forty-and-eight were still two unopened cases of C rations, one of which I ripped open, stuffing as many cans as I could into my pack, throwing aside the turkey stew, beef stroganoff, and chicken something, saving all the pork and beans and corned beef hash, the only two that were really edible. I talked another man into helping me carry the unopened second case by thrusting an old broomstick I found by the tracks under the metal bands around the case. It was heavy and awkward, and my pack was already sagging under the weight of the C rations.

When we lined up, our sergeant called the roll and announced we would be marching into the town of Gotha, about three miles away, and would have hot chow. Hot chow or not, I was convinced the C rations would be worth their weight one day.

Gotha was the first German city we saw up close, the first we observed away from a railroad or marshaling yard. It was odd to be marching through this old, historic city with its cobbled streets, medieval buildings and archways built alongside the modern buildings. There had been a war here just few weeks before, but now everything seemed so normal that it was really abnormal. Entering, we saw a wide and cobbled street shaded by large trees and a stone arch, but there was not a car in sight. People along the sidewalks beneath the trees stopped and watched as we marched through the town in our columns of twos. Our uniforms were wrinkled and dirty from the long train ride in boxcars, but they were still new and un-faded, and the steel helmets we either wore or hung from our packs were unmarked. Then too, we were all fuzzy, downy-faced cherubs compared to the older men occupying the town. We passed through a large stone gateway into a courtyard of an old castle-like building then climbed a series of stone stairs and settled down in a large upper room. The interior passageways were dark, lit by narrow-slit windows, archers' firing ports, I thought. Men ahead of us dropped out on unoccupied floors, but our platoon, the same platoon of gunners' mates, kept moving until we reached the top floor, a large empty room with a heavy-beamed ceiling, lit by narrow-slit windows. Someone asked about the "hot chow." And the NCO who had led us to the top floor said we could leave our gear there in the large room and go back to the courtyard where they were serving. My friend and I found a spot against the sloping roof near a window and dropped the case of rations then our packs and stretched out. When a voice from below shouted that the so-called cooks were passing out hot C rations, we shook our heads and mumbled, "Nothing doing." It was four flights back down to that courtyard and four flights back up. I dug a can of pork and beans out of my pack and tossed it to my friend Wally Goldberg who smiled. "Well, you know I'm not a very good Jew, Joe, but would you mind eating the beans and give me the corned beef?" We laughed, traded and opened our cans.

"Another day of cold C rations won't hurt as much as that trip all the way down and back," I said. The rest of the platoon stormed down the stairs as I pulled out a book and began to read and spoon beans into my mouth.

These would be our quarters for the night, they said, so I unrolled my sleeping bag and stretched out, and I slept well that night; the floor, my bed, neither bumped nor rocked, and no clatter of wheels disturbed my sleep. They rousted us out at 0600 and served us a hot breakfast of scrambled (powdered) eggs, hot bread, and coffee, the first hot coffee in almost a week. After breakfast, we found all our duffel bags stacked in the courtyard and a long line of six-by-six trucks ready to move us to our units. We hadn't seen the bags since we left Fontoy six days before—it seemed like six weeks. I rummaged through my bag and found my little library intact—Durant, Modern Library Shakespeare, plus several of the Armed Services paperbacks I had stuffed in the bag before leaving Fontoy. A sergeant was calling off names and assigning us to trucks, telling us to stay with the truck until we reach our outfit.

"It's going to be a long day," he shouted. "You'll have piss break every fifty minutes. Fill your canteens now. Remember, you get separated from your truck, you're AWOL. If you're lucky, you'll have real chow for lunch."

"What if we aren't lucky?" someone shouted.

A voice answered, "Then it's tough shit."

Before I could ask him the name of the outfit we were joining, he had moved up to the lead truck, and we were off. No one took bets that we would be lucky. Seeing new country from an open truck speeding along broad highways is entirely different from seeing it through the open door of a rocking forty-and-eight. I had planned to make myself as comfortable as possible and read one of my books, but watching the country race by was too interesting. We were on the autobahn most of that morning but had to take detours and pass through small towns because the Wehrmacht had blown up the bridges and bypasses in their retreat. Most of the farm villages we passed showed few signs of the war, blown bridges on the autobahn, the main reminder of the war along this stretch from Gotha south. One farming village, however, was virtually burned to the ground, reminding me of our sergeant during maneuvers who told us never try to flush out a sniper if we could avoid it: "You don't own no Kraut real estate. Burn it all down."

We arrived at the division headquarters just in time for the hot chow we had been promised. There, to my great surprise, painted on a large billboard beside the division CP were the words

WELCOME TO THE

102 INFANTRY DIVISION

YOU ARE IN OZARK COUNTRY

On either side of "102 INFANTRY DIVISION" were the yellow and blue insignia of the Ozark Division. Inside a yellow circle on a blue field was a yellow—some say gold—Z, beneath it a yellow arc, in other words "Oz-arc."

Of all the divisions in the ETO, the 102nd Ozark Division! How could it be? And why an ASTP division? I told the guys in my truck about the 102 being stationed at Camp Swift near Austin when I was at UT and about my knowing a number of men in the division. They admitted it was weird and a small world and all that. I didn't expect to see anyone I knew at division headquarters, but I looked around, hoping I might see a familiar face. I couldn't remember the names of anyone who had spent weekends at the house. I had actually talked to only a couple, the ones who advised me to check the V-12 box on the application.

They fed us a hot meal from a real kitchen, and we actually sat at tables with china mugs and plates for the first time since leaving Camp Kilmer, a sure sign we were in the rear echelons, someone remarked. First, I looked around and saw that we were all there, the gunners' mates from the *Louis Pasteur*, and I was satisfied now that we had not been chosen at random but picked delicately by some card sorter that read our punch cards. There's a destiny at work here. *"His eye is on the sparrow" and me*, I thought happily to myself, but later, I told Wally Goldberg who was assigned to the same truck as I was he should stick close to me. My life was charmed.

Back on the road, our numbers diminished now as the replacements for the other regiments turned off in different directions. Late in the afternoon, our three lead trucks turned off the main highway and into a small town that appeared to have been bypassed by the war. Not a bullet mark or shell hole or any sign of destruction was visible anywhere. In the town where we had stopped for lunch, there were signs of considerable fighting, but here, we saw no sign a shot had been fired. Aside from a few houses on the roads in and out, there were only a school, a city hall, and a *gasthof*, a large tavern or inn but nothing so grand as a hotel. Our trucks drove into a cobblestoned courtyard and parked side by side before a large L-shaped farmhouse. Acrid odors of cow and horse manure filled the air. A GI with a carbine slung on his right shoulder stood by a doorway, above which a sign read, I BAT, 406 INFANTRY. Our sergeant got down from the lead truck and told us to stay put, that we'd be on our way in a few minutes. There were only six of us left in my truck, about the same in the other two. For the first time, we knew the regiment and battalion we would be in. *It wouldn't be long now*, I thought.

The PFC by the door, who looked no older than the rest of us, walked out to where we were parked and asked the usual questions: When did we get overseas? Where did we do basic? When did we leave the States? Where in the States were we from? When I said I was from Texas, he asked where, and I said I was from Corpus Christi but had been in Austin when the 102 was at Camp Swift outside Bastrop. He looked amazed and said he had gone into Austin every chance he had and asked if I'd been a student at the university. I told him I had and had known a few of the men from the 102 but was unable to remember their names.

"I got to knew one guy pretty well," I said. "He came to our house almost every weekend, but all I can remember is his first name, Bill. He had curly blond hair and did card tricks."

"You mean Bill Dahlquist!" he shouted. "He's my platoon sergeant, Special Services Platoon. He's just inside."

It was impossible—Dahlquist was the one who had told me to check the square for V-12. I could hardly believe that the first person I talked to in the division would know someone I knew. The other men in the truck were as amazed as I. The PFC turned and ran back into the building, and a minute later, Bill Dahlquist exited the door, called out my name, "Joe Gilliland!" Before I knew it, he was shaking my hand and was asking how I managed to get there. Over a year had passed since the division had shipped out from Camp Swift. They had landed in France in September and moved into the line on October 1. Then he told me he was in charge of Special Services, troop entertainment "and any shit detail the CO can think of. I'll get you in my platoon if you want."

I told him I had gone into ASTRP right after leaving UT and then to basic after only one term. I thanked him for the offer, but our sergeant returned before I could answer, and Dahlquist asked him where our truck was going.

"B Company, Engerda. Why?" he asked.

Dahlquist explained he had known me in Austin when they were at Swift. "I used to stay at his house every Saturday," he said.

"No shit! Small world. We've gotta go, Bill," he said and got back into the truck. As we pulled out of the courtyard, Dahlquist said he would look me up.

The 102 was created when the army discontinued ASTP in 1943. Four new infantry divisions—102, 103, 104, and 106 and under strength outfits like the 28 Division—absorbed the "college boys" like Dahlquist. In the four new divisions, they filled out the numbers with regular army cadre gleaned from other outfits and with draftees. Almost a third of the men in this division had at least two years of college; some had their degrees—it was not your typical infantry division. The unfortunate 106, or Red Lion Division, the most recently arrived in 1944, had gone into line just two weeks after landing, had slipped into Ozark Division holes while the 102 moved north into line near the British. The high command considered the quiet 102 Division sector to be ideal for the untested 106.

It was just two weeks before the German winter offensive of 1944, better known as the Battle of the Bulge. All but a regiment of 106 ceased to exist after the first shock wave of panzers hit, but contrary to popular belief, the untested regiments slowed the panzer charge and threw it off timetable in spite of being heavily outnumbered and confronting some of the most experienced fighters in the Wehrmacht. The loss of two of its regiments was less a factor, however, of their failure to perform than a failure of intelligence at the highest level. The Twenty-Eighth Division and its ASTP reinforcements also performed well before the Bulge was contained. Fortunately for the 102, it had been pulled out of the line and moved north to hold a line ordinarily supported by a corps. Paul Fussell's memoir of the war, *Doing Battle*, describes the fate of 103, which like the 102 proved that well-educated, well-trained men "worked a transformation in the infantry," and in the opinion of the commander of all ground forces during the war, Gen. Leslie McNair, they would be outstanding.[3]

In my experience as an instructor at Cochise College in Arizona in recent years, I have seen how the modern American professional army benefited from the World War II experience with college-educated infantrymen. Perrett in *There's a War to Be Won* points out that "it [takes] intelligence to be a good infantryman, and until the experience with the ASTP in the Second World War, the army personnel policy was likely to push the dullest, least enterprising men into ground combat."[4] Perrett is too generous in a way. The army's policy was based on the ancient assumption that common soldiers were expendable. Even generals have been known to consider them mere numbers. According to the men in my platoon, Patton once demanded that the 102nd Division extricate his tanks from an apparent trap. When the commanding general of the 102 told him that a number of his own infantrymen were also in danger of being encircled, Patton was reported to have said, "To hell with those men. Save my tanks. We can always get replacements." Ah yes, *replacements*! Apocryphal it may be, but the sentiment was real, and there was a kind of truth in Patton's remark. There was indeed a plethora of men in the theater who had not seen any fighting and were obviously available but . . ..

The coincidence of my joining an ASTP division after having been in the program myself seemed unbelievably lucky. But now it seems we were picked less by chance than for a purpose: we would most likely fit in easily as gunners' mates and to fill the 102 spaces with college boys. Out of all the divisions

---

3   Perret, Geoffrey, *There's a War to be Won: The United States Army in World War II* (Norton, 1991).

4   *Ibid.*

in the ETO, to find myself assigned to one of the two in all the theater was remarkable. But even more astonishing was that I would find such a needle in the haystack as Dahlquist. Though I had forgotten his last name, I had remembered him well. I recalled that he had attended DePaul University in Chicago before the army and had entertained in nightclubs with card tricks and a comedy routine to pay his way. Of the men who had spent time at the house, he was always welcomed and the one we most enjoyed.

At dusk, the six of us in my truck arrived at B Company headquarters, another farmhouse on the edge of a still smaller village. Looking us over, the company first sergeant made no effort to disguise his disappointment.

"How old are you, men?" he asked.

"Eighteen," we answered.

"Goddami*t!* Why us?" he groaned loudly.

I wondered. *What did he mean, why them?*

"It's OK, Walsh," a softer, gentler voice behind said. "Welcome to B Company, men. Don't mind Sergeant Walsh. He's not as rough as he sounds. We just weren't expecting *any* replacements."

The captain nodded to the first sergeant then left. Sgt. Walsh, sounding resigned to the reality, told us to empty our duffel bags, dump all our gear in front of us, and then he began to read off a list of items to toss into a pile: gas masks, snow packs, and all manner of gear that had been at the bottom of the duffel bags, greatly reducing the amount we had lugged with us. I had a number of books, cans of C rations, a personal OD sweater lying there.

"Stuff that shit back into your bag. Where did you get those rations, for God's sake?" He looked over at Wally Goldberg's pile and noticed his cans too. I told him about the extra boxes when we got to Gotha.

We had heard that replacements were generally unwelcome in combat outfits, but the war here was over. What difference could it make? To the officers and men of B Company, however, it made a great deal of difference, I learned. We lowered the average points of the entire outfit and made it more likely the division would ship out for CBI or the Pacific, maybe even Okinawa.

While the supply sergeant was reading off a list of the equipment we had been hauling in our duffel bags, telling us to stack it beside him, a tall, first lieutenant joined him, saying he would take over. We saw no salutes, heard no one call us to attention.

The lieutenant introduced himself and then asked, "Is someone here from Texas University in Austin?" he asked. I said I was the one. He looked at me and smiled. "We got a call from Dahlquist. What's your name?"

"Gilliland, sir."

"Well, welcome to B Company, Gilliland, and welcome to the rest of you men. It's a good company."

After we had turned over about a third of the equipment we had hauled with us from Camp Kilmer, the sergeant told us to repack our gear and to keep our M1s, though some of us might exchange them for carbines. He read off four names and told them to stand aside then told Goldberg and me we would be taking a jeep to our platoon.

"Have you men had chow?" he asked. We said we hadn't eaten since we stopped at division HQ. "Shit! Lieutenant, nobody's fed these men. Why didn't somebody at battalion tell us these men hadn't been fed?" It was the first time he appeared concerned for our welfare, but to me, it was a sign that we were about to begin our service with noncoms and officers who cared for their men, even those who were too "goddam young."

Wally Goldberg and I and the others stood there silently, feeling now more depressed than we had felt since arriving in the ETO. It was supposed to be like arriving home when you joined an outfit. The lieutenant apologized that the kitchen was closed. Someone muttered that this was really some chicken-shit outfit we'd gotten ourselves into. Well, we *had* been told about the queen of battles, so we shouldn't be surprised.

When the jeep drove up, the first sergeant told Wally and me to get in then told the driver to take us to Engerda where the second platoon was billeted. "Maybe they'll have some chow left, but I doubt it. I'll call ahead." Then in a tone thick with sarcasm, he said, "Oh yes, welcome to B Company."

Neither Wally nor I felt we had a right to complain; neither of us had been through anything like a war. Besides, I still had over a case of C rations stashed in my pack and duffel bag. I was happy to be there; after all, Sgt. Dahlquist at battalion HQ and later Lt. Lance at B Company had personally welcomed me.

It was quite dark when a very young Lt. Patterson welcomed us into the large farmhouse and apologized for not having chow for us, admitting that things in Engerda weren't any better than back at "company." The platoon sergeant added that the chow hadn't been much anyway. I told him Wally and I had some C rations we salvaged from the train.

We dropped our bags and packs in the large main room of the farmhouse, found a place to sleep and made ourselves comfortable. There were no beds left, but I hadn't expected one and didn't mind particularly since I'd been sleeping on the floor of a French boxcar for the last four or five days. Four men were playing cards at a table in the middle of the room, two more were stretched out reading dog-eared magazines, and one lay on a ripped and sagging couch; another was propped against a wall under the light of an ancient floor lamp. Only one nodded a greeting then turned back to his reading. Wally silently lugged his bag and pack into an adjoining room. I broke the silence and asked where the latrine was. The man who had nodded got up from the floor and said he'd show me. On the way, he asked where I was from, how long I'd been in the ETO. He joined the platoon only a week before the cease-fire, he said, and had transferred in from an antiaircraft unit after returning from the hospital in England.

"I had pneumonia," he said. He told me how, on the way back from England, he learned his outfit had been deactivated because there were no more German planes to shoot at. All personnel in his outfit had been dispersed among combat infantry units. "Fortunately, the war was over," he said. "I never even fired an M1. I still haven't."

Like Wally and me, he had not been welcomed either, he explained, because the old-timers could see the 102 becoming a casual unit for the army's own brand of "displaced person," men shifting from unit to unit as their own unit deactivated or rotated back to the States. Since the 102 had arrived in ETO later than most combat divisions, it lacked the status of older outfits that looked forward to returning intact as a unit. No one knew whether the 102 would remain intact at all, not even as an occupation unit.

I slept well and woke to the sound of boots scuffling and to the smell coffee overlaid by a heavy odor of manure. The sun was coming weakly through the windows with the smell of rain joining the odor of manure. I sat up, grabbed my boots, and rushed out to the canvas privy where I had to wait my turn.

As I stood there in silence, one of the men looked at me then spoke, "You come in last night?"

I said I had.

"Where you from?"

"Texas," I replied.

He tapped the man's shoulder in front of him then said, "What's your name Texas?"

"Gilliland," I answered and thought, *Well, now, we're getting somewhere.*

Before I could ask his name, he said, "What's your first name, Gilland?"

"Joe," I said

"Well, fuck you, Joe." He laughed and punched his friend's shoulder.

"Ignore this asshole, Joe," the friend in line said as they moved together still laughing into the enclosure. *So much for a welcoming committee,* I thought. It was colder—the weather and the welcome—than I thought it would be in

May, cold enough to see my breath, and the steam rising from the fresh piss in the trench. Could be that was the odor. Back inside, I smelled the coffee again and saw a tall man with a canteen cup steaming in his hand.

"Where's the coffee?" I asked, digging in my gear for my canteen cup.

"This coffee's in my cup. You want coffee, you boil your own water, *soldier*," he said. This was Oravecz, the tallest man in the platoon and oddly regarded as the best humored, though at that moment I couldn't see how.

My friend from the night before, Perkins, said there was a stove and boiling water in the other room, but if I didn't have my own coffee, I would have to wait until the chow truck came from the company. I rummaged through my pack and produced a handful of Nescafé packets and threw him a couple.

"Let's make coffee," I said. Then I had a thought again and I grabbed a dozen or so packets from my hoard and said, "Let's make a *pot* of coffee. Is there a pot big enough in the house?"

He laughed and followed me. Pretty soon, the others from my room were up and flopping around in unlaced combat boots, muttering curses about all the snoring and farting. One of the card players grumbled he was going to kill the fuckin' rooster and eat him for waking him up. One of his partners said he'd kill him, but no one had the teeth that could eat "that tough old sonavabitch." It began to feel like home. Someone asked my name and then said, "You, no shit, got some coffee?"

I was tearing open the packets and emptying them in an ancient steel pot. "My name is Gilliland, and yeah, I have some coffee, Nescafé. It'll be ready when the water boils."

"OK, Gillan, Nescafé's close enough to real coffee, I guess." He laughed.

Most of the men in the room where I slept were men who had joined the company after the first of the year. The old-timers, or those who'd come to the ETO with the division, were mostly upstairs in rooms with beds or straw mattresses. By the time breakfast arrived, I had gotten to know nearly all the men in my room, the instant coffee having helped ease my way in.

Over the next few days, I learned much more about the division from PFC Givner, an old-timer who had been with the platoon when it was created out of ASTP. He wasn't all that old for a so-called old-timer, but he was welcoming and seemed not to resent my arrival. When told by the platoon sergeant, Culpepper, to pick a man for roadblock duty, Givner had picked me, by name no less, to join him on the 2200–0200 shift. I noted it was only the second night, and already, someone called me by name—remarkable. But then I would learn that Givner wasn't a typical old-timer. He was well-liked by everyone, had a rich sense of humor and a sense of the absurd, considering himself the most absurd of all. Givner had a BS degree in chemistry from Johns Hopkins, and he spoke a fair amount of German.

As we reached the roadblock at the edge of town and relieved the two on guard, he explained there wasn't really any need for roadblocks anywhere since the German civilians didn't go anywhere at night anyway, but those who did were routinely passed through without any questions. He supposed it slowed down the traffic that was mostly foot or horse cart; no one had cars or the gas to run them.

"They have to find something for us to do, I guess," he said and laughed. "Lt. Patterson even has orders from our company CO to send out patrols during the day."

"Aren't there supposed to be some Hitler Jügend organizing wolf packs or something?" I asked.

"We heard something like that. The war's over for these people."

The next morning, when I was assigned to a squad, I moved to a room at the back of the house with three other men and four army cots. The odor of pig shit permeated the room, a stench like none I had ever smelled. I was amazed that no one seemed to mind, and since no one complained, I didn't either. As if to warn me, someone mentioned a pigsty just out the door, urging me not to open it.

In the days that followed, a few of the men in the squad began to speak to me a little, but when I dumped almost a case of C rations on to the floor and told everyone in the room to help himself, my value as a human being rose like mercury in a steam bath thermometer. They marveled that I had lugged the rations all the way from the train at Gotha. They divided them among themselves and thanked me. One man told me that the Germans traded poontang for C rations.

Someone shouted, "Yeah, fraternization will get you a seventy-five dollar fine and thirty days in the stockade." They laughed. "If you get caught!"

"It'll get you a dose of the clap too," another chimed in.

It took only two new replacements, Goldberg and me, to convince the lieutenant that the second platoon's "quarters" would not suffice. I refused to complain about the stench of the pigsty, and Goldberg agreed that we really had nothing to complain about, and the several men who had preceded us felt pretty much the same, although Perkins and another had been in action with other outfits briefly before their antiaircraft units became obsolete. Morale was *kaput*, as they would say. Some men rarely left their beds upstairs, except to use the latrine outdoors, and the story got round that they were even avoiding the latrine and using the forbidden toilets in the house, the really repulsive indoor pit-type toilets the medics had made off-limits. Since Patterson, a combat commission, had served with the platoon since the division was formed in Camp Chafee, he was reluctant to discipline his old buddies and let them shit where the pleased. For months before V-E Day, the division had been on the move, had stayed nowhere for any time. Even when off the line, their "quarters" were only temporary, a tent city in the rear or houses in a village or town, never a place called home.

This large farmhouse in a small *dorf* of no significance was less than adequate in every sense. Meals that arrived from the company kitchen were often cold and almost always short. Separated from the company, the men felt free to do what they wished and no longer felt any need to "keep up appearances." The war was over. Because German civilians never refused an order from the military government, there was nothing for an infantry platoon to do in time of peace, except what our second platoon was doing: sleeping, getting drunk, selling cigarettes on the black market, stealing eggs from the farms, killing a chicken for the pot now and then, and fraternizing with the women.

Givner had explained how he made his life worth living there in Engerda by fraternizing with the enemy. Since entering Germany, he'd made use of his college German fraternizing, not by seducing the women but by entering the homes of locals and telling them right off he was a Jew, "allowing" them to welcome him into their homes where he could relax and share his rations or cigarettes.

"Anything to break the monotony of life in a rifle platoon," he said, chuckling to himself. "They always claim no dislike of Jews, assure me they never approved of Hitler or the Nazi party. There's a family here in Engerda— I'll introduce you if you want—I visit there every day and share a meal." He laughed. "I just eat eggs or chicken and *kartoffel*, potatoes, never sausage."

Fraternization was *verboten*, he said, and if he were "caught," he could be fined seventy-five dollars and might even get thirty days in the brig. "But no MPs are about, no officers around to press charges. Seriously, would they arrest a GI who'd been in combat, for associating with civilians?"

It was absurd, as was everything I saw in the platoon there in Engerda, even the two patrols I went on with Garfield, my squad leader. On one "patrol," we walked out into the countryside along small lanes or trails, visited farmhouses, knocked on doors and asked in GI German if they had any weapons stashed, then left and moved on. We chatted about nothing in particular, while PFC Remington played tunes on the fine harmonica he had looted before V-E Day, mostly pop tunes like "Sentimental Journey," or "I'll Be Seeing You."

Remington and Garfield were from the same town in Indiana. Once in a while, he and others would break out in a bawdy GI version of "Lily Marlene." Garfield was a few years older than the original ASTPers, had never been to college, but had been with the 102 since Chafee, he said. Like everyone else in the squad, I liked him right off because he had spoken to me early and seemed to have no Kraut animus or any animosity toward anything. A high point man because of the length of time in service and several dependents back home, plus the battle stars and a Purple Heart for a minor injury that had not sent him to hospital, he had good reason to be a cheerful leader.

The second patrol was even more ludicrous. Garfield drew together eight of us, some real vets and other noncombat replacements like me. It was never clear that Patterson had actually ordered the patrol since Garfield never explained why the night patrol was necessary. He laid out the plan with an old guy acting as point guide and with Remington bringing up the rear with his harmonica.

"Gilliland," he explained in all seriousness, "watch Rem and learn how to keep a look out on our rear." Since all the others were taking his orders seriously, I did too. "We'll stay on the road then cut cross the field and use that little bunch of forest for cover. Now let's jump off." Remington's harmonica went silent the moment we left the dirt road.

After only ten or fifteen minutes out of town, we reached an ordinary well-lit farmhouse, perhaps a little larger than most. The owner and his wife were waiting at the door when we stopped. As Garfield approached, the husband opened the door, and then Garfield, with his stumbling GI German, asked if they could make a small supper of bacon, bread, and eggs.

"*Ei und Shenken, mit Brot für acht Soldaten.*" He said he had Deutsche mark to pay.

Die frau answered in English, "Yes, come in." And in we filed. He handed her a handful of Nescafé packets and said, "For us," then another handful, "For you."

Remington was smiling, as were all the others. Garfield turned, faced us, and said, "Give me a Kraut mark each, no script, just marks. C'mon, this bacon here is unbelievable."

When we finished our eggs *und Shenken*, we rose and thanked the hosts who, at first, pushed back the marks but relented in the end and thanked Garfield for the Nescafé. On the return, we took the main road back to town, singing as we "marched." Garfield said nothing more, never explained why, but he looked pleased with himself and I figured his joy had nothing to do with the meal we had all just enjoyed. Later when I got to know him better I intended to ask him what it was all about, but I didn't, feeling I should just leave it at that. Fact is I found the platoon to be full of unanswerable questions.

Two days later, Lt. Patterson had us fall out after the company breakfast jeep had left and told us to get our gear together and to look for any of the guys who might be missing—one or two always managed to find other sleeping arrangements—and tell them we were moving out at 1000.

"Colonel Schott's bringing all the companies into Rudolstadt," he said.

No explanation followed, but everyone seemed to know what was happening, or perhaps didn't care, and went about getting gear together— just another troop movement, I figured. And that was my week in Engerda.

Chapter 8

The One-O-Deuce

It came as no surprise. We had heard the rumor, and Paterson confirmed it: the battalion, all four companies, was moving into Rudolstadt. First Battalion HQ had already moved into the city with the 406th Regimental HQ. From all appearances, Rudolstadt was sparkling clean, so free of rubble it was obvious both ground and air forces had bypassed the city. As we moved into town, I was struck by the sudden silence, the guys in our truck apparently impressed by the absence of any signs of combat.

The battalion assembled in a large theater even before moving into new billets, and it was pretty obvious we were not gathered there for a USO entertainment. Suddenly, a voice on the PA system shouted us all to attention, and Colonel Schott entered and mounted the stage, his staff following in grand procession. Today he began right off lecturing us for our lack of discipline and our "un-soldierly conduct in the villages."

"I get daily reports," he began, "from MG that you men are stealing eggs, killing chickens, milking the cows, and doing something with the women."

The last remark brought audible if restrained chuckles, along with muttered warnings from sergeants and officers. Colonel Schott ignored the laughter, announcing that all the companies that had been billeted in the villages would now be moving into the comfortable quarters in different parts town and would be under the eye of battalion HQ.

"Military Government," he whined, "reports many infractions of the anti-fraternization laws issued by SHAFE. You all know how I dislike being scolded by a bunch of MG lawyers." He paused as if to let the seriousness of the comments sink in.

"This is serious business." His voice became a whine. "Military Government can bring charges against the whole battalion, so I suggest we cooperate. I'm not going to get my ass in a sling for a few unruly companies out in the countryside. We're moving all of you into housing where you *will* be required to have inspections, training, and work details." He paused, became conciliatory, and continued, "We, the staff and I, wanted to allow you men some privileges, give you a rest from garrison duties, because you've deserved it. But if you don't want to play ball we'll just have to do it the army way. I'll not have the MG complaining about the conduct of my troops."

As we filed out, most agreed that his warnings were "no big deal" or that nothing had changed or would change. We preferred regular hot meals and better quarters to whatever "advantages" the countryside offered regarding eggs and milk or women. It was a reasonable trade-off. Sleeping next door to a pigsty had gotten old. Truth told, everyone figured it would be easy garrison duty; guard duty and KP would be rare, especially KP, because German civilians and discharged soldiers were eager for the job. It turned out that garrison duty amounted to little more than keeping our billets clean and doing an hour or so of close-order drill and calisthenics at roll call every morning.

Battalion HQ assigned each of B Company's platoons an entire four-story apartment block, our squad occupying an apartment on the top floor. The German tenants had left all their furnishings, so by comparison to our farmhouse at Engerda, these were five-star luxury accommodations—lace curtains; sturdy, attractive couches and easy chairs; carpeted floors; polished birch dining furniture. Since there weren't enough beds to go around, they scrounged German army cots from somewhere so everyone slept on a mattress. Though none of the apartments in the block had its own bathtub or shower, each apartment had a modern flush toilet with lavatory. There was a shared bathroom in the basement with a real tub for soaking. Displacing families was common after the division crossed over into Germany.

Rudolstadt was an interesting city. Schopenhauer had settled there after his studies in Gotha, someone said, and I was impressed, even though at the time I wasn't sure who Schopenhauer was, but I found out when I looked him up in Durant. Near the town's center was a castle that looked more modern than the one in Gotha where we spent the night.

A few days after we settled in, I pulled a two-hour shift of guard duty at the castle watching American civilians, whom we had been ordered not to speak to, packing and crating machinery that turned out to be IBM calculators and equipment that had been left when the war started had been used all during the war by the Germans.

Nothing was going as I had expected. Beginning my army career in college, I had moved on to basic infantry training where the majority of the men had not graduated from high school—a few like Gaston had not even finished grade school— and now I was in a company where the average man had more college than I. Just sitting around after chow or any time of the day, I could join bull sessions talking about local history or the architecture and would overhear men discussing books they were reading or even discussing current political events at home and in Europe, not the usual topics in a typical infantry platoon. My world centered around two men whom I came to know best at the time, Givner and Knowles, *real* college men, one a graduate of Johns Hopkins University and the other a junior at Harvard. Givner had been the first man in the platoon who had condescended to speak to me, the only man who seemed not to consider replacements anathema. Right from the beginning he spoke to me as if he had known me all along. I found out later after he rotated back home to Baltimore that, although he was an old-timer and well-liked by everyone, he was in reality something of an outsider like me.

Then there was Knowles, also one from the early ASTP men and something of an outsider himself. He just seemed to come out of nowhere one day. I was lounging on the large couch in the parlor reading when he dropped in my lap some pages torn from a book. We'd never spoken before that; he just dropped the pages in my lap and said, "Here, read this, Gilliland. You might find it interesting," then moved off.

I looked down and saw it was all poetry and noticed that the Ardennes was mentioned, the dense forest where the Battle of the Bulge had taken place last winter. The 102 had just missed it, had been pulled out of the line, turned their positions over the Red Lion, 106th Division and moved north under Montgomery. Later, when I asked him about the pages, he told me that his father had sent them with instruction to read them and share.

"My father's always tearing pages out of old textbooks and sending them for me to read. If he finds a poem or anything that mentions some place where a battle's been fought, he sends it and suggests I share them."

"What is he, a teacher?" I asked.

"He was a professor of English at Harvard but resigned over some department row," he said. "He's teaching at St. John's College in Annapolis now, you know, the great books college. I heard you talking about it somebody the other day" He paused as if the line of thought no longer interested him.

"The stanzas he sent are from Byron, 'Childe Harold's Pilgrimage,' where Harold describes his journey through the same country where the 102 passed last winter."

He said he'd seen me reading a poetry anthology from Armed Services Editions, and thought I might find Byron interesting. And, as a matter of fact, I was talking about St. John's College a few days back. It had been mentioned in one of the books I'd saved from a carton of Armed Services editions. This was a different kind of army, for sure, but then the war in Germany was over and everything was different, wasn't it?

"The only things of Byron I had read," I said, "were short lyrical poems like 'She Walks in Beauty' and 'So We'll Go No More a Roving.' I've heard of 'Childe Harold' and 'Don Juan,' but I haven't read them." I never imagined, ending up in an outfit where I would be reading Byron and talking to a guy whose father was a college professor; but all around me were men who talked intelligently about everything, the German people, Japan, Roosevelt, about anything.

When I asked how far along he was on his degree, he said he had finished his second year at Harvard before entering ASTP and managed to finish most of his junior year before he was "transferred" to Camp Chafee. I had known guys who liked to read, who even read poetry just because they liked it, but not many. Knowles was different though, a junior at Harvard *and* an English major, and for some reason, he'd picked me out to pass along the canto of Byron's "Childe Harold." I tried to read poetry from the time I began reading but found most of it too puzzling. Kipling was different; like Shakespeare's dramas, his poetry told a story. Missing a word or line here and there didn't matter so much because you would eventually catch the line of thought. Mostly, it was the sound and meter that got me and held me.

Once, in Ms. Cobb's class—of all places—we read aloud Wordsworth's "Lines Composed a Few Miles above Tintern Abbey," each one reading a passage until he reached the end of a sentence. I recall my segment was longer than most and that I loved it, not the meaning so much because only a few places made any real sense, but it moved so easily that you wanted it to go on and on. I thought about the poem, especially the language that wasn't all that "poetic," and for a long time, I tried to find a copy so I could read it again. And then I did, and when I reached the passage I had read in class, I stopped and read it over and over and over again.

> And therefore am I still
> A lover of the meadows and the woods
> And mountains all that we behold
> From the green earth . . .

It went on and on. I memorized it and would often recite it to myself because it felt magic even if I didn't get it all. So when Charley told me he had read the Harold stanzas just as his father had told him, I think I understood why it was important. I read the "Childe Harold" selections and thanked Knowles and asked if the passage was about the same country the 102nd Division was in about the time of the Bulge. He explained the division had been pulled out a week or so before the panzers attacked. It was close.

How weird! How strange it all was, I thought, finding myself in a place like Rudolstadt, reading poetry. I realized how poorly read I was. I remembered a selection from Byron was in my senior English text, but we had not even glanced at it. So I wrote Jane immediately one of the V-mail forms, and I told her about Knowles and the passages from "Childe Harold" and told her about the Untermeyer anthology I had picked up and how I was serious about wanting to read more poetry.

Jane was good about sending books, usually good used copies or inexpensive Modern Library editions. When Knowles suggested I should be reading Tacitus's *Germanicus*, I mentioned it in one of my letters, and she sent it, a new copy, along with some other books: Maugham's *Moon and Sixpence* and *Ariel*, the Andre Maurois biography of Shelley, along with a book on formal logic, which I specifically asked her to send because I was thinking about taking philosophy when I returned to UT. I immediately read the *Germanicus,* amused to read how little the people had changed since the first century AD. What a great idea, I thought, reading the work on site. God, I thought, how much I had changed since leaving home for Austin: reading Tacitus and then reading almost every poem in the ASE anthology *Great Poetry from Chaucer to Whitman* because I wanted to.

Just as I opened the box from Jane Knowles passed by and grabbed the Tacitus.

"Oh good, Tacitus!" he said, opening and glancing at it, and then just as abruptly, he snapped it shut and said, "It's in English! We read it in Latin in high school."

He had, of course, gone to the Boston Latin School. Though Knowles, I assumed, was well on his way to becoming a scholar, reading during all his free time, he was, all in all, one of the least snobbish guys I ever knew. He loved to talk about what he was reading and what others were reading, saying what he liked and disliked but without a superior know-it-all attitude. He recommended things I might enjoy, mostly poems I never heard of, but things he assured me were "important." Often he asked me what I thought about whatever it was I was reading, and then he would ask why. He never actually said I was wrong; he just said what he thought and left it at that.

Charley was never pedantic and never chattered a lot of critical jargon. He took good books and ideas for granted, I think, never speaking down to anyone. Once in a while Sgt. Culpepper, who was our platoon sergeant, or one of the ASTP old-timers would joke about the "study sessions" Knowles and I carried on and would ask if Charley gave hard exams or if I had a term paper coming due for Professor Knowles. Later, after I returned to Austin, I told my roommate, Mullins, another English major, how Knowles put me on to so much good literature. Mullins was aghast I had been around so many well-read and well-educated people in an infantry outfit.

I saw few outward signs of envy or resentment from any of the replacements or non-college men toward the ASTP guys, nor did they assume a higher-than-thou attitude toward anyone. College men, like Knowles, Culpepper, Wojtkewiezc (nicknamed "White Cabbage" then just "Cabbage"), and Givner had basic and advanced infantry training along with regular draftees and they had all spent time sharing foxholes and patrols, and had learned to respect each other. I tried to keep it all in perspective, neither hiding nor flaunting my own college and ASTRP credentials.

One afternoon up in our flat I was reading one of the books Jane had sent me. Besides me, there was Sgt. Warren, the oldest man in our platoon, one of the late replacements probably in his late thirties. They said he had transferred in from a defunct Triple A outfit. I don't think we had ever spoken. He was sitting at the other end of the large table leafing through my *Formal Logic* when he asked me, "Don't you think those books, the Tacitus and this logic text are a bit over your head?" This *Logic* gets very advanced."

I agreed, "The *Formal Logic* is *'a bit,'* especially the section dealing with something called the 'calculus of propositions,'" I replied. But I found his tone offensive and condescending. No one, not even Givner, had even hinted I was out of my depth. I told him he was probably right, especially about the last half of the text. I explained, "It is way too advanced for me. I really wanted an introduction to logic."

Then in a quasi-fatherly tone, he said, "You know, Joe, I think all you're doing is just trying to impress your elders. That's true now, isn't?"

"No. Why'd I do that?" I asked. "Who do you think I could ever impress in this outfit? I'm trying to get ready for when I go back to the university. Impress who? Nobody here cares what I read. Why should you?"

"You know," he sneered, "I don't believe you one bit." He closed the book and pushed it toward me.

I hadn't noticed that Knowles had come in and had overheard us. I was about to reply when Knowles interrupted, agreeing the logic portion of philosophy was often a beginning student's Jonah, and then he blithely added, "Gilliland's smart to be reading it now. I hated the logic portion of my philosophy class." Warren just smiled, got up, and left, and that ended that.

Knowles, who rarely talked about others, said I should ignore him, everyone else did. "Warren came to the outfit looking down on all infantrymen as dumb-ass soldiers, but the truth is, he knew nothing and was as out of place in the platoon. He has no command experience. Those are technical stripes."

Later Knowles said, "He had age and that ack-ack specialty that gave him the stripes of a staff sergeant, but he was totally ignorant of anything about the infantry, even the weapons. They let him keep his stripes and the money, but he remained a rifleman like everyone, and that made him bitter."

I told him Warren's remarks didn't bother me. It was strange hearing Knowles go on like that. He was the least "GI" or "military" guy in the platoon, but it explained why Warren always kept to himself..

"It just pisses me off," he said. "That asshole confronting a piss-ant PFC with a book he admits himself he can't read." He laughed.

Reading became a passion for me that year in Germany. A few souls like Perkins read little if at all. But many who had never seen a college campus became avid readers for lack of anything else to do, men like Burdick and Smitty, who was a late-comer in the outfit, a farm boy from Wisconsin and, according to the others, a helluva BAR man. Smitty discovered westerns and read them with a passion.

We all had too much time on our hands, and reading was important. I always had a book stuffed in my jacket pocket in case we were forced into waiting. A minor miracle had occurred in the publishing world early in the war that may have saved many men from going bonkers. The Council on Books in Wartime, one of the civilian agencies organized to promote the war effort, created the Armed Services Editions. A committee chose titles that covered classics and rubbish, treasure and trash, though as Paul Fussell said, there was no out-and-out trash. Titles included a whole herd of horse operas, along with sword and bosom historical novels by writers like Thomas Costain, Kathleen Winsor, and Thomas Shellabarger. There was a horde of sentimental message novels by Lloyd C. Douglas and A. J. Cronin, along with whodunits of all levels. But mixed in with the lot were works by Fitzgerald, Steinbeck, Wolfe, James, and Shakespeare, Boccaccio and Balzac, and those Louis Untermeyer poetry anthologies I had found. Erskine Caldwell's *God's Little Acre* was probably the most widely read book of the lot, certainly the most dog-eared and annotated, particularly those passages regarding Darling Jill's "risin' beauties." Major history titles and books about language, also appeared, along with works dealing with education, philosophy, humor, horror, but mostly there was just plain reading. Fussell describes the little books as fitting into an OD shirt pocket; it was more like the skirted, filed jacket pocket with an extra-large edition fitting the long thigh pocket of green fatigue pants as well as the lower field jacket pockets. *Look Homeward, Angel*, one of the larger format editions, still required editing even after Max Perkins's labors had made it publishable. I read my first Dorothy Parker and Ring Lardner stories in that format, along with my first John O'Hara (*Butterfield 8* and *Pal Joey*). When Kathleen Windsor's lubricious *Forever Amber* hit the streets, it came out simultaneously in the Armed Services Editions. Some outfits had to create waiting lists to give everyone a chance to read it.

I have often heard former GIs recall their years in the service as being a total waste, but my two years and three months, if I count my time at Texas A&M, came at an ideal time. Those two years matured and focused me, and they gave me the time, leisure actually, to choose and examine, study and learn, a whole new world of learning that would become the foundation for a career in teaching. The learning and teaching began when I arrived at A&M—no surprise there—continued all through IRTC. Later with the "One-O-Deuce," though my studies were disorganized and unplanned, they moved ahead with "teachers" like Knowles and Givner and a library supplied by Armed Services Editions.

Shortly after the platoon had settled into our billets in Rudolstadt, Sgt. Culpepper came to me with a special assignment that he said was a job right up my alley.

"I figure, Gill, that with all that mail you get every day, you must write a lot of letters, so this assignment is going to be easy." He told me a Gaston story about a man in the platoon who had received a hated "Dear John" and needed the help of a letter writer.

"Perkins's girlfriend wrote him she had a new boyfriend, an air corps guy home and soon to be discharged, and she says since Perk doesn't write, she's going to start seeing this air force the guy."

He explained quietly that noticed Perk was down in the dumps and need help. I told him I understood and gave him a brief account of Gaston's success. Perkins, from Macon, Georgia, had been the man who first spoke to me after I arrived at Engerda. While he was a friendly guy like Gaston, Perkins was *not* a Gaston. He had gone to high school, though he hadn't graduated, and he knew how to write, but he didn't know what to write, and he believed quite literally that he *couldn't write.* I followed with Perkins the same process I followed with Gaston and asked the same questions: what did he do yesterday and the day before, and what was he planning to do tomorrow? I told him to read her letters and see how she fills up the space with just ordinary things. Like Gaston, he could hardly believe she would want to read about our platoon or what we did during the day. I insisted otherwise: Helen James would have been proud.

Then I asked him if he read aloud those trivial happenings in her letters. When he did, he understood immediately.

"Hell, Perk, tell her what we have for chow, and tell her anything. The important thing is this: tell her you think about her *all the time*. That's true, isn't it? That's why you'd be disappointed if she stopped writing and started going out with other guys, isn't it?" He smiled sheepishly and agreed.

We got a V-mail and a pen, and he began to write, mostly those things he had mentioned himself. The details—Ah, bless you, Dr. James! Like Gaston's first letter, it barely filled the page, but unlike Gaston, Perkins wrote a clear and legible hand. Also, unlike Gaston's case, I plotted a two-pronged strategy, one to overwhelm her by numbers and the other to get him into the habit so he wouldn't need help after the first week. The V-mail format was ideal for writers who thought they had "nothing to say." It was limited to the one small sheet and got filled in a hurry.

"Write her every day for a week," I said. "You don't have to write much, just often, then next week every other day. Spoil her. She'll think she's a goddam queen," I said.

"Every day? I can't think of anything to say *every day*," Perkins said.

"Don't worry we'll do it the way we did it today. I'll help, but you'll write. But fill her in with details about what we do every day and keep telling her you think about her. Perk, that's all true. You told me how you felt, you can tell her. Hell, man, that's how we all feel, and that's why she wants you to write her. Put her in the picture. Tell her what it's like in the One-O-Deuce. Then repeat her words, show her you've read her letters. Write it out first, and I'll check the wording and spelling. Then you can copy it over on a V-mail form."

He got her letter in return mail, which for V-mail was less than two weeks; it was replete with assurances and promises that she would continue writing and never see the air force man again. Culpepper praised my craft and subtle art, and I praised Perkins for doing what he did. It was my second success as scrivener, and I really did feel pleased with myself. Later, when I told Knowles how good it made me feel, especially since English composition had been a disappointment as a freshman, he puzzled me, saying, "No one can teach anyone how to write. You either know how or you don't." I had heard that pedagogical canard before and had thought the speaker an ass posing as a wise man. I knew I had not really "taught" Perkins how to write so much as helped him over an obstacle.

I wrote Jane about the Perkins's letter and recalled how I'd done the same for Gaston earlier, mentioning how ironic since I had such a struggle in freshman composition, but mainly, I was writing to tell her how much I missed Austin and the university, how much I actually missed being in class. I wrote, for the first time, that I was no longer a chemistry or premed major and said that when I got out, I would return to Austin and the university and would never leave but would spend my whole life on the campus, taking courses and going to class. I, of course, wasn't serious, or at least I didn't think the tone of the letter sounded very serious. I even said I didn't care what I studied so long as I was at the university. I concluded by admitting the letter might be just a reflection of the company I was keeping.

Then suddenly, the division received orders to vacate Rudolstadt. One day, we were all settled, actually enjoying warmer weather and the freedom of walking about a real city. Then suddenly, orders came, giving us just two days to pack up and leave the city to the Soviets. In the weeks we were there, the people of Rudolstadt had tried hard to remain aloof and ignore our presence, but when they realized the Russkis were coming, they suddenly changed. Frauleins, who had been careful to keep their liaisons secret, were all about the place, begging GI "friends" to take them along, or at least as far as the new border. Men with more or less steady girlfriends would return to our rooms telling horror stories of what the *mädchen*'s families were expecting when the Russkis arrived: rape, pillage, murder. They spoke of reprisals and confiscations. Women and young girls were begging to be allowed to travel in our trucks as we moved south. Most of the men felt pity, even those without Frauleins, but they also admitted that Russian desires for revenge weren't exactly without cause.

Our trip from Rudolstadt to Klingenbrünn in the southeast corner of Bavaria took two days, passing through the ruins of Nuremberg and Munich and through some absolutely incredible scenery. Detouring around the destruction took us through narrow streets of small, well-preserved medieval towns, and one of the men in our truck gave a running lecture on the architectural features of the town halls and churches we passed, explaining the probable dates or pointing to buildings that were nineteenth-century reproductions. He grew excited every time our convoy had to creep through an arched gateway into a large *platz* where a *gasthof* or a steep-roofed *Rathaus* would rise. Once, Burdick asked how the guy kept all "that shit" in his head, to which another remarked: "That's all he's got."

Culpepper leaned toward me and said, "Rogers was just a semester shy of his degree in architecture," then said loudly to Rogers, "Go on, Rogers, Gilliland here's taking notes." When the company was finally settled in Klingenbrünn, I felt for the first time I was a member in good standing, no longer just a dumb replacement.

Our new home was smaller than Engerda and infinitely more beautiful. A long forested ridge rose to the east of the village, and to the west, the land rose and fell in a broad expanse of valleys and hills, all green and brown checkerboard, with here and there a deep green square of tall conifers planted generations before in neat well-maintained plots. The buildings were so white that the village itself seemed to sparkle. While the town had a few large farmhouse compounds, walled and fenced, most of the larger buildings looked like official government structures. A large *gasthof,* a high-pitched civic hall, a small church, and a large school dominated the town center. Scattered about the edge of the "city center," facing the plowed fields, were smaller houses.

The school compound became B Company's new billets. Each platoon had its own area consisting of three whitewashed squad rooms, brightly lit by large casement windows, each holding five double bunks with straw mattresses and a large library table stood in the center of each room. I heard only one complaint: it looked too permanent. Sgt. Culpepper said he felt really uneasy when he saw the showers and indoor toilets. Most old-timers still hooped that the 102nd Division would go home intact and would march in parade down the street. Knowles smiled and said how too much comfort meant the likelihood we would become too permanent. They all would have preferred temporary quarters with no amenities. Permanence meant the division would not be returning stateside as a unit but would become a "casual" division, a temporary home for men being rotated home or shipped out to Marseilles and sent east to the Pacific or to CBI (China-Burma-India). In early July, the Battle of Okinawa was still raging.

Indoor toilets were fantasies, and soon after, the showers lost their charm. A large sign on the door of each squad room announced that the unsanitary non-flushing indoor toilets were off-limits, that the showers had no hot water. We, therefore, would use an outdoor slit-trench latrine enclosed by tall canvas walls, the regulation GI design approved by our division medics. Officers' billets in the local *gasthof,* on the other hand, had fully operational flush toilets and hot running water.

Three hot meals a day served in a large comfortable dining room at the large *Gasthof* that also billeted the officers would compensate for the lack of hot water. Added to that was the promise of light duty, no twenty-four-hour roadblocks, no KP, only one guard at the CP, and one night guard at the kitchen. When I walked into the platoon office, Culpepper was saying, "Calisthenics and close-order drill every morning, but that's all, and for that, we get hot chow every meal. Oh yes, every fourth week, the second platoon will furnish two squads for a border patrol up on the ridge of that mountain, volunteers accepted."

Shortly after arriving, the company clerk posted announcements for German language classes, along with classes in college level math, history, and composition. But German was the only class that had enough signers to make it worthwhile, and even German folded when the first high pointers began to receive orders for the States. Most would be rotating home too soon to make language lessons necessary, but I signed up and stuck it out for a couple of weeks, thinking that German would be the language I'd use to satisfy a degree requirement when I got back to UT..

Then a few days after the class postings, at morning roll call formation, the First Sgt. announced that any man wishing to transfer to an "active theater" could sign up in the CP. I was standing next to Givner in the front row of the platoon when I saw him step out and start for the orderly room. Surprised at first, I followed. Here was this guy, I thought, who had been through everything since the division arrived in the ETO, and he was volunteering for more combat, actually volunteering for the invasion of Japan. All the invasion stories predicted the heaviest casualties of the war, yet I believed, "If Givner goes, I should too."

He had often expressed his belief in the war and what it meant to him and what it should mean to all of us. I had missed the shooting war so far; why, I asked myself, shouldn't I try for the one in the Pacific? My reasons are still a muddle. Melville had it right: "All wars are boyish." Beyond that, I recall feeling shame for arriving too late, for having missed the war, for "wasting" all that good IRTC training. Perhaps it was only boyish jealousy and envy. Whatever it was, I followed Givner into the orderly room.

As soon as we walked through the door, Lt. Lance barked, "You get outa here Givner! Turn around! That's an order, Givner."

His tone of voice reflected Lance's honest respect for Givner and made me all the more envious. Actually, it was just the tone of voice you would expect from a man like Lance. The war was over for him and men like Givner and he knew it. Although they were not close friends, they had known each other since the early days of the division at Camp Maxie and Camp Swift; now, as an officer, Lance could prevent his friend from making a foolish decision, and he did. However, when I approached the desk, it was different; the First Sgt. pushed a sheet forward and told me to sign my name and print my name and serial number under it.

Later, Knowles said I was foolish, just that and nothing more, except that he was sure the war in Japan would be over before I was ever called. Givner asked if his gesture had made me do it and apologized in case it had. He hadn't tried to dissuade me or question my reasons, thankfully. I wouldn't have had an answer. By that time, I had such immense respect for him, for his having been the first to speak to me, for being so bright and being one of such integrity that I silently wished for his approval. There was never any pretense about Givner. He always volunteered for such details, partly to kill the lie that Jews never take personal risks or accept their portion of the load and partly because he thought it his duty as a fervient antifascist. He was a "lefty," he told me, a bona fide socialist but not a Communist, either lower case or upper case, or a Stalinist. Places like Belsen and Buchenwald and the Polish camps had all been reported in great detail in *Stars and Stripes* and several from our platoon had walked through Belsen in the early days.

Klingenbrünn was down in the southeast corner of Bavaria just a few kilometers from the Czech and Austrian borders. Patrolling the border would be our chief occupation duty while we were stationed here, the CO announced. The Soviet zone began at the border with Czechoslovakia, the wooded ridge to the east, and it was our job to see no one crossed without proper papers. Each week, two squads would take off for a large hunting lodge high on the ridge. Our platoon, like the others, was at two-thirds strength and consisted of only two full squads.

After a week, we took off for the *Schützhaus* on the ridge and relieved the squads from the first platoon. The building itself was an architectural marvel straight out of a vampire movie or a Graustarkian novel. Its three stories rose like a step pyramid, each floor set back on all four sides from the floor below it. The top story had a steep slate roof, the four corners ending in tall, spear-like lightning rods pointing three or four feet skyward. Every corner of the lodge held one of the sturdy rods. A wide covered porch raised four to five feet off the ground by large foundation stones covered three sides of the building. On the ground floor was a large main room used for gatherings and dining and took almost the entire first floor. Off it was the kitchen with its large table and wood-fired stove. A shallow cellar entered just off the back door acted as a cooler of cold storage room. Steep narrow stairs led to the second floor and four rooms, each with two double bunks with real mattresses. Snow, Burdick, and I took the smallest of the top-floor rooms, barely large enough for three canvas cots. Again, the indoors privy were off-limits, thus the outdoor slit trench surrounded by waist high sheets of canvas. Another slight inconvenience: every morning, we had to fill the large Lister bag with spring water and treat it with the halozone tablets changing the pure clean spring water to regulation GI chlorinated water. No other water was allowed for drinking; though washing outdoors at the long table by a pump was permitted.

I had never seen any place quite like it, nor had anyone else. For at least a century, it had been the hangout of rich Bavarian hunters and, for the last few years, Nazi Party functionaries. Tall, thick grass grew up close to the house and almost obliterated the gravel path that led down to the end of the jeep road a little less than four hundred yards. Our only duties were the daily patrols, one to the north and one to the south, usually four men, two ranging south and two ranging north, each lasting two to three hours depending on the length of time our rest periods lasted. I hadn't noticed or even thought about it, but the others did right off; we had no "handy-talkies," portable radios, for the patrols in case we encountered an illegal crosser. Culpepper laughed, said it was all a sham anyway, just some kind of job to make it seem more like an "occupation" for the occupiers. All talk of Nazi guerrilla activity, the mythical *werewolf* fighters, had been talked to death in the first days or week after V-E Day. Had such things been true, this would be the place to jump off and begin the guerrilla war. But we did set out with extra ammo in our ammo belts.

Tall pine and fir trees covered the ridge and only from the small balconies at the gable ends of the third floor could you see over the tops of trees to the valleys beyond. A few yards to the east of the lodge was a small rocky peak with what appeared to be a fire lookout cabled to the rocks. The lookout gave a better view of the valleys on both sides of the ridge. I thought myself lucky to be in the first tour. Except for Burdick, Perkins, Sgt. Snow, my squad leader, Oravecz, and me, all men there at the lodge had been with the original company when it trained at Camp Swift. They had crossed the Siegfried Line, the Roer, and the Rhine each crossing requiring a battle. Except for Burdick, Snow, and Oravecz, we were all ASTP alumni. Culpepper posted a duty roster every morning, and somehow duties were performed without any further announcement. In fact, no one announced anything, but everything got done. I noticed from the first day I arrived that the college men did not congregate solely with the college men, nor did the non-college create their own group; friendships cut across all lines.

Twice a day, either Culpepper or one of the other noncoms reported back to the company by radio, but there was nothing much to report since none of the patrols on our first tour up there ever met anyone attempting to cross. Patrolling the Czechoslovakian border was the only detail of importance for the month and a half we were in Klingenbrünn and, from what I could tell, was the only reason we were there. After having served our first tour on the ridge, we all were eager to be back below. I made two trips to the top before the 102 got orders to move north. That first tour was most memorable and came at a time when I felt I had been accepted pretty much as an equal, that is everyone called me by name, shared snapshots from home, even asked about my family.

A light shower came almost on time every evening after supper, and one night, one of the showers was accompanied by lightning and thunder. Our only light after dark in the old lodge was candlelight or a couple of Coleman lanterns for the kitchen. Amid the lightning and thunder that night Burdick, Snow, and I had turned in up in our third-floor aerie. That evening I was trying to read by candlelight, my candle perched on a small shelf above my cot., The paperback was an ASE anthology of horror stories so heavily over-written they were more ludicrous than blood curdling. But I felt they fit the circumstance: high up in an ancient *Schützhaus* in a lightning storm, bolts crackling about the roof striking the lightning rods. I pictured myself as having just been admitted to Count Dracula's castle somewhere in Transylvania. Several guys had been trying out their Bela Lugosi accents during supper while the storm raged outside. Once I read aloud a blood-freezing passage to Burdick and Snow just to illustrate the awful prose; they thought it sounded good and handed me their candles, insisting I read entire the story. Naturally, I was happy to; when had I ever refused an audience anything?

As I began reading the gory story, I could feel them listening. Pitching my voice lower, imitating the voices of radio actors on shows like *Lights Out* or *The Shadow*, I read while the thunder clapped. The story told of a young scientist who had begun working for a "once highly respected" great man, now fallen like Faustus to necromancy and those "forbidden" investigations into the "nature of life itself." The young man worked long hours, going to his bed every night exhausted and doubt-filled regarding the old man's strange manner and the purpose of his research. Every night, the young scientist would hear strange sounds like claws scratching up through the dark hallway outside his door. Then one night, frightened and sweating, he leaped from his bed, flung open the door and stared down the hall but saw nothing though he heard a crab-like scuttering. The next night, he waited until the sounds approached his door. This time he grabbed a lantern, flung open the door, and saw two human hands crudely cut from their arms, "festooned with greenish gray decaying flesh trailing behind pieces of jagged bone." I recall clearly the word "festooned." As the light hit them, the first hand shriveled then turned and ran on its green decaying fingers out of the light. All night, he sat in his room unable to sleep but heard no other sounds. His employer the next morning refused to answer any questions. The young man later learned of the disappearance of the scientist's previous young assistant, and he learned they had quarreled frequently those last days before his disappearance.

I had read of the second sighting and began reading a third—these appearances somehow always occur in triplets—but before I could begin the third, Snow suggested we take our mattresses and blankets down to the main floor where the lightning strikes were less noisy. Burdick agreed. Alas, I thought, they are listening indeed.

Downstairs, the floor of the large room, lit by a hissing Coleman lantern, was already crowded with guys from the upper rooms, but Burdick, Snow, and I found comfortable spots near the light of the lantern. Two guys who had been listening from the room across the narrow hall upstairs followed, and when we got settled, the crowded room grew quite. I found a chair, leaned it back on two legs against the wall just under a shelf holding the lantern.

"You men won't mind if Gill reads the story, will you," Snow asked.

When no one objected I began reading, and Snow asked me to back up to that first time the hands ran away from the light. This is great, Snow is an aficionado of horror, I thought; and they all had really gotten caught up in the story. More than that, I was elated that anyone would want me to read such stuff aloud.

The claws once more began to scratch and crawl. This time I reached the part of the story where the young man, petrified with the knowledge that these same claws were perhaps dismembered joints of the previous assistant now seeking some sort of revenge or—no, it was too horrible to describe. For now, the antique doorknob began to turn, and the heavy oaken door, with its deep baroque carving, creaked open, and the verdigris flesh appeared as . . ., I never finished the sentence. I looked up to see the heavy steel door leading to the porch slowly opening with a loud creaking sound and a large hand appearing slowly in the eerie light of the lantern. Someone yelled, screamed, hollered. We never learned who. A large object flew across the room, slamming into the metal door with a loud clang, followed by a sheathed bayonet. My chair slid from under me. I crashed to the floor, banged my head hard against the floor, and let out a loud moan. Just then, Oravecz stomped his foot, slapped his knee, and roared with laughter.

The rain pounded outside, the flashes of lightning had moved on. There was silence for a moment then loud cursing, as someone groaned out, "Goddam you, Oravecz! You sonofabitch!"

Knowles laughed, Burdick cursed, some groaned, and when I propped my chair again, preparing to take up where left off, someone moaned, "Knock it off, Gilliland, and get some sleep."

I didn't argue, nor did anyone insist I continue. I picked up my mattress and returned to the aerie. The next morning, no one mentioned the reading or the door or Oravecz, but after that, I read no more aloud up at the *Schützhaus* on the Czech border, and from that night on, I thought Oravecz to be a comic genius.

In the weeks of waiting for the call to pack my bag and get on the truck, the Battle of Okinawa ended, and the war in the Pacific turned into a war of B-29s. We read the stories in *Stars and Stripes* and waited.

Then it was August, and the day after we arrived at the hunting lodge on the border for our second tour, the call came, a brief radio message ordering me to return to the company for reassignment. The next morning, I hiked down the road and met a jeep that took me back to the company. It was strange, no one said good-bye, good luck, or anything, and the jeep ride was just as silent. When I reported to the orderly room, the First Sgt. simply looked up, thought a moment as if he were struggling to recall why I was there, then said, "In the morning, 0800, Gilliland, a truck from battalion will be here to take you to a repple depple." That was all. Nothing more.

I hesitated to ask but finally got the courage, "Sergeant, did anyone say where they take us when we leave the division?"

He shook his head and said no one told him anything and went back to his paperwork. It was August 6.

A few hours later, back in my squad room, I heard it over the Armed Forces Radio: A bomb, a "new device" of some kind, had been dropped on the Japanese city of Hiroshima, totally destroying the entire city, a single bomb. As soon as I heard it, it all came back, Uncle Benny's lesson about the energy in the nucleus of the atom. Several other men listening also said it: "Atomic energy!" Being in a unit with so many college men, it was inevitable. If anyone would know, they would, and in those days, almost everyone had taken at least one course in college chemistry or physics. I doubted that any other division in the ETO would have reacted as quickly as the 102 did.

The next morning, I took my duffel bag to the orderly room to wait, but the First Sgt. said that all troop movements were temporarily on hold.

"It's over Gilliland," he said. "Unpack your duffel bag. You're staying here."

Two days later, the bomb at Nagasaki ended it for sure. When we heard the final news of the surrender, there was only one long sigh, no celebration, no fireworks, only relief. I unpacked my bag and waited for the platoon to come back off the mountain, and for three days, I had my squad room to myself, no duty, nothing. I saw the sergeant once in the corridor. He had always ignored me ever since we arrived new and dumb in the night.

Now he stopped, called my name, "Gilliland, have you unpacked yet?" He smiled then added, "You're one lucky bastard, you know that?" He actually smiled, but I knew it was nothing personal.

The rest of my tour in the ETO was free of great events. Oh, two truckloads of us rode into Passau and saw Jack Benny and Ingrid Bergman, along with Les Brown and his Band of Renown with "Liltin" Martha Tilton who sang "Sentimental Journey," our favorite song of the war. Another trip took us to see Bob Hope, Jerry Colonna, and Francis Langford. In our B Company truck, it was unanimous: Jack Benny was better, and Bergman was gorgeous. She performed a speech from Maxwell Anderson's play *Joan of Arc*, the final speech at her trial. We had good seats, saw her and Benny really well, but years later, when I saw the movie *Joan of Loraine*, I was disappointed. It was much better the first time with Culpepper and Knowles and Dzonweick and the rest, all marveling at the incongruity of a Bergman Joan of Arc in a giant field house filled with roaring GIs. But on second thought, it was beautiful.

In September, the division moved north to Wunsiedel, a much larger town still close to the Czech border and close to the border with the Soviet zone. Our division HQ was in Bayreuth and the regiment's was in Hof. Gradually, the high-point men began to leave and men from other units replacing them. The original composition of the ASTP troops had changed, only a few of the youngest like Knowles remained. We were down to only two officers, Lance and an executive officer who had been with the company prior to my arrival. Our duties had changed little: regular morning close-order drill and calisthenics, occasional guard duty at roadblocks, checking IDs and papers of discharged German POWs, usually afoot. No one complained about any of it. We had an occasional lecture covering such subjects as duties of occupation soldiers and the Nuremberg war crime trials that were just getting under way. We even had a weekly I & E discussion which, being voluntary, few attended. These discussions were pale in comparison to the lively arguments that had been so stimulating in our Klingenbrünn quarters. Morale in Wunsiedel was good. Our executive officer supplied the enlisted men with funds to open our own beer hall. Prodigious purchases of the light pilsner and delicious rye bread rolls and occasional cheese kept it operating at a profit. The B*ier Stübe* employed a few Germans who claimed to have been anti-Nazis. One woman, middle-aged blonde who occasionally worked there behind the bar, and mostly hung out with us drinking the pale pilsner, had an honest claim to having been anti-Nazi. A journalist by profession she had spent time in a political concentration camp before the war and again near the end. At first, the *Stube's* rule was that no German civilians would be allowed as guests, but the men simply ignored the order and brought their girlfriends, and soon, other German civilians arrived, men as well as women, so that by the time I left Wunsiedel, our beer hall looked like a typical German *Stube,* anti-fraternization laws having gone the way of the war.

I really enjoyed the place and spent what was probably an inordinate amount of time there drinking beer and eating rolls, but mostly I enjoyed the talk and the music— accordion mostly but sometimes a saxophone and piano, playing German pop hits from the thirties. My friendship with Knowles and Givner made all the difference that summer. I missed Givner after he shipped out for home and university. I never knew men so intelligent, so well-read, and yet so easy to talk to or so willing to talk to me. They were men of totally different interests and backgrounds, one a chemist and a Jew and the other a product of Boston Latin School and Harvard Yard. Because Givner was the first man in the platoon to speak to me, ask me questions about myself, take an interest in my ASTP connection, I would have followed him anywhere, which partly explains why I stepped forward when he did and volunteered for the "active theater." We talked about chemistry mostly, the courses he enjoyed most and least and courses I should watch out for—if I stayed a chemistry major. We found we had many interests in common. He too, caught the bug when his father gave him his first Gilbert Chemistry Set.

Shortly after we arrived in Wunsiedel, Knowles lucked into a week's R & R pass to the UK. Most men in the company chose Paris or the Riviera, but Knowles understandably chose London for the literary connections; he confided that if he went to Paris and his father found out he had passed up London, he might as well not go back home. When he returned, after overstaying his leave a full week, with no complications, he found he was on shipping orders for home. Being a combat veteran and AWOL was no big deal in late August 1945. Lance and the First Sgt. held his orders for rotation, and said nothing. I would miss him.

Knowles was a quiet intellectual rebel, a comfortable nonconformist, who was always able to get away with whatever variety of nonconformism he was working on at the time. In countless stories coming out of the army, there always appears a bright, often brilliant iconoclast who is almost never in proper uniform, always late to formations, constantly irreverent, and persistently recalcitrant, a true individualist swimming in a sea of conformity. Like Knowles, this individual is rarely insubordinate, considering out-and-out insubordination a waste of time. Knowles was never in trouble, never broke serious regulations simply because it wasn't worth the agony of confrontation, but for platoon sergeants and squad leaders he was a quiet pain in the ass. When he left, for me, the company changed entirely; it became duller and more predictable. For instance, when he returned from England, he told marvelous stories about bookshops, and walks in the city where Dickens had walked, about the parks, and his favorite place of all, the British Museum, its collection still largely dispersed. Ordinarily, Knowles didn't act or talk like a literary scholar. In fact, he had honed his vulgarity and profanity to a sharp and witty edge. Culpepper, laughing, had said that Charley turned GI slang and vulgarity into an art form. But when he was describing to me the main reading room of the British Museum, he was downright reverential. "You know how many great men used that place?" he said and read off to me a list of names, most of whom I'd never heard of but whom I would hear of and would study in years to come.

When he showed me a thin very old edition of Oscar Wilde's "The Ballad of Reading Gaol,"

I read the title aloud, and he said, "It's *Red-ding*, not read-ing, Gilliland. And it's pronounced *jail*, not *gale*."

He had memorized the more macabre, overcharged, sentimental verses, so heavy with irony he admitted the whole thing was entirely overdone, but that he loved the ballad meter and said it would amuse his father. Then he showed me a slender book of four poems by T. S. Eliot that was titled *Four Quartets*, and reminded me it was the same poet who had written about that "patient etherized upon a table." He let me read the volumes, which he said he'd bought as gifts for his father, especially the Eliot volume. I found Wilde wildly interesting but the Eliot far too esoteric for me. When he asked me what I thought about the poem "Burnt Norton," I told him I was thoroughly stumped, even when I reread it aloud. "I liked the sound, the echoing of the word 'time,' but I have no idea what it's about.'"

He agreed and said he thought it had some connection to Vedic thought because Eliot had studied eastern philosophies and religion at Oxford. The poem stayed with me for years, the Vedanta-like chant of time past, present, and future echoing and later leading me to take a class in eastern thought. Charley made much of Eliot's *Four Quartets* being a first edition, or a first edition as a collection of four earlier poems. He quite gleamed when he pointed out the date, 1943, and said it was just the gift he'd been hoping to find for his father at St. John's.

I copied out several pages of "Burnt Norton" and held on to them for more than a year, never knowing for sure what they meant but mesmerized by the sounds and rhythm of the lines. Charley may have known what he was doing, maybe not, but he was teaching me to "read close," a critical term I knew nothing about for years, but that's what it was. I would later think of this time and see myself as Charley offering the same good services to a young reader as he was offering me. He had begun my tutoring back in Klingenbrünn; I had been reading aloud Whitman's "Out of the Cradle." I'll never forget it. Since then I've read Whitman aloud whenever I could do so without disturbing anyone. Those experiences with Knowles and the poetry he put in my path were the reason I took the poetry course my first semester back at UT. What attracted my attention quite early were the incongruities of character and spirit he demonstrated, the unexpected elements in his character and interests. The first time I noticed it was the morning after my reading horror-laced prose in the hunting lodge. Charley spoke about the "really bad prose style of Lovecraft," the author.

"People really believe all those long, Latinate words are signs of intelligence, of real intellect, which is nonsense. You want to hear something really horrifying? Read Robert Browning's 'Porphyria's Lover.' Do you know Browning?"

"I like the 'Last Duchess.' It's in that anthology I was reading," I answered.

"That's good, but listen to this." He began:

> The rain set early in tonight,
> The sullen wind was soon awake . . .

And from memory, he spoke Browning's lines smoothly and clearly, not performing or embellishing with an actor's style, but easily, as if he were simply describing a scene in prose matter-of-factly and then suddenly:

> The moment she was mine, mine fair,
> Perfectly pure and good; I found
> A thing to do, and all her hair
> In one long yellow string I wound
> Three times her lovely throat around
> And strangled her . . .

He stopped there then continued and finished,

> And thus we sit together now,
> All night long we have not stirred,
> And yet God has not said a word.

"Well, what do you think?" He just sat there and smiled, knowing I felt the shock. I couldn't say anything at first, trying to assimilate it, understand it, somehow figure out the meaning while still virtually mesmerized by sounds, rhythms, images.

"W-w-why?" I stammered.

"There's no *answer*, it just is."

"Who the hell is Porphyria?"

"*Es macht nichts,*" he smiled, "It's poetry. Remarkable, isn't it?"

We later talked about "Prufrock" and its sounds and pictures, rather *images,* of etherized patients and ragged claws and then rolled trouser bottoms and walks upon the beach. Those short talks, I'm sure, meant more to entertain him than to teach me, for we never, he never, concluded anything, just walked away content with what he'd started.

Under the influence of men like Knowles, who treated me as if I actually might know something, I moved ahead in my mind to a place I might never have found easily on my own. He often spoke about the day when he would return to Harvard and how he hoped to finish his BA and begin graduate studies as soon as possible. When Knowles got the news that he was eligible to return, I decided it was time for me to leave too, even though the army thought otherwise.

By the fall of 1945, the army faced the loss of so many men it appeared it might not have the troops required to carry out the occupation. Every once in a while, the army brass conceives a plot that makes so much sense you wonder where it came from—ASTP was such a thought, I believe. In order to ensure the army had enough men to carry out the peace, the army offered one-, two-, or three-year enlistments in the regular army, each enlistment period having commensurate rewards that included furloughs, bonuses, mustering out pay—the longer the enlistment, the larger the bonus and longer the guaranteed furlough in the States before reassignment. The furloughs ranged in length from thirty days to *ninety days*, depending on the length of the reenlistment period. Some of these men would reenlist eventually anyway, men who were the regular army or men who had been serving before the draft began in 1940. Some were men whose entire adult life had been spent under the control of first sergeants and COs, either from CCC days or early days of the draft; they had neither made a commitment to a civilian career nor understood its problems.

One of my good friends in B Company, Daniel Smith, fit that category. He was a junior high school dropout, straight off a farm in Wisconsin, a good soldier who became a man and reached adulthood in every sense in the infantry, most of it in the One-O-Deuce, which he often spoke of with love. He had "found a home in the army," and was liked, admired, and trusted by all levels in our platoon and company, and he loved and trusted them as well. Of all the men in the platoon, I believe Smitty truly loved the men he served with. An early replacement in the fall of 1944, they had given him the cumbersome BAR because he was tall and sturdy--a lot like Gaston in many ways--and then because no one else had wanted it because it drew enemy fire and weighed too much. He carried it proudly and, apparently, from what I heard, used it well and came through the entire war unscathed. Smitty never resented the ASTP men, never felt they acted superior or snobbish (because they didn't as far as I could tell) as some older regular army men had, and in turn, he was genuinely respected. Though he had no formal education beyond the seventh or eighth grade, he was not stupid, merely unlearned in any formal sense; and like almost everyone in the platoon, he was a reader, belonging to the Max Brand, Ernest Haycox, and Eugene Manlove Rhodes club. He liked to hang around with me for some reason, perhaps because I made him laugh. He said he liked the way I talked, though I was never sure if he meant it was my Texas accent or if it was something else—I still don't know; nevertheless, it flattered me since I had come late to the platoon, one of the pariah class, too young, too dumb, and too late. Dannie always saved me a place at his table in the company beer hall.

At first, when Smitty suggested I look into "re-upping" with him, I said no. Then I counted up my points and saw I had virtually no chance of returning home much before December of 1946 anyway, the date I would be discharged if I chose the one-year option. He honestly did not look forward to returning to the Wisconsin farm, he said, and had no understanding of nor belief in a GI Bill's benefits for him. Our enlisting now, he said, would get us "home for Christmas," a soldier boy's dream. He reasoned we would end up in the same unit if we enlisted at the same time, and I never questioned his logic. He took the two-year option, I took the one-year.

Several days before my nineteenth birthday, Smitty, Quinn, and I rode into Hof, our regimental HQ, for an interview with the Battalion CO to see if we possessed a suitable personal character for the new peacetime army. Others said the interview was to determine if we were in our right minds. Knowles had earlier insisted again and again that the act of enlistment or reenlistment was an admission of mental incompetence. All the way to regimental HQ, Smitty agonized, first, about his class A uniform then about the polish on his combat boots that never took a polish and, finally, about his not having even gone to high school. I assured him he would pass on all points; his combat record alone made him a find, I explained. We all "passed," of course; the army was not in the business of turning down anyone at that time.

The morning after our return from battalion was our day to hunt deer in the forest around Wunsiedel. It was also October 25, my birthday. German farmers in the area, pestered by a deer population that was eating their wheat and barley, begged us to thin the herd. They begged us to shoot anything, bucks or does, not a sportsman-like activity we thought, though the prospect of killing a young grain-fed doe was tempting. Sportsmanship had nothing to do with it, conservation of grain crops did. We all checked out M1 carbines that were lighter, though less accurate some said, than the M1 Garand and also less likely to tear a deer to pieces. Each group of four would hunt only its assigned sector. This was not in any sense a sporting event, more like the guaranteed hunts ranchers provide rich Texans nowadays. Many of the GIs that fall were experiencing their first dear hunt—I was such a hunter.

Early that morning, a nip was in the air, and our breaths produced vapor clouds. Altogether, six of us were out. Our "squad" of four—Burdick, two others from the first platoon, and me—set out in a skirmish line, four abreast, making sure no one stepped out too far and got caught in a line of fire. The other two, one a sergeant in charge, went down several hundred yards to a wide fire lane and waited for any deer we skirmishers might flush out.

The forests were second- or third-growth trees neatly aligned, all of the same age and size, pretty, but unlike a real forest, more like a tree farm. We were all carrying between five and ten rounds in the fifteen-round clips, hardly sporting since we could squeeze off as many rounds as we wanted as fast as we pulled the trigger.

We took off in our sector in "a line of skirmishers" and had walked perhaps twenty yards when Burdick shouted, "Deer!" Two does jumped directly in front of me a little over ten yards perhaps. I sighted quickly and opened fire at the running targets, without one good well-sighted shot, just a hail of .30-caliber slugs, five rounds, all I had in the magazine, all squeezed off rapid fire, not by any sporting man's rules. But I got my deer, as they say, though she hadn't fallen clean. At first, I wasn't sure I'd hit anything, but we found her about another thirty yards into the trees with one round in the neck another in the chest. She was dead when we got there.

"Good shooting, Joe," Burdick said, his voice expressing no sign of enthusiasm.

The other deer made it to the fire lane. We heard the crack of a carbine. One of the men waiting got her as she moved into the clearing. She had two holes in her plus his. Since I was the only one spraying fire at the time, we assumed that Gilliland had gotten one and a half deer that day. I was not proud, felt none of the elation of the hunter, felt much the way Burdick had sounded. I was happy we got the meat, however, and happy that we were able to share it with a German family. It was my first deer hunt and my last and was the last time I would fire a rifle of any kind. The sergeant, who claimed the second doe as his, helped us string the deer and gut them. The others expressed no disappointment in failing to get a deer and showed no wish to continue. Burdick, whom I ordinarily might have expected to insist on continuing, for the first time I can recall, looked quite sickened and said he'd never hunted like that. "Sorry, Gill, it just don't seem right. But good shootin' anyway." I agreed and thanked him.

The sergeant's deer went into the company's cold storage locker while mine went to a woman and her family living near our billet. She cooked the back ribs and a small rump roast for the platoon and served it with gravy, potatoes, onions, and carrots, along with small rye rolls. The rest of the kill was hers for her trouble of cooking my birthday feast. She thanked us vociferously, promising to give us some of the sausage when it was ready. To go with it, we got a small keg of pilsner from our company beer hall and set it all up in the large room on the floor above our second platoon area. Most of the platoon showed up for a taste and a stein of beer, and a few from the other platoons dropped in. It was my birthday. I was nineteen, and that night, after the party broke up, we had the first real snowfall. These deer had fed so well on the grain of the fields we tasted hardly a hint of wild venison.

It was only the second real snowfall I'd ever seen, the other *real* snowfall being that one at Camp Wolters the night before our long LMG problem. Some of the guys stared out at the white stuff, large flakes that covered everything, expressing real hate and recalling the terrible winter of a year before, voicing feelings of despair that orders for home would never come. Stories began to roll out of the previous winter, the winter of the Bulge.

Once in the shooting lodge, I heard tales of the winter of 1944. Knowles lost all his mirth as he related the long days in freezing foxholes, sometimes wishing for any action to break the tedium. The 102nd Division was holding a corps section to the north of the line while the Battle of the Bulge raged to the south; there was so much distance between foxholes they could hardly hear each other. Without fires, except for the burning K ration cartons, the holes were like deep freezes. He tried to tell the story jokingly about how he wished at one point he could stick his foot up in the air and have it shot off. Someone nodded and said he had thought about it too. But no one in B Company lost a foot that way. Knowles then laughed how everyone treated

Givner as if he had lost a foot when machine-gun fire shot off the heel of his boot. "German snipers wouldn't have done us the favor," he said. "They only aimed for your head."

Two weeks after the deer hunt, Smitty, Quinn, and I said farewell to B Company, 406th Infantry, and to Wunsiedel. It took Danny, Quinn, and me over a week from the time we left the regimental HQ at Bayreuth for us to reach Camp Lucky Strike, the replacement depot in Le Havre, the same camp where a company of "gunners' mates" replacements stayed on the way from England. The boxcars from Bamberg to Le Havre, the forty-and-eight cars, were less crowded than they were on the trip to Germany, and much colder. Our train stopped once, on Thanksgiving Day, at the siding called Tours, and we detrained for "a turkey dinner with all the trimmin's." Ike had announced that every man in the ETO would have a traditional American Thanksgiving, but by the time we reached the long chow line, all the turkey was gone and all that was left was cold canned turkey or chicken and cranberries, tepid gravy, and canned yams with small squares of pumpkin pie. I can't recall anyone complaining or much caring because we were heading in the right direction. We did "enjoy" the luxury of eating off real plates and drinking coffee from real mugs, not tin canteen cups, and we sat at long tables inside a semi-heated mess tent where German POWs poured steaming cups of joe, the kind "that's good for cuts and bruises and tastes like iodine." As long as we were moving, you would hear no bitching, but when the train pulled into a siding to wait for a train coming in the opposite direction, a great howl would rise along the line of cars; three quarters of the men moving toward Le Havre were on their way home to be discharged, the rest, re-uppers.

I had caught a miserable cold on the slow trip from Bamberg to Le Havre that tuned into a miserable hacking cough, the forty-and-eight boxcars much colder in November than they'd been in April. Before we embarked, we were to do two important things: turn in all our money, occupation script, and deutsche marks and get influenza shots, the latest medical miracle. Ours was the last shipment home that allowed everyone to cash in *all* his cash, meaning all black market profits. In the rail yards outside Frankfurt, I had sold a carton of Raleighs and a carton of Pall Malls that came to a total of thirty dollars. Lucky Strikes or Camels would have brought twice that much. By November of 1945, the black market was awash in these less popular brand cigarettes; Lucky Strike, Camel, and Chesterfield still brought twenty-five to thirty-five dollars a carton, a carton that had cost us only five dollars in the PX at Bamberg. Many exchanged ten or a hundred times the amount I did. As it was, Smitty had to lend me ten dollars to buy the two cartons at the

Bamberg PX since I was flat broke, most of my paycheck going home in the form of savings bonds every month.

The flu shots presented a potentially serious problem since the order came down that no one with a cold or with fever would be allowed to have the shot, and no one would be allowed to ship out without the shot. I blew my nose thoroughly, did all I could to suppress my cough, and sneaked through the inoculation without detection. That evening at the Red Cross Club, a very nice elderly Red Cross lady admonished me for possibly endangering my health, but I felt no guilt or fear, only gratitude. Smitty and I had hung together since leaving the company, but now we learned we were in different shipping companies, his group slated for a camp in Wisconsin and my company slated for Fort Sam where I had been inducted. When we separated just after leaving the boxcars, we exchanged addresses and promised to write. It was sad, parting from my new "old friend," actually sadder than saying good-bye to Knowles. Though we had known each other for barely three months, our last weeks together had been very close. Once again, I felt like an *isolato* as I climbed into my bunk on the converted American Fruit Company cruise ship. I knew no one in my shipping company.

Our ship had none of the amenities we had enjoyed on the *Pasteur*, with one exception—the food served by the army transportation corps was far superior to any we had eaten since leaving Bamberg. One other fact about that crossing that I felt was historically significant was that all the shipping companies, even ours headed for Fort Sam Houston, were integrated, probably the first time this Texas boy had ever been *allowed* to travel in racially mixed company. From the first draft in 1940 until November 1945, the army had observed the rules of segregation but not now. Our casual company held a sprinkling of Negro soldiers with remarkably no complaints. Also, perhaps of minor significance, our noncom in charge of the company was an Indian from Oklahoma, a tech sergeant, three stripes and a pair of rockers, who informed us when we were first assembled that he would be addressed as "Sergeant," that he never wanted to the called "chief," which was "OK in the navy but not here." The emphatic order was never forgotten. I filed his comments and the desegregation policy for future use in case I found myself enrolled in Dr. Mac's anthropology class someday, a day I hoped not too far off.

Another more telling experience made the trip most memorable, well, made it one that deserves telling. Our company boarded light, sans duffel bags, and we shuffled rapidly and eagerly through the passageways to our forward bays, raucous cheers celebrating the fact that we were homeward-bound. Two men in front grabbed the lower berths, and I threw my light pack up to the top rack which, I saw, was half covered by a ventilating shaft, and next to the canvas rack across a narrow open space was another rack with an early occupant lying stretched out, looking quite comfortable, his rack without a shaft. As I pulled up and glanced across, he looked straight at me. We stared at each other a moment, and then he said in a flat matter-of-fact tone, "You want me to move?"

He was black. "No," I replied in as noncommittal a tone as I could find, "unless you want to sleep under a ventilating shaft."

"Just askin'."

I stretched flat and then said, "Well, no tossin' or turnin' this trip for sure."

He laughed and turned away. But it galled me, angered me that he asked almost automatically as if it were expected that a white boy would not wish to sleep next to a black man. I would file this one for sure. It might even become a topic for an essay, I thought. My thoughts shifted back to a conversation in B Company about Negro soldiers who like all minorities were often singled out as slackers, rear echelon dandies. Other than the Negro infantry divisions and armored units, the African Americans were drivers of trucks in the Red Ball Express, the major suppliers of ammo, fuel, food, and mail, often without armed escort and, in the fall and winter, under frequent Luftwaffe attack. Snow himself had sworn he'd far rather spend time in a foxhole than driving a two-and-a half–ton, six-by-six full of ammo. From all appearances, the men in my hold returning stateside on the American Fruit Company troopship felt the same.

We made the crossing in only five days, sailing through the tip of a storm so severe that the USS *West Point*, America's largest troop transport, was forced to stop in mid-Atlantic and wait it out while we steered south around the edge. Our arrival, just before dusk on the last day of November, like the entire journey, appears in memory now as a scripted production straight from MGM or RKO. Even though the war had been over for more than three months, we were greeted everywhere in the grand manner as "conquering heroes." As we arrived just at dusk, an "escort" of fire ships appeared, spraying water cannons in great arcs while blowing horns and whistles. All ships and tugs passing in or out blasted whistles or sirens, and as we passed the Statue of Liberty, her lights came up suddenly, though probably only because it was that time. As I said, it all seemed scripted by a studio. Debarkation was an even greater surprise. Unloading went smoothly with little or no hurry-up-and-wait, and when we arrived at Camp Kilmer, we were sumptuously overfed with steak and ice cream, though some of us complained the apple pie was seriously not Mom's.

Processing at Kilmer went swiftly, and the next day, our train for Fort Sam left before sunup. It was so strange. Alas, no forty-and-eight freight cars but regular Pullman cars with sheets and porters. We all could feel it; the army wanted "shut of us." As our troop train passed through small towns, people at the crossings would wave and honk their horns. The stations and city lights burned brightly, and streets glowed with Christmas decorations, sights that for a moment silenced laughter and stilled the roughhousing. When I had passed this way nine months before, a brownout was still in effect, more for conserving energy than for fear of bombing raids, but now everything glittered as if it were illuminated just for us; we knew we were only one troop train of thousands that had passed on these tracks in the last three months. Most of the men in my car were combat veterans or men who had been a year or more overseas. Homecoming for many was tearful and emotional. I had been over there with a young division, mostly with replacements and young draftees, and had forgotten there were men who had been in since the first draft in 1940, or men in their thirties when drafted and now, five years later, had crossed the big four-zero. A few men on our train had been with the first troops in England in 1942. To me, it was all terribly moving. But it was also a time filled with the unexpected, particularly concerning those who had seen the worst.

As we would slow down and come to a stop, waiting for a clear track ahead, several of the men would jump from the train and take their chances looking for a telephone or a liquor store. One man was too late in getting back and the train left without him, but we picked him up at the next town. A civilian had seen him miss his train and had driven him ahead, and the station had flagged the engineer who had slowed down and let him jump back on. It was an unusual time. The joys of homecoming superseded all military protocols. Our car commander, a major, closed the door to his compartment and ignored everything, considering all rules suspended for the duration, in this case the duration of the men's service. He opened his door only when an orderly from the kitchen staff brought him his tray. One man left the train in St. Louis where the train had to lay over from midnight until dawn, and he didn't get back on the train until Texarkana when his wife, in a "new" used Buick convertible, delivered him smiling and spent. They had resumed conjugal relationships, he reported, in the backseat while a sister-in-law drove them south, thus he had the record for the one who would first fulfill the famous promise: "The first thing I'm going to do when I walk in the door is make love to my wife and the second thing is drop my duffel bag." It was SOP.

The air was full of Christmas cheer and booze. During our layover in St. Louis, most of the men left the train and crossed the tracks into town or to the station's bar. I, not surprisingly, had been given KP.

An older vet from the Ninth Division sharing my Pullman berth explained, "They're playing army with Joe. The one with the least army time, it seems, is always the loser. It's easy, goes like this, 'Let's play army, Joe. You lie down and I'll shit on you.' But I don't mind. Nothing personal."

I was the youngest and least "scarred" by service overseas. In other words, it was situation normal all . . .. My job was simple: crack all the eggs, sixty dozen eggs, in the case into the large pot for breakfast the next morning. After an hour of cracking, one of my comrades, actually a total but caring stranger, filled with the joy of the season and the blessings of forthcoming discharge, came to the car and brought me a large glass of whisky, raw and cheap but so consoling that I could recall only about the first forty dozen eggs that eventually made it into the pot. The rest of the trip from Texarkana to Dallas was all a haze, and when I woke, the train was at rest on a siding just inside Fort Sam Houston—back where I started.

They separated us who had reenlisted from the men being discharged, the first group a mere handful, and began the processing immediately. I could hardly believe it when they *promised* we would be free by 1600. When had anyone promised us anything like that? I got to a phone and called home with the news and asked if I should try to get a bus or stay over at Aunt Kate's. Mama said she was leaving at that minute and would be there to meet me, and she asked where she should go. I told her to meet me at the Main PX about four o'clock. I had no idea where the Main PX was, but I was sure there was such a place, and I knew someone would be able to direct her to it.

The processing was simple; it included picking up our discharge from the army—I have two army discharges—and receiving my two months' back pay, mustering-out pay, reenlistment bonus, travel pay to and from Corpus Christi, plus a per diem allowance, that last highly irregular for enlisted men on leave but one of the incentives they used to get us to sign up, and that was it. Finished with everything before the deadline, I shouldered my pack, hitched up my duffel bag and took the bus marked Main PX. When I stepped down, there she was, just as we had planned so carefully in advance.

Corpus at Christmas and home for the holidays, a soldier boy's dream, and with nine hundred dollars in pocket, I felt richer than all the princes of Araby. How odd, I thought, right then I had more money than I had made all that summer of 1943, enough for a full year of college without working. But the joy of being home dissolved any lingering knot of anger I had felt the year before. Almost exactly a year before—only a year?—I had left home for Camp Wolters, Texas. I thought, *"O earth, what changes hast thou Seen!"* But all I could think of was seeing the house; petting Butch, our giant Angora cat; calling Bill or Luther or Harvey and Jerry, if she were in town. These old friends from high school days, what were they like now, where had they been, and what had they done? I had been to Germany and France, walked the Czech border; the others had remained in the States. But they were out now or getting out. Don Vaughn had been in the navy sailing to Iceland and the Caribbean, transporting the "goods of war: toilet paper, Kotex, and kitchen supplies," he had written jokingly in the only letter I'd gotten from him.

But there was still another year to go, another full year that began the day I left, again waving to Mama with me standing at the bus stop at Fort Sam Houston's Main PX.

Chapter 9

Korea

The furlough passed quickly, and for that, I was grateful. My life had taken a new tack entirely, one for which I was deeply content and happy to be on. It had taken me into a realm of ideas and experiences that I could not explain to anyone. I could barely explain it to myself. More than two years had lapsed since we had all been so close; now I felt closer to men like Smitty and Snow, Knowles and Givner, or almost any of the "Asstrapers" at A&M, especially men like Dykes and Lovejoy. It was happening to everyone all over the country.

Shortly after I arrived in Corpus, I returned to Austin for a long weekend and stayed in the fraternity house. It was something I would never have thought possible before, but I had money now, my mustering-out pay, reenlistment bonus, and two months' back pay. The room where I had lived all alone that last month now held three men, and all the rooms in the house were overflowing. I envied the men who were back and reenrolled, and briefly, only briefly, I wondered whether I had not been too hasty in reenlisting even though it was for only a year. I had made up my mind not to look back on what might have been. Lines from Eliot's "Burnt Norton" came back:

> What might have been is an abstraction
> Remaining a perpetual possibility
> Only in the world of speculation . . .

I had memorized the lines early and kept them close; they sounded wise as I repeated them to myself. As much as I wished to be back living in the house, I still felt I was not ready.

I spent Friday morning wandering across the campus, looked in on a class of Dr. Mac's cultural anthropology. He gave me a nod and a smile as I took a seat on the back row of the tiered lecture hall, but I knew he did not recognize me; he had grown accustomed to former students dropping by and sitting in. I was in uniform, was wearing an ETO ribbon, along with the WWII Victory ribbon and one for Occupation of Germany; those with my gold overseas bar made me welcome. Later, I took the Tower elevator and stopped off on Dr. James' floor and found her in her office with a student. When I turned to leave, she called me back, by name, and invited me in. The student was just leaving. When she saw my ETO ribbon and overseas bar, she seemed surprised. I was happy she remembered my name and remembered that I had been in her comp class two years before. When she asked if I was returning to the university, I told her I had another full year before I would be back and explained my reenlisting, confessing I was uncertain what my major would be. So far, she was the only person I'd told. It felt good talking to her. She listened as I told how I had missed the fighting, and then I told how the Bomb had saved me from going to the Pacific.

"You seemed so young the last time I saw you, Joe. It comes as a shock to see you now in uniform with ribbons." She smiled.

I told her, as briefly as I could, about enlisting in June '44 and being sent to A&M, repeating freshman comp and algebra then transferring out. I wanted to tell her how much her class meant to me, but I didn't know how to say it without sounding like just another sycophant. But I did tell her about teaching Gaston and Perkins to write their girlfriends and about how much I had read and how much I enjoyed reading and how the Armed Services Editions had kept books in my duffle bag. The really impressed her I think, and she was especially impressed when I mentioned men like Knowles and Givner.

When I rose to leave, she told me she appreciated my stopping and wished me luck. I had seen the two people who meant the most to me, marveled that one was an English teacher and the other anthropology, neither were in chemistry or zoology. That brief visit with Helen James was a high point of my furlough. The rest of my time in Corpus was all anti-climax, even New Years Eve with Reiss and Vaughn; we just didn't have much to say.

On the day after New Year's, Mama, Don, and I drove back to San Antonio and visited Aunt Kate for most of the day, said hello to some Gillilands I felt I hardly knew and then drove to Dodd Field right up to the barracks where I was released a month earlier. Just one street over from the barracks was the tent city where Dykes, McNair and I had been inducted into active service, just a month over a year ago. I was surprised how relieved I felt when I stepped out of the car. I was no longer angry with Mama about anything; she had done everything she could to make my thirty days at home pleasant, had cooked all my favorite meals, baked apple pies, welcomed my friends when they stopped by. I had changed, and she knew it, but she said nothing, thankfully.

When I walked into the darkened barracks, a light came on, and a sleepy corporal rose slowly off a cot, glanced my papers, and pointed me to the barracks room, muttered something about a roll call at 0800 then went back to his cot. He was fully dressed but looked as if he had slept in the same clothes for weeks. As I walked into the barracks room, I had the oddest feeling that I was at home here, that the month in Corpus had all been unreal. Had I indeed "found a home in the army"?

When I didn't hear my name called at the 0800 formation, I found the corporal who had greeted me the night before and told him. He admitted he hadn't seen my name on his roster for new arrivals and wondered if I hadn't come to the wrong place. When I showed him my orders and furlough papers, he agreed I was in the right barracks then remarked that I wasn't the first left off roster.

He laughed and said, "You would have simplified *my* life if you hadn't come back, but it sure as hell would've fucked up yours. Don't worry, they'll find your records someday, but if they don't find you when they do find your records, you've had it."

Almost a week passed, meeting formations, hanging about the service clubs and the library, waiting to hear my name called. Then one day, on the bus into town, I had a semi-Dahlquist moment when I bumped into an old platoon mate from Camp Wolters. The last time I had seen him was the day we "graduated" from infantry basic. He had orders to report to Fort Benning for paratrooper training. We were both incredulous meeting there on the bus. When I asked about jump school, noting that he was not wearing a paratrooper's badge or the shiny jump boots, he told me he had flunked out the first week, ending up in Okinawa where he was wounded his first day in action. It was a minor wound, but it got him a Purple Heart and a "ticket home." He too had re-upped and was now assigned a clerk's job at Dodd Field.

They finally called my name the next day along with fifty or so recent enlistees, not a draftee in the bunch. Our orders were to ship out that afternoon for Camp Pickett, Virginia. I was sure it meant we were slated for Germany. The miserable ride through the South in a ratty Pullman without a working toilet and the long stopover in Shreveport after our car had been disconnect from the regular passenger train and a shorter one in smoky Birmingham was proof that the war was over, that active duty troops were surplus commodities. Camp Pickett in January was a bleak, forlorn camp of red soil and scraggly pines and no different from hundreds of army posts created during the war. We were a mixed bag of ranks from buck privates through six-stripers, from short-timers like myself to twenty-year regular army men, half of whom had been overseas in the ETO, mostly Germany and France, a few from Italy, the rest stateside desk jockeys. The prospects of our getting orders to move on to a POE seemed about as hopeful as had been our prospects at Fort Sam.

At first all ranks below sergeant fell out for "riot drill" and orientation lectures on "occupation duty." When a few of us old-timers—that is, those who had already been overseas—realized the people in charge had no idea what an occupation army was expected to do, we told them that the Germans we had seen were less likely to riot than were the troops stationed here at Pickett. Several who had been in Japan agreed. The second morning, when they called us out for "riot training," three of us took off for the service club, just over a small hill. Every morning after that, the same "AWOLS" would arrive at the service club, would loll around reading in the foyer, waiting for the doors to open, at which point we would go to the coffee bar and get our free cup of Red Cross coffee and two sinkers then disperse, some to the pool tables, some to ping–pong, others to the club's library. For all its faults, Pickett had one great feature: an excellent service club library. The Red Cross ladies were always cheerful and pleasant and liked to chat. Only the librarian, a civilian volunteer, seemed suspicious of my regular appearance and asked me one day how it was that I spent so much time in the service club, didn't I have some duty, and wasn't I supposed to be in training classes. I answered, "No, ma'am," and left it at that. But when I told her she had one of the finest fiction collections I had seen, she thanked me and never asked another question, except about my choices of books: George Meredith, Henry James, George Gissing, Aldous Huxley. I had started with *The Good Soldier* by Ford Maddox Ford, partly because of the title, I suppose, but when I found it was not about soldiering, I turned it back in and checked out Huxley's *Antic Hay*. I had read about Huxley somewhere and had heard of his *Brave New World*, which I did read and liked. But it was Meredith's *The Ordeal of Richard Feverel* that really enthralled me. First, the title was intriguing, specifically the word "ordeal," which I thought portended a struggle. But, in the end, it was Meredith's amazing prose that hooked me. I had heard of Meredith. One of the poetry anthologies I came across in Germany had a selection of Meredith's sixteen-line "sonnets" from *Modern Love*, which I found dour but readable. I had read enough in the last year to appreciate the bitterness and heavy irony. It was Meredith's romantic poetic prose that set him apart from the others, I thought. His plot, a combining of comedy and tragedy, seemed to cancel out a lush sentimentality of a love story that his prose style suggested—at first--and seemed to be the antithesis of what I thought romanticism was all about. I read *Feverel* slowly, savoring the poetic passages, so slowly in fact that had not finished it when we got our orders to ship out, so I took it with me and planed to give it up at the next army library I found.

On the day our orders came down, three of us were headed for the service club, when we were stopped by a second lieutenant fresh from OCS. As we passed the company orderly room on our way "over the hill" he stepped out and called to us:

"Shipping orders are coming down from post headquarters in a few minutes. You might want to be there when they call your names," he said as sternly as he could. He looked even younger than I and, apparently, wanted to sound as military as he could. Then he added, "I think we'll all be shipping out this evening, so you better get ready."

Get ready? My duffel bag was always packed and ready.

A little while later, when the same lieutenant read off the names of the men who would be shipping out and announced our destination was Fort Lawton, Washington, a low moan arose throughout the formation. Most of us, especially those of us who had re-upped in Germany or Italy, expected to return to the ETO and assumed, since Pickett was practically on the East Coast, that it was the logical repple depple for the ETO. We were wrong. We were even more disappointed when we learned that our final destination was to be Korea and not Japan. It wasn't that we *wanted* Japan especially but that no one seemed to know where or what Korea was. Some thought it was in the South Pacific, a few had a vague idea it was "near China," and only a few had even the foggiest idea what Korea had to do with the war. Not everyone had been as lucky as I was; I had Mrs. Hilliard for geography, and I remembered meeting Korean missionaries on Missionary Sunday at the First Methodist Church in Beaumont. In B Company, 406th Infantry, there would have been no question about Korea's whereabouts, but here, even our lieutenant was vague about where it was.

I had been looking forward to learning German and to applying for one of the college programs the army was offering occupation troops. So much for best-laid plans. What I knew about Korea was what I had learned years ago in Sunday school when Methodist missionaries from Korea visited classes and showed us their magic lantern slides and told us all about "the Land of the Morning Calm." They showed us pictures of life in villages and pictures of the quaint dress of the old men. I had read a little about Buddhism and Confucianism back then, but what I had read I hadn't understood until I read McGovern's book about Tibet or books like James Hilton's *Lost Horizon*. Even then, it seemed a contradiction of everything I understood. Pearl Buck wrote in detail about Chinese culture and Confucian philosophy, but that world was still far removed from the sort of things we studied in high school. The *Why We Fight* films we watched in basic had precious little information about Asia that wasn't slanted, and the films told us almost nothing about Korea.

That evening at a siding on Camp Pickett, we loaded on to really good sleeping cars designed for transporting troops, sleeping cars which were far more comfortable than the Pullman cars. Bunks were stacked three high and arranged in L-shaped units; the bottom two bunks became benches with backs during the day and two single bunks in the evening while the top bunk remained in place and made up for sleeping. Grabbing a top bunk, I heaved my pack up and climbed in after it. The cars, triumphs of design and function, held twice the number that Pullman cars did, and from my top bunk, I could read undisturbed or gaze out through the small clerestory window. The year's experience had taught me to grab a top bunk and to avoid the easier, noisier, and more traffic-plagued lower bunks.

After breakfast the next morning, I reached into my pack, found Meredith, and settled back to read when the GI in the upper bunk that made the L connecting mine remarked, "So far all you've done this trip is read and stare out the window. What's that you're reading now?"

"There's nothing better to do," I told him, showing him the novel. "I'm a poor poker player, and besides I'm too poor to play."

He asked with just the slightest sarcasm if I were a "college boy or something." I told him about my year at UT and the semester at A&M and ASTRP.

He laughed and said, "I was in the Asstrap too. That's what we called it at Penn State, and I had a semester at Muhlenberg before that."

I laughed and asked him why he *wasn't* reading. We talked about college and agreed we wished we were back and then talked about what we'd do after the army and what we would study. He said he would probably, like his father, go on to law school, and I said I had no idea what I would do, but I doubted that I would continue in premed.

"You read so much, maybe you should be an English major," he said. Then he told me how much he liked English when he was in high school.

I told him my sister was finishing her BA in English at UT and that she wrote about not wanting to teach, although she had thought about it. If I ever taught, it would have to be in college, I told him. When he asked me why I had changed my mind about going to medical school, I told him I wasn't the one who changed his mind, "They changed it for me. They called my bluff." It was getting easier to admit it every day.

"What's that patch on your shoulder?" he asked.

"The One-O-Deuce, my outfit in Germany, one of those ASTP divisions." I liked boasting about the 102nd Division. "There were more college men in my platoon than probably any outfit in the army, several from Penn State, and schools like Harvard, Johns Hopkins, and Cornell too. It was an education just being in that outfit."

"God! You were in Germany? Did you see any combat?" he asked.

I told him I was too late and explained why I had re-upped. "I was a bit jealous when I went back to the Lambda Chi house before Christmas and saw friends already out and enrolled, but I don't feel that way now. I'm actually looking forward to Korea for some reason."

Prutzman came from a well-to-do family outside Allentown, Pennsylvania, not far from Muhlenberg where his father also had attended. Prutzman would be in the same casual company until we reached Seoul..

Fort Lawton, Washington, like Fort Meade, was a replacement depot and nothing else. But there were huge differences, the major one being Meade's dilapidated tarpaper barracks used by the replacements in transit. No one was ever there long enough for the army to concern itself with the quality of accommodations. We had nothing to do there after the initial formations and the announcement of our departure time. During the war, none of this information was ever given out, but now they told us everything. Right off, Prutz and I went to the post library so I could return the novel I had borrowed at Pickett. First thing, the assistant librarian began scolding me for not turning it in at Camp Pickett, even as I was explaining that we had shipped out before I could get to the post library. All the while Prutzman was laughing at me for bothering to even talk to the woman.

Down at the other end of the desk was another altercation between another librarian and, of all people, Dave Brown, an Asstraper from A&M. Brown, the brightest man and the youngest in our unit, was one of the few men, everyone agreed, who could out-bullshit Gilliland. Now, there he was, rattling away at the end of the counter. I think we saw each other at the same time and instantly broke off our discussions about books due and overdue. I hurried down the counter to meet him, and he ran to greet me, shouting, "Gilliland! Goddam! Gilliland! You sonofabitch! Guess who's here! Guess!" all in one breath and so loud both librarians went into shock.

"Here at Lawton?" I asked, shaking hands, and without stopping to think, I shouted, "Carlos Lovejoy, the Russian!"

"Right! He's here, and he's a second john in charge of a company shipping out tomorrow," He replied in the same loud tones he had always used at A&M. Carlos Lovejoy, truly an original, one-of- a-kind. Of all the crew in Duncan Hall, was the one person I would most have wanted to see. Prutzman looked on in surprise and dismay as we shook hands and ranted. I introduced them then found a place where we wouldn't disturb others in the library.

Brown said Carlos was CO of a company shipping out for Korea on the same ship as we.

"You *are* headed for Korea, aren't you?" he asked. "Don't call him 'Russian' when you see him. He told me the army's not amused by his nickname."

Brown exuded enthusiasm, as he always had, but now even more so, the idea of our sailing for Korea on the same orders seeming to overwhelm him. To me, our meeting was just another Dahlquist event I was betting accustomed. Eccentric, bright, witty, and probably the least GI soldier in the army, he would, I predicted, drive some CO into a Section 8 discharge before he rotated home. I wished we would end in the same outfit. It was hard to imagine Brown going through IRTC. Brown had the intelligence for much better things.

I saw Dave the next day just as he was coming aboard the USS *Gen. LeRoy Eltinge*. As he passed on his way to his sleeping bay somewhere in the bowels of the ship, he told me Lovejoy followed in the next company and that he wanted to meet me. So I waited to one side as the troops came aboard, and when Carlos arrived at the top of the gangway, I waved but didn't call him "Russian," though I was tempted. He looked every inch an officer, complete with his shining brass bars, natty trench coat, an officer's musette bag and clipboard. I envied him the officer's stateroom and officer's mess but not his job. He said something to the MP at the gangway and came over to where I was standing.

Instead of shouting Lovejoy, I called out, correct and formal, "Lieutenant Lovejoy, *sir*. A moment, please, *sir*!"

"Goddam, Gilliland!" he said, stepping over to where I was standing and shaking hands with me. He turned to Sergeant Clipboard and told him to hold the line coming up the gangway.

He began, "Brown told me you were shipping out with us. Quick, where's your deck, and what company are you in? I'll get in touch as soon as I'm free."

I handed him a slip of paper with my deck and bay and the number of my company. It was good meeting him. I still couldn't get over how easily I met friends I'd made earlier in the army. How could it happen so often?

We were at the bottom of the *Eltinge* in a stuffy, cramped hold, but then so was everyone who wasn't an officer. The *USS LeRoy Eltinge* wasn't so bad as troopships go, not nearly as comfortable as the HMS *Louis Pasteur*, but better designed as a troopship than the ship from Le Havre to the States. Just as I'd done on the American Fruit Company ship out of Le Havre, I volunteered for permanent KP, and that was a mistake. Permanent KP on the army transport had worked well for everyone but not so on the *Eltinge*. Two days out of Seattle, two days free of those corkscrew currents of San Juan de Fuca, nearly everyone in the racks around me down on D deck had adjusted to the calmer, more regular swells of a peaceful Pacific.

Twice, once after morning chow and once after evening chow, the ship's loudspeakers broadcasted loud and clear: "Now hear this! Now hear this! The following men lay down to the master-at-arms shack . . .." The voice, for two days straight now, had read off the same six names, the second name, loud and clear, being "Gilliland, Joe D.."

"Three racks down a voice shouted, "That's you, Gill, that's your name!"

Then a another voice," They gotcha, man. They gonna court-martial your ass for desertion. You'll be walking that fucking plank before we ever sight land."

I looked over at Prutzman who was grinning bizarrely. I continued reading. Fact was I had indeed deserted my post two days earlier, right when the USS *Gen. LeRoy Eltinge* was literally screwing the hell out of our guts. Easily, three quarters of the men on the ship were retching everything they'd eaten that day and the day before.

"He's right, Gill." Prutzman added, "They're 'going to court-martial your ass,'" his tone a perfect impression of the voice from below. "You volunteered, man, and now you're a deserter, you and those other five guys."

I replied, "They've got to find me first. I'm not ever going back on that stupid-ass KP. I un-volunteered two days ago."

I'd thought it through. If they had wanted my skinny ass, they'd have found me. "Besides, who's going to court-martial a vital replacement?" I said.

Prutzman was right though. I had volunteered for permanent KP, again, just like the time sailing home from Le Havre last November; that KP duty allowed me to eat when and how often I felt like eating. Yeah, back in November, on the way home from the ETO I served well, willingly acting as an angel of mercy—I'd served not only the mess sergeant but all the sick GIs on my deck—bringing them bread and fruit, biscuits and gravy, and anything they could hold down. Hell, once a day, I worked in the galley's supply room and moved canned goods and loaves of fresh bread forward. And with my KP pass, I took meals whenever I felt like it, along with the other KP volunteers. Food was great too. So, I thought, why not do it again on the *Eltinge*?

That was then. The *Eltinge*, was entirely different. No supply room detail for army KPs. Instead, a fat-assed chief petty officer handed us steam lines and pointed to the steel tables where GIs stacked used trays, and then he pointed to the garbage cans below the tables.

"Hose down the tables, keep 'em clean, then swab the deck in your area. When the cans get full, put a new one in line and don't let no garbage pile up. I don't wanna see no garbage pilin' up on them tables. The steam'll do it all. Got it?"

God, I cleaned up garbage and vomit that whole damn shift. It sounded so simple before we cast off, before that first meal, before that corkscrew current of San Juan de Fuca—Fuca! You could say that again! When we headed out of Puget Sound, the corkscrewing began. No simple pitching up and down, no simple rolling from side to side, only a slow combination that churned and ground away in the guts. Hell, after those two trips across the Atlantic, I'd thought I was immune to seasickness. Not so!

That first meal, I scraped, swabbed, and steamed my station and added my own serving of navy beans, roast beef, and canned peaches—involuntarily—to the can below the hole in my refuse table; it was my first time for me ever to have any seasickness. When my shift ended and I'd steamed the steel table and swabbed the deck, along comes this one guy staggering with the ship's pitching and screwing. I waited for him to knock off the remains from his tray and watched him sway with the ship's motion, wobble and waver over the shining steel, then puke it all back up, not in the can as others had done but all over my polished table and my spotless floor.

He turned and smiled a greenish shit grin. "Sorry, Mac," he whined, "can't help it." Then he slithered off, slipping and sliding in his own puke.

"OK, soldier, hose it down and clean it up!" the petty officer shouted.

I did as he said, then turned off the hose, coiled it, and left—never to return. I had been in the army a month over a year, and now I had, ignominiously, if not treacherously, deserted my post "under fire," so to speak. After that, I sneaked into chow lines, always mixed with other companies, always behind and never ahead of my schedule mess call, figuring that someone in charge might be checking IDs for an AWOL KP. But no one checked.

The master-at-arms, who or whatever that was, was requesting interviews with all five or six of us "deserters," all puke steamers, I assumed. Prutzman would laugh every time the loudspeakers horned in and requested my presence at the shack. I actually enjoyed hearing the navy's jargon blare out: "now hear this," "lay down," "master-at-arms shack," so quaintly historical it was almost literary. Imagine a "shack" on a modern troopship.

"They'll court-martial your GI ass, Gilliland," Prutzman grinned.

"No sweat, Prutz, no sweat!" I barked back. "After they hear how that son of a bitch puked his guts on my table, no jury would ever convict me. Besides, I'll tell them I'm a regular army volunteer, a veteran of the ETO *and* an Asstrapper! No, I'm waiting here for one of those giant marine SPs to come for me."

Prutz laughed. "Go back to your book. Don't worry, we'll hide you."

I reopened the heavy volume I'd found in the ship's library and began to read. Like Prutzman, I'd grabbed the top rack in a tier of five, right under a lamp that gave me plenty of light. The shaded and dark lower racks made reading impossible. Besides, lower racks got more than their share of puke from above. Prutz and I'd grabbed the top bunks on the troop train from Camp Pickett, mainly to be out of traffic, and we'd done the same here, thrown up our packs and climbing into the canvas racks while others elbowed and fought for the lower racks that were easier to reach. I had discovered on the Le Havre to Manhattan trip the real advantage of the upper racks was freedom from the spewing of half-digested meals, as well as freedom from traffic. True, the fetid air redolent of all the pukes and farts and the stale odor of the unwashed would rise, but it would also drift away with the occasional rush of air from overhead vents.

The book I balanced on my chest, *A Treasury of Satire*, more than compensated for the foul air and crowding. Many of the names in the table of contents were of writers I'd heard of before like Chaucer, Rabelais, Shakespeare, Swift, Fielding, Twain, and Thurber, from the earliest times right up to the twentieth century. Although I'd heard or seen the names, most of them I'd never actually read. That second morning after the fateful chow, I followed the arrows to the "Troop Library," and there it was, a small room just below the main deck packed with books of all kinds, carefully arranged by genre and alphabetically by author. After browsing the shelves, I found it: *A Treasury of Satire*. I had a pretty good idea what satire was, knew that it was a kind of humor that aimed to ridicule the pompous or sacred, but it had not been a big part of my English class with Helen James. The introduction explained why satire was important and not always funny in the usual sense and that intrigued me.

No mistake, *A Treasury of Satire* was some kind of textbook. I flipped to the piece by Rabelais, remembering what Bob Varner told me about this giant Rabelaisian character, Gargantua, a giant boy, not the famous Ringling Brothers gorilla. Here it was: "Gargantua's answer to Grangousier's question about what the giant young man used to wipe his bum after moving his bowels." Wow! People actually *studied* this crap (no pun)?

Back up on my rack, I began reading in earnest, and all I could think of aside from the sheer absurdity of the whole thing was the question, do people really get college credit for this? As I read, I began chuckling, softly then louder, and then guffawing, finally roaring: "The neck of a goose!" Laughing, I went back, and reread the passage again: *"But to conclude, I say and maintain, that of all the torcheculs* [a new word] *arsewisps, bumfodders, tail-napkins, bunghole-cleansers,* and *wipe-breeches, there is none in the world comparable to the neck of a goose that is well-downed . . .,"* and there, in print, all those new words for toilet paper.

Prutzman shouted from his rack, "What's so damn funny about the neck of a goose?"

I asked him if he had ever heard of *Gargantua and Pantagruel.*

A voice bellowed from below, "Sure, that giant gorilla in the circus, but I never heard of *Pant-whatsit.*"

I didn't realize anyone was listening. The low hum and vibration of the engines, I thought, damped the sounds of voices that deep in the ship. Then the same voice from below came again, "If it's so funny, read it aloud, Gilliland. We wanna laugh too."

"Yeah, there's nothin' to laugh about down here, except your farts!"

"You heard 'em, Joe," Prutz said. "Read!"

Why not? So I began from the beginning and explained how Gargantua, the giant boy, not the famous gorilla, came about and about his teacher Pantagruel and his noble father Grangousier who asked his son about his personal hygiene and about the object he found most comfortable as an ass-wipe or "torchecul" or whatever.

"Strange question for a father to ask," came a voice from below.

I explained, this was written back in the Middle Ages, probably, but not much different than here in the *bowels* of the *USS Gen. LeRoy Eltinge,* where the main topics of conversation, next to poontang, were puking, shitting, and farting.

"What?" another roared as I explained. "This is about wiping your ass?"

I read on. The list of items Gargantua used and found wanting included the most discomfiting items one could imagine. From below and from ranks of racks further down the aisle, loud groans and laughter accompanied my reading. Before I reached the end, the number of listeners had grown many fold. When the Rabelaisian list reached the end and Gargantua declared his favorite bum wiper to be "the neck of a goose," all the troops groaned and laughed. One lower down objected loudly and seriously that only a twisted mind would even want to print such garbage. Prutzman rolled his eyes, grinned, and lay back, shaking his head and chuckling.

The next night after second chow, I read more, and this time I had to stop reading and explain what satire was, explain why writers were "always saying one thing and meaning something else." I was mainly repeating what I'd read in the book's introduction, often explaining it to myself for the first time as well as to the listeners below and down the aisle. It was interesting that none or only one or two would complain about the readings or my explanations. We had never really talked about satire, irony, or humor in high school English classes, and Dr. James in freshman comp passed over it all pretty swiftly (no pun). In fact, what I knew about satire was concerned with what I knew of Swift and Twain and perhaps the little Thurber I had picked up on the mall before the Tower.

At A&M one night, Carlos Lovejoy had regaled us all in his dorm room with Chaucer's "The Miller's Tale," telling how his high school English teacher had assigned them the tale, along with the "Pardoner's Tale," which was in their text. His teacher, even though it was senior English class, was almost fired for reading "The Miller's Tale" aloud in class, though he read it in the original Middle English. Lovejoy could hardly stop laughing when he told how much better so-called naughty bits sounded in Middle English than in modern English.

The Treasury of Satire had only "The Nun's Priest's Tale," by comparison pretty sanitary entertainment that hardly bore reading to my scatalogically-obsessed audience down there on D deck. To my surprise, I found the *Canterbury Tales* in modern English and Middle English in the ship's library and checked it out and began reading it several nights later. It was a revelation to me, as well as to them, the richness of the descriptions, the characterizations of the pilgrims, and the sense of timing as near perfection as was Jack Benny's. I wondered why we had not read Chaucer in high school. Carlos told us how his teacher would stop after a particularly bawdy passage and repeat the lines in Middle English. It was always funnier in Middle English than modern English, especially that passage describing how Nicholas breaks wind in the face of Absalom, the monk. It was too rich to pass up. Giving the modern English between Chaucer's English so I was able to prepare them for the punch, I read,

> *And therewith spak this clerk, this Absolon,*
> And then spoke this clerk Absalom
> *"Spek sweete bryd, I noot nat where thou art."*
> "Speak sweet bird, I know not where thou art,"
> *This Nicolas anon let flee a fart,*
> *As great as it had been a thunder-dent . . .*

The last two lines needed no translation, for a roar arose without it, several in fact admitting they understood entirely what had happened, echoing the words "let flee a fart" and "thunder-dent" again and again.

It was, for that evening below decks, my *pièce de résistance*, and it worked. Prutzman rocked, they all rocked, and even the voice of the moralist from the bottom rack agreed that Chaucer's English was funnier, though he insisted, "But shit! Nobody never read nothing like that in my high school English class," to which another added, "If they had, I might a stayed in school."

Absalom's smiting Nicolas's ass with the hot poker and Nicholas's screaming for water and, finally, the cuckolded carpenter's fall from the roof exceeded any comedy we could recall on radio or recall ever having seen in the movies or at the Gayety burlesque in Baltimore.

By the third night, the readings had become "required readings." Someone would shout, "What's for tonight, Gilliland?" And I would start reading from the treasury. Usually, I chose a selection at random from the table of contents, though some of the satire wasn't all that funny, not by the measure of my listeners' taste or interests, or of mine either for that matter. Everyone had heard of *Gulliver's Travels*, the Lilliputian episodes, but none had heard of the later darker voyages, and at first, the tales from Laputa and from travels among the Struldbrugs earned nothing but silence, so I'd skip ahead. Once in a while, I was unable to explain satisfactorily what Swift was really getting at, even though I'd read the editorial comments. Earlier, I had read about Swift's darkest episode among the Houyhnhnms and the Yahoos, so when I gave a mini-lecture about satire's darkness, my listeners' interest deepened when they caught a description of a type we all recognized, the Yahoo.

One bellowed, much in the style of a Yahoo, "What the shit is that all about?"

Another shouted, "Shut up and let him read!"

Reading "Voyage to the Houyhnhnms" earlier to myself, I became quite depressed (as I still do to this day) and thought it not funny at all, and later, when I ended with my reading to the listeners that shadowy paragraph describing Gulliver's "reconcilement to the *Yahoo*-kind," a voice, subdued and soft, barely audible, spoke, "Tain't funny, Magee. That's too true to be funny." I looked over at Prutzman who raised his eyebrows in agreement and nodded. *Someone,* I thought, as I felt Prutzman also thought, *is really, truly getting the point.* I never knew who spoke those words from his own lower depths. It was the first time, I was sure, he'd even uttered a sound. Thinking back now, I wonder what he might have said had I read "A Modest Proposal." A few others chimed in and agreed there was less need for laughter.

"Right," I added, "Swift didn't think it was funny either. He hated cruel and stupid people, who for him meant most people, I guess. You ought to read all of *Gulliver's Travels*."

Then from Prutzman came, "It really isn't a children's book, you know."

Silence, then "oh." That was all, just "oh."

Another blanket of heavy irony, living satire I should say, assailed our ears during our entire passage from Seattle to Incheon, Korea. Twice every day the announcement on the PA system would blare, ordering five men "to lay down to the master-at-arms shack." The same five names. As far as I could tell, no one was running down or "laying down" or lying down or standing down to or at or before the master-at-arms shack. I never even bothered to find out where the so-called shack was. Then one day, when I returned from the head, Prutzman told me that a tall second lieutenant was looking for me.

"He left his name, Gill. Here, I wrote it down, 'Lovejoy, Lieutenant Lovejoy.'" He handed me a slip of paper. "Guess they finally caught up with the KP deserter. He probably saw the wanted poster."

"I expected him to show up," I said. "Really, it's the same Lovejoy who told us about 'The Miller's Tale' back in ASTP."

Prutzman shouted, "You're shittin' me!"

"I couldn't shit you, Prutz, if I tried, you're—"

"I know, I'm too big a turd," he came back.

I reminded him of Brown whom we'd met at the Lawton Library and reminded him Brown had told us Lovejoy was aboard.

Lovejoy's note asked me to meet him "topside by the ladder to the aft portside gun pit" and gave a time after evening chow. When I arrived, he was there, right on time. I popped a salute, and he did so back. We shook hands then climbed the ladder and hunkered down out of the wind. The gun pits were empty now. The Oerlikon stanchions, identical to the ones on the *HMS Pasteur*, were all that remained of the ship's armament.

As we stepped down into the gun emplacement, Carlos sighed, "This is great!" He looked over the top of the gun pit, at the huge expanse of the gray, lead colored Pacific then leaned back against the steel parapet.

"Man! Meeting you and Brown--this ship--the water—god, it's great!" He settled back, smiling. He looked like a happy man. Then he continued, "Brown told me you'd re-upped for another year. Why, for god's sake?"

I explained how I was low man in points back in the One-O-Deuce, low man on everyone's totem pole, how all my friends in the division were rotating home, and then I admitted, probably out loud for the first time, "I guess I wasn't ready to get out." I laughed. "Don't say I found a home in the army. Mainly, I guess, I had no idea what I'd study when I got back to UT in Austin. I know now I'm no premed, certainly not a chemistry major anymore, so . . . who knows what? Who knows? I had no idea when my points would come up. Hell, maybe . . . a *home* in the army after all?"

He laughed. "Still reading?" I nodded. Then he said, "You know, you really got me reading that summer, almost made me flunk out after you started me on Dos Passos. I read *Three Soldiers* and *Manhattan Transfer*. You were right about *U.S.A.*, and I can see why the regents at UT wanted to ban the book. It's a great book. I'd never read anything like it," he paused, dug deeper. "All great books are dangerous, aren't they?"

As soon as I'd heard about the student uprising at the university in Austin that fall, I had read all of *U.S.A.* but hadn't read anything else by Dos Passos. I told him about the Armed Services Editions, about Thomas Wolfe, Whitman, about the reams of poetry I'd read, about this Harvard guy who introduced me to T. S. Eliot. Then I told him how my sister had sent me Tacitus and that I'd read the *Germanicus* while I was *in* Germany and told him about the 102nd Division was made up largely of college men, ASTP men who read voraciously and talked about everything.

"Not much like basic training. The guys in the 102 were in the original ASTP and were all transferred to the infantry. They were to be replacements for the D-Day casualties, I guess. I met guys there I'd met when they were stationed at Camp Swift near Austin. Can you believe it? I mean, same college men who stayed at the frat house in Austin." And I told him about Dahlquist.

We sat there quietly for a while, looking over the parapet at the lead gray water and the matching sky.

"After Dos Passos," he said, "I discovered James T. Farrell's *Studs Lonigan*. God, what a book!" He paused. "They don't approve of us liberals in OCS, you know. I had to drop the nickname 'Russian' when an officer asked if I was a commie."

There was a long silence. He rose over the steel parapet, looked off across the ocean, sat back down. "Water looks like molten lead," he said. He looked back. Our eyes met.

"Good simile," I said.

He was silent for a moment then said, "You made a difference, Gilliland, you know." He looked back over the parapet, sat down again. "I thank you all the time." That touched me deeply, mostly because Russian had always impressed me. "I thought a lot about our talks about books and things." He paused, embarrassed. "After you left the program we missed you at those bull sessions, you know."

His confession had embarrassed him. It would have me as well, I thought, but I was too pleased and proud. No one had ever really spoken to me like that, not that I could recall. In high school, only Reiss and I ever talked books and music seriously, music mostly.

"I missed them too," I said. "There were some bright guys there, some real *stupidos* too," I said. "It was all fun. A&M was good, even after a year at the university in Austin it felt good. That freshman reading room was great. It was better than Baylor! God, we could have been sent to Baylor!"

We both laughed and sang the old refrain,

> "Don't send my son to SMU,"
> The dying mother said.
> "Don't send my son to Baylor U
> I'd rather see him dead,
> But send my son to Texas U,
> It's better than Cornell.
> Before I'd send him to A&M,
> I'd send him first to hell!"

I said, "Classes at A&M, especially Eckfeldt's English comp, were damn well taught. You know I hated English in high school, not the subject, just the teachers. They didn't know diddly poop about how to teach. They used to 'chap my bongy,' as Hayes would say." I stopped, and then said, "I saw him at Wolters once, dumb as a Louisiana cracker, even if he was from New Orleans and rich as hell. No shit, best classes I had at UT and at A&M, too were English classes. Especially Eckfeldt's, those classes made me want to read everything, and I almost did in the One-O-Deuce. That's all we did, read and pull occasional guard duty. Nearest I came to war was guarding a pair of SS prisoners." I saw him look at his watch. "What are your plans after the duration?" I asked.

"Architecture, my plan all along. Now the GI Bill will make it easy. Are you going back to Austin?"

"Yep, but I've thought about smaller schools. I have a friend down below, Prutzman, went to Muhlenberg College in Pennsylvania, one of those small liberal arts colleges the East is full of. Sounds like the kind of school I'd like. UT is going to be huge. But I don't really know. I'd like to study philosophy or psychology or just anything as long as I can stay in school."

I told him about my sister still at UT, how she would send me books, a logic text, Tacitus, writings of Bertrand Russell. "I still carry Durant's *Story of Philosophy* everywhere. But just the idea of being at the U is all I really care about now. I think Korea will be interesting. Another entirely different culture. I'm glad it's not Japan."

"Why not Japan? Why wouldn't you want to go there?"

"We bombed the shit out of it. I saw Nuremberg, Munich, Münster, and Cologne—nothing but shell holes and broken rubble. Talk about destruction! Korea wasn't in the war. I had an anthropology course at UT, read a lot of Ruth Benedict, *Patterns of Culture*. I'd like to see other cultures, maybe learn the language. Who knows?"

He rose, straightened his snappy new trench coat. "I better get back. They don't approve of officers fraternizing with enlisted types, especially KP deserters."

"Yeah?" I asked.

"Don't worry, I won't tell. It'd look bad on my fitness report."

We shook hands warmly.

"Fraternizing meant something entirely different in the ETO," I replied, sounding only a little like a real veteran, "involved Fräuleins, not officers."

We both laughed. "Russian," I whispered, "we're all proud of you."

That was the last time we spoke. Three years later in Austin, I did spot him with classmates outside the Architecture Building, and we chatted, recalled our meeting on the *Eltinge* but seemed uninterested in renewing the old acquaintance, and I understood—life goes on. But that meeting high up in the gun pit had meant a lot, especially his recalling the bull sessions and the books. Those ties bonded well.

Below decks, the nightly readings continued. New listeners joined us, and no one, as far as I could tell, drifted off. The sessions never lasted long, less time than it would take to teach a class: fifty minutes? Prutzman teased me about it, claiming I was hooked, that I was enjoying it more than they were and wondered if I ought to be on the radio. My hat size grew.

That is until he said it, "Yeah, Gill, you ought to be on the stage. There's one leavin' in five minutes."

The last reading before landing wasn't a funny one and brought about the most discussion of all, mainly because it wasn't funny. How did it classify as satire, someone asked, and one who had caught the seriousness of the passage insisted it was the best of the lot, better even than the pieces from Thurber's *Sex ex Machina*. I agreed. The passage was from *Huckleberry Finn*, where Huck fights the demons of his conscience and chooses to go to hell rather than surrender Jim. Is it a win or a loss? Who knows? All the ambiguity arrested me as much as it did the others. I read *Huckleberry Finn* in high school and enjoyed it, but we didn't discuss it much. We missed the depth and breadth of it. We thought Huck's life was more joy than pain and had not seen, as anyone who knew how to really read would have known, that there were light-years of differences between Tom and Huck. As often happens, my own understanding grew by what it fed on, the reading and the talking.

"Hell, Gilliland, it's just a story. No kid like Huck would damn his self for a nigger," someone said.

"Maybe there *is* no kid like him, and that's the point." I tried to explain. "He's talking about justice on the river, friendship, loyalty, and the injustice and the sin in slavery."

"He's right. Twain's right too," Prutzman remarked. During my reading, he hadn't said two words all during the crossing. Then *de profundis*, he muttered, "But shit. It's just a story" and was silent.

"Yeah, some story. Read us some more of those dirty Italian stories next," came the voice from below, along with laughter.

I dearly wanted to own it and was tempted, but *A Treasury of Satire* was too large and too heavy to pack away in my duffel bag. Desertion from KP duties, I thought, was crime enough for one passage, so I dropped my *Treasury* off in the return slot at the library.

Next morning, I awoke to a silent ship and realized at once we had arrived. The *Eltinge* was perfectly silent, "dead in the water," a sailor would say. I pulled on my pants and buttoned my shirt and buckled my combat boots then rushed topside to catch my first glimpse of Asia. As soon as I stepped through the hatchway onto the deck, I looked out at a perfectly still glasslike sea flooded with a brilliant light, but there was no land in sight. I quickly moved through the narrow passageway to the port side, and when I did, a blast of freezing air hit me square on, cutting right through my field jacket and wool shirt. But there it was: the coast of Korea and the port of Incheon not far away. I stood for a moment, contemplating the barren and blasted landscape with hardly any vegetation or sign of human habitation. What had I expected? More than this friendless and forbidding desolate landscape surely. For a few seconds longer I stood and gazed, Korea, Chosin, yeah, "frozen Chosin." Reminding myself that I had now crossed two oceans and was about to set foot on the Asian landmass, I thought, *Lord, who else did I know that had done the same?* I went below, dug out my long johns underwear and the heavy cumbersome overcoat, and told those around me to prepare for "frozen Chosin."

By the time our company was called to disembark—we were first on and now last off--every man had donned his long johns, heavy overcoat, wool knit caps, and gloves. Somehow we managed to balance duffel bags and make it down the long gangway to the floating dock, then on to a slowly bobbing landing craft for the long ride to the shore. The last off had the advantage of the shortest time standing around waiting for the roll call and the march to the shabby rail cars. Still, no one had mentioned the miscreant KPs or the mysterious master-at-arms shack. All day, I had waited, listening for my name or for a master-at-arms to appear and clap me in irons. Prutzman had moved on up the landing ramp, along with the others, avoiding the crowd of young Korean boys begging for cigarettes and chocolates. When I reached the familiar faces of our company and plopped down, as much out of the cold blast as I could manage, I reached into my coat pocket and pulled a paperback copy of a collection of *New Yorker* pieces by E. B. White, a little Armed Services Edition that I'd lugged all the way from Wunsiedel, Germany.

"More satire, Gill?" someone asked.

"Something to pass the time," I said. "Hey, listen up. Here's a bit of living satire. I've been called a sonofabitch by a little kid in England, by one in France, and now Korea."

"Hell, Gilliland, you're well known!" someone replied.

"Really, in Liverpool, a little kid asked me for a cigarette. When I told him I didn't smoke, he called me a sonofabitch, same thing in Le Havre as we marched away to get on our 40&8s. Then just now, that kid down there on the ramp called me a *sun u ga ditch*. I guess that's Korean for sonofabitch."

"Hell, Gilliland, it proves one thing. They know a deserter when they see one."

Then it happened, and it was as satisfying and gratifying as it was unexpected. "Well, Professor," someone said, "I hope we get into the same outfit. I really enjoyed listenin' to them stories." It was that voice from below.

"Me too, professor," another said.

Professor? They were looking across and smiling, the same old stinking group of them, and Prutzman was too, smiling or smirking, I don't recall which, but it felt good.

Then a voiced called out, "Gilliland did someone say? Which one of you men is Gilliland?" It was a lieutenant with an armband but not an MP, thank God. Maybe this was the master-at-arms.

No one answered, but all faces pointed toward me.

"Fall out of over here, soldier. Come with me."

I rose, slipped my pack on, hefted the duffel bag, and followed the lieutenant and four others then waved at my audience, my . . . class.

"Don't worry, Gill," Prutzman called. "They have libraries in Leavenworth."

I waved back.

The important thing was I knew something I hadn't known when I boarded the USS *LeRoy Eltinge* two weeks earlier in Seattle, and it had nothing to do with KP, dereliction of duty, desertion, AWOL, or the master-at- fucking-arms shack. I felt it deep, felt it "along the blood," though I would not know what it really meant until years later. Years later, I would read Gorge Steiner's memoir, *Errata*, and here, he would say it for me, describing a similar moment among men he had talked to about a piece of great literature: "I knew, now, that I could invite others into meaning. . .," and from then on, from the depths of D deck, "the Sirens of teaching sang for me," and I would never harbor a doubt what I would do for the rest of my life. Whatever happened from that point on, I knew something important had happened. "I could invite others into meaning."

Our arrival in Korea was as inauspicious as possible. There was neither an army band nor a welcoming party, only the ubiquitous gaggle of children begging for candy or cigarettes. Our company was the last to come ashore. The others had waited on the wind-swept quay all day. For all of us, the only meal that day was a box of K rations—canned cheese, crackers, powdered Nescafé, one hard cookie, and two cigarettes—which, I guess, I should have shared and would have avoided being called a *sun a ga ditch*. Since there was no way to heat water, the Nescafé was useless. More demoralizing than lack of food was the waiting and the cold dry wind. When the troop train did arrive, we were shocked at the condition of the cars. The French forty-and-eight cars were Pullman coaches by comparison. Broken windows, missing floorboards, narrow wooden benches with straight backs designed for smaller Japanese and Korean passengers made the slow bone-chilling train ride into Seoul an ordeal. When we reached Seoul, we had to wait on a freezing, dimly lit platform for an hour while names were called and trucks assigned. The last called were names of six deserters. Being last, waiting longest was our only punishment.

I recognized no one in my truck or any of the trucks, Prutzman and all the men in my sleeping bay having been called shortly after we stepped off the trains. It was well past 2300 when my truck finally reached a huge field house with ranks of GI double bunks. Miraculously, the moment we entered the huge space, a loudspeaker ordered us to line up for a hot meal, our first of the day. How often had I been in such a place? In the last batch of names called on the platform, I found myself with another totally different set of men. I never saw Prutzman again or any of the men I had shipped with from Camp Pickett.

The next morning, before sunup, we five deserters loaded again into a truck and headed for our new assignments. It took us all day, from before sunup until after dark, in open two-and-a-half-ton trucks across icy mountains and through biting winds to reach the headquarters of First Battalion, Thirty-Second Infantry, Seventh Division in Samcheok on the coast. Since arriving in

Incheon, we had traversed the Korean peninsula and were now facing the Sea of Japan. In all that time and distance, no one spoke to us, except to call our names and point us where to go. Here, we had another hot meal, our second since landing. Afterward, a sergeant directed us to an ice-cold barracks, once a small warehouse, where we picked up heavy quilts and then were told to bed down on the concrete floor using one thick quilt for a mattress and one for a cover. The sergeant, feeling sympathy, apologized for the sleeping arrangements, explaining that his quarters weren't much better. Then for the first time since we arrived, someone spoke to us with the consoling news that we'd be on our way to our companies first thing in the morning where things would be better.

"I assure you, gentlemen, that the line companies are better housed than we are here at battalion," he said.

We were too tired to complain. The so-called quilts were Japanese-army-issued *futon* stuffed with lumps of kapok and were too short for even the shortest of us. I put on an extra pair of socks, rolled out the wool sleeping bag I'd stuffed in my pack then wrapped my feet in my GI overcoat, and pulled the Japanese *futon* up to my chin. The mattress was also Japanese issue and just as short as the *futon*, but we were so tired we fell right to sleep.

The sergeant returned just before sunup and ushered us to the chow line, telling us to stay together, that we'd be getting orders to move out at 0800. Hovering over us through chow more like a mother than a sergeant in charge, he assured us we'd be in our companies before noon. I believe he felt our disappointment, but knowing that nothing he could say or do would make it better, he kept his silence and joined us at the table as if to keep us company. I asked how long he had been there. " I been with the Seventh Division since Pearl Harbor," he said. "I'm a lifer, regular army." he said, and then asked me about the Ozark patch.

I told him how different his greeting was from the one I received as a replacement when I arrived at B Company in Engerda, Germany. He looked at me, smiled, and thanked me for my remarks and recalled how it was when replacements joined the division on Okinawa. The other men listened to us chatting but said nothing. I told him I arrived at B Company too late to see any combat, that I understood why the old-timers were reluctant to welcome new replacements.

"Well, I'll say this, you guys are sure as hell welcome here. Replacements mean some of us get rotated home."

It was the best breakfast we'd eaten since leaving Fort Lawton—plenty of eggs, steaming hot cereal, *and* pancakes—and it was served by friendly accommodating cooks, almost as if they were trying to atone for crimes committed against innocents. Their thoughtfulness was appreciated, but I had a sudden moment of fear that their solicitations were precursors of some evil to come or that we were being fattened for the kill. I had noticed in all my peregrinations through the army replacement system that the closer one got to an outfit, the more accommodating and less officious were the noncoms and officers. They actually seemed concerned for all the agony and pain we'd been through; these were men of the proud Seventh Division, proud of the First Battalion.

In his history of the European war after Normandy, *Citizen Soldiers*, Stephen Ambrose devotes a full chapter to the replacement system. Like Winston Churchill's famous description of democracy as the worse system of government, except all other systems, the system of the replacement depots was the worst possible system, except that it worked well enough to win the war. When the war was over and the need for reinforcements was no longer critical, but the replacement system was left intact. While new, raw infantrymen were in no danger of losing their lives on first arriving, they often found themselves in limbo. I had gone, as stoically as I could, through the initiation of non-acceptance, to be finally accepted and finally named; but I don't know how I would have felt had I gone through it while the war was going on.

Most movies made during and after the war omit that experience of displacement the replacement knows, largely because neither writers nor directors ever had such an experience. Replacement scenes lack drama, but in the movie *Battleground*, Marshal Thompson, who plays the part of a new replacement in the 101st Division, conveys the feeling of an outsider joining a closely knit group of combat veterans. It is told realistically and poignantly, expressing sentiment without sentimentality. Thompson's fellow replacement, played by Scotty Becket, and he arrive full of enthusiasm for their new outfit but are received with indifference and hostility, much as Wally Goldberg and I were treated those first days at Engerda in Germany. Thrust into a combat situation without a moment's orientation or even an introduction, Thompson's character is confused and disoriented but survives. The morning after the firefight, Thompson's character learns that his friend's platoon is on their flank, and when he finds the sergeant of the platoon next to them in the line, he asks for his friend, only to discover his friend was killed in firefight during the night. It comes as a shock to Thompson and to the audience, especially when the sergeant learns the name of his friend for the first time. I knew people who saw the film and criticized that bit when Thompson returns to his own platoon and tells Van Johnson his name as unrealistic and mawkish. The fear of anonymity echoes a fear of dying alone and unmourned. This small episode expresses that feeling of loneliness and alienation better than any film out of Hollywood. It seemed a minor touch, but it was real, but when I saw the movie—on Armistice Day 1949—I recalled every detail of the acceptance-rejection I'd felt when I joined second platoon company, B Company, at Engerda, and recalled how good it felt when PFC Givner pronounced my name when he told me I was to go with him out on a roadblock.

The younger the soldier, the stronger the need for this sense of identity; a shoulder patch establishes identity. Even when I was no longer on the rolls of B Company, 406th Infantry, 102nd Division, my Ozark patch announced I had a unit, my own band of brothers, somewhere. Those patches that identified a soldier as being a member of the ground forces, Eighth Service Command, the Transportation Corps, or some paper command encompassing service areas assigned no identity, or about as much "identity" as *Homo sapiens* assigns an individual. How I envied those men whose patches said that they were members of elite or special units no larger than a regiment. With the blue and gold Ozark patch, I had some identity, no matter where I was. Still, I felt I was nowhere until the weapons carrier delivered the four of us to C Company, Thirty-Second Infantry, Seventh Division in Mukho.

"Stay put, don't leave the truck." How many times had I heard that? We had arrived, and I had no reason to do other than what he said. The wind had stopped, and a winter sun warmed us, albeit weakly. Circling inland and south from Samcheok, we had come through a bleak and barren countryside in the grip of winter, but here on the coast, it was warmer now because the sun was out and the wind had stopped. The weapons carrier had stopped before a row of uniform, well-constructed houses. Across the street was a silent factory of some sort, with no smoke issuing from its stack. Behind the factory, not much higher than the stack, was a small hill with a row of larger houses along the crest. Several young boys wearing cut-down army fatigues "policed" the company street, picking up pieces of paper, cigarette butts, and other trash. They stopped what they were doing and stared at us. Our driver returned accompanied by the usual T-5 in well-pressed ODs, his pants bloused neatly over polished combat boots. He carried, the symbol of clerical authority, a clipboard, and waved to us cordially.

"Well, men," he said smiling, sans tones of command, "you're finally here. Bring your gear and follow me."

He stepped off in the direction of the buildings, asking where we were from and where we'd done our basic training, the same greeting I'd heard many times before. We shouldered our duffel bags and followed him into the building. Above the entrance was a sign that read "C Company, CP." Dropping our bags outside the entrance, we stood waiting in the foyer. A first lieutenant passed through and, before we had a chance to brace to attention, ordered us to be at ease and take seats on the benches lining one wall. Then a master sergeant came through the sliding main door and closed it behind him, told us the CO, who had just passed through, would talk to each of us before assigning us to our platoons. I was the only PFC; the other five were still buck privates, obviously fresh from basic training. I'd never seen any of them before we loaded onto the trucks in Seoul. It was the first time I could recall that I ever outranked anyone. The First Sgt. looked at me and the patch on my field jacket. "You'll have to remove that patch. What is your name, and what is that outfit?"

I told him it was the 102nd Division, an ETO outfit. He looked surprised and asked if they were sending replacements now all the way from Germany. I told him I had reenlisted for a year and had been reassigned to Korea. He shook his head as if he were unable to comprehend anyone reenlisting or being assigned to Korea or both.

"OK, Gilliland," he said, pronouncing my name on the first try, "you outrank these guys, you be first."

The interview was brief, mostly about my outfit in Germany. The lieutenant asked if I'd been in combat. I said I hadn't and explained I had joined my outfit just days after the war was over. Then he asked what I had done in my company in Germany.

"I was in the weapons platoon, LMG section, sir," I lied. It just came out without my thinking, but it turned out to be the right answer.

"Were you a gunner?" the sergeant asked.

"No, Sergeant. We didn't see our guns after the war ended. They stayed in the supply room with the armorer artificer. But I qualified on the LMG1917 in basic."

"Put him in the fourth platoon, Sergeant. Give him to Barker," he said. "You're dismissed, soldier. Tell the next man to come in."

My lie about having been in a weapons platoon had come to me in a flash. And it was a brilliant stroke. It meant I would be issued either an M1 carbine or a sidearm instead of an M1 or the heavier BAR. But more important than my weapon, my wandering had finally ended, which meant I had a little more than nine months of army life left. Those months would pass swiftly. I could endure anything for nine months; a year from now, I would be in class at UT. It was now the middle of February; since the day after New Year's, I had been on the move, my enlistment time eroding away in travel and idleness. I much preferred having a permanent address and some kind of work that would make the time pass more quickly.

As I was leaving the company CP, Staff Sergeant Barker, my section leader, met me and guided me to the fourth platoon's quarters. Barker, who wore a combat infantry badge, was medium height, stocky, young, very serious, and had been in the army only two months longer than I had. There were three kinds of men in the company: first, a few *very* old-timers who had been in Alaska, the Philippines, and Okinawa; second, those who had come over as replacements just as the war was winding down; and third, a group who had joined the division after September. Since the latter were all fresh from basic training, that put me into a separate category, an "old-timer" from the ETO without combat experience. As a nineteen-year-old old-timer, I was an anomaly.

As we walked to the fourth platoon, I remarked that the company was housed a lot better than I expected. Barker explained that they had taken over the houses of the Japanese who'd all been shipped back to Japan. "They operated the coal company and the port. As far as I know, there're no more Japanese in Mukho."

The fourth platoon had two small houses, a pair of duplexes, one house for the two light machine gun sections and one for the .60-mm. mortar sections. With the platoon two-thirds under strength, he said, there was plenty of room. An LMG section usually had two squads of men with six men in each squad. Each house in the duplex had a small kitchen and a toilet and two rooms or one long room once divided by sliding paper doors. The one large room had twelve cots, two of which were unoccupied.

Barker showed me my bunk and a place to stow my gear then introduced me to the men in the room. They all looked quite young. Barker was the only man in the section wearing the combat infantry badge, which meant the rest were replacements, who'd arrived late. When I had stowed my duffel bag and arranged my library on a shelf above my bunk, Barker asked Sgt. Quessenberry, my squad leader, to take me to the supply room to draw a weapon and the usual supplies. John Quessenberry, who was about my age, had joined the company just after the Battle of Okinawa and had been in the army a shorter time than I had.

As we headed for the supply room, he asked if I was a gunner. I told him no, that I hadn't fired a machine gun since I left the depot outside Thionville, France, and said that our guns had been stored in the company supply room. He admitted he hadn't fired one since basic training and that we weren't likely to take them out as long as we were in Korea.

"We really don't do anything here, except some close-order drill and calisthenics every morning and go on patrols in towns. When it gets warmer, 'they say,' we'll do some hikes along the coast."

Sitting on the supply room counter lay a shiny new helmet liner, a well-used carbine, two empty ammo clips, a web belt and clip holder, a first-aid pack, a canteen and cup with canvas holder. The supply sergeant said, "You get a carbine here. The CO don't want nobody carryin' a .45. You better get that patch off your shirts and sew these on."

He handed me a half dozen red and black hourglass patches of the Seventh Division. I told him I had a canteen and cover but no web belt and that I still had my mess kit. Next, he piled on the counter a thick army comforter and two GI blankets, a pillow, and a fart sack.

"This is sheer luxury," I said. "All the time I was in Germany, I didn't see a fart sack or, for that matter, a GI mattress to put it on."

When Quessenberry asked where I had gone through basic and how long ago it had been, I told him I had finished basic at Camp Wolters, Texas, the last of March a year ago. The supply sergeant said a sergeant in the second platoon named Hansen had done his basic at Wolters too, probably about the same time. I told him a Hansen had been in my platoon in basic. "He went to jump school at Fort Benning."

"Same man. Hansen went to Benning but dropped out the first week and got to Okinawa just in time for the last big push. He's a good man."

It was unbelievable. As we walked back to the platoon, I told Quessenberry about meeting Dahlquist when I got to my outfit in Germany and now the coincidence of meeting Hansen again. We talked about our arrivals overseas and what it felt like to be a replacement. "It's a lot easier this time than it was the first," I said.

Quessenberry said he'd arrived in Okinawa just as I had in Germany, only a few days after the Japanese defeat. While I had never heard the proverbial shot fired in anger, he had. Even after the cease-fire on Okinawa, there were pockets of resistors, he said, but he'd never been shot at nor had ever fired a shot.

When I asked what they did to keep busy, he admitted they didn't keep busy. When they first got to Korea in September, they had been stationed on the Thirty-Eighth Parallel, he said, but for some reason, just before Christmas, they had moved down to Mukho.

"We have better living quarters here than we had up on the border, and there's almost nothing to do here. There's hardly any KP, very little guard duty, a couple hours of close-order drill, and some calisthenics every morning, but that's about all. We never have inspections. There aren't any passes because there's nowhere to go. Kyong Song, or Seoul, is too far, and there's not much there, even if you get a pass. You can go into Mukho, where there are a couple of bars, but there aren't any girls. They keep 'em all locked up. The movies we get are all old, and the projector keeps breaking down. But other than that, we have a good time." He laughed.

All menial tasks, such as cleaning the squad room, making beds, polishing boots, and even washing and pressing our uniforms, were relegated to "house boys," the young boys I had seen policing the company street. He said they were kids, mostly thirteen and fourteen, from poor families, who had come begging for jobs when the company arrived in Mukho before Christmas and had quickly attached themselves, working for whatever food they could get from the leftovers "and packs of cigarettes the guys pitch in."

"We started taking up a collection and began paying them with cigarettes, which they sold on the black market. But now we all chip in and pay them in Korean money, no cigarettes, except those some guys give 'em. They are smart kids," he said. Because they had learned English so quickly, they were used as translators. The two, who worked for the LMG section, Sylvester and Kim, slept in the unused kitchen. He added, "I give Sylvester a package of cigarettes whenever I can.

The army had never officially sanctioned hiring the boys, but by the time I arrived, they had become a regular fixture, each platoon hiring at least two or three. Even KP was hired out to Koreans, their pay coming from monthly donations that the men were eager to give in the form of Korean currency acquired from the black market sale of cigarettes. It was all *sub rosa*. When inspectors or brass from regiment or division came down, the boys vanished, along with the KP staff. Hiring Koreans for these tasks was actually an act of charity, a form of GI public welfare that helped the local economy, though as most well-intentioned social programs, the "generosity" had its down side for the GIs as well as the Koreans.

We had no training program aside from the close-order drill and an hour or so of calisthenics each morning, and guard details were so light you could go weeks without being assigned to a patrol or a shift guarding the supply room or the CP. Quiz, which he preferred to Quessenberry, said he'd heard we would start doing some forced arches to get us into condition when the weather got warmer.

I was astonished when I first arrived to see how comfortable our quarters were. The squad rooms were large, airy, and warm, heated by the sun during the day and fuel oil drums during the coldest nights. All the houses in the compound faced south, and all had sliding glass doors enclosing small verandas separated from the main rooms by paper sliding doors which, when opened, flooded the sleeping area with sunlight. Quiz explained that these were typical Japanese houses, just like ones they had seen on Okinawa. The army had removed the straw tatami mats and had covered the raw lumber flooring with cheap linoleum and had closed down the pit toilet in each house, just as the medics had ordered done to the indoor privies in the Klingenbrünn school. There were central flush toilets and communal showers and a large Japanese-style bathhouse building in the center of the compound where the company kitchen was located. We could use the showers but not the bathhouse. The offices of the managers became command post and supply room, and a large meeting hall became our mess hall and kitchen, but no one ever used the mess hall, preferring to bring food back from the serving line to the squad rooms. The sergeant in Samcheok had not exaggerated; we were indeed well housed.

Down the hill from our fourth platoon quarters was a large shed-like building housing the company's rec room, which Barker and Quiz said no one ever used. It had two ping–pong tables and a well-worn pool table, along with cues "untrue" and, I supposed, "elliptical billiard balls." The large, drafty room served as the movie theater or chapel, but I recall seeing only two or three feature films all the time we were there and never a chaplain. Along one wall were shelves holding the company's "library," a five-by-ten-foot bookcase of Modern Library hardbacks, book club editions, and paperback reprints. Most of the hardback editions were water-damaged but readable, and the paperbacks were mostly Armed Services Editions. But I saw right off some good hardback selections, *Madame Bovary, Arrowsmith, Tess of the D'Urbervilles, Grapes of Wrath, Tobacco Road, A Tale of Two Cities, Henry Esmond, The Way of All Flesh*, along with a copy of *The Decameron* and short stories by Balzac, Maupassant, Poe, Hawthorne, Steinbeck, and even novels by Fielding and Sterne. However, most of the books were standard Westerns and detective novels with a number of historical novels by writers like Thomas Costain, Shellabarger, Anya Seton, Hervey Allen, Rafael Sabatini, H. Rider Haggard, and the du Mauriers. I had read some of these when they appeared in Armed Services Editions.

Quiz came down to the rec room with Credo Bisquerra, a late replacement, who preferred to be called "Bisket," and me and said we could take whatever we wanted so long as we returned it. "No one's ever used the room, except when a movie was in town, and that's pretty rare," he said.

"Do people read these books?" I asked. "Where did they come from? I'm amazed! It looks like the entire Modern Library list is here."

Bisket said, "No one ever reads in this outfit. You know about books, are you a college man or something?"

I detected that same note of disapproval in his voice that I had heard before. I pulled a book off the shelf and held it out. "See, Modern Library, standard inexpensive classic, great books, major titles. Well, almost everybody in my old outfit in Germany read something. Those Armed Services Editions boxes are full of all kinds of books. Here's something for everybody, not only college men. How do people pass the time?"

"You didn't answer my question. Are you a college man?" he asked again, his tone even more disapproving, so I ignored it.

When I told them that *Bovary* was about seduction and infidelity, that *Tess* was about a woman who's seduced, has an illegitimate child, then murders her seducer, they began to show an interest. Finally, he asked how I knew so much about the books. I told him I really didn't *know* that much about books, not as much as I wanted to, but I liked to read and said that the only thing I had done since I left basic training was read. When he asked if I had been in ASTP, I said I had one term with ASTRP at A&M. He had taken the exam to get in the program too, but it had already shut down when he was drafted. We talked about college for a while and what we planned to do after the army.

Finally, I said, "They called us 'college boys,' not men."

Bisket said he had been the top of his class in high school and had been the cadet commandant in high school ROTC. He had wanted to make a career in the army, but being a Filipino, he felt he'd have no chance for a commission. The best chance for a commission, he thought, was through a college ROTC program. I told him I had never had any experience with racial prejudice toward Asian Americans, being from Texas and the South.

He laughed. "Yeah, you Texans have our hands full discriminating against Mexicans and Negroes."

I admitted it was pretty bad and wanted to say I had no prejudice but knew it would sound lame and was probably not true. Dr. McAllister had once remarked that too often, the person who has to deny he has any prejudice is either lying or deceiving himself. Like the queen in *Hamlet*, he "protests too much." I asked him if he had to face a lot where he lived. He said he did, not physically; there were no race riots like the ones against Pachucos and Latinos in Southern California or against Negroes in East Texas.

"Filipinos are heroes now, so they allowed me to be cadet commandant. The war isn't all bad. But no one would want me to marry his sister." His cynicism was thick and real. Fact was, Credo Bisquerra was one smart Filipino.

It was the first time I had ever had a frank and open conversation with a victim of racial discrimination. That night, I would write a letter home about this conversation. Credo Bisquerra was indeed the brightest man in the platoon. He spoke well and was interested in everything he saw, and more than any man in the platoon, he appeared to understand the Koreans' attitude toward the American army, which was beginning to change from the early days of the occupation. I could believe he was at the top of his class and imagined he might have resented me and the ease with which I had moved through the system; I had the preferred skin color and an acceptable surname. When we were alone, I asked about Quessenberry's and the other men's attitudes toward race. He said they were OK. No one ever made any open remarks racially, but they called the Koreans gooks, a name the army had always preferred when referring to Asians, even Filipinos.

He laughed and then said, "Hell, I even find myself calling them gooks." Then he added, "I wouldn't call Sylvester or Kim a gook. What's really funny," he continued, "*Nam me-gook saram* is Korean for I am an American." He laughed and repeated *me-gook*.

I browsed through the shelves and took *Madame Bovary* and Boccaccio's *Decameron* back with me. Later, when we began to get boxes of the ASE books at irregular intervals, I noticed that, unlike the men in the 102, few in C Company showed any interest in the books, not even in the Westerns or mysteries. Whenever the box of books reached the fourth platoon, I'd remove and set on my shelves the titles that looked most interesting or those by authors I'd heard of. At first, Bisket and I were the only ones who took an interest, though after a couple of weeks, Quiz began reading books I recommended. Barker read the Westerns, and *Bovary* made the rounds. The library and the ASE books were a godsend for me and gave me the chance to read reams of trash I would never have read otherwise, not because my "taste" had evolved so but only because I might never have had the opportunity or time. The major works stood out, however. Some titles made a major impact on me, works by authors I heard of but never read, such as Thomas Wolfe's *Look Homeward, Angel*. The ASE edition was slightly condensed, but even so, it was printed in the giant format that fit the large pocket in our fatigues or field jacket.

My bringing books back to the platoon and my talking about them, I believe, turned the LMG section into readers—well, some of the section, not all. Quiz became as serious as anyone about books after that visit to the rec room, and we would sit and talk about what he was reading for hours with Bisket joining in. Gradually, several others picked up on the conversations, men like Aleman and Rendo Stowell, both Mormon boys from Arizona and Utah who had finished high school and apparently had done well.

On the second day, as I was leaving the mess hall, I ran into Hansen on his way to chow. We recognized each other immediately and shook hands. I saw he had the three stripes and rocker of a staff sergeant, the rank of a squad leader, though I had heard he had just been made a platoon sergeant. I asked about Fort Benning, and he replied he had twisted his ankle badly on his first jump from the tower, was lucky it wasn't a sprain. It had put him back a week in the training cycles, giving him the option to transfer out. The medics said he would have to rest it and would miss too much training. He shipped out in time to get to Okinawa.

"You were lucky, Gill. Two of us washed out that first week. One guy in our platoon broke his back." I told him I had heard about it while I was in San Antonio.

Aside from books and letters from home, there was virtually nothing to relieve the monotony or boredom of life in Mukho. Quiz and I took a walk through Mukho, which turned out to be much smaller than it looked when I first rode in from battalion. He showed me the route we covered on patrol assignments.

"There's really no reason. The gooks have their own police force that's a lot tougher than anything we have."

Passes to Seoul did not exist, and there were no recreational areas as there were in the ETO that could have relieved the debilitating ennui. Female companionship, licit or illicit, was also rare to nonexistent. Korean custom and the language barrier, which was huge, prevented normal social relations between native and occupier. Racial prejudice discouraged anyone from learning Korean or even trying to understand the culture. Korea, having suffered a brutalizing colonial experience at the hands of the Japanese, had barely entered the twentieth century technologically, a fact that few American troops understood. The result was that most GIs viewed the lack of modern technology as proof of the Koreans' "inferiority," and this consequently deepened the average GI's prejudice and ignorance. I thought to myself how McAllister's anthropology taught me to see everything differently from how I might have seen, how reading *Patterns of Culture* prepared me for Korea in ways I had not expected.

Every squad had a radio, tuned constantly to the Armed Forces Network stations in Tokyo and Seoul. We passed many hours listening to the radio for news and music. We also listened to records on an old wind-up portable gramophone supplied by Special Services, exactly like the one we had up on the Czech border. It was amazing how those wax 78-rpm disks of Spike Jones, Glenn Miller, and Tommy Dorsey had made it through all the way from Okinawa. We had them on the turntable whenever the radio was silent. Somehow a few twelve-inch wax and newer plastic classical recordings of Ravel's "Boléro," Sibelius's "Valse Triste" and "Finlandia," Mendelssohn's "Fingal's Cave," Tchaikovsky's "Nutcracker," and Liszt's "Les Preludes" had made it into our collection. Once in a while, you'd hear "Fingal's Cave" or Ravel, the first one because it had been theme music on an old radio show and "Bolero," I suppose, because someone liked it. No one ever criticized anyone for his taste or complained when AFR Tokyo broadcast classical music.

When I first got there, I noticed that in the evening, when the AFN began its hour of classical and semi classical music, someone would always turn off the radio. When I turned it back on and said I liked it and asked for "equal time," no one protested. Because I listened to Country and Western music, they allowed me to have regularly symphonic or musical show tunes during our evening meal. Until I began to tune in to the "classical" hour regularly as part of our equal time agreement, no one had ever listened to the classical records in our collection. But that gradually changed. Later, in the evening, it wasn't unusual to hear a Liszt or Mendelssohn or Sibelius recording coming out of our squad room. No one ever admitted to *liking* what he heard; still, no one openly complained when it was on. It was a case of a new listener fearing someone might think them effete or effeminate if he revealed an interest in anything highbrow. One of the men, shortly after I arrived, challenged me with the wisdom that "the only people who listen to that shit are women or queers." I laughed and told him he was full of shit, that everyone in my old outfit listened to it and they had been through a lot more combat than he had or anyone in the fourth platoon had. They certainly weren't "effeminate," though I had no idea if any of them were queer. He couldn't believe that, he said. Credo also told him he was full of shit; his father listened to classical music and he wasn't a woman or a queer.

One man, Givens, exclaimed that Ravel's "Daphnis and Chloe Suite" had the same name as a Spike Jones's comic piece, "Chloe." It came to him like a revelation. When I told him the story of the legendary love affair, he was amazed, but at the same time, he insisted there was no connection between Ravel's music and the story I told. I agreed and told him I couldn't see it either but explained that Ravel's music was for a ballet that retold the story by way of dance on stage. He laughed and said he'd sure like to see that.

"How do you know all that shit, Gill?" he asked, laughing and shaking his head in bewilderment.

"I don't really know that much about it," I tried to explain. "It's just the kind of entertainment I got used to as a kid."

After that, Givens would hang on every story I told, and we became good friends from that day on. I had always enjoyed telling stories, but I never enjoyed it as much as then. Having a ready and appreciative audience, like the one in D hold on the *Eltinge*, had a lot to do with it. Givens liked it most when he could interrupt to embellish and improve the bare outline with sexual elaborations. A semiliterate former cab driver from Miami, Givens, had been quite unaffected by urban life, though he had lived most of his life in a busy metropolitan area. I told him evening after chow that had never heard of such creative profanity, such imaginative vulgarity, such bucolic obscenities from anyone, and when I told him, we were sitting in a circle of guys in the platoon. Even Stowell, a conservative Mormon moralist, was moved to head-shaking wonderment, and Givens smiled with pride and explained how he had developed it all driving his taxi in Miami just to amuse his Yankee passengers and himself. He said he had cultivated his qualities on purpose because there was money in it. He couldn't have been more than a year older than I was, perhaps two, but his view of the world was ageless. He explained it once when I asked him in a state of awe how he had gained so much wisdom about people. "When you drive one of them whorehouses on wheels, you can't help but get educated," he said. "But you have to keep your eyes and ears open."

My being a college boy impressed him not a bit, though my writing so many letters did, letter writing and reading being my chief occupations, a letter every other day to my mother and, in between, letters to friends—not long letters, only two or three sheets from a letter pad was enough. For Givens, anything more than a postcard was a tome. Planning what to write consumed time and helped pass many hours. Others in the platoon wrote occasionally, usually a weekly letter home, maybe slightly more. Mail call in Mukho was as important as it was in Wunsiedel or Wolters or anywhere else, perhaps more. Korea was farther from home in more ways than miles. Letters from the States were, therefore, essential, we thought, and I knew the surest insurance for getting letters—as Gaston and Perkins learned—was to write often; therefore, my writing habit was really a defense against boredom. Having communication of some sort in almost every mail call was my reward. Givens always got at least one letter every mail call, but I can't recall his ever writing anything but postcards.

From Barker, I found out that Givens had seen considerable action as a gunner on Okinawa; he had had logged more combat time than Barker, more than anyone in the platoon, except Ricobene, our platoon sergeant. The question I wanted to ask, but didn't, was why he hadn't been rotated back? I assumed that he might have picked up bad time along the way, time in a guardhouse for some infraction, and that this was holding up his rotation. It wasn't something a replacement would ask about.

Givens and I made several daytime patrols in Mukho together, and I found him good company. He liked the Koreans and got along well with the people we met on the street. He had a good sense of humor, though there was a kind of sadness about him, as if he were always homesick. He liked to ask me about my letters and would sit looking at the little album of snapshots I had begun collecting while I was in B Company, pictures of our house in Corpus; of Jane and Don, Mama and Albert; the cat; and a couple of girls I dated, Jerry and a girl, Emily Folda, whom I dated only twice but whose picture I kept because it always brought admiring comments. In a short time he knew all the names and could recite the stories I told as if he had joined the family. It was touching to hear him tell others about Jane and me being at the university at the same time. But he spoke only sparingly of his family in Miami, a wife and young daughter born shortly after he was drafted, and his mother, all subsisting on his wife's salary as a waitress and his allotment check.

The album was already showing a lot of wear by the time I reached C Company, though I had had it for less than a year. It was the center of attention in our half of the house, guys like Givens and Aleman slipping it out off the shelf then sitting on my bunk and slowly, silently leafing through it as though it were theirs. Aleman also knew the names of everyone now, even guys like Burdick, Snow, Smitty, and Knowles from B Company, men he'd never seen but whom he knew now and could refer to as "Smitty, the farm boy from Wisconsin" or "Burdick, the horse trainer from New York" or "Charley Knowles, the Harvard man." Givens knew them too and could make corrections if Aleman got a name wrong. I gathered it was a measure of their homesickness or some great desire to connect with a world outside C Company.

I have a picture of Givens and me in the middle of a street where we patrolled in Mukho. Around us are Korean children who followed us through their neighborhood, sometimes for a stick of gum but usually just to watch us or listen to us speak our foreign gibberish or watch us laugh, which invariably bring them to laughter. It had been a special occasion for Givens that day of the picture, though when we set out that afternoon on our usual patrol through the waterfront area, it seemed like any other day. Halfway along the route, Givens led us off the main thoroughfare into a narrow side street leading back to a cluster of shops and small houses. I asked him if he was visiting a friend, but all he would say was that I would see.

Joe and Givens on patrol in Mukho

Finally, stopping at the entrance to a small shop with a sign showing that photographs could be made within, he told me, before he rotated home, that he wanted a picture of just us two on patrol, in Mukho. He went into the shop and returned with the photographer carrying a large studio camera and tripod. I told Givens that men in the platoon with cameras would be glad to take our picture, but he insisted he wanted a "real" photograph of us on patrol. And it is a "real" photograph in sepia tone with everything in sharp focus. In the picture, he stands like an *ephebe* or like the Kritian Boy in a classic *contra posto,* his carbine slung over his right shoulder and his helmet liner hanging from his left hand. I'm standing, legs apart, in a semi-parade rest, my helmet liner cradled against my hip. My pose is less artful, my carbine slung properly on my right shoulder. We're both smiling but looking quite soldierly with our trousers perfectly bloused over the tops of combat boots. Convinced that any day his orders would be coming through, he was anxious to have a good picture of himself and "the man who got me my discharge," a charge I denied but by then had become reconciled to.

A few days before we had the picture made, Givens showed me a letter from his wife telling him that all he had to do to get an emergency "hardship" discharge was to write the adjutant general's office in Washington and request it using the Red Cross case number she had written. The neat legible handwriting told him what he had been hoping for. He told us repeatedly of the hard time his wife was having making ends meet on his GI allotment, especially since he was also supporting his mother who was ill. We had urged him to apply for an emergency "hardship" discharge. If anyone deserved it, we said, he was the one. When I read the letter, I gave it back and said I was sorry to hear how bad it was.

"Hell, Gill, I got to get back home and make some money. I should've been outa here a long time ago," he said. "You write that letter for me. She wrote the address and everything."

I read the letter again. She explained how she had spoken with a Red Cross caseworker and how the caseworker had investigated and approved her request. Unless, however, he made a formal request to the AGO, he would not get it. Too many men had no desire to return to hasty marriages, and the army wanted no part in aiding and abetting women who might have tricked a soldier for his allotment check. I told Givens that letters to the AG were supposed to go through channels, first through the company commander then on up the chain of command—that was the army protocol. I explained it was one of the first things they taught us in the so-called military science class we had at A&M. Enlisted men were forbidden to communicate directly to the AGO or anyone outside their company.

"Technically," I told him, "you'd have to get permission from Sergeant Barker just to send the letter through the CO, Lieutenant Singer."

But he insisted her letter said that *he* should write directly to Washington. I honestly didn't have the heart to argue with him and agreed that it was a lousy system. It wasn't that Givens was stupid; he wasn't. He simply and very rationally refused to accept the rigid forms of the military, especially now that the war was over. His claim was legitimate, and our CO was chicken shit and probably would let the letter sit for days before endorsing it.

"All right, I'll write—no, I'll *help* you write the letter, but you have to copy it in your own handwriting. It has to be from you," I said and pulled out my writing tablet and set to work. It was the third time in the army that Joe, the scrivener, would oversee a letter of importance. The army ought to make an MOS for scriveners, I told myself.

"Let's keep it simple," I said. "Simple and direct is always best. Now answer this question: Why are you writing the AGO?"

"To ask for a hardship dis—"

"No, you say it in full sentence, simple and direct."

"OK. I am writing you to ask for a hardship discharge," he began.

"Tell him why."

"Like it says in the Red Cross case, is that OK?"

"Givens, that's perfect!" I handed him the paper and watched him print out the words he had spoken. Then I made a minor correction, closing with "Red Cross case number . . .," and added the number his wife had written.

"Now rewrite it in your own handwriting. That way, they know it's from you."

I watched him carefully print the letter and felt a deep pang of sympathy as he labored trying not to splatter the ink. The ink frightened him most. He wanted to use a pencil, but I insisted on pen and ink. What was so easy for most of us was an exercise in agony for Givens, but he persisted and even rewrote it to make it as neat as possible. When he finished, he signed his name and wrote his serial number under it and "C Company, Thirty-Second Inf., Seventh Division." I told him to address the envelope too and gave him an airmail stamp.

From that moment on, he lived in a state of high expectation, certain that any day his orders would come through. Our photo in the streets of Mukho followed soon after. Bisket, Quiz, Barker, and I tried to explain that the red tape would take weeks, maybe months, but he insisted he would be getting orders any day, thus the rush to get our photo made on patrol. And he was right. To our surprise, the orders came through in two weeks, in less time than turnaround for mail to the States. And it came to Givens during the morning roll call and formation; the first sergeant called out his name, told him to get his gear ready, that he was shipping out for home in thirty minutes. He had to be ready when the courier returned to battalion HQ.

Givens let out a whoop, "Gill! We done it! We done it!" and was gone. The first sergeant glanced quickly at me and told me to go help him. The letter had nothing to do with his orders, I insisted. It was just a coincidence; besides, the orders had come too soon for the letter to have an effect, I told him. It would have taken a miracle of Lazarus rising proportions for the Pentagon to work that fast. As far as I could see, that letter constituted no miracle.

When he closed his duffel bag, I rejoined the platoon for close-order drill. He was back on the street with his bag in ten minutes and was standing beside the battalion jeep, still proclaiming my genius. I was sure the first sergeant was aware that there was a letter that had *not* gone through channels and that he deduced instantly that I, or someone, had helped or had even written the missive.

We were in the middle of our morning drill, and Barker was counting cadence when Givens broke in and said, "I gotta talk to Gilliland, give 'em a short break, Barker."

Barker halted the platoon and told us to take five and nodded to me to go talk to the happy man. The platoon was all-agog, pumping air with fists, infantry sign language for double time.

"Goddam, Gilliland, you smart son of a bitch, you wrote one fuckin' goddam good letter!" he shouted. "Anytime you goddam come to Miami, remember you got a free fuckin' ride anywhere in my fuckin' taxi, I promise you, no shit! Ya hear?" He grabbed my hand and shook it. "I mean it. God dammit, I mean it!"

I tried to explain again that it was probably the normal rotation orders, though I honestly believed it wasn't that sure. I had mixed feelings, hoping, on the one hand, it was the normal procedure and proud; on the other, I had done my bit to flaunt the protocols around a chicken shit CO. The platoon was enjoying Givens' excitement, pleased that one of ours had been "chosen." They were proud that "the letter" had worked a miracle, that a lowly enlisted man had bucked the system and had come out ahead. It was as if each of us in Company C had had received orders. Aleman was especially appreciative, laughing and congratulating Givens and me for writing a successful letter. I kept telling him it was just a coincidence. Mail didn't travel nor did Washington work that fast. But he insisted it was my letter.

"Remember, you got free cab rides all over Miami." I backed into my squad, and Barker continued counting cadence as the jeep and Givens drove off.

Another wave of orders for rotation came through shortly after Givens left and company strength fell precipitously. For a few weeks, our company had only an *acting* first sergeant, an Okinawa veteran, who agreed to take the job only until a replacement arrived. Ordinarily, a company at full strength has a complement of six officers—a CO, an exec, and four platoon leaders—but we had only two officers, our CO, First Lieutenant Singer, and the exec, Lieutenant Steinfield. Credo and I, because we had passed the NCO exams, became acting squad leaders in the LMG section. Promotions didn't mean a thing since it would take a month for them to go through. Besides, all ranks were "frozen until further notice," according to the CO. The "squads" we were in charge of were down to only three men each, a machine gun squad ordinarily holding six. Ours were indeed paper commands. As acting squad leaders, we would no longer be required to pull KP—there was never much KP anyway—though we would still walk patrols in town because the company was so short of men. Anyway, I could write home that I had been promoted, even though was I still a PFC, and was in charge of only three men. The table of command showed Gilliland as an LMG squad leader. Instead of KP, it meant I would have to pull duty in the orderly room as a charge of quarters about twice a month. CQ meant sitting in the orderly room, four on eight off, just to answer the telephone and run errands for the first sergeant; someone had to be in the CP at all times.

Lieutenant Singer got the bad news while I was sitting my first CQ. The mail clerk delivered the CO's mail that morning, putting it all on my desk, and said I should take the CO's mail in right away because there was a thick important-looking letter from battalion HQ for him. Ordinarily, the first sergeant would take it in, but he was out. When I approached, the lieutenant was sitting at his desk listening to the news on AFN. I dropped the bundle of letters and memos on his desk. He thanked me, and I left, but I had barely reached my desk in the anteroom when I heard the first shout.

"All right! Who did it? Who wrote it?" His voice echoed through the building and probably across the waterfront, all the way to the center of town. Ever since he had assigned me to the fourth platoon three months ago, I'd not heard him speak more than a dozen words and then never above a normal tone of voice. Three or four times that morning, he'd passed my desk without speaking, just as he usually never spoke to anyone, except the first sergeant. I jumped to my feet as he stormed into the outer room waving a sheet of paper, asking the same question, "Who wrote this?"

Years later, I would sit in a theater in New York and watch Henry Fonda in *Mister Roberts*, and I would hear the captain shout in that same tone, asking the same question, and I would flash back to that happy day in Mukho when Lieutenant Singer discovered Givens had written directly to the adjutant general in Washington DC, and had not "gone through channels."

"I want to know who wrote this letter for that son of a bitch Givens. That dumb bastard couldn't sign a payroll. Somebody wrote this letter. Gilliland, you knew that son of a bitch. I didn't think he could write. Who wrote this letter? Somebody wrote it!"

It was the first time he had ever addressed me since assigning me to fourth platoon. He thrust the letter at me. I saw it was the letter itself, written on paper from my own letter pad.

"No, sir, that's his hand writing, and that's his signature," I said.

By that time, the acting first sergeant was back from his break, and Singer had calmed a little. The sergeant stood in the doorway and asked what had happened.

"That son of a bitch Givens went over my head and requested a hardship discharge. He wrote directly to the AG's office in Washington, and now I have to write a goddam letter of endorsement every thirty days for as long as I am in this fucking army, explaining why his letter didn't go through the goddam channels. They assume I *denied* him the right to request his hardship discharge. Hardship! Hell, I'll give him hardship! Every thirty damn days! That puts a mark on my fitness report, the only mark in *all* the time I've been in the army." The word *all* sounded a prolonged moan of agony. He paused to catch his breath then looked straight at me. "Some son of a bitch wrote that letter, and I'm going to get his ass in a sling if that's the last thing I do. Then I'm going to Miami and beat the shit out of that little asshole! What did he need a hardship discharge for anyway?"

"He *could* have written it, sir," the first sergeant said after glancing at the paper and looking straight at me. "Givens really isn't stupid, sir, just illiterate."

Well, I could see the Lieutenant Singer was put out about it, so I decided it would best if I not offer any explanation or even try to explain the need for a hardship from Givens's point of view. What did Singer, the heir to an East Coast manufacturing fortune—refrigerators, vacuum cleaners, sewing machines, whatever—know about the hardships of men like Givens? It was a joyous day, and I silently sang "ca-loo, ca-lay, oh frabjous day." Even the acting first sergeant thought it amusing and a well-deserved mark on a perfect asshole's perfect fitness report.

I looked at the first sergeant, he at me, and we shrugged. I knew he knew I had helped Givens write the letter. I knew he had heard Givens thanking me the morning he got his orders. His saying nothing more about it to me or anyone else convinced me he would have made a very good permanent first sergeant. I would hate to see him go, which he did soon after. If Singer hadn't been so aloof, or had he ever come down out of his officer's house on the hill and mingled with the men as the officers in B Company had done, had perhaps eaten in the mess hall instead of his little chalet on the hill, they might have felt some sympathy for him, but it was aloofness that forced Givens to resort to a direct appeal. He doubted the legitimacy of Givens' request because he didn't know Givens and didn't want to know him. They had been in combat on Okinawa, but the army's caste system, added to Singer's own class attitude, had kept them strangers mainly because Singer had never believed it should be otherwise. It would never have happened in B Company. I believe that we all felt the mark on his fitness report was fair. Givens, henceforth, was our David, our Joshua.

I had done nothing in the army up to that time that I was as proud of as I was in helping Givens, Perkins, and Gaston write letters that changed things for them. For someone who had to struggle just to get a B or C on freshman composition, this letter, consisting of only one sentence, was my, as well as Givens', triumph. I was bursting with pride. And to see "my" letter in Singer's hand and to see his face turn red with fury was a vindication of English 1. If only Dr. James or Dr. Eckfeldt could know, they would be proud too. One clear, coherent compound-complex sentence had done it all.

In early April, C Company received orders that for the first time had some relationship to the war and its aftermath. Our task involved no more than a dozen men of the fourth platoon, four shifts of three men each, and it lasted for only one day and one night; however, its importance outweighed many times its brevity. I look back now and see that this episode and several like it that followed had an immeasurable influence on me and contributed directly to the life I describe in this memoir. For years, I have felt that these two years in the army reached a point of clarity and meaning in the duties we performed that night, though at the moment there was no light of revelation or even any remarkable act that made the episode stand out from other events.

One evening, instead of the pointless patrol along the waterfront, Quessenberry, Candelaria, and I were told to guard a large warehouse near the docks and to prevent anyone from going inside. We were so shorthanded at the time that even squad leaders and section leaders had to pull a shift on guard duty. That the guard was assigned to Quessenberry and me, both noncoms, on the first shift suggested it had some importance. The building, about the size of a large field house, was filled with Japanese families, mostly women and children, no male members, between the ages of sixteen and sixty. These were Japanese repatriates I had read about, families of civil servants, plant managers, engineers, supervisors, and military men, all dependents of men who had lived and worked in Korea during the period of the Japanese annexation, a better term would have been Japanese exploitation. The five hundred women, children, and elderly represented only a tiny percentage of almost six hundred thousand Japanese who would return to Japan that first year after the war. They were the Pacific War's displaced persons, but there was no real similarity between the Japanese DPs and those DPs I had seen just a year earlier in Europe.

Here in the warehouse in Mukho was a vast difference. Here were whole families still intact, well-dressed and secure, cooking meals of rice and fish supplied by the American Forces Pacific Theater, sleeping on comfortable pads, warm and protected, and safe in the knowledge they were returning to their homeland and not to a DP or labor or concentration camp, returning perhaps to relatives, hometowns, or villages. To be sure, some would find entire cities leveled by the B-*ni-ju-ku* (B-29) raids on Tokyo, Nagoya, Kobe, Osaka, and all the prefectural capitals, and finally, of course, Hiroshima and Nagasaki. They were heading home while those we had seen in Europe lived in a state worse than a limbo, some hoping *not* to return to their homes for fear of reprisals there. "Slave laborers" under the Nazis, they would become "collaborators" under Stalin and would be rewarded with a bullet in the head or at best a long-term in a Siberian gulag. These families in the

Mukho warehouse were DPs with a difference. Camping out now in the damp and drafty warehouse, they had been the oppressors and the exploiters, the beneficiaries of Japan's Greater East Asia Co-Prosperity Sphere. Nearing the end of their displacement and agony, they were doing so under the benevolent guidance of their conqueror. Quessenberry, Candelaria, the relief guard, and I had orders to assist, to give aid when requested, and to protect the families from Korean reprisals. I knew we were seeing history that might not ever be recorded or discussed in the sweeping studies of the Second Great War, except possibly as a footnote in the chapter on the Potsdam agreements of 1945. Few in the platoon understood or cared about what was happening, understood that in the history of the world, no defeated people had been so carefully protected from harm as these. I told Quessenberry what I was thinking, and he understood, but for some in the company, it was just another job. It would have been different in B Company.

In the summer of 1945, the *Stars and Stripes* and an overseas edition of *Time* reported that the U.S. had agreed to repatriate all the Japanese military and civilian personnel living in the liberated territories in Asia. We'd talked about it in our platoon in one of those I & E sessions and had discussed the terms and the meanings behind the terms.

A cheerless cloud hung over the entire scene, yet still, the sense of tragedy here did not compare to those scenes in the DP camps of Europe. Here, families, without fathers or older brothers, gathered in tightly knit units, eating, sleeping, and speaking together, while in those camps in Europe, all I saw were crowds of strangers thrown together with little or no sign of hope of ever meeting again a mother, father, husband, or wife who was last seen being forced into the backs of army trucks or through the doors of boxcars.

Any feeling of triumph seeing these people here was long past. They were hardly the enemy, merely the flotsam and jetsam of four years of war and thirty years of aggressive colonialism, and I doubted then guarding was as necessary as we were told it was. The Koreans in the neighborhood seemed unconcerned of what the warehouse held. Although they had despised the Japanese annexation, when the war ended, no wave of reprisal or revenge arose. It would have been understandable had there been. Perhaps it was the presence of the U.S. XIV Corps in the south and the 225,000 Soviet troops in the north that prevented such an uprising. But even before the Americans arrived in the fall of 1945, no attempts at reprisal had occurred. While we walked our tour at the warehouse, no one from the outside approached or showed the slightest interest. Inside, all was quiet, as each family settled down for the night to await their transport in the morning.

Only once while I walked between the neat rows was I approached. A woman's voice spoke from behind in perfect American English, "Excuse, sir, may I borrow your torch?"

I turned and looked into the face of an attractive middle-aged Japanese woman dressed in the strange bloomer-like pants, or *mompei*, and short kimono most women her age wore. Still startled, I handed her my flashlight. She said she had lost something and needed a light. I followed her to the little square reed matting she and her small family had organized and watched as she searched among the packs and satchels. When they found it, a bottle of vitamins, the woman returned my "torch" and bowed slightly, amused perhaps at my curiosity.

"You speak very good English," I said.

"Yes, I was born in San Francisco and lived there until I was sixteen. Where do you come from?" she asked.

"I come from Texas. Where are you from in Japan?"

"I have been to Japan only once, to my grandparents' home on the island of Shikoku." Then she bowed again and said, "So sorry to disturb you. Thank you very much."

I felt the hairs stand on the back of my neck stand up on hearing her words, "So sorry," the familiar cliché we all repeated when discussing the Japanese during the war. When I got back to the platoon around midnight and turned in, I lay awake recalling the scene, wondering what it would be like to lose a war, to lose your home and your place in the world.

The next morning after breakfast, I wrote a long letter home describing what I had seen, but that letter today conveys none of the feelings I've just attempted to relate, comparing and contrasting the two groups of people, nor does the letter begin to suggest the importance it still holds on my imagination. Perhaps at nineteen, I could see only what my buddies saw, and the meaning of those memories etched as if by acid on a plate I had saved to contemplate at a later date.

Today homelessness is an idea that invades all our awareness, not only the homelessness of refugees in far off lands but also the homeless within our own cities. As a nineteen-year-old product of Middle America, I had never experienced anything more alienating than a rare tramp begging at our kitchen door during the Depression in Beaumont. I recall Grandmother inviting into the house a young man who had "raked leaves" for a bowl of homemade chili and rice. For all his loneliness and desperation, his plight did not come close to that of the families in the warehouse or the stricken faces I had seen behind the wire of the DP camps in Europe after the war.

In the ETO, I had just barely missed getting into combat, and had briefly resented my good fortune, ashamed that I hadn't shared the fear or danger that my friends had faced, but now, almost a year since the signing of the armistice, I realized the war was still with us, that all across the world, people were still searching for families and homes, still hoping for a full belly and a place to sleep, warm and free of rats and vermin. It was there in that cold damp warehouse I began to realize, for the first time since arriving in Korea, that we were doing something important, I mean *we*—Quiz, Aleman, Stowell, Bisket and all of Company C—though at the moment, it was actually nothing more than quietly walking among those families.

At the end of April, the first battalion moved from the coast inland to a new posting north of Seoul, and C Company had a new assignment.

Chapter 10

A Darkling Plain

The long truck ride from Mukho to Pocheon had taken us through Seoul and only one other city of any size, Uijeongbu. We skirted our new "city," a mostly thatched roof collection of houses with few two- or three-storied buildings, and took a sharp right over a narrow bridge spanning a small creek and left the town behind. Now, stretched out before us was a long tent city, one long street of twelve-man squad tents, quite a shock after the comfortable Japanese houses and the neat layout of the company in Mukho. But hell, this is the army, right? Mukho's quarters were the anomaly; the line of twelve-man squad teams was the army! The real question was, what was there about Pocheon that had made our moving so important?

We climbed down out of the trucks and hauled ourselves into the tents, dropping our gear then assembling as ordered in a neat hillside amphitheater with a large white movie screen. Lt. Steinfield, our new CO and the First Sgt were standing on a raised platform waiting for the tiers to fill. Steinfield was smiling and talking to the guys already seated, unlike the old CO, Singer, who never deigned to speak to any enlisted man below sergeant. The question was, why the move and how long would we be in these tents?

When the last man found his seat the CO began:

"OK, why are we here?" He paused and began again, "We're going to be pulling guard duty at the Thirty-Eighth parallel. That's about ten kilometers notch of here. As you all know, that's the border with the Russkis. Every two weeks, I'm going to send a couple of squads, twenty men plus noncoms and a cook, up to the parallel to pull guard duty and run patrols. We've got two jobs: to secure the border and to regulate the traffic between North and South Korea, between the Soviet zone and the U.S. zone. Some of the farmers up there have to cross back and forth daily; they live on one side of the border and farm on the other. But that's no problem. All we do is check their permits. The Russkis are doing the same. The main difference between now and last September and October is there'll be no fraternization with the Russkis, so we get no vodka."

Groans and laughter.

"But the most important thing we'll be doing is regulating the traffic of Japanese refugees." He paused again, then began, "This is serious shit, men.

All those Japanese who've been occupying Korea and Manchuria are moving south through our area for repatriation to the home islands. Thousands will be on the road, and our job is to inoculate them, dust them with DDT, and guard them from the Koreans." He paused, paced back and forth. "Remember that warehouse in Mukho? Well, they were just the forerunners. There are thousands more. *But!* We're not at war anymore, so there won't be any molesting or harassing. Got it?"

Everyone was stone silent.

"This will be the most important duty we have here. It was part of the Potsdam agreement. Any questions?" He paused and paced slowly back and forth waiting. "That's really why they moved the whole first battalion up here to the Parallel. Let me repeat, this will be the most important duty the company's had since we left that shit hole Okinawa."

He turned it over then to the first sergeant, who began, "We've got a lot of work to do here to get C Company shaped up. The engineers left us some materials for showers, and they will be putting a roof over that giant latrine you see over there, the only twelve-holer in the Far East."

Our first view of Pocheon had been a shock, so different was it from the coastal towns of Samcheok and Mukho. All day, our convoy had wound its way through a countryside marked by small villages, tiered rice paddies, and barren hills. When we finally reached Pocheon, we barely had a chance to see it before our convoy crossed over the long narrow concrete bridge spanning an almost dry riverbed. All we had seen of Pocheon was just a cluster of thatch-roofed houses and a few concrete two-story buildings that appeared to be school or government structures of some kind. Even with the paved streets, it looked like something out of a nineteenth century travel book, right down to the old men in their white skirts and strange horsehair hats.

The tent city lay alongside a long, earthen dyke that screened us from the dry riverbed and from a view of Pocheon that lay on the high bluff just above the river. Unless we climbed the dyke, we had no sense that we were even near a town, our main view being the low, tree-covered hill to the east. I took no time to move in, make up the cots, and stow our gear. Supper that first night was cold C rations, but that first morning, we had flapjacks and bacon.

Staring out at the wooded hill then looking back at the long earthen dyke, Rendo Stowell reported how the engineers had made a serious flaw when they planted the company smack in a riverbed.

"That the bridge connecting us to Pocheon," he said, "goes way beyond that dike and the company street," which he pointed out. "That means our tents are right in the flood plain." Rendo laughed and said, "If we ever get a good rain, that river's going to fill the riverbed, and we'll be lucky if that dike holds. The levee's not compacted, just a lot of loose silt pushed up out of the riverbed by the dozers." He sounded as though he knew what he was talking about. "A good three-day rain'll raise the river as high as the dike and wipe us out."

Coming as he did from a small town in Arizona on the Gila River, Rendo knew whereof he spoke. The Gila, he said, resembled the Pocheon River, except during the monsoon or in early spring when the snow melted in the Gila Mountains. Then it rose to flood stage. "These rocky riverbeds are all alike," he said. "They flood easily unless you have real well-built dykes, and this one is *not* well-built."

I glanced over to Aleman, who was from Utah and lived in the same kind of dry rock country Stowell did.

Someone remarked, "why would anyone build a town here if the river floods every year?"

Stowell laughed. "People build towns all the time on flood plains back home. They build in dry cycles then watch their homes float away in the wet. But Pocheon's on a high bluff, not here in a flood plain."

He pointed at the wide, gradually sloping field that reached up to the low wooded hill to the east of us. "That's a field for planting. It floods and silts every year, and I bet they plant just like the farmers on the Nile in Egypt."

He was right. Stowell didn't talk much, but when he did, he made sense. His Mormon heritage had taught him much about reading rivers, fields, and nature's cycles.

A week after we arrived in Pocheon, twenty of us from the fourth platoon loaded into two six-by-sixes with all our gear and rode off to the Thirty-Eighth Parallel. It was the first time since we had guarded the Japanese in the warehouse that I felt we were doing something of value. In the Mukho warehouse, we stood guard to make sure no one harassed repatriates while they waited to board an LST in Mukho Harbor. This was different and would be the most important assignment our division would have all the time I was stationed in Korea.

Yungmun-yi, the village on the parallel where our outpost was parked, was much smaller than Pocheon, only a dozen or so small thatch-roofed houses, almost identical to the ones we passed on our way cross country. This was the real Korea. Before, in Mukho, the Japanese company housing and the entire Company C compound was not at all Korean, and even Mukho itself, or the parts we saw on patrol, was not really *Korean* but a product of Japanese colonialism. My thoughts flashed back to Dr. Mac's anthro class and back to the Reserve Reading Room at the Main Library; I should have spent more time reading Benedict's *Patterns of Culture*. God, I felt I was standing in the middle of a class in cultural anthropology, and I wished I'd "borrowed" the copy of Ruth Benedict's book I'd seen at the Camp Pickett library, along with *The Ordeal of Richard Feverel*.

No wonder so many men were always bitching about "dumb gooks;" they never understood what they were seeing or what they were trying to deal with. In Mukho, we were living in a foreign cocoon. This was really Korea, but moving into real houses and into an environment not much different from the familiar world of Western norms, we remained insulated from Korea. It was different now.

If the engineers had erred in planting our tents in a floodplain, they had really goofed here at Ynugmun-yi planting our Quonset hut directly on the border between North and South Korea. That's right, they had stuck it squarely on the Thirty-Eighth Parallel, our living quarters in the Soviet sector and our kitchen and mess quarters in the U.S. It was a lovely spot, however, a little hillock overlooking the river or creek, or whatever it was. The view that reminded me of one of those scroll paintings of hills, streams, and twisted pines, the kind Japanese call *san-sui*, mountain and water paintings. Aesthetically, it was ideal, but politically, it was a disaster. Steinfield, who had driven to the parallel with us to see that we got set up properly, stared at the hut shaking his head in disbelief.

Across the road from the Quonset was a small lean-to guard hut, and a few yards to the north of the hut were the remains of a bridge that had once spanned the shallow rill that ran parallel and a little north of the border. The guard hut stood on our side just overlooking the collapsed span, the road running north and south ending at the approach to the bridge. The lieutenant stared down into the gulch shaking his head then looked up, turned to face us, and said dryly, "There *was* a bridge here last week when I drove up. It looks like the Russkis don't intend to have any traffic passing through this checkpoint. I'd call this a pretty good roadblock. It sure simplifies matters here." It was true—no trucks, cars, or carts would be passing through our border check.

Standing in the road at the north end of the collapsed bridge, less than fifty yards from our lean-to, a lone Russian soldier stood looking across to where we were standing and kept glancing back toward a cluster of buildings fifty or so yards from where he stood. We waved and beckoned for him to come across. He shook his head and saying, "*Nyet!*" then shouted, "Good-bye!" in English and Russian. Several of our men offered him cigarettes, but he shook his head and repeated his good-byes. Finally, he turned and walked back on the road north. It was the last time we would see him or speak to any of the Russians until later in the summer when I pulled my last duty on the parallel. The Allied High Commission, apparently, had more pressing issues to consider than a poorly placed Quonset or a blasted bridge, and so until the end of August, we continued to use the Quonset where it was and ignored the blasted bridge. Later in the summer, after most of the Japanese had departed for the home islands, our engineers returned and moved the Quonset to a proper location south of Yungmun-yi.

It was good duty there. We had no drills or formations; everyone pulled guard at the little hut or went out on the patrols, but no one was on guard or patrol for more than two hours during the daylight hours, and no one had to spend more than a day on KP in the week we were there. When I was not at the hut or out on a patrol that took us deeper into the countryside beyond roads fit for trucks or cars, I spent most of my time reading, writing letters, and just gazing out at the countryside. The villagers in Yungmun-yi, like those in Pocheon, were friendly and welcomed us to sit and smoke and drink tea in their *matang*. It was probably the first time any of us had ever tried to speak Korean to someone other than our houseboys in Mukho. They laughed at our mispronunciations and corrected us, which we struggled to reproduce. I know they found us a strange lot and were mystified by our patrols out into the valleys and hills surrounding their little village. In truth, they weren't the only ones mystified, for the patrols that often went deep into the southern reaches of our sector had no mission or goal other than being seen. Though they were friendly and responded to our greetings, we noticed that none of the households allowed the young women outdoors when we were around. It was as if all young girls above the age of eleven or twelve had been shipped out or locked up. Even the wives and young mothers were careful to avoid eye contact or to linger in the *matang* when we were around. The old women, often toothless and always stooped with an infant strapped to their backs, would socialize and chatter away when we visited in the shade of the veranda. They gladly accepted cigarettes and pieces of candy, usually breaking up the cigarette and stuffing its tobacco into tiny brass bowls of their long-stemmed pipes. But the language barrier was always there, and only a handful of us ever picked up enough of the language to carry on a conversation. My Korean was not even rudimentary, though it was better than most.

A few days before our first group of Japanese was scheduled to arrive, battalion HQ called and told us that an inspector general, a bird colonel from MacArthur's headquarters in Tokyo, was on his way for a visit and would arrive in a little over an hour. It was the first we had heard. Although we had just over an hour to get ready, no one seemed to panic. Ricobene, our platoon sergeant who was in charge of the operation, called the CP in Pocheon to tell Lieutenant Steinfield that an IG from Tokyo was on the way. He had only just heard of the IG's visit himself. These inspections were supposed to be surprise visits, but because Ricobene had good friends at battalion HQ, we got the warning in time to get ourselves in order.

Until that call came through, we had assumed that the people in MacArthur's headquarters in Tokyo didn't even know we existed, but it seemed perfectly reasonable that the high command in Tokyo would want to know whether or not Fourth Platoon C Company was up to processing thousands of Japanese while, at the same time, guarding the Thirty-Eighth Parallel. We were a callow lot. Few of us were over twenty, and only a handful had been in the army for even as long as I had, which was barely a year and a half. Fewer still had seen any combat, and only two of our noncoms had ever really commanded troops. Such was the unit that had been given the responsibility of maintaining order and processing the repatriates. No one had commanded a unit on a frontier post far from the seats of command; in addition, no one in C Company had ever been in charge of processing and caring for thousands of civilians on their way back to a devastated homeland. If our mission impressed no one else, I was impressed. We *deserved* an IG's attention. I had been wondering for weeks what value our occupation force in Korea really had and why we were not doing anything of importance. Now I marveled that I was involved, if only tangentially, in important events.

I had wondered when a medical team would arrive and set up a system for administering shots or when a military government unit would arrive to handle paperwork or at least instruct us on what we should do. Now the IG was arriving and would find us totally unprepared and, moreover, sleeping every night in the Soviet zone. I marveled that Lieutenant Steinfield stayed at the company CP, but neither Ricobene nor Barker showed much concern. Ricobene assured us there was nothing to get worked up about. But I suspected his complete aplomb rested more on his imminent departure for the States than his belief in our ability to impress the IG. Barker, next in line for platoon sergeant, had told each to make sure his weapon was clean and set us to policing the area around our Quonset.

So we were all bending over when I heard Ricobene shout, "Gilliland, get your ass over here!" He and Barker were standing beside the guard hut talking to Aleman who was pulling his hitch of duty.

"Gilliland," Ricobene said, "go put on a clean shirt if you got one. I want you to relieve Aleman at the checkpoint before the IG gets here."

When I asked why me, he said it was because he wanted someone who could talk and who wouldn't freeze up when the IG asked questions.

I glanced at Aleman who shrugged. I said, "Aleman can talk as well as I can."

"Aleman says he's never talked to a colonel before, and I know the colonel will talk to the man on at the hut. You ever talked to a colonel?"

"Once or twice." I said and almost said I once had supper with an admiral, but I didn't.

"Since you talk all the time anyway, Gilliland, now you can do your stuff." He smiled and said, "That's an order. Now get that shirt on, the one with that Ozark patch."

I was amused and mildly flattered, surprised that Ricobene knew me that well. My clean shirt was at the bottom of my duffel bag and looked pretty sorry, but it was clean and as presentable as the others in the platoon. I never worried about these assignments and found it amusing that my tendency to jabber was considered so unusual. Even in Germany, among older and more experienced men, I would often be assigned to guard posts where I was likely to meet high-ranking officers because I could and would answer questions without stammering—all thanks to Ms. Fife at Dick Dowling.

We heard them coming long before we saw the dust cloud, and soon, they were roaring through Yungmun-yi, three jeeps and an old prewar open command car, with a stout little colonel in the backseat, and we were impressed: the IG was not riding up in a big army Buick or one of the six-wheeled armored cars that most of the generals loved to run around in. Of course, our IG was only a bird colonel. Ricobene, who was good at this sort of thing, greeted the colonel as he stepped down from the command car, popping a proper salute, and standing straight without bracing. The short stocky little colonel with a waistline problem was wearing rough, unpolished regulation combat boots with his pants slightly bloused and a conventional unpolished helmet liner marked by a stenciled eagle, not a silver one. It was obvious he was a no-frills, old-fashioned field soldier and proud of it. We had seen too many colonels and generals regaled in polished paratrooper's jump boots, fancy pistol holsters, and brightly painted helmet liners emblazoned with eagles or stars, more in costume than uniform, but this colonel's outfit was all GI, which meant he'd be either very good and easy or the epitome of chickenshit regulation. We'd found that those who had come up through the reserves or National Guard were more likely to design their uniforms like Custer at Gettysburg outfitted right from the racks of Abercrombie & Fitch complete with riding crop, polished boots and all, even a shoulder holster. But this colonel was strictly GI. His aides emulated the "old man." Not a "ponset box," or swagger stick, in the group.

It was a warm day, and already, I could feel the tickle of perspiration running down my back and could see a dark ring under the colonel's armpits. He would likely want to be on his way as soon as possible. From where I stood, I could see Ric listening, nodding, answering questions. The colonel was smiling, his aids laughing, not at Ricobene's jokes, I thought, but at the colonel's wit, right out of the West Point witty remarks book. As they entered the Quonset hut at the north end, I heard someone shout attention and heard feet hitting the floor, and I wondered if the colonel was aware he had invaded the Soviet zone when he stepped into the front end of the Quonset. From where I stood, I could see through the windows of the hut and watch the entourage walking from north to south, watching the colonel speaking to men along the way. He passed quickly through the kitchen and left by the rear door. There would be no lingering in the mess; no one in Tokyo wanted to hear about the really lousy chow we were eating on the Thirty-Eighth Parallel. It had taken hardly ten minutes to move from one end of the hut to the other. I waited at parade rest, glancing sideways to see if he was going to approach the checkpoint. Clustered near the rear entrance of the hut, the colonel and his aids once again spoke to Ricobene who was answering questions, making wide sweeping movements with his arm and pointing back toward me. Then the colonel looked toward the checkpoint and headed toward me, leaving Ricobene and the rest of his party back by the jeeps.

I came to attention and saluted, holding the sling of the carbine tight with my left hand. He returned my salute and asked right off, "Who gave you permission to wear the Ozark patch, soldier?"

I told him no one had; I had served in the outfit before being sent to Korea, so I sewed it on according to regulations. He told me to stand at ease then asked me what regiment I had served in and who my CO was. When I told him I was in B Company, 406th Infantry, he said he and the former CO of the 406 had been roommates at "the Point." I think I uttered, "Small world." He asked how long I'd been in the ETO, and I told him I had joined the division just a week or so after V-E Day. Then small talk aside, he said, "Tell me, what your job is here, soldier."

I realized then that this was the reason for the inspection: Tokyo wanted to know if anyone here understood the mission. I answered, "My job is to stop all traffic from the north and check the ID and crossing permits, sir. There's only foot traffic here now, sir, since the Russians dropped that bridge span there."

"How can you tell if the permits are legitimate? Can you read Korean?" he asked as if it were a real question, and I wondered just how much *he* knew of the whole operation.

"The permits are in Russian, Korean, and English, sir, and have an official U.S. Army seal stamped on them with the other seals. If I'm in doubt, or any guard is in doubt, sir, we hold the person or persons until someone comes up from military government."

"Have you ever restrained anyone?"

"No, sir. The only people I've seen, that goes for the other guards as well, are people from Yungmun-yi or the North Koreans who farm on this side. We know them all now, but we check their permits anyway."

"Good. What other jobs do you have while you're here?"

I told him about the patrols and about processing of Japanese repatriates. For a moment, he seemed to be thinking about what to ask next. He walked around the hut, a flimsy structure that must have served at one time as Korean police box, then returned and stood in front of me again and said in a quiet voice, more relaxed than the official tone he'd used in the other questions, "Tell me, son, what do you think about being stuck out here in nowhere?"

This sounded like a genuine question. I told him I thought it was interesting, more interesting than doing guard duty at corps HQ like we did in Bamberg. I told him we had handled DPs in Germany along with a few former POWs returning to their homes in the Russian zone. Then I said, "But now we're helping to repatriate the Japanese who occupied and worked in Manchuria and occupied Korea for more than thirty yeas. This is a historical and important job, sir. I like it, and I'm glad I'm here," I said and then said to myself I'm talking too much.

"You are right, it is important. You're regular army then?"

"Yes, sir."

"Very good. Carry on."

I came to attention, saluted, and he returned it. He was really all West Point, even though he looked more like a bank president than a bird colonel. He did an about-face headed rapidly to his command car and signaled his retinue to follow. I really liked the old fart, not a phony bone in his body, and I'd bet that the enlisted men who worked for him liked him too. Ric stood beside the colonel's car, spoke a few words, saluted, and backed away. The whole business had lasted less than half an hour. When they drove off, Ric came over and relieved me and asked, "What in hell were you two talking about?"

"He wanted to know how my old CO in the 406 was doing, and I told him he was fine the last time I saw him and mentioned he'd put on a little weight and said that he ought to get out more, and, I asked how his wife and kids were —"

"Go to hell, Gilliland. You must have said something he liked, but so did everyone he talked to in the hut. I think he left happy."

Duty on the Parallel turned out to be my favorite duty while I was in the army. I loved those mornings when we were on the Parallel. I would awake an hour before the whistle blew and take a book and walk out along the trails between the rice paddies until I reached a spot that overlooked the valley, "the Land of the Morning Calm," they called it. I'd heard it first at one of those Missionary Sundays at First Methodist Church in Beaumont. It truly was a land of calm mornings, even though most of my buddies spoke the slogan derisively. It was Wordsworthian, as I see it now, as I came to see it when I began to read the Lake poets, not because this part of Korea resembled Lake Grasmere or Keswick—nothing resembles the lakes—but because this place still comes to me as the River Wye and Tintern Abbey and the golden daffodils came to Wordsworth. It was all because I was nineteen and I had come through the war untouched in my body but not in my mind, and to be young in a far country, away from home and living among these men and these people was indeed a very heaven for me.

Years later, when I would sit in "pensive mood" and let my mind slide back to a spot where I had been most at peace, it would slip into that place where I took my book to read. If it is true that "nature never did betray the heart that loved her," in my mind's eye, this was the nature the line was speaking of.

My most poignant memory of those two weeks on the Parallel was the sight of that first long line of Japanese moving south past the Russian outpost, climbing slowly down over the crumpled bridge and back up to our guard hut. We had been told to expect large numbers of Japanese, whole families, maybe entire communities, all on their way from the factories, mines, mills, and cities of Manchuria and North Korea on their way to the home islands. I can't forget the sight of that line moving inexorably on, so slowly at first, though not as slowly as it could have been, considering the number of elderly and the number of small children in the long lines, many of whom were tied papoose-like to the backs of older sisters, grandmothers, and even little brothers.

We had expected thirty or forty at the most, but this crop numbered several hundred. They were moving steadily, with only two or three lagging further to the rear. At the checkpoint, the guard and Barker directed them to a large open field we had enclosed by a single strand of barbed wire to keep them from spilling into farming plots near the border. Sergeant Ishihara, the interpreter from military government in Uijeongbu, had waited until the last family entered the area then spoke to them as they assembled off the road south of our guard hut. They listened silently to his instructions and explanations, never raising a question or speaking back. Then each family went about making small family camps, spreading their inevitable reed mats on the ground in neat patterns, always settling their infants and old people first. Once they had arranged their households, they set about making tea or preparing pots of soup on little kerosene stoves. We furnished nothing; they carried everything they needed. Small children never strayed far from their mothers or older sisters. There were no boys over twelve or men under fifty. The few older men wore dark suits or jackets and fedora hats. Their coats or trousers were dusty and wrinkled, but no one appeared in rags. These, after all, were the families of middle-class Japanese businessmen and civil servants who had been running the occupied territories. The women all wore *mompei*, the same strange balloon-shaped pants tied close at the ankles we had seen in the warehouse in Mukho. They wore an overlapping kimono-like upper garment stuffed in at the waist. Some of the older women wore kimonos with the wide obi at the waist, and on their feet were *zori* or *geta*, straw thongs or wooden clogs, some so worn you could hardly see their elevating blocks. A few men who had been on Okinawa could even speak words of greeting or issue simple commands, but no real communication took place, except through our interpreter, Ishihara.

In the mess hall at the end of the Quonset that night, Ric reiterated that our job was to make sure they were not molested or harassed by the Koreans. "We know how the Koreans despised the Japanese," he said. "Remember that lecture we got last winter?" He went on to say that a year ago, he damn sure despised the Japs. "But you know the war's over! No one can screw this operation up!"

A few heads nodded in agreement. He posted a guard roster, listing two pairs each shift walking back and forth along the road just to make sure no one disturbed them. The next day there, I saw no signs of anger or hate expressed by anyone.

When I sailed out of New York for the ETO aboard the *Louis Pasteur*, I had been retreaded as an antiaircraft gunner and a look-out, and now I was being retreaded again, this time into a medic here on the Thirty-Eighth Parallel. Shortly after the IG left, a detail of medics came up and taught us how to give the shots and vaccinations. None of us had ever given shots, but we learned quickly, apparently so well that none of the Japanese ever complained of our technique, but then it would have been dishonorable to complain, would have dishonored Japan and all repatriates, though we did see a number of blood-streaked arms because we used the same needles again and again, dropping the needle into a beaker of alcohol after each use. To avoid stabbing anyone too viciously with a hypodermic, I got myself assigned to smallpox vaccinations that required only a small scratch with a tiny lancet that came with each dose of the vaccine.

None of us had ever seen anything quite like it. The morning after they arrived, families lined up along the road and rolled up sleeves or removed their shirts or blouses and silently passed between the men inoculating them for typhus, cholera, and smallpox. A few of the guys found it quite difficult to concentrate on the smooth upper arms of young women who had nonchalantly removed their blouses and all their upper garments. We did as the medics had shown us: one man filled the syringe from the small bottle of serum and made sure there was no bubble of air in the needle, another took it and jabbed it in the bared arm, then another took the syringe and dropped the needle in a beaker of alcohol and the syringe in another beaker. Another man picked up the used needles and syringes and returned them to the head of the line where still another reassembled the needle and syringe and passed it to the man who repeated the process. After the inoculations, we sprayed them with DDT, stuffing long tubes down backs and inside their trousers until clouds of insecticide billowed above and below. No one was aware at the time that DDT might be toxic for humans, but had we or the Japanese known, I doubt it would have made a difference, so happy were they to be rid of the vermin carried all along the way. The final step in the process required the head of each family group to turn over all currency to Ishihara and his assistant who gave them receipts that would be redeemed when they landed in Japan. The reasons for confiscating the money were twofold: first to exchange the Korean and Manchurian currency, which was worthless, and then to prevent their being hijacked along the way. I assume the U.S. made good of the Manchurian currency.

That evening, after the Japanese had left on trucks, we sat around and talked about what we had seen and what we had done. Ishihara said he had spoken to a few of the Japanese. Some, he said, had traveled part of the way by rail, boxcars mostly, but the last stretch of several hundred kilometers through North Korea had been on foot. A few elderly grandparents had died along the way, mostly of pneumonia, a few of exhaustion, spiritual and physical, he said. No one had talked about it much, he said. We had done all we could to alleviate their fears and anxieties, and they had been grateful; a few had thanked us, he said. We listened as he told what a giant step down each had been forced to take by the defeat and then the trip back to the home islands.

Many of these people, Ishi explained, were members of a "ruling class" in a government and industry that had ruled harshly, so harshly that the people in Korea were not likely soon to forget. The financial losses they suffered were huge but nothing close to the loss of self-worth and family honor. Suicide had been common in the days and months before the diaspora began. Then Bisket reminded everyone that these people had been the overlords and could not be considered entirely as victims.

Ishihara, a graduate of the University of Washington, had seen his own family, all American citizens, herded by the United States government into "relocation centers," euphemism for concentration camps, shortly after Pearl Harbor. He, like thousands of young Nisei men, had volunteered for the service, and because he had studied Japanese and was virtually bilingual, he became an interpreter-interrogator. He smiled and noted that although he was a college graduate, the highest rank he was able to reach was sergeant, while white boys, whose Japanese was a lot less fluent, were commissioned second lieutenants. No one asked him how he felt about his family's internment because none of us knew much about it, and we knew almost nothing about it because the stories had not been widely printed. No one was interested.

Over the next three months, C Company processed thousands, some passing through in large groups, some in smaller groups of fifty or so. It was the most important duty I would take part in all the time I was in the army. Whenever I could, I talked with Ishihara about what it meant to him; I tried to get him to explain what the relocation centers were like, but he very politely let me know he wasn't ready to discuss it.

I would have enjoyed telling Dr. Mac about the experience, about how we tried to make the whole process as painless as possible, and how we tried to avoid using insulting or disparaging gestures or words. Ishi was always there not just as a translator but also as someone who could interpret the patterns of Japanese culture to us because knowing those patterns made our job easier. Ishihara told me he visited Japan as a student fresh out of high school in the summer before he began college and told how he had seen firsthand the way of life he heard his parents speak of. He said he understood for the first time why they had immigrated first to Hawaii and then to Washington State. They were traditionalists, he said, but had never wanted to return to Japan. It had pleased them that he had studied Japanese at the university, but they were afraid he might want to return. Ishi laughed. He was too American to ever want to go back and stay, though he had enjoyed his prewar visit.

"You know, Japan claims that all Nisei, people like me, are automatically Japanese citizens wherever they happen to be born. If I'd been in Japan on

Pearl Harbor Day, they would have drafted me. I had a cousin who got trapped like that," he said.

Ishi was never confused about who *he* was, never sympathized with their situation any more than we did, and that I found even more interesting. That Ishihara was able to explain to us so much of the culture of these defeated travelers was a conundrum. At the same time, most of the men in my platoon still vigorously resisted any effort to learn about the Korean culture around them. Of course, men like Quiz and Bisket, a fellow named Lansfear, and Stowell and Aleman were all eager to learn all they could, but most simply pined for home.

Later that summer, when we took our turn on the Parallel, the size of the groups had begun to decease sharply from the peak of our first two weeks, and they began arriving less frequently. By August, the largest group we had was less than a hundred; it was still a sad and depressing sight. I recall we had worked steadily most of the afternoon without shirts, and most of the Japanese had stripped to the waist, even the old people, men and women. When we finished work that afternoon, I was convinced we were actually doing something of value, something far more important than the pointless patrols through the farming villages along the Parallel. It was past four o'clock in the afternoon when the last person finished at Ishihara's desk. We had worked fast so the "visitors" would not have to sleep another night in the field and could leave on the trucks that evening, even if it meant riding all night down to a seaport, probably Mukho, on the East Coast.

Satisfied with ourselves for moving them through so well, we were lying on the embankment below the hut when we saw the small dark figure of a little boy fifty yards or so up the road barely moving, limping along so slowly you could almost feel his pain. His pace was so determined, so painful, we felt an urge to run to him, even though he was still inside the Russian zone. My first impulse was to rush down through the rubble of the bridge and get him, but we had strict orders never to cross the line. Three of us ran just as far as the line and watched as he carefully made his way to the rubble of broken concrete. As he stumbled down through the concrete rubble, two of us clambered down and met him, lifted him, and carried him up to the checkpoint. Hardly five or six years old and more bones than meat, he looked at us with stark fear in his eyes, too weak to protest or cry out. The only sound he made was a soft wheezing noise. He was wearing a thin, black pullover shirt and black cotton pants several sizes too large. Over his shoulder was a small leatherette bag that he clutched as if it held something of great value.

When I sat him down on a table in the kitchen, Ishihara spoke to him softly and gave him a cup of water, which he drank and asked for more. The little canteen in his bag was empty. Ishihara asked if his mother or family were with the group that we had just processed. He said no. They had left him days ago. He continued to look with fear at those of us crowding around, and Ishi quietly asked us to move back, which we did, and he gradually relaxed. Someone brought a small oatmeal cake crumbled in a cup, and he took it, nibbling slowly.

"They left him to die," Ishihara said, his own voice trembling as he rose. Then he shouted, "Someone hold the trucks!"

Stowell ran out shouting the Korean word for stop. The room was stone silent. A hundred questions raced through our minds. What kind of mother would desert a child? Who was the leader that would have allowed it? If that wasn't his group in the trucks now, why had they passed him, left him alone, and why would the Koreans have allowed him to continue stumbling all alone up the road, and how had he, so obviously ill and so weak, been able to continue? What must he have felt? In his eyes was the same look we had seen in the photographs and newsreels of faces staring through barbed wire at places like Belsen or Buchenwald. This was the extremity of war, impossible to conceive, not an atrocity conceived and committed by an SS guard or a holocaust engineer, more horrifying than the bombed-out cities, the dozens of wrecked stations and rail yards we had passed through chasing the 102. I had read of the piles of gold fillings accumulated at Auschwitz, how camp guards had made lampshades of human skin, of the bundles of human hair, floors covered with eyeglasses, but those stories were abstractions. Here was an atrocity we could see and touch, one not committed by the ideologues and dogmatists of extinction but one committed by the disease of war itself, by fear and desperation that wars bring in their wake. This boy was a casualty of a fifth horseman, perhaps the most horrible horseman of the apocalypse. Almost a year had passed since the last shots were fired, but still, the war continued to reverberate and kill not by the enemy but by desertion, by being left behind.

Ishihara lifted the boy and carried him to the trucks just outside Yungmun-yi. When some of those in the truck saw us coming, they turned away, and when Ishihara asked whom the child belonged to, they continued to avert their eyes. No one spoke even as Ishihara, ordinarily so calm and patient, raised his voice and spoke in sharp, angry tones. No one admitted knowing or having ever seen him. A few villagers came out to see what was causing the commotion around the trucks and stood around looking curiously at our angry interpreter. By now, it was clear we were all angry about something. Ishi and I went to the lead truck where Ishi asked the driver if he spoke Japanese.

He said he spoke a little. Ishi explained that the boy would ride in the cab with him, that he would telephone the next checkpoint and the checkpoint after that and told him that an American military government officer would be looking for the boy, and the boy had better be riding in the cab with him. The driver vigorously nodded in agreement. Then Ishi delivered the same message to the people in the truck. They bowed their heads in agreement. He had apparently gotten through to them. When we returned to the Quonset, Ishihara cranked the phone and got through to his CO in Uijeongbu, telling him what had happened and of the orders he had passed on to the driver. We were all shaken.

"You shoulda been on Okinawa," someone said softly. "It was like that at the end, abandoned kids, dead kids. Hell, it made you sick. Parents and kids committing suicide together."

No one responded, none had been there, but then I forced myself to reply, "There's no comparison. It isn't pretty or easy being forced to walk all the way from Manchuria, or wherever they started. These people are being cared for, being treated with respect and kindness, not threatened with death or prison. Look! For God's sake, they're getting a ride, a fucking ride, to the seaport and a boat home."

I was just noise. It was beyond comprehension, beyond explaining. I knew then I would never forget the sad, frightened, tearless face of a lost child left behind by a mother afraid that stopping or carrying might lessen the chances of her other children. Questions whirled like the maelstrom as I searched for reasons, some answer, any answer. Late into the night, I kept hearing the last few lines from a poem I'd read just a few days before. I couldn't recall the poet or the title. Opening the anthology, I read the lines and repeated them over and over to myself and understood them now in a new way:

> For the world, which seems
> To lie before us like a land of dreams,
> So various, so beautiful, so new,
> Hath really neither joy, nor love, nor light,
> Nor certitude, nor peace, nor help for pain;
> And we are here as on a darkling plain . . .

That's for sure, I thought, *it only* seems *beautiful and new.* Only minutes before I saw the boy on the road, I had basked in warmth of a satisfying accomplishment, complimenting myself and all my friends in the platoon for a job well done and for a summer that had made me proud. We were proud—too proud?—that we had felt no anger toward the people who for four years we had been taught to hate, proud that our humane treatment of these thousands was proof that the war was over; but seeing the boy, feeling those bones, seeing him tearless and lost, that look on his face—the war was not over. It would never be over for the mother who must have felt compelled somehow to abandon him, sick and dying, perhaps afraid that he would hold them back, would jeopardize the lives of her remaining children. They call it triage but a decision no parent should ever be compelled to make. There were *no* certitudes, and there *is* no help for pain.

In the years to come, whenever I assigned the poetry of Arnold—and "Dover Beach" would always be part of that assignment—that scene would return like a lesion that refused to heal, and sometimes, not often, I would feel I had to tell the story and hope the listeners would understand that which still embraces as the great enigma.

* * *

While the people in Pocheon were much friendlier than the people in Mukho, language was still a serious barrier to making friends. The army's phrase books helped us with basic Korean, but few of us managed to get beyond the first pages. We could order one, two, or three beers and ask where the bathroom was, but the only beer in Pocheon was our GI beer ration, and no one in Pocheon seriously cared whether you used a bathroom or the street. John Quessenberry and I made friends with the local electrician and radio repairman when our radio went on the blink. He had visited the tent to make repairs on our electrical wiring and had suggested we bring our radio to his shop when he noticed it wasn't working. That he spoke more than a few words of English was a surprise, but that he generously invited us to his house was an earthquake. He told us he had been studying English since he was a boy and had attended a mission school, but Japanese discouraged Koreans from studying foreign languages. We had tea and cakes in the *matang* and visited with his wife briefly. It was the first time we had been invited into a Korean's home. We would visit his house a number of times and always feel welcome. We were not the only members of the company to break the ice in Pocheon.

By the end of June, several of us had made trips to Seoul where we browsed the shops in Bung Chung Street, the major shopping district for souvenirs, but we found the prices so inflated by the GIs stationed there permanently we grew discouraged and returned to Pocheon. John Quessenberry and I visited the bookstalls, where I collected a handful of cheap German texts with

Japanese glosses, along with older Armed Services Editions I hadn't read. The fine Korean ceramics and paintings in the little antique shops were far too expensive for us. Had we hoarded our cigarette rations, we might have had the money to barter with, but like country cousins visiting the big city, we were ignorant of the ways of this world, and our trips to Seoul served mainly to convince us that we were better off in Pocheon. With the advent of our large gasoline-driven "reefer," we found the beer in C Company was colder and cheaper than the beer in Seoul.

Now that our radio was working, thanks to Pak, Armed Forces Radio broadcasts from Seoul—and on good days from Tokyo—did more than anything to alleviate the boredom, particularly for the men who didn't read. The radio was turned on every morning at reveille and played continuously until lights out, regardless what was playing. There were moments during a Jack Benny show or a Red Skelton broadcast when I would almost imagine I was home. Radio dramas, quiz shows, variety hours were all recorded transcriptions of the stateside network shows; in place of commercials were occasional official announcements, but the major interest was the music. But even the radio grew boring after a time, and my only relief was the same as it had always been, the books, those I had brought with me, the ones Jane or my mother sent, and the reliable Armed Services Editions. By this time, I no longer discriminated between trash and treasure. Out of sheer necessity, I read everything that came through, works I would have refused to give a second look at any other time. Ironically, many of the works I would have ignored were classics, works like *The Decameron*, *The Odyssey*, and serious short works like Henry James's *Daisy Miller* and the poems of Robert Frost, some of which I had read in high school but had not recalled.

Unlike B Company in Germany, the average educational level of the men in C Company was only a bit higher than it had been in basic training. The fourth platoon's average IQ was measurably higher than the other platoons because heavy weapons, mortars and machine guns, required a different kind of intelligence than the rifle platoon. I often found myself explaining the meaning of certain passages or simply retelling a plot line or explaining a character or identifying a locale. That they read and were interested enough to ask questions told me that, inside, there was a latent intelligence that might be tapped. Had these men not reached the nadir of boredom, they might never have decided to read any of the free books that were at their disposal. And had they not read, they would have had no questions. I learned that a lack of formal education did not denote a lack of intelligence. It was an idea I had heard and repeated often myself, but I had never quite understood what it was about. That I knew these men well, that they were now my friends, made me look deeper and with greater empathy. Every day my eyes were opened by men who had, in the beginning, declared they never read; now they were reading as much as I was and questioning more.

One of the most popular novels was a true potboiler, Elizabeth Gouge's *Green Dolphin Street*. Men who had never read a complete novel would read it, apparently enraptured by the exotic New Zealand passages. When *Forever Amber* was making the rounds or *Captain from Castile*, questions inevitably arose about its historical authenticity or about details that had nothing to do with the plot or the conflict, which was just as well, since there was nothing original or arresting in either. When Amber St. Claire saves her lover's life by lancing the buboes in his groin during the year of the plague, the men who read it questioned whether such a thing could really happen. I explained that swelling lymph glands were symptoms of the plague and that it was caused by accumulation of dead white blood cells or puss. They were amazed that anyone would know such a thing. I said that I really didn't know much about it but that I had read about it in medical encyclopedias out of curiosity. I then explained that the buboes was where the term *bubonic* came from, and that the old term for one form of venereal disease, "blue balls," was probably a corrupted cognate of buboes, not from the plague but from syphilis. After that they, singly or in pairs, would come to my bunk quietly and would ask me to explain "difficult" passages. Even works like *Forever Amber* that were written for mass audiences contained subtleties too opaque for some readers. I felt an over powering exhilaration when I had a chance to explain these passages, though most of the time, my explanations were sheerest guesswork.

I would recall the pleasures of D deck classroom on the *LeRoy Eltinge*. One novel really disturbed them, not because of violence or salacious sex or the plot. "Disturbed" is probably too strong a word to describe what they felt. I heard comments about it for weeks before it came my way, and when I finally read it, I was surprised at how beautifully written it was, but I understood why it unsettled some of the men, and I wondered why the selection committee had picked the title.

I had never heard of the author and wondered why I hadn't. It was so "well written," the general term we gave anything that was both easy to read and enjoyable. They asked me in mumbled disbelief if it was about "homos" or "queers" or what. Someone would remark how "well written" it was, and then he would say, "But I don't know if I like it." Like Mr. Roberts in Heggin's novel, I distrusted that praise, "well written," for like Ensign Pulver, it often meant the author had written graphically about sex or written slavering descriptions of a Darlin' Jill's "rising beauties." Homosexuality was taboo in the army of 1946, taboo almost everywhere, though I never knew anyone harassed or abused because of it. We knew it existed, but the fact was very few people understood it, and taboo was manifested more as an embarrassment than anything else. I don't recall righteous Christians denouncing it.

Now as I look back, the reaction to William Maxwell's *The Folded Leaf* bears out my contention. The story of two boys and their affection and love for each other is central to the plot of the novel, though Maxwell, as I recollect, never mentions the word "homo" or "queer," and no overt homoerotic scene occurs in the novel. Their friendship never crosses the line, nor is there a clearly "feminine" male. It is about a successful and very masculine schoolboy and his admiring much less masculine friend and about the nature of their devotion and loyalty to each other. Damon and Pythius, David and Jonathan, there are numerous pairs for which a case may be made. And I suspected, though never explored it, that those most disturbed by the question likely had experienced a strong friendship that made them question themselves--silently, of course.

Remember, the men in this platoon were quite young, even the few combat veterans who still remained, and most were unsophisticated sexually, in spite of boasts, and many were afraid to raise questions about homosexuality. In the end, most said they liked the novel and understood the friendship, bonding it would be called today, without feeling any discomfort. I am convinced today that whatever the relationship Maxwell intended—and I believe he did intend a homosexual attachment if not an active physical attachment—the young men who read the book accepted it because it was so "well written," which in the case of *The Folded Leaf* meant more than the ease and flow of language but because of its essential honesty and humanity. "Well written" meant to the men in fourth platoon that it was easy to read, to enjoy, and to see and feel--you know--Conrad's aim in the preface to *The Nigger of the "Narcissus,"* which is, in the end, to Maxwell's great credit. As Oscar Wilde stated, there are no "bad books," only badly written books, or something to that effect.

And in the end, these books performed a service far outweighing their importance as diversions or entertainment. It was impossible for anyone to read such writers as Mann, Huxley, Faulkner, Thurber, Lardner, O'Hara, Dorothy Parker, Fitzgerald, and Thomas Wolfe and not be affected by a world beyond the strictures of one's own mind and world. Many of us, because of the little ASE editions, had already read more since we had been overseas than many of the men would read in a lifetime. Max Brand, Luke Short, Ernest Haycox, along with Raymond Chandler, Earl Stanley Gardner broadened and deepened our lives by giving us another dimension of experience to explore the world about us.

Our discussions were not one-sided affairs but were real dialogues, sometimes quite searching. I learned many lessons about teaching and learning that summer, but mostly, I learned how to listen. Most of these men, really boys, had never read fiction seriously, and many had not read a book all the way through until they reached Charley Company. That they were now regularly reading books "from cover to cover" was largely because there was nothing else to do and because there was a reliable supply of books to read. Several guys in the platoon admitted to me, privately, that they might never have read anything if it had not been for me. I believed them and took pains not to allow their confession to go to my head.

Of all the writers in the collection, Erskine Caldwell was the favorite and *God's Little Acre* the favorite of all, but the much less raucous *Tragic Ground* was a close second. Those men, who came from the South, where poverty ruled like the poverty in Caldwell's books, swore that Caldwell had not exaggerated the conditions. Many of them were also fond of a small novel by George Sessions Perry, whose *Hold Autumn in Your Hand* had reached the bestseller lists before the war. His earlier and less well-known *Walls Rise Up* treated the Brazos River folk humorously while telling profound truths of people impacted by sad economic conditions. It is a minor classic by any standard. I had not heard of it before nor have I heard of anyone who has read the book since; I consider it a measure of the intelligence of the selectors that it was included. My fellow readers recommended the book highly for its accurate descriptions of the people. It had flavors of Steinbeck and Caldwell with a touch of Faulkner in his lighter mood.

I had no thought at the time that I would one day make a living teaching literature, that I would be speaking to classes of freshmen and sophomores in pretty much in the same way I talked about it in that fourth platoon squad tent across the river from Pocheon. My college classes would be a little more organized and slightly better planned. I would raise questions more often than the guys in the tent did, but I listened to their questions and learned where the doubt and disbelief originated just as I would one day in Introduction to Literature. In the long run, the discussions didn't differ all that much.

I look back on those literary seminars in the weapons platoon as my practice teaching, the only difference being that I had no supervisor and got no college credit, but I firmly believe it to be as pedagogically sound as most courses now offered in colleges of education. Since I never took a methods course, nor had to do a semester of supervised practice teaching, I cannot vouch that what I just said is true, but I know my platoon asked questions more freely, suggested answers more willingly than the regular freshman or sophomore college student. Their bullshit detectors were far sharper than the ordinary freshman college student and a few graduate students.

Two things sustained me through most of my second year in the army: those book discussions we had that summer and my growing interest in Korea and the people. Today I credit the Armed Services Editions with pointing me in a new direction, along with the generous-minded men in my platoon who tolerated me and my tastes in music and joined with me in the impromptu seminars, for they taught me, simply by asking me their questions, to think more critically. Also, they were not afraid or ashamed to say, "Gilliland, you don't know what the shit you're talking about." I often had to agree. Their curiosity forced me to think about literature as pleasure and as a way of understanding "the human condition" beyond the tent or the classroom. It was the generosity of spirit in that handful of men in my section that allowed us to have the dialogues. Without these elements working together the less than inspiring intellectual atmosphere that generally prevailed in C Company would have been torture. In Germany, under the influence of men like Charley Knowles, I had just begun to enjoy the pleasures of intellect, without which life would have been a virtual Sahara of the mind.

I was appalled when, in 1951, I read Shaw's *The Young Lions* and read his description of how the NCOs tormented and harassed the main character for wanting to read, for even having a book—Joyce's *Ulysses,* I think—in his footlocker. My situation was entirely different from character's in Shaw's novel: no one criticized my footlocker library that contained Durant's *The Story of Philosophy* and my Modern Library *Five Great Shakespearean Tragedies.* My serious reading happened while I was an established member of a platoon, not a trainee, but I seriously doubt that Ortiz or any of the cadre would have found a reason to deride anyone's reading. I never encountered any men, all the time I was in the army, like those on Shaw's novel. What I might have done had I joined a typical rifle company when I arrived in Germany, I can only surmise. When I joined C Company, I had been in the army over a year, longer than many in the platoon, and I had served overseas, so I was not put through a trial period in which I had to prove myself. My taste in books, music, and conversation was never seriously challenged, simply because of my earlier experience overseas in an infantry outfit, simply because of the Ozark patch I wore when I arrived, though I was often characterized as being a "highbrow," which I took as a compliment, and was encouraged by the willingness of the men in the tent to take part in discussions about *books!*.

The rainy season began in Korea early in July. Coming from East Texas, I was familiar with days of rain but nothing I had ever seen compared to the rain that fell that July 4 in Pocheon. Several of us had taken the truck into Seoul, hoping to spend a three-day pass, eating, seeing movies, and sightseeing, but the rain in Seoul was just as bad as it had been in the company. So we found a truck returning to Uijeongbu and took it back that far, and Quiz wrangled us a ride to Pocheon.

All night, we could hear the soothing tattoo of rain on the tent. But in the morning, when we heard the sounds of reveille and the rain still beating down on the tent, Stowell's prognostications regarding our levee took on significance. It had been raining off and on for over three days this time. By the time we returned from breakfast, we were beginning to worry that Rendo had been right about the earthen dike; already, the river's level was higher than the level of the company's street, and some claimed it was higher than the entrance to the tent. If the dike gave way, we'd all end up in the Russian zone. Quiz, Bisket, and I didn't wait for orders from Gillespie who went about his business oblivious of the rising waters. Steinfield clambered to the top of the dike and returned calling the noncoms to the orderly room. After breakfast, Bisket, Quiz, and I had already organized the fourth platoon and had begun carrying our footlockers and cots to the high ground above the company amphitheater. When Barker returned from the CP, he ordered everyone to move all the gear to high ground then told the three of us to organize a detail and begin taking down the tents before the water got any higher, but we had already begun to pull the pegs.

The river was already cresting the bridge that connected us to the highway. In some tents, the duckboards were afloat. Without being told, men all along the line began pulling tent pegs and collecting those already washed loose by the rushing water. Somewhere upstream the river breached the dike, and water, almost knee deep, filled the space between the tents and the dike.

All up and down the company street, people were pulling floating boxes, footlockers, cots, and the furnishings from inside the tents up to higher ground, but there was no panic, no pointless rushing to and fro. People were either hauling masses of canvas and poles up the hill or were carrying supplies. I saw Lieutenant Steinfield carrying a cumbersome file cabinet and supervising the removal of the orderly room. The bulldozer that had sat idle almost from the time since we first arrived was dragging pallets of crates from the supply tent to higher ground, its tracks churning through the mud and water. No one counted the number of trips it made carrying whatever it could up the hill and back. I was resting for a moment on the side of the hill when I suddenly realized Steinfield had no one to help him move the officer's tent. It was standing alone, next to the spot where the fourth platoon's tents had stood and was beginning to sway. He had been so busy moving the CP records and equipment that he'd neglected all his own stuff. Quiz, Bisket, and I pulled together half a dozen men from the fourth platoon and began collecting all his belongings and stashing them on the hill above the high watermark. Much of his gear was soaked, but we saved it all, even his footlocker of booze, the treasure trove about which many stories had circulated since I first arrived in Korea. Incongruously among the GI equipment was an old, now water-logged easy chair looking like a piece of flotsam, sad and forlorn. Steinfield must have salvaged it on one of his trips from a furniture store in Seoul.

I have no idea how long we took to empty the tents and carry them to the high ground; it seemed like days, though it couldn't have been more than a couple of hours. Had we started immediately after reveille, we would have lost nothing. Even so, we lost very little, only the mess tent and half a drum of gasoline, the most expendable things we had. In less than two hours, the river had transformed our perfectly aligned company street, our neat little tent city, into a rushing river the color of creamed coffee the width of a football field. Debris of all sorts—tree limbs, timbers, fragments of fencing—floated by. There was not a trace of the company street or the tent sites the engineers had so carefully aligned. I heard Steinfield tell the first sergeant to call the platoon sergeants together and to meet with him in the latrine that was now the CP; the giant twelve-holer was still intact. Miraculously, the engineers had erected it above the flood plain.

By early afternoon, we had set up our two squad tents among the trees on the hill. I was frankly in awe of the men in my section. Once I mentioned that it would be a good idea to get the tent up so we could be under cover for the night, they all began laying out a rectangle along the most level section of our part of the hill. No one issued an order or told anyone what to do. They just set about doing it. Although no one in the fourth had ever pitched one of the monsters, it went up with ease. I could see others were as amazed as I and twice as proud. Quessenberry was laughing, Barker smiling, and I was overjoyed when one of the crew that had saved Steinfield's tent produced a half-filled bottle of brandy. Most of our equipment had survived without a soaking; even my small library had been spared. In the rush to get our things out of the tent, I had forgotten that I had dumped all my books in my footlocker and had covered it with a poncho. Barker went to each man and checked like a good mother hen to see if anyone had scrapes or scratches that would need first aid. He passed the word that floodwaters are dangerously contaminated, and we had all been wading, some up to our waists. As he passed each cot, he examined feet and legs and thanked each man for his efforts. It had been a hell of a day, but at the end, throughout, the company morale was the highest I had ever seen it. And it wasn't Steinfield's brandy we were high on.

The next morning, the cooks who had worked all night reshaping their kitchen and mess tents served a hot breakfast. They, along with volunteers from the platoons, had stayed up most of the night arranging their cook tent, reassembling the hastily dismantled stoves so that they could serve a hot breakfast on time. The company bugler even blew chow call that morning. Most of the water had receded. It was hard to believe that, less than twenty-four hours earlier, there had been a busy company street and a long line of squad tents in the flats before us. All the topsoil moved in by engineers to make the company street was washed down to the original gravel and rubble of a wadi. Nature had already taken it all back. The river raged in its original channel, entirely free of the offending dike. "Something there is that doesn't love a wall," I said, quite out of context, but it seemed to fit.

Nothing epitomized the American occupation of Korea so clearly as the sight before us. Writing this from the distance of fifty years, one can see how we had landed in Korea and attempted to bring about change but had only placed our stamp on the surface of an existing culture. For centuries, that river had flooded year after year with such regularity that no one had ever built in its flood plain, and so no serious damage had occurred, no disaster struck to alter life. We could see the collapsed span of the bridge now, the washed-out pillars, and on the opposite shore, the people of the Pocheon standing, gazing at our company. We waved, and they waved back. It would be several weeks before trucks would cross the bridge but only days before the villagers had erected timbers across the space so that we could visit the little village. I doubt that the engineer who planned and executed the construction of C Company asked anyone in the village about the river's habits; then I also doubt that anyone in the village volunteered what they knew about the river. We all wagered that if the people of Pocheon *had* offered advice, a captain or a major would have ignored it.

A week after the flood, we were still cut off from the battalion, except for the news and orders of the day that came by radio. The lieutenant suspended all special details and all but a single roadblock guard south of the village. With a span of the bridge washed away, we had no way of receiving supplies from battalion; no other roads connected us to our base. It took only a few days before we had exhausted all our food supplies. One day, a line of villagers from Pocheon made its way across the temporary footpath over the bridge and delivered us bundles of rice, small potatoes, and onions. Unlike our Soviet counterparts to the north, the American forces had never relied on the Koreans for food supplies but had imported everything from the States, but now Korea was our only supplier. It is testimony to the character of the Koreans that they generously gave us these bundles before we even requested them. We assumed that the goods were being sold to us, but Steinfield said they were delivered without a request for payment. Potatoes, rice, and onions would not suffice, however, and Steinfield urgently requested an airdrop.

Two days after the gifts of rice and potatoes, battalion radioed that Air Transport Command would drop us emergency food and mail at 1400. The C-47 was right on time. The company gathered on the hill to watch the two cargo planes fly in from the north and swoop down over the fields barely two hundred feet off the ground, cargo doors gaping. On the first pass they waved to us made a climbing turn and circled back to the north. On the return, they were so low we could see the faces of the men as they kicked out the heavy bales of food. The first bundles came tumbling out the wide door and landed dead center on the target we had etched just beyond the company area. On the second and third passes, the bundles missed the target and bounced and landed further south, one barely missing our precious reefer. On the last pass, their "aim" was much better; the bundle hit the reefer dead center without a bounce, smashing the sides of the box, sending insulation and parts flying in all directions. A great cry rose from the gathering on the hill, a mourner's keening expressing our great loss. It was as if the flood were not bad enough. Why did we have to lose our beloved reefer and all hope of cold beer in Charley Company? Early on flood day, we had been most concerned that the dozer save the giant reefer that meant frozen meat and cold beer. The dozer driver, without an order, put a chain on the skids somehow and pulled it to high ground then ground his way back to help salvage the supply room equipment. He was, at that moment, an anointed hero, but now it was all for naught. What made it worse was the news a few days later that the airdrops had earned the pilots and crews letters of commendation from our corps commander, General Hodges. There was no mention of us, the stranded companies that had saved all their supplies and a precious reefer, with no loss of life or serious injury. It was ever thus, someone said, and I recalled Lieutenant Banks' assessment of the infantry as the earth's lowest order of life and was reminded of the dour welcoming speech at Camp Wolters informing us that the infantry was the queen of battles and of the rules of the "army game." It was a fact of a soldier's life going back as far as Napoleon—no, further back to the Roman legions. The more abuse or neglect one heaped upon him, the more impervious he becomes to the next abuse. It molds and builds character so well that, eventually, one's pride in his survival transcends the slings and arrows of all fortune.

The squads that had been guarding the parallel had remained there all that time, securing supplies directly from battalion. The Quonset hut was high and dry. As far as they knew, there had been no flooding, except from the flood of Japanese that passed through. When they returned and related the stories of the fine food that battalion had furnished, no one would believe them, nor would they believe the horror stories we related.

A few weeks after the airdrop, army engineers appeared on the far side and repaired our bridge, allowing us to receive supplies regularly. The repairs might have been made earlier, but all trained combat engineers had rotated home, and the ones who effected the repairs had to be flown in for that purpose alone. Until then, we subsisted on C rations and whatever we could buy from the farmers in Pocheon. But in an odd way, the flood had been a blessing: it had furnished us with the task of rebuilding the company, a job that would occupy us for several weeks and would mitigate the boredom and monotony we would otherwise have to contend with. It took weeks to clear away the flood's debris, to realign and level the new company streets high above the flood plain, and finally to pitch again the squad tents, not in a single line but in three rows forming a neat square tent city.

While we were busy laying out the new streets and leveling the ground for the tents, a new second lieutenant fresh from OCS joined the company, allowing Steinfield to return to the States. Steinfield had become a familiar fixture now, securing for us a beer ration and even joining bunches of men for bouts of drinking. We hated to see him go. Though no one ever really got to know him well, we had become accustomed to his style, and we knew what to expect and not expect. In the weeks after the flood and during the restoration of the company, Steinfield had come out of his shell and had worked closely with us. As soon as the bridge was repaired, he made numerous trips to battalion to try to get better rations and a replacement for our bombed-out reefer.

The new lieutenant, Francis Foote, just out of OCS, looked more like one who had just graduated from high school, and though he was friendly and worked closely with us as we finished the restoration, we cynically assumed he would change when Steinfield left. We were wrong. Foote was different from any of the officers we had in the company, and that was, as it turned out, a serious problem.

By the time the tents were reset and the new area established, we lost all combat veterans of the division, except the handful who had reenlisted under the same deal I had, some having requested return to their original outfits. When the last of the old-timers returned home, our company strength fell below fifty percent of its normal strength.

Quessenberry became platoon sergeant, though everyone knew it would be only a matter of weeks, maybe a month at the most, before he too would receive orders. A handful of fresh replacements joined us, a few barely eighteen and fresh from a much shorter basic training, the absence of war making extensive live ammo training superfluous. As Quiz moved up the ladder, I became the LMG section leader; we had no need for squad leaders since there were not enough men to form more than a squad. Work details came to a halt when the company was replanted and guard duty in the company area was confined to a single roadblock south of Pocheon and a company guard post.

Lieutenant Foote continued two daily patrols to the outlying villages for no other reason than to announce our continued presence. Shortly before the flood, our excellent first sergeant left, and we inherited a twenty-year man who came to us with the rank of corporal. Someone asked, "Twenty years, and only a corporal?" One had to wonder. His longevity immediately earned him the promotion, that and the fact that he was regular army with a three-year hitch guaranteed assured him of the position of top soldier. At first, we believed him when he said he had been up the ladder and busted back by a "chicken shit" West Pointer. It took us only a couple of weeks to find out that he'd taken twenty years and a wartime emergency just to earn the two stripes.

Gillespie was large-bellied, tall, full of bluster and unearned pride, a yahoo. According to our company clerk, who had to cover all of Gillespie's mistakes, he was practically illiterate and had virtually no schooling. The company clerk, Corporal Rich, had to teach him everything just to keep the company from caving in. But no one cared as long as he stayed out of the way, which he did.

By August, things began to return to normal. Our platoon returned to the parallel with John Quessenberry in charge. It was John's last trip to the parallel, his orders coming while we were on the border. Since the flood of refugees had slowed to a mere trickle, Foote decided that we needed fewer men to do the job and cut the number from two squads a week to a single squad and reduced the number of patrols we would make. He would have abolished them all together, but we asked him to keep them on the duty schedule; without them, we would have had nothing else to do but stand watch over the checkpoint that needed no watching. When we arrived at the Parallel, our first trip since before the flood, we saw that the Quonset was, alas, no more. The division engineers had dismantled, dragged, and stacked it back south of the hundred-yard limit. They had pitched a pair of squad tents, one for the kitchen and mess, the other for sleeping quarters, high on a promontory overlooking the river and the Russian encampment. The new camp was about two hundred yards back from the Parallel in a little forest of twisted pines, the kind so often seen in lovely misty Chinese and Japanese scroll paintings. This time they had chosen a perfect spot, high enough to catch whatever breeze there was and a few yards from a swimming hole still technically off-limits for swimming. All the time we were there, no Japanese passed through the border crossing, and so we confined our activities to watching the local farmers pass back and forth to their plots of rice or vegetables and making a daily patrol along through the outlying farms along the border, which both Jon and I saw as good will patrols or public relations, maintaining close relations to the people.

Although we were noncoms—John had gotten his third stripe, and I was made a corporal—and were not required to perform guard duty, John or I would go with the patrol every other day just to break the monotony and to get away from the dull routine of the outpost. But by that time, military protocol had worn so threadbare that a noncom on patrol was never noticed.

John was a good person, easy to be with, and quite intelligent; in that period after the flood, we became good friends. Unlike most others, John showed a real interest in Korea and even made an effort to learn the language. It was John who accompanied me—or rather, I accompanied him—when we went into Pocheon to visit Pak and his family. He enjoyed talking about the books we read and was thinking about going to college under the GI Bill when he got back, though he said he had no idea what he would study. He explained that he had never intended to go to college because it never seemed necessary; his family owned several orange groves in Southern California, and while they were not wealthy, his future was financially secure, but the more I talked about returning to the UT in Austin, the more appealing it sounded to him. When he asked what he could study, I suggested he sign up for classes in business or something to do with growing oranges, but he said he hated the business courses he had taken in high school and he was not interested in going to an ag school. His father could teach him all he and his brother would need to know. John had made fine pencil sketches of our houses in Mukho, and once in Seoul, he had bought watercolors and had begun painting scenes of Pocheon and our river camp. They were more than "quite good," I thought; therefore, based on the sketches I'd seen and his watercolors, I suggested he study art. I told him I thought he was very good.

"What good would it do me? I don't plan to become a commercial artist," he replied.

"Well, it probably won't do you any *good* as far as making a living, but it wouldn't do you any *harm* either. You can still pick grapefruit, and you might enjoy it more if you had your art." I told him a lot of men take up art but never intend on becoming full-time commercial artists.

"I'm biased, I guess," I said. "For me, education—a college education—is everything I ever wanted. I used to think about it only in terms of making a living as a doctor or a chemist. Now it's nearly all I ever think about. If I ever get back on a college campus, I'll probably never leave."

John laughed and said, "Yeah, I can see you as some college professor a whole lot more than seeing you as a doctor." He had no idea how good it made me feel to hear this unprompted endorsement of my great desire. Then he admitted his father didn't need him full time on the ranch, that he could get a degree if he wanted, especially since there was the GI Bill.

Before we finished our tour of duty on the parallel, Quiz got his orders to return, but he finished out his week and said goodbye the day after we came off the Parallel. I hated to see him go. He was the last man I would have a close connection with, the last to whom I could talk and listen to. When he got back to California, he enrolled at San Francisco State College and majored in art. We corresponded for a couple of years, but I think he was disillusioned by the experience, and though his letters were interesting, still full of curiosity, they came at longer and longer intervals until they finally stopped. I have always regretted losing the connection.

Credo Bisquerra, one of the brightest men in the company, might have taken John's place as close friend and confidant, but our interests differed. We had a good connection, however, and talked a lot, and I found he had a sharp critical sense. Then there were Stowell and Aleman, both slightly younger than I, who, along with Bisket, were the best-educated men in my platoon. There were no real dodoes in the platoon. All were men of great good humor who solidly supported me when I became platoon sergeant. Stowell and Aleman were also Mormons and figured later in my collection of Dahlquist moments.

In the fall of 1947, my first fall back in Austin, Aleman showed up one day, a real surprise when Mama called me from Corpus to tell about a young man who bounded up on the front porch one day and rang the bell asking if Joe Gilliland was at home. She told me how he talked about knowing me in Korea and about having been in the same platoon. When she asked him how he had found out where I lived since our telephone was listed under Delsman, my stepfather's name, he said he had recognized the house from the picture in my photo album. She found it hard to believe that he could remember a photograph after all that time. But Aleman said it was easy; he had looked at my album over and over again and had listened to my stories about Corpus Christi, about Jane and Don and the big white Angora cat, Butch, names he actually recalled. That rang true. I did talk about them a lot and remembered how Aleman and others would often pull out the album from my books and leaf through it. Mama told how she had asked what he was doing in Corpus, and how he had hedged his answer, and she remarked that it disturbed her somewhat. I laughed and explained that Glenn was no longer the "jack" Mormon he had admitted to in Korea, that he was back in the fold and on his obligatory mission, one that had been delayed by his service in Korea. When she said there were two other young men dressed in black trousers with white shirts and black ties standing on the sidewalk across the street waiting while she and Glenn chatted on the porch. She noticed the shirts and ties weren't the usual attire of young men in Corpus Christi in late August. She told me on the phone she had given Glenn my Austin number.

We met. Aleman called and we had lunch together, talked about Korea and the platoon, and I realized really for the first time how important how he, Bisket, Stowel, and Quiz had been for me then. But I was foolish and met him with several friends from the house where I was living; we should have been alone or with his friends so he could have told me what he was doing and what his plans were. It was shallow of me and very thoughtless. Glen Aleman had been an important figure and a steady friend, especially after John left.

I recall these men—John, Rendo, Glenn, and Bisket—because of their innate goodness, because they shared a time in my life when I truly began to change, if not fully understand, my view of the world and my place in it. I will admit to regrets for friends I've let slip away, men like these who still abide deep in my consciousness. What was it Polonius told Laertes about "hoops of steel"?

Chapter 11
Winding Down

When Quessenberry shipped out, Lieutenant Foote made me platoon sergeant of the weapons platoon. I had gotten my second stripe for taking over the LMG section, so it came as no surprise to me or anyone else. I had more time in the army than the others and was now, at nineteen, an "old-timer." No one else in the platoon had shown much interest in the job, except Credo Bisquerra, who was mortar section leader and could have done as well as I, perhaps better. I had made no serious errors and managed to get on well with everyone in the platoon. I had the backing of men like Aleman and Stowell and probably Wilson and Wynand, whom we called the "Behemoth," because of his size and his deep voice. I had also the backing of Bustamante, Barbera, Gutierrez, Solomon, and the two Candelarias, the Latinos, which was odd, my being an Anglo from Texas and all. Their support stemmed from a simple fact: I could pronounce names like Bustamante and Gutierrez and once openly criticized Sgt. Gillespie for not trying to pronounce their names correctly. Foote, being from California, had no problem with Spanish, also making him a friend. One day, after he had been company first sergeant for months, Gillespie came into our tent asking for "Bust ta mant" and "Gut-rez." Neither of them answered, even though they were sitting on their cots only a few feet away. He shouted their names again and called them "Goddamn Meskins."

Angered by his gross stupidity, by his total disregard for them as men, I jumped off my cot, I wasn't a noncom then, and said, "If you ever tried to pronounce their names, you dumb ass, they'd answer you." My anger shocked even me.

"Look, I don't give a shit when you mess up, Gillespie, you're just dumb, most people mispronounce Gilliland, but I bet you didn't know that I've never heard a Mexican guy *mispronounce* Gilliland." I recall Gillespie said not a word, just stood there. There were times I felt sorry for Gillespie, almost felt compassion for his stupidity, but this was not one of those times. When Gillespie turned and left the tent without the two, they turned to the others and me and smiled, just nodding with no other comment

Like his namesake, Solomon stood out as a leader among the Mexican GIs in the company. He erroneously became convinced that I could speak Spanish.

He saw me laugh once as he muttered half under his breath that Gillespie was a *"pinche caballo capón."* The truth was I didn't really understand it, but I knew, from living in bilingual Corpus Christi, that *pinche* could be a seriously unflattering epithet and figured that *capón* was a castrated chicken, which meant Gillespie must be a "fucking" horse without balls. It fit. The other thing that "endeared" me was my sharing the canned Mexican food Mama sent me regularly—the chili con carne, the tamales, and refried beans. Once, I got a double-size can of Gebhardt's canned chili, my favorite San Antonio brand. We were all on the Parallel when it came in, and I got the cook to boil a big pot of rice—I loved chili and rice—then invited Solomon and the others to join me and passed around a can of jalapeños. That's when I acquired the nickname of *Pato,* more often *Pinche Pato,* because of my fair imitation of Disney's Donald, and *pinche,* in this case, not the negative epithet it had been in the case of the gelding. That I had earned their respect, I could never honestly swear.

Foote actually apologized for giving me the honor, assuming that command positions were as odious for others as they were for him and perhaps because I would not get the three stripes or the pay until I had served thirty days in each rank between corporal and technical sergeant, which would take four more months, by which time I hoped to be back in Austin, a sophomore at the University of Texas. And a week past my twentieth birthday, my orders to appear at Yung-dung-po, my last replacement depot, came, before the third stripe came down the chain of command. And therein lies a tale of which I am too proud to admit.

A month or so before the order came to "rotate" me home I took my last tour on the Parallel with a squad, leaving the platoon with Credo. I knew it was getting close to my time and was aware that the post on the Parallel might be closed for the season. Thinking like an old-timer, I sorely wanted to visit the Parallel for the last time, so much had happened there that pushed me closer and closer to the place I wanted to be in life that I regarded it as a celebration of sorts. God, listen to this crap! I was only nineteen.

The weather turned bad shortly after we arrived, early October as I recall, and already, signs of the "Frozen Chosin" were taking control of the Land of the Morning Calm. Patrols were in the cold and rain, and life in the poorly heated squad tent was miserable. But a legitimate cause for bitching only confirmed our military status, I told Stowell, "A grunt without a gripe ain't not grunt at all." I said my farewell at the end of the week and, in a slow, cold drizzle, returned with the squad to the company.

After chow that evening, I hit the sack covered by the one luxury we had, the warm, soft quilt everyone called a "Maryann." I was reading by a candle, and most of the men were bundled and sleeping when I heard Gillespie outside.

"Gill, you gotta send a couple of men down to the roadblock. Fourth platoon's got the duty."

"Go to hell, Gillespie, we just got off the Parallel. We don't get the duty til next week," I answered back through the tent flap. It wasn't a screw up, I knew. The company clerk would never have put us down for the roadblock.

"I checked with Lieutenant Foote, and he OK'd your platoon."

I rose, looked down, and saw a row of immobile forms that I knew were men cringing at the thought of standing a two-hour shift at the miserable hut south of the town. *Why? Why send out men on a roadblock to wave at the passing traffic? Passing traffic? What traffic?*

"Gilland, you gonna—"

"No! Get someone else!"

"Lieutenant Foote said get you."

"FUCK FOOTE!" I shouted. It was stupid, I knew, the second I said it, but I liked the alliteration.

Then another voice issuing from the neighboring tent said, "Sgt. Gillespie, find someone else. Corporal Gilliland, see me in the CP after breakfast."

The mounds stirred silently.

Foote was at his desk as I walked in unannounced. Gillespie's hulk had vanished. No one had seen him, not even the company clerk. The lieutenant told me to sit and offered me coffee from his pot then got right to it.

"Sorry about the mess last night." That was the thing about Foote, he apologized when he was wrong, even to an enlisted man. "I gave Gillespie the OK without thinking, but this morning, Rich said Gillespie had tricked me. Dumb me, tricked by that moron." I listened, he paused to think then said, "Everyone in the company heard you, and so I have to hold up that third stripe a month. Sorry."

"Don't apologize, Lieutenant. I should be the one. Sorry. It was more the sound of it that made me say it, not the meaning. You know, alliteration. The best profanity has a lilt about it."

Within the week, Foote was gone and replaced by a captain who had just arrived at battalion HQ, over age in rank with nowhere to go. Foote, like myself, had blurted the wrong words to the wrong colonel at the wrong time and place. Another IG visited Charley Company to investigate complaints a congressman and a senator received about the food from two line companies in the division— Charley and Dog, we think—the two companies in the Thirty-Second Infantry that were last in the food chain and were supplied the worst chow in the army.

This visit from MacArthur's IG was no surprise; we knew it was coming when the mess sergeant announced frozen chops had arrived with fresh lettuce and vegetables. That meant a colonel would appear and see we had no reason to write letters to congressmen. The truth was, no one had written the letters; only a parent had.

The next day, the colonel and his entourage that included our own battalion CO appeared in time for noon chow. With the aroma of fresh beef grilling, filling the kitchen and mess tent, it was obvious to the IG and his entourage that the complaints were all unfounded. Peak, one of the newest replacements, and I watched while we cut our chops and noted how the colonel's aid had taken position to check the waste bin for uneaten chop or salad.

Peak moaned, "Gill, they piled my plate with more than I can eat. I been feeling sick a week almost, 'n' I told 'em to leave it off, to gimme a small piece."

He offered uneaten chop around, but his admission that he'd been sick discouraged any takers. I followed him with my empty tray and watched him scrape half a chop and half the potatoes into the can.

"There! There! I knew it!" the aide exclaimed. "Soldier, you're wasting good food. Lieutenant, this happens all the time—"

Foote was about to speak, but I chimed in, "Sir, this man's been ill. He asked for a smaller portion."

"Did I address you, soldier? Lieutenant, is this an example of—"

Foote interrupted, "Sir, the corporal was explaining." Looking at me, he told me to go to my tent and take Peak with me, sounding as though he would discipline us in our tent. Because tent flaps were rolled, the sound spread, and we could hear some of the exchange and were proud of Foote's defending his men. Typically, a lowly second lieutenant would not speak out in front of witnesses, a fact that colonels and their aides relied on. But the "damage" that led to his being relieved of command of C Company came later after the IG inspected troops and quarters. From the mess tent, the IG passed through company tents and found only neatly swept duckboards, well-made cots, tightly rolled tent flaps, and well-shaved men. The damage occurred right there in the company street in front of fourth platoon tent, and we all heard it. Our tent was the IG's last walk-through, and when they exited, they all assembled in the street. Remember, all the flaps were tightly and neatly rolled so we could see it and hear everything clearly.

First, the colonel: "Lieutenant, your men have clean and orderly tents, but I have looked hard ever since I arrived, and there's one thing I *don't* see—a training program."

Silence, and then Lieutenant Foote, who had been standing more or less at attention relaxed, dropped a shoulder, bent a knee, and slipped into the classic *contra posta* then lifted his right hand with forefinger pointing and shaking in a characteristic schoolmarm waggle. "Colonel, sir, you just don't get the point. We are so seriously under strength that most of the men are performing regular company maintenance programs and guard duty at the roadblock, as well as duty on the Thirty-Eighth Parallel."

"I can't believe that, Lieutenant. These young men ought to be into weapons training or intensive infantry training!" Now he was blurting. He turned, faced Sergeant Gillespie. "See this man here. He tells me he has more than twenty years in the army. He should be in charge of the program. Ask him, he can tell you what these young troops need!"

Foote was silent, I assumed shocked by the raging absurdity, and from the stands, the tents bracketing the company street's arena came gasps and laughter when the colonel spoke of "this man's years of experience." We could hardly believe what we were hearing. We knew Foote was shocked into silence by the farce taking place. Who inspects an inspector general?

The colonel and staff wheeled, made for the command cars, and with only a cursory farewell to the battalion CO, not Foote, they left. The chatter from the tents began. Gillespie and his boneheaded sycophants—every company has a few—headed for the orderly room as we watched the major and Foote enter the officer's tent that was almost flush with ours.

When neither Foote nor the major moved to lower his flaps, we were surprised, but I understood immediately: Foote didn't care. He had been right, and he knew it. From the defense of Pike in the mess hall tent to his testimony in the street, he had spoken truth to power, and power had come away the fool. But this was the army.

"Lieutenant Foote," the major began, "how do you ever expect to make first lieutenant by talking to IG colonels as you just did?"

"Major, I really don't want to make first lieutenant. I just want to go home. Sir, you know that no company in the first battalion has a training program." Foote was silent.

"Well, son, you know I am going to replace you, have to replace you now." The CO sounded sad, almost, almost fatherly.

"I understand."

"Be ready to move the day after tomorrow."

I knew then it was time for me to rotate home.

A month later, on my way to the replacement center at Yungdungpo, we stopped at battalion for transportation, and I looked up Lieutenant Foote again. He was acting communication officer and tied up in an equipment mess and quite unhappy. He admitted that his being relieved had a lot to do with his having become too friendly with the men, not difficult since he was the only officer.

"It's the same through the battalion, Gilliland." He sighed.

I told him the new CO would never have that problem. So far, as I knew, he'd never spoken to anyone but Gillespie and the clerk. We said goodbye, and we wished each other luck.

I turned twenty just two weeks before I got orders for home. The year before, when I had just turned nineteen, orders came through to report to Camp Lucky Strike; I was elated then but not as delirious as I had seen other men in the company when their orders reached them. Now it felt odd, and I couldn't explain it. I had looked forward to it, had thought about the day I would leave and return to Austin, but now a big part of me was mixed up with the company and with Pocheon and Yungmun-yi. It had been just a little over nine months since I had arrived in Korea; for most of the time, I'd been living in tents, eating subhuman chow, bathing infrequently, but surrounded by a platoon of decent men filled with humor and growing curiosity about a strange and peculiar world. To say my feelings were mixed is trite understatement. I had entered the army willingly, filled with hope and high expectations, and I was never disappointed. Of my two years in the army, I had served eighteen months of them overseas, the most important eighteen months of my life.

A week or so before I got my orders, a new company clerk arrived fresh from basic training and clerk's school, one of the same special schools they'd offered me at Wolters. He was already a T-5, a corporal with a T under two chevrons. I had been in Company C since February, a platoon sergeant since the end of August, and was still a two-striper. He had been in the army five or six months and was already a T-5. For a minute or two, I was resentful and assumed he was some kind of brownnose artist, but he had gone to clerk's school right after basic, he said, and had been assigned to a unit where he got his stripes almost immediately. I knew I had no right to be resentful; after all, I had been offered signal school and driver's school and would have gotten the stripes had I wanted them. He had the training, and they needed his skills, so why shouldn't he?

I sat across from him at lunch his first day, and we talked about the company. He told me he had met Gillespie and asked how he had managed to get the six stripes of a master sergeant. I laughed and told him it was the question we all asked.

"You shouldn't ask," I said. "I'm bitter because you arrived with *two* stripes. I've been here for nine months and still don't have my third, and that cretin has six, and he can barely read. But I'm leaving here in a few weeks. My enlistment's up in December," I said, explaining my situation. "What are *your* plans? Gillespie thinks you're regular army."

"That's not likely," he said. "I enlisted because I wanted to get the GI Bill. No one's likely to start a war before 1949, are they?"

"Who knows?" I asked. "They better not. No one in this company has fired a weapon since basic training, and I'm not sure they know how to even load a light machine gun or how to fire a .60-mm mortar. Have you seen those machine-gun emplacements we dug on the other side of the hill? They're a joke."

He shook his head and sighed. "Well, I'll get four years of college with a three year's enlistment, maybe more. If I get more stripes, I'll stay in the reserves and collect some more."

I thought of men in the 102 who had earned their four years of college by crossing rivers, sitting in winter foxholes, and being shelled by barrages of German .88s. He and I were truly the lucky ones, I said. I asked what he was planning to study and where. He said he was planning to be a psychologist, that he had finished a semester at Ohio State before he went in, and that he was reading all the books he could on psychology. He said quite seriously, as if he were passing advice to a young man, "You ought to go to college too."

I smiled, sounds like me a little, I thought. I said, "I plan to. I'll have three years on my GI Bill, more than enough to finish my degree. In fact, if I can manage it, I'll never leave college," I said.

"You've had some college too?" he asked, sounding surprised.

I told him about my year at UT and the term with the ASTRP. When I asked him what he was reading at the time, he looked at me patiently as if he knew I would not know what he was talking about.

"I'm reading Sigmund *Frood*. It's about psychoanalysis and the interpretation of dreams," he said.

"How do you spell that? *F-r-e-u-d*?" I asked.

"Yes. Do you know about Frood?"

"A little, I've read most of Freud's basic writings. I have the Modern Library edition translated by A. A. Brill," I told him.

"No, that's Frood, I'm sure," he replied.

"No, it's Freud. It's a German name, and it's pronounced 'Fro-id.' I was in Germany for nine months and studied the language before I left."

"Well, I've heard it pronounced Frood."

"So have I, and I've heard Gutierrez pronounced Gut-i-rez."

When I said that, Bustamante, who was sitting beside me, laughed. I said, "And I've heard Bustamante pronounced Buss-tu-mant. By the way, speaking of pronouncing names, here's a bit of good advice. Learn to pronounce every man's name correctly and you'll be a prince. Every man likes to hear his name pronounced correctly, whether he's Spanish, Portuguese, German, Polish, or Scots-Irish. Gillespie still can't say Gilliland or Gutierrez. Don't worry about it, but learn. Just go up and ask and explain why you want to know. Right, Bustamante?" I said. Then I told him about the number of Polish names we had in the 102nd and how our noncoms could spell and pronounce each one. "But if I were you, I'd read some basic psych texts first, you know, men like William James, authors like that. Freud's fun, but psychoanalysis ain't psychology."

For a man planning three years in Charley Company, he had a pretty good library, I thought, and he'd be giving Gillespie *the* headache if Gillespie lasted that long. Surely, literacy had some importance, but I doubted Foote's replacement would be the one to call the bluff. He didn't look as if he'd be going to the trouble or appear much more capable than the lump of lard with six stripes.

Though he had taken over Charley Company with orders to set up "intensive weapons training," he gave us less to do than Foote did, which was ironic but surprised no one. Foote had been relieved ostensibly for failing to organize a training program; in reality, he had been relieved because he embarrassed an IG. The new CO had not organized anything before I left. He turned the company over to Gillespie as the general had suggested right there in public, right there in the company street. In essence, that was the same as turning it over to the company clerk and the platoon sergeants.

Captain Walker slept late and never spoke to anyone in the company, except in line of duty. He wasn't as bad as singer, did not openly disdain the lower ranks as Singer had, but he appeared to have no idea what an infantry company commander did. Since there were so few duties, that meant he rarely spoke to anyone, and I don't believe he ever learned anyone's name, at least not while I was there.

His case was a living example of the sad state the army was in a year after the armistice, but since he offended no one and was offended by nothing except an occasional inconvenience, no one ever found anything to complain about and he stayed where he was. At the time that happened, I had less than a week in the company, my orders having come through, but I still had duties as platoon sergeant.

Early in November, the temperature dropped precipitously, enough for water to freeze in a canteen left outside the tent and it was becoming more and more obvious that the company would not move into the Quonsets before the first freeze. When I went on charge of quarters the last time, the four-to-six shift in the morning, the man I relieved told me the CO had left orders to have someone to light his potbellied stove at 0550.

"He hates to get up to a cold tent. There's a can of kerosene outside his tent. Pour a cupful in the stove and throw in a match," he said. "Poor SOB can't light his own fire."

I never minded the 0400 shift. The stove in the CP really did warm the tent that now boasted a good wooden floor. I could read undisturbed in the warm tent or doze off if I wished. The CQ at that time of morning was just there to answer a phone that never rang. It must have been close to freezing that morning. I went to the kitchen as soon as I heard the cooks moving about and got a cup of their coffee that was always perked and not boiled, and we chatted for a few minutes. Since the incident in the chow line with the IG, the cooks had always looked on me as a friend. The CP was next to the kitchen tent, close enough to hear the telephone if it rang, which it never did at that hour. Then at 0550, I went to the back of the officer's tent and found two jerry cans beside the entrance, poured a cupful in a steel helmet sitting beside the cans then quietly made my way into the dark tent and found the stove. His cot was so close to the stove that he could almost brush it if he rolled over in bed, and I wondered if it was really too close for safety, but it was his choice. I quietly lifted the lid of the little round steel stove and poured in the liquid, which seemed then to have the wrong viscosity for kerosene at that temperature. It was odorless in the cold air. I waited a few seconds then dropped a match on to the paper and wood. There was a bang and a loud *whoosh*. The damper flew open, blowing ashes all through the tent. I had obviously poured a cup of gasoline, not kerosene. I retreated quickly and returned to the orderly room.

My relief was waiting with two cups of coffee.

"God damn, Gilliland! What was that explosion? Here's some hot coffee," he said smiling.

"I just lit the captain's fire. Blew the sonuvabitch sky high! I hope." We laughed and waited. When he didn't come in, I took off, my shift being over. The guys in my tent were laughing when I walked through the tent flap. They had heard the *boom* and *whoosh* and realized what had happened.

Years later, when I was living in New York City and saw the play *Mister Roberts* and heard Ensign Pulver explain how he had saved fulminate of mercury for a "firecracker" which he planned to put in "the old man's overhead," I roared louder than everyone, as I recalled the bang and *whoosh* and thought to myself that gasoline does the job just as well as fulminate of mercury. I'll say one thing for the laziest captain in the Seventh Division: he never said anything to me about it, and I knew he was aware who lit the small bomb in his stove.

A week before I got my orders, a letter came from Hollis Porcher, my old friend from Corpus Christi High School and UT. His letter said he expected his orders soon and recalled that my enlistment was up in December. Having seen a shipping schedule, he knew that the chances were good we would ship out together. Since I ought to be getting my orders soon, he said I should be sure to call him if I got to Seoul before he left. In Seoul, I had to stop at the regimental HQ to sign out and to pick up my final papers, separating all connections with C Company and the Thirty-Second Infantry Regiment. As the clerk at headquarters pulled my file, he called me Sergeant Gilliland. I said, "No, it's Corporal Gilliland," and pointed to my sleeve.

"Gee, that's too bad. Take this back to your CO, and you can go out a sergeant. He has to sign it." He showed me the orders promoting me to sergeant. I could have gone back and still made it in time for shipping out, which was not for another week, but I had no wish to go back up the road to Pocheon, then hitch a ride back to Seoul, had no wish to give someone a chance to lose my precious service records. I thanked him and told him I needed the discharge more than I needed the other stripe. Before I left the regimental HQ, I called Hollis, but his buddy said he was on his way to Yung-dung-po.

"Yung-dung-po," I had always liked that name, and I said it over and over, rolling the scatological sounds around in my mouth. It sounded like one of those made-up names we used to utter as kids, dirty ditties or titles of books or authors like *The Constipated Chinaman* by Hung Chow. But now the name had a beauty that transcended all such lewd connotations.

The replacement depot was also a rotation depot, and the POE for all the ships sailing for San Francisco. Unlike the cold barn we had spent the night in almost a year ago, the depot now had warm and dry barracks, good chow, and a great rec room with an excellent library, one that rivaled Pickett's. For a week, we waited for the *USS Marine Fox* to dock and disgorge its replacements. I "volunteered" for a half-day filing job in the headquarters building just to have something to do. The rest of the time, I spent at the service club in the library, writing letters and browsing the shelves. I found a copy of Hudson's *Green Mansions*. I had read about it a great deal, saw it mentioned a lot, but had never read it. When I did, I found it disappointing, missing the allegory completely, so I put it aside. I was getting tired of fiction.

The library's nonfiction section was impressive, books on psychology, history, even philosophy, and several volumes of Durant's *The Story of Civilization*. I checked out the volume on Greece and immediately became so absorbed in the chapters titled "Advancement of Learning" and "The Conflict of Philosophy and Religion" that I seriously contemplated liberating it and taking it home. Had it been smaller, I probably would have found a place for it in my duffel bag. Instead, I checked out Irwin Edman's *Philosopher's Holiday*, along with Hudson's book, and like *Richard Feverel*, they left with me. I could not depend on the troopship having as good a collection as the *General Eltinge* had.

Edman's book had a positive effect on me, though it is not a profound book, more about the pleasures of philosophy as a vocation. Ever since high school, I continued to read Durant's *The Story of Philosophy*, carrying it wherever I went. Edman's book, like Durant's, introduced me to a way of thinking about thinking.

Before I left home in 1944, I had subscribed to the Classic's Club, a book club offering selections of "great books," works by Lucretius, Plato, Homer, Aristotle, Marcus Aurelius, Epictetus, Erasmus, and many others, all bound in a conservative beige buckram with gold stamping. I had read and reread a number of chapters in *The Story of Philosophy*, particularly the ones on Spinoza and Nietzsche, but it was Edman's *Philosopher's Holiday* that made up my mind. Edman's chapter called "Intimations of Philosophy in Early Childhood" reminded me that, for a long time, I had been asking myself many of the so-called big questions. When I discovered the book and that chapter that echoed so much of my own early experience with "big questions," all still unanswered, still encroaching on old certitudes, I was still struggling with memories of the child painfully stumbling to our guard post on the Parallel. I was sure that somewhere there were answers to the questions Edman raised.

Edman's breezy style barely disguised his book's serious undertone that, for me, a beginner, was like a magnet pulling me further and further into his thought. When I had read Durant, sometimes finding its thought muddy, such as the subchapters on Spinoza, I would put it down, wishing I had someone with whom I could discuss the passages I had finished. Edman's little book was an entertainment loaded with ideas I could assimilate, especially the two late chapters on the intimations of philosophy in early childhood and the fashion in ideas. They both echoed the thoughts I discovered when I was thirteen and fourteen, about the time when my high school friends, Luther and Henry, and I set up our science club, which required us to prepare topics for discussion and questions for examination. Inevitably, our discussions would lead to questions about first things and underlying causes.

When I read that Edman too had first learned the rules of syllogistic reasoning in his classes in geometry, I was "made glad" that I had learned the principles of logic the same way. Later, on board the *Marine Fox*, I would read those chapters over and over, gleaning the ideas that we had in common. How I wished I could meet him, hear him talk. Later, during my year in New York, I did meet him, though only briefly, when he appeared on a panel of speakers in town hall. He was a dandified little man whose wit and sense of wicked irony reminded me a little of Dr. McAllister, though he was never as acerbic as Dr. Mac. I went down to the stage and introduced myself and told him I'd stolen his book in a place called Yung-dung-po, that it had led me to take a minor in philosophy. I wanted to shake his hand and thank him for helping me make up my mind. He smiled, thanked me for my "kind words," and apologized for having to rush off. The book made a great difference to me at the time; therefore, being able to tell him so gave me sense of satisfaction. In his description of a friend's father, a businessman, who first stirred the philosophical juices in him, Edman suggested that the study of philosophy did not necessarily lead to a life as professional philosopher or academic.

I lost that paperback copy of *Philosopher's Holiday* after I left the university. One day, I began looking through the small library of books I carried with me whenever I made a move, and one day, it simply wasn't there. I hadn't looked into it in a long time. I had since put aside Durant and had begun reading the primary sources, like Russell, Santayana, and Bergson. I felt the loss more out of a sense of disconnectedness with my past, with that time I made the discovery, than with any sense of intellectual loss. Edman was a part of my youth, that time when a "new" idea sparks a "shock of recognition," of a sense of unity with the great chain of thought running through all things, something akin to the *logos* or *Dharma*. Edman echoed Wordsworth, a poet I had admired since high school when I first heard and read "Tintern Abbey," in his chapter titled "Intimations of Philosophy in Early Childhood." The book had things in it I "understood" because they were more "felt along the blood" than thought out in the processes of intellect. I was just a year from retirement as teacher of philosophy and humanities when I found a hardback copy of Edman's book in almost mint condition, a 1938 printing. That it no longer seemed as deep or serious as it once had came as no surprise or disappointment. Its charm still held, and now I see why it had attracted me so easily to a life in teaching philosophy if not as a philosopher.

A few days later, we left Yung-dung-po in trucks for Incheon. Close to the same spot where I'd come ashore with my "class" in introduction to satire, we assembled and collected around signs indicating points of induction, assuming that these would also be points of departure. I dropped my duffel bag near the Fort Sam Houston sign and began to look for Hollis. I had missed him at the depot in Yung-dung-po, but his buddies assured me he was shipping out on the USS *Marine Fox,* the same troopship I was. While I was looking for him in the crowd around the Fort Sam sign, an announcement came over the loudspeaker directing all Regular Army men to assemble by the Camp Beale sign. I ran back to Fort Sam's sign and began looking for my bag. At first, it seemed to be nowhere, and then I noticed someone sitting on a bag occupying the spot where I was sure I had dropped my bag. He was also holding another bag in front of him. I touched his shoulder and asked, "Is that your bag you're sitting on?"

He turned and shouted, "Joe, goddam, Gilliland! Where the hell have you been? I've been looking all over hell for you!" My life in the army was a linking of Dahlquist episodes.

"Well, Hollis, goddam, Porcher! I'm here, and you're sitting on my bag."

We shook hands, slapped each other on the back, and roared with laughter. He swore he had no idea he was sitting on my bag, the block letters spelling my name turned to the ground. So it happened again, another case of the proverbial needle in a vast army haystack: Dahlquist, Hansen, Porcher, it continues.

The *Fox* took two weeks to make the passage from Incheon to Oakland, California. Only three days elapsed from the time we landed until I received my discharge on December 4, 1946, two days short of two full years after I began my active duty in 1944. My leaving the army was much like my arriving: long lines, long waiting. When my turn finally came, I approached the desk, saluted the officer, gave him my name, rank, and serial number, and waited for him to find my name on the list. When he pushed in front of me a sheet with a list of names and spaces for signatures, he repeated the pay-call litany, "Sign your name above the line. Below the line is red line." I signed my name exactly in the space provided, as I had done every month for two years, then watched the captain count out the bills and change: two months' back pay, travel pay to Corpus Christi via first-class Pullman with per diem allowance, and the three hundred dollars mustering-out pay stacked in a neat pile. Alas! It was too much. I had received the mustering-out pay, supposedly a one-time payment, when I re-upped a year ago. I almost interrupted, but I didn't, less out of greed than a desire to get on with it. It would have taken a millennium for them to sort it all out, and there was always the chance that someone would lose my service records. I scooped up the stacks of bills and change, did a sharp about-face, and left. It felt very good.

Chapter 12

The Happy Time

If home is truly where the heart is, then I was not at home for the month and a half after I returned from Korea. While waiting to register for spring term, my thoughts were all in Austin. I got a wonderfully warm and happy welcome when I stepped off the plane from San Francisco, where Chuck Safford, a friend whom I'd met on the *USS Marine Fox,* and I spent two marvelous days riding cable cars, eating at great little restaurants, and simply absorbing the beauty of a great city. Of course, I was glad to be home, glad to sleep late, and glad to enjoy home-cooked meals, but I missed C Company, and at times I felt uncomfortably out of place. A letter from Bisket was waiting for me when I got home, describing the new Quonset huts and the miserable cold. He told how he had received orders as had several others, including Stowell and Aleman. The letter helped me break away and helped me to put Korea aside, file it, so to speak, knowing I could pull it back when needed.

I spent some time buying new civilian clothes, writing letters to old friends, reading, listening to some old albums, and admiring my new library of classics that arrived while I was away. For the first time that I could recall, Mama didn't worry that I had my nose stuck in a book, nor did she think it odd I moved into Jane's old room and left Don to himself. She showed me my stash of Victory bonds deducted from my pay, almost a thousand dollars' worth, as if to assure me she hadn't cashed and spent them.

That first week after I was back, I took the bus to Austin and found the Lambda Chi house so crammed with returning brothers and new initiates that they had opened an annex across the street in an old, decaying Victorian mansion that a prewar brother had bought to restore to its Victorian splendor but had decided not to begin repairs until after the chapter returned it to him. Most of the brothers living there were on scholastic probation, those failing to make a 2.0 GPA and were thus unable to live in the chapter house because of the university's ruling. A few of the veterans had not made a smooth transition back to student life, some arrested in a civilian no-man's-land where marathon poker games and beer binges triumphed over classes. Back at the house, I found a bed in the attic—the new guest room—that turned out to be a quiet retreat from the constant melee below. It was a cheerfully welcoming house filled with strangers far less homogeneous than I believed was the typical frat at UT. Few matched the Greek stereotype, or frat rat, and that pleased me. It continued to reflect the chapter that I knew before I left.

My main purpose for the visit was securing a room for the spring semester. Living space in the university residence halls and rooming houses was so scarce in January of 1947 that many men were living in garages and attics or any place where a landlord could cram a desk and a cot. In the early fall, when I received a letter from old TOS friend Harvey Dunne, now a Lambda Chi, telling me how serious the housing shortage was, I immediately wrote and reserved a space in the house. When I left campus in '44, the enrollment was just over seven thousand; and when I returned, it had grown to over seventeen thousand. The enrollment at the time of Pearl Harbor had been around eleven thousand. Almost all the increase was due to the GI Bill.

While I was still doing time in C Company, I had dreamed about moving into a quiet little space near the campus, perhaps Mrs. Carter's house on Pearl Street, but no such spaces like that were left in university town. I had even thought I might take up inactive status in the fraternity, a veteran's option. My visit confirmed my reservation and cancelled any thought I may have had of living elsewhere or not returning to active status.

The day I arrived back at the house and found my old room ready for me was a happy day indeed. One of my mother's friends, Helen Stewart, asked me to drive her daughter's new Oldsmobile to Austin for her. Patti, whom I had never met, was staying in an elegant old Austin mansion that had been converted into an elegant women's boarding house just around the block from the Lambda Chi Alpha house. I was happy to do so, of course, because it meant I would be able to carry my library of classics and all the other books I had bought while I was at home as well as the small classical record collection I had accumulated since my return. It was a great way to start again, so different from my first arrival dragging my father's old Gladstone suitcases.

When I walked into the room at the head of the stairs, my old room, two roommates there already, one I'd known from my days in '44, the other I'd never met. Bill Dirks had returned in the fall, fresh from the navy, and he was now beginning his last semester on his petroleum engineering degree. The other man, Bill Mullins, turned out to be the finest roommate one could ever have. A bit older than Dirks and I, Mullins was finishing a bachelor's in journalism and at the same time a bachelor's in English! When I walked in, Dirks was at his desk, and Mullins had just finished stowing his stuff in the closet behind him. Dirks' desk, facing the wall, was smack in the middle of the room, and separated my part of the room from theirs.

Dirks got up and grabbed my hand. "Where've you been all this time?" he said. "I heard you'd reenlisted."

How man times had I heard the comment issued in the same note of disbelief?

"You two guys must be the last ones back home and out."

Mullins echoed Dirks, "You reenlisted? You found a home in the army?"

After I explained my reenlistment and added that I spent most of my time in Korea, I asked about their service. Dirks said he'd spent about a year in the islands of the Pacific and the rest in San Diego, like me, missing all the shooting. Mullins said he'd been in medical administrative corps, first on Guam in medical air evacuation and then for most of a year in Japan. Dirks and I had been enlisted men, he a petty officer and I a corporal. Mullins said he'd been discharged as major, which really impressed Dirks and me.

"Well, I wasn't really discharged," Mullins said, "just released from active duty. I'm still in the reserves."

For the rest of the afternoon, after I delivered Patti Stewart's Oldsmobile, we talked about our majors and traded war stories, mostly about how Mullins and I had learned to love our last assignments, his in Japan and mine in South Korea, both expressing strong desires to return someday, more sooner than later. Dirks was incredulous, wondering why anyone would want to return; he'd seen all he wanted of the islands and the people.

When I brought my boxes of books up to the room, I noticed an equal number of books stacked by Mullins's desk, and the next day, when I got back to the room after registering, I saw that Mullins had found a large five-by-nine-foot metal bookcase that he'd bought at the army-navy store. After we attached it to the wall across his side of the room, we shelved all our books. The bookcase covered the entire space on Mullins's side of the room.

When Dirks saw our books all shelved, he exclaimed, "You guys won't need the library over there on campus! Not with that collection."

"That's the point," Mullins replied.

I had thought long about my classes for the first semester, determined to take only classes I wanted to take, only classes reflecting interests I had developed over the last two years: philosophy, literature, history, psychology. I had studied the catalog Jane sent while I was in Korea and the spring schedule of classes, but when I walked into Gregory Gym to register, I was sure of only one thing: I would not start back with a load of lab classes and would not register for math. My registration packet, I noted right off indicated I was still listed as a premed and my advisor as Professor Breland, the same advisor who had handed me my freshman schedule with three lab courses. This time I selected my classes without consulting anyone: Beginning German, Introduction to Philosophy, Introduction to Psychology, Introduction to Poetry, and . . .. There I stopped and wavered. I had spent much of the morning trying to decide which literature to sign up for. UT, like all state colleges, required two full years of English for all bachelor's degrees, regardless of the school or college, whether fine arts or pharmacy, education or engineering; it was all the same. The problem was which sophomore lit class should I to take. For me English had become a major consideration.

All the sophomore survey courses had fifty or more sections, and the spring schedule listed "staff" as the instructor for all sections. I had talked to several men who had been in my freshman class, and they told me staff indicated either a graduate teaching assistant or a part-time instructor, most of whom were pretty bad; also, most sections enrolled forty or fifty students. I searched the schedule and found only two sophomore-level classes, Introduction to Poetry and Introduction to World Literature, each taught by a named professor. Both sounded perfect, but each stipulated: "For Plan II students or permission of instructor." Plan II was the university honors program that required an invitation, a 3.5 GPA, or ranking in top five percent of the student's high school graduation class. I saw no possibility except by permission of Dr. Fletcher for the Introduction to Poetry. It had to be Introduction to Poetry. Even though I had read reams of poetry the last two years, I still needed to fill the gaps, the seas of confusion and doubt I continued to feel when I read a totally new poem. Because Dr. Fletcher had to initial the box on the registration card for the poetry class to indicate his permission before I could register, I was not at all sure that he would give permission; nevertheless, I set out for his office in the tower. On the way, I decided what my fifth class would be and picked up the registration card for it. It just might, I thought, just convince Dr. Fletcher I was serious. It was Beginning Greek.

The line at Fletcher's office was long and moving slowly. When one young woman came out smiling, obviously pleased, I asked her if she'd asked for permission for Intro to Poetry. She smiled and said yes. And when I asked if I could look at her card, she handed it to me.

"Thanks," I said, handing it back. "See you in class."

When she turned and left, I scrawled Fletcher's initials "TF" in the space provided.

Mullins and Dirks wondered what the hell my schedule had to do with premed, and I told them it had nothing to do with it because I was not planning to be a doctor.

"Breland signed off on my schedule without even looking at it, and two years ago, he advised me to take three lab courses—a freshman, three lab courses. Figure it. They don't care what a person signs up for," I said. "They just want to be sure they have bodies in the class."

Because of the GI Bill, I no longer weighed each course in terms of its cost or how well it fit into a degree plan but only whether it interested me. The kind of degree was itself of no importance. I knew that something would turn up. Moreover, I no longer concerned myself with—sounds strange today— keeping a high GPA since I no longer planned to apply to medical school. The original critics of the GI Bill—it had passed the U.S. House of Representatives by one vote—had cited cases like mine in support of their opposition to the whole business, arguing that the bill would encourage those who had no aim or goal other than living well on a government handout. They saw the GI Bill as a dangerous socialist experiment that would turn a generation of veterans into a generation of educated bums. The greatest bloc of opposition was the southern anti-Negro cabal that feared the bill would elevate the Negro or simply give him the idea of equality. No arguing the point, it was an experiment in socialism, which contributed directly and materially to the enormous growth in American wealth and power.

Unlike many veterans, time to me was not a factor. I was barely twenty when I got my discharge. I had no family obligations nor any prospects or plans of acquiring any. The ratio of men to women on campus that spring made the prospects of acquiring family responsibilities either by accident or intention unlikely. Again, the accident of my beginning school at the age of five proved a major benefit, outweighing all the negatives of being too small or too young, that had dogged me earlier. All I wanted was to be at the university and to stay as long as my GI checks lasted and longer if I were lucky enough to find a job that would support me in any style in which I was content to live. By contrast, my roommates had no doubts about their class schedules. Bill Dirks had only one more semester on his petroleum engineering degree and was considering an engagement and marriage before the end of term. Mullins was so far along toward a degree that he never had to think, *what next?* Had I listened to Mullins at the time or even to my own interests, I might have decided to major in English just as Jane had; but even though I loved to read and had consumed a modest library of greats, I still held the erroneous belief that mostly women majored in English. Although I learned much about writing and reading in Helen James's freshman composition, the mediocre showing I made in her class decided me against even considering English as a major. I refused to take advantage of the free counseling services the VA was offering when I returned, partly because of the viciously satiric treatment of academic advising in Max Schulman's *Barefoot Boy with Cheek* and partly because I was afraid the interest inventories would direct me where I didn't want to go. One of my new friends, Phil Mounger, was just such a victim. Because he had worked on the railroad and had a working knowledge of machines before joining the Marine Corps, the VA counseled him toward an engineering degree. He almost flunked out the first semester, not because he lacked the intelligence to pursue the engineering curriculum, but because he lacked the interest. He loved working as a fireman and engineer of both steam and diesel engines, but he did not love the study.

I was aware then that if I followed the path I was taking, I might never *finish*, might end as a perennial undergraduate, thus fulfilling the dream I'd written to Jane in Rudolstadt. Looking back on that semester now and considering what I taught in college for more than fifty years, I see my unplanned selection was the ideal preparation; in academic parlance, mine choices became a pre-humanities major, if such a thing existed. But I was not thinking about humanities at the time; I doubt I had ever considered it even had I known what it meant or entailed at that time. My aim was to explore an education in the liberal arts that I first encountered when reading Mark Van Doren's book by that name. Few colleges or universities offered courses titled humanities. Fewer had humanities departments or offered degrees in the humanities. Columbia University at the time was offering a course on the major books taught by two men who became two of America's leading teachers in the field, Jacques Barzun and Lionel Trilling; their ideas would have a great influence on me later as a teacher of humanities. But in the spring of 1947, I was, more for my own interest and pleasure than with any expectation of teaching in the area, just beginning to explore what was meant by the term. Such an idea was out there floating in an amorphous cloud and would, sooner than I realized, begin to take shape, actually evolving into a calling, a vocation.

From the beginning, everything except German went smoothly, though I would begin to enjoy the class once I got over my erroneous belief that the German I acquired in Klingenbrünn and Wunsiedel would get me through. Frau Bodenheim did compliment me and several others on our German pronunciation, explaining that many returning GIs sounded good because they, we, had learned to speak mostly by ear and not by books, as one should. Her goodwill and wit saved many of us, I believe. Fletcher's poetry class did for me even more than I expected. Using the Brooks and Warren's text, *Understanding Poetry*, more as a handbook and guide than a gospel, we learned to read poetry as we found it without the baggage of literary history or biography, though Fletcher never considered biography or history to be baggage, and I still don't. Charley had quite informally taught me to focus on image and metaphor as the essential language of poetry. In Fletcher's class, we were able to concentrate on the poem as a work of art, employing whatever came to hand. When it came to the New Criticism of the that era, Fletcher was not dogmatist, never tied the class to any specific critical method, and urged us to use whatever we could to illuminate the poem's meaning or experience. Contrary to postmodern ideologues, we were not indoctrinated into the rigors of metaphorical analysis and were never instructed that larger contexts were necessarily irrelevant to full appreciation.

About a third of the way into the semester, I experienced a moment of fear when I suspected Fletcher had found out I was in his class under false pretenses. On my first critical paper, he had scrawled C+ and a note asking me to see him after class. From the moment I saw this, I suffered a "sickness unto death," apologies to Kierkegaard. The grade was not bad for me. Most of the others had written B or A papers, which was to be expected in a Plan II class. But it turned out the note was to remind me to make an appointment for a conference to discuss the paper.

Younger than he appeared, Fletcher often looked stern, even unfriendly. The truth was quite the opposite. When I stopped at his table, he explained quite cordially that he wanted to point out some problems he thought I should attend to and made an appointment.

"Be sure to bring your paper with you, Mr. Gilliland," he said as I walked away.

I was sure then he was aware that I was not a Plan II student. My writing showed that, and when I arrived and took a seat by his desk, I realized that I had overstepped the line when I forged his initials.

He asked right off, "Mr. Gilliland, why are you taking this class?"

I wavered between telling him I was searching for a class not taught by a teaching assistant and trying to explain the more difficult reason: that I wanted to learn how to read poetry with more understanding and insight. I told him the awkward truth that I liked reading poetry, but I didn't always know why I liked it. When he asked why I thought I liked it if I didn't understand it, I told him that I read a lot of poetry while I was in the army, and it awakened me to what I didn't know.

"I had a friend who offered me a lot of poetry to read, poetry by Eliot, Browning, and Wilde and Shelley." And I told him how Knowles' father had sent him bits and pieces torn from textbooks. I told him I'd read poems in connection with Shelley's life, *Ariel*, and then I mentioned Byron and the Ardennes and the stanzas in *Childe Harold's Pilgrimage* that describe the area the 102 passed through. I explained how reading the poetry made my experience in Germany mean more, and finally, I mentioned reading the Whitman I found in the Armed Services Edition. I recall his nodding, saying he had heard about the little books, and he sat there quietly listening.

But I couldn't tell if he was really hearing until he asked, "What Whitman did you like and why?"

I mentioned "Out of the Cradle Endlessly Rocking" and "When Lilacs Last in the Dooryard Bloom'd" and admitted I wasn't sure, but from the first, it was the sound of the opening lines that grabbed my attention. They echoed over and over in my head for a long time, and I thought that the alliteration of the *l*'s in the opening lines was the saddest, one of the most beautiful lines I had ever read.

I said then, "'O Captain! My Captain!' was one way to write about the death of Lincoln, but 'When Lilacs Last . . .' said what he really felt, what a lot of people must have felt."

I admitted there was still a lot in the poem I didn't get. Then I apologized for talking so much and admitted I really didn't know what I was talking about.

I remember exactly what he said then, for his words were most encouraging. "You said it quite well, Mr. Gilliland, really quite well. I think you know exactly what you're talking about." He paused for a moment and then said, "And I think what you said about your army experience was interesting."

Fletcher was not noted for his warmth, but that day, that very moment, I found him to be a very warm and very kind man.

"Mr. Gilliland, you allow a very careless English style to get between your good thoughts and your reader. You really should be more careful."

I had expected it, and I told him I had expected it.

We met twice more, and the last time we met, we talked about George Meredith and the poetic prose of his novel *The Ordeal of Richard Feverel*. He had assigned several of Meredith's sixteen-lined sonnets from *Modern Love*, poems I had come across in the Untermeyer anthology; and after class, I asked him what he thought about *The Ordeal of Richard Feverel*, asking if he didn't find Meredith's prose unusually poetic.

"I found the prose in the novel to be almost like music."

He agreed quite vigorously, "Oh yes, there are passages that are pure poetry."

We talked about Meredith beside his desk and ended our chat only when the next class began to come in. That kind of brief informal conversation never happened with either my psychology or philosophy professor. Those classes were too large and consumed by lectures, and when the classes ended, the professor always rushed away. Blodgett was a good lecturer, clear, well organized, and quite easy to follow; and in the end, I usually had no questions. He seemed a nice enough man, but he made it clear that he had no time for questions, implying that we sophomores were fortunate to have such a distinguished man teaching the Introduction to Psychology. I was disappointed that I was unable to engage Blodgett in conversation as I had Fletcher. It was the same with Dr. Mitchell in philosophy. His lectures were interesting and clarifying and appeared to be coming right off the top of his head. He never carried a sheaf of notes, only the textbook, and then he never consulted it except to assign readings for the next class. A year and a half later, Dr. Mitchell's upper-division social philosophy, with its heavier reading assignments and exams that demanded long essay answers, had much more give-and-take, but still he never allowed us to "engage" him in talk. That was reserved for his graduate students.

George Laban's Beginning Classical Greek was *all* give-and-take, something I initially thought impossible, but it worked easily with his help and encouragement. And in German, Frau Bodenheim expected exchanges— *auf Deutsch*. But that was different. My only problem that term was still not having even the glimmer of an idea which way I should go. I did much better in Laban's Greek class than I did in German, thoroughly enjoying the readings in classical authors. Much better, though, meant only the difference between a C+ and a C-. Laban pleaded with me to take the second semester with him in the summer, but I was afraid that the class would be too compressed—I was wrong. I see now it was a serious mistake not to continue with Greek, which would have added greater depth to my teaching humanities; but at the time, the idea of concentrating on humanities or becoming a classics scholar did not interest me. Laban's class in Attic Greek might have tipped the scales.

The spring term had many exciting moments in the classroom, but unlike most of the men in the house who were committed to their majors—chemistry, accounting, music, architecture—I was still far from focused, enjoying too much the freedom to "strive, to seek, to find" whatever it was that was out there to be found. Bob Woods was burning it up in premed and showed no anxiety about whether or not he would be accepted in medical school. The most directed man in the house was Bill Mullins, my roommate, who, at the end of the spring term, was less than a full semester from his degree in journalism until he found that a second year of Spanish and would earn him bachelor's in English. He could have finished with a light summer and a light load in the fall. Instead, he decided to do the BA in English and leave with two degrees at the end of the '47 to '48 academic year, and he admitted that halfway through his BJ, he found out that he preferred English to journalism. I was still conflicted, however, and at least partly hooked on the idea that the purpose of higher education was finding a good job.

I took a total of four classes in the summer session: comparative anatomy, human heredity, physiological psychology, and flight training with ground school. The first three more or less speak for themselves and illustrate perhaps my reluctance to change directions. The aeronautical engineering classes? Mullins and Andy Anderson, the man across the hall, convinced me one night at the Tavern that earning a private pilot's license was the best thing I could do for my future happiness and inevitable employment. Both Andy and Bill had served time in the army air corps but had never flown, both washing out before they finished primary training. Mullins had ended up in OCS and qualifying for the Medical Administrative Corps, while Andy moved into gunnery and mechanics schools. Both were motivated to finally win their wings and satisfy their need to fly denied them by the air corps flight instructors. I went along for no other reason than lacking a good reason not to.

Although I signed up for both zoology classes mainly on a whim—I liked zoology—I believe that I had a good reason for enrolling in physiological psychology, which lasted the full twelve weeks extending across the short terms and meeting only four times a week. Physiological psych was an upper-division course and required permission of the instructor because I was still classified a sophomore. Having done well in introduction to psychology, I felt confident that I should move on to more advanced courses, and physiological psych was such a class and was the one I believed essential because it laid what I thought a solidly physical science foundation for the theories taught. Too much of the psychology I had read since deciding to major in the subject had *seemed* more intuitive than empirical—that to me was the basis of scientific understanding. It was clear, I thought, that most of Freud's conclusions, as interesting as they were, were far too intuitive for them to be seriously scientific. Dr. Blodget only skimmed the surface of Pavlov's experiments and hardly examined the neurological bases for psychological reactions.

It was curious why physiological psych was not required for the degree, why it was not required early in the progress toward the degree. This time, I got permission; and in the end, I did well as far as the grade was concerned but still was not convinced there was a clear connection between physiological and behavioral psych. At the end, I was not totally convinced I was making the right choice of major.

Fortunately, at the end of term, when I went to see my grade, posted on the departmental bulletin board, I ran into Caesar de la Garza, a close friend from TOS in Corpus and also a psych major. Caesar, a senior, had just learned that he had been made the undergraduate assistant to Prof. Austin Foster. I congratulated him and then told him I had switched from chemistry to psychology but was already haunted by doubt. He was quite surprised that I had switched and wondered why I had begun to doubt.

"I just finished the physiological psych class and feel now it was a great waste of time," I told him. "I came close to changing my major again. It may have been the instructor, but I'm not sure."

"Don't worry about that dumbass in physiological. You're good to have that behind you. The department has some great people. Just stay away from instructors who are also PhD candidates."

"What about Blodget?" I asked. "He never has time for questions."

Caesar smiled and looked around. We were obviously too close to the office of the departmental secretary, so I changed the subject and suggested we go for coffee.

"What does an undergraduate assistant do, anyway?" I asked as we headed to the union.

Caesar replied that Professor Foster had just hired him, and he still wasn't sure what the assistant did. When I asked him to recommend a good fall psych class, he insisted I take Foster's class in personality. "Psychology of personality was my favorite class and is the polar opposite of experimental and physiological. As I said, it's good you have physiological out of the way."

At the union coffee shop, we talked mostly about his plans for graduate school and when we parted I felt much better about my choice of major. I would see Caesar off and on over the next year, but after he graduated, I would not see him again until our fifty-fifth high school reunion in 1998. At that time was a retired professor of psychology at Texas A& M University, Corpus Christi, with a doctorate from Rutgers.

Anyone examining my spring and summer transcript would conclude that the motley conglomeration of courses were leading nowhere, and if he or she added my freshman transcript to the spring and summer, it would look even more confused. It was, and I loved it. The five hours of aeronautical engineering, consisting of flight training and ground school, looked most absurd and could easily have served as proof that the congressional opponents of the Serviceman's Readjustment Act, the GI Bill, had a valid argument. I was not intentionally pursuing a degree, was instead consciously pursing an education. True, without he luxury of the Veterans' Readjustment Act, it would not have been as easy, but I would have followed the same path. My fall selection was only slightly more focused than the spring or summer.

I registered for Foster's Psychology of Personality, as Caesar recommended, along with German, organic chemistry, philosophy, and one hour of flight training, the latter because the flight program had run short of qualified flight instructors and had to put off the last few hours of dual instruction that prepared us for the FAA licensing flight check, which I passed and received my pilot's license; Bill and Andy once again dropped out. Where was the planning and what was the rationale behind such an oleaginous mess? There was no rationale other than personal whim, though today I can see a pattern. However, one significant consequence did ensue: I ended my pursuit of science, claiming they had called my bluff, and I never enrolled in another science class, though I would preach the importance of including history of science in the teaching of general humanities. Psych class with Professor Foster and a philosophy class with Dr. Brogan, the graduate dean, set me clearly on the path of a major and a minor.

A tragicomic final examination in organic chemistry was instrumental though not decisive in my final break with science. In the mid-term exam I made a disastrous grade of 45 that threw me into a deep depression. Organic had from late junior high school been my favorite brand of chemistry, and I could not believe I had gone so far off my original track. Apparently over half the class was undergoing the same agony, until Professor Hatch apologized for the exam and for his absence from class for several weeks. Before anyone had a chance to express dismay and sorrow at the exam, he apologized and offered to give a makeup exam for all those making below 70 or below their lowest mark on any previous exam. It was the first time anyone had ever heard of a professor grading himself F. The two weeks prior to the exam that many bombed so badly, a graduate assistant had lectured in his place while he was away consulting. To be honest, the substitute was not entirely the reason for my failure. But I accepted the chance to take a makeup, and I did by doing an all-night cramming, and it worked: I made 86, erasing entirely the 45.

When the final exam week came, I crammed again, and that was where the tragicomic events occurred. Once more, I crammed all night. The 85 on the makeup had proven Mullins's famous philosophy for successful exams: "Play vigorously all semester and then cram hard the night before every exam if you wish to succeed and stay off of scholastic probation." At Scholz's, one night, when Mullins first proclaimed his philosophy for success, I countered with the wisdom that cramming only works for passing, not for learning or retention.

"Once you've taken the exam, all is forgotten, all is lost," I asserted.

"Of course," he said in rebuttal, "that clears the mind for the next semester."

But cramming had saved my average in organic, assuring me I would could leave science on the crest of a wave and not in the trough. All night I reviewed the course, worked out all the equations from scratch, checked my results, tested myself on every principle Hatch had emphasized in lecture, and at 7:00 a.m., I left the house for the exam scheduled for eight in the large lecture hall. I planned to arrive early, take my place at 7:30, and cram just as I had done so successfully on the makeup exam. There was a problem, however. I recognized none of those already seated, and instead of a half-full lecture hall, I saw only a handful.

"This is organic chem. 820, isn't it?" I asked before I sat.

"No," one said, "Bio chem. 440." They all nodded and smiled. For them it was comedy, for me tragedy.

I left, desperate to find the exam's venue. I was twenty-four hours early and was a victim, not the beneficiary of Mullins' Philosophy of Cramming 101. Alive and ready, all senses tuned and taut though less then taught. I was too well-prepped and soon to lose all I'd crammed, so my mind would be empty and free and ready for the next cramming. Next Crammed, Coffeed, No-Dozed, and tuned so tight that more turning of the tuning peg and I would have surely snapped, so tense and tightly tuned, I could not sleep or rest and could not re-prepare, though I did sack out and lay there half sleeping, half waking through lunch, and then at last rising only to return to the notes I'd crammed twenty-four hours before. Mullins and the brothers, aware of my impending tragedy, stayed clear of the room, regarding the case as one too delicate to offer sympathy or aid. Mullins would insist later that it was not a failure of the cramming philosophy, but of its application. By midnight, I crashed, leaving a note in large red letters for a wake-up call at seven. Hatch's exam was a gift of the testing gods; almost all questions were those I had quizzed myself with during the cram. He had thoughtfully posted lab grades, average grade in the class, and the score we'd need in order to make the grade we wanted. I needed a 71 to ensure a C, an 85 to ensure a B. Never greedy or one to overachieve, I made a 72 and said farewell to chemistry for all time.

When I first returned from Korea, Mama told me Arthur Dykes had called and had written, asking when I might be coming home. I had lost Art's address and had not written about my reenlisting or about Korea. Although I had run into old Astrappers like Dave Brown and Carlos Lovejoy, my failure to stay in touch with Arthur had been a real loss to me, so now learning that he was already enrolled at UT and working toward a degree in architecture was good news indeed. As soon as I got to Austin, I called him and invited him to the house. He pledged the fraternity and moved into the house in the fall and was initiated soon after the term began. The house was filled to overflowing at that time, and by the fall of '47, the university was settling back into a prewar mold. Many veterans who had never intended to become college students or those who held only a tenuous commitment had dropped out or were on their way out. While most stuck with it, some found the routine of classes, assignments, and exams too rigorous and confining. Many were excellent students. That fall, the house looked younger and more like a prewar house than ever, but there were still veterans. Having lost Dirks as a roommate to graduation and marriage, Bill and I faced the task of finding a suitable replacement. We agreed the new occupant should have at least as good a library as we had. Dirks's books had barely filled one shelf of his bookcase. During the summer, Mullins bought a used record player—this was before LP records—and began to collect a number of ten-inch and twelve-inch records, mostly semi classical and big band. I began laying the foundation of my Red Seal Victor recordings, mostly singles of great tenors like Jussi Bjoerling, Beniamino Gigli, and a fine new tenor named Giuseppe Di Stefano, and great divas like Licia Alabanesa, Hilda Gueden, and Erna Berger. My taste leaned decidedly to the lyrical and Italian singers and away from Wagnerian. Bill insisted the new member of the library at the top of the stairs should have a good record collection along with books. The last qualification, on which Bill insisted, was that he must wear a 9 ½-size sock and a 15-½/33 shirt. He said he was tired of washing socks and complained that my shirts were too small and never clean in sufficient quantity to serve the two of us.

Unfortunately, our winning candidate qualified on only one item—his books. But Phil, or Iwo, Mounger measured up in ways that exceeded all other categories. When Iwo moved in, the intellectual level of conversation in our room rose considerably and became decidedly more liberal. Phil had been severely wounded on the second day of the Battle for Iwo Jima, a Japanese mortar round killing his close friend and wounding him so severely he was at first assumed KIA. At the hospital in San Diego, they found the mortar fragment in his heart, about the size of the nail on his little finger, was inoperable. When he was able to travel, he was furloughed home to Smithville, Texas, sent home to die by the way he told it. But he lived and still lives at this writing. Mounger, or Iwo, was attending the university on the special bill for wounded veterans called Public Law 316. When he arrived as a freshman from Smithville, Texas, the VA counselors gave him a battery of tests to determine the best course of study for him. Phil's father and brothers were all railroaders, engineers, conductors, and firemen. When the war began, his father, an engineer, was able to have him qualified as a fireman on steam engines before he was eighteen. Because his father and he had lied about his age, he had been able to spend a year working on the railroad, riding the left seat in a steam engine for the MKT before entering the Marine Corps in time for the invasion of Iwo Jima. His VA test results came back as one might expect: they show him to have a high aptitude for engineering. But after a semester, he dropped out, discouraged by his lack of interest in all engineering classes.

When I first met Phil, he was living alone in a room very poorly made from an old garage behind someone's house near the campus. Having dropped out of engineering, he was studying economics and anthropology along with Russian and had dived into his new subjects with enthusiasm. Even though Phil's politics differed markedly from most of the brothers—then as now, most Greek fraternities were strongly conservative—he was held in the highest regard, partly for his service during the war but mostly for his steadfast honesty regarding his convictions. That he held markedly different views regarding the sacred cow of capitalism from the majority of the men in the fraternity made no difference. So when Bill Dirks graduated and Mullins and I were looking for a suitable replacement for the fall term, our votes went with Iwo. He was exactly the maverick needed. Mullins, one of the brightest men in the fraternity, had no apparent political leanings; or if he did, they were the most moderate. His East Texas origins bespoke a loyalty to conservative Democratic ideals, which he rarely voiced for the sake of harmony. He tolerated my outbursts of liberal ideals on race, religion, economics, and other subjects that would crop up, but he neither supported nor disputed my views. His tolerance was all the proof I needed of liberal leanings. Others on the second floor were less tolerant. On racial issues, Bill would have been regarded as a liberal since any form of bigotry or know-nothingism was anathema to him.

Phil spoke with studied authority and offered himself as my ally, though in truth, it may have been the other way around. His brand of left of center politics was more influenced by New Deal social economics than by Marxist doctrine, though Phil had no fear of socialism or Marxism as scare terms, knowing that few if any of those who opposed his views understood the real meaning of either. His dislike of racism was as strong as my own. He brought with him a highly sophisticated library in economics and anthropology, but our association as roommates lasted barely a week into the semester. It was a severe disappointment when he decided to leave.

I was with Phil as he was completing his registration in old B Hall, the ancient men's dormitory that housed the offices of the Slavic languages department. Phil couldn't understand how he could have made an A in Russian 1a. He said that he still could not speak the language and could hardly read a periodical or newspaper with any facility and wondered how Dr. Miçek could have given him an A. To assuage his doubt, he decided to sign up again for Russian 1a as an auditor while at the same time taking 1b. His VA program allowed him to retake whatever classes he wished at no extra cost. As we coasted through the halls, we ran into Professor Miçek; and Phil, believing Miçek would be pleased, told him he would be taking the 1b and would also be auditing 1a. But Miçek, rather than being impressed, angrily demanded to know why, taking Iwo's remarks as criticism of his teaching and grading.

I stood aside and listened, knowing for sure that Professor Miçek would grow even angrier when Phil refused to drop 1a. Phil never took matters of principle lightly, especially when opposing arguments were so lacking in principles of their own. For Phil, the purpose of studying a language was to learn to speak and read it; ergo, what harm was there in repeating a course, especially if one could without cost? Most students at the university back then took a foreign language only because it was a degree requirement. When we left, Phil asked what Miçek's anger was all about. He had, in Miçek's mind, virtually accused the man of being a poor teacher and a sloppy grader, I said; the more Phil insisted he had *not* insulted Miçek, the angrier *he* got.

That night, the eve before classes began, the three of us repaired to Scholz's for the usual schooners of beer, and Phil spoke angrily about his meeting with the Russian professor and declared he was dropping out of school as a protest of Miçek's protestations, and the more beer we drank, the more we—mostly Bill as I recall—agreed we would all three drop out in protest. When we returned to the house, Phil began packing clothes, books, everything he had set up in his room. In the morning, when he returned to Smithville, we were shocked that he was so adamant. He declared that he could pick up twenty-five dollars a day driving a switch engine in the Katy yards outside Houston even while drawing a 100 percent disability check for the tiny mortar fragment still lodged in a heart muscle. We tried to dissuade him, arguing that Miçek was not worth it.

Losing him was a bitter disappointment. In the few weeks I had known him, he had begun to have an influence on me in much the same way Dr. McAllister would by asking questions like a young Socrates, by demanding a basis for my opinions, and by pointing out inconsistencies in my arguments. When they called him a pinko, he laughed it off, knowing his accusers understood nothing about anything he professed and perhaps knowing even less about what they themselves believed. He was proud of the epithet—as proud, I believe, as he was of Iwo.

For me, Phil epitomized the worker as intellectual; reading widely and deeply in his two fields of interest, economics and anthropology, he searched constantly for the answers. McAllister's name had passed back and forth across the dinner table at the fraternity house, both in praise and condemnation. Phil, unable to resist an opportunity to find where the truth lay, signed up for Dr. Mac's cultural anthropology and soon became another of Dr. Mac's devoted acolytes, while he would become, at the same time, the source of chagrin to McAllister and other professors. Seemingly on a whim, Phil would drop in and out of school and would return to his job on the railroad where he would continue to read serious works in his major fields. Some at the house assumed he was doing it for the pay, twenty-five dollars a day, a lordly sum in the 1940s. I knew otherwise.

When he dropped back in a year later, I hoped Phil would move back into the room at the fraternity house, but instead he chose the strange old Victorian Gothic relic we called Wuthering Heights for its picturesque windows and steeply sloping roofs. Behind St. Austin's parish house, the place was just a block off the campus and was home for several other brothers. Phil settled into a room of his own away from the noise and commotion of the house but always welcomed visitors. He preferred the long, quiet hours for reading that Wuthering Heights offered him to the noisy comings and goings of the Lambda Chi House. At the same time, I always felt welcome when I would drop in on the way to campus. In my senior year, desperate for a quieter environment, I too would move into the house.

To replace Phil, Bill insisted we stick to our plan to select only the most qualified; so contrary to fraternity policy, we advertised for applicants to share our room at the top of the stairs. Bill's journalistic skills got us around the house manager's objections to our unbrotherly and elitist criteria. Dirks had been almost the ideal roommate for the two of us, quiet, studious, reserved, and tolerant of all manner of bullshit that caromed off the walls. We would not tolerate anyone who complained when the precious bullshit misfired. Secretly, we did not want a business admin major, law school student, or an engineer. A law school student was acceptable only if he studied in the law library when or if he found the atmosphere of the room too discordant. Bill distrusted journalism majors, being one himself, and Andy Anderson, journalism major, resided across the hall, and that was close enough. Bill claimed his second bachelor's in English diluted Andy's journalism toxicity. Since I fit no category yet, I was acceptable and could be molded by association. His goal, our goal, was to promote the idea of a true liberal education as the only salvation.

With that criterion, we recruited Tom Bunge, a young, recently initiated, nonveteran (new blood, Bill claimed, was like hybrid vigor) who had transferred from Transylvania College in Kentucky in order to follow a favorite history professor—an extremely positive sign we felt. He was also the son of the Dutch consul in Galveston. Quite the opposite of Phil in most ways, Tom added class to the library at the top of the stairs, with his large collection of books covering European history as well as an excellent classical record collection. Topping it all off, he was a top student, not quite a fly bait, but just what we needed, someone between Bill's straight-A average and my solid C. Tom impressed me mightily; I had never known anyone to transfer from a college just to follow a favorite professor. Bunge had left Transylvania, which he adored, he said, to study European history under the famous Professor Riker. I assumed he was planning to follow in Dr. Riker's footsteps, but he said he had no intention of becoming a professor or a teacher. In other words, Bunge was simply real student.

Dr. Austin Foster's Psychology of Personality was like nothing I had taken up to that point. Nothing so resembled my idea of a real university class as did that class, both for content and for method. He was a brilliant teacher and thinker and conducted the class in a most informal manner, close to a Socratic dialogue in the Stoa. He never or rarely lectured. Thinking out loud, we called it, he allowed us to experience his thought processes. He would shift and change his mind, contradicting his original thought, and then turn and come back with new arguments, welcoming us to join his journey through a problem, insisting we join. He would listen to a student expand on something she might have read in one of the two texts he recommended (never required) and then turn to a classmate and ask if he had anything to add or question. So unlike the weltering ton of flesh from the summer, he would pause and then explain, offering us new routes to follow. He urged us to read both recommended texts, one by Gordon Allport, the other by Roger Murphy. But there was no condition: read or else. I read all of Allport, little of Murphy, when it applied to the question of the day, but I can't recall his ever lecturing from a set of notes or any kind of prepared material. On the first day, he began by asking the class to define a number of terms we had used for most of our lives, words like *self* and *person*, which, of course, no one answered to his complete satisfaction, though he never discarded our attempts but used them as spring boards for discussions. By the end of the first week, when he had convinced us that all our preconceptions were only that, if not quite wrong, he began suggesting readings in Allport and Murphy. He would later add a recommended reading list from which we were to choose works that would be the bases for critical papers, two papers of modest length and one a longer paper applying ideas gathered from class and readings from Allport or

Murphy. The third, a longer more detailed paper, would act as substitute for the final. He would give no quizzes or even a final exam.

I read more, wrote more, and enjoyed the lectures more than anything I had taken outside the class with McAllister when I was a freshman. His class resembled a philosophy class more than one in psychology. The Socratic method disturbed a number of the senior and graduate students, and I could understand their anxiety, for in the beginning I felt as though I were swimming in very deep waters, often out of sight of shore. When I saw Caesar once and told him how uneasy several of the seniors felt, he explained they were desperate for an A and found the search for answers on their own rather too risky. Most admitted they were more comfortable having straight lectures from which they could take notes and produce correct answers when exam time rolled around. Once when I was scribbling frantically, Foster stopped and asked what he had just said. Rather than reading back my notes, I tried to paraphrase what he just said.

"Good! Now stop scribbling and listen and think," he said. "I wouldn't swear, but I would guess that your notes aren't as good as what you just said." He paused, looked around, and then said, "Folks, let's listen, let's talk to one another. I don't give exams so you won't need to take notes." That really frustrated the seniors. I should have known: he had totally dispensed with the examination by regurgitation.

The board of regents and the new president never acted directly as censor or dictator, but there was a residue from the turmoil surrounding Rainey. The psychology department toned down much of the purely speculative aspects of the study of human behavior and began to emphasize safer areas of research, such as psychometrics and behavioral theory that trended away from the humanistic toward the computational; the speculative, the questioning, and doubting gave way to safe mathematical certitudes. Turned away from what Jerome Bruner characterized as narrative in favor of the computational, statistical.

Foster was not constrained, certainly not that fall. Instead, he challenged us to rethink all our earlier concepts of consciousness and self. The two texts offered us a background of two different views, and Foster's long reading lists of books and journal articles, which we were encouraged but not required to read, gave us more to think about. My two major papers drew from Karen Horney's major work of the day, *The Neurotic Personality of Our Time* and two of Freud's later works, *Beyond the Pleasure Principle* and *The Ego and the Id*. Horney's book was popular at the time but never slipped off into the world of pop psych. I had read most of the A. A. Brill translations of Freud in the

Modern Library Giant edition. It was the first time I was required or allowed to write critically and speculatively about such substantive matter. I had never written papers like these before and approached them with some trepidation. When Caesar told me that Foster had read my Karen Horney paper with great interest, I relaxed and actually faced the papers on Freud with more pleasure than anxiety, and his comments on my paper based on *Beyond the Pleasure Principle* quite startled me.

I have not looked at that paper since that fall of 1947 and do not recall what I said to earn such comments. I did rework the paper for Brogan's class, and he found it quite acceptable (meaning it earned a B), but I was sure he or his grader saw it as a rework. But I do recall that *Beyond the Pleasure Principle*, at least for me, seemed less a work of science than a work of metapsychology, brilliantly intuitive and creative but lacking in what I thought was scientific rigor, and I am sure I stated so with examples. I was pleased and amazed that he accepted my view and did not discount them or fault the paper. The paper earned me an A. I am sure my commenting on Freud's speculative and highly intuitive approach allowed me to rework the paper for Dr. Brogan's class.

His classes were exciting, exploratory dialogues that often extended beyond the class period moving on to his office or an empty classroom where we would debate definitions and struggle to keep up with Foster's mind. *We* is not quite accurate; I rarely spoke during these sessions out of class and almost never made a comment in class. There was so much I didn't know.

I was deeply disappointed in Dr. Brogan's Philosophies of Life class, which professed to focus on philosophies that emphasized values and ethics in a broad social and historical context. Brogan, being the graduate dean, often turned the class over to one of his doctoral candidates who talked and discussed more than lectured but was often out of touch with the readings Brogan had assigned earlier. We had few tests and only one paper. For my final paper, which was supposed to discuss some philosopher or contemporary thinker and his contribution to contemporary thought, I handed in a discussion of Freud's *Civilization and Its Discontents* and got an acceptable passing grade, though I was sure Brogan's grader had not read much beyond the title page and very likely had not read *Civilization and Its Discontents*.

Halfway through the fall term of 1947, something happened that interrupted the smooth progress I had begun to make in all my classes, even in organic chemistry and German. I became smitten. From the time I enrolled in the spring of '47 until the fall term, I had had few dates. With the GI Bill, the stipend now seventy-five dollars a month, and my two years of savings bonds, almost two years of the fifty dollar bonds, I had enough money, but

I found no one I was sufficiently attracted to ask out. The ratio of men to women made getting dates a problem. But things changed, and it was largely the fault of Scholz's Beer Garden and the vows Bill urged us to make after the second or third schooner of Scholz's excellent lager; normally, vows at Scholz's required a third round. One night, dateless and soaking up the suds, we swore we would both find a girl, get pinned, and never be without a date when we needed one. No more picnics as loners, he swore, no fretting about whom to take to the winter formal. And so it happened.

Fall is truly the most beautiful time in Austin, particularly in the environs of the university. Fall had it all over spring as a time for the turning of one's fancy. It was the time I recalled most vividly while I was overseas and aching to return. It was that time of year when I was first liberated from the jesses of home and Mother. The first cold snap of autumn clears the air, brings out the color in the trees, and litters lawns with scudding yellow, brown, and orange leaves. Walking to and from campus, through the falling leaves beneath the overarch branches—sycamores, hackberries, pecans—was always a stimulus. It was autumn, not spring, that stirred the sap for me. The Delta Gamma sorority, following prewar tradition, thought it meet to introduce two of their pledges to our men in the fraternity (and possibly observe their social skills?), and so the Lambda Chi and Delta Gamma social affairs officers arranged a weekday dinner for the two pledges and their chaperone or sponsor or whatever she was called. Both were extremely attractive, one a freshman, the other a senior, one an English major, one a biology major; both seemed happy to be on show appeared to enjoy the attention.

I've never understood why young women and young men of normal breeding require instruction in the rules of social intercourse; I always thought it was something learned at one's mother's or father's knee. But that evening, a member of Delta Gamma Sorority—a friend of a brother—brought two pledges to our house and introduced them almost as though she were placing them on the market, exposing them to the world of masculine virtue for the first time. The mock ritual was a form of hazing the sororities employed in preparing the pledge for a formal initiation into the sisterhood. They were being tested, no doubt, to see how they might handle the attentions of strange men (or boys). At the same time, it was a chance for the brothers to observe the pledges and determine which would require more demanding instruction. All in all, it seemed pretty stupid, but it worked. The brothers and the sorority pledges were indeed on their best behavior and greeted the young women cordially sans effusive gesture or speech and helped them to their places at dinner and carried on conversations consisting of fatuous small talk, apparently prescribed for the rite of passage. The Dee Gees were a "good house," they said, not the top on campus, but then Lambda Chi was also only a modest outfit, neither house having premier cars like Cadillacs, Lincolns, or Chryslers parked out front, nor placing members among the Goodfellows in the *Cactus*, the University of Texas yearbook.

As I mentioned earlier, I had not met many women since returning to campus; the number of dates I went on could be counted on one hand, with fingers left over. Even in my senior year in high school, I had dated only two girls, only one often enough to call a "girlfriend," and that was *les Jarbeaux* the flyer. The two young women that night were well dressed and perfectly coifed, charming, intelligent, talkative, friendly, and were fortunately possessed of a sense of humor about it all. One had brilliant copper-red hair combed naturally in soft waves that accented her best features. At that moment, I recalled my pledge at Scholz's and managed to get a place at a table just across from where she sat; and in the conversation at dinner I learned she was a biology major, which suggested we might have something to talk about on a first date if it got that far. In the past I had not done at all well in the area of first-date repartee, which might have explained the difficulty I was having when asking for a second date. After dinner, when a dozen or so of us sat or stood about in the living room making more small talk, I found she was not presently attached or committed and learned that her birthday was a few days hence and that she was remarkably only a few weeks younger than I. Her name was Barbara, and she was a recent transfer from Oklahoma City University, a senior, which seemed strange since pledges were usually freshmen or sophomores. But I was done with dating freshman women, I told myself, and silently thanked DG for their autumn ritual. The next day, I sent a dozen red roses to the Delta Gamma house along with a card wishing her a happy twenty-first birthday. It was a brilliant strategy: members and pledges would all know she had an admirer, and that knowledge would gain her, still a pledge, a modicum of respect. It worked. I did not even have to make a follow-up call. Instead, she called to thank me; and when I hung up, I had a date to the fraternity Western dance on Saturday night. Western dances in those days meant hiring a hillbilly or country dance hall and a country-western band out in the hills west of Austin. It also meant you dressed *down* rather than *up*. It was cheap and far enough out in the hills west of Austin's mainstream so that underage drinking was safe.

My social life since returning had been minimal until then, but I found Barbara talked easily about a wide range of interests: pop music, movies, hometowns, and her major, which was biology. She was from Fort Worth and had a brother at the university who was an ex-GI and a physics major. We found common grounds of interest in her major and in my former major, making noxious small talk unnecessary. Our first few outings were quite successful. It was as much the pressure of convention that drew us together over the next few months, as it was an overwhelming attraction. While we found we had many things in common and enjoyed each other's company, no grand passion emerged, though it finally reached the point where we were "seeing" no one else. A formal commitment of our "going together" or being pinned did not occur. Dates consisted of going to informal fraternity parties or a movie and dinner at a Mexican restaurant or coffee and "study dates," with walks along wooded parkways. Twice we sat in a park or a secluded angle on the campus and listened to the Saturday afternoon Texaco opera broadcast from the Met over a portable radio she had borrowed. She found my knowledge of the operas interesting and unusual, particularly that I should know the names of the artists, the story lines, and even the words (in Italian) to the arias. I, of course, basked in her wonder of it all as well.

At the time, I felt I was living the ideal life although the university held less meaning for her than it did for me. She had no interest in graduate study but was instead looking forward to graduation and a job, a prospect I declined to discuss; she found it odd that anyone would major or minor in philosophy, neither being reliable preparations for work after college. For me, the university had just begun to take on the meaning I had always dreamed it would. I was barely a junior and still hoped never to graduate, and that idea separated us. It was a topic we never or rarely discussed. It was as if we occupied separate realities, different planets, and that our meetings were like those of two aliens in space agreeing to meet on a neutral orb. We entertained each other. Other than the new friendship and the pleasant companionship, the most notable change in my life was the maintenance cost. Until I began to call her regularly, I had not cashed any of my war bonds. But once we began "going out," I began cashing them, first at the rate of one a month, then two, and then more. Movies, small dinners with wine, flowers even, began the drain. By the end of February, they were all gone, and I was once again wholly dependent on my GI check. While it was enough for single bliss, it was not enough for two. If Barbara was an intelligent, career-oriented young woman, she was not in the least liberated in any real sense. Women did not share the costs of courtship, nor were they expected to, nor were their swains inclined to allow them to. For two semesters and the summer, I had enjoyed the luxury of not having to work, but now halfway into the spring, I had to get a job if I intended to continue anything resembling a courtship. It was not our original intention to see the relationship progress to its more or less logical conclusion. But by the second half of the spring semester, the normal laws of inertia had taken over, and familiarity began to breed a kind of content. We had even signed up for a class together—abnormal psychology—and would meet between classes to talk. In the end, it became more than a pleasant infatuation but an exhilarating extra that made the classroom experience even more satisfying. Still an inherent weakness in the relationship raised its head: my own lack of a clear and strong commitment to a major. She could not or would not understand my apparent lack of purpose, and I could not or would not explain it in terms she understood. I was still unable to understand it fully, but for me, it simply was the great adventure I had envisioned in Rudolstadt.

One evening while we were studying together in the library of the Delta Gamma house, I was proofing a paper on Josiah Royce for Dr. Gentry's contemporary philosophy class, and Barbara was studying notes from her human physiology class. Everything was going well. Study dates were common tactics that allowed couples to meet their academic and romantic commitments without doing serious damage to either. We had the sonority's library to ourselves until a half hour or so before the time for all dates to leave. Barbara had offered to type my Royce paper and was waiting for my final proofing when the matter arose. She looked at what I had written and asked me what it was really all about, saying that it made no sense whatsoever. In defense, I admitted that Royce was not all that important to me either, nor was I sure just what he meant; but I was beginning to understand his idea of absolute idealism and thought the paper might explain it. She was incredulous, wanting to know what difference it would make if I did explain it. I answered rather off hand that it made the difference in whether I understood or didn't understand. Then she said it all seemed rather silly and asked why I didn't major in something that made a difference. I told her that I believed philosophy might make *all* the difference and speculated that I might want to teach philosophy some day. That statement, I think, surprised me more than it did her. She typed the paper anyway and then apologized. No harm done, I said, but we both knew I was wrong, both knew that it could not be undone.

One happy result was a well-typed Royce paper, my first paper ever to earn an A+. When I showed it to her, she was incredulous. I explained, half-joking, that it was really her typing that made the difference. Gentry's grader, I said, couldn't have possibly understood what I was writing about since I didn't either. She stared at me, uncomprehending, and I realized then, for the first time, that she lacked a sense of humor; it was obvious she had missed the irony I intended. She admitted, rather sadly I could tell, that she lacked a real sense of humor, that the only things she found "humerous" were upper-arm bones. I felt that my lack of seriousness in contrast to her solemn commitment eliminated any possible continuation of the affair beyond June, when she would graduate; we knew it. Neither of us considered that she should wait for me to graduate since neither of us had any clear idea of what she would be waiting for. In her mind, my future was so clouded with my lack of decision it would have been foolhardy for either of us to make plans for the future. I still regarded my indecision as a journey of discovery. The longer the journey, the more eager I was for it to continue. What I was studying and learning at the time was valueless to her and to her mother, who was the great arbiter of intellectual values in her family.

Two visits to Fort Worth to meet her parents revealed my weaknesses when her mother asked me outright what my plans were for the future. I told her I had no plans except to finish a bachelor's degree, though I suggested that graduate school was a strong possibility. At the crux of it was her mother's open disapproval of my choice of a major. Psychology she seemed to consider as barely permissible, but philosophy was out of the question. I had not committed to either philosophy or psychology and was still at the point when it could go either way. I frankly felt inadequate in both and was aware that neither major would get me a job; getting a job was to Barb's mother as of major importance. I had friends whose psychology degrees played no role in the jobs they got, good jobs with major corporations, though not jobs that I saw myself capable of performing for life.

To me, the thought that I might want Mrs. W's approval for anything was odious in the extreme. Neither Barb nor I had ever spoken of marriage or any commitment other than the idea that we were committed to going together and enjoying each other's company. The campus was swarming with young women intent on getting husbands who were on their way to the top, talented and intelligent men eager to make up for time lost during the war, men with focus and determination to cash in on the fruits of victory in a growing economy, etc. It would have been the deepest folly for them to do otherwise. But may apparent lack of focus, vision, or determination was Mrs. W.'s chief concern. I lacked interest in anything other than the quest itself, and Barbara knew it, and she also knew that I would not change for her sake. In 1948, none of the studies of men in the gray flannel suits or organization men had come out. Important or seminal works like David Riesman's *The Lonely Crowd* or *Individualism Reconsidered* were years in the future, and no serious sociological analysis of the postwar GI Bill generation had been published to tell us who and why we were who or what we were. The criteria of the prewar years were eroding but were still the only criteria we had. It was too early for sociologists to detect trends that would dominate the studies of the fifties. Nor were there studies or writings about the growing society of bohemia or the later beatnik trends. But ineluctably, the new patterns were taking shape as Levitt Towns and suburbia began to grow, all fostered by the flood of BA, BBA, and BSc degrees. I was never concerned that my vacillating and my searching was out of step with the times, though all my friends were finishing their degrees and moving on to jobs in engineering, accounting, advertising, or on to medical school or law school. Only a few were heading to graduate school or toward teaching. There is a strange and interesting irony, perhaps too narrow a sample to base a sociological theory on. While Barbara's mother was suspicious of my love of academe, Barbara said her father, a biochemist, and her brother, a physics major at UT, thought highly of me and approved of what I was doing, or failing to do, or unable to do, or not wishing to do. Barbara and I continued to see each other and correspond for almost a year. After she graduated and returned to Fort Worth, we wrote and talked long distance and saw each other occasionally that summer and on into the fall and winter. But in neither case did absence make either heart grow fonder, but simply more absent.

The real benefit that came from all this was my job in the main library of the university. When all my accumulated wealth in war bonds evaporated and I was forced to get a job, I learned that there was a life in academe after the GI Bill. It paid little but gave me the spending money I needed to get by. More than that, it proved I could continue indefinitely taking courses even after the Bill went dry, and it introduced me once more to the inner world of a library, this time, one of the truly great libraries in the country. It also introduced me to an area of academia where I could work, could earn a living—though small—while reaching for a higher degree. More important than a job or future job, as an employee of the library, I could check out books for indefinite periods. It also provided me a private study carrel in the stacks. Only graduates or seniors working on special projects normally had carrel privileges, but Miss Lorena Baker, the librarian, let me have an unused carrel on the top floor of the stacks. After that, I did my heavy studying high above the campus in unsullied isolation, often working past midnight. Twice I was warned by the night watchman not to stay past midnight, but their warning was pro forma, and I stayed.

My great enthusiasms that spring were Applied Anthropology with McAllister and Dr. Gentry's contemporary philosophy for which I wrote a well-researched and probably my most mature term essay. Dr. Gentry was one of the department favorites, and his contemporary philosophy was by far the most engrossing philosophy class I had taken up to that time, but it convinced me that philosophy would not be a major field of study for me. Dr. Gentry was a dynamic lecturer and easily held our attention, but he rarely opened the class to free exchange of ideas. He avoided the existentialists, Sartre and Maritain, considering them too much a part of the mainstream, pop culture and preferred to explain his favorite contemporary philosophers, many of whom he knew or had known personally: Royce, James, Santayana, Bergson, and Russell. He mentioned Dewey briefly and assigned a good deal of Dewey for reading. We had no exams in class, only papers on general topics and long critical reviews of works we chose from his list of recommended articles or chapters. My paper on Royce, which I worked on more diligently than on any of my papers, received the highest grade of any paper I had written at the university and had an accompanying comment from Gentry remarking on its clarity.

In addition to Gentry's class, I signed up for McAllister's class in applied anthropology, occupying the same desk I had occupied as a freshman. It was a small class, less that twenty, made up mostly of returning veterans, only two or three women, nearly all former students. The course, I learned later, was a McAllister invention. Few had attempted to teach anthropology as a utilitarian exercise, but McAllister had always seen cultural anthropology as a field having significant practical applications. Using Commander Alexander Leighton's work *The Governing of Men*, Dr. Mac led the class through a critical anthropological analysis of the government inside the Japanese relocation centers of World War II. A guest physical anthropologist lectured on the fiasco attending the army's development, rather attempted development, of a gas mask intended to accommodate the physical requirements of the highly diverse population in the U. S. Army. Dr. Kelly, took us through the detailed story of the research and development, its failures chiefly, announcing in the end that the mask they adopted was no better in design than the masks already issued. Both topics illustrated Dr. Mac's critical approach to the study of anthropology and showed clearly that anthropology consisted of far more than interesting explorations of the various patterns of culture or variations in facial dimensions.

The pleasures of academe that semester were broad and deep, and for the first time since I was back in school, my studies began to take on a pattern and coherence that had been lost somewhere along the way; however, it was not a pattern that reflected a conventional major or minor. At best, the hodgepodge was beginning to reveal a pattern of humanistic studies: abnormal psychology and developmental psychology, contemporary philosophy, anthropology and U.S. history. There were interesting overlaps, but there was still no concentration or focus.

When the semester ended, I remained on campus for the first six weeks, taking a German literature course in which we read, I should say in which I attempted to read, a seventeenth-century German classic by Eichendorf, *Auf dem Leben eine Taugenichts,* printed in the horrendous Gothic font; I made my first F that summer. The other class, American History, a core requirement for graduation, was a disaster. Taught by a teaching assistant who told us the first day that his specialty was military history (he wore a seersucker jacket with tie to class even on the hottest days so he could wear his Bronze Star rosette in the jacket lapel's buttonhole) and that we would deal mostly with the wars. By the end of the fifth week, I had burned out completely and, for the first time since returning from Korea, longed for a rest. Had I been able to work full-time at the library I would have stayed on and lived at the fraternity house, but there were no full-time jobs for students that summer. It was a measure of my exhaustion that I gladly returned home to Corpus.

Even so, living at home presented a frightening prospect. Mama was unhappy that I had dropped out of premed and even unhappier that I was not looking for a job. There were jobs, of course, but not for students on a six-week summer break, and I refused to apply for a job because I refused to lie to any potential employer that I was *not* returning to Austin in six weeks, although neither Mama nor Albert saw any harm in my deceiving a prospective employer. I tried to convince her that I had been going to classes around the calendar and now needed time to recoup. I also told I them I needed time to read and time to write a long paper for the contemporary philosophy class and explained that my professor had asked us *not* to hand in our final essays at the end of term but to take incompletes so that he could leave early for his guest lectureship in Cambridge.

They relented when I assured them I had returned with a small nest egg I had saved from my library job at the university. When she suggested I contribute rent that summer, I said I couldn't and left it at that. I understood that Albert was urging her to demand I pay up or return to Austin. I finally said what I had bottled up since I left for Austin in 1943. I told her I believed it wrong for Albert and her to even ask for rent and board because she had kept nearly all my earnings from AMSCO that summer of 1943, money that I, a boy of sixteen, had earned for my tuition, room, and board for the year. I told her that holding my money had required me to work far off campus and that it had affected my grades and may have been the one factor that forced me to drop premed studies.

"But if you insist," I said, "I'll go to Austin now and I'll find a job."

Then I added the stinger, "The sons or daughters of your well-to-do friends would never be asked to pay for their room and board." I hated, well, almost hated, what I had said, though I had wanted to say it for a very long time. The air grew cool. She was silent, turned, and left the room, and no one ever mentioned it again.

When I learned that Del Mar College was offering both semesters of my required government classes for the grand sum of twenty-five dollars, which I had, I decided to sign up. The classes met back to back from 8:30 to 12:30, and since the college was in walking distance of the house on Clifford Street, it was a welcome excuse for getting out of the house.

At night, when I wasn't reading, I would bang away at the old Royal portable, writing the paper for Gentry's class. He had given us a wide a scope as possible, by requiring us to deal with contemporary social, economic, political, or psychological issues from a philosophically critical point of view, preferably some subject related to our major field if we were not philosophy majors. In my job at the library, I came across a wealth of material in psychiatric journals, mainly the *American Psychoanalytic Quarterly*, dealing with concepts of sexuality, which was not a widely discussed topic of the day though not nearly as taboo as it might have been before the war. My thesis had been stimulated by McAllister's lectures on race and was based on scientific findings that sexuality appeared to be less a result of moral choice than a natural or inborn propensity. McAllister's cultural anthropology had an important influence on my choice of topics in that it raised the question more than it established a firm scientific basis, and I used the ideas about nature and culture he had pounded into us as well as material I had read about sexual customs and mores among so-called primitive peoples or those peoples not governed by Judeo-Christian moral strictures. Although it was not definitive, research into nonhuman animal behavior revealed other species showed crossover sexual tendencies and identities in much the same way that humans showed them. Homosexuality was not a major subject of research in the late forties, and sexuality, while not taboo, was not yet a common topic in academia. The famous, for some *infamous*, Kinsey report, *Sexual Behavior in the Human Male*, published that year would soon bring discussions of sexuality to the forefront and would shock a nation. My thesis was that natural tendencies, biologically caused phenomena, were beyond the purview of moral or ethical judgment, but I still was a long way from "don't ask, don't tell." When Mama inquired into my topic, I explained as gently as I could, and she was shocked, though not nearly as much as I had expected her to be, that I would choose such a "distasteful" topic—her word. When curiosity got the better of moral indignation, she persisted in asking me for more details throughout the summer, particularly details concerning the behavior of a neighbor's son and certain women she knew, and I explained I was not an expert, though I did not believe that their behavior was immoral or even "unnatural." I told her how we had learned in abnormal psych that homosexuality was a natural stage of a person's psychological development, and its persistence was viewed as a form of grown-up narcissism. I perhaps belabored the semantics of terms like *natural* and *unnatural.*

It was the first time I could recall we ever had a conversation that even bordered on what I was studying, and it felt good, felt almost as if we were no longer conflicted about our roles regarding parent and son. I suggested that if she were really interested she should read *The Well of Loneliness*—that had sat on my shelves for years unnoticed. I warned her, jokingly, that the novel might convince her that reading novels had been my downfall and was the reason I had dropped out of premed studies. Earlier, she and Albert had noticed I was reading *The Way of All Flesh* and had asked if it was a required reading and if so why, the title suggesting something lurid. That the tone of our dialog on sexuality had remained light and had not descended in moral indignation was a relief. For the first time I was able to explain that my reading, Jane's and Dorothy's as well had always been a road to learning and was not ever a "waste of time." Before we broke off I added that I believed books to be far less corrupting than the moralists claimed. I quoted Oscar Wilde's comment about "bad" novels and "badly written" novels. My mother's and popular opinions aside, I was able to write a creditable paper that received a high mark from Gentry and his reader; even though I may not have proved a point absolutely, it did make some valid and strong suggestions.

The government classes at Del Mar College met every morning five days a week for six weeks: Gov.10a, U.S. Constitution, from 8:30 until 9:45, State and Gov. 10b, State and Local Government, from 10:00 to 11:15. When I walked into the 10a classroom the first morning and found only seven students enrolled, I asked if there were more, afraid it would be canceled, but they assured we were the full class and that it wouldn't be cancelled. I remarked that it would be at UT, saying that only graduate and senior-level classes were allowed to go this small. I took my seat at the large oval table with the others and asked what year they all were. All but one were beginning their sophomore year; the other, a young woman, was finishing her second year at the college and planning to transfer to Texas A&I College in Kingsville. None, remarkably, were veterans. That meant I was the only UT student, the only veteran and the only senior. I relaxed and asked if they knew who was teaching the section, wondering if it was someone I knew or had heard of.

"Mr. Agee," one answered.

"James A. Agee?" I asked, surprised to hear that the assistant principal from Corpus Christi High was now in the classroom.

"Do you know him?" some one asked.

"Do I? He was assistant principle when I graduated from high school in '43. How long has he been teaching at Del Mar?"

The young woman who was heading to Texas A & I College answered, "He's been here as long as I have. I had him for US History."

I wondered if he would remember me; it had been five years. When he walked in and took his seat at the middle of the long table, he glanced around the table and nodded good morning and then said, "Well, Joe. I'm glad to see you're here for your government requirement."

I nodded and thanked him for remembering me. He began by calling the roll and then made an extensive reading assignment due the next class period and then handed out a list of readings on reserve in the library. Compared to the reading assignments at UT, his were more extensive.

"With a small class like this," he started, "I won't be lecturing but will be calling on each of you to carry on discussions over the reading assignments. We'll have three essay exams, one of which will be the final, and you'll have two papers, one a short paper based on your reading and the other a longer paper, which will be an analysis of the presidential campaign of one of the four political parties—Republican, Democratic, Progressive, and Dixiecrat." He said we could argue why the party will or will not or should or should not win. Then he asked us to introduce ourselves and tell what we are majoring in and what we plan to do after Del Mar.

He looked at me, "Joe, why don't you begin since you are the oldest." *That was a first*, I thought.

He didn't really lecture that first day or any other day but asked us how much we knew about the Constitution, when we had last read it or any part of it. Then he warned us to be sure to read it through again even if we had read it before; that was in addition to the earlier assignment.

"Most of you read it in high school, but that was some time ago. Read it again," he stopped looked around the class, then continued, "In this class we avoid making broad, generalized statements, so be prepared to cite sources. That means you should come prepared with your notes."

Meeting more as a seminar than a lecture class, we found ourselves giving brief reports on topics he assigned and often leading the class discussion while he acted the gadfly, teasing, contradicting, insisting on the source of an opinion, and irritating! I told him one day after class that he was very much like J. Gilbert McAllister, always irritating us out of complacency. He smiled and said he had heard it before and thanked me for making the comparison to McAllister. I had known Mr. Agee as the tyrant of the main office, assistant principals traditionally serving as the school's disciplinary officer. And since I was never sent to the principal's office in high school, I had rarely spoken to him. By the end of the first week, I realized I had missed much by not knowing him and felt that his gifts as an instructor had been squandered by holding court in the high school.

Unlike Agee's class, every seat in Gov. 10b, State and Local Government, was taken. The young instructor, a recent PhD, seemed unperturbed by the size of the class and began calling the roll while a student handed out reading assignments and class procedures. When he began lecturing, speaking easily from the podium, not even glancing at the notes on the lectern, all my preconceptions of the junior college vanished. I could tell by their expressions that the students liked him. He rarely went to the blackboard but moved easily around the lectern, showing that he was not tied to his notes. Because of the size of the class, we had no long papers, just his weekly exams that always had at least one short essay question.

Of all my undergraduate courses, the best taught and the most effective was Agee's American Government. He was not my greatest teacher—that would always be McAllister—but next to McAllister, he stands out over all the rest in my years as an undergraduate. He changed my idea of what the junior college—in 1948 it was not yet called "community college"--was and what it could be. If anyone in my undergraduate years influenced my classroom style or method, it was Mr. Agee. What impressed me most was not style or method, but his command of and his respect for the subject, his love for it and his wish that each of us would love and respect it. Having never taken a course in teaching methods, I had never learned "how to teach" except by watching the best professors or instructors like Agee, McAllister, Foster, Helen James, and George Laban, each one quite different from the other. Through them I learned what to do and, to some degree, how to do it, though the art of teaching they imparted was not replicable.

Chapter 13

An Ending And A Beginning

A few weeks before the end of the junior year, every student at the university received a summons from his dean, requiring him or her to fill out a degree card declaring a major and minor and projecting a date of graduation. When I had accumulated eighty-five credit hours, just five hours short of the official senior level, my summons arrived in the mail. At the end of the summer I would have ninety plus hours. Until I received my degree card, I had not thought seriously about my standing or my major and minor, so it came as a minor shock. That I might actually graduate the following June was a remarkable feat for someone who had so assiduously avoided the reality of graduation, for someone who had wandered happily through the catalog of wonders, taking what interested him while generally ignoring degree requirements. I found myself in a quandary. I was only twenty-one and had served two full years in the army, yet I would be graduating the following year at a ripe old age of twenty-two, finishing my BA in less than four years of study. It was happening too fast. I wasn't ready to graduate. I didn't need to graduate, and I could not stay on as a graduate student because I had no idea what I wanted to study for a master's. So I ignored the summons. I figured if I had no declared major, I could not graduate; if I could not graduate, I would not have to leave. Ergo: I could avoid that Rankian trauma of parturition and remain forever within the nurturing womb of alma mater.

When I returned to Austin from self-rustication in Corpus, I was no closer to knowing what I was going to do, how I was to make a living, than I was when I got back from Korea. Having done so well in the government classes with Mr. Agee—he had praised my work in class and my term essay, faulting me only on my failure to proofread carefully—I wondered what it would be like to get a degree in government or political science. Changing my major at this stage would ensure at least an additional year; the GI Bill would see me through, if not the U.S. GI Bill, and then certainly the Texas veteran's bill, which promised to pay tuition for as long as I lived, and I knew now I could find a job that would keep me going.

Mrs. W., Barbara's mother, was not the only person to question me about my future plans with a degree in psychology; my mother and several of her friends had asked the same question. Out of desperation, I said I was planning to go to graduate school and would probably teach psychology on the college level, and in order not to sound too grand I added most likely at a junior college. That pleased Mama. It gave her something to repeat without embarrassment. It was bad enough having me end my premed studies for teaching, but having an undecided and drifting son was almost a disgrace. She did not know that beginning college teachers, though respectable, were near the bottom of all wage charts. One of her friends, Mrs. Wunderlich, had a son who had doctorate in psychology and was noted as a specialist in acoustical research. It was only after she learned of Dr. Wunderlich's success that she began to approve of my choice of major. It sweetened somewhat the bitter tea of disappointment she felt when she learned I had given up on medicine or rather medicine had given up on me.

When I returned to Austin, a second summons to the dean's office awaited me dated the last day of the first summer session, informing me I had failed to acknowledge the first summons. It warned that my failure to reply might result in my being sent down, automatically. Confident that my original plan would work, I put it aside and began reading a letter from Jane, who was now living and working in New York City. She wrote that she wished I was there and described her life briefly, the galleries, Broadway shows, concerts, and plays and her writing class at the New School for Social Research in Greenwich Village. It sounded great. As I was reading her letter, the morning's mail arrived at the house, and in it was another summons from the dean, this one printed on a card colored a bright burnt orange and repeating the warning that my failure to reply would result in automatic dismissal with the additional word *immediately*. So, *immediately,* I dialed the number on the card and got the secretary to the Dean of Arts and Sciences. When I told her who I was, she asked me to wait a moment and then came back, announcing that I should be in the dean's office at two o'clock that afternoon. They had been expecting me to call, she said, and then hung up without waiting for a reply. It was less than an hour away. *They're really serious*, I thought. The threat of automatic dismissal made me shudder: a year's rustication in Corpus Christi, a year at home? Never!

My roommates Tom Bunge and Mack Jacobs were just arriving as I was leaving for the meeting. When I told them of the orange card, they said I was lucky; they had heard of people being kicked out of school for failing to answer any summons from the dean's office. It was clear. In the fall of 1948, the University of Texas was filled to the hatches, overflowing at the gunwales, bursting at the seams, and needed to graduate or rusticate the surplus.

I arrived five minutes early, and at exactly two o'clock, Dean Parlin himself emerged from his inner office and called my name. I rose quickly. He smiled cordially, extended his hand as I approached, and asked how I was, calling me by my given name, something virtually unheard of in those days, especially in a dean's office. No instructor or professor at the university had ever addressed me as Joe before. McAllister always referred to me as Gilliland, never Mr. Gilliland or Joe. But here was the redoubtable Dean of Arts and Sciences himself calling me Joe. It made the other one in the waiting room look up from his book to take note of the unusual familiarity, and it made me wonder.

He pointed to the chair beside his desk and asked me to have a seat and then asked, "And how *is* Jane these days?"

There it was again! All through school in Beaumont and even in high school in Corpus, I was known as Jane's little brother, later more kindly as her younger brother. Now here in the fall of '48, five years after high school and after two years in the army, I was still Jane's brother. Noticing my surprise, he explained that he had noticed my name, had read that I was from Corpus Christi and assumed Jane was my sister. I told him how I had been reading her letter from when I got this final notice. She was in New York, I said, writing and editing publicity for the Methodist Church and attending writing classes at the New School for Social Research. That seemed to please him. He said she had been a fine student and had worked in his office as a typist, and then he asked me to remember him to her.

Seated and holding my folder, he asked in a light satiric tone why I had ignored his invitations, and before I could reply, he supplied the answer, saying he thought it must be because I was afraid to graduate. I said it was something like that: "Not afraid so much as reluctant."

"Well, it's not unusual, but we need you to graduate and make room for those coming behind. Now, first, what is your major? It says here you are a premed, but I see no premed pattern in your transcript since the summer of 1947."

He waited for me to speak. I told him I was considering psychology but had not spoken to anyone in the psychology office. When he asked why I hadn't, I told him that the one time I went by to talk to someone, everyone was too busy, which was true. I had, in fact, gone by several times with the same results. He suggested I could as easily do a philosophy major. He was sure that the philosophy department would welcome me, though it would push my graduation into the summer, probably as late as August. I thought for a moment, asking myself, *what does a person do with a BA in philosophy?* Jobs were uppermost in everyone's mind. But then I thought, what *does one do with a BA in psychology?* This was all many years before colleges and universities organized career days to prepare graduates for life in the real world.

Boldly, I asked aloud, "What does a person do with a BA in psychology? Go to graduate school? I know," I said, "getting a job is something I know we all must do, but . . .," I paused.

He spoke, "I understand. You really want to stay."

I sighed. "Put me down as a psychology major and a philosophy minor." I paused and wondered if I should tell the tale. "Dr. Parlin, a couple of summers ago, in Germany, I wrote Jane and told her that when I got out of the army, if I had a choice, I would never leave the university. I'm not a great student. I guess I'm the gentlemanly C variety, I admit, but I love college, love going to class, love studying and writing papers."

He listened and said he understood.

Choosing psychology was more a toss of the coin than a carefully thought out decision. I handed him the selection of classes I had tentatively made out on the way to his office. He read it over and asked what I would be taking in the spring other than psychology, and I told him I would be taking a sophomore English survey, a freshman math, sophomore history of the U.S., and my second semester of sophomore German; only one course in the five was a senior-level class. He raised his eyebrows and smiled, shaking his head at the oddity, probably wondering how I had managed to have a sister like Jane or, more likely, how she had managed to have a brother like me. He did some quick calculation and then said if I passed everything, which he was sure I would, I would graduate in June. I was stunned to hear it spoken with such certainty and finality. He chided me for my tardy appearance in his office, but he was just as everyone had described him, cordial and pleasant. When I tried to explain why my last semester would have so many lower-division classes, he smiled and insisted he understood. The fall semester looked good: Theory and Construction of Tests, Primitive Religions (anthropology), Social Philosophy, Reading Biological German, Government and Politics of the Far East, by far the most interesting collection of courses I had taken thus far. He said that he understood, that I shouldn't worry too much because I had actually put together an interesting collection of courses. I asked what class Jane had taken from him. He told me it was the nineteenth-century British novel course.

"I know you're busy, Dr. Parlin, but two of my best friends, MacDonald Smith and Bob Wood, took the British novel course with you and loved it." I told him that they had enjoyed reading the novels and hearing his lectures, and on their recommendations, I'd bought used copies of the books they were reading that semester and had read them all: Austen, Eliot, Dickens, Bronte, Gissing, Meredith, Hardy, and Wells, especially enjoying *Tess* and *The Ordeal of Richard Feverel*, which I couldn't resist telling him how I had borrowed the Meredith novel from the library at Camp Pickett.

"It was almost as if we had our own seminar talking about the novels," I aid.

"I'm glad to hear that, Joe. You should have taken my course. You liked *Feverel* then?" he asked. I told him it was one of my favorite novels, that I had read it just before going overseas to Korea in 1946. Then aware that others were waiting in the outer office, he excused himself and said he had others like me to speak to. As I left, he asked me to say hello to Jane. As I left I though, *God! What had I missed?*

To accumulate enough hours to graduate, I signed up for an eight-hour psychology course called Theory and Construction of Tests although I had little or no interest in the subject; and of all the classes I signed up for that fall, it was the one I enjoyed the least, but I learned a very important thing about myself and one even more important thing about standardized testing. Neither was good. A senior or graduate-level course, it sounded too much like something out of the college of education. The only interesting part of the class was Dr. Blake's lectures and discussion of testing theory that consumed most of the first semester. Unfortunately, he convinced me that I was not a psych major and convinced many of us that standardized testing was a highly over rated system of diagnosis. The bulk of the course consisted of taking a battery of tests and something called item analysis that had to do with the tests' validity. Back in the spring, Jim Smith, a close friend living in the house, had suggested we take the class together. He had already finished a BA in zoology and had started an MA in psychology while awaiting admission to medical school. I had said I would consider it, but now with Parlin's urging, I decided to do so, though by the time I got back to the house, I regretted not choosing philosophy for my major. It would have guaranteed my staying on through the summer.

Theory and Construction was a two-semester course granting eight hours credit and consisted of three hours of lecture with four hours lab every week. During the first semester, lab consisted entirely of taking a battery of tests that included all the major intelligence and aptitude tests, personality tests, and interest inventories. In the second semester, we took more tests and submitted the class results to item analysis. Unknown to me at the time, psychological statistics was a prerequisite, which, of course, I had not taken, though no one seemed to care when I registered. That meant I would need to learn all about mean, median, mode, and standard deviations before being tackling the item analysis portion of the curse. When I asked Jim why he didn't tell me he had already taken psych stat, he said he assumed I had already had it since he was told by his counselor that statistics was required for all psych majors. I shouldn't worry, however, that he'd teach me all the stat I would need or I could take a freshman stat course in the spring and that would satisfy the math requirement for the degree.

Our major assignment in the second semester was to assemble an annotated bibliography of all journal articles on an assigned test. My test was the 1937 Terman-Merril edition of the Stanford-Benét. The dreariest and most uninteresting assignment I had ever done, our annotations had to be typed on Ditto masters (BX, before Xerox) so that Dr. Blake could have copies run and distributed to everyone in the class and to his colleagues across the country. Although the Terman-Merril Stanford-Benét was, at the time perhaps the most highly regarded of its kind, mine was the 1937 version and therefore quite out of date. While the assignment was informative, it was also highly redundant; its main value was supplying students of testing and professors a valuable reference tool. Today in the world of computers and databases, all our energies would be wasted; but in 1949, the only way to put together such a bibliography was through the painstaking gathering and reading of hundreds of badly written and crashingly boring articles. In connection with the class, Blake gave me an additional two hours college credit for an undergraduate library research assignment analyzing literature regarding IQ testing of subjects suffering from schizophrenia, brain damage, and mental paresis. It earned me an additional two hours of B and some understanding of IQ testing. Only Jim Smith's presence in the class and Dr. Blake's light offhand manner saved the class from being a constant bore.

I had been back less than a month when I awoke to the fact that I no longer found it comfortable to be living in the fraternity house. Lambda Chi Alpha had suited me perfectly when I pledged as a freshman; it gave me a decent place to eat with a decent and congenial group of men who were not the usual frat types. Though we had members whose families were well off, we were not a rich house. Many of the men had jobs, some out of necessity, others because they, like me, wanted the extra cash. More than anything, the Lambda Chi chapter appealed to me for its lack of snobbish pretensions in dress, language, and transportation. We had old Packards and jalopies, Jeeps and Model As parked out front. I enjoyed the camaraderie at meal times, and the food was excellent, but I had outgrown the house itself. Close friends

Arthur Dykes and Bill Hart had moved out, and Mounger was temporarily back on the railroad. Bunge and Mack Jacobs were the good roommates, but everything seemed to have changed since Mullins left. With Mullins gone, the size of the library at the top of the stairs was seriously diminished. I would miss the record player Bill had left, but that was all I'd really miss.

I did not wish to become an inactive, that is, sever ties entirely, but I did want a place away from the noise. Old "Wuthering Heights," where Mounger had lived, had a vacant space—a large comfortable room—with Charley White, a studious, quiet engineering brother with quiet habits and a good sense of humor. The lovely corner room with large floor-to-ceiling dormer windows had a perfect view of the tower and the lawn around Sutton Hall, and it was less than half a block from campus. I thought it would be a perfect place to end my college career at the university; moreover, the rent five dollars a month less than the house rent.

The fall semester of '48 was my best and happiest time as an undergraduate. Free from all entangling alliances, I began to learn what a real academic life could be. I was taking, except for psychology, only those courses I really wanted: social philosophy, primitive religions, government and politics of Asia, and scientific (biological) German. I was still working in the main library and was able to keep my carrel, now legitimately because I was a full-fledged senior. In the past, my unrequired reading took me far afield; but this semester, almost everything I read that was assigned and related in some way to my classes. As for a social life, it was much less involved than it had been in the spring and curiously more satisfying than I expected. When two of my closest friends in the fraternity, Bill Hart and Gene Dixon, invited me to attend meetings of the Canterbury Club, which met every Sunday evening after vespers at the little All Saints Episcopal Church, I surprised them and myself by going and becoming a regular. That fall unaccountably, the fraternity had three pre-theologs, all Episcopalian. Gene, whom I had known in Corpus Christi and who preferred Anglican Catholic to Episcopalian, warned me that attendance at vespers was obligatory if I wanted to partake of the free evening meal in the parish hall—unless I had attended a morning service, which he insisted on calling mass. A Southern Baptist convert to Anglicanism, he was as high church as an Episcopalian could reach and not be Roman. All Saints, situated on the west end of the campus, looked much like a small village church in the English countryside with its perpendicular Gothic style, the light patina of old mold, and the shade of ancient live oaks. The only thing lacking was the cemetery with rows of mossy leaning tombstones. No one ever mentioned my becoming confirmed, taking for granted that I would ask if I were interested. When Father Joe Hart, the student chaplain at the small church, asked me once why I, a Methodist, had chosen the Canterbury Club instead of the larger and more influential Wesley Foundation, I explained the Wesley group was too large, and I knew no one there, that I had been made to feel more than welcome the first meeting; besides, I said—and this surprised him—I liked the Episcopal liturgy better, and "weren't the Wesley brothers both Anglican priests?

"After all, it is the Methodist Episcopal Church," I said. "Also, you have to admit it, the Book of Common Prayer reads awfully well." He, of course, agreed.

The upshot was that I began attending a church service—sometimes two—every Sunday, all because of Dixon and Hart. Father Joe, who years later was named Bishop of Arizona, became a good friend. Of the two organizations, the Wesley group was politically far left compared to the Canterbury Club, but both groups were strong advocates of civil rights and both opposed the peacetime draft, though the Wesley Foundation and the great Reverend Heinsohn were more outspoken. The Canterbury Club was rarely outspoken about anything except the right to serve beer and wine at their picnics.

As the year progressed and as I became more active, I believe I became more attached to the Canterbury group than I did to the fraternity. It was ironic that as my interest in the fraternity faded, in the spring of '48 I was asked to hold office for the first time and was elected pledge trainer, or more distinguished, High Gamma, whose job was to prepare the new pledges for membership into the brotherhood, making sure they understood the history of the national fraternity, the philosophy of Pan Hellenism—which meant memorizing the Greek alphabet—and that they had a clear understanding of the chapter's scandal in the basement of the old house resulting in the chapter's suspension for most of the 1930s. My election to pledge trainer placed a subversive in the very office that was intended to maintain Greek solidarity, a subject I consciously avoided, mostly because it reeked of clannish attitudes such as those spelled with a capital K.

It was an election year, my first chance to vote in a presidential election, and I was having serious arguments over election politics with a few of the brothers, not over the fine points of Harry Truman's platform but the larger questions of civil rights. I had proclaimed that since all hope was lost for Truman being reelected, I was voting for Norman Thomas, the only man campaigning on true principles. When Truman, who had been initiated into Lambda Chi Alpha, though he never attended college or university, passed through Austin not a single fraternity brother consented to go with me to the station when his train stopped. I went alone and stood in the cheering crowd, too ashamed of our lack of representation to send a note to his handlers that a Lambda Chi member was in the crowd. My disappointment, at least in part, was one of the reasons for my moving out and into Wuthering Heights.

I became even more discouraged with the brothers and their policies of indifference that fall. Dykes knew it was a losing battle to oppose the outright racism of many, not all, so he retreated into chagrined silence and then moved out. There was no noticeable diaspora of liberals because of the long waiting list for rooms. We liberals got our revenge, however, when the University Campus Chest, much like the Community Chest in those days, began its campaign to raise money for its collective charities. In the past, the chapter had voted one hundred fifty dollars for the good of the cause; but this fall, when I made the motion that we should raise the sum to one hundred seventy-five, the motion failed. The raise not only but vote to support the original amount failed. I was stunned that there would be so many mean-spirited men in the chapter; we could easily afford it according to the house manager and treasurer. I should not have been surprised. In spite of men like Arthur and Iwo and Jim Smith, the mood of the fraternity was turning quite conservative and was clearly against giving money to any pinko-red-lefty-Marxist organization. The Campus Chest had no political agenda as such, but it did support the YMCA that was gaining notoriety as a forum for liberalism, particularly the free speech variety, by offering a platform for debates where every shade of the political spectrum could be heard. The Y had also been active in the student protest during the Rainey and Regent controversy, which most fraternities had opposed at the time. The YMCA previously been host to Wendell Addington, secretary to the Young Communists organization on campus, but later it welcomed as a speaker William F. Buckley who had written *God and Man at Yale* and was founder of the *National Review*. He and Ronnie Dugger, publisher of the far left *Texas Observer*, would also debate at the YMCA.

A year earlier, I had gotten into a heated argument with PH, one of the newer members, over my lending a typewriter to one of our Negro porters. During the flush period when our revenues from room and board were flowing in, we had hired a pair of porters who made beds, waited tables, and vacuumed the rooms, a luxury common to many houses and for which we were often criticized by the non-Greek houses and cooperatives. One of our porters, a premed student at Huston-Tillotson College in Austin, a Negro college, asked me if he could borrow the old Royal portable he had seen gathering dust on my desk. Houston Jackson was a year younger than I, a short, stocky, well-spoken guy who would often stop by my room and chat about the courses we were taking. He had made it through his first year of premed, he said, with a strong B+ average for which I congratulated him, noting I dropped out of premed because I had *not* maintained a B+ average. Bill Mullins or Dirks would often come in while we were chatting and seemed to think nothing of Houston's taking a break from his usual chores and even joined in. When he asked if he could borrow the Royal, I said he was welcome to it and told him there was no hurry in returning it. I had just finished typing a paper for Dr. Foster's class and wouldn't need it for a couple of weeks.

The next day, PH came to my room and asked if I knew that the "nigger Houston" had taken my typewriter. I said I did and asked why. Pete used the *N* word constantly along with all the other racial epithets common those days, and I had more than once told him not to use the words in my room or around me. He said he believed in free speech and that we had just fought a war to protect that right. I told him he hadn't fought at all, not any more than I had, and had not even been overseas, even though he was in the marines. He said it was wrong to let "these niggers" borrow our stuff because it gave them the "delusion" that they were as good as we were. I knew it was as much about baiting me, a liberal, as it was about keeping *them* in their place; but I responded automatically, that he might be surprised that Houston *was* better than some of us; he was on the honor roll, was working his way through college, was on the GI Bill just like Pete, and, as far as I could see, was not a stupid bigot, at which point I asked him to leave my room again. Then Pete blew up and asked why I didn't go to Huston-Tillotson if I loved the niggers so much. I laughed and asked if he was listening to himself and to how irrational he sounded. I explained my choice of university had nothing to do with whom I loved and whom I didn't.

"What connection is there between my lending a typewriter to a Negro student and my enrolling in his college? Hell, Pete, I might even lend my typewriter to you if I thought you knew how to use it," I said.

Someone broke it up about that time, for our rancorous exchange had broken a rule of brotherhood and the frat house. Pete screamed that we should go outside and end it now, claiming I was hiding behind the fraternity rules against fighting, which I probably was, but I told him he was a fool if he thought beating the shit out of me—which was highly probable since he outweighed me at least thirty pounds—would make him any less a stupid bigot. No one took sides in the argument since it was all so pointless, and the only reason it went as far as it did was that I had baited Pete as much as he had baited me. I'm sure more brothers supported Pete's side of the argument than mine, but they didn't join in on Pete's side because it simply wasn't worth it, and the fraternity frowned on and discouraged controversies in the common rooms like the dining and living rooms. But the main reason no one joined his argument was that, while bigoted, they were basically pretty decent types and would never have considered Houston a "nigger."

I began to feel I was outgrowing the house and found myself a maverick, more and more on the outside of issues at a time most of the brothers rigorously adhered to conformity and were striving for the norm. Aside from the usual political arguments, I openly opposed a hazing activity that brought me into opposition with older members, who held a kangaroo court to censure one of the members who had concurred with me and had acted openly to stop what was happening. Between Christmas break and final exams in January, the brothers decided to conduct one of their infamous pledge walks, an exercise in foolishness that had the potential of inflicting serious harm on the pledges, most of whom relished the opportunity of being placed in harm's way to prove their solidarity with the brotherhood. Vestiges of primitive rites of passage still lingered. A pledge walk consisted of driving blindfolded pledges far into the hills west of Austin, usually after midnight and usually on a moonless winter night, and leaving them to find their way back home. All those who owned cars were made to forfeit keys to avoid their calling for help as soon as they were able to reach a telephone. This walk occurred during dead week, the week before final exams, a time set aside for the cram, but what made this effort different from all other recent acts was the makeup of the pledge class: it was the first class since the war having only nonveterans. No sane membership would have attempted to carry on such a piece of nonsense otherwise. I opposed it, as pledge trainer, on the grounds it was dangerous, much too cold, and during the week when many were cramming for finals. I wrote my protest and filed it to be mailed to the national office when it was all over. One other member, Bill Reick, also opposed it and quietly told me not to worry; he had a plan. When the brothers returned from dumping the fifteen or sixteen freshmen, Reick left with a pocketful of spare keys. In half an hour, all the pledges returned to the house warm and safe. Reick had picked up those who owned cars, and they in turn retrieved those dozen or so who could not squeeze into his car.

What followed proved to me that I had remained too long at the fair. One member, a deeply religious, or rather violently religious, brother from Port Arthur called for a trial to publicly censure Reick, implying that the judges might even ask him to resign for going against the will of the brotherhood. We often ridiculed the tradition of the Texas aggie "Bull Pen" in which a wayward aggie was forced to submit to a public denunciation of some fault or weakness, a favorite tool of all tyrants from the Inquisition to the Stalinist show trials of the thirties, not unlike the lynch mobs of the not too distant pass and still in mode in the minds of many. Now we had our own Torquemada and Inquisition. JA, I'll call him, boasted he was a graduate of the Jesuits and professed his strength lay in his knowing the difference between right and wrong. When the officers of the fraternity and I informed him that his kangaroo court had no standing in fraternity law or any other, he said he knew that, but insisted he had to follow a higher law. All he wanted to do was extract a confession and an admission from Reick that he had violated the trust of the brotherhood. I pointed out the inquisition he planned was more clearly a violation of the fraternity's rules than anything Reick had done. I told him, for a Jesuit, he had completely lost his hold on logic. JA hoped that in deep contrition Reick would offer to resign at which time JA would forgive him and welcome him back with love and fellowship. It was sickening, redolent of witch trials and star chambers and reminiscent of the worst excesses of the Spanish Inquisition to borrow a line from Monty Python.

Bill Reick made a perfect target for the glib and polished style of JA's religious zealotry: he was overweight, shy, and inarticulate except when producing work in his darkroom or completing an practice set in accounting. He was now faced with a number of angry members who wanted revenge for their foiled sadism. It was more than sickening. When I demanded, as High Gamma, to speak first, JA allowed me to make a statement. I explained that Reick was not alone, that he was in fact carrying out my request, which had official standing, as I was the only fraternity officer consulted in the matter. If they wished to persecute—"prosecute" was not the appropriate term, I said—they should start with me; but if they did, their efforts would be futile since I, not they, had standing, and I had no intention of repenting that which I had not done. They quickly voted to forgive me and moved on to meatier prey, pointing out quite accurately, since the court had no standing, there were no rules to govern it. Bill allowed it, sitting there for almost an hour while witnesses testified to his sins and crimes. JA was a parody of the inquisitor, and his circle egged him on until a voice suddenly boomed from overhead.

"Why are you all are here, boiling in your righteous indignation? Because one man of you showed compassion and sympathy? Hasn't this gone far enough? Aren't you satisfied that you have tortured one of your own brothers? You ought to be ashamed. This is not a trial! It is a lynch mob!"

It was Phil Mounger, the one man for whom there was no greater respect or higher regard. Phil was the one man who relished his position as an outsider, the one who could never be harmed by an inquisition or a kangaroo court. At that moment the meeting ended, dissolved almost immediately, before Bill Reick broke, but not before I learned a serious lesson about the power of demagogues and self-righteous zealots. I had disagreed with brothers like JA and PH many times before, but it had never reached this point of total disenchantment. Now, for me, the well was poisoned: too many of the brothers had gone along willingly, and many had gone along even though they disagreed—they were the more venal. After final exams, I went inactive for my last full semester as an undergraduate, and I announced in the monthly meeting of the chapter that it was in part due to JA's inquisition and the number of brothers who supported the kangaroo court, which violated the oaths they had taken during their initiations. The fact that the national office and the university outlawed hazing was nothing compared to their zeal.

My floor-length window looked out on the southwest corner of the campus, and every morning, I would wake to the Westminster chimes from the Tower, the top of which I could just see rising from an expanse of oak trees and the tiled roof of Sutton Hall. Even though I took my noon and evening meals at the fraternity house, I began to spend less and less time there. The spring term was not nearly as demanding as the fall term had been, and the result was as might be expected: my grades were not as good. Three of the courses I signed up for were sophomore level—German, history, and world literature—and one was freshman math, statistics.

That semester I had one great highlight experience that outshone all others and was unlike any other experience I had while at the university: It was performing the role of the Archangel Gabriel in Goethe's *Faust I, auf Deutsch*. Every year, the drama and German departments produce a play in German; this year, it was Goethe's masterpiece. One Sunday evening at Canterbury Club a friend of Bill Hart's majoring in German asked me to try out for one of the minor roles in *Faust*. She had heard me mouthing Hamlet's most famous soliloquy in German, "*Sein, oder nicht sein, das ist die Frage*," when she made the suggestion.

"You're not serious?" I said, at the same time thinking that I would very much like to.

She insisted she was very serious and said she had a small part near the end and quoted several lines in an excellent German accent. Dr. Michael, who was directing that spring, was short of actors for the small parts, she said, assuring me I'd not have more than a dozen or so lines. So I let her drag me to an early read-through where Dr. Michaels had me read a speech from the "*Prolog im Himmel*."

"That is good," he said. "Where did you pick up your German, in the service?"

"Yes, sir, a few years ago."

"I thought so. OK. You will be the archangel, Gabriel." I was cast on the spot, an archangel.

I had been missing something important, I knew, something more important than rambling through the catalog. By confining myself to the fraternity and the small circle of comfortable friends, I had missed out on a wider world of the university. Now, just as I was nearing the end I was beginning to learn about a world I had missed. The Canterbury Club introduced me to another kind of student and began to play a significant role in my university experience that spring, unlike any experience I had before. And although I did not consider it at the time, being a part of the *Faust* production and of Dr. Steffan's world literature class significantly expanded my experience in the humanities—a term not in wide usage in colleges or universities in those days. That I had already read many of the required readings in Steffens's world lit made it easier for me to keep up with the pace he set for the class, which, as in Fletcher's poetry class, was intended for the honors program. Steffans's lectures and our discussions brought them into focus in ways my earlier reading had never done before. It reads differently now, of course, reads like something I should have known before, but I did not know then how truly important my seemingly random romps through the catalog was preparing me for a future.

For the first time, I began to think more seriously about life after college, ruling out any thought of continuing in psychology even if I were to apply for graduate school; but there was no other field I had done sufficiently well in to consider as a possible graduate major. The thought of majoring in English had not crossed my mind, or I should say not seriously; and for the first time, I began to question the random romp. I was on the verge of graduation, if not the end of May, then certainly by the end of summer. I would have a bachelor's in psychology. So, shortly after the spring semester began, I wrote the Methodist Board of Missions in New York and asked about the possibility of a teaching job or any job in Korea, or even China, that my army experience or my degree may have prepared me to do.

About the same time, I got a letter from my brother, Don, who had recently followed Jane to New York City to pursue an acting career. He had found a job with Time Inc., was attending acting classes at the New School for Social Research, and was set up, he said, in small walk-down apartment in Greenwich Village. Suddenly, I was faced with options, though the idea of living in New York and sharing a bohemian life with Donnie had never entered the picture. At Christmas, Jane and Don had managed a trip to Corpus, and at the time, she suggested I think about New York, but she did not mention anything so specific as Don proposed. However, she added that if Don was able to get a job supporting himself, surely I could also.

When he graduated from high school, he refused to enroll in Del Mar College, had stayed at home in Corpus, and worked as a draftsman with the gas company, making and saving enough to pay his way to the New York and to finance himself until he got a job. By the summer of '48, he was settled in Greenwich Village, had a good job with Time Inc. and was studying acting at the New School. When he invited me to come to the city and share an apartment with him, assuring me that I would be able to find work, it was a pleasant shock. We had not been very close growing up, and I had no idea that he would want me to live with him; it touched me deeply that he had thought of me. Don wrote that he knew I loved the opera and the symphony orchestra, the theater and books, just as he and Jane did. He wrote and suggested I could attend the New School as well. The letter became as important a source of thought as anything; I believe my speaking the lines of an archangel from the stage prompted him to consider me as a roommate.

The Methodists replied that there were no positions in China, that most positions were being closed because of the march of the Communist forces against Chiang; however, the letter did mention a three-year short-term missionary program in Japan and Korea that would reopen for new applicants in the spring of 1950. The letter urged me to keep this in mind.

When I did not graduate in June because I had dropped my statistics class, I faced one more term, one more class of freshman math—trigonometry, which I signed up for and audited a seminar in metaphysics. When I took the room at Wuthering Heights, I had promised the landlady I would be out by June, and she held me to my agreement, having committed to let the room to another student. The fraternity had bought the old Kappa Alpha Theta sorority house that spring and needed tenants badly for the summer session, so I moved in for six weeks. Having quit my job at the library, I had more time now than I ever had and was able to read further afield, mostly in English literature: Waugh, Greene, Huxley, Wells, Hardy, more Meredith, Austen, Brontë, Bertrand Russell and Locke. Steffan had introduced me to modern French and German literature, which I also began to read, principally Remarque, whose *Drei Kameraden* I read in the original that summer and more or less amazed myself, making up, I felt, for dropping the German lit class where we—they, I should say—read Eichendorf's *Auf dem Leben eine Taugnichts*. While I attended the seminar in Hobbes, Descartes, and Locke, I offered to read no paper and only sat and listened, knowing that the participants were all graduate students. Dr. Miller knew what I was doing, that I was using the course to fill out the minimum requirements for my GI Bill, and for that reason, he never called on me to participate, though he did allow me to interject a thought once or twice, providing none of the bona fide students wished to talk.

Because the new house was not serving meals that summer, a group of us found a boarding house nearby serving good meals at a reasonable price that was willing to take us on, reserving a large, round table in one corner of a spacious, well-lit dining room for us. It was the same group every day: Phil, Jim Rutland, a jolly DeWitt Magee, Willis Tate, one or two others, and myself. Tate, now dean of students at SMU, had lived in the old house the summer before and was finishing his doctorate in education; the rest were seniors or graduate students, and the table talk was almost always stimulating, often zeroing in on politics, current movies, sometimes sports—UT had just won the NCAA Baseball title—but usually some issue in world affairs. It was our round table seminar.

Near the end of the term, I announced at dinner that I was not only going to pass college trig and graduate, but I actually was assured a B in the course. They had made much of the fact that I was a senior and still hung up on freshman math, but now they were all congratulatory. I said I was sad to be leaving, probably sadder than I had ever been in my life. Then I said, with tears in my eyes, that this table meant more to me than they could know; their talk, always bright and filled with wit, was as intelligent as any talk I'd heard at table in all my years in Austin—even when they disagreed with me—which was more often than not. I said they made me see what the word "collegial" meant and what it was like when good friends and scholars dined together. I said I hoped that in a year's time I would be abroad, somewhere in Asia, probably Korea. Willis asked what I planned to do there. I said I had no idea but hoped to do something for the Methodists. Willis and his brother Bob Tate were Methodist ministers and Lambda Chis from SMU. He was quite interested when I told him about the short-term missionary program I was looking into.

At that point then, he said, "If any of you need a job reference, you're welcome to use my name. I'll have PhD after my name, and I have just been promoted from dean of students to vice president for academic affairs." The promotion, he said, was his reward for completing the doctorate.

We thanked him and assured him we would use his name.

When I arrived in Corpus with no clear commitment and apparently not worried that my future was undecided, Mama and Albert were more than a little concerned. In Mama's mind, it was as if I had purposely avoided getting an education that would prepare me for the world of work, as if I had indeed lived up to the wish I made after my first day of real work at AMSCO. Perhaps she was right. I understood but could not sympathize with them. Albert had never finished his degree, though he had worked hard at Northwestern University to prepare himself for the CPA examination and had continued to study for it most of his life. Finding a job as an accountant just as the Depression hit made a degree seem superfluous, and it probably was. Because he was capable, intelligent, and worked hard during the Depression, he was never out of work nor was ever caught in dead-end jobs. He had never ventured out of his field of specialization, never lost focus. A university degree, my mother felt, as did most people she knew, had value only in proportion to the quality of job it prepared one for. It was bad enough that Don had refused to go to college, that he had gone to New York just as he turned eighteen for the purpose of studying acting and only acting, but for me to have taken a degree in psychology with no intention of becoming a psychologist was beyond comprehension. Hell, I hardly understood it myself.

Somewhere in the back of my mind, I was certain that I would one day enter graduate school. In spite of my mediocre grades, I was sure that I would be admitted on the basis of the Graduate Record Exam, although in those days a BA from UT automatically guaranteed admission to a master's program at the university in Austin or any of the state colleges. A doctoral program was different; it required a GRE. For the time being, I felt I needed more realistic goals before setting out for a master's in psychology or philosophy or anything I might randomly consider. A year's hiatus in New York would not be a bad way of discovering what I should do. Don's suggestion offered the best of all possibilities. When I told Mama that I was going to New York, I believe she was relieved. I would be out of town and no longer a reminder of my failure to continue in medicine. She agreed that I was sure to find something interesting that would pay enough to support myself while I decided what I really wanted to do. She made two suggestions, however, that I found reasonable and easy to follow though. I was sure neither would produce the result she desired. First, she suggested that I should speak to President Harvin at Del Mar College and find out what I needed to qualify as a teacher in a junior college. She had assumed rightly that I would be happy as a college teacher. The other suggestion was to stop in at the Veteran's Administration Employment Service just to see what they might have in the area; she had heard of several recent graduates who had found good positions through the VA. I agreed to both.

Dr. Harvin was cordial, welcomed me into his office, and congratulated me on my degree. Like Dean Parlin almost a year before, he asked how Jane was doing and then asked what I had taken my degree in. When I told him, he said, as I expected, that I needed at least an MA for a full-time position; but if I wanted to hang around and take my chances, he might have one or two part-time introductory classes.

My visit to the VA was no more productive, but it was more interesting. When I arrived for the interview, the employment counselor greeted me with a handshake and congratulations on my degree. He still wore the "ruptured duck," his gold discharge pin. We chatted briefly about my branch of service, where and when I had served, and in what outfits. People were always impressed I crossed both oceans and that I was so young and looked even younger. For a few minutes, we exchanged war stories, and then he asked where I had gone to university, what I had majored in, and what my degree was. He was in the act of opening a large file drawer behind his desk when I told him that my BA in psychology would be awarded in August in Austin at UT but that I had completed all the requirements. He slowly closed the drawer and turned to a small four-by-six file box on his desk and pulled several printed cards. There were no openings in Corpus, he said, but there were two openings in Austin, one in testing and another in counseling. Both required a state civil service exam and require either a major or minor in psychology, but neither would begin until October. The starting salary wasn't handsome, but it was better than a school salary, and it came under the state civil service. He was about to hand me the cards but laid them on his blotter and asked me what my minor was. When I told him it was philosophy, he looked downright dejected. I was spoiling his day. Finally, in desperation, hoping to salvage something and to save face, he asked, "What work experience did you have before you went into the service?"

I told him about the four months in the AMSCO Refinery as a lab assistant during the war and the eight months driving an ambulance while I was a freshman and working as a morgue assistant and about the year with the library.

"Do you need a job right away?" he asked.

"Well, what do you have?" I asked.

He reached into the top desk drawer, pulled out a small business card, and said, "I have here a roustabout job on a wildcat rig. It pays better than anything in your academic fields. Do you know where the Top Hat Café is on Highway 9? If you meet Mr. Ike Roberts there Monday morning, he's picking up men for a drilling crew, you know, roustabouts. It's really good pay," he said and handed me the card.

I thanked him, and we shook hands. As I left I turned and said, "Look don't feel bad. I don't. I'm leaving for New York City the day after tomorrow. I really didn't expect much. If nothing happens in the Big City, I'll look into those state jobs if they haven't closed on them."

"Oh, they won't close until after the testing date." I had relieved him immensely.

Bill Reiss was home for the summer, a full semester from a BS in geology, and had accompanied me to the employment service. When we left, we were both laughing at the man's dilemma, but Bill remarked how far I had drifted since the time he and I brewed a batch of bromine in his lab off his garage and how we ducked our faces in buckets of water to wash out what was in essence tear gas. We had several beers at the dim old Oyster Bar just off Water Street, a dive that seemed a fit place to say our farewells. When we were kids, we had often dreamed of walking through the doors of the Oyster Bar and taking a seat among the bums and whores. It was the only sawdust restaurant with oyster shells that I knew firsthand, and I told Bill it seemed even more fitting than one of the clean, well-lighted places farther up the street. I talked about reading the "Love Song of J. Alfred Prufrock" for the first time in Klingenbrünn and how I recalled the Oyster Bar in Corpus Christi when I read those opening lines the first time. Sadly, they had stopped serving beer on tap, and we had to share a large quart bottle of Lone Star. "There it is, Bill," I said, "the oyster shells *and* the sawdust. I'm surprised the health department allows it."

I told him that Don had written me in the spring, suggesting that I come to New York, and assuring me that I would find a job paying well enough to do those things I wanted to do: going to plays and the opera, attending concerts, visiting the great museums and galleries. Jane had suggested it at Christmas and mentioned that I could enroll in classes at the New School for Social Research. It had been at the back of my mind for some time. Bill agreed it was a good idea. Most of my friends with new degrees that summer had taken executive trainee positions with large corporations in Houston, Dallas, or Chicago. The jobs paid well and promised much; even those with BA degrees in history and sociology had had no trouble finding good jobs. Of course those with engineering and accounting degrees fared much better. Never before had business and industry enjoyed such a supply of well-educated young men who had matured during the war and were eager to take on responsibility. They were ambitious to get ahead, loyal, and well-disciplined. I had interviewed for several positions in the spring before graduation but hadn't pursued any of them because I really didn't see myself fitting into a corporate structure as a manager or as an executive. I told Reiss I knew only three people besides him who understood my reasons for *not* taking these jobs: Bill Mullins, Phil Mounger, and possibly Jim Smith. Mullins, planning to make the army a career, had returned to active duty, taking an assignment as a writer with the Army Institute of Pathology in Washington DC. Phil was still dropping in and out of college, working as an engineer on the MKT and switching cars in the Houston rail yards while reading Korzybski's *Science and Sanity*. At the time I left Austin, he was back in summer school, looking as if he might stay a while this time and maybe even complete his degree with a double major in economics and anthropology. Jim had finally been accepted at UT Medical School. And old friend, Dykes, was moving through the school of architecture. Everyone was fitting into his niche with such ease and comfort that anything seemed possible. For me, in spite of all the talk of creative freedom and unlimited opportunity, they seemed dead-end jobs.

No one in the fraternity, except Arthur, would have understood why I would want to leave the booming and expanding land of opportunity for the odors of the Orient. Bill Reiss understood and of course Mullins. One night at the beginning of the summer session, a group of us from the fraternity house were soaking up many steins of beer at Scholz's and were winding our way back to the house. We passed the house where Bill and Pat shared a large comfortable ground-floor room. Having lost track of my old friend from the days of the Texas Order of Science, I had quite forgotten where he lived. Suddenly, Bill appeared before me on the sidewalk outside his house. He pulled me off the street, laughing, saying that he had recognized my loud voice as it echoed though their open windows, disturbing their study. The others continued down the street, but I stayed there several hours, talking and renewing an old and dear relationship. Bill and I had always enjoyed long—and we believed intelligent—conversations. Of all the survivors of the capsized *Wench*, Bill was the only one who read widely outside his narrow field. Art, music, and ideas dominated the talk that night, and I became aware how much I had missed by not keeping up. I said I had waited too late to move out of the fraternity house, and he agreed. Both he and Pat had become inactive in Alpha Tau Omega and, in doing so, had entered into the wider world of the university. That night, stimulated by a prodigious quantity of Scholz's Pilsner, I tried to explain my desire to get back to the East. Once at the fraternity house, several brothers had gathered in my library at the top of the stairs, discussing a *Life* magazine article about the graduating class of 1949. Most of the graduates said they were going into business or science, but one, a Cornell man, said he hoped to work in China or somewhere in the Far

East, not as a missionary or a teacher, but as a businessman with the hope of improving the lives of people who suffered longer than anyone the effects of the last war which, for them, began ten years before it came to us. Mao had just chased Chang off the mainland onto Formosa (Taiwan), so the young man from Cornell said he might have to wait. I told Bill and Pat how one of the brothers remarked, that he was a fool and was wasting an expensive Cornell education. I had thought it a stupid remark and had asked where the waste lay and had insisted he explain.

"It really made me angry," I said. "The others were silent, said nothing, and I suddenly felt alone there." Bill and Pat listened, agreed. It was good stopping here and seeing them both. Neither Mullins nor Mounger would have voiced such cynical sentiments nor let them pass. Talking to the Reiss brothers, I would get arguments but never cynical ones. Bill had stuck to science and would finish his BS in geology the following January. I envied Pat who had shifted from chemistry to a business degree in foreign trade and a second degree in French. After graduation in June, he planned to use up what was left of his GI Bill and study ecology at the Sorbonne.

All in all, I was optimistic as I made plans to join Jane and Don. Even the economic downturn that began that summer did not seem serious enough to cause me any anxiety. A week after the Oyster Bar with Bill, I was with Don in his new apartment at the Paul Revere Arms, a dingy, small, overheated, noisy place two flights up on the corner of East Forty-eighth and Third Avenue. Every morning, except Sunday, the uptown and downtown expresses together with the uptown and downtown locals hit the corner at the same time, making wake-up calls or alarm clocks redundancies. He welcomed me apologetically and somewhat sheepishly, which was unusual for Don. I never knew my brother to be sheepish about anything.

The first night, he and Jane planned a welcome for me at her place on West Eighty-first Street. She shared the two-bedroom apartment with three other young women, two of whom had been suite-mates in the Scottish Rite Dormitory at the University of Texas. The fourth member of their group was a graduate of U of Minnesota; like them, she had come to the Big City to seek her fortune, not necessarily a mate. They were all working as writers or editors in some area of publishing. None had such grand salaries, but they shared and got by with enough left to buy tickets to plays, concerts, and the opera, providing the seats were in the balconies. That apartment with those marvelously bright people became a safe harbor in the midst of what in the early days appeared to be a world of disorder. I doubt that I would have survived so easily had it not been for Don and Jane and her friends,

Pat and Betty Ruth, or BR as she preferred. All three had quite early learned the ways of the city and had become New Yorkers, thus able to pass on their understanding of the city. That night after we had eaten, I felt I had arrived when we all got on the subway for Lewisohn Stadium and a free concert with a young Leonard Bernstein conducting.

Chapter 14

Wonderful Town

The *Times* classified section had columns and columns of help-wanted ads, but no ads for anyone with a BA in psychology or for any of the varied talents I described in the application forms. After the first week, when I had found nothing, Don began to get a little anxious, though he tried not to show it. Only a year out of high school, he had found a job within a day or two of arriving. It wasn't much, a messenger in the offices of *Architectural Form*, a Luce publication and part of the Time, Inc. organization, but it paid well and led to a job in the transportation department of *Time* magazine that also paid well and had normal working hours. Delivering messages to people like Henry Luce himself and members of the Republican Party hierarchy during the Dewey campaign in 1948 was a most interesting part of the job. Don was a strikingly handsome young boy of eighteen, extremely black hair and eyes, the Iberian-Irish roots showing I suppose, and he moved easily in a cool, somewhat upstart manner one would expect in an aspiring actor. When the summer job ended and he moved over to the *Time, Inc.* building, pay improved, and he continued as a messenger from time to time.

I had allotted myself two weeks to find a job and settle in, and I made it just under the wire, largely because of the generosity and the imagination of a Mr. Wilson, the acting personnel manager for the Bowery Savings Bank. An employment agency where I had gotten several tips called the Paul Revere Arms late one afternoon and left a message asking that I come in first thing Friday morning, the Friday before Labor Day, which was my deadline. If this didn't result in a job, I would be heading back to Corpus or Austin on the Greyhound and taking the Texas civil service exam as a tester or counselor. At the agency Friday, the clerk gave me an appointment slip and said the interviewer was a good friend of hers, a nice man, and she was sure this would be something I would like. The position I was interviewing for was for bank clerk, the most entry-level position the had, other than janitors and maids, at the Bowery Savings.

After reading my application, Mr. Wilson reacted much as they all had up to that time. "I'm afraid you are way *overqualified*," he said apologetically.

"I don't think I'd ever heard that word used to describe me before I arrived in New York," I said. "But I can count on one hand and have fingers left over the number of times an interviewer *hasn't* used it. Frankly, a person who needs to eat and pay rent can't be too overqualified."

Don and Jane in the wonderful town

He smiled and nodded agreement and seemed to be less disturbed by my over qualifications than the others I had spoken to. He said he thought that with my education, I would probably find the job too boring after a few weeks. I could feel a polite refusal coming. He paused. "But if you want to try it, we would be glad to have you."

He was unlike all the other managers or personnel men I had spoken to, far more relaxed and certainly less impressed with himself or his position than the others. I told him I was definitely interested in the job, and I would gladly take it. "As far as being bored," I offered, "I don't see how anyone can be bored living in this city."

We continued to chat, mostly about my degree and my background, and he seemed in no hurry to end the conversation. From his questions, I could tell he had only scanned my application. When he learned I was a veteran, had been overseas while the war was still going on, he voiced surprise and looked back at the application.

"You don't look twenty-two," he said. "You look too young to have been overseas and have a college degree."

I told him I was almost getting used to hearing that and that one day I would probably appreciate hearing it a lot more than I did then. He laughed. He had been too old for the service, he said, still in no hurry to wind up the interview. Then casually, almost as an afterthought, he asked if I had ever thought of going into personnel work and explained how the Bowery was planning to reorganize its personnel system when he retired within the year. With my degree in psychology and some additional courses in personnel management, he thought that I might be a good person for the new department.

"I don't have any background in personnel," he said. "I just came up through the system, started as a clerk years ago, and I'm just temporarily in the job until I retire. We've always contracted out a lot of our personnel counseling and testing. But I think with your background and with the experience you will get on the floor, you might work out quite nicely, that is if you'd be interested in that sort of thing. And, of course, it pays a lot better than a clerk or even a teller."

I told him I was indeed interested. I told him I thought my degree had prepared me for just that sort of thing, and I asked for him to keep me in mind. Then I added, "I would be certainly willing to take whatever courses that would be of help."

He nodded and said he was about to suggest just that and said the bank would probably help pay any costs for the classes at NYU or Columbia. It was amazing how frank and informal he was about it all, how totally lacking in pomposity or self-importance. Though he offered me the job early in the interview he was still in no hurry to send me on my way. While I sat there, I looked around the office to see if I could tell by the furnishings where he fit in the company's hierarchy. It was plain but expensive in a conservatively unostentatious way. The whole suite of offices, carpets, and wall decorations fit what I had read once read about as "quiet opulence." The chair I sat in was covered in soft, comfortable leather. His desk was of a fine wood, its surface uncluttered, the pad and blotter clean but not spotless, *and* he had a window shaded by tastefully simple drapes. I'd heard that a window in a New York office signaled status. Mr. Wilson was surely the most skilled of all the interviewers I had met in the last two weeks, eliciting from me far more general and personal information than any of the others, and all without a pad and pencil or a formal list of questions to refer to. His tone of voice had never wavered from an easy, familiar and relaxed tone of an old friend, his questions appearing to be ones a person might ask of any new acquaintance.

"Wait here a minute, will you, Joe?" he said. He picked up his phone and pressed a button, waited, and then spoke, "Agnes, is he there? I wonder if I could speak to him for five minutes . . . No . . . Thanks, I'll be right over."

He hung up and smiled. "Come with me."

I followed him into a long corridor, indirectly lighted and hung with framed oil paintings of the city, the floor carpeted in a light-green pile. We passed through tall mahogany doors reaching almost to the ceiling and into a long room, obviously the main boardroom of the Bowery Savings Bank. It was like a movie set, and I half expected a frowning Raymond Massey to be enthroned at the far end. Instead, a tall heavy-set man with a ruddy complexion and sparse hair entered from the far end, his hand extended to Mr. Wilson.

"Harry, how good to see you. You're looking well," he said as he and Wilson shook hands. His voice was cordial, just a degree off familiar; but nevertheless, he sounded like he was genuinely glad to see his old friend.

"I'm much better, Mr. Schwultz, thank you. I'd like to introduce you to one of our new clerks, Joe Gilliland. He says he was born in Dallas just like you," Wilson said and beckoned me into the presence. "Mr. Schwultz is president of the Bowery, Mr. Gilliland," he said.

I wondered, *is this the normal thing at the Bowery Savings Bank?* Mr. Schwultz acted as if it were. We shook hands and chatted about Dallas and how long it had been since either of us had been there. He asked where I had gone to school. His manner was charming. There's no other way to put it, and for the moment, I felt he was really interested in my background and me. He asked when I would start to work, and Mr. Wilson said they wanted me on the floor the day after Labor Day, next Tuesday. Then he said, "I'm thinking we'll work him into the new personnel department, Mr. Schwultz, when we teach him what the banking business is all about. He just graduated in psychology from The University of Texas."

All that, right here in the boardroom of the nation's largest savings bank. Mr. Schwultz smiled and then wished me luck and said he had started at the bottom too and then returned to his office.

As we walked back down through the corridors of power, Mr. Wilson said, "Mr. Schwultz is the president of the bank. You know, the Bowery is the first billion-dollar savings bank in the world. By New York law, we have only four branches, but we are the biggest. Mr. Schwultz is a fine man." I believed him. As we stopped outside his office, he handed me an envelope and said, "Take this to the doctor at this address today and get a physical exam. It's only a formality for the insurance company. My secretary has made you an appointment. Now we'll see you at the Thirty-fourth Street branch Tuesday morning, nine o'clock. They'll be expecting you."

We shook hands. I had a job. It had been so easy, so easy to like this good man and tell myself that if he were typical of the people in charge—well, I was just plain lucky. At that moment, I felt that 1949 was the best of years to arrive in New York City for the first time. I was a few blocks from Rockefeller Center and the Time Inc. Building, where Don was working. The job and my meeting with the president of the bank would make a good lunch topic, and I had just enough money to buy lunch for us both this time. When I told him I had the job, starting at thirty dollars a week that included noon meals and an evening meal on Friday, when the bank stayed open until seven, he smiled.

"We'll make it easily. It's great!"

Don was relieved and happy for me, especially when I told him I was not starting at the entry-level salary but the next step up. I thought it strange that the bank would serve meals to its employees, but Don recalled hearing how the New York banks did not allow employees leaving until the workday ended, except in emergencies. After some quick arithmetic, we figured that between us, we could afford a better place. He told me then that in a month, he was planning to quit his job at Time Inc. in order to have time to take acting classes. The famous teacher and actress Stella Adler of the old Group Theater had accepted him as a student after a long interview and an audition and offered him a fifty percent scholarship. He was sure, he said, that he could find a couple of part-time jobs that together would pay as much as the job at *Time* was paying. After searching for two weeks and finally finding a thirty-dollar-a-week job, I was in awe of Don's insouciance, his utter nonchalance. Just that morning, when I left him at the corner of Fifth Avenue and E. Forty-eighth, I told him that if I didn't find a job today, I would be leaving for Corpus or Austin on the bus the next day. Though he had wished me luck, neither of us was very sanguine about my prospects. I had an interview the first thing, but it would surely be like all the others, I thought, and I was certain he thought so too. We talked about it, about how ironic it was that he, with only a high school diploma, had found jobs waiting for him, even had people come to him with offers.

But then it wasn't so ironic. In high school, he had taken the classes that prepared him for the real world: bookkeeping, drafting, typing, along with the general studies classes that prepared him for college. In other words, he was immediately employable, whereas I was . . . merely overqualified. Then Don had always been the most remarkable fellow. His reason for coming to New York was to become an actor; he could have enrolled in classes at Del Mar College and studied drama at the university, but he preferred to go directly to the heart of the theater and try. He had told me of how a few weeks after arriving in the city he was standing in line to register for acting classes at the New School when he was approached by someone who asked if he was an actor and right there offered him a chance to read for a small part in an off-off-Broadway play, just a small part, a walk-on with a few lines. Most aspiring actors stand in lines, wait for auditions, and never or rarely get called.

"That would be enough to give anyone confidence," I said to Jane after repeating the story.

"Don't kid yourself. He arrived with a truckload of confidence," she shot back and laughed.

He was only nineteen the summer I arrived and supported himself, studied and worked for a year with no support from home or encouragement of any kind. I was more than a little impressed when he said he would quit a job that already paid him better than my job at the Bowery, that he would do this in order to take classes from the famous Stella Adler of the old Group Theatre. I had not the slightest doubt he would do it.

The day after I landed the job, we left the noisy Paul Revere Arms and moved into the strange apartment in the west seventies, just off Central Park West. A Lambda Chi I knew from Austin, Dick Glover, insisted the three of us find a place together. Don agreed, though without enthusiasm, but Glover found the place and grabbed it as soon as I told him I had the job. Don's apathy was barely disguised.

I had already begun to enjoy the manifold pleasures of the city: the galleries, the cheap movie theaters, free tickets to radio or television broadcasts, and, of course, the glorious museums. Even after the most disheartening interviews, I would find comfort and solace at the movies. A week after I arrived, I saw at the Metropolitan the largest Van Gogh retrospective ever assembled. Glover, who took me to see it, assured me that such things were not unusual.

It was impossible to live in New York and not discover a world of new ideas. Every morning, when Don and I left the apartment, I would feel a quickening of pulse and a heightened awareness as I walked over to Broadway to get the subway or over to Central Park West for a bus that would deliver me to a stop in front of the Bowery Bank. I would stand there at the bus stop, looking up and down, quite overwhelmed. Such streets actually do exist, I told myself, wondering when the feeling of awe would finally fade. I felt more than elation, felt something akin to triumph. Though all I had was a job as bank clerk, making less per week than I made at sixteen as a lab assistant, fresh out of high school, I knew I was secure and settled for a time at least. I was able to pay for a seat in the family circle at the Met, the real Met, or the high balcony at Carnegie Hall. And 1949 was a great year for the theater. *Street Car* was still playing and so was *Kiss Me Kate* and *South Pacific* with Pinza and Martin, and then there was *Death of a Salesman* with the original cast of Lee Cobb, Mildred Dunnock, and Arthur Kennedy; Henry Fonda was *Mr. Roberts*, and Joyce Redmond was Anne in *Anne of the Thousand Days* opposite Rex Harrison's Henry VIII, and Mae West was doing *Diamond Lil* again. Then there was Sinatra on radio for Chesterfield with Marlene Dietrich as his guest, and Don and I had tickets for the broadcast. In those days fifteen minutes was all it took to sell toasted lungs on radio—Don got the tickets and we saw *La Dietrich*. It was marvelous. No less marvelous was Fort Tryon Park and the Cloisters, where the Middle Ages stood intact above the wide Hudson with the Merode Altarpiece as clear and bright as when Roger Campin painted it.

A week after the job began, the day after Labor Day, I enrolled in night classes at the New School for Social Research in the Village, taking classes in psychology, anthropology, and Russian literature, all crammed into two nights a week, Monday and Tuesday from six until nine forty-five. Of the three classes, the only disappointment was Social Psychiatry that dealt entirely with Sheldon's somato-typing of personality, all about endomorphs, ectomorphs, and mesomorphs—medieval-sounding concepts that echoed to me the spurious sciences of phrenology and astrology. J. Gilbert McAllister himself had blasted Sheldon's somatotyping of personality based on physical measurements as he had blasted all pseudoscientific justifications for racism. It sounded like so much quackery, and I wondered how Harvard could have given a snake oil salesman the pulpit to preach such a canting science. The class was filled with auditors like myself, mostly suburban types, well-heeled, middle-aged clubwomen, the kind that read a chapter of *Interpretation of Dreams* and immediately become deep analysts and experts on human sexuality. Sheldon had a snappy style and either dyed, shiny black hair or a very bad rug, and he directed most of his attention to the well-heeled and well-coiffed ladies on the front row.

The other classes, however, were excellent. Professor Tartak in the Russian lit class had a thick Russian accent but looked too old to have been a recent refugee. The course covered early Russian literature: from Lermontoff through Pushkin and finally Gogol. He gloried in Pushkin and told wonderful stories of his life and writings, pacing up and down before the class, quoting passages from Longfellow from memory, first in Russian and then translating into English to prove, he said, that the Russian was better. Even English poetry, he insisted, sounded better in Russian; and when he read the opening lines of Longfellow's "The Song of Hiawatha" in English and then in Russian, we agreed.

When we got to Gogol, I checked out the *Inspector General* from the branch library and read it along with his discussion; and when he talked about

Dead Souls, I bought it. Never more than a few questions came from the class because no one wanted to interrupt the brilliant and easy flow of wit and poetry that poured from his mouth. After class, we would approach the desk and ask our questions, and he would always take time to answer, often trailing crowds of listeners into the hall as the next class came in to occupy their seats. Once he was so involved in an answer he didn't notice the next instructor had begun lecturing while he was waxing eloquently. The new students and their instructor listened too, enraptured by his wit and persuasiveness.

The anthropology course was a study of modern race relations and was in essence a course in applied anthropology. The instructor held degrees in anthropology and law, and at the time, he was teaching the course represented by the B'nai B'rith, the Urban League, and NAACP. Debunking the pseudoscientific bases for racist philosophy, the early lectures covered much of the same material Dr. McAllister's lectures covered in the freshman course I had taken in 1944. The latter half covered civil rights cases and efforts to bring about change. His lectures dealt with specific cases, mostly in the South, but avoided famous cases, such as the Scottsboro boys and others from that period. He welcomed our questions and participation, using students' comments as springboards for wider discussion. Our texts were a government publication entitled *To Secure These Rights*, a collection of essays on the progress of legislation that broadened human rights, and a recent work by Oscar Handlin. I had expected the class to be filled with strong civil rights advocates and people conversant with the history of civil rights in America but was surprised by the ignorance, even naïveté, of most of the class, particularly the younger ones. When the instructor began to discuss Jim Crow laws, they were shocked but quite ignorant of the more subtle forms of discrimination in the North, where race laws were unwritten. The instructor constantly led them into the trap, allowing them to make claims and then showing them their own image. Once when he said, "Jim Crow by any other name is Jim Crow," they did not understand. When they began making blanket statements about *all* Southerners, *all white* Southerners in particular, he politely and quietly showed them they were making the same kind of error the so-called white Southerners were making. I sat near the back of the room directly in front of a very large Negro man—*black* was not the politically correct epithet of the day—who chuckled to himself every time a young lady on the front row would make a comment or a suggestion as to how to wipe out all prejudice. I raised my hand and said I had encountered almost as much outrage about integration in New York as I had in Austin, Texas, and gave an example of the place where I worked.

"I'm not naming the bank where I work—it's on Fifth Avenue—but there are no Negroes working in any positions except as messengers, couriers between the branches who are large, impressive men, the kind that few thugs or criminals would mess with." Then I told how one of the Irish guards, a retired NYPD officer, told me how sad it was that "they" were allowing "coloreds" to play ball with the whites. I told him how he even suggested that we in the South knew how to handle this stuff.

The instructor explained how discrimination in this case served a purpose for the bank and the employees, and he agreed that it would probably be difficult for a large, mean white man to get such a position. Since the couriers always traveled in pairs, the ingrained prejudice of New Yorkers in the mass would find it unusual, even improper, for a mixed-race pair to be traveling together. The large man behind mumbled, "Amen!"

During a break one day in class, I asked him what he did during the day. He was always dressed in a neat, dark three-piece pinstripe, though he looked as though any minute it would burst at the seams. He said he was a stevedore and worked the wharves not far from the New School itself. I could tell by his accent he was not a New Yorker but more likely from Louisiana or Mississippi. At first I was reluctant to let anyone know I was from Texas, afraid I would be stereotyped and therefore have anything I said automatically discounted by Yankee prejudice. But the front row, mostly young women with heavy Brooklyn accents, finally got to me when they insisted it was impossible to change the views of people in the South. I finally asked her if she had ever known anyone from the South or if she had ever been in the South. She said she didn't and she hadn't. I asked her if she considered Texas a Southern state, and she said she did.

"Then did you know that last spring in Austin at the University of Texas the student government took a straw vote to see how many students, graduate and undergraduates, favored integration of the university and the public schools? There was a lawsuit of a man, Heaman Swett by name, who had applied for admission to the law School because there was no 'separate but equal' law school in Texas. The state immediately established a law school at Texas Southern U in Houston, but he claimed it was not equal, and of course, it wasn't. It was not in the interest of The University of Texas Law School to be judged equal to a newly established law school attached to a Negro university. Well, the voters voted overwhelmingly to open the university to people of all races."

The instructor listened and took notes. Then I went on and told about the protest march in November 1944, when the majority of the students marched to the capitol, protesting the firing of Dr. Rainey, who advocated integration. "I know," I said, "because I was there, and I marched even though I was in the army at the time. So it isn't true that *all* are opposed to integration. In some cases, not even *most* are opposed," I pause. Then as calmly and as carefully as I could, I added, "It's sweeping generalizations like *all* and *every* that I hear every day up 'Nawth' that tell me prejudice and bigotry are not confined to the South."

She sat silent. The instructor asked me to see him after class; he wanted to get some more information about the straw vote, which he had not heard about. After class, I told him I would look up the story in the *NY Times Index*, and I'd give it to him next time. I admitted that the straw vote was not definitive since fewer than fifty percent of eligible voters took part—better than the national average in presidential elections. He said he realized that, but assuming that those violently opposed had voted and the equally violently in favor had also voted, it gave you a pretty good idea how people felt.

More important to me than my classes and far more important than the job at the bank was the impact Jane, Betty Ruth, and Pat made on me. New York was everything I thought it would be and, if possible, was even more stimulating and exciting than I expected, but it would not have been had I not had them to guide and teach me. They had all majored in English or languages and had jobs as writers where they were in constant association with interesting people. Our talks at the apartment always revolved around the theater, books, motion pictures, music, and all the arts. The *New York Times Book Review* (when it was still an honest reviewer of books and not a promoter of editorial bias), *Saturday Review of Literature*, *New Yorker*, *Theatre Arts*, *Partisan Review*, *New Republic*, and other "little magazines" were always there on the coffee table and were required reading. Someone, Pat or Betty Ruth, was always recommending something for me to read, gently pointing out my areas of ignorance. The conversations on W. Eighty-first Street stimulated and challenged me intellectually more than any of the discussions in my classes as an undergraduate, with the exception Dr. Gentry's philosophy or McAllister's applied anthropology. Because of Phil Mounger, I began reading the *New Republic* and *Nation* in Austin, and I much earlier had read the *New Yorker* in its overseas edition while I was in Germany and Korea. The *New Yorker* was a premium in Germany, and often by the time our squad got one, it was worn and tattered, but in Korea, no one wanted the *New Yorker*. It was too highbrow. I often found the short stories rather limp, but "The Talk of the Town," the cartoons—which were either hilarious or incomprehensible—, the long critical reviews and the profile essays carried me to a land I'd never been. "The Talk of the Town" was even more interesting and amusing because I was in that town. I had told myself then that someday I would go to New York, and then I would be able to appreciate better the quiet wit of the pieces. I didn't know who E. B. White was then, except through a little collection of his stories called *Quo Vadimus* that I carried with me for a long time in the pocket of my field jacket. I was aware that it was probably the best English prose I had ever read, and I longed someday to imitate its smooth, relaxed style. When I would read one of his short pieces aloud in the tent, someone would always complain that they couldn't see why I spent my time with "that stuff"; nothing ever happened, they would say. Now that I was in the city, walking the streets, riding the subways, taking those trips down Fifth Avenue atop the bus, I would tell myself I knew it all, recognized it because I had read it all in the *New Yorker*; it gave me a feeling of belonging. Jane and Betty Ruth and Pat were the real catalysts. It was bizarre because the clerks and tellers at the bank, except for one named Anne Modr, were as oblivious of their surroundings or as indifferent as the guys in the weapons platoon in C Company were of the wit and wisdom in those little E. B. White pieces that I read aloud to them.

Now the conversations on West 81st Street ranged far beyond a casual encounter with new ideas; they actually laid the foundation on which I would later build when I began to read writers like Trilling, Wilson, Howe, and others. No one in the fraternity house except Mullins or Mounger—and after the first year, Mullins was gone and Mounger was absent much of the time—was ever interested in or capable of having such conversation. In a large sense, this was the beginning of my *liberal education*, for it opened new worlds of ideas and revealed to me how worlds of politics, science, art, and literature were all intermeshed. It was almost as if my sojourn through the language had been scripted, for in the early days, I bathed in the sharp wit of Mr. Roberts and felt at home; and in the near the end of my stay, it was the ironies and allusions of Eliot's *The Cocktail Party* that tested my growth.

Everyone seemed to have read more and to have understood more than I; even Don seemed to be more aware of the connections between things, but my foundations I saw were sound. I was wrong, of course; I had crossed both oceans, seen marvelous and hideous things, read constantly, and sought out experience and ideas as avidly as they. But they made all the difference in my reading and my thinking about reading. At one time, I had been amused that anyone would take literature so seriously that they could argue for hours about meanings or about the significance of a word or passage or a scene, argue so seriously and passionately that it seemed they were not discussing a work of *fiction*. Through a kind of intellectual osmosis, I began to develop new way of thinking and, out of self-defense, began to take part in those discussions and in doing so I felt passion grow out of a new reality.

I should not give the impression that I believed I was a complete ignoramus when it came to great books and ideas. My undergraduate years from the freshman days of Dr. James's comp class through Dr. Steffan's world lit laid an unexpected foundation. In the spring of '47 and '48, two films came to Austin that tipped the scales for me once and for all: Olivier's *Henry V* and his *Hamlet*. They "blew me away" as they say today. Barbara, whom I was going with at the time, remarked once that *Henry V* was the most beautiful movie she had ever seen, and she had agreed to see it with me a second time when it was being shown at the Varsity Theatre on the drag. It surprised and pleased me at the time since her tastes often went to bathetic pseudo-dramas in the movies like the execrable *Green Dolphin Street* or *The Fountainhead*. Her appreciation of Olivier's *Henry V* might have been due as much to its Technicolor spectacle as Olivier's interpretation of Hal. It was *Hamlet* that really startled me. Two years before, I had read the play on my own, which means outside of class, and was awakened by the language and by Shakespeare's ironies. Finding I could read such a play on my own was liberating. I knew that with a little bit of extra effort, I might read *anything*. But I had read it mainly because I had read Ernest Jones' *Hamlet and Oedipus* and needed to go to the "source." In the movie I found Freud's touch was everywhere. When I saw *Hamlet* the first time at the Paramount Theater in downtown Austin I was sure Olivier had read Ernest Jones' little book.

But it made no difference. The play, rather the movie, *was* the thing that hit me. It was being shown as a road show, that is, all seats were reserved, and no one was admitted after the film began. Bill Hart and I bought the last two seats in the house in the center of the first row. To say that it was an overwhelming experience is no exaggeration. Any film might easily overwhelm when seen that close, but it overwhelmed me in every other sense as well. First, I had never heard English spoken so beautifully and clearly, had never been able to follow the meaning of Shakespeare's language so easily, and never found the plot so easy to follow. What enigma? I asked.

When I first read the play, I concentrated on the major speeches, the big scenes as most readers do, I suppose. But this was different. The next day, I cut a class and went back and saw it from the first row of the balcony; it was as overwhelming from that angle as it was from the first row. The next day, when the film moved out to the Texas Theater on the Drag—at half-price—I went back and saw it a third and fourth time, not leaving the theater but sitting there and waiting for the film to begin again. By now I had committed to memory all of the first soliloquy, most of "To, be or not to be" and all of the Gravedigger's dialogue—both parts—as well as Fortinbras' (Horatio's in Olivier's version) charge to the soldiers in the final scene. On the fifth viewing, I came away with "Get thee to a nunnery" intact, all without reference to the printed text. Seeing the film led me to read and reread other plays by Shakespeare over the next months as well as a number of major critical essays. I convinced myself there was no mystery enveloping Hamlet's delay or his character unless you happened to see a poorly produced version. I understood it all. Hadn't Olivier made it all clear? When we read *Oedipus* and Aristotle's *Poetics*, in Guy Steffan's world lit survey, it became even clearer, so by the time I joined into dialogue with Betty Ruth and Pat, I was not totally insensitive to the nuances of great literature. I understood now why people would major in English.

I occasionally read *Partisan Review*, bought it at the newsstand on the corner of Fifth Avenue and Forty-second Street, and though the allusions often baffled me as *New Yorker* cartoons had earlier, I stuck with *PR*, knowing that "use *can* change the stamp of nature." The *PR* essays also made me think and compelled me to read more. Knowing was so much nicer than not knowing. I would always associate my walks up and down Fifth Avenue or my rides down past the Flat Iron building to meet Jane after work with reading *PR*. Years later, when I read Alfred Kazin's memoir, *New York Jew*, I recalled that excitement and confusion I began to feel then; it was the same excitement he described in one marvelous sentence: "I went between my home, my publishers at Lexington and Twenty-eight and the *New Republic* at Forty-ninth and Madison [Don and I lived just two blocks away at Lexington and Forty-eighth] in a *dizzy exaltation mixed with direst suspicion of what might happen next.*" (My italics) A "dizzy exaltation!" How apt!

Jane's apartment became my Eighty-first Street seminar, and I rarely attended a meeting of the seminar when someone didn't insist I read a particular article or review usually related in some way to a film, a play, or an exhibit. At one meeting, Pat gave me Arthur Miller's essay "Tragedy and the Common Man" and insisted I read it since I had recently seen *Death of a Salesman*. The essay's clarity was stunning, and today, many years later, appears in almost every major publisher's school anthology of modern literature. My reaction to Miller's thesis, I believed, surprised her as much it surprised me. I found it consistent with Aristotle's rules of tragedy explained so succinctly—and with equal clarity—in the *Poetic*, which surprised her— that I had read the *Poetics*, that is.

I did not come to Miller's play or to his essay unprepared; I had read Sophocles' *Oedipus* in world lit, and had read Freud's *Totem and Taboo* and *The Savage Fear of Incest* and all about the Oedipus complex. I had even read the part of Aristotle's poetics dealing with the theory of catharsis. And because of Olivier's *Hamlet* and my interest in Freud, I had also read Ernest Jones. So Miller's essay fell into place, made enormously good sense—it still does—but more important, his essay showed me how well-written criticism could open windows of understanding and how literature and drama could explore psychological and social issues more concretely and more succinctly than most psychologists and sociologists. I recalled how most of the works we read in world lit lent themselves to psychological interpretations, works written centuries before the advent of psychology as a science, and I recalled how Freud said his teachers were not men of medicine or science but Sophocles and Shakespeare. I could see more clearly now the connections, which I had only intuited before, between psychology and literature, anthropology and literature, history, biography, social movements, politics, the entire world, which the surveys of literature had barely grazed. It wasn't that I had missed so much, but that I had not seen the ideas expressed so clearly before and in contexts that were themselves richness itself. Images of eternity in a grain of sand, or of truths that lie too deep for tears, all these I began to see now as more than artful images. These were the true shocks of recognition that brought about a protean change that would in time become me.

I lived in two different worlds, a world of ideas and a world of work. Of the two, the first had a greater impact than the second did. Working alongside me at the bank were people much younger than I, mostly recent high school graduates preparing themselves for careers in banking or business. Some would accept the bank's offer and take special classes to prepare them for careers in other branches of banking. I was something of an anomaly, a college graduate. Though I never thought of myself as being over-prepared, only prepared for other things. I liked the job and was never bored to the point where I thought I had to move on to something else or go mad. At the time, I didn't see my job at the bank as conflicting with the other world of the arts and ideas. One of the young men who had been hired straight out of high school was a pre-law student in night school at City College, which meant that he was in at least the top ten percent of his high school class. City College, in those days, like the other colleges of the city, Queens College and Brooklyn College, were highly selective and tuition-free.

But one of the clerks also attending college was a young woman who was majoring in Latin and minoring in French at Barnard College. She was clearly not planning on a career in banking. Anne Modr had been working full-time during the summer, but when Barnard College's fall term began, she shifted to part-time on Thursday and Friday evenings. On my first day at work, the chief clerk, Mr. Simpson, asked Anne to show me around and explain my duties to me, how to enter the deposits and withdrawals, how to figure the daily interest on the customer's account records, how to prove up the tellers' transactions, and how to assist the tellers during the rush periods. There was no mistaking it. She was the most intelligent and most capable of all the clerks, and the young men knew it. We had been going through the routine when right off she said it seemed odd that I was starting to work as a mere clerk. She implied no disrespect for the other clerks but wondered why I had taken the job since I had already finished college, and clerking didn't require a bachelor's degree. I agreed but explained I had to eat and pay the rent, and I described to her the agonies of being told constantly that I was overqualified, which I said was, in the words of my grandmother, the same as an "educated fool." I explained the city was swimming in a sea of college graduates from schools outside New York, people like me who had come to sample the excitements of the great city, and I told her about my friend Glover and others who had arrived without influential contacts. But I said nothing of my desire to return to Korea. She admitted she had actually met very few people from outside the city.

I hadn't spoken to anyone about why I was there and what I was planning to do. No one asked. The dozen or so clerks who assisted the tellers treated me with a strange kind of deference. Somehow they learned I was a college graduate; not even the chief clerk Mr. Simpson had a college degree, and virtually none of the tellers had attended college or banking school for more than a few years. On top of all that, I was from Texas; they were all from New York, Brooklyn, Queens, or New Jersey. So far as I knew none of them was interested in any of the things I believed were important. One of the tellers—a really nice guy—even thought it weird that I read the *NY Times*; they all read the *Daily News* or the *Mirror*, he said. I replied that the *Times* cost just three cents; the others were a nickel. That was when New York still had five or six papers including the far left *PM* and the *Sunday Worker*, the old *Daily Worker* having just gone weekly. I was an anomaly, and though they were all polite, sometimes even respectful, they treated me as a stranger, which added to the feeling that I was living a double life. That's "parallel universe" in today's parlance. I liked it. One world existed on the floor of the 34th Street branch of the Bowery Savings Bank, the other touched W. 81st Street's world of arts and ideas that I began to explore the minute I stepped out on 5th Avenue at three o'clock every afternoon. Anne Modr became the link connecting the two worlds.

There wasn't much time to sit around chatting, but one day on our afternoon coffee break, we talked about my reasons for being in New York. She seemed to be genuinely interested, and I was glad to have someone to talk to who I thought would understand. I told her I was still looking for something but didn't know for sure what it was and that my degree in psychology was only a preparation for graduate school, though I was still undecided what I would major in. I told her how I had changed my mind while I was in the army, and I mentioned Mr. Wilson's suggestion about the personnel department.

"Aside from all that," I said, "I'm just happy to be in New York, where I can see plays, go to the opera, visit galleries and museums." She smiled, amused, I thought, that a boy from Texas was so excited about the Big City. "This job is fine, for now. I get off at three every afternoon, have time to read, see movies, go to an occasional concert, and even take a few classes at the New School. It's great," I explained. "I won't do this forever."

I tried to explain to her, a native of Manhattan, what it was like for an eighteen-year-old Texan who had never been anywhere to stand in a 20-mm. Oerlikin gun pit and watch the skyline of Lower Manhattan fade from full color to a purple haze and then watch it gradually vanish as the troopship plowed its way all alone through the Narrows. I explained what it was like nine months later, to see it suddenly come into view just at dusk and then, as if a stage manager had thrown a switch, see all those lights come up, creating a great black-and-white silhouette more like a backdrop in the theater than the outline of real city. When I asked her if she had ever known anyone from Texas, and if she had, what did she think, she smiled and said during the war, she and her mother had met a Texan about my age, but he wasn't as enthusiastic as I was.

Anne Modr and I began a friendship right then that lasted until I left for good in May of 1950. She was very bright—a NY Regents scholar—and was interested in most of those things I found great in the city: the galleries, the opera, the theater. She couldn't imagine what it would be like not to have everything New York had. More important than the link between the worlds I shared with Don and Jane and my work, she was a link to New Yorkers I would never have met otherwise.

She and her mother lived on East 71st Street just off Lexington. I was the only person at the 34th Street branch who was not a native New Yorker and only one of three who actually lived in Manhattan. All others commuted from White Plains, Jersey, Staten Island, Brooklyn, and other places. I could rise at eight, shower, shave, have breakfast, and be at the door of the bank before nine. If I rose half an hour earlier, I would take a bus so I could gaze at the streets, the people, and all the traffic and know I was really there. To do that, I would gladly take the thirty dollar-a-week job and wait to see if anything would turn up. Anne was not only a native of the city, she was also a second generation, both parents having emigrated from Czechoslovakia when they were children. All her family were still closely linked to the old country. Though she spoke only smatterings of Czech, her mother spoke it as her father did and her uncles, who were members of the solid, professional, upper-middle class who lived in the mid-seventies off Lexington, Madison, and Park Avenues, well-to-do and comfortable by any standard. Her father, an attorney, died a few years before and left her and her mother comfortable enough, though Anne, even with the Regents' scholarship, felt she ought to work. Hers was a milieu I would never have known had I not met her.

The clerk's job was almost insanely routine and that was not a bad thing; the routine ended abruptly every day at three and was the only job I would ever have that I could leave after work and not think about afterward. Monday through Wednesday, the bank closed sharply at three o'clock; on Thursday and Friday it closed at seven. At closing time the clerks and tellers went to work "proving up" the cash drawers, rarely taking more than half an hour and most of the time taking even less, which allowed us to leave early when we did. My job was simple.

It was a pleasant place to work once you got used to the hard New Yorkers' façade that each of my fellow workers affected. There was no browbeating the clerks; I never saw a teller shout or demean a clerk. Though they were often unbelievably rude to customers, I learned that what I thought was rude was, in New York, ordinary customer relations, and all in all, surprisingly free of pressure, except at noon, when office workers from the Empire State Building across the street would flood into our cavernous neoclassical temple to mammon and deposit or withdraw money. Our transactions were limited to the simple transactions of a savings bank; all other services, investments and loans, were conducted at the main branch on Forty-second Street across from Grand Central Station, where I had been inducted. Of all the banks in New York, it was the safest and most profitable. It had been so even in the depths of the Depression. Even though I was as low on the banking totem pole as one could be, I always felt I was in the center of the business world of Manhattan. The Empire State Building was across 34th Street, across 5th Avenue from the famous B. Altman's department store, and up a block or so was Lord & Taylor's, while west on 34th Street was Macy's, where the Christmas miracle occurred.

Two parades passed while I worked there. President Harry Truman, riding in a grand open convertible, was in the one going up; the one going down was a rodeo parade with real rodeo cowboys on its way to Madison Square Garden. In both cases, Mr. Simpson, the head clerk, pulled me from my station and said, "Leave what you're doing, Tex. You'll want to see this."

A New Yorker showing an outlander his town was always in his glory. I did want to see the president, whom I had admired especially now since he had won the White House on his own, but the rodeo was another thing. I never enjoyed rodeos as much as I should have, being a Texan and all, but I watched mainly to please Mr. Simpson and the others who thought all Texans must love the broncos and bulls. Each Western state was represented by a cowboy slouched in his saddle, holding a state flag. Flags of Wyoming, Colorado, Utah, Arizona passed, and then a palsied chuckwagon slowly rolled by, pulled by a pair of sad mules, pans and pots dangling from the chuck box on the rear, a pair of rodeo riders on the driver's box, reins hanging limply from their hands, the Lone Star flag held by one of the riders wafting in a light breeze. The other clerks stood by me at the tall window, with Mr. Simpson watching as it passed.

In the thickest East Texas accent I could muster, every word a polysyllabic drawl, I said loudly: "Thathurs jus' th' way ah us'ta raad t' schooool." They believed it and loved it. I almost believed it myself.

Only two people seemed concerned that I had a college degree and was starting as a clerk. Anne and a youngish man named Al, who seemed more or less in charge of the clerks. He roamed the floor, filling in at times as a teller, overseeing the X-mas Club cage, watching to see if we needed assistance. The first morning, when I took the mandatory fifteen minute break, he asked me casually why I had I applied for the job, and I explained my degree, my coming to New York, and Mr. Wilson's suggestion that the bank was planning to create a personnel department. Al was satisfied, and that was the last time he mentioned it. I wondered, after my conversations with Annie and Al, if I was ever the subject of curiosity. Mr. Simpson, the chief clerk and, next to the branch manager, the highest-ranking man on the floor, quickly named me Tex, and the others followed except for Anne, who agreed not to call me Tex if I agreed not to call her Annie.

I had been there just over a week when Mr. Schwultz passed through on a routine visit. I heard murmurings among the clerks and tellers that Mr. Schwultz was on the floor and assumed it was normal occurrence, but you could feel a mild frisson in the air suggesting that visits from on high were rare occurrences. I was bent over figuring interest cards, penciling the correct amounts when I felt a hand on my shoulder. "Hello, Joe. Everything working out?" a voice said.

I turned and saw Mr. Schwultz smiling down. "Oh, Mr. Schwultz, hi. Yes, sir, it's fine. Thank you."

"Well, fine, glad to see you."

"Thanks. I'll be seeing you," I said and returned to the figures as he passed on around the tellers' positions. Danny, a tall, blonde young clerk from Brooklyn, more or less the local character whom everyone was fond of, slid in beside me and asked *sotto voce,* "You know him?"

"Sure, he's president of the bank, Mr. Schwultz. He's from Texas too, you know," I replied.

"Oh, then you knew him before?" he asked.

A light went on. They think that's why and how I'm here. They think I'm an old friend of the family. I thought and almost laughed out loud; instead, I decided it was best to answer straight, no heavy denial, just a simple explanation, which I surmised would convince everyone I was not lying.

"No, I met him a couple of weeks ago for the first time." I realized then that the other clerks and a couple of the tellers were listening. Diplomatic Danny had been selected to be the one to ask.

"You met him?" Danny asked, incredulous. I nodded.

It became for me a question of whether the hand of the maker or the devil had touched me. Later that afternoon, during our coffee break, Anne asked me if I had known Mr. Schwultz before I applied for the job. I told her I had never met him before the day I applied for and got the job, but I could tell by the tone of her voice and her manner that she suspected I had deceived her about why I started work as a clerk. She said everyone thought it strange that he would stop and chat with me as if he knew me. I said I thought it was strange too, but I just assumed he was a nice man who wanted to say hello, and I slipped into my East Texas accent and said, "Down home, it's the sorta thang people jus' do." Anne didn't buy it, accent or no accent.

After three months, Don, Glover, and I went our separate ways—Don to a cold-water flat in the Village and I to a room in an elderly couple's elegant apartment on Riverside Drive. The Horlichs had advertised the room, more a monk's cell it seemed, with bath, for a college student at an amazing seven dollars a week. It was an easy move, only a short walking distance from our place just off Central Park West. What was nice was being able to see yet another facet of the city. The building was a large, elegant apartment building on Riverside Drive with an entrance out of the wind in the west seventies complete with a uniformed doorman and elevator operator, both of whom helped me get my gear off the sidewalk and into the building. This was less out of courtesy than an agreement with the Horlichs not to let the other tenants know they were subletting their former nanny's room. Within a week Mrs. Horlich had adopted me. Every night, when I returned to my room after class, I'd find a glass of milk and a saucer of cookies or cake sitting atop my chest of drawers. She always asked what movies I was seeing, what plays I had gone to, what concerts I had heard, and insisted I "take a concert at Carnegie Hall," which I did. I rarely saw the old man, but once when I came straight to my room after work, he asked me to sit a while with him in the large living room with its curved, plate glass window looking out on the Hudson. It was like a movie set. I had never seen a large curved pane of glass in a private living room before, a living room furnished in fine antique pieces with floors covered by Oriental rugs. We sat there in silence for almost half an hour, I looking out the window across the great Hudson River, Mr. Horlich smiling, nodding at my remarks but never speaking. Finally, I rose and thanked him for the lovely view. He nodded and smiled.

I enjoyed the quiet of my little room and having a place to retreat to. I often met their son as I left the subway. He was interested in my reasons for coming to the city, about where I had gone to college, and why I had chosen the New School. He often spoke of his parents and how glad he was I had moved in. I mentioned that his father had asked me to sit with him, and that I'd enjoyed the view of the Hudson through the spectacular curved glass window. It pleased him.

One of the driving forces behind my decision to join Jane and Don was the opera. Grand opera had been a passion ever since I saw Gounod's *Faust*. Anytime Lawrence Tibbett, Lily Pons, Rise Stevens, or Robert Merrill performed on radio, Jane or Don would call me to come in and listen, and it was a rare Saturday that I missed the Met broadcast. Just a week after I arrived in New York, Jane announced she had tickets for a performance of *Don Pasquale* with the great basso Salvatore Baccaloni; it was glorious. I knew nothing of opera buffa, had no idea what to expect, couldn't understand the Italian, but I loved it. Salvatore Baccaloni, whom I had heard often on the Saturday broadcasts, sang the Don's role. But I yearned for the *grand* opera at the Met.

My first opera in New York was *La Traviatta* at the NY City Opera with a very pretty young Czech soprano, Eva Likova, making her American debut. The singers at the City Opera, they said, were always younger, prettier, or handsomer and finer actors than the stars at the Met, and some even better singers. The acoustics in the theater were excellent and sight lines were good, but the shallow stage looked cramped, especially ballroom scenes like the opening act of *Traviatta*. When Violetta sang her big first act aria, "*Ah fors e lui,*" Likova danced and whirled beautifully, but her wide bell skirt struck a small table and sent it rolling, wine bottle, glass, and all. In spite of the collision with the table she finished to roaring bravas. Likova possessed all the vocal qualities the role demanded and the acting skills as well. But the cramped stage, the ill-placed table, and her wide skirt, things of no importance really, put a crimp in Act 1. But it was nothing. Her voice was perfect. The night's tenor was far more than adequate, and at the end of Act 1, I was feeling quite grand. Her second act duet—my favorite duet in all opera—redeemed it all, and at the final curtain, I truly had something to write home about. This, indeed, was why I had come to New York, and the great Metropolitan was still to come. Likova's notices the next morning in the *Times* and the *Herald-Tribune* were excellent.

When the Met season began, for some reason, I felt awkward walking up to the box office window and asking for a single ticket, just for myself. I didn't know where I should sit, balcony, family circle, where? The first time at the Met required a good seat, but the orchestra seats were so expensive, more than six dollars, a fifth of my weekly salary. Since standing room was only a dollar seventy-five, I'd stand. But when it finally happened, it was far different from what I imagined or planned. First, I wasn't alone. Anne Modr was with me. I told her I'd seen Likova, which seemed to impress her. And then quite on the spur of the moment, I asked if she would mind standing at the Met for *Rigoletto*. It was Friday night, late night at the bank. We had both eaten, which meant I would not have to treat. She agreed to go if I carried her books; she had come to the bank directly from her classes as was usual every Friday. I would have carried her I was so excited. I told her it would be my first visit to the Met, something I had looked forward to since I heard my first Saturday afternoon radio performance. The cast had Leonard Warren, Giuseppe Di Stephano, and Hilda Güden. Again, I boasted, telling her I had Güden's recording of "Caro Nome" and had collected Di Steffano's recordings when the first ones went on sale.

We walked from 34th Street up to the Metropolitan, talking about opera, the crisp autumn air, her classes at Barnard, and my classes at the New School; but when we arrived, we found that the last standing-room ticket had been sold. She moved away as if to leave, but I asked for anything in any balcony, and the ticket seller reported that the last two tickets in the house were in the dress circle at four fifty each.

I said, "Good! I'll take them."

Ann said, "You're mad! That's a third of your salary!"

"Right! But it's dress circle! Let's go." *I won't eat supper next week*, I told myself.

As we moved up the grand staircase past the Diamond Horseshoe level and far, far, far down the dress circle, she kept calling me mad, crazy, wild, and insane, and I kept agreeing. I was indeed mad, just as she said, but that madness, I believe, sealed a friendship. And *Rigoletto* was great, "Caro Nome," "La Donna Mobile," the quartet, everything.

When I say it sealed a friendship, I mean it led to a Thanksgiving dinner in her uncle's Park Avenue apartment (well, just off Park Avenue) and a meeting with Eva Likova, the diva herself! Dr. Tuma was a successful dentist whose large apartment in the east seventies was between Park and Madison, with windows on Madison Avenue, not a bad address. They were all Czechs. Mrs. Tuma was the sister of Anne's mother. The Tumas and the apartment exuded culture, not pretentiously but comfortably sans snobbery. Dr. Tuma's son, a pre-veterinarian student at Penn, was there, quiet, almost sullen. He looked and spoke like a typical Ivy League sophomore who lacked the assurance of good grades. In fact, from what I gathered, he was soon to be "sent down." The good doctor was a happy, generous-natured man who made me feel welcome, gave me the name Joe Tex, and offered me a drink before lunch. Then he announced that our guest of honor would be Eva Likova, the soprano. He told us of her difficulty in entering the U.S., getting out of Czechoslovakia right before the Iron Curtain descended, and that she was now unable to leave the U.S. unless she returned first to Czechoslovakia. Her defection had made her an outlaw. Dr. Tuma and several others were sponsoring her and helping her to get a start.

When Anne told her uncle I had seen her debut, something none of the others had done, he asked me what I thought. I described the table incident in Act 1 and described how nervous she seemed, quickly adding that after that, she was marvelous, remarking especially about the glorious second act duet and her *"Addio del pasato"* in the last act. He listened intently and applauded my final summation, thanking me.

When she arrived, I was quietly transfixed; I'd never met a bona fide diva and certainly not one singing lead roles nor one so beautiful. She seemed taller on stage.

Dr. Tuma began, "Joe Tex here says your first act was a mess. You were nervous and knocked over a table, Eva, but he thought the rest was quite good."

Anne laughed as I tried to insist that I had praised the performance to the skies, trying my best to extricate myself. Anne told me later her uncle was always doing things like that. Likova, of course, was gracious and said I was right and thanked me for my words about the duet and the last act solo. When I asked her who the baritone was, she showed her really gracious side by praising him as one of the best she had ever sung with, that it was he who made the duet go as well as it did, and then she said he was singing several days a week the lead baritone role in Gian Carlo Minotti's *The Consul*, which I had also seen earlier. I was pleased that I could talk opera with her or rather that she would talk opera with me. After dinner, she sang several Czech songs accompanied by Dr. Tuma on the violin. As a young man, he had worked his way through dental school playing violin in the pit orchestra at the Winter Garden. This was indeed a very unusual family. I would see Uncle Tuma several more times and under most interesting circumstances.

I saw Likova in three more performances that season, all major roles and all beautiful: Giuliette, the Venetian courtesan in Act 2 of *Tales of Hoffman*; Nedda, the wayward wife in *Pagliacci*; and Liu, the slave girl who loved the Calif in *Turandot*. As Nedda, she astonished everyone by performing a real ballet on points while singing.

There was more than the opera, of course: the Metropolitan Museum, Museum of Modern Art, and all the other galleries. There at the Met that year was the great Van Gogh exhibit, paintings and drawings, and at a private gallery in the fifties was a Rembrandt show. At MOMA, I saw Brancusi's "Bird in Flight," Picasso's "Guernica" and "Blue Guitar," Mondrian's "Broadway Boogie Woogie," and Duchamp's "Nude Descending a Staircase." I became a walker of galleries, reading everything I could about everything I saw.

Shortly after I arrived in New York and received from Glover E. B. White's *Here Is New York*, he directed me to a piece in *The Crack-Up* in which Fitzgerald describes how he felt about New York in the early years of his success before *Gatsby* and after *Beautiful and Damned*. I had fallen in love Fitzgerald's titles, and always felt his titles were as great as anything he wrote: *The Beautiful and the Damned, Taps at Revile, Flappers and Philosophers, Tender Is the Night*, but of course, the latter belonged to Keats's nightingale. For me, Fitzgerald's prose flowed as smoothly as Bombay gin. The New York piece was heartbreaking, even though critics found it self-pitying, though much less so than his essay "The Crack-Up" that details his loss of power. For me it was only an imagined loss, for all the writing in that collection was still true and as sharp and clear as the earlier pieces. How I envied his rides in cabs through the city and all the crazy, rude, and thoughtless things he seemed—only seemed—to get away with. I was about the same age as Fitzgerald when he broke upon the big New York scene and began his career as a novelist, and at that moment reading from *The Crack-Up*, I wished I had been there to see it. But the moment was fleeting, and any comparison I may have imagined, never a real comparison, ended. For I knew then I was living a life I had never thought I would know, my classes at the New School, the visits to the Metropolitan and to the opera and concerts at Carnegie Hall, and meeting a real diva of the opera while at dinner just off Park Avenue. The aura of Fitzgerald gave it all a most special feeling.

Anne later asked me to escort her to a Christmas concert and ball at the Waldorf Astoria. Uncle Tuma, a member of the University Glee club that was giving the annual event, had asked Anne to bring an escort. It was a formal black-tie affair beginning at eight in the evening, with the concert followed by supper and the Christmas ball. Anne and I, her mother, her aunt, and Anne's cousin and his date shared a box high above the ballroom floor. To visitors in New York from the West, the Waldorf Astoria was, along with the Plaza, legendary; though not nearly as elegant or exclusive as the Plaza or Sherry Netherland, the Waldorf stood out for most of us as the model of a grand hotel. I felt quite as though I had made it in the world as I escorted Anne, her mother, and her aunt to our box. When the singing stopped and the ball began, Dr. Tuma, who was singing with the glee club, would join us later at our table below, just off the dance floor.

The concert lasted just over an hour and consisted of college songs, choruses from opera and musical comedy, and a medley of Christmas songs. The voices were better than good or even very good, the sophisticated arrangements reaching beyond the predictable dynamics of Fred Waring's Pennsylvanians, who, in those days, were the standard that most college glee clubs aspired to. When the concert ended, we descended to the ballroom floor where Dr. Tuma had arranged a table with cocktails and hors d'oeuvres. We danced until two in the morning, and then Dr. Tuma took us all to breakfast at an all-night restaurant on Lexington Avenue. Miraculously, I got to work only ten minutes late the next morning.

The Christmas dinner and the concert ball, I realized, had been testing grounds for Anne's beau to determine if he were suitable, though I seriously doubt Anne thought of them in any other context than what they were—ordinary dates. We had become good friends, but neither of us saw a relationship developing much beyond that. I had spoken too often of my wish to return to Korea, to enter graduate school at some point, and never expressed a desire to apply to either Columbia or NYU or any other university in the

East. It became clear to me that her uncle, nominally head of the family, was seeking a husband for the only eligible female, all the other cousins being male. The final party of the season with the Tumas was New Year's Eve dinner at the apartment of a friend. Dr. Tuma, Mrs. Modr, her sister, Anne, her cousin, and I were all invited to the Park Avenue apartment of what in popular novels is called a society doctor, in this case the anesthesiologist who assisted on Wally Warfield Simpson Windsor's most recent face-lift. Anne's mother, a tall, slender and rather elegant-looking woman described the little man as satirically as I had ever heard anyone speak of the rich and famous, or almost famous. Uncle Tuma was not in a good mood that evening as it started out, though he mellowed after his second old-fashioned, an odious drink he also foisted on me. The gas-passing doctor—who, like Dr. Tuma, addressed me as Joe Tex believing, I am convinced, that it was my real name—saved my life by taking from my hand the sweet old-fashioned Uncle Tuma had pressed on me and replacing it with a twelve-year-old single-malt Scotch, my first and last for many years, promising it would do me much less harm than the odious fruit salad mixture Tuma loved. The supper began shortly after midnight, was served by two uniformed servants in a long narrow dining room and lasted until after two. Several wines, including champagne and later more scotch, locked the events of the night in a sealed vault of my memory, the combination to which I lost around four that morning and have not found it again. I woke around noon in the spare room of the Modr household, my tuxedo neatly folded on the chair beside me. From all reports, I did nothing to shame the Gilliland name or myself; for according to Anne and her mother, the good uncle had said my company delighted him, though he was puzzled by what I planned for my future. As I said, Anne and I had a warm and comfortable friendship based on our mutual likes in books, music, and theater. Other than the extravagance of our first visit to the Met, all other theater or musical performances were made possible by half-price tickets and seats in the highest balcony.

My final encounter with the good uncle, and I supposed the final check on my ability to appear in public, was a black-tie dinner and University Glee Club concert—all male—at the Yale Club, where the then-president of Columbia University, Dwight David Eisenhower, late of SHAEF, greeted members and guests with a brief informal talk and then left. It was during a lull in the affair, between dinner and the short concert, Dr. Tuma asked me point-blank what I intended to do with my career, implying that I surely wasn't planning to remain with the Bowery forever. I said I had no fixed plans, that I was spending the year in New York with my brother and sister mainly to see what I had heard about all my life, the opera, museums, and theater. I mentioned the outside possibility that the Bowery might offer me a position in a new personnel department, and I said I had thought of going to graduate school, perhaps back to the University of Texas. He asked if I would go into psychology, and rather than beat around that bush again, I said yes but that I would have to return to Texas, where I could take advantage of free tuition the Texas GI Bill offered. He asked why not Columbia or NYU, and I said I didn't have the money for either and would have to bone up especially hard to pass the GRE for Columbia.

"I can take care of all that for you. Just let me know, Joe Tex, when you are ready to go graduate school. Just let me know when you want to make the change." He smiled and laid an avuncular hand on my shoulder in lieu of a handshake.

I thanked him, though I was in some shock and a bit frightened that I had either misheard him or that I had indeed heard him correctly. My mind replayed the Faust and Mephisto scene of the compact with the devil, and I could hear the base tones of Italo Tajo, or was it Norman Triegle laughing and singing about calves of gold? I had drunk only one martini and a glass of wine all night, so my head was clear. Dr. Tuma had taken me around the room, introducing me to a vice-president here, a chairman there, and other balding and graying men of substance, men who had success written across their brows. It was a shame, I thought. I liked Dr. Tuma and admired Anne and her mother, but other plans were taking shape, plans of my own choosing for once and which I looked on with a good measure of excitement. I doubted that Anne had approved of his initiative, though she must have wondered why he had invited me to the black-tie affair. It played too much like a novel of the twenties and was redolent of old world ways. I reflected on Anne's knowing only because this was the way of those people living in the east seventies between Madison and Park Avenue.

The bank offered to send me to a banking school in the city, a proprietary school that specialized in training people in the business of banks. They had not made it go or else, and I told them I would think about it when the term at the New School was over. I was also scheduled shortly after the New Year to begin working directly in one of the tellers' cages, first in the Christmas Club window and then alongside one of the older tellers during the rush hour, after which I would get my own cage under the supervision of a senior teller. I was beginning to make the rounds described by Mr. Wilson. The other clerks, younger men who had been clerks before I arrived, noticed my advancing and showed no sign of envy. It was as if it were expected, my college degree and my friendship with Mr. Schwultz, what else? After a month in the windows, Mr. Simpson said I would see a small increase in salary, and I would be getting my own cash drawer.

One afternoon shortly before Christmas, when I got off at the bank, I drifted down Fifth Avenue to the Methodist Building to meet Jane. I often got to her office shortly before quitting time, but that day, I was a half hour early. While I was sitting, chatting with her, she introduced me to Dr. Mel Johnson at the Board of Missions. Dr. Johnson had answered my letter inquiring about jobs in China and Korea almost a year earlier, and he and I had talked briefly about the short-term missionary program mentioned in his letter. Jane spoke to him regularly when he passed her office and had mentioned I was still interested.

"I am glad to see you, Joe," he said. "We're accepting applicants for the program in Japan, Korea, and one in Latin America."

I told him in clear terms that I was interested in Korea and repeated I had served there during the occupation in Korea in 1946 and had always wanted to return. He said he would appreciate it if I would think about it.

"Think about it? I'll think of little else," I almost shouted. Not long afterward, Jane handed me the application forms that I immediately filled out and had Jane give to Dr. Johnson personally. *Perhaps this would help me to decide*, I thought, even though by then I had decided. When I spoke to Dr. Johnson that afternoon before Christmas, he dangled the idea of a long-term missionary teaching English and said the Mission Board would finance my graduate studies at Teacher's College Columbia if I decided to go that direction. I could not believe people could offer anyone virtually cost-free graduate study so cavalierly, especially to universities that traditionally were so selective and expensive.

In February, Don asked me to move in with him in the apartment in the Village. He needed someone to share the rent, he said, and thought it would be fun having a Village address together. His place was more convenient than the Riverside Drive address. Nearby, there were small, cheap restaurants, neighborhood grocery stores, small butcher markets, a laundromat, two bars, an old-fashioned drugstore with a soda and lunch counter, and a subway station that gave me a direct, nonstop, no-change express ride to Penn station only two long blocks from the bank. I could wake up at eight, shower, shave, and dress and be at work by nine; no other employee at the Thirty-fourth Street branch could make that claim. I would also be enjoying the added cachet of living in the Village; it would be something to write home about, "to tell my grandchildren," Don said.

With my promotion to Christmas Club came a small salary increase. Mr. Simpson's assistant, Al, who was my immediate boss, explained quietly that I was being placed there as part of the training I needed before moving on to the new personnel office. It was a matter of weeks before I moved into another position. After several weeks in the Christmas Club, Mr. Simpson moved me to a teller's cage, where I worked under the supervision of a teller. During the heavy periods of the day, I stepped aside and gave the cage back to its original owner and took over a clerk's duties that required me to operate the large NCR calculator for him. At closing time, it was my job to make the final tally and make sure the clerk's figures balanced with the transactions I had made. I was not sure whether I liked it or not, especially the responsibility for a drawer containing thousands of dollars. A very small part of me found it exhilarating to be in charge of a teller's cage, counting and balancing thousands of dollars of withdrawal and deposit slips and making them all jibe with the tens of thousands of dollars in the cash drawer. But always flitting around in my mind was the possibility of a position as a short-term teaching missionary in Korea.

In the first week of February, I returned the completed application to Dr. Johnson. I listed some good names as references: Mr. McCauley, one of Albert's closest friends, the same gentlemen who loved to argue politics; the chairman of chemistry and faculty advisor for Lambda Chi Alpha, Dr. Robin Anderson; Father Joe Hart, the students' chaplain of All Saints Episcopal Church; and for balance, I listed Dr. Willis Tate, vice president of Southern Methodist University; finally, almost as an afterthought, I added Dr. Hall of the Wesley Bible Chair. A few weeks after Jane delivered my application, I met him again outside Jane's office as he stepped off the elevator. Pulling off his gloves, he extended his hand and said with a knowing smile, "You listed some *very* good names for references, Joe."

I thanked him. When I found out later that Willis Tate had just been named president of Southern Methodist University, I thought that he had more than balanced the Episcopalians on the list. On the first of March, a letter came, saying my application for the short-term missionary program in Korea had been accepted, giving me a date for an interview with the committee and laying out a schedule of events that would follow if I passed the interview. According to the plan, I would meet the committee in just two weeks; and within ten days after the interview, I would hear whether or not I had been accepted to the program. When I asked for the time off for the interview, Mr. Simpson quickly agreed and seemed rather to have expected that I might be looking for another job. He said it was no problem. I could take off the whole day if I needed it. I agreed it would be a good idea since I had no idea how long the interview would take. I offered to work both the late shifts on Thursday and Friday, and he said that would be fine. When I told Anne that afternoon that I was interviewing for another job, she seemed no more surprised than Mr. Simpson did. But when I told her where I was interviewing, she was surprised.

"Then you really did it?" she asked. "When will you be leaving?"

"I'm not sure I'll be accepted, so don't tell anyone yet," I said. Shortly after the dinner at the Yale Club, I had told her that I might apply, but I had not spoken in detail, only saying if accepted, my appointment would be for Korea. She had not commented on it one way or the other. Since the black-tie dinner at the Yale Club, we had not been going out as much. We had seen the last performance of *Born Yesterday* a couple of weeks earlier, but nothing since. When she said that she wasn't sure I was serious about it, I detected nothing in her voice to indicate that she was either happy for me or disappointed and I was relieved. I added that I hadn't been sure myself that I would go through with it until I finished filling out the application. We were having coffee in the lounge during my afternoon break when Al, my supervisor, stopped in and told me that Mr. Simpson mentioned I was interviewing for a job and asked what kind of job I was applying for. I told him it was for a teaching job overseas, in Korea.

"Where? Korea? Why? Everyone I know who was in Korea hated it. Were you ever there?" he asked.

I told him I had been in Korea for nine months and liked it, that this was a chance to go back. I didn't tell him the job was as a short-term missionary; the effort to explain just wasn't worth it, I thought. Being a missionary would separate me even more than I was already as a college man, as a Texan— enough was enough. Happily, Anne said nothing.

"Most of the people who were in Korea hated it," he repeated.

"Yeah, I know, I did too at first. It's the call of the East," I said. "You know, like Kipling, Somerset Maugham, and all that."

"I *don't* know about *all that*. What will you teach?" he asked.

"English mostly. I'll be taking a crash course in teaching English as a second language this summer. Look, I may not get the job," I said, not wanting to get into the K3 business.

I asked, "Is it like this all the time, everywhere? I mean Mr. Simpson, everyone, is so accommodating, so generous." I felt myself shaking. "You know this is a great place to work."

Al smiled and said, rising, "No, the Bowery isn't like other places. It is a good place to work. Let me know how it goes as soon as you can." Then he got quite serious and explained that Mr. Simpson needed to know so he could take me out of the other cage and give the spot to one of the other clerks. I told him I understood.

It was a Friday, and ordinarily, Anne and I walked out together after the evening shift; but that evening, I wanted to take the news up to Jane's place and tell Pat and Betty Ruth. They had all been interested and supportive. I hated the idea of leaving these friends who had taught me so much. I hadn't told Don yet either since he left before I picked up the mail on my way to work that morning. As I walked to the subway, I thought how much they had all given me, especially Don, and how little I had given back. Jane was always interested, asking questions about everything, and it was that interest that bolstered me, assuring me I was moving in the right direction for myself. She and Don never let me swim in doubt. But Don? How could I pay him back?

Jane and the others were, of course, elated and congratulated me, assuring me as people are wont to do, that the interview was simply a formality, that I was a shoo-in.

When I got to the Methodist Building on Monday morning, I found one other young man waiting for his interview. He had taken the bus up from Drew Theological Seminary in New Jersey, he said, and asked if I was being interviewed for the short-term missionary program too. I said I was. We were both nervous and admitted we had no idea what to expect. I said he would have no trouble, being a seminarian and all, and I mentioned I had no theological training, except for Brother Gray's Youth class at the South Bluff Methodist Church and two Bible classes as a freshman. I didn't mention the Canterbury Club. He said he hoped it helped but was told seminary would make no difference. I asked if he would finish his degree this spring, and he said he would. He had his BA already and would be getting the bachelor's of divinity. I was glad he was there, I said. Waiting all alone would have been a kind of hell. We both laughed. He agreed the metaphor fit.

They called me in first, and I was asked to take a seat at a long, wide, oval table around which were seated *twelve* interviewers. I almost made a joke, that if there were twelve of them, what did that make me, but I didn't. When they introduced themselves, I recognized only two, Dr. Mel Johnson, who sat on my left, and Dr. T. T. Brumbaugh, who was an old Korea hand and whom I had met earlier in the application process. On my right was a small gray-haired man who was introduced as Dr. Eigelhardt, the senior Methodist missionary to Japan. The person sitting opposite me at the far end of the table began the questions, asking me to tell them why I had applied and what I thought I could do as a short-term missionary in Korea. I decided earlier to avoid religious clichés because they would surely see the hypocrisy coming from me, so I began by saying that my motives were more humanitarian than religious. I said I had spent nine months in Korea and had developed a deep respect and interest for the people and the country and that I wanted to return to do whatever I could to help them overcome the years of Japanese oppression, blah, blah, blah. Teaching English, I believed, would help them, particularly to improve their lives because English was now the new lingua franca—I even used the term. I admitted to having had a typical upbringing in Methodist Sunday Schools and Epworth League activities, but I was unsure of having a deep religious calling and, for that reason, was more interested in the idea of serving as a short-term missionary. It seemed to me my reason was consistent with what I knew of the Methodist Social Doctrine that makes service to one's fellows the highest priority. I even alluded to the doctrine as reason for applying. I admitted that I had not been an English major at UT but was confident I could master whatever techniques were required. The more I spoke, the easier it became. Most of their questions dealt with things I had done at the university, about why I had chosen to major in psychology, if I had planned to work in a bank. That question gave me a minor shock that must have registered because T. T. Brumbaugh asked why I looked so surprised.

"Well, the truth is I was also surprised that I ended up working in a bank, but it was the only decent job I could find, and when Dr. Johnson said that, it reminded me how many prior interviewers asked if I had planned to be a mortician, and I said it was because I needed a job when I was a freshman at UT." There were a few soft chuckles and Brumbaugh laughed with a big guffaw.

Then inevitably, someone asked why I had joined the Canterbury Club instead of the Wesley Foundation—someone mentioned knowing that the Wesley group at Texas was a highly successful organization. I explained that I had attended several of its meetings but found it too large, and since I had several close friends in the Canterbury Club, I felt more comfortable. Then one interviewer asked bluntly if I actually read the *Saturday Review of Literature*, *The Nation*, and the *New Republic* as it said in my application. I couldn't help notice a tone of incredulity in his voice and wondered what the problem was.

"It's not that I doubt you, Mr. Gilliland, it's that so few of the young people we interview read magazines like that," he said. He was the most elegantly spoken man in the room, his words resounding with a clear upstate New York accent recalling the cadences and timber of a Roosevelt. Jane had told me about one of the interviewers, a third son of an ancient and wealthy

New York family, one whom she had met when she first began to work for Dr. Stoody at Methodist Information. He would stop by her desk and always ask what she was reading and would invariably comment on the book or article's content and even on the style. He even spoke as if he knew several of the authors. It amused her, she said, to see such wealth in such a humble calling. Years later, he would come to mind when I was teaching the monk in Chaucer's *Canterbury Tales*.

I told him I did read them and that I began reading them in college, more often since I had moved to the city. I blamed my waywardness, I said, on my sister Jane and her friends who read them regularly. It had become a habit since I arrived in New York. Then he asked what courses I had taken at the New School. I could see they were trying to sketch a picture of personality and character. It was not at all the kind of interview I had expected; aside from the question about the Canterbury Club, there were hardly any questions dealing with my Christian beliefs.

Then at last, Dr. Eigelhardt asked point-blank, "I see in your application that you rose to the rank of a corporal and commanded a weapons platoon in Korea. How is it you could serve as a corporal and keep a Christian tongue in your mouth?" I would have felt better had he asked the question in another tone, one more ironic.

There was a sudden stillness around the table, though I noted smiles on the faces of several as I began, "Well, I probably *didn't* always manage a Christian tongue, but," I paused.

Dr. Brumbaugh at the other end of the table broke in, "Dr. Eigelhardt, he was only a corporal. You're thinking about sergeants."

He broke into a loud laugh and the others followed. Dr. Eigelhardt put his hand on my arm and said softly with a smile, "I think Joe knows what I mean. You've answered my question, son." I loved the man instantly. The irony was the *absence* of irony, I realized, and calling me "son" made me want to hug the man. I thanked him.

What decent, humane folk, I thought. Finally came the question of my religious beliefs and my definition of Christ. I waited, thinking, and summed up briefly what I said above, admitting that though I understood that Christ was the personal savior of all human kind, I did not understand fully what that meant, but that I believed one day I would, after more study and thought. There was a long silence, and then Dr. Johnson asked if there were any more questions. No one spoke. He rose and thanked me and then escorted me to the door where we shook hands, and he whispered, "Very good, *very* good." *What a kind man he is*, I thought and recalled his comment a few weeks back.

It was over, and now the wait.

I closed my eyes and muttered a soft "thank you" to whoever might be listening. My friend waiting in the anteroom looked anxiously toward me. I assured him the room was filled with good Methodists, meaning, I said, a room full of generous-minded, humane, and essentially Christian men and women. Then I said, as if to assure myself as well as him, "They are probably the best people you'll ever meet, all there in that one room."

He smiled and thanked me. I waited, talking with him until he was called, and then I went down stairs and relaxed in Jane's office. She asked how it was, and Dr. Stoody came out and shook my hand warmly, assuring me I had won. God! I loved the world.

"I think I did it," I said. "I think I just became a short-term missionary, and I feel better than I have felt in a very long time. Probably feel better than I've ever felt!"

As I took the bus down to Washington Square, I recounted each question and went over each answer, thankful that I had not tried to anticipate their questions or tried to prepare answers for them. They would have found me a fool and a fake, which I probably was anyway; but by answering the questions spontaneously and as honestly as I could, I had given them the chance to accept me or reject me as I was. From the nods and smiles and the laughter at the end, after Brumbaugh's attempt to save me from embarrassment or from a lie, and from Mel Johnson's reassuring remarks as I left the room, I felt I had passed the test. It was strange how well it went, how good I felt as I left, more strange in that I felt I had learned more about myself and the reasons for my applying than they had. When it was over, I was more convinced than ever that I wanted to work in an organization that would be led by such people as they.

A week later, it arrived. I had done the right thing; I knew then I had made the most important decision of my life. A feeling of urgency and impatience to get on with it swept over me. On Friday, Al asked if I had heard the results, and I told him I hadn't; but on Monday, just a week after the fateful day, I stopped at my mailbox as I left for work, and there was the letter. As soon as I arrived at the Bowery Bank, I told Mr. Simpson and asked if it was all right for me to finish out the month and leave about the first of May. First, he congratulated me and said I could stay as long as I wished, and then he said, "May I ask what you will be doing and who you'll be working for?"

"Yes, sir. I'll be teaching English in Korea for the Methodist Board of Missions. I'll be what they call a short-term missionary for three years." I said it at last, relieved now that it was out. I knew he would be surprised and would begin to defer to me the way normally polite and nonreligious people do solely because of my religious connection.

"Tex, I had no idea you were a religious person," he said with a note of awe in his voice.

"I'm probably not any more religious than most people. It's really a teaching job more than a religious job," I said.

All day, people from my section would stop by and speak softly as if I were entering the priesthood. I called Jane and gave her the news as soon as I was free to call, and then that evening, I wrote Mama and told her that I had applied for a position as a short-term teaching missionary in Korea and had been accepted. I described to her the interview and outlined briefly the things that would happen in the next weeks and months ahead and that I would probably be sailing for Korea sometime in August. I knew she would be surprised, probably even shocked, so I explained that I planned on returning home for a month before going on to the seminary in Hartford. I emphasized the fact that it was a teaching position, that I would be working with young people, and that I had been thinking about a life in teaching for some time, perhaps ever since Germany. I tried to explain that I had not written earlier because I was not sure I would be accepted.

A few days later, I got her reply and was pleased when I read she was not really as surprised as I thought she might be. Chuck McCauley, the friend whose name I had put down as a reference, had mentioned getting a letter from the Board of Missions, asking for a recommendation. Her letter said that she was surprised and a little embarrassed when he told her, mainly because she knew nothing about it. "My children never tell me anything anymore, I had to say when he told me the news," she wrote. She had been saying that for years.

At first, I thought I would feel sad about leaving New York. Living with Don in our cold-water walk-up in the Village had been a joy, my best time in the city. I had read about the bohemian life in the Village, about the writers and artists, actors and dancers, about the cozy bars, small cafes, and coffee shops; and until I moved in with Don, I had seen little of that part of New York. I just touched the edge of it several times, walked through Washington Square, admired the old houses that lined the park on the north and read Henry James's novel of the same name. I saw Olivia de Havilland in *The Heiress,* based on his novel, but I had not really been a part of it all, still wasn't. Until I moved into the old run-down apartment just off Abingdon Square at West Eleventh Street and Houston, I was like Fitzgerald when he first visited his lost city: "I had come only to stare at the show, though the designers of the

Woolworth Building . . . and the producers of musical comedies and problem plays could ask for no more appreciative spectator, for I took the style of New York . . . above its valuation."[5] In the three months from January to March, I had become a denizen and a familiar face around my neighborhood. It was as though Greenwich Village were a true village with neighbors and shopkeepers who knew who you were and where you lived. I understood that when one Saturday morning, I was wakened by a loud knock on my door. When I answered it, a young man in a white apron informed me I had a telephone call across the street in the drugstore.

"Your sister asked me to call you to the phone. I'm from the drugstore," he said and left.

Don and I had stopped phone service to save money, but Jane was able to get the message to me. I hardly ever walked into the place, but the counter man had seen Don and me and was able to find where we lived. It was no big deal, he insisted, when I tried to thank him for his trouble, just the neighborly thing to do. The result was I made a point of stopping there for breakfast coffee and a roll several times a week. I had only just begun to learn what it was like to live in this town, not really a big city at all. I would miss it. It had been a marvelous nine months.

---

5   F. Scott Fitzgerald, *The Crack-Up* (New York, 1945), 24.

Chapter 15

Seminary

The Hartford Seminary Foundation (Hartford Theological Seminary) bore a remarkable resemblance to a Hollywood movie set for an English public school. Its pseudo-Gothic buildings and broad, tree-shaded greensward was right out of a black and white movie of the '30s. The half dozen buildings arranged in no particular order around a wide-open area could have been one of those schools where issues of empire were settled. It would not have surprised me to see C. Aubrey Smith or Robert Donat approach me as I alighted from the taxi in front of a large, neo-Gothic structure. As I entered, a number of people, men and woman my age, were milling about the foyer of what must have been a residence hall. Dr. Mel Johnson, whom I had seen last at the interview, came forward, shook my hand, told me where to put down my bags and then introduced me to Ms. Mildred Huggins, seated at a small table and signing in people as they arrived. In the large halls on either side of the entrance, a host of people like me were gathered, shaking hands, reading name tags, laughing, and talking enthusiastically. Ms. Huggins gave me a tag with my name and hometown and then instructed me to check in at the men's residence hall across the wide playing field.

"You're in the tower with Burt Housman, another K3," she said, smiling. "After you've settled in, come back here and meet the rest of your group, and welcome to Hartford." She smiled warmly. "We'll be having an orientation meeting here in about an hour. Glad to see you here, Joe." She knew me already. It felt good.

The men's hall was a slightly larger version of the women's residence and main building—as it turned out, Old Main—where I had registered. One large wing of the men's residence was a dining hall with a high timbered ceiling and tall, peaked Gothic windows—sans stained glass—that gave the room a light airy feeling while also giving it the hallowed look of a monkish hall. The other wing consisted of large, comfortable dormitory rooms. My room was in the tower that rose between the dining wing and the wing of rooms. At the top of the landing were two doors opening into spacious quarters. I assumed at first that I would be sharing the large room with the K3 Ms. Huggins had mentioned, but when I opened the heavy door, I noticed there was only one narrow bed, hardly more than a cot, a single desk, and lamp and a tall bookcase. The bare wooden floor and the narrow-leaded, diamond-shaped windowpanes gave the place an air of a monk's cell, and it was so peaceful I had a sudden feeling that I could stay here and never leave.

"You're here. Welcome to Hartford Seminary," came a voice from behind me on the stairs. "I'm Burt Housman," he said extending a hand. "They put the two K3 men up here in the ivory tower, it seems. I'm across the hall from you."

We shook hands and I introduced myself. He followed me into my room and explained that he had arrived half an hour earlier. He said we were the only men assigned to Korea, and all together there were only six of us.

"What do you think of this place?" he asked.

"Well, I've never actually seen a place like this, except in a movie, Gothic arches, ivy-covered walls, and leaded panes. I feel like Chaucer's clerk of Oxenford." I answered. "I could get used to this."

Hausman was a head taller than I, built like an athlete, and had short, curly hair. He said he was from La Jolla, California, and had just graduated from Oberlin in Ohio. When I asked if he planned to go into the ministry, he said he was undecided, that the three years in Korea would help him make up his mind, and then asked me what my plans were. I agreed: three years in Korea would also help me to make plans. "Before I was accepted by the board, I was working as a bank clerk on Fifth Avenue," I told him. There in the atmosphere of a cloister a clerk on fifth avenue sounded almost exotic.

On the way across to the women's hall, we talked about our reasons for choosing Korea. Predictably, he was surprised that I had been in the service and had served in Korea. He'd been drafted right after the war was over, had served less than a year, and had enrolled in Oberlin right off. I was surprised he was younger than I, barely twenty-two. Burt exuded enthusiasm and spoke with an intensity I had rarely heard. When I asked what he majored in, he said something about sociology, but I took it that he was in an honors program of some sort and sociology was more an emphasis than a major. Whatever it was, I was sure it was something substantial. He was so serious and so intense that I felt for a split second I had joined the wrong program. But when I met others at the main hall, I understood: Burt was the exception. He seemed almost a parody of the YMCA man down among the natives.

Mel Johnson greeted us as we came into the hall and mentioned he had personally seen we would get the rooms in the tower; as K3s, we would have an excellent opportunity to practice Korean language while we were here. Most of those in the hall were headed for places in Latin America, he said, and the others for Japan while one was on his way to Portuguese West Africa and would be studying Portuguese with the half dozen or so assigned to Brazil. It was exhilarating listening to him name off the countries where we were all heading. I felt a great satisfaction knowing that I was part of such a group and was more certain than ever I had made the right decision. When I stepped out of the cab in front of Old Main I wondered how I would fit in at a campus full of seminarians; but after meeting Burt, an Oberlin man, and after walking among those gathered, I could not pick the theologs from the gen eds.

No one I met fit the stereotype I had in mind when I got on the train for Hartford. Even though we were not enrolled in the seminary classes, I felt I was treading on more or less hallowed turf and so expected the others to fit a stereotype of a typical seminarian, whatever that was. Well, I was wrong. I saw the man I had met at the interview, and he was no longer a trembling leaf, but an outward, jovial, talkative chap. Most had attended Methodist colleges or universities, schools like Emory, Syracuse, USC, Illinois Wesleyan, and all the other Wesleyan schools—many of which I learned were Methodist in name only and held their religious connection tenuously at best. A few had studied at seminaries like Drew or Scarrit College. The bathed-in-the-blood Christian missionary was the exception. Most represented the left of center Methodists for Social Action with backgrounds in social work and political civil rights movements. In other words, they (we?) were forerunners of those who joined the Peace Corps in the sixties. The fundamentalist and theologically conservative members of the group were the exception.

As I was introducing myself to one of the J3s, Martin Pray, I heard a voice behind me say, "Are you Joe Gilliland, the one from the University of Texas?" I turned and faced a stranger, a man my age with a slight Texas accent. "I heard your name when you introduced yourself," he said. "Anne Modr and her mother told me to look you up and introduce myself."

Out of chaos emerges a pattern—again, here, even here, a Dahlquist moment! All chaos, after all, is order misunderstood, according to the poet. Anne and her mother had spoken only once of meeting a young Texan during the last year of the war, a Bob Tate, who had been, like me, coincidentally a student at the University of Texas. Tate graduated from Texas the year before me and moved on to Vanderbilt University, taking an MA in sociology. That we would cross paths just now, barely two months since I told Anne and her mother both farewell, that *he* would be here, *he* on his way to South America and I on my way to Korea, seemed too improbable to grasp. In Asian thought, such coincidences are not considered remarkable or worthy of wonder in themselves, but this was Connecticut, the East to be sure but not the Far

East. I could not help but wonder at Ann and her mother's surprise when Tate called them and told them he was on his way to somewhere in Latin America as a short-term Methodist missionary and was heading up to the Hartford Seminary Foundation.

I asked him how Anne and her mother were and how long he had stopped in New York before coming on to Hartford. He was as amazed as I, at the probability we would meet, especially since he had neither written nor spoken to Anne and her mother since seeing them in the last months of the war and had only called from a pay phone at Grand Central as he was passing through. After talking to Anne, he decided to take a later train and had taken the subway up to East Seventy-first, he said. They were well, he said, and seemed eager that he look me up. I told him how I had met Anne and about getting the job at the Bowery on what would have been my last day in the city had I not gotten the job. We marveled at the serendipitous nature of it all.

When I said goodbye to Anne and her mother and left New York in May, I had assumed I would not see them again or even hear their names. They were surprised at my decision to join the K3 program since I had never mentioned my wish to return to Korea. I did not want to go to the trouble of explaining a desire many, especially ex-service men, considered bizarre. Korea was still a vast unknown to most Americans. I had told no one other than Jane, Don, and Jane's friends in the apartment. When I did tell Anne and Mrs. Modr, it came as a shock. Because I had visited them frequently in the apartment on East Seventy-first Street, I believe they assumed I would have been more sharing with my plans for the future. Now I wondered what Anne and Mrs. Modr must have thought about meeting two transplanted boys from the wilds of South Texas, two young boys or men with virtually nothing in common except a university—and a very large university at that—and military service, who would themselves cross paths there in the Hartford Seminary. These coincidences would happen again under even stranger and even more improbable circumstances, though none of these coincidences would have an influence on my life in the long run. Tate and I chatted a while, and then after we had exhausted the surprise, we parted. Neither of us pursued the connection since our assignments would place us on opposite sides of the earth, and in spite of the small size of the group, we would not run into each other more than once or twice during the six weeks there. But this once was quite enough to shake me. I had assumed that bridge had burned.

The mixture was about evenly divided between male and female, all in the twenty-two to twenty-seven-year age range, most in the lower end as I was. That first evening before dinner as we mingled, waiting to go into the large dining room, a special radio news bulletin reported that North Korean troops had invaded the Republic of Korea and that the city where several of us were most likely to work, Kaesong, just south of the Thirty-Eighth Parallel, had fallen to the invader. The first reports were sketchy and some said that it might not be a general invasion, but only a local incursion. These incursions had happened before, and some suggested that the trouble might be over by the time we were to leave Hartford. Just two weeks before, I had spoken to the Methodist Youth Fellowship in Corpus Christi about Korea, its government and its people, basing my talk on material I had used in writing my term essay in Government and Politics of the Far East under Dr. Henry Wu. I had hurriedly "up-dated" the paper with information I gleaned from a recent *Time* magazine. Almost everything I spoke about concerning the new Republic of Korea was wrong, as were the stories in *Times* the week I made my little talk. My data at the time I wrote the paper was recent, 1948, and as up to date as possible, but neither *Time* magazine nor the *NY Times* had kept up with what was happening north of the Thirty-Eighth Parallel. No one had.

As far as that goes, neither had Louis Pietsch, rather Colonel Pietsch, my cousin Frances' husband who served with the Korean Military Advisory Group. When I visited Dorothy in Beaumont the weekend before heading to Hartford, she had gathered the family together to bid me farewell. Louis and Frances were there. Recently returned from Korea, he insisted that Korea was "safe from any invasion from the north," so well trained and equipped were the ROK troops. I thought *so much for academic research and so much for the oxymoronic military intelligence of the day.* I had told the Corpus meeting that, according to all news sources—presumably from our own State and Defense Departments—South Korea had the most modern and best-equipped army in Asia at that time. In less than a week, that army had disintegrated.

The six of us assigned to teach in Korea began our Korean language lessons the next day, knowing it was highly unlikely we would see Korea in the near future, if ever. Radio reports that first morning described a rapid disintegration of the ROK forces, one of the earliest reporting the fall of Kaesong, the place where I had thought I might be sent. After a few days, T. T. Brumbaugh called the six of us together and offered us an opportunity to resign and go home at the Board's expense or to continue as participants in either the J3 or a new one in the Philippines. Burt and I chose to join the J3s while the four women chose the Philippines. As more news came through, it was clear that the war would be longer and more difficult than reported. Many of us, still under twenty-four, wondered what part we would be expected to play, nearly all being eligible for the draft. A month before leaving for Hartford, I received my discharge from the inactive reserves. Several of the men in the program received ROTC commissions upon their graduation from college and expected to be called to active duty—Martin Pray, soon to be my partner in Japan, being one of them—but no such calls came. The Board of Missions pled that their importance to the program far outweighed their usefulness as new second lieutenants. I remember laughing with Marty Pray, a J3, that anyone who had served in the army in World War II knew that new Second Johns were all useless, and especially those from ROTC. We joked that their being released from their military obligation was a tacit admission that second lieutenants had never proved much use anyway—which, of course, was not true, as we all knew. Bill Asbury, soon-to-be publicity man for the United Church of Japan (*Kyodan*) was a navy lieutenant JG reserve and had served in the navy in the war; he too was excused. Had his second language been Korean rather than Japanese, he most likely would have been called.

For the first few days, I found it impossible to concentrate on the classes in teaching English as a second language; my thoughts were constantly on the ugly news that came out of Korea. But once Burt and I made the decision to continue as J3s, I was able to concentrate on the English classes in the morning and Japanese classes in the afternoon. It was good to be back in the classroom, the place where I had always felt the most comfortable; I loved the routine of lecture and discussion and even the ordeal of cramming for exams and preparing papers. The difference here was the absence of all exams or term papers; our exams would come, we were told, when we walked into our first classes and would begin applying what we had learned. Not having to work while going to classes, as I had done my last years in Austin and the semester at the New School, was pure luxury.

In the late forties and early fifties, TESL was a relatively new discipline and not very widespread in schools of education or English departments. The University of Michigan and Teacher's College Columbia were the leading centers for preparing teachers in latest methods of teaching foreigners to speak English. For the two weeks of intensive lessons in teaching the language, the Board of Missions had assembled a team of specialists under Dr. Kitchens of Columbia's Teacher's College. Kitchens had been a student and colleague of the pioneer in the field, the famous Charles Fries of Michigan, and had prepared a two-week program that would cover the same materials she ordinarily covered in two semesters at Teacher's College. Her two assistants were doctoral candidates at Teachers College. Our text that summer was Dr. Fries' *The Structure of English*, which was still in the developmental stages, our copies being inexpensive mimeographed copies of the work that would come out in hardback later in 1952. It was an entirely new approach to the study of language for most of us. Even the English majors in the class and those who already had their teaching credential had never heard about Fries or his new concepts of teaching or any of the concepts Dr. Kitchens and her crew were imparting. The lectures covering Fries' theory were, Kitchens insisted, far less important than the demonstration and application. We were assigned readings in the text and expected to familiarize ourselves with the theory, but it was the classroom application of theory to method that took precedence over everything. In the second week, each of us was expected to perform and demonstrate our understanding of the methodology of sentence patterns, substitution frames, intonation and pronunciation drills as well as the use of phonemic spelling.

In those first two weeks, we met five mornings a week from eight until noon and for two hours in the afternoon. During those first two weeks, afternoon hours from one to three were given over to laboratory or practice teaching sessions. From three to five was language study, mostly Spanish, for those heading to Latin America, and a small group in Portuguese. The rest of us, twenty-two or twenty-three, were in an intensive conversational Japanese class with Ms. Rose Sawada.

Having no examinations, homework, or papers for the TESL classes—Teaching English as a Second Language--we moved rapidly, learning the phonemic alphabet, normal intonation patterns, and the use of substitution frames to introduce new vocabulary. She lectured on practical methods rather than linguistic theory, such things as how to introduce conversational techniques, how to carry on pronunciation drills, how to deal with sounds not native to certain languages, how to describe intonation patterns, and how to use "juncture and stress." We were taught to make lesson plans that tackled specific problems. Dr. Kitchens and her cohorts taught the Fries method as if it were gospel; in those days, it was. Like all new pedagogical theories TESL had evolved its own dogmas, and departure from them could subject one to excommunication. Dr. Kitchen and Ms. French and their male partner—his name long forgotten—were excellent presenters and convincing preachers of the Gospel according to Fries. They were also honest purveyors of truth, which meant they were not afraid to admit the Gospel's imperfections; for some in the program educated in the schools of orthodox religion, that seemed to be irreconcilable.

They would admonish us, "If it doesn't work, don't use it," or "find your own way." That final truth was the only absolute we had to know; the rest was useful so long as it wasn't followed too rigidly. Today, looking back at fifty-plus years of teaching in disciplines other than TESL, that advice became the only pedagogical dogma I would ever follow and explained whatever success I had in the classroom. For the students in our group trained in orthodoxies, it seemed like heresy.

None of us would be teaching literature or ideas unless conducting Bible classes. Religious liberals dominated the J3 pack and agreed that teaching Bible in English was a travesty. Our Japanese Bible students, we preached, most likely would be in class primarily to learn English and to hear it spoken by an American. Few of the dedicated Bible teachers looked on teaching Bible in English with relish, but since they were not likely to speak Japanese well enough to teach Bible effectively, they accepted the fact that their students' interest in Holy Scripture was incidental to learning English. A few patently refused to use their Bible classes for teaching English and were told they should do as they chose. A few—I was one—begged off from teaching Bible at all for the simple reason we didn't know the Bible well enough to teach it and believed there was enough error professed and/or preached floating around already. We too were excused without argument.

Shortly after checking in that first day, I realized that I was one of the few in the program who was not fresh from graduation. Within a few days of the session, most of us had selected the group of friends we would meet with most often. Other than Burt, who occupied the other room in the tower, my circle of friends consisted of only three other people: Marty Pray, Bill Asbury, and an attractive young woman from Texas named Bettie Crumpton. We were a curiously mixed assortment. In the first draft of this memoir, I called us mavericks, but when the term became so diluted by television pundits who called anyone who walked his or her own path a maverick, I decided it didn't fit any of these wild cards. Marty and I met early that first day and found we had a number of things in common, the principal thing being we had served overseas in Asia—he in Japan and I in Korea—which was a rarity in the group, only a handful having served anywhere overseas and only a few more having served at all.

Asbury, something of an anomaly, a star really and perhaps the best-looking man in the group, was also the most unorthodox in that he was not slated to teach but to act as the public relations specialist for the United Church, or *Kyodan*, in Tokyo. He could already speak, read, and write Japanese, having passed through the navy's intensive language school during the war and having served as an interpreter and investigator at that time. Bill told us his Asbury name placed him in the historical line of Methodists,

Bishop Asbury, the first Methodist bishop in America, and he claimed that his collateral descent from the great bishop had guaranteed his acceptance to the program, piety having nothing to do with it.

Marty, on the other hand, had the least or thinnest connection to the religious orthodoxies, even thinner than my own, since he was not a Methodist at all but an Episcopalian. John Wesley's Anglican origins established a thin connection for Marty, but it was the liberal attitude of the Methodist Board of Missions that granted Marty a place among the others. Marty's desire to return to Japan was the most fervent of all, even more fervent than mine to return to Korea. He believed that it swayed the Board to accept him. He also spoke Japanese freely and without hesitation, albeit a GI street Japanese. A recent graduate of Syracuse University with a major in anthropology with an emphasis in Japanese studies, he was also an ROTC second lieutenant, one who was in doubt at first as to what he should do when the war started. All three of us—Marty, Bill, and I—considered it something of a miracle that we had been selected, none of us having ever demonstrated a record of religious piety; I think we were properly humbled by the Board's generosity and tolerance and impressed by its refusal to rest on dogma. We also were aware that there were members of our group who considered this a mark of the Board's weakness.

The fourth member of or group was Bettie Jane Crumpton; she abhorred her middle name and insisted we drop it. I was immediately attracted to Bettie, partly because she was from Texas, partly because I was struck by the sound of her voice, by her talk, and partly because she was physically the loveliest person in the group. Her accent and tone of voice were not like any I had heard, and at first, I couldn't believe she was from Wichita Falls. I was convinced she had lived abroad. Her accent wasn't practiced or forced, but natural and clear and a bit self-conscious but in the positive sense like one who knows she speaks well and wants others to notice. But mostly I was attracted to her because that first day in the hall, I found her company entirely agreeable, and she apparently found mine agreeable as well and didn't drift away or make excuses when I approached her. Moreover, she listened as I spoke. That there were others who found her equally attractive and interesting was not surprising. She was uncommonly direct, frank, earnest, and often disconcerting, particularly her remarks regarding the proceedings. Many probably agreed at least in part with her candid observations, but they were too attuned to the mood and mode and resisted the impulse to strike even the weakest spark. Ms. Crumpton didn't, perhaps couldn't resist (no *perhaps* to it I would later discover). I wasn't sure, but I was prepared to find out. To say her remarks were candid or unguarded would be an understatement; they often amused and sometimes even disturbed—angered is too harsh—some.

And then there was the added attraction: she talked about books—all kinds of books—literature, anthropology, travel, history; and she talked about theater, which she had studied and admitted to once wanting to act upon the stage and study drama at Northwestern. After graduating from Harden Junior College in her hometown, however her parents insisted she attend Texas State College for Women, where she majored in speech and minored in history. Her father was a postman and her grandfather a rancher, yet she spoke like Catherine Cornell without a trace of a Texas accent or common idiom of the range. The upshot was simply that I fell in love with her and, after a week, could not think on not being in her company. That was that!

Our interests were so much alike that, without a prompt, we all four asked each other, "What are you doing here?" Of the three, Bill had the most extensive work experience, having left a well-paying job as a writer and editor of a California journal. He was immensely attractive, witty, arch, sometimes bordering on bawdy which made his presence among the missionaries even more interesting. Some thought he lacked seriousness, but Marty and I did not consider a sense of wit and style necessarily a sign that he lacked in seriousness.

Marty was much like Bill in his wit and intelligence, but he, unlike Bill, could radiate gravity and efficiency almost at will and could turn it off just as deliberately. He had learned Japanese during the occupation, serving as an MP at the Sugamo Prison in Tokyo, where the major war criminals were held. Of the two, Marty was clearly the true Japonicaphile. His aim was to return to Japan and live as deeply immersed in the culture as he could manage, in one sense becoming a contemporary Lafcadio Hearn. His devotion to every aspect of Japanese culture became legendary among the J3s, but that singular devotion often drew the harshest criticism from some, who disapproved of his "going over to the other side," which to them bespoke paganism that had to be extirpated with adoption of Christianity. We doubted that disapproval ever bothered him, though he frankly admitted there were things he could not do, and he resisted completely acculturating to Japan as had Lafcadio Hearn.

Burt and I were the only two men in the program assigned to private rooms; we even had a semiprivate bath. I appreciated my room in the tower and enjoyed the isolation of my position. Though I admired my friend in the tower, he and I had little in common. He had no interests aside from the program. I was still caught up in the reading I had set for myself while I was in New York and was immersed in Trilling's *The Liberal Imagination*, which I had given to Jane for her birthday in April but had held onto until I left

New York for Corpus. When I gave her back the book, I picked up copies of works by authors who appeared in Trilling's table of contents. I had brought several books with me: Fitzgerald's *The Crack-Up*, paper copies of *Dubliners* and *Portrait of the Artist*, William Carlos Williams' *Selected Poems*, Gogol's *Dead Souls*, and the same Modern Library edition of Shakespeare that I had carried since I first went overseas. After one old sergeant in the army said no one ever went wrong by reading the Bard, I regarded it as a talisman, a good luck charm. I had carried it with me to the ETO and to Korea and on every trip I had taken since and felt I could not safely leave it behind.

Having no one to disturb me at night nor having anyone I could disturb, I read late into the night, not necessarily works the Mission Board had given us, but my books. It was always the same with my "unrequired readings." In spite of our divergent interests, Burt and I, isolated in our tower, became friends. Of all the young men I met at Hartford, I believe he had the strongest sense of mission and would make a great difference someday. Unfortunately, I lost track of him almost from the day we landed in Yokohama.

It became clear to me early that these weeks at the seminary would become a deciding factor in the course my life. Although our time at the seminary was strictly regulated with classes, regular meals in the grand dining hall, early morning watch, evening vespers, even scheduled recreation, it never felt forced but offered a comfortable rhythm slowly and comfortably ending in the quiet tower with my books. There were a few of us like Marty Pray and me, who had no prior seminary experience or small Methodist college background, so it was rare to hear anyone grumble about the piety. I never complained, nor did Marty; I knew that I was preparing for something important that was a light-year from anything I had experienced before. Teaching? Of course, but what else?

The six weeks raced by. After the TESL classes ended, our afternoons were filled with language study, and the mornings were filled with classes in culture, Bible study, philosophy, and lectures on modern Marxism, as it was manifest in the areas where we were going. Rose Sugiyama, our language instructor, had taught the first J3s who had passed through two years before. She drilled us in common Japanese phrases and sentence patterns, teaching us Japanese using the same general techniques we had studied in the TESL classes with Dr. Kitchen. She even used the basic U.S. Army Holt Language Series, which required her to make extensive revision. She was able to bring us along remarkably well in the short time we had. Though we were not able to speak more than the most common phrases in Japanese when we arrived in Yokohama, we had acquired enough vocabulary and practice with the sounds of the language—and the all-important sentence patterns—that we were able to continue learning after arriving in Japan. Several became quite fluent during their time there, and Marty astounded us all by writing and publishing a small book in Japanese before his three-year commitment was up. For me, the most interesting classes dealt with our studies in Japanese culture and history taught in part by Dr. Floyd Shacklock, who taught culture and history of Japan in the first training session in 1948.

I began to see my haphazard selection of course paying off in ways I'd never suspected possible. My semester in McAllister's applied anthropology class prepared me well for Dr. Shacklock's talks about Japanese society and culture. At least a third of applied anthropology class had been devoted to Alexander Leighton's *The Governing of Men*, which examined in detail the Japanese relocation camp outside Poston, Arizona. I had read much of Ruth Benedict's *Chrysanthemum and the Sword*, which Bill Mullins had insisted I read in the spring of 1947. Although I had no idea at the time that I would be teaching in a Japanese university or even visiting Japan, my term research in the primitive religions course grew directly from Bill's interest and our discussion of Shintoism, both state Shinto and historical Shintoism. But my real introduction to Japanese culture relied on our interpreter, Sergeant Ishihara, on the Thirty-Eighth Parallel during the repatriation of Korean and Manchurian Japanese. All the time we were processing the Japanese families for repatriation, Ishihara was there to answer questions and explain the people we were passing through and quietly revise our views previously based on the racist wartime propaganda. My research into the government of South Korea had shown the Japanese in a most unfavorable light. In addition, my conversations with the few Koreans I met in Po Chun had led me to believe that the Japanese were uniformly cruel in their administration of Korea over a forty-year period. The picture began to change in the summer of 1946. Everything I had learned from Ishihara, from Leighton's book, from Ruth Benedict, and from my friend Bill Mullins confirmed the impression I got from the dignified and courageous people I met that summer on the Thirty-Eighth Parallel. Everything I saw built an understanding, even the enigma of the abandoned boy contributed to my understanding. When Shacklock and Rose spoke of the paradoxical nature of Japanese character, I understood immediately, though no one fully comprehends the paradox, according to Rose, not even the Japanese. Marty often tried to explain his immediate attraction to the country and its people. Arriving with occupation forces shortly after the cease-fire had been signed on the USS *Missouri*, he was assigned to Sugamo Prison as a sergeant guarding the most notorious of the war criminals. Nevertheless (paradoxically?) he never felt appalled by the duty or by the men he guarded. Contrarily, he felt attracted and consumed by a desire (his words) to understand the culture. And I had encountered the paradox dramatically and tragically in the summer of 1946 in the person of a small,l lost child struggling down a dusty road, trying to find his mother. My confusion and doubt surrounding that experience, the lost boy's struggle and abandonment, in some inchoate way, was the reason for my being there at the seminary. Over a year before arriving at the seminary, I had written an essay on religious and national Shintoism for an anthropology class called Primitive Religion. And that same semester, I wrote for Government and Politics of the Far East an essay on postwar government in Korea, the early part, which I discussed in some detail the oppressive Japanese colonial policies in Korea before the war. I had no expectations at the time that either essay would have any other value than fulfilling a course requirement and satisfying my own curiosity. As a result, however, I believe, I was as well informed in Japanese culture as any member of the J3 group, except for Marty and Bill. And by the summer of 1950, I felt I was as free of damaging prejudices as anyone could be. That I was for six weeks in the close company of men and women of unparalleled tolerance and generosity of spirit contributed much to my continuing effort to understand Japan and its people.

My greatest weakness as a J3 missionary I felt lay in my shaky background in Bible study. The typical Methodist Sunday school student, unlike his cousin in the Southern Baptist schools, does not get a heavy or thorough dose of the Bible's "inerrancy." My Sunday school teachers followed lesson plans strongly influenced by Methodist Social Doctrine rather than one steeped in the inerrancy of scripture. I knew the major stories from the Old Testament, Adam and Eve, Cain and Abel, Joseph's coat of many colors, Noah, Jonah, Daniel, the fiery furnace, and Job, but I had missed many of the doctrinal truths that guided them. The Minor Prophets, the postexilic philosophers, were a blank. And the real meaning of Abraham and Isaac meant little until I chanced upon Kierkegaard in Dr. Brogan's Philosophies of Life class. I had taken two New Testament course as a freshman, the Harmony of the Gospels and the Journeys of Paul, and had done well in the first, less than well in the second. The point is that the message of Jesus came through in the idea of the historical Jesus far more clearly than it did through the letters of Paul and the writings in the Gospels. That made me less than effective material for the mission field, I'm afraid. Therefore, I looked to the Bible lessons in the Hartford session with eagerness and hope. But I got little from them. While it was easy enough to follow Coleridge's prescription to suspend my disbelief while reading poetry, I failed miserably when it came to the reading of scripture whose teachers proclaimed its truths in both the abstract and the concrete. Several teachers were notable as storytellers and teachers, but others were inclined more to exegesis than to explanations of how to teach ideas emanating from the texts. One of the lecturers from Illinois Wesleyan University spent a week lecturing, or rather speaking informally, about teaching specific Bible stories and demonstrated, to my astonishment— and therefore demonstrating my lack of experience in the field—that even among the Methodists, there were disagreements as to the authenticity of the story. For example, he demonstrated how one might teach the story of Jonah as extended metaphor, emphasizing the dramatic elements while pointing out the enduring truths, not in the occurrences themselves but in the central wisdom of the story. After class, several said they were deeply offended when he suggested the story was a work of fiction and not a report of an actual occurrence. When I asked if the approach did not depend on the sophistication or the educational level of the hearers, I was told by the inerrancy advocates that truth was truth, and we had no right to shade it. The professor from Wesleyan was silent on that point. It was strange that here in a seminary, we were gathered to prepare ourselves to carry out a Christian mission, and there was so little agreement regarding the meaning of the word that was central to that mission; but such is the history of all religion.

We had far less difficulty agreeing on secular issues we were likely to encounter; the LA3 group became deeply immersed in the politics of our own U.S. brand of colonialism. I cannot recall anyone at Hartford standing on the conservative side of political issues. The few true fundamentalists had no political views, at least not then, though today's fundamentalist is often as much a political dogmatist as a religious one. When I left New York for Hartford, the Hiss trials were just getting under way. Senator Nixon, soon to be joined by Senator McCarthy, was searching out un-American activities; and the *Reader's Digest* was about to print an article titled "Methodism's Pink Fringe" that dealt with the Methodist Committee on Social Action, a liberal, perhaps even Marxist leaning group, however, more guided by the Methodist Social Doctrine than by Marx and the manifesto. It was a group championing social justice and expressing the belief that Christians, Methodists especially, had an obligation to seek social and political justice along with religious transformation of the soul. No one I met at Hartford would have argued with that idea. One of our speakers, Dr. Matthew Spinka, a specialist in the theology of the eastern European Berdyaev and a full-time professor at the seminary, gave us four or five hours of lecture on the Christian response to Communism. Spinka, a bona fide intellectual, spoke to us as if we were politically mature and free from the bondage of right-wing ideology. For almost a year, the press had been dominated by a vicious anticommunist Cold War rhetoric. Spinka's lectures on the basic tenets of Marxist and Stalinist philosophy—they are not identical—were measured and rational. Few in the group had been so fortunate to have these concepts placed before them so reasonably. It convinced me at the time that the Board of Foreign Missions of the Methodist Church were under no false illusions as to what many of us were about to encounter as we went overseas or likely to encounter again when we returned. Since we were sharing the campus with a large number of LA3s and one person on his way to Angola, there were also speakers who treated specific problems they might encounter not from non-Christians, but from other Christian denominations, specifically the Roman Catholic Church. Direct pointing at rival denominations disturbed a number of the short-termers, even when they were told that centuries of religious domination, virtually free from any outside interference, had created powerful theocratic societies reinforced by military dictators who were in turn constantly aided and abetted by our foreign policy. Conflict among Christians, Protestants, and Catholics smacked too much of the Klan doctrines in this country, they said. It was shown that Protestant churches in some of the South American countries were forbidden by civil law from placing crosses on their churches or displaying them outside the church sanctuary. The liberal spirit that inhered in my colleagues did not rest easy, accusing other Christians. One of the LA3s remarked to me that I was lucky going to a country where all Christians were regarded pretty much in the same light; he thought it wrong for the Mission Board to bring men from the field who tried to inspire the new missionaries by disparaging other Christians.

The atmosphere at the seminary was heavy with ideas and ideals, but it was not all thought, work, prayer and meditation. We had many hours to ourselves, and from the first week, Bettie and I began "keeping company," though there were no words spoken—not for the first six weeks—sealing our relationship, no plighting of troths. Our futures were committed to the programs, and neither was sure, after only six weeks, that what had grown was more than it seemed: a summer affair. We had much more in common than our state of origin. The books she cited, her plans for her future, her interest in the theater, and her desire to travel were all things I could understand. The one thing I loved, which she had not experienced, was the opera, but she insisted she was open to finding out about it. We filled all our free time in our excursions into town with movies—usually Westerns—and with walks through the grand parks and lawns of the insurance companies of Hartford and even a clandestine visit now and then to the Ratskeller and authentic German *bierstube,* which were within short walking distance of the seminary. Sometimes Marty and Bill accompanied us to the Ratskeller. Usually we went alone, and by the end of the session, we were rarely apart.

In the last days before we left Hartford, we learned of our overseas assignments. I expected to be assigned to one of the mission schools in Tokyo or some other large city and could hardly believe my luck when I learned that Marty Pray and I would teach at Wakayama University, a Japanese government university. The university was located far to the south of Tokyo, an hour's ride by train from Osaka, Japan's second largest city. Burt had hoped he would be stationed in a large metropolitan area where he might be allowed to do social work among the poor in addition to teaching conversational English, but he too was assigned to a government university on the far west side of Honshu. He and I talked about our assignments that last evening in our ivy-covered tower, and he explained how teaching English was not what he expected to be doing, that he was still disappointed we were not going to Korea, that he had heard how much work there was to do among the Korean Christians after three decades of Japanese rule. I agreed and said my initial motivation was to return to Korea and work with the people, that it made no difference if they were young or old, but I did believe that the original reason for the short-term missionaries was embodied in the original title of the program: the Fellowship of Reconstruction. English was a means for the ordinary man and woman to rise from the old system of economic exploitation; it was liberation from constant dependence on the upper classes, the power elite. We both felt that Christianity was tied so inexorably to human rights; economic justice gave validity to both religious and social issues. He agreed but admitted he had envisioned something more dramatic. Burt had served only a brief hitch in the navy at the end of the war and had never been overseas. He said he envied me my experiences, especially since they had not been life-threatening either for the enemy or me. His Oberlin years had turned him into a militant pacifist, he said.

Marty was as elated as I that we would not be in a mission school, speculating that we had been chosen for the Wakayama post because we didn't fit the mold of the proper missionary school teacher. I wasn't sure whether it was a compliment or a censure. He said it made no difference, adding that Wakayama was an important historic city, the home of Tokungawa Ieyasu, the first shogun. Other than receiving our assignments that evening, there was nothing more said by Drs. Shacklock or Brumbaugh. We had expected someone to explain what the schools were like. There were thirty-one of us, all teachers, but for one, Bill Asbury, and we were scattered all over the chain of islands, from Kyushu in the south to Sendai and Hokkaido in the north. We would all be sailing together on a president liner, though the name of our ship and the date of its sailing were not then known. Bill Asbury, who knew his assignment to be the main office of the Kyodan in Tokyo, was not scheduled to leave with us but would remain in New York for a month to receive special instruction in setting up the publicity office, which he wanted to rename Public Information Office.

Aside from her strikingly good looks and her voice, the one thing that attracted me to Bettie was her genuine interest in the things that interested me most. Her major in college had been speech and drama and her minor history, though she claimed no interest in speech and took it simply because she had as a child taken so many "expression" classes, something which, in an earlier era, would have been called elocution. But there was never a suggestion in her tone or pronunciation that her diction was forced or somehow "made up." That first evening at Hartford after supper, I found her sitting off to one side with a book. When I approached, she put down the book and smiled, insisting I was not disturbing her. We inevitably talked about the books that interested us or had influenced our thinking and agreed that as children, we enjoyed reading Richard Halliburton, whose travel and adventure books strongly influenced our desire to see the world. She admitted she had not traveled as much as she had wished, that she and her parents rarely traveled beyond the boundaries of Texas. Though after graduation, she had been as far as Mexico City and Puebla and had visited Teotihuacán and the excavations of the great pyramids. She told how she took a bus from Nueva Laredo alone and abandoned it halfway to Mexico City to ride the rest of the way with two young men, hairdressers, in their open convertible. I asked if she hadn't been taking a chance, taking off like that with total strangers. "It didn't seem so at the time, but I never told my parents." She laughed. I listened, quite enraptured by her enthusiasm. I could see her, free and independent, bold, striking out like a female Halliburton.

I envied her spirit, admitting that I had never gone more than a few miles beyond the borders of Texas until I went into the army. I made up for it, I said, being one of the lucky ones, I believed, crossing both oceans and never having to fire a shot in anger or fear. I was amazed the we had both read William McGovern's book *To Lhasa in Disguise*, that until I met her I knew no one who had even heard of the book. I had found it by accident while working as a volunteer in the high school library and figured it was one of those titles on a list of books recommended for high school libraries. She had found it browsing the shelves of the Wichita Falls High School Library just as I had in the Corpus Christi High School Library. Finding a perfect stranger—and perfect she would be when it came to leaving the seminary—like Bettie, someone who had also read *To Lhasa in Disguise* leaped to the level of a Dahlquist meeting.

Her major interest at the time was India and Nepal, particularly the region around Everest. She had, she said, always been fascinated by the stories of the men who had climbed and failed to reach the summit. One thing led to another; imagination and curiosity steered her into the unusual corners of the globe and to remote historical periods. I had found someone as addicted to books as I was, someone who could pursue her own interests independently; and for the first time, I knew a person who openly approved of such a propensity rather than merely tolerating it.

She did not simply tolerate it—she believed it—and said she completely understood how my love of books may have been the reason for my backsliding out of my original plan to study medicine. I told her how I began reading Jane's Book of the Month Club anthologies and found those three amazing works, "Babylon Revisited," "The Short Happy Life of Francis Macomber," and "That Evening Sun Go Down," that began my downward spiral into literary debauchery, spelling ruin to my career in medicine. I told her I had long ceased to blame my reading habit for that failure and had learned to accept the fact that I could not resist temptation, that now, up in my Gothic tower, I would read until my eyes ceased to focus. She said she understood.

I had never met anyone whose own single-minded interests could so easily shut out the rest of the world, but Bettie knew she would not be teaching English, either as a second or a first language. She was going to one of Puerto Rico's leading girls' schools to teach social studies and took no interest in the classes given by the Colombia Teacher's College group, though she attended them regularly, nor did she study Spanish with enthusiasm since she knew her students would be fluent in English. Instead, she read her own books about the Himalayas, rarely mixed with the other J3 or LA3 short termers, but would spend hours telling me how she longed to see them. When I asked her why she was at the seminary, she replied it was because she didn't want to be in Wichita Falls and thought it would be fun to visit the Caribbean and be paid to do so. She never echoed the pious clichés of others, and I found it refreshing. She had been raised conventionally, she admitted, which meant she went to Sunday school as a child and attended church with her parents and grandparents. Her paternal grandfather, Absalom Crumpton, whom she never knew, she said, had been a circuit riding Methodist preacher in Texas at the turn of the century; and her father's middle name was Wesley, but that was about the only connection she could claim to Methodism as such. In her interview, she had acknowledged her lack of deep religious faith. Bettie was not connected to the Board of Foreign Missions, but to the Board of Home Missions, whose director visited her school in Laredo and saw what she liked and offered her a job at a girl's school in Santurce, Puerto Rico. To placate the Foreign Missions, the director agreed Bettie should attend the summer program at Hartford. Through her eclectic reading, she inhabited her own more interesting and more satisfying world and appeared to need no one outside that world. Even though I had just met her, I was determined to invade her private domain and take up residence; and after a short siege, she admitted me to that world that previously only her students had entered. It was a credit to that pious institution, the Methodist Board of Home Missions, that it possessed enough imagination and originality to hire such an individualist to teach in one of its mission schools.

She was a naturally gifted teacher. Like me she had taken none of the education courses that would certify her to teach in public schools; therefore, so totally lacking in any formal teacher preparation, she began her career teaching in a private Methodist school on the Texas-Mexico border. In one semester of teaching junior high school geography and history, she made a name as an outstanding teacher whom the children loved. I could envision her—tall, strong, startlingly attractive, charming them with her looks, her mellifluous voice, her enthusiasm for the subject, sharing bits of essential as well as arcane knowledge gleaned from her unconventional readings. How I envied them. A latter-day Ms. Hilliard with great good looks, I imagined.

When the session ended in Hartford, we moved en masse to Manhattan and checked into an old hotel on Broadway not far from Times Square. I moved up to Eighty-first Street and, for a week, slept on Jane's living room couch. For two days, we attended lectures in the Methodist Building, detailing the workings of the mission services, how we would be paid, what we were expected to do to keep the Board and our supporters informed of the progress we were making. We also bussed en masse out to the United Nations at Lake Success on Long Island and watched the *UN in Action*. Bettie and I spent the first evening with members of the Hartford group just walking the streets of the Big City. I suggested we take a trip on the Staten Island Ferry, crossing over just before dusk and return just as the lights came up in Lower Manhattan. I told them Don and Jane had declared the ferry trip to be the greatest bargain in the city and said I had taken the trip across and back once before in the early afternoon one fall day, shortly after I had arrived in New York; I also said I had seen the lights of Manhattan go up in 1945, when I had just come back from the ETO. It was a spectacle unlike anything they had ever seen. It seemed fitting that summer of 1950 that we take that trip across to celebrate our leaving. Of the entire half dozen or so in that little group, I was the only one who had been abroad. In a few days, they would be shipping out to South or Central America or to the Caribbean. I was the only one heading to Japan. It was an emotional moment, especially as the ferry headed back and the lights came up just as we passed the Statue of Liberty. The next morning, we said good-bye to our friends in the Latin American group. The second evening, Bettie and I rode the subway up to Jane's apartment, where I proudly introduced her to Jane and her friends Patsy and B. R., who welcomed Bettie warmly to the apartment where I had learned so much. We had a delicious supper and excellent talk afterward, Bettie joining in as if she had been there always.

There were moments when I felt that last week was entirely unreal. It was not dreamlike or *surreal*, but logically, rationally, it seemed impossible. Those six weeks at the seminary passed quickly and pleasantly; the new friends, the studies, and then the most unbelievable of all good fortunes, meeting and falling in love with Bettie, all came together and informed me in a way I'd never known before. How could it all have happened and why, now that both of us were so firmly committed, she for teaching in Puerto Rico and I for Japan? It was maddening. Neither of us was prepared to say good-bye, so rather than linger in Manhattan—I had no intention of leaving New York as long as Bettie was still in the city—we decided to take up Bill's offer and take the train down to DC, where we would visit the monuments. It was fitting, symbolic, we thought. I told her how, while I was at Fort Meade, just a day before I shipped out for the ETO, I had gotten a pass and spent a whole day walking the same streets seeing the great monuments.

I was now intensely in love but was helpless to do anything about it. Neither of us had made a commitment to the other regarding the future. We had made a commitment to the Board of Missions, and neither even suggested that we not follow through. I least of all felt I was able to make such a new commitment. Six week was too little time on which to base a lifetime together and, knowing that, we avoided mentioning the future except the work that lay ahead. Yet neither of us was ready to say goodbye, so we took the train out of Penn Station for Washington. Bettie had a room at the Roger Williams Hotel; I planned to camp out in Bill's apartment nearby until she, not wanting to be alone those last days, insisted I stay with her, and I found no reason to argue. With no plan or itinerary, we let our instincts guide the long walks to the city's most famous sights, the National Gallery, the Lincoln and Jefferson Memorials, the White House, still closed for renovations, and, of course, the Capitol, all the sights I had visited before shipping out for Germany in 1945. We spent a long afternoon walking through the National Gallery, discovering that we had the same tastes in art and thus convincing ourselves we had enough in common to spend a life together. If there had been any doubts before then that we had fallen in love, those doubts vanished on the train back to New York. It was the greatest dilemma of my life.

That day in March, when I opened the letter announcing that I had been accepted as a short-term missionary to Korea, everything in my life appeared to be finally settled for at least three years. But now chaos had come. In the end, I finally spoke the words I had avoided, telling her how difficult it was to see her leave but how impossible it was to do otherwise. I think we took the subway up to Fort Tyron Park and the Cloisters. Ever since I left Korea, I had dreamed of a chance to return to the East. I was certain, I explained, that my entire future was tied up with what I had planned for the next three years. Yet if I lost her for good, that future, I said, would be meaningless. But if I were to give it up now and ask her to stay and give up her plans, I would have nothing to offer her. She understood, she said, and assured me she was in the same dilemma as I. She agreed we would wait. Neither suggested it was really for the best; it simply was. We both refused to dress it in hollow platitudes or clichés. We would write letters and wait; something was bound to turn up.

The next morning, we said good-bye at the midtown terminal where she boarded a bus for the airport in Newark. Later that afternoon, after I had picked up my footlocker and box of books at the apartment on West Eleventh Street, I went by Jane's apartment to say goodbye. Jane and Pat and B. R. had liked Bettie, my Bettie, and I was glad they had all met. I regretted that Don had not been there too so Bettie could have met all the people who had been most important to me that year in the city. I would miss the gatherings and the talks we had of books and plays, of galleries and everything that had shaped my thoughts and aspirations. Jane and B. R. went with me to Penn Station to see me off to Corpus. More than fifty years would pass before I would return to the wonderful town where "people travel in a hole in the ground," but I knew my thoughts would never be far. Those nine or ten months had changed me, opened my eyes and my mind, and had set me inexorably on another course, though just where it would lead, I still had no idea. Saying goodbye to Bettie had not been easy, but I knew, we both knew, that it was inevitable and necessary. It had been unspeakably sad to see her board the bus that would take her to Newark thence Puerto Rico, yet at the same time I was unspeakably happy to be on my way. Something magnificent lay ahead, and at the moment, I knew a joy I had never known.

Betty Ruth and Jane lingered, laughing and crying with me beside the train, waiting for it to leave. I tried to tell them how much the year had meant to me but nothing came; I was oddly speechless. So we kissed and hugged, and I turned to leave just as the train began to move. When I turned to wave, I felt like the young Daedalus welcoming life and encountering "the reality of experience," though still not knowing just what "*I* would forge in the smithy of *my* soul."

Chapter 16

Departures And Arrivals

When I arrived at the pier in San Pedro and looked up, there hanging over the rail of the SS *President Wilson* was a line of J3 short-term missionaries, waving and calling my name. They had gone aboard the night before in San Francisco; I was the only one who would embark at LA. At the head of the gangway stood a smiling Marty Pray and Burt Housman.

Marty gave me a friendly embrace and handshake and said, "Last night, some of us were placing bets that you had backed out, that you and Bettie had gone back to Texas to run cattle."

"It was close," I replied.

Burt added, "I knew you'd be here."

Others crowded in with greetings as I headed toward my staircase.

Burt was very excited. "I got us a table and a great dinner companion," he said. "I'll introduce you to him. He's a professor of Japanese."

Then Marty said, "Go stow your stuff and meet us back here to say goodbye to the U.S. of A. You're the only one with a cabin all to himself. The rest of us are three or four to a stateroom. Several even have large suites."

My cabin, more like the tiny cabin the Marx Brothers shared in *A Night at the Opera*, was on the lowest passenger deck, practically in the engine room from the sound of it. No doubt this level was originally second class, but now the *Wilson* carried only first and tourist class. It suited me perfectly, for it meant I could keep whatever hours I wanted and could read as late as I wished. I was not ready to enjoy the *gemütlichheit* with its enforced fellowship that the others seemed to find impossible to live without. My mind was still too full of those days and nights in Washington and New York. I looked forward now to the meals and promenades, lazy hours just watching waves and gazing out to sea.

As I punched the elevator button to return to the main deck, I could not help laughing at the difference between this sailing and the one on the USS *Leroy Eltinge* out of the narrows of San Juan de Fuca. I wondered if the *President Wilson's* ship library was as good as that on the *Eltinge*. As I stepped from the elevator, several of the group came running, still filled with the excitement of departure.

411

"We're getting ready to shove off," someone said. "Hurry, let's wave goodbye to land."

They were brimful of the excitement of their first ocean voyage, describing their cabins, the ship's manifold luxuries and pleasures, and the unbelievable food. It felt odd not being able to share that excitement, especially since I had looked forward to it ever since the news of my acceptance came through half a year ago. Even though I stood there along the rail with them all, I felt apart. Marty, a few places down from me on the railing, was chattering excitedly with Dave Reed, his Hartford roommate, telling him what it had been like when he had crossed the Pacific the first time, how different it had been on the crowded troopship.

After we left sight of land, I returned to my cabin in the lower decks and stretched out on my bunk. I opened Gogol's *Dead Souls*, which I'd started months before for Dr. Tartak's class, thinking I should put it down and begin the Japanese language text. No, now I would finish Gogol and then check out the ship's library. What I wished for was Trilling's *The Liberal Imagination*.

In April, I had given Jane Trilling's *Liberal Imagination* for her birthday but had taken it back immediately afterward. I'd not heard of Trilling until the bookstore manager at B. Altman's had recommended him over Bernard DeVoto's collection of "Easy Chair" that was no longer in stock.

"If she likes DeVoto, she'll love Trilling," he said, adding that Trilling was a much more "substantial writer than DeVoto."

The table of contents looked impressive, far more literary, and more substantial than anything I had seen recently. On the bus down Fifth Avenue to the Methodist Building, I began reading the essay "Freud and Literature" and discovered Trilling's argument to be lucid and quite unlike anything I had read about Freud and literature. By the time I was at her office, I couldn't give it up. Later after my trip to Corpus and when I stopped off at the apartment on the way to Hartford, she let me take her copy with me. It seemed entirely appropriate that I should read his essay "The Meaning of a Literary Idea" up there in my elevated isolation of a pseudo-Gothic. His essay on Tacitus convinced me I should have continued reading him. I had only skimmed the essays about Fitzgerald and Sherwood Anderson. I would have loved two weeks with *The Liberal Imagination*.

Now alone in my own cabin, I was once more an *isolato,* and I gloried in it. Was I making too much of it all? No, it was obvious to others as well. Before we left Hartford, someone had told Marty that a small group in the women's hall had held a prayer vigil for Marty, Bill, and me the night before our leaving. They were afraid we had drifted apart and lacked commitment to fulfill our mission. There must be something, I thought, in the mind of the truly committed that abhors isolation. On hearing of the prayer vigil, my first reaction was umbrage at their presumption, but second thoughts persuaded me that they were sincere and were deeply moved by that sense of fellowship expressed so often at vespers. I was touched that they felt compelled to help us along.

Just as we passed out of sight of land and before I headed back to my cabin, Burt found me and told me about securing a table for us with a Professor Yamagiwa, explaining how we would be able to practice Japanese now all the way across—not a happy prospect, I told myself. Then shortly before we went into dinner, he introduced me to the professor, a rather rotund, soft-spoken Buddha-like man, with a ready handshake and a cordial smile, probably in his late forties. It was hard to tell. I was surprised when he had handled the *l*'s in Gilliland so well, the Japanese having no *l* in the language. Rose Sugiyama had written my name on the board in katakana, the Japanese phonetic script used for foreign words and names, and it came out as Gi-ri-ran-do. Trying to avoid sounding as though I were condescending, I mentioned briefly that he handled my name very well for the first time. Burt was pleased with himself for nabbing Yamagiwa sensei for our table, along with a Mr. Ito, who spoke almost no English, making sure we would have an opportunity to practice Japanese at all meals. That Ito san spoke almost no English would make our lessons even more of a challenge, Burt enthused. He loved a challenge. It seemed like a good idea at the time, I told him, but I was disappointed. I had looked forward to playing the tourist, to eating and enjoying the meals in the first-class dining room.

The last to take a seat at the table, I opened the large impressive menu and asked Burt and Yamagiwa san what they had ordered. The sensei (Burt had begun by using the honorific, and I followed along) said he had chosen to take it all and that I should do the same. His English was impeccable, I thought, and I wondered how he had acquired such a clear Midwestern American accent. I decided that he must have studied in the States before the war. Many Japanese had. Halfway through the soup, Yamagiwa san—he asked us not to call him sensei—asked me to pass the salt and again pronounced Gilliland perfectly. When I handed him the shaker, I said I hoped he wouldn't consider it rude if I complimented him again on how well he pronounced *Gilliland*, adding that it was a difficult name to pronounce correctly the first time, even for most Americans. Dr. Kitchens and her crew had insisted we not speak slowly or in an artificially intoned manner to our Japanese students because they might think we were condescending or speaking like a teacher, or worse, they would pick up our manner of speaking. We should always speak at a natural speed and use only normal speech patterns, she insisted, but I was concerned that the professor understand every word, so I elocuted as I spoke.

Burt looked at me oddly and then remarked about the many homonyms or homophones in Japanese and how easy it was to confuse words. The professor agreed, pointing to the flowers in the center of the table and then to his nose and repeated two barely distinguishable *hanna*s. Burt and I repeated the sound, pointing first to the flower and then to our noses and repeated it again. The professor smiled. I got it just the opposite the first time but corrected it and was complimented on my second try. Again, he said Gilliland with all the *l*'s clearly enunciated. Again, I complimented him.

A few minutes later, looking down at his plate, he said softly, "You know, Mr. Gilliland, this will be the first time since 1942 that I will miss the first home game at the University of Michigan." He laid down his knife and fork and sat back, looking straight at me with a smile of extreme self-satisfaction.

I was stunned. "You mean . . .?"

"Yes, Mr. Gilliland. English is my native language. I didn't begin to learn Japanese until I was twenty years old. I was born in Chicago. You see, my parents insisted we speak English in our home." Now he laughed and explained to Mr. Ito what had just transpired. Ito laughed and shook his head. Burt said he thought he had told me that Dr. Yamagiwa was chairman of Oriental Languages at University of Michigan. I apologized again, confessing that I hadn't been listening when we were introduced, that I was too busy greeting and being greeted by my friends and was probably too excited about crossing the Pacific again.

He said, "Oh, then you've been to Japan before." I told him I had crossed the Pacific but not on my way to Japan and explained briefly about my Korean experience. And predictably, he commented about my seeming youth and about Korea not often being an ex-serviceman's object of choice. After that, all Japanese lessons ended, to Burt's chagrin.

During the meals that followed, Dr. Yamagiwa and I had conversations over a wide range of topics, most of which were only tangentially related to Japan and its culture. The pronunciation of *hanna* was our last Japanese lesson at table as I recall. I had gotten the impression quite early that Dr. Joe—he preferred that to the ultra-formal sensei or the full Dr. Yamagiwa—did not relish the idea of tutoring us in Japanese for two weeks. He let us know that first night at dinner that he was on a working sabbatical, but for the two weeks on the *Wilson*, he was looking forward to all play and no work. I would see him walking laps around the deck or sitting and reading, and when we reached the warmer latitudes, I would see him at the small pool leisurely and effortlessly swimming short laps.

The third day at lunch, he asked why he never saw me taking part in any of the tournaments or games the ship's social director set up, pointing out that Burt and Marty took part in everything. I replied I disliked games because I wasn't very good at them and thought it a waste of time on a voyage like this and said my favorite pastime is to let time pass and then said, "Because I disliked losing, I avoided the opportunity of doing so, and I admit I'm uncomfortable around people like social directors, particularly when they tried to make sure I'm 'having a good time.'" Burt said it was their job, and I agreed, but I didn't believe that pleasing them was a condition of travel. I told him I was spending my time reading, that I had just finished reading *Dead Souls* and had started *War and Peace*, which I had found in the ship's library. "That's my goal now, to finish it before we land."

"You are fond of Russian literature then?" he asked.

I said I had taken a course in Russian literature at the New School from a wonderful teacher named Tartok and had enjoyed it but was not *especially* interested in Russian literature. I was enjoying *War and Peace* and added that I had recently read *Death of Ivan Ilych*, probably the best short novel I'd ever read. He seemed genuinely interested and asked what I liked about it. This was extremely pleasant, I thought, to be talking books and eating fine food, and I regretted that the Methodists frowned on wine with one's meals (though I couldn't have afforded it if they hadn't). I told him I wasn't sure. I would have to read it again. I thought that Tolstoy had made Ilych's final suffering seem so real and so loaded with meaning, I was sure there was an underlying meaning even more profound than his final recognition of the importance, even beauty of life, ironically, at the end of it. In a way, I said, it reminded me of the line in *Macbeth* about nothing so becoming someone's life as his leaving it.

"Cawdor," he said. "It was Cawdor whose leaving became him. You read Shakespeare too?"

"Not much nowadays, but I carry a Modern Library collection of the tragedies wherever I go, the same one I carried in the ETO *and* Korea." *Now I'm showing off again*, I told myself. Burt shook his head and kept on eating.

He seemed interested in the Russian literature course and asked me about the other writers I had studied, continuing to show interest in my reading. There I was, I thought, talking to the head of Oriental Languages at the U of Michigan, almost as if I knew what I was talking about, and the thought struck me how lucky I was. I never spoke more than a few sentences to any of my professors in Austin, even the ones I admired most; none of them ever showed as much interest in what I knew or what I thought. This was truly an exceptional man. When he asked who my favorite author was, I said I supposed it was Fitzgerald, "*The Great Gatsby*, not the *Rubaiyat*. I've read almost everything Fitzgerald wrote, well, all but one of the novels and dozens of short stories." I could see Burt was anxious we get on with our Japanese conversation and appeared to be bored by the talk of books and especially talk of my reading preferences, which had nothing to do with the reasons we were aboard the SS *President Wilson*. The truth was I had no interest in learning to speak Japanese at that time. To me, there was nothing more stimulating than good conversation over an excellent meal.

Dr. Yamagiwa's interests, like those of many truly brilliant and gifted scholars, ranged far beyond his specialty, Asian literature. I felt not even the slightest suggestion of condescension in anything he said or the questions he asked, and I had the feeling from the beginning of our acquaintance that he must indeed be a fine teacher. Once, while we were on deck chatting, he asked me how I had become interested in Japan and teaching as a short-term missionary. By his tone of voice, I sensed that he considered it a personal question and assumed I might prefer not to discuss the subject in a group of fellow J3s. I told him about my failure to progress through premed and about my term the army and finally my choice of major, psychology, and finally how my army experience in Korea had been the reason for my joining the program. Then I mentioned how my months in New York with Jane and Don had opened up to me a whole new world: the theater, opera, literature, and the arts in general.

"You asked me earlier about my favorite writer, and at the time, I was thinking in terms of novelists or poets. But the writer who interests me most right now is Lionel Trilling. I bought his *Liberal Imagination* last April and gave it to my sister for her birthday. I'd never read anything like it, especially the essays on Fitzgerald and Freud, but I had to give it back before I left and so never finished it. I have never read much serious criticism before, only book reviews in magazines like the *New Yorker*, *Saturday Review*, or the *Nation*."

He said, "Well, that is interesting. If I can get to my hold luggage, I'll dig out my copy and let you read it."

"You know the book? You have a copy too?" I asked. Having never heard of Trilling until I bought his book for Jane, I foolishly assumed he was as unknown to others as he had been to me.

"Yes, Lionel gave me a copy last spring while we were at Kenyon College," he said. The voyage suddenly took on an entirely new meaning.

Once after dinner, Dr. Yamagiwa asked what I was reading in Trilling, and I said I was rereading one of the essays on Freud. When he asked what I thought about Trilling's treatment of the great man, I admitted I wasn't sure, and that was why I was rereading first the one titled "Freud and Literature" and then "Art and Neurosis." I told him I had read a lot of Freud, or what I thought was a lot, most of the Modern Library's *Basic Writings*, "Beyond the Pleasure Principle," and *The General Introductory Lectures*, and the work on Leonardo and a number of other late writings. I said I thought I pretty well understood Freud, but now I wasn't so sure. Trilling was making me rethink a lot of what I had earlier believed I understood. But that was what I liked about Trilling. Dr. Yamagiwa said he found it most interesting that I would take the trouble to find out and wondered if I had made any serious plans about what I was going to do after I finished my three years' obligation. I said I had no idea but hoped it would be something along the lines of what Trilling did. He had explained earlier about Trilling's being one of Columbia's great professors, and agreed it would not be a bad thing to follow Trilling's example and added, "I think you would be good at it." I was quite pleased, thinking as we sat there about Jane's reply to my Rudolstadt letter, saying that she *too* had considered teaching in a college. My thoughts had never been so focused on that possibility, as they were sitting there and chatting with Dr. Joe Yamagiwa. Teaching conversational English was not the same.

Our last day at sea was our only day of bad weather in our two weeks at sea. The ship rolled and shook, spray blew across the boat deck and waves crashed over the bow. The sea had that look of molten lead Lovejoy had noted when we met that time on the *Eltinge*, and I wondered if this last day was a portent of things to come or just the tail end of the typhoon that had preceded us into Yokohama. I told myself that I was perhaps reading too much and was seeing the world now only as metaphor. Early that last morning a sudden silence woke me just as it had when we dropped anchor off Inchon in 1946. I dressed hurriedly and made my way topside, recalling that morning in February when I stepped out on deck and gazed at the windswept landscape of Inchon. I was not the first on deck this time. Nearly all of the J3s were lining the windows on the promenade deck looking off to the port of Yokohama.

Anchored about a half mile out along with a number of freighters off-loading their cargoes of armored half-tracks, six-by-six trucks, and jeeps, I was suddenly back in the real world, not the world as metaphor. There was a war going on not too far away as a crow might fly; for two weeks we all seemed oblivious that people were being killed in a war that was not going well. The SS *President Wilson* was an anomaly there in the midst of warlike bustle.

Although the ship's newspaper had issued bulletins about the war's progress, few aboard had discussed it. Now here, we were aware that not many miles away, a war was raging. A kind of hush had fallen over the group standing there, realizing for perhaps the first time since leaving Oahu that there was a war not far from where we lay at anchor. We knew it was going badly for the U.S. forces. Though a number of us were veterans of the last war, few had been overseas, and none as I recall had been old enough to have seen combat.

I returned to my cabin, set my one bag in the passageway outside my door, and then returned to the main deck and waited with fellow missionaries and other passengers, waiting to take a lighter ashore. The air was heavy with anticipation. I saw Dr. Joe sitting in a corner of the lounge surrounded by Japanese reporters and answering questions. Marty told me that we had been traveling, apparently, with a well-known scholar. They were asking him questions about the University of Michigan study center at Okayama, where he was heading, and one reporter had remarked to Marty about Dr. Joe's elegant Japanese pronunciation. When the interview broke up, the doctor rose and came toward Marty and me and wished us luck. I told him how much I had enjoyed our meals together and our conversations on deck and thanked him for letting me read Trilling's book. He asked us if we had an address in Wakayama and said he would like to keep in touch just to see how we were getting on. I had memorized it—*Komatsubara dori, 5 chome, Wakayama shi*—and wrote it down for him. It was the address of Dorothy and Louis Grier, the Presbyterian missionaries who would be our contact in Wakayama and our hosts until we settled in at the university.

When we finally disembarked from the lighter, we passed through customs quickly, and quite suddenly, Marty and I found ourselves all alone in the customs shed. Welcoming parties had whisked all the others away, but no such party from Wakayama University awaited us. Only Dr. and Mrs. Igelhardt, who had acted as head of my interview committee and was now the senior Methodist missionary in Japan, were still there waiting. We did not have to wait long. Coming across the empty parking lot was a round figure in a wilted seersucker suit, looking like someone out of a short story by Maugham. He greeting the Igelhardts, who immediately recognized him, he then directed them to a large black limousine and then moved toward Marty and me.

"You are Gilliland and Pray, I take it," he said, offering us his hand. "Which is which? So sorry to keep you waiting. I got hung up at the office in a meeting"—he laughed—"always meetings."

He explained he was from the Kyodan, a name we would be hearing often from then on, and explained we would be delayed in Tokyo until Louis Grier in Wakayama called to let us know when they were ready for us. The storm, typhoon Jane, had passed through Wakayama prefecture the day before and had torn up the house Marty and I were to occupy, he said, and the Grier's were getting a room ready for us in their home until our house was repaired. On our way to the limousine, he explained we would stay the night at the Manse, a hostel there in Yokohama, where missionaries in transit often stayed, and then we would move into Tokyo, where he had made reservations for us at the YMCA in the Kanda District. Marty told him he knew the area well. It was near the building where he had earned his black belt in judo back when he was in the occupation.

He offered to help us make arrangements with the Nippon Express to have our heavy luggage sent on to the Grier's address, but Mary said he'd do it and ran off to the express office across from the customs shed. Back at the car our greeter told the Igelhardts he was very impressed by Marty's lack of hesitation and his ability to handle the language—so was I. As we climbed into the car, I mentioned that I had given my last ten dollars to the room and bath steward and that I had no money to change for a train ticket into Tokyo. He laughed and pulled a wad of Japanese yen from his pocket, peeling off several ¥1,000 notes.

"I expected as much." He laughed, writing the amount he had given me in a small notebook. "That will get you to the Kyodan and maybe buy a meal or two, but that's about all. It's not as much as it looks."

Everything seemed to amuse him, or nothing seemed to disturb him. I wasn't sure whether he was naturally happy about everything or he was trying to put us at ease. Whatever it was, it was infectious. "Don't worry, we'll get you some money tomorrow when you stop by my office at the Kyodan," he said. Then we drove off, the three of them—Dr. and Mrs. Igelhardt and our host—chatting about old friends and the changes taking place everywhere.

Our drive from the pier took us through a heavily bombed section of the city up to a bluff where the damage was less obvious. The Manse, just outside the perimeter of the most devastated area, had been the rectory of a large Methodist church that burned down during an air raid. It was now being used for missionaries in transit. That night, we joined the Igelhardts for supper and talked about plans for the future. I reminded the doctor that he had been on my interviewing committee, and he said he recalled it and remarked with a wry smile how he had enjoyed putting me on the spot. I had told Marty and Bill earlier how Dr. Igelhardt had put it to me and how T. T. Brumbaugh had saved my soup. Now the good man was home again. In the second year of the war he had to be tied to a stretcher when he and other missionaries were loaded onto the *SS. Gripsholm* to be repatriated.

Waiting to get word from the Griers that they were ready for us was not a waste of time. Marty introduced me to friends he had made during his days in the occupation, an officer of Nippon Bank and a family living near Sugamo Prison, where he had spent his time as a sergeant guarding several war criminals. He also took me to Tokyo's *Kabuki-za*, Japan's premier Kabuki theater to see if I passed the test. He believed an appreciation of Kabuki was the mark of a person's ability to survive the culture shock of living in Japan.

"There's nothing like it anywhere," he said. "If you like Kabuki, you'll have no trouble acculturating."

He was correct. The Kabuki drama we saw was one of the most moving, most operatic, most theatrical experiences I could recall. When I explained to Marty how the music, costuming, dancing, and language—of which I understood not a word but was never an impediment to my understanding of the drama—all came together and conveyed an overpoweringly emotional story that I had no difficulty in following from beginning to end. At that, he pronounced me fit for duty.

But the days grew long, and our patience wore thin as we awaited the call from Wakayama. Several times, we met members of our Hartford group for lunch and listened to them wax on about new friends and the jobs they were already beginning to perform. Our stay in Tokyo convinced me that I did not wish to spend my three years in a large Japanese metropolitan area. In the fall of 1950, Tokyo still showed signs of the devastating firebomb raid that killed more people than the Hiroshima bomb. Traffic was insane and the weather abominable, noise overbearing and crowds impossible.

At the end of our fourth day, we received a note from the Kyodan telling us Dorothy and Louis Grier were ready for us and that the office had made reservations for us on the night train to Osaka. The train was carrying only Americans, mostly officers and dependents and a few DACs, department of the army civilians. All other men on the train our age were in uniform and bore insignia of either officers or noncoms. With the special fast express trains soon returning to the main line between Tokyo and Osaka, this would be one of the last special trains for army personnel to run between major cities. The train had the appearance of those days of the British Raj when the West ruled the East and when the trains, clubs, hotels, and residential compounds were off limits to native peoples. The only Japanese on the train were conductors and white-coated car attendants. Marty grumbled that he would have preferred to take the day train, even if it meant taking a third-class seat in an non-air-conditioned car for thirteen hours, but when we arrived the next morning in Osaka, he admitted it was not as bad as it seemed.

Miraculously, Marty was able to get us from Osaka Station to Tennoji, where we made the connection to Higashi Wakayama. To me it was a maze of disorder and confusion, but Marty's Japanese worked well, and we were able to step off our car and change directly to the local circle train with no difficulty. By the time we arrived at the platform for the train that would take us to our final stop, the heavy rush of commuters had departed, and we fortunately had to wait only minutes before the Wakayama train was due to leave. It was an interesting ride along the coastal, through mountain villages surrounded by rice paddies and small forests, like traveling through the pages of *National Geographic.* The farther from Osaka, the deeper we receded into the past, saw fewer automobiles and trucks and more carts pulled by animals or men, more motorcycle trucks, more bicycles carrying loads that towered precariously over the heads of their riders. Occasionally, we passed swiftly through hamlets that had not changed since the days when Hokusai or Hiroshige made their block prints. The war had not visited these towns and villages. By sheer luck, we had grabbed an express and not a local, and so we sped through most of the stations along the way. But at each stop, passengers coming aboard would glance toward us and then away, do a quick double-take, then stare or glance surreptitiously in our direction. *Gaijin*—foreigners—were still uncommon on the train to Wakayama, we surmised.

From the station to the Grier's house, our taxi ride took us through a severely bombed section of town and past much new construction. Signs of the one devastating firebomb raid in the last month of the war were still visible. By comparison to what I had seen in Tokyo, where whole sections of the city, greater in size than all of Wakayama, still lay in rubble, the destruction in Wakayama seemed much less severe, even though eighty percent of the city, we were told, had been severely hit in one raid. Marty chatted with the driver in rough familiar Japanese all along the way, translating the running commentary about the firebombs and the *"B-ni-ju-ku,"* or B-29s. It was obvious Marty was home and enjoying every mile of the trip. As we left the center of town, curving around the gently sloping stone walls and the moat of old Wakayama castle, the destruction was much less marked. After a few blocks, the signs of the raid disappeared entirely; and for the rest of the ride, we saw no sign that any raid had taken place. It was as if the castle were the boundary of the raid. South of the castle, the major residential areas were intact. But there was something out of date there, something entirely out of time. The streetcars were tiny versions of the Toonerville Trolley, and all the houses and shops appeared from an age long passed. The cars—including the cab that we picked up at the station—were all prewar American cars held together it seemed by the proverbial chewing gum and bailing wire. All the way through town, Marty remarked on how fortunate we were and kept up a running dialogue with our cab driver about the places we passed. I agreed with his estimate of our good fortune mainly because we had escaped the madness of Tokyo and Osaka.

The Grier's large, actually rather sumptuous, old mission house was at the end of a narrow lane outside the bombed area of the city and only a short walk to Wakayama University's *Keisai* or Economics Campus. As our taxi pulled up to the gate, Dot and Louie came out to welcome us and immediately made us feel as if we were home. Louis, he preferred Louie, looked like a Hollywood casting of Robert Louis Stevenson with a long narrow face, large moustache, and bright-red hair in need of trimming, and Dot, somewhat taller than her husband, was quite blonde and genuine Minnesota Nordic. After we settled into our upstairs guest room, Louie told us how typhoon Jane swept through Wakayama and ripped two entire window casements out of our house along with a number of roof tiles, causing extensive water damage to the floors and interior plaster. We were welcome to stay with them, he insisted, as long as it took the university to make the repairs. Our classes at Wakayama Dai Gakku (University), would not be starting for almost three weeks, which would give us time to adjust to our new life and to meet groups of university students whom Dot and Louie had invited to the house. Neither Dot nor Louie regarded our camping out with them as an intrusion. We broke the routine, Dot insisted, and created a friendly social atmosphere especially when Louie was off on errands among the small rural communities outside Wakayama.

They were in their third year in Japan, spending their first year entirely in language study in Kyoto. Dot was an RN and a graduate of Carleton College in Minnesota. She and Louie had met while he was at Yale, finishing his master's in divinity, and while she was immersed in language study, preparing for a missionary post in China. Louie, also preparing to enter the foreign mission field, was also studying Japanese. They arrived in Japan about the same time the first J3 and K3 missionaries arrived in the East and had been living and working in Wakayama for only a year, taking over a prewar mission house and picking up where the previous missionary left off when the war began. Their first child, Steven, was born during their year of language study, and Norma Jean arrived after they moved to Wakayama. Though Dot had her hands full with the children and her regular duties as a missionary and a wife, she seemed happy to be hosting Marty and me; more important, she enjoyed teaching us the ways of Wakayama and correcting Marty's GI-Japanese while doing her best to encourage me to renew my language studies, which had lapsed during the voyage over. Neither Louie nor Dot fit any missionary stereotype pictured in films or novels. Truthfully, hardly any of the missionaries we met fit the stereotype I had fixed in my mind when we arrived, and Marty agreed, but I learned early, in spite of their wide interests in arts and ideas—that great world I had only begun only to appreciate—their real interests lay in the Japanese churches Louie was working with. In a sense, Marty and I and our world appeared as comic, if not bizarre, relief.

As soon as we stashed our suitcases in the guest room and returned to the living room, Marty asked how far the university was and if our house was nearby. Louie explained it was quite close and gave us directions and then told us President Itoigawa san would arrive here at the Manse after one o'clock and that Inoue sensei, head of English at the university, would come by shortly afterwards. We set off immediately to check out our house.

The university compound, or *kansha*, where our house was located, was only a few minutes' walk from the Grier place, and what we found was nothing like the simplicity and beauty Marty had described nor anything like the comfort I recalled of C Company's simple Japanese housing in Mukho, or the houses Mullins so often described. We imagined the sliding paper walls and doors, the walled gardens, and quaint entranceway or *genkan*. As we approached on the narrow dirt street and saw the wall, the long tiled roof, the large roofed gateway, we were quite impressed. Then as we turned into the gate we found not a Japanese-style house but a long, strange-looking clapboard building painted in something resembling army olive drab. It was huge and resembled no recognizable architectural style past, present, or future, north, south, east, or west. Instead, it was a style that someone may have once *assumed* to be the style of a Western domicile circa 1920. We entered on the north through a *genkan*, a typical Japanese entrance with *getabako*, a shoebox beside a step where you could doff your shoes and slip into slippers before entering the main hall. Alas! It only looked like a Western-styled house, but the principle was pure Japanese. Its one feature that really made sense was a southern exposure on the back of the house away from the street. Large south-facing windows set to gather the sun's rays on wintry days ran the length of the house; it was a feature that was simply an adaption of traditional Japanese houses. Along the south side of the house, large rooms were arranged in a row opening off a long hall that ran from he genkan the length of the house. The genkan opened into a large room, possibly thirty-by-thirty, with a bare wooden floor where once linoleum lay.

Marty clapped hands and announced, "I've figured it out. Look, the long windows will let in lots of sun and air, and we'll have them lay in tatami in all the large rooms and do away with all this ratty linoleum. We'll heat with hibachi and like the Japanese we'll carry them from room to room."

Marty was an enduring surprise; so long as he was able to translate anything western into Japanese style he was happy, and here he found everything in the house adaptable to a Japanese style of living. Tatami would negate the need for Western-style furniture, of which there was none. He had already opted for futon in his bedroom, and I would follow or adapt. Two rooms, a comfortable south-facing room for dining and a small, low-ceilinged study with a built-in desk and bookcases set into a small south-facing bay window, would remain tatami-free. There was also a bay-windowed entrance from the garden on the south that he suggested we use as an extra guest room. Mine was a small room on the north that unaccountably was furnished with a large armoire, and equally unaccountable a pair of iron hospital-style beds with mattresses that we later learned had been shipped to the university by the Kyodan. Marty planned it well. Rather than lay out money for custom made futon—my height required the custom made ones—I opted for one of the iron beds and mattress.

"Ten rooms aren't bad for a pair of bachelors," he said. "Look, a kitchen with gas stove, a Western-style toilet that flushes, and even a septic tank, a real hole-in-the-floor *benjo*, too, for Japanese visitors who don't like to sit and shit."

But the one feature that really cheered him and would me when I learned more, was the wood-fired *o-furo*, a square room with a large, steel cauldron set in a brick fire pit. "A real bath for soaking and thinking." For safety, the firebox for heating the bath water opened outside the house.

"We've got it made, Joe Tex!" Marty clapped. "It looks like a foreigner's house only on the outside."

The workers who were re-plastering the walls watched and listened, amused at Marty' ebullience and his GI Japanese. Asking of the workers for the man in charge, very much like the lord of the manor, he explained which rooms were to be fitted with straw tatami mats, which to be left without— only the kitchen, the study, and the dining room. Another tatami room off the kitchen was perfect for a maid or cook or both, he said. Marty's enthusiasm quieted any doubts I might have had, and when we trudged back up to the Grier manse to tell Dot and Louis about our good fortune, we talked of which rooms we would choose and how we would furnish the dining room and study. Just as we arrived, a car drove up with the president of Wakayama Dai Gakku, whom we followed into the house.

Itoigawa sensei resembled a very dapper, middle-aged bank manager right out of an old silent movie, wing color and all, but that impression soon gave way to an entirely different reality. He was fluent in English and, unlike his counterparts in other institutions, was also quite candid, admitting right off that he was more than a little surprised—I would have said dismayed—at our extreme youth. We had been told in our Japanese culture class at the seminary that it was quite rare for polite Japanese to speak candidly and frankly to new, especially professional, acquaintances. It often takes years before a person is willing to state openly an honest opinion. Not so with Itoigawa sensei. Not realizing that Marty spoke any Japanese, he committed a *faux pas*, a kind almost unheard of in Japan by a man of his station.

Marty and I understood that the deference shown to us by older Japanese had nothing to do with our real station in the world of academe. Any courtesies we received from the older men on the faculty were the result of the U. S. victory over Japan, but that aside: What had he said that second Louie Grier introduced us?

"*Ah, sono hito wa aka chan, desu ne!*"

I, of course, did not catch the meaning, but I saw by Marty's reaction that he did had caught it and he whispered right off: "The president said to Louis that we were babies, but Louie told him we both had university degrees."

Louie smiled and assured him were older than we looked, and that both of us had served overseas in the last war. I was reading body language and facial expressions, missing the verbal exchanges, and I could see that Louie's last comment surprised the president.

"*Ah soo desu ka?*" he said and nodded in our direction. Itoigawa sensei excused himself quickly and then turned to us and listened as we explained, in English, how we had undergone training in teaching English as a second language by professors from Columbia University, a name we knew would impress him. With that explanation, he relaxed and became quite cordial. Neither Marty nor I looked on his surprise as a lapse in manners, for we understood: he had a good reason to look surprised. I asked Louie to tell him people often assumed both of us were younger than we actually were. Louie admitted later that the president's remarks were unusual but not too surprising since he himself was shocked when we first stepped out of the taxi. By the end of the interview, which was carried on in English after Itoigawa's *faux pas*, I had the feeling that the president was well satisfied; he had, after all, *not* gotten two proverbial pigs in a poke after all.

MacArthur's ministry of education had created several universities like ours in Wakayama by combing smaller *semmon gakku*, or higher schools, into a single entity, in Wakayama's case by combining a business college, a normal school, and an agriculture school. By doing so the Ministry of Education (*Mumbu sho*) opened higher education to a much larger population than before the war. Before the war, only the upper classes were able to send their sons (and a very few daughters) to the universities. Before 1941, Wakayama *Keisai Semmon Gakku*, or Higher Business School, had always employed several foreign instructors, usually from England and America and either Germany or China. The imperial universities and several large, better-known private universities hired foreign faculty, usually well-known writers or scholars. The new universities like Wakayama University had to do without. President Itoigawa was justifiably proud of the old higher school and was eager to make sure the new Wakayama Dai Gakku would attain the same level of high regard. He explained that the last graduating class of the semmon gakku would receive diplomas in January and that all the classes that followed would be *Wa Dai*, Wakayama University, classes. Marty and I would be teaching the last of the old and the first of the new.

Roughly an hour after Itoigawa san left, we met Inoue sensei, the chairman of the English department. Warned what to expect, he did not evince as much surprise as Itoigawa san had, but he was slightly taken aback, and he said so quite frankly with a smile. Less concerned with the issue of public image than the president, Inoue sensei's job was much easier; all he had to do was make sure that we knew something about teaching English as a foreign language. Right off, he asked Marty and me how we would go about teaching conversational English, and we told him that everything we did would be experimental, that we had only just begun to learn the techniques of ESL that were also still in the development stage in the U.S. One thing was certain: we would not teach formal English grammar. I explained that our method depended heavily on students who were willing to speak up.

"Conversational English classes require heavy student participation," I said. "There is some rote memorization, of course," I said, "but mostly we depend on speaking and repeating patterns of English." Marty added that we expected the students to converse with us, and explained that there would be a lot of repetition and recitation and would seem monotonous and even boring at times. Neither Marty nor I had ever been "interviewed" by such compliant bosses or by anyone so willing to accept our views. It was not natural, I felt. And when Inoue sensei said he understood I relaxed and silently rejoiced and any doubts I may have had before the interview suddenly vanished when, rather than expressing dismay at our infancy, he said he thought we would have an advantage because we were so much younger than the rest of the faculty, that we were on average only three years older than our students.

After that, the conversation became an informal discussion about our personal interests, about what we had studied at university, about books and authors we enjoyed reading. Inoue spoke excellent English with only the slightest Japanese accent. He had never been out of Japan and had learned all his English in school. He told us he was a graduate of Kyoto Dai Gakku, one of the three Imperial universities. I was impressed at how familiar he was with modern American literature, particularly twentieth-century authors, such as Steinbeck, Fitzgerald, Hemingway, and Faulkner. Considering that all these authors had been banned during the war and strongly discouraged in the decade leading up to Pearl Harbor, he was extremely knowledgeable. Clearly his main interest lay in teaching and studying literature, not in administering a department or the teaching of conversational English. Before the meeting ended, he asked a personal favor and insisted that if we said no, it would not be an insult or be taken badly, for he knew we would be busy with our classes and any other work we would be expected to do for the church.

He asked, "Are either of you familiar with the plays of Eugene O'Neill?" We said we were.

"He's America's greatest living playwright," I said and added that I'd read *Desire Under the Elms* in college in my senior year and had just finished reading *Strange Interlude*, *The Hairy Ape*, and *The Emperor Jones*.

"I can't believe it," he said, excited. "Except for the *Strange Interlude*, those are just the plays I have been working on. I am translating Eugene O'Neill into Japanese. I am the authorized translator for all his plays into Japanese. May I ask you to read the plays and help me with his American slang? I have difficulty understanding what he means. I understand it is impossible to translate slang, you know. But I believe you could help me find he best Japanese equivalent."

We agreed. I said that many people, critics and scholars, had found O'Neill's slang to be stagy and more art than actual American usage, probably dated though effective. He said he was relieved to hear that. I repeated what I had learned in the 81st Street seminars, that O'Neill's language is always a little artificial, even though he was regarded as an American realist. I told him that I believed him to be more of a poet than a realist in his dialogue. He nodded agreement and vigorously thanked us, said he would bring copies of the plays for us, and made dates to discuss the plays.

Before we parted, he invited us to tea on campus so that we might meet the other members of the department. "We will give you your class schedule at that time." Then as he left through the entrance to the house, he turned and asked, "I almost forgot. Would you agree to teach a night class two nights a week for non-university students? You call it adult education, I think."

I looked at Marty and he at me then and said we would. I asked. "One of us or both of us?"

"We can work that out," he said, thanked us, bowing rapidly, and then left, wheeling his bicycle out into the driveway.

I liked him immediately. I was elated with what I had seen and what I had heard. Think of it: *Eugene O'Neill!* He was obviously an intellectual, though in no way a pedant. We all agreed he was probably a very good teacher. He asked questions and waited for answers and asked them again if he didn't hear the answer or if we were vague or indecisive. At dinner that evening, the four of us talked about the two interviews and came to the conclusion that Itoigawa's apprehensions were not our concern. Louie and Dot pointed out that as a president, he had to face problems of public images all the time while Inoue was concerned only that we could teach; Louie said he seemed not to be worried on that score. I talked about his remarks that our age was an advantage, and Louie agreed, saying we were more likely to get our students to respond than their Japanese would because traditional Japanese teaching depended on the lecture and regurgitation, with the regurgitation coming only on the written examination or essay.

After our meeting with the faculty, I felt more confidant about the task ahead, although by comparison we were indeed *aka chans*, the other faculty all past the age of forty. As far as Dot and Louie were concerned, we were also closer to aka chan than to sensei.

As we expected, the faculty were friendly and welcoming, and, except for one, reflected Inoue sensei's easy informality and friendliness. The one stiff and formal member of the department, ironically, had been born in California and had come to Japan with his parents when he was in grade school. He spoke English free of any accent (pronounced "Gilliland" with ease) but littered with the solecisms you would expect of a small child. One, Tadokoro san, had a bachelor's degree from Earlham College in Indiana and spoke a clear Midwestern American English. The fourth member spoke very little and then very slowly and cautiously correct, but he was, we learned, the most popular among the students.

When we saw that our weekly schedule consisted of twelve one-hour classes, we explained that it was completely impractical, that no one would learn the least bit of conversational English meeting only an hour a week. Inoue and the other instructors had theorized that having two English instructors, the students would have an opportunity to hear two American accents, which would make it easier for them to understand. It was not a bad idea we explained, but since Marty and I did not have drastically different speech patterns—most people hardly recognized any trace of a Texas accent in my speech—there would be less advantage than continuity two classes from the same instructor could provide. Unless Marty and I coordinated our classes perfectly or followed a rigid outline, our classes would lack such continuity. Each freshman and sophomore spent five hours a week in English classes: an hour each of formal grammar, composition, and reading, and two hours of conversation. It seemed like an excessive amount of language study, particularly since it was a requirement for all students regardless of their majors. Japan early realized that the English language was the key to their survival in a world economy, for English, at mid-century, was the major language in the world and would continue to be for generations to come. We suggested that we meet our students two hours a week, that we each have six classes, meeting a total of twelve hours. They all agreed. Half of my classes were on the old *keisai* (economics) campus, the other half on the *gakku gei* (liberal arts) campus, where the former teachers college had its classes. All of Marty's were on the *gakku gei* campus. It was not a crushing schedule.

Joe and Martin Pray at the meeting with Inoue sensei

Just as the regular university class schedules presented a problem, so did evening classes that were to begin immediately. Inoue suggested that the classes meet two hours a night, two nights a week for eight weeks, Marty taking the first four weeks, I the second. When I asked how many were registered, he said there were thirty in the class, perhaps more. As soon as we heard there were thirty students in all, we suggested we split the class into two sections of fifteen each for the full eight weeks.

"Why not divide the class into two sections of fifteen each, beginners in one and more experienced in the other?" I suggested.

Marty added, "We will switch classes at the end of the fourth week, if you believe the students would benefit from having two teachers. In that way, they get the experience of two *gaijin*."

The other instructors looked at each other silently, shaking heads as if it could not work, and then Inoue said, "Ah, so, but you see we can only pay one salary."

"It makes no difference," I said. "Marty gets half, I get half. It's all the same. Fewer students, less work." The fact was Marty and I would not get the pay anyway, I explained, because our salary came from the Kyodan, and any money from Wakayama University went directly back to the Kyodan. As it was, we had only twelve hours a week in class; the additional four was not a stretch. So if indeed Itoigawa got a pair of pigs in a poke, he got two for the price of one in this case. I insisted we were not being overly generous, just practical. Thirty students in a conversational class were far too many, I said. Marty agreed and added that there were bound to be beginners along with advanced students. I recall his looking straight at me, smiling; we were both amazed at how parallel our thoughts ran. It was indeed a partnership, I thought, and we found it would remain so for the duration of our time together. The men at Hartford who made the assignments were wise beyond all expectations.

That's when Inoue asked if we would try to spread the word in our classes, if that was indeed the reason we wanted to spend more time with our students. I was amused that Inoue had picked up on the proselytizing cliché. Neither Marty nor I had ever discussed in detail our personal motives for becoming J3 missionaries. There had been a sort of tacit agreement that we were pretty much in the same boat.

I told Inoue that I was speaking for myself, that I was not an evangelical missionary but a teaching missionary, and I was there to do whatever I could to help Japan return to normal, whatever that was, and to develop a freer and more open, more democratic society, especially for young people. Teaching English seemed to be important at the time, for our students and for Japan; and since it was the only thing I could do at that time that might help this younger generation to move ahead, it was what I had to do. "Education is everyone's salvation, I believe. That is my 'mission,' if you will." Marty agreed and added that he had come to love the people and the country and wished to do whatever he could to help Japan recover. At the same time, he wished to learn from his students as much as he could. We both believed that the more we learned of each other's language and culture, the more everyone would benefit. It sounded trite even then, but it was simple and it was true, if naive.

Inoue seemed satisfied. I added that our evening students, in having four hours of English a week, were actually getting a better deal than the university students. He agreed and thanked us.

When we returned to the house that afternoon, we agreed what we had said sounded more than a bit pious and idealistic, but we insisted we were sincere. Honestly, I had never met a person like Marty Pray. In style, we were quite different; but in underlying motive and philosophy, we gibed. That neither of us was accustomed to "testifying" or "witnessing," missionary parlance we readily admitted. We had not articulated earlier our reasons for joining the program, either at Hartford or afterward; we both had felt the less said the better. That's when Marty said, "You know, we're a lot more alike than appears on the surface. You were thinking my exact thoughts in there." Both Dot and Louie looked on, smiling and amazed that neither of us had discussed any of this, and they too marveled at the wisdom of Shacklock and Mel Johnson.

I agreed and said, "I hate sounding pious. Because I am not. But I wonder what those men thought when they heard me talking about helping Japan to return to 'normal'? God, that must've galled them. The white man's burden and all that Raj shit." Marty agreed. The truth was that the original mission of the first J3s was embedded in the program's title: Fellowship of Reconciliation. I believed in the mission and strongly believe it was a turning point for both of us. Though we differed markedly in our approach, I never doubted Marty's dedication, and I believe we truly trusted each other implicitly.

The first night of class worked with ease just as we planned, the class dividing exactly fifteen and fifteen as we had hoped. Marty took the beginners because he had enough Japanese to help the weakest over the dead spots while I took the more advanced. Inoue san emphasized that we should not use Japanese in our classes, but Marty made an exception for his beginners, vowing to use a word or an expression from time to time only in order to get the beginner back into the mainstream. Not having any texts, we needed leeway in introducing ideas and new forms. When the class began, Marty led off, introducing me in Japanese and English, and then turned the class over to me, and I introduced Marty—in English. We had no handouts or texts, so we wrote everything on the chalkboard. Marty printed key words while I spoke, and I did the same for him when he took over. Then we stopped and had the class repeat in unison all words written on the board, repeating them until their pronunciation began to approximate standard American English. For a half hour, we drilled sounds and familiar phrases, mostly greetings and responses. Then we stopped the repetition in unison and went through the class student by student, calling each student by name and checking the student off as either advanced or beginner.

We explained that we were dividing the class into beginners and advanced or those with some English ability. Marty explained in his best Japanese, which amused and interested everyone; gaijin Japanese was often amusing. When we were sure they understood and approved, we divided the class according to our notes; and like the Pied Piper, Marty led off his half while I stayed in the room with mine.

I had prepared a dozen or so conversational gambits, questions and answers and greetings and responses, all of which I printed on the chalkboard. At Hartford, Dr. Kitchens and her crew had stressed the importance of using the International Phonemic alphabet, one that most closely approximates American-English pronunciation, instead of the twenty-six letters of the common alphabet, which often does *not* come close to modern American English. But we learned first thing that it would not work for our students. Because everyone could read English and had learned the vagaries of modern English orthography, spending time with the fifty or so symbols, one for each distinct sound, cost us time we did not have. I pronounced everything I wrote on the board, "trippingly on the tongue," and insisted the class repeat it every time. And in doing so, I violated a basic tenet of the Fries method: I spoke slowly and enunciated clearly, avoiding my own speech patterns. Again, it was a factor of time. The theory was good, but theory was based on daily classes, frequency of drill and practice. Our students had work schedules that did not permit such frequency. I theorized on my own: as they began to develop their hearing of English, my speaking would become my natural way of speaking. As I read off a line, I motioned for the class to repeat it after me, and then I would point to an individual to repeat the line several times. When everyone had repeated each of the phrases, I asked two students to speak to each other using the phrases and then another pair. The technique was to keep up a steady flow of question and response so that their ears became accustomed to the sounds of English. This meant moving about the class, waving arms, beating out the rhythm of the language, and intonation patterns, always keeping their attention, performing, joking, and praising. A few already had excellent English sounds, but most did not. However, in an hour and a half, I began to hear improvement in them all.

At the end of the period, I was exhausted, physically wrung out, partly because of the configuration of the classroom, from walking up and down the aisles and back and forth from chalkboard to the front row and back. The class was a classical European-style lecture hall with rows of desks on tiers arranged in a semicircle around a large lectern raised on a dais in front of the blackboard. At the beginning of the class, the students demonstrated a universal student tendency to avoid the front rows. After running up and down the terraced rows a few times, I asked them to move to the first two rows and occupy only the center section. I tried to explain in measure English phrasing that I could remain at the large lectern, but to create a conversational atmosphere, I thought it better that I approach each student and speak directly to him or her. It was, I understood, a teaching manner entirely new for them—for me as well. But they assumed I had been doing this for years and followed where e'er I went. Ninety percent of teaching conversation is performance, is showbiz. I learned that in my first class—only slightly less in conventional teaching. And in the years that followed I learned that a very large percent, if not ninety, of all teaching is performance.

I had planned to begin using substitution frames, conventional sentence patterns in which I could add or substitute new vocabulary to familiar patterns. But I decided to build about a dozen common conversational exchanges and ask them to copy them and memorize them. As Dr. Kitchens had preached, I made no attempt to translate them but suggested they use their dictionaries when in doubt. By having them discover the new vocabulary themselves, they would more likely make it their own. Mainly, I tried to use phrases that I could translate by acting out. I said they should memorize these phrases and practice them at home or at work. Finally, I asked how many had radios at home. When they all said they did, I suggested they listen to an Armed Forces Radio broadcast for at least one hour every day to help them become accustomed to hearing normal English—"not sensei English," I said—spoken at normal conversational speeds. Understanding in the beginning was not important.

When the class was over and they began leaving the room, each paused, bowed, and thanked me for teaching them. Each laughed at his inability to say the *l*'s in Gilliland. Three hung back in order to be the last, two whom I noticed had spoken the clearest and most fluent English. One was a young woman and the other a slightly older young man. The third man was standing and chatting softly to the young man. At last, there were only the three. The young woman motioned for the men to go ahead as one would have expected, since well-bred young women insist males go first—and less well-bred also insist that their betters go first, for everyone in Japan knows her place. But the two young men insisted she speak first. I was exhausted and eager to meet Marty and to stop at the Aka Dama, a nice beer joint we had found, and have a tall bottle of Asahi beer. A cool beer and the scratchy phonograph with old

Dorsey and Miller records would help us to unwind. If Marty were wound as tightly as I was at that moment, it would take two or three tall beers to unwind. I nodded and beckoned her to step forward. She was the age of the university students but was not wearing the white blouse and pleated navy-blue skirt they usually wore. Her hair was cut straight just below the ears with straight bangs, framing a perfectly round face with the classic Japanese slender nose and very narrow eyes. She bowed quickly and spoke in slow but precisely enunciated English.

"Thank you for the lesson tonight. I like it very much Mr. Gil i ran, Gillilan, excuse me my pronunciation. Your name is hard for Japanese." She smiled. "My name is Takehata Chieko. I speak a little English. I am graduate of Kobe Women's *Correge*, College. It is two-year college. I want to become good speaker English, *prease*. I like your teaching. It is very good, I think, for learning *conva sa shun*."

I tried to interrupt several times, but I could see she had worked up the courage to speak her speech and wouldn't be stopped. When she finished, I complimented her on her clear and accurate pronunciation and her command of the language.

"Ms. Takehata, I think you had very good teachers at the Kobe Women's College," I said.

"Sank you, Mr. Gill i land." She smiled, getting all the *l*'s properly. "I would very like to be intimate with you."

I swallowed hard and began, "Thank you again, Ms. Takehata. But may I correct your usage? You may say that you would like to be friends, or you would like to know me better, but it is not correct to use 'intimate' in that way, not in modern American English. The word 'intimate,' I believe, has a different meaning from what you want." She listened intently and said she did not understand.

I could see the taller of the two young men smile broadly as if he clearly understood the connotation that "intimate" carried. She thanked me again and then repeated my last suggestion about wanting to know me better. I asked her if she was attending Wakayama University. She said she was planning to take special classes later.

When she bowed again and left, I nodded to the two young men, and they came forward, but neither bowed in the formal way. Instead, one spoke up casually without hesitation as if he were accustomed to speaking with Americans.

"I am Yamagami, and this is my friend Madenokoji san, but we call him Made san for short. I wanted to say I enjoyed your class very much. I like your teaching method," he said. "It is not the Japanese way, and that is good."

I thanked him and complimented him on his English. "I don't think you need a conversation class, Yamagami san. Your English is nigh perfection," I said.

"*Nigh*? Does that mean near?" he asked with an ironic grin as if he knew I was using an archaic form on purpose.

"Yes, that was a test to see how well you know English." I smiled. "It is rather old fashioned, rather literary. You *are indeed* a good English speaker."

Made san said Yamagami was the best speaker of English of all his Japanese friends.

Yamagami, still smiling serenely, said, "We graduated Kyoto University last year, and now we are working in the management section of the Shin Fuso Steel works across the river. Do you know it?"

I said I had seen it, but I had never been across the river. "Are you sure that you want to attend the class? It may be a waste of your time," I said. "You are welcome to attend, if you wish"

"I would like to attend to hear American English. I think you have a good accent. It is easy to understand, but a little different from Pray san's accent, isn't it?"

As we walked out, I explained Pray was from California and I from Texas and that his accent was more like a standard American English, if there was such a thing. Marty was expecting me, I said, and they followed along.

Then he said, "I am like Ms. Takehata. I want to know you better. I have never had an American friend. May I call you Joe san? I can say Gilliland, but Joe san is much easier."

"Of course, Yamagami san. As I said to Ms. Takehata you are welcome to visit my house in the university housing, the *Daigakku kansha*."

When we met Marty I introduced them, and Marty urged them to come to see us. When we parted at the tram stop outside the university gate—the class was held on the gakku gei campus—we bowed *and* shook hands. I told Marty about Ms. Takehata's desire to "become intimate" with me. He agreed laughing; it was probably for the best I explained what intimate connoted and then suggested she probably already knew what it meant, being a graduate of Kobe Women's College. "She might have really meant what she said, Joe san," he said, "you old dog."

At the Aka Dama bar—literally Red Ball, a sobriquet for the national flag—we sat and drank our beer and discussed our classes and the feelings of success we were enjoying. The feeling I'd gotten from the students' responses and from my own energies elated me.

"That was my first class ever, but I never had a moment of stage fright," I said. "It felt like the most natural thing I have ever done. There's a lot of show business there, you have to be *on*, and I mean *on*, but it works, and I am exhausted. It's like running a mile in five minutes. I was exhausted when it was over, but I loved it."

I was ranting rapidly out of control, and Marty was smiling and then laughing, agreeing with me. "It was good, I agree, but not that good."

Back at the Grier's, I ranted on and on to Dot and then again to Louie when he came back from the country church, and they both listened. Marty explained I hadn't allowed the engine to idle since leaving class and teased that it was because one of the young women had announced she wanted to be "intimate with him."

"It happens," Dot said with heavy sarcasm.

The next morning after breakfast, a call from the business office at the university said that our house was ready and that we could move in anytime. We were overjoyed when the news came. I had begun to feel, and Marty more so, that we had stayed much too long with the Griers. I was restless to get into our own place, out from under Dot's protective wing, although there were, I found, compensations living there. The meals were excellent, our hosts bright and stimulating, always helpful, and Louie had a fine library crammed into the little study just off the entrance. I spent many hours those first weeks comfortably ensconced in a broken-down old easy chair, rereading *Desire Under the Elms* and *The Hairy Ape.* Our night class had broken the ice and we were under way. We were more eager to get started than ever, and being in our own place, with whatever inconveniences, seemed preferable to camping out with the Griers. When the news came that next morning, it was as a coda to the overture.

Neither of us imagined we would be living in such a sumptuous palace. As soon as we heard that it was ready, Marty and I rushed off for a look, mainly to see what we would need to set up housekeeping. One of the compensations for the delay and for living under Dot's wing was never having to plan a meal or worry about who would prepare it. We had no idea what we would need to get started or how well the house had been furnished. Dot and Louie joked about our bachelor life and how poorly we would fare on our own, but I was not in the least apprehensive, having managed well those months with Don in the Village. But when we saw the size of the house and the empty rooms devoid of any furniture except a small gas cooker in the kitchen and a tiny primitive ice box in the pantry—ice box, not refrigerator—we knew there would be some slim times ahead. Still, it was an adventure.

Greeting us when we reached the house were three university students who introduced themselves without the formal bows, which was a relief. All three spoke excellent English. Miki Tanaka, the shortest of the three, who appeared to be their spokesman, explained that President Itoigawa thought we might need help moving in, so he had asked them to do whatever they could to help. Tanaka san was at once the most fluent of the three and the most congenial. He told us his nickname was *Buru* or Bull, which he said was appropriate because people said he looked like a bulldog. Marty and I said it was a gross exaggeration. The other two, Kameoka and Nishikawa followed Miki and introduced themselves, speaking English almost as well as Miki. All three were for more relaxed and easily familiar than the young Christian students we had met at Dot and Louie's house. I assumed when Miki first introduced himself and explained their mission was to assist Marty and me that he had worked with Americans, possibly the military, in some capacity, and later on when I asked if he had, he said he had for a short time when he was in high school. All three had been regular listeners to the Armed Services Radio.

Itoigawa's anticipating our need for someone to answer questions and run errands was a stroke of genius, I felt. All three were second year students, probably twenty years old and virtual contemporaries of both Marty and me. While they were courteous, none seemed overly awed by our presence in Japan, as the students we had met at the Griers' house. I got the clear impression that all three were determined to speak perfect English.

They walked through the house with us asking if there was anything we needed, and said that the president had told them to inform the university business manager of any problems. At one point in our tour Miki said hesitantly, "I think this is a very strange house. It is not a Japanese-style house, and I don't believe it is an American-style house either. I think it is what a Japanese carpenter thinks an American house is like. It must be strange for you."

We laughed and agreed, but said emphatically that is was going to be very comfortable for us. I liked this young man immediately. He was bright, had a sense of humor, and knew how to talk without the forced formality and excessive politeness Japanese often seem to feel is necessary when first meeting foreigners. I told him I thought it was much too grand for two single young men, and Marty admitted that he had expected a small Japanese-style house with a garden. They agreed. Then Nishikawa said he believed this was a house for the foreign teacher before the war.

Neither Marty nor I were used to such refreshing candor from someone whom we had just met. We had not met anyone thus far who was so at ease or so frank from the very beginning. Only Yamagami san from my night class had been as relaxed as these three were, and I assumed it was our age that made them at ease.

There were a few items we would need immediately, such as a few chairs for the little English-style study. When Nishikawa asked if we would not need furniture for the dining room, Marty said we would eat Japanese style, using *zabuton* (large flat square cushions) and sitting on the floor. He laughed and said he thought that would be much too uncomfortable for Americans. I agreed.

"President Itoigawa said the university would buy furniture for all rooms, but I think that will cost too much. I think it is a good idea to follow Japanese style," he said.

We agreed but only in part. Marty explained that because the large rooms had new tatami mats on the floor, we should not use Western-style furniture in those rooms and they agreed, though they were surprised that we would not find the Japanese custom of sitting on the floor too uncomfortable. Marty explained how he had lived in Tokyo just after the war and had learned a lot about Japanese customs, which he added was one of the reasons he had returned to Japan. We admitted, however, that the little English-style study with its built-in shelves and desk would need chairs and lamps. Then Nishikawa—he preferred we call him by his nickname, Saigo--then Saigo asked if we planned to get a maid and someone to cook our meals. I said we would have to think about it and explained that most Americans, single men teachers particularly, were not accustomed servants unless they were rich, which we were not.

"A cook is a good idea," I said. "I don't think Pray san would like my cooking, and I probably wouldn't care for his."

It took us no time to move in and claim our rooms, Marty taking the room on the southeast corner of the house, while I the one on the northwest corner, the room we called the refrigerator, or the *aisu bokusu*, when winter came. Later that day, Mr. Sato, the university's business manager, came by and discussed the items we said we needed. At first, he apologized for not speaking English and then for not having everything ready for us when we moved in. He explained that no one knew what furniture we would need and that the university would have the furniture made for us to our specifications.

He spoke slowly in an effort to make sure we followed him, and even I was able to understand most of what he said. The president had told him that Marty's Japanese was quite good, but we could tell that treating with foreign instructors, two Americans *aka chan*, was an entirely new experience for him and we tried as much as was possible to follow Japanese rules of etiquette in order to make it easier for him. In the hierarchical system of the university, his being an administrator gave him a degree of status, though not as much as he might have in an American institution where the teaching faculty—except distinguished professors or tenured faculty—do not have the prestige or power of deans and business managers. As Americans, victors *and* teachers, we automatically enjoyed considerable, albeit unearned status.

The room was suddenly silent, and Sato san seemed quite ill at ease, as if he had intruded on our privacy or as if he were about to ask a favor. Then he asked if we had hired a maid.

Marty told him no and asked if he thought it necessary pointing out we were not rich. He nodded and explained the *rusoban* system that required a person's domicile to be occupied at all times in case of fire—a frightening reality in Japan with its closely built tinderbox houses. Following a string of formal apologies, he ventured a suggestion: he had an older sister living with him, a widow in her sixties, who would like to apply for the position. It was not his place to praise her, he said, but she was capable and in good health. Marty nodded, thanked him, and asked how much we should pay her. He said she didn't need much, just her room, meals, and ¥1,000 a week (at the time, the dollar was worth ¥360). He knew how much we were paid and said it would not be too much, he thought. We agreed and asked when we could meet her. He bowed low and thanked us and said he would send her right over. Her name was Tonai san, but it would be fine if we called her Oba san, or Aunty, he said smiling. Obviously relieved that he had accomplished everything he had set out to do, he rose, bowed and thanked us, though we both had the distinct feeling it was we who should be thanking him. We agreed to speak to her and thanked him. So began our housekeeping days.

Meeting Tonai san for the first time was one of the most exquisite experiences I can recall. She was very small, clad in a lovely kimono in very subdued shades of gray and blue; she looked her age, sixty-five, which she offered almost as soon as we met. One of the first things she did was to apologize for not speaking any English and to say she did not believe she could learn the language. Marty patiently explained she would not need to because he spoke some Japanese and I was learning to speak it. Then he said one of her jobs as Oba san was to teach us to speak better Japanese. When she laughed at the idea we knew she was the right person for us.

The next day, with Oba san's help, we were completely moved in and had even hired a cook, an older woman whom we would call "Obaa san," the Japanese word for grandmother. She came to us highly recommended, having worked as a cook at the Brazilian Embassy in Tokyo in the early days. She was quite elderly, though she claimed to be in her early sixties; we later learned that her *daughter*, a retired Catholic nun living in Hokkaido, was sixty-five.

Obaa san was a fitting name, Tonai san said, telling me in confidence shortly after the old lady moved in that she, Obaa san, was old enough to be *her* mother. Marty and I not only found ourselves in charge of a staff, but we also discovered we had become the care providers of a human artifact of the old Japan. That she could shop for the best bargains and could cook, there was no doubt. We never complained about the food she served, and our bills at the *nikku-ya* (butcher shop) and the *pan-ya* (bakery) were never out of line. But the two old ladies never really got along, Obaa san always assuming the prerogatives of age and status, cooks being traditionally superior to maids in the upstairs-downstairs world of service.

We had been in the house barely a week when day classes began at the university. I was never sure how Marty felt about his first day of classes, whether or not he was as anxious to get on with the business of teaching as I was. Though neither of us had ever taught a class until we walked into our night class, I don't recall either being anxious or uneasy. On the morning of our first classes, I recall only a mild case of stage fright, light frisson, a heightening of the senses that goes with moments of expectation. Don had told me how he always felt a wave of nausea before he walked on stage before an audience, and I had read about the fear that grips some teachers before they begin classes, how, even for experienced teachers, standing before a room filled with students, was analogous to performing on stage. Inoue sensei had said he would go with us to our first class and would introduce each of us to the students, and I was glad that he offered to say a few words to break the ice.

The English faculty had warned us that Japanese students differed drastically from American students. They were always reserved and less responsive, they said, but we should not be disappointed if we found it difficult at first to get them to respond. It was the custom in Japan. Tadokoro san, who had studied at Earlham College in Indiana before the war, said our students were accustomed to sitting quietly, never moving except to scribble notes. He told how wonderful he thought it was when he was an undergraduate at Earlham, to be able to address a professor in class, even to raise a question and disagree.

"You won't find that here at Wa Dai, Joe san. They are very bright, but they are shy, always afraid someone will ridicule them," he said. "When I first began to teach, I tried to imitate my American professors, but my students disapproved as did my colleagues. We hope you will not try to be like us."

The others agreed and added that Tanaka, Kameoka, and Nishikawa—whom they all knew—were not typical of the kind of student we would find in our classes.

When we arrived that morning, several members of the English faculty were already in the faculty commons, standing around with Dean Iwasaki, who had joined them to wish us luck on our first day. Dean Iwasaki, one of the most dignified and scholarly gentlemen I ever met, spoke a few words of greeting in Japanese *and* English, saying how happy he was that Wa Dai now had two young American teachers. He bowed and wished us luck. We sipped cups of rich green tea and accepted everyone's best wishes. I realized then how important it was for the university to again have two foreign instructors; it represented a return to normal conditions, and I felt at that moment I was part of something important. Echoing Tadokoro's comments, Inoue had warned Marty and me not to expect the students to respond as willingly as students in the States; he regretted that Japanese students were unused to speaking out in class, but he assured us they would be polite, perhaps too polite. Just before nine o'clock, the sensei and I walked together to my classroom and stood waiting outside while the students filed in, each bowing quickly as he passed. He had planned to say a few words to my students and would introduce Marty in his class immediately after. As we stood there waiting for everyone to file in and take a seat, he reminisced briefly about his first day before a classroom of gakku sei and admitted he had been petrified that first day. When we walked in, the entire class rose and bowed, waited for Inoue and me to return their greeting, after which they all sat quickly and quietly in their seats. While he made his short statement, first in English and then in Japanese, the students sat at complete attention. I could understand a little as he explained I was their instructor of conversational English and was a recent graduate of the University of Texas; he told them to give me their full attention, to speak when they were spoken to, and not be shy or afraid of making mistakes. "You must take chances and not to be ashamed of making errors or mispronouncing words," he said. He paused and then turned and bowed his head quickly and extended his hand, fingers closed, palm flat, pointing me in the direction of the lectern.

As I stepped up on the platform and stood there looking down on their faces, the old cliché of the inscrutable Orient came to mind. Their faces appeared frozen and expressionless. Row after row of dark navy-blue uniforms with an occasional white shirt in the midst stretched before me. Inoue sensei moved to the door and paused, waiting for me to begin.

I thanked the sensei for his remarks and then turned and said, "Good morning," which they repeated loudly and clearly.

"You all speak very good English!" I said, looking surprised. There was a moment of silence followed by a burst of laughter. They had grasped my irony. I was off and away. I began by explaining hand gestures I would be using: raising one hand or two hands palms up meant that they should repeat what I had just said, lowering the hands palm down meant they should listen or remain silent. When I pointed at someone, I explained, I was not being rude, but only asking the person to repeat or answer my question. The gesture I would use for requesting an answer was moving my hand, palm up, and pointing to myself. Inoue slipped out as I explained. I realized then that I had reached another level—I was alone with my class of university students.

We practiced saying "good morning" and "how are you?" Then I printed several sentence patterns on the blackboard, conversational gambits from the beginning lessons found in most conversational guides. At first, their response was scattered and ragged. But by placing my cupped hand behind my ear, I let them know they were not repeating vigorously enough. When their responses came back full and loud, I applauded and said "Good! Thank you," which they echoed loud and clear, and I jumped with a start, acting shocked. A ripple of laughter spread through the room, and I knew then that the icy reserve was beginning to thaw. Dr. Kitchen had preached that our first priority was to appear relaxed, establish rapport, and, most of all, to avoid an authoritarian teaching mode. Not a difficult task for someone who had never adopted such habits. Already, I could feel in their spontaneous laughter and their smiles that whatever I was doing was beginning to work.

I went to the board and wrote my name in large capital letters and pronounced it.

"My name is Gilliland, Joe Gilliland," I said. "If you can say Gilliland, then you do not need this class." I waited, heard a few chuckles, soft mutterings across the aisles, and then more chuckles as translations passed along from one to another. Then I asked the class to repeat my name. They tried, but what I heard was "Gi ri ran." I cupped my ear with my hand and gestured with the other for them to repeat. It came louder but was "Gi ri ran" again.

"I think you misunderstood. This is what you said." I went to the board and wrote the katakana[6] for Gi ri ran do and said, "I am sorry, but this is what you said."

---

[6]   Japanese may be written in four different forms of script: romaji, kanji, hiragana, and katakana. Romaji is the Latin alphabet and works well only for non-Japanese. Kanji is the pictographic system borrowed from Chinese and is used both phonetically and pictographically. The latter two are phonetic systems, the first a cursive script used for Japanese words, verb endings, prepositions, and forms for which the Kanji is too cumbersome. Katakana is used most often for foreign words or phrases adopted directly from the original language and rendered more or less in the original. Thus, 7^XW] approximates Gilliland.

They laughed again and nodded. I pointed to my name and repeated Gilliland slowly. Then I wrote a number of words on the board with *l*'s: *lily, like, listen, little, lazy, love, loose, lovely,* and then in large capitals, *LALAPALOOZA.* During the war in the Pacific, GIs had used "lalapalooza" as a sign or countersign to catch Japanese infiltrators; and when I heard the first sounds come from the class, I understood why they had done so. It came out "raraparooza." A low moan rose through the class. I demonstrated placing the tip of my tongue behind the dental ridge and made the sound *la,* signaling the class to repeat. I heard mostly *ra.* They laughed, and I laughed with them. We tried again and a few genuine *la*s came forth. I left the podium and began walking up and down the aisles, as I had done in the night class, repeating the *la*s as notes on a scale, and they began to sing along with me. Once back on the podium, I turned and applauded them for their effort. Their faces seemed to come alive with satisfaction. "Good!" I said, and they came back with a loud "Good!" I jumped, and again, they laughed. It was really performance after all, not an unpleasant feeling. I followed the *l* drill with other consonants and vowels, walking up and down the aisles, pointing to individuals, applauding even the near misses.

Then I wrote a short exchange on the board: "What is your name? My name is _____. How are you today? I'm fine, and you? Thank you, I'm fine too." They repeated each line as I guided them through it, and then I stepped down from the podium and walked up the middle aisle, pointing at students randomly. I got full cooperation, although I had to signal for some to speak louder. When I pointed at two students and asked for them to speak the lines to each other, they immediately responded.

When I pointed to a young man at the back and gestured for him to speak to me, he stood up and bowed and said, "Excuse me. What is your name, sir?" He was the first to break the mold and add words. I answered. Before he sat down, he said, "Where are you from?" The class turned toward him and stirred. He was stepping out of the pattern into new territory. He was daring to be different. I had an ally.

"I am from Texas. Where are you from?"

"I am from Sakai, near Osaka," he said. This was good—a breakthrough on the first day. One student refused to follow form, and the sky did not fall. I wanted to shake his hand, thank him right there, and had I been in a class at home, I might have; but I had learned to move slowly, that too much praise could embarrass him and force him back into a normal reticence. Instead, I complimented his English and asked him where he had learned to speak it.

He bowed quickly and said, "Thank you, Mr. Giriran. I studied English in high school."

"You had a good teacher," I said and moved on.

The next student repeated the new pattern, and so it went until we had only ten minutes left. I thanked them and said they had done well. Then breaking Dr. Kitchens' rule again, I spoke even more slowly, enunciating each word carefully, saying that we would try to leave ten minutes every day for questions, any kind of question.

"Who will be first?" I asked.

There was total silence. I took a chance and called on the bold student at the rear of the class who had been the first to depart from the script. "Mr. Watanabe, do you have a question?"

He rose and said loudly, "Yes, *sah*. Do you speak Japanese?"

"I speak a little Japanese," I said, emphasizing *little* and pointed to the word I had written earlier.

"Can you speak Japanese now?" he said smiling. The class chuckled. They recalled Inoue's words that I would only speak English.

I said, "Inoue sensei said I should speak only English, but I will try." I looked over my shoulder as if checking to see if the sensei was there, then I said as clearly as I knew how, "*O-benjo wa doko ni arimasu ka?*"

There was another rumble of laughter. Borrowing one of the common phrases from the army's beginners guide to Japanese, I had asked where the bathroom was, assuming correctly that Japanese gakku sei humor was as toilet-oriented as American student humor. They laughed again and looked at Watanabe san and then to me and back again.

Watanabe, still standing, answered in English, "It is outside."

I bowed and said, "*Dom arigatoo gozaimasu*," making a mad dash to the door. The loud laughter let me know I had them and, they had me, and I had made it through the hour.

At that moment, the bell rang. The class rose and bowed, and when I bowed, they filed out, several stopping at the podium to thank me just as the evening students had done. Watanabe san stopped and said, "I like your teaching, Mista Giriran," and laughed. I thanked him and returned his bow. As I stood there watching them leave the room, I felt relief and joy that everything went well. Making them laugh was easy and relaxed all formality, destroyed the tension.

If I had mugged, pretending to be shocked at their sharp replies, it was to make them relax and to enjoy the experience. I did not teach them anything they didn't know already, but I began to erode the natural barriers, convinced that I *could* teach, convinced that I could do whatever I needed to do to help them learn or rather want to learn.

Back at the house, Marty and I compared our triumphs but admitted that future classes would require more planning, and we agreed that we had begun at least to bridge the so-called cultural gap, that our fears of rigid traditional classroom procedures inhibiting our students' willingness to participate were groundless. I wasn't sure, I said, whether I had gotten them to cross over into my territory or I had crossed into theirs. Marty said perhaps we had met them somewhere in between. We knew from everything we had learned at Hartford, and from our own stumbling efforts to learn a foreign language in college, that two hours a week was not enough time to make real progress. They needed more exposure than the two class meetings, especially for those who wanted to learn to speak English well. Not all were as eager to work as hard as others or even believed they needed English, but since it was required, they would take it and do the best they could.

Wakayama U. Keisai students with English faculty

Several students like Miki, Saigo, and Kameoka clearly wanted to master conversational English. With this in mind, I suggested we have open house on Tuesday and Thursday afternoons, Marty hosting one day, I the other. He said he was on the verge of suggesting it himself. We would invite both groups both days and would encourage everyone to speak English, though at first we understood it was better to lay down no rules and simply make everyone feel welcome. Marty added his condition that he be allowed to use Japanese if it came naturally. The open house would extend our teaching beyond the classroom and partially, at least, fulfill our mission by allowing students to ask questions about our beliefs and about ourselves. They had already shown great curiosity about our families and the places we lived.

In the weeks that followed, classes continued to improve as I outlined lesson plans in greater detail and prepared mock conversations that stressed pronunciation problems and introduced new vocabulary. These became more structured and less spontaneous, particularly the pronunciation drills and substitution frames. I regretted the loss of spontaneity and tried to return from time to time to the more open-ended and ad-libbing method, but it was exhausting. We had no copy machine, no way to duplicate materials, no texts or printed guides at that stage. Fortunately, most students preferred an unrehearsed responsorial method and would take part willingly. But I knew that a number of students were not taking part, allowing less inhibited and more interested classmates to carry the class. It was same apparently the world over.

Later, I began by borrowing passages from their reading assignments in other English classes. *Tom Sawyer* in the freshman classes and the *Autobiography of Benjamin Franklin* in the sophomore classes provided a framework of both vocabulary and subject matter. I would "translate" passages of Twain and Franklin into contemporary colloquial English to give them a contemporary English conversational tone. Dr. Kitchens would not have approved my using literary sources because they did not follow "natural" conversational usage, but I thought they were as natural as the phrases I had invented, and it put their academic English into a street-worthy context. I used these passages only when there was a lull in the normal exchange, and after the novelty of having *Girirando* in class wore off, we had lulls that needed filling.

Usually after the opening warm-up, we would launch into Q & A time. I would use their questions as a basis for the sentence patterns and substitution frames. Sometimes a student would write on the blackboard a question concerning something he or she had read in the newspaper. We would note new vocabulary, repeat each of the words in context. Then I would go down the rows, having each repeat the question and the student opposite answer the question. If the new word was too difficult to pronounce, I would break it down on the blackboard, and then we would all repeat it, emphasizing the intonation pattern, in and out of context, basing the markings for stress and pause on the schemes learned in the Kitchens' classes.

Having no formal text worked as long as I was able to hold their interest with new patterns. It was not always easy and required frequent injections of humor or personal stories suggested by their questions about the sentences we were working on. For weeks they were too shy to ask me to repeat a difficult word. Interrupting a sensei required great courage, and it took time to convince them I expected and welcomed questions. Inoue and the other English teachers had warned of this. But after a few weeks, even shy ones began to catch on and would interrupt to ask meanings of a words or phrases.

While telling a story, I would write key words on the blackboard, pause, and lift my hand, palm up. They would repeat the word, fixing the sound in their minds. Or I would stop the story, repeat a sentence frame, raise my hand, and have them repeat. Then I would continue. The story became a given, and if I failed to "digress"—a word they learned to pronounce early in the term—they would insist I "make digression."

One day after we had been working long on pronunciation drills, one of the bolder students raised his hand—I had insisted that interruptions were permissible—and asked, "Mr. Giriran, please, will you have digression now?"

The class started and then smiled. I bowed and said in the mock seriousness of a samurai movie—I had told them of my fondness for the *chambara* samurai films—"*domo arigatoo gozaimashita.*" The expression *chambara,* came from *cham cham, bara bara,* supposedly the sound of swords clashing—*cham cham*—and the sound of samurai running across wooden bridges. That simple act of teaching the teacher an essential amused them and brought us another step closer because they had learned how to avoid boring drills. While the digression had not been a lesson plan offered by Kitchen and crew, I began to use it regularly, following it with conversational gambits borrowed from the stories, always printing new words on the chalkboard behind me. The first time I heard a student use a phrase from a story, I knew I had made a mark. Several times, I expanded on a story that I had used in one of the open-house sessions.

At the end each class session, especially the good ones, I would be completely drained and would rush to the faculty lounge for the cup of green tea that was always ready when I got there. The poor sessions, those where the repetition grew weary, stale and flat or the responses were slow in coming, were even more exhausting than the good because they drained me psychologically as well as physically. When the good things worked, I was impelled and moved on to the next; but when the bad things failed, my mind was always burdened with self-doubt and questions about what went wrong, thus I would leave the class feeling frustrated. The word got around that our classes were entertaining and exciting. I would hear students making remarks about something Pray had said in class, and he would hear in his classes things students would say about my classes.

At first, I was worried when Inoue sensei told us he was jealous that our students appeared to enjoy our classes so much more than his, worried he might mean my classes lacked substance and that I was on stage performing more than teaching. The alternative was to avoid the digressions and jokes, but I was reluctant to move to a rigidly prepared script. Both Marty and I needed the relaxed atmosphere and the classes' participation. We depended on their willingness to follow. It would have been pedagogical suicide to succumb to the traditional way of teaching. When Inoue insisted he was complimenting us, not criticizing, I stopped worrying and continued as before.

"We like what you do," he said. "It is sad, but we can't do it. Japanese teaching methods are too formal, too dull, I think."

It was always like that. Inoue supported almost everything we did or tried to do and rarely found fault.

Our open houses went so well I was convinced we were accomplishing more with them than in the classroom. Sometimes the large room would be packed and would overflow into the hall and the little study. Unlike our colleges and universities, Wa Dai had no convenient gathering places for students to meet informally on or off campus. They, of course, had dormitories and no doubt had rooms where they could meet, but I never saw students just hanging out in the vicinity of either the liberal arts or the economics campus. Every Tuesday and Thursday afternoon, between three and five, crowds of students filled our large tatami room and crowded into the small English study where they would leaf through our magazines and photo albums—I had brought the one Aleman and the guys in C Company had seen.

The open house became the most important part of our so-called mission to the students; the simple act of inviting the students to the house broke the traditional barriers between student and professor. In a more practical sense, the open houses helped our classroom teaching by furnishing us with ideas for conversational lessons. And I suppose the absence of a text force us to be liberated and free to invent. When the discussions grew heated, in Japanese as well as English, you would see them whip out pocket dictionaries looking up new words and then sigh deeply over something one of us had declared. While the major topic of conversation was American movies, it was surprising how quickly they picked up on issues in American politics and how familiar they were with the names of congressional and political party leaders.

Once, Oba san complained that they ate too many of our *simbe* (rice cakes), and she insisted Marty and I couldn't afford to buy all the cookies and fruit they were eating. Dr. Shacklock had told us to deduct such expenses when we mailed in the salary we received from the university, but I wasn't sure these activities would qualify since no one ever mentioned the Bible or the church at these gatherings. The question became moot when they began bringing boxes of simbe or sacks of sweet *mikan* (tangerines) that Wakayama Prefecture was famous for. Oba san, we later learned, had scolded several of the boys, telling them they were eating too much, that the two sensei couldn't afford to feed them. There was even an occasional package of green tea in the offering. Oba san had become far more the aunty than we realized; they listened to what she said. What's more, the students loved her.

Chapter 17

Class Time

Compared to the other short-termers, both Marty and I felt we were not doing well by our obligation to the mission program. Although Marty corresponded regularly with his roommate, Dave Reed, who was working near Nagasaki we rarely saw any of the J3s who came over with us. Dr. Shacklock never made demands on any of the J3 group, always telling us we should let our personal convictions direct us. Marty, Burt, and I were the only short-termers with mission assignments that separated us from mission schools and senior missionaries. Our only missionary contacts, Dot and Louie Grier, rarely if ever commented on our activities or lack of activity in the program. We had learned at Harford that our mission was to teach and set examples by living a Christian life and was not to proselytize. Few of us had attended seminary; even fewer considered themselves future pastors. We assumed that those who had attended seminaries and who had received their degrees, were about their proper tasks. Dr. Shacklock and the others at Hartford told us again and again that any commitment to act was our own, and for the majority, even the seminarians, commitment grew from a personal desire for social action consistent with the idea of reconciliation or reconstruction. When I voiced my concerns to Louie, he would listen, offer a sympathetic ear, and when I was free would take me with him to rural parishes where he met with pastors and their flocks; but I was simply a body, my lack of fluent Japanese making me inadequate for any substantive task. I always felt I was along for the ride.

Early in my first semester at Wa Dai I met with the Student YMCA, the student Christian group having no affiliation with the International YMCA, to discuss finding and furnishing a regular meeting place and reading room. When we first met at Louie's house, we talked of building a small library of basic Christian writings, and I told the group then that I could use my Wa Dai salary to lay the foundation for that library. The nominal leader of the group, Hayashiguchi san, handed me a list of twenty or twenty-five books they hoped to buy someday, which I ordered through the Kyodan and suggested they use my office on the liberal arts campus for a meeting place. I had an office on both campuses, which I rarely used, preferring students to call on me at the house than meet in the cavernous space. They were astounded that I would relinquish it, but I explained I also had an office on the economics campus, and that I used the liberal arts office only once or twice a week. Dean Iwasaki, I told them, had agreed the YMCA was a good use for the space. Nothing we requested within reason was denied us by the university administration, so the office became the Christian Students Center. I met with them from time to time for tea and cakes and whenever they wished to consult with me about the organization. Since I spoke little Japanese and they were reluctant or unable to discuss religious matters in English, I was able to do little in the way of religious instruction even if I had been qualified to do so. This they understood completely.

Early on, when I explained that my Japanese was too poor for any instruction or Bible study, Hayashiguchi san smiled, as did the others in the room that day, and said they all understood, and I suspected they regarded my inability to teach Bible was not entirely a lack of fluent Japanese. In effect, I made it easy for them, anticipating their request that I not attempt to teach or preach. What they meant by that polite understatement was that they preferred I *not* instruct. However, my conscience still troubled me, though later, Dr. Shacklock reasserted his earlier admonitions: we should do only what we believed we *could* do best and hinted that in my case it would probably be better were I *not* to venture forth into Bible study.

CONFESSION: Truth was I spent far more time writing and thinking of Bettie than I did my so-called mission. Her letters were filled with her thoughts and experiences in Puerto Rico and were more than I could have wished for. The news occasionally disturbed me, made me fearful and often a little jealous, spurring long, detailed responses from me that apparently worked, for it was rare when a week passed without at least two good letters from her.

Almost as important as my duties in the classroom was the work I did with Inoue sensei on Eugene O'Neill. All that autumn, twice a week, the sensei would visit the house, and we would discuss O'Neill's plays, first *Desire Under the Elms* and later *Emperor Jones* and *The Hairy Ape*. At first, he was concerned only that he find the best Japanese equivalent for the slang or stage idioms that I tried to explain were either extremely dated, before my time, or were O'Neill's invention. His highly effective language, I thought, was not necessarily authentic New England American slang but whatever it was, it worked. Essentially a poet, the language was theatrical and not intended to be an exact recording of naturalistic colloquial speech; and the sensei agreed, assuring me that it was his intention to render it into a Japanese approximating O'Neill's intentions. When I would apologize for my shortcomings he assured me our conversations were helping him to clarify most of his questions. When our discussions touched larger universal themes, I would return again and again to certain passages to make sure I understood what the playwright was driving at. We had read *Desire Under the Elms* in Dr. Steffans' survey of world literature but had not dug as deeply as Inoue insisted we do. It was the first time I had ever probed so thoroughly any work of literature. The pleasures I found in these sessions would be shaping factors in my decision to study English on my master's, though at the time the pleasure of participating in the process was sufficient reason for doing it. At one point I considered writing to Guy Steffans, telling how I was "helping" my chairman Inoue sensei translate *Desire Under the Elms*, how the world lit class had been of great help in the enterprise, but I did not. For one thing, I lacked the nerve to present myself as a collaborator on such an enterprise. I would, however, one day have an opportunity to tell Steffans face to face how it had gone.

My Japanese study was chiefly limited to Tonai san's corrections and an occasional lesson from a woman Louie Grier recommended. Because the text my instructor used was in the phonetic hiragana with increasing numbers of kanji as the lessons progressed, I felt I was really progressing. I moved slowly from one lesson to the next and gradually picked up a conversational-level Japanese that got me through most social situations although I was never able to go much beyond polite small talk; surprisingly, I was beginning to read. For a long time, I felt guilty for not studying Japanese as Marty did. I envied his concentration and dedication, but I could not put aside my interests in literature. I told myself that those students who seemed as deeply interested in literature—American and Japanese--as I justified my interest. I wasn't, however, entirely neglectful. I read everything I could find in English about Japanese culture and religion, particularly about Buddhism, and when I was able to find English translations of major Japanese writers recommended by Tanaka or other students, I read them. The Wakayama University library furnished me with a work in English by a Mrs. Rhys Davids called *Manual of Buddhism for Advanced Students*, and Professor Taniguchi, who taught religion and philosophy and who spoke fluent English, directed me to other readings. Taniguchi sensei visited Marty and me several times and invited us to his home in Hashimoto, not far from Wakayama.

Early in November, a fateful conversation with Miki Tanaka forced me to take another tack in my journey through books and ideas. He asked me what I thought of William Faulkner, who had won the 1949 Nobel Prize for literature. I said I had read "That Evening Sun Go Down" and the novel *Sanctuary* but admitted I had read little else, and I suggested he check out *A*

Rose for Emily and Other Stories that I had seen in the Wa Dai library in the little Armed Services Edition. He was reading a collection of stories at the time, forcing me to dig out the university's ASE anthology. I read *Sanctuary*, probably for the same reasons the character Ensign Pulver had annotated his copy of *God's Little Acre*, though I found *Sanctuary* far more substantial than its so-called X-rating suggested. Miki had asked about my opinion of Faulkner because he was writing a short article about the Nobel Prize for *Orange*, the English Speaking Society's newspaper. Our discussion of "That Evening Sun" and "A Rose for Emily" was almost as demanding and as stimulating for me as Inoue's questions about *Desire Under the Elms*. Miki was surprisingly familiar with Southern attitudes toward race and family and had no difficulty following my remarks on the subject that were drawn from having been raised in East Texas. The thought occurred to me at the time that I would relish an opportunity to teach the writings of Faulkner along with Fitzgerald and even O'Neill.

I couldn't help it. My interests kept shifting back to Trilling's *The Liberal Imagination* and to all the reading I felt I had missed along the way. At first, I suffered hours of guilt and a few sleepless nights for not getting on with the business at hand, that is, improving my teaching of conversational English. But ever since New York City, I had felt a need to catch up on all that I had missed in the world of arts and ideas. It was like a compulsion, and ironically it was Miki who prodded me to begin exploring it all again. The broader mandate of the J3 program, I rationalized, was set forth in the original idea conceived as the "Fellowship of Reconstruction." The original forty or so short-term missionaries were to go out "to teach English and serve as leaders in a variety of activities."[7] In that sense, I believed—finally—my digressions into O'Neill with Inoue sensei and my long discussions about American writers fulfilled at least in part that mandate. Several other students were reading modern American writers and were steering me deeper and deeper into the canon. Marty had admitted quite early that he had only a passing interest in and little knowledge of the main currents of American literature. During the open houses, a group would form around me to discuss their readings of writers such as Steinbeck and Sinclair Lewis. How they came to read them I had no idea. Some had found translations while others, like Miki, were attempting to read them in English. I discovered that I was doing for them what I had been doing for Inoue with regard to O'Neill, not translating so much as interpreting and explaining what I believed to be the essential themes

---

[7]   William Mensendiek, ed., *With Uncommon Kindness: The Story of the 1948 J-K3s*, 1990.

and ideas. I was beginning my study of modern American drama and fiction and at the same time learning how to teach it.

When Miki submitted a short essay on Faulkner's achievement for the, *The Orange*, I was pleased, first that it was well written and second that it contained language and ideas that came up in our discussions. Although his major was economics, literature was a serious secondary interest. In Japan, businessmen, engineers, physicians, people of all professions, often develop wide interests in the arts and sciences independent of their occupation or calling. (Since beginning this memoir, I have corresponded with Tanaka san via e-mail and have, some fifty years after our discussions of Faulkner and Steinbeck, been able to offer advice regarding his translation of *Land Below the Wind* and *Three Came Home* by Agnes Newton Keith). When I found that the university's library was well stocked with standard editions of nineteenth-century British and American writers and a smattering of twentieth-century writers in Armed Services Editions--left behind when the army moved out of Wakayama in the early years of the occupation--I was able to fill in the gaps in my reading while encouraging my students to look into these works as well as popular fiction.

I often visited Dot or Louie, hoping to borrow a book from Louie's well-stocked library or to find Dot willing to talk about her reading. She usually began by chiding me for not studying Japanese more assiduously or for not attending meetings of the Christian students' group, but after her initial reprimand, she would relent and allow me to ask what she was reading for pleasure and would admit that there was more than one way to fulfill an obligation. Louie also agreed that there was more than one way to reach out. Approaching students through secular literature was not entirely outside the realm of our mission. Such rationalization from Louie made me feel much better.

My bookshelves in the study were slowly filling. Before leaving New York I ordered a number of books through the Methodists that I thought might help me at the university, works by major American writers: *Complete Poems of T. S. Eliot, Complete Poems of Carl Sandburg, Mizener's* biography of Scott Fitzgerald, *The Far Side of Paradise, The Selected Stories,* and a two-volume text-book anthology of American lit. I also located several books on English grammar and the teaching of English, the most interesting of which was Charles Fries' *American English Grammar* (1940). the work that had been the foundation for his later work on the teaching of English as a second language. Though I was becoming book-obsessed, I still had not made the logical connection between my bibliolatry and a life in teaching. In his book

The Pleasures of Academe, James Axtell, professor of humanities at William and Mary, wrote that "the one magnet" that draws people into teaching the humanities is the love of books, not just reading, but the love of books themselves. I agree. Then, however, I did not see the connection between my own love of books and scholarly ventures. Early in my high school years, I began to collect used books and to build a library, mostly books on science; and all the time I was in the army, I continued to collect books, even when I had to lug many extra pounds in an already heavy duffel bag. Years later, when I was in graduate school, I discovered lines of Chaucer from another prologue that spoke my feelings exactly to the letter:

> *On bokes for to rede I me delyte,*
> *And hem yeve I feyth and ful credence,*
> *And in myn herte have hem in reverence . . .*

Books were indeed my delight, and while I might take exception with Chaucer's claim to have full faith and full credence in everything they say—Chaucer's tongue was deep in his cheek on that line—I did hold books in great reverence and continued my collecting while I was in Japan. At the time, I did not relate a wish to teach to my love of books. Teaching English conversation was only a job that I was beginning to like very much; my love of reading was one thing, teaching another. The connection between books and teaching would come later.

Marty's case was quite different. He was well on his way to becoming a master of Japanese culture, studying to become a formal tea master, studying the Japanese harp, the koto and more. My reading, I believed, was for one purpose, my own pleasure. Time, "the subtle thief of youth," had stolen on its wing my four and twentieth year, and I was still in a quandary as to what my real life's work should be or would be or even could be; I was sure it was not conversational English. What possible relevance could Mrs. Bennett's anxieties for her unmarried daughters have to do with my teaching conversational English to Japanese university students? At various times as an undergraduate, my love of reading almost proved my undoing, and it was only when my reading, rather my choice of books, coincided with the courses I was taking that I did well as far as grades were concerned. Likewise, I began to suspect that this obsession was the chief distraction from my purpose as a J3.

A few days after my twenty-fourth birthday, near the end of October, a package of books from Jane arrived. I was hoping she had sent *The Liberal Imagination.* Instead, I found Frank Swinnerton's *The Georgian Literary Scene* and Edmund Wilson's *Classics and Commercials*. I had never heard of Frank Swinnerton and assumed his book must be about the Southern agrarians or the "fugitives," whom I had read about somewhere. I knew there was a revival of literary creativity in the South; Faulkner, Penn Warren, Allen Tate, John Crow Ransom, and, more recently, Truman Capote were all Southerners and were the focus of considerable attention. I had no idea that Georgia even had a literary scene, but then there was a lot I didn't know about writing in America or anywhere else. Of course, the literary scene referred to in the title referred to George V of England and writers, such as Joseph Conrad, Ford Maddox Ford, Henry James, Virginia Woolf, H. G. Wells, and others. I had read some of these authors but had never thought of them as *Georgians.*

It was the second book that made a difference: Edmund Wilson's *Classics and Commercials*, subtitled: *A Literary Chronicle of the Forties*. It would have almost the same impact on me as Trilling's *Liberal Imagination*. I knew of Wilson as editor of Fitzgerald's *Crack-Up* and the unfinished novel *The Last Tycoon* and as the author of the scandalous *Memoirs of Hecate County*, but I had no idea that he was, in 1950, considered America's most most respected man of letters. *Classics and Commercials* was a revelation. A year before, this collection of essay reviews would have meant little, but not now. Under the collective guidance of Jane, Betty Ruth, Pat and my friend, Dick Glover, and because of my own desire not to be left out in the cold, I had read many of the writers and works he reviewed during the 1940s. In those early days, I could admit without embarrassment that I read to avoid the stigma of illiteracy as much as I had read for pleasure and diversion; but as I read more and acquired a certain glibness in discussing what I had read, I began to claim I was reading for more profound reasons, and in part it was true. I've said earlier that the year in New York City was like a year of postgraduate study in the arts and humanities, perhaps even more valuable than a comparable time enrolled in seminars and lectures. I would learn later that I was not the only college graduate to discover that he had passed through college only to come out a semiliterate at best. In spite of the great variety of courses I had taken, a few with some success, I became aware of how little I really knew. My good fortune was my association with Jane, Pat, Betty Ruth and Don. Night classes at the New School had helped, but the seminar on West Eighty-First Street helped the most.

Wilson's reviews covered a wide range of reading. In each essay, he alluded to and commented on a world of ancient and modern literature that he assumed his reader knew sufficiently well in order to understand and appreciate his allusions. They were not dropped to impress the reader or to solidify his reputation but to give breadth and depth to his critical observations. Partly because of his emphatic style uncluttered by polite or judicious qualifications or the puddery of critical jargon and partly because of his genuine erudition, Wilson's style spoke with authority. From the moment I read him, I felt as if he was aiming the reviews directly at me, convinced that his ideas deserved consideration. For example, in the essay called "The Boys in the Back Room," he treated the works of James M. Cain, John O'Hara, John Steinbeck, and William Saroyan with high seriousness. These were writers I had read earlier for sheer entertainment, unaware that they had anything more to offer than absorbing plots and characters. Dick Glover had insisted I read Cain's *Serenade* after I had told him I'd read *Double Indemnity* and *The Postman Always Rings Twice*, racy adult novels with what we considered in those days explicit sexual scenes barely outside pornography. Wilson wrote seriously about Cain, taking time to analyze and to criticize his writing for adopting the marks of Hollywood. It was possible, I learned, to critique a work seriously noting its strengths without approving or disapproving—providing it adhered to some criteria. But I was appalled when I read the essay on O'Hara, an author I liked a great deal, especially *Appointment in Samara* and *Butterfield 8*. *Hope of Heaven*, which I had read not long after reading Bud Schulberg's Hollywood novel *What Makes Sammy Run*, had been a disappointment. Schulberg's novel was truer than O'Hara's relatively shallow *Hope of Heaven*. I had seen that for myself and understood the difference lay to a large extent on Schulberg's writing about Sammy from his life within the industry, while O'Hara's stemmed from his relatively short life as a screenwriter. Wilson cut away any pretense of discovering a redeeming literary quality when he stated simply that O'Hara "does not quite know what he is doing." It pleased me that a man like Wilson confirmed my view of O'Hara.

Wilson's reviews and critical essays appeared in magazines like *Esquire*, *New Republic*, *Nation*, and *New Yorker*—not all of them magazines with mass appeal, but neither were they scholarly journals or "little magazines" aimed at a highbrow coterie. His style was quite different from Trilling's more academic style. I had read similar reviews, perhaps even his reviews in magazines lying around Jane's apartment. His frankness and willingness to express his personal bias were refreshing, but most important, his lack of equivocation or any attempt at balance aimed at pleasing as wide an audience as possible, forced me to reexamine earlier conclusions I had drawn, and forced me to think, even disagree, but disagree from a base of knowing rather than an illusive taste. Wilson's reviews, in a very true sense, were a variation of McAllister's theme: "Education by irritation." His opinions were shaped by a politically liberal point of view as Trilling's were, but more important for me at the time was his range of allusion to works I had not read but had seen referred to time and again. These allusions would constitute my personal required reading list, for they offered me a key to a deeper and broader understanding, appreciation and pleasure.

I made up my mind that I would read something by every writer mentioned in the reviews, good or bad, mediocre or outstanding. I wanted to know what he knew, so I began a journal listing authors and works I would have to read. I had no clear purpose for doing this; all I wanted at the time was to increase my own capacity for enjoyment. I still have that copy of *Classics and Commercials* on my shelves along with practically everything Wilson published in book form, often in duplicate. Like the Gideons, who pass out little green New Testaments on college campuses, I pass to students and younger colleagues works by Wilson I find in used bookstores. My copy of *CC* is dog-eared, spine sprung, and ragged from having been with me on many trips. To say that it changed my life as Trilling's great book did is an understatement many times over. It made a difference even though at the time I had no idea what that difference would be or that it would lead one day to my teaching literature and humanities.

I have often wondered how it might have been had they sent me to a mission school in Tokyo or Kyoto or Nagoya, or if I had been able to take up my post in Kaesong in Korea. I doubt that I could have ignored the mission school routines and persisted in my readings so easily. I am fairly sure I would have studied Japanese with more dedication. I cannot know for sure. But I am certain that having a clear routine within the scope of the J3 program, I might not have been able to carry on with my personal interests as I did. Marty and I both departed, I believe, from the intended path of the original program: he into a penetrating study of the art and culture of Japan like no one else in our group and I into a quest for deeper understanding of contemporary literature. Ironically, my meetings with Inoue sensei and our discussions of O'Neill were no longer confined to O'Neill's slang, but were concerned more with an inquiry into general cultural questions raised in the plays, opening up for me a way of seeing the plays I might never have seen. It was nothing like Dr. Steffans' class, where we hurried through Ibsen and Chekov and Hauptman in a week. Inoue and I spent months on *The Hairy Ape* and *Emperor Jones* and a year on *The Iceman Cometh*. Inoue was extremely well informed about American social mores, particularly about the world O'Neill portrayed; he seemed never to rest until he corroborated every detail. How I helped him gain further insight into these questions or how this knowledge influenced his translation or the notes he supplied in the translation, I'll can't say. When Inoue's translation of *Desire Under the Elms* came out, several students in the English Speaking Society on the economics campus told me Inoue sensei had acknowledged in his prefacing remarks my contributions to his effort. My contributions were, however, minuscule compared to his contribution to my own development as a student. Perhaps those hours closeted with him might have better been spent with my students in appropriate missionary activities. What those activities might have been I have no idea, even to this day; although I'm sure that fellow J3s like Dave Reed, Ben Sawada, or Paul Linde had no difficulty finding work more suited to their roles.

I was spending increasingly less time preparing for the classes and more time seriously looking into whatever Japanese authors I could find in English translation. My students found my interest in Japanese novelists Soseki and Akutagawa curious and were amazed that I had found in the Wa Dai library two novels written by an American expatriate named Shaw about Japanese soldiers in the Chinese campaign: *Mud and Soldiers* and *Rice and Soldiers*. When I asked Inoue and Tadokoro about these works, they admitted knowing them more as aberrations, Japanese literature written in English by an American living in Japan who considered himself a Japanese very much as had Lafcadio Hearn years earlier. There was nothing like them available in those days. The novels were poorly printed on cheap paper and had no publication date. I could not imagine their coming out in English during the war, and there was no indication that Japanese translations existed or that these were English translations of original Japanese. I've learned recently after reading Dowert's *Embracing Defeat* that in the years immediately after the war, occupation censors prohibited the publishing of Japanese works about the war, curiously even antinationalistic and antimilitaristic works. That was fifty years ago, and my memory of the works is cloudy, though I do recall Shaw's novels were frank, realistic works with a strong bias toward the common soldier, similar in that sense to Bill Mauldin's sardonic bias.

As my teaching conversational English continued to improve, or as students became more willingly conversant it understandably came more easily, and I spent less time preparing for class and writing out mock conversations. For as long as they lasted, I used my evening classes to try out material for the day classes. Evening students were always more eager to participate, since they were all volunteers. Chieko Takehata, who had earlier expressed a desire for intimacy, improved rapidly and had few of the timid mannerisms of the average Japanese young woman; her eagerness to take part did much to encourage the others.

Yamagami san, the young man with whom I walked out with on the first night, continued to attend and visited the house often, usually on weekends. He was deeply interested in American society and culture, in family customs and religion, not because he was in any way interested in becoming a Christian, but because he was interested in the culture of the occupying country. I didn't realize how transparent was my misplacement in the J3 program until one day he said he did not believe I was as religious as most missionaries were. There was nothing accusatory in what he said or in the way he said it. It was just a typical Yamagami observation of fact leading to something else, I thought. But it did say something about how far our friendship had progressed. I admitted he was correct. We were told, I explained, that many students in Japan were suffering from a malaise, from a depression of the spirit that swept over Japan as a result of defeat. Yamagami san and I were in the study. I built a little fire in the grate to take the chill off and closed the sliding shoji, shutting off the big room. I was quite cozy and very quiet. He told me about his entering Kyoto University shortly after his discharge, about studying literature and not knowing what he should do. I admitted that I was going through the same dilemma and that my coming to Japan was largely the result of having no plan beyond college, and I told him how I had wanted to return to Korea but had not been able to because of the war.

"I'm really not a teacher. Well," I stopped, thought then said, "I never planned to become a teacher."

Then he said something that pleased me a great deal, something that I have thought about many times over the years. "I think you must be very happy being a teacher because you enjoy it, I think. I have never seen anyone teach the way you teach. You make students feel comfortable and not afraid to speak."

It was my first student evaluation, and I was happily stunned. At that moment, I learned that statements like Yamagami san's would be my chief reward over the years; and for the first time since I arrived in Japan, any doubts I may have had about my contribution to the J3 program began to fade. I told him that I thought many teachers in America taught the same way I did, that all I tried to do was imitate my best teachers.

"Then, Joe san, I think there are many lucky students in America," he said.

Though I wanted to, I could not believe I was as good as he said I was. All I did was what I thought would get my students to respond, to talk back. I wanted to believe him, and I eventually accepted his remarks as having at least a degree of credibility. When Nishikawa later made a similar remark, specifically that my students all believed I enjoyed teaching, I believed Yamagami might have been right, for Nishikawa was most sparing in statements of approval. Of the three, Tanaka san was the least sparing. But the simple fact was I could not see myself becoming a teacher of English as a foreign language. TESL would become a major department one day in American universities, and my experience in Wa Dai would give me an advantage over American graduate students, I was sure. The idea of teaching it day after day when my real interests lay in the literature, ideas, and everything I learned in classes with Fletcher and Steffans (and in the Eighty-first Street seminars), was untenable. I recalled the seminar in satire aboard the *Leroy Eltinge* and the thrill—yes, thrill—I felt when a question would come from below. Somehow conversational English was *not* teaching, clearly not teaching as I conceived it, and now, reading Wilson, Trilling, and other authors I'd found in the USIS library in Kobe, Alfred Kazin and Irving Howe, Van Wyck Brooks, I began to think about asking Inoue sensei if I could offer a different kind of class to advanced students who planned to become English teachers. *Hell, it was Inoue's fault*, I thought; *asking me to dig into the plays of O'Neill distracted me from my conversational tasks.*

When Marty received from an aunt Ford Maddox Ford's *Parades End*, I read it straight through, almost unable to put it down, while he ignored it after barely making it through the first novel of the tetralogy; Marty's interests and mine outside the classroom took off in completely opposite directions. Fiction, poetry, prose nonfiction, unless it dealt with Japan, interested him not at all. I could not understand his indifference at first, but later I understood. My absorption in literature and philosophy had become such an obsession that I failed to recognize it for what it was. When I heard him every evening practicing koto in his room or watched him doing calligraphy at the low table in the big room, I envied him his concentration, and simultaneously I began to understand and respect him even more.

Although our interests moved on separate tracks, we shared much. He took me with him to tea ceremonies and would pass along books he thought I might find interesting or helpful. Marty passed on Sansom's *Short Cultural History of Japan, which* was a tremendous help, and he found English copies of Soseki's novels *Botchan* and *Kokoro* that deeply expanded my understanding. We went shopping together for *kakemono*—scroll paintings--and lacquer ware and whatever Japanese objects d'art we could afford. His dedication to all things Japanese influenced my learning about Japan, and I appreciated his efforts to refocus my own efforts. From Sansom's book and other works Marty lent me, I began to develop a deeper interest in Buddhism. For my anthropology class in primitive religions, I wrote a term paper on Shintoism, its mythology and practices, but my knowledge of Buddhism when I arrived in Japan was limited to what I had read about it when I was in Korea. Sansom only discussed Buddhist thought when it entered Japan and its influences on Japanese art but his *Short Cultural History* did not delve into the philosophy. Because my students seemed uninterested in discussing their own attitudes or understandings of Buddhism, Shinto or the teachings of Kung Fu Tze, Confucius, I was reluctant to broach the subject except in the most general way. It was bad enough that I refused to teach Bible; it seemed quite inappropriate that I, a short-term Methodist missionary, should be interested in such matters. I was wrong, of course. Wakayama city was close to two of Japan's most sacred Buddhist sites, Mount Koya and Kimiidera. Ironically, Marty was not interested in the foundations of Buddhist thought, only in the ways it applied to such things as tea ceremony and Japanese art.

When it came to teaching conversational English, we were in complete accord and shared everything. Our classroom styles were not the same, his being more formal than mine and better organized, though not as rigid as the traditional Japanese style. Our open houses worked well, bringing us into closer contact with our students than the YMCA club or Bible classes might have. At the request of the students who attended the open houses we organized, English Speaking Societies on the two campuses and invited all of our students to participate, even those who would not be enrolled in the classes. Marty sponsored the ESS on the liberal arts campus and I on the economics. Several times a year before the war, the ESS at the old Semmon Gakku published the *Orange*, an English newspaper, that my ESS members were eager to get it back into print. The name came from the prefecture's leading agricultural product, the small seedless tangerines or *mikan*. Marty's ESS, not to be outdone, decided to publish the *Green,* thus giving Wa Dai two English publications. After the first two issues, neither Marty nor I had anything to do directly with layout or editing. We checked errors in grammar, punctuation, and usage, but we felt it best that we not become rewriters, allowing all but the most egregiously twisted idioms to stand, to be corrected later on. We would critique the papers at the first meeting after publication, explaining common usage and suggesting alternate ways of expressing ideas. There was no way to correct every error in style or usage without casting a pall over the entire enterprise. All in all, the *Orange* and the *Green* were a credit to their instructors I composition and were far better than we had reason to expect as the papers were the first serious student attempts in Wakayama to publish in English since before the war. In the first issue of the *Orange* were articles on William Faulkner, American movies, the two new American instructors, and the open houses.

By Thanksgiving, both Marty and I began to feel confident that we were doing the right things in class as well as out of class. In addition to the open houses, we had a constant stream of visitors, a few who were total strangers unrelated to our teaching, people who were curious and bold enough to see what the foreigners were like. Several news stories had appeared in the local edition of the *Asahi Shim bun*, which encouraged curiosity. The two reporters who were at our first interview, young men our own age, dropped by from time to time and asked us out for noodles and sake, and they introduced us to Japanese samurai films, beautifully photographed and costumed epics with plot lines straight out of Hollywood horse operas.

Shortly before the Japanese holiday, *Bunka no hi,* National Culture Day, that coincided with our Thanksgiving we received a letter from Dr. Joe Yamagiwa, asking if we were planning to be at home during the long weekend. He was in Osaka, he said, and asked if he could drop down to see us. We were delighted. Marty suggested we invite J3 friends to the house for the long weekend, and I agreed. He had stayed in touch with his Hartford roommate, Dave Reed, who was teaching in a boys' high school on the island of Kyushu, and we both had kept in touch with Bill Asbury who wrote that he would be coming down and bringing a friend of his brother, an air force officer and fighter pilot in Korea. We immediately began making plans for the holiday: a tour of the seaside resort of Wakanoura, just down the road, a dinner at a restaurant in the party district of Wakayama, perhaps a trip down the coast to Kimiidera. It was just the sort of thing Marty did best. We expected it would break us financially, but the idea of such a gathering outweighed all other considerations. In the end, our guests insisted they contribute to the cost of the grand meal, complete with two local geisha as well as the meal at the resort.

Seeing Dave Reed gave us an opportunity to compare classes and to see how far we may have strayed from the path of Dr. Kitchens' teaching. Bill's guest, Captain, later Major, Clark Sykes had been a reconnaissance pilot in the South Pacific in the last war and had recently flown missions over Korea, but more recently he had accepted a post as an intelligence officer in the Dai Ichi Building, where MacArthur had his headquarters. We virtually had no contact with the military while were in Wakayama, and except for the Armed Forces Radio programs; we knew little about the war in Korea. Sykes rarely mentioned the war during the visit, though Bill spoke of his brother's visits to Tokyo and admitted that the war news was rarely the subject of conversations even in Tokyo. Sykes was a most interesting addition to the company that Thanksgiving and showed a genuine interest in everything Marty and I were doing as well as in all things Japanese. Marty and I attributed his relaxed, unmilitary manner to his air force affiliation, which in our experience meant he never displayed a normal, heavy-handed GI attitude, and he seemed as impressed as the rest of us with center piece of he week end, Dr. Joe Yamagiwa.

Dr. Yamagiwa's visit, more than anything else, gave that holiday its special character, at least as far as I was concerned. We had good talks about books and things, much like the talks we had aboard the *President Wilson.* I can't explain the full extent of his effect on me at that time, but it was considerable, for he continued to encourage me in my reading, at a time I was still unsure of what I should do on down the road. He admonished me slightly for not working more on my Japanese, and he shared with us one afternoon wonderful insight into the Japanese poetry, or *waka*, that had been written about Wakanoura, the lovely seaside resort built along the bluffs overlooking Wakayama Bay, which had recently been voted by the Japanese as the nation's most beautiful seaside resort area. We were all rather in awe of this most humane, scholarly man who had chosen to visit us for Thanksgiving. His visit lead to our receiving an invitation to spend Christmas with him and his students at the U of Michigan Study Center in Okayama.

Neither of us knew what to expect at the U of Michigan center in Okayama, but we realized that it was for each of us an honor to be invited to spend time with such a distinguished scholar. Half of the students studying at the center were completing research for doctorates in anthropology, the others in literature and languages. Dr. Joe's position was to advise the young scholars and make sure the center's logistics provided the necessities. There were eight people completing masters or doctor's degrees, all young men in their late twenties, two with wives. As one would expect, they all spoke Japanese, though none claimed to be truly fluent, and Dr. Yamagiwa concurred but said their language was more than adequate and improving all the time. During the day, he drove Marty and me around the countryside and through the fishing villages that two of the men were studying. It was cold and overcast most of the time we were there, but the views along the Inland Sea were lovely and reminded me of *san-sui* paintings, usually gauzy monochromes of sea and mountains. In the evenings and after meals, Marty and I sat and listened to the scholars talk about their projects, discussing the difficulties they were having as well as the discoveries they thought they might have made. Dr. Joe listened, answering questions and raising a question now and then; but most of the time, he listened. While we were there, they suspended all fieldwork and everyone was enjoying the holiday away from labs and books, but the talk continued to be about their work. I had the feeling that from this study center would eventually come important monographs, and the people here would one day hold important chairs at major schools.

From Okayama, Marty and I went on to Tokyo to visit Bill Asbury and to renew old acquaintances from Hartford. It was cold and blustery and far too expensive to spend more than a few days in the city with its crowds, heavy traffic, and the interminable trips on the elevated trains. Marty was occupied most of the time with old friends from his days in the occupation. Since I knew little of Tokyo and had never developed close friendships with any of the J3s at Hartford except for Bill and Marty, I really had nothing to do or anywhere to go. It was quite another world from the provincialism of Wakayama. I enjoyed going with Bill to interesting bars and small bistros in the Ginza, where bright neon lights turned the streets into a gay, carnival-like midway. The Ginza was a spectacle, but I never felt in tune with it. Bill and I met Clark Sykes for lunch one day at the British officers' club in Motomachi, near the Imperial Palace. The food and wine were excellent. It was a world so far from the world of Wakayama it was hard to believe I was still in Japan. Clark had invited an RAF officer and his wife to join us, or perhaps we were his guests since it was a British officers' club. Bill introduced me as a professor of English at Wakayama University, a fact the captain's wife found unbelievable because I looked too young to be a university professor—and of course I was. From the way they spoke to Bill, it was clear to me that they knew him as a publicity man working with Japanese journalists and apparently had no idea he was connected to the United Church of Christ in Japan. Since I was seated next to the captain's wife and Clark and the captain seemed occupied with shoptalk, I found myself speaking to the "veddy" British lady who spoke a "veddy" proper U brand of English, which meant she spoke of everything and everyone with marvelous condescension.

"You can't possibly be a professor at a university," she said, dripping elegant disdain. "How old are you anyway?"

I replied, "You are right. I am not a professor, but I *am* an instructor, and it is my first teaching job, but it *is* a university, and I *do* teach English to Japanese students."

"But do you have a degree?" she asked. I told her I did. Then she asked how I managed not to be in some branch of the service. Bill sat back amused looking on as if expecting her to carry on an inquisition. He had met her before and had watched the same performance with other Americans. After getting over my initial irritation, I relaxed and began to enjoy her performance as grand dame of the British Raj. Her husband, obviously accustomed to her rudeness, ignored everything happening on our side of the table and remained in deep conversation with Clark Sykes.

Answering her query about my not being in the service, I repeated my favorite cliché when explaining to strangers my not being in the service while there was a war going on. I said, "I have an agreement with my draft board in Corpus Christi, Texas. They call me only every other war. Actually"—and I imitated the best British dialect I could—"they didn't draft me in the last one. I volunteered." She wouldn't believe that was possible either. From the food and wine and the gay atmosphere in the dining room of the club, there was no sense of war anywhere, except the plethora of uniforms and splashes of ribbons and wings across the chests of the men.

She looked at me, her eyes narrowed. "You can't be old enough to have been in the last war *and* have a college degree."

Bill interrupted, "He was, and he served in both theaters."

"Good Lord!" she said. Then she took off on another topic, one even more disagreeable than the other that I had thoroughly enjoyed since it was chiefly about me. She could not understand, she said, how we Americans could be so friendly toward Japanese or why we treated them *almost* as if they were equals. She, however, found our treatment of the Negroes in America disgusting. She herself had no prejudice toward dark-skinned people—the British had always treated their blacks with kindness, she said—but she had never considered Orientals, especially the Japanese, as decidedly inferior.

Asbury looked at her now with the disgust I felt, but he said nothing; however, I couldn't resist replying. I was certain by now that Asbury and Sykes had set me up.

"First, the war is over. Persisting in the same racial hatred as we had during the war is stupid. It was stupid then, but I suppose it was natural. It makes it easier to kill people when you hate them." I was echoing the lessons I had learned in applied anthropology, as well as ideas we had just discussed at Okayama. "Second, there are a lot of Americans who agree with you about the treatment—as you put it—of the American Negro. We are not all in agreement about civil rights in our country, even many of us from the South where racial bigotry is virtually an institution—and I am *from* the South. But your history of relations with the dark-skinned people isn't much better than ours. Isn't the favorite British word for brown-skinned people 'wogs' or 'niggers'? Even Kipling said you didn't treat the Fuzzy Wuzzies fair when you 'sloshed them with martinis.' I've found the Japanese highly cultivated, extremely sophisticated, and very intelligent, just as I find many Americans or British, red, black or brown. The Japanese culture, in general, especially, the art, architecture, drama, is exceptional."

When I stopped to take a bite, I noticed that Clark and the captain were watching and listening. The captain said, "For god's sake, Sheila! Are you on that race business again? Ignore her, Joe. She's an awful snob," and then turned back to discussing whatever it was he and Clark had been discussing. Bill and Clark later admitted they had expected her to take off on the subject, apparently her favorite topic and the only thing she ever talked about around Americans. I was appalled, not at what she said, but that it all fit so neatly the worse caricature of the stuffy, colonial Brit. I had assumed it was a breed long extinct. They found it amusing; her husband found it irritating.

The trip to Tokyo turned out to be nothing like I expected. I saw little of former classmates from Hartford but spent most of my time visiting Clark Sykes and his friends at the *Gun Jin Kaikan*, or Soldier Hall, one of the major officers' billets in Tokyo. I had been months now in Japan, and only now was I aware that there was still a war going on in Korea. In October, after the landing at Inchon, it looked as if it were over and that I might be allowed to go to Korea. A headline in *Life* magazine had spoken of "Hard-Hitting Troops in Mopping Up Operations," and an editorial that same month had urged the UN to reunite the Korean peninsula. But no one seriously thought that short-term teaching missionaries would move back in anytime soon; the country south of the Thirty-Eighth Parallel was devastated. In October, the real war had been won; and by early November, it was only a question how far the UN under MacArthur would advance. But by December, the war had changed again, and that change was visible on the faces of all the men around Soldier Hall. It was the first time since I landed that the war was a palpable presence. Wakayama, with only its small contingent of CIC officers and noncoms, could have been somewhere in south Texas for all the war we experienced there. "Bugging out" was the new jargon of the moment, and it was repeated around the mess and quarters in somber and gritty tones of shock and frustration. Bill's brother joined us one evening briefly, back from flying ground support missions, weary and dejected, but no one spoke in details, only in the practiced phrases of the official releases. It felt strange sitting there among them, knowing I was still of age and not in uniform. Bill and I mentioned the odd feeling, but only when we were alone. Everyone associated with Clark Sykes had served in the other war, some had stayed on in active duty, some like Bill's brother had been called back, but none asked why I was not back in. Bill himself held a reserve commission in the navy and his navy ID admitted him to officers' clubs and PXs. It was that strange.

Though I was enjoying Bill's company immensely—he was by far the most interesting and amusing of the entire J3 crowd in Tokyo—I felt I had to return to Wakayama. Clark and his friends offered to put me up in the *kaikan*, and the few missionaries I encountered also offered me a place to stay. But since my money was running low, returning home to Wakayama for the New Year seemed best. The Japanese traditional *Sho Gatsu*, or New Year, lasted five days with parties, visitations, and gatherings at Shinto Shrines. In big cities, modern times have reduced the five to three; but in Wakayama, five days was customary. Marty stayed on, however, catching up on old friendships.

Back in Wakayama, Mrs. Uehara—she said she preferred I call her Frances—had planned an all-night vigil for New Year's Eve and asked that I come and welcome it with her and several friends of her daughter Ann, and Miki Tanaka's parents invited me to spend January 2 with their family in the country. Kameoka's parents asked me take part in the New Year's ritual of pound steaming rice into *mochi*, a thick paste-like substance rolled into tasteless, glutinous balls and placed as New Year's offerings to the household gods before familys' Shinto shrines. Chieko Takehata from the evening class invited me to a family party on the third of January. Her father, manager of the local *Teikoku Genko* (Imperial Bank), where Marty and I banked, had invited us to his home several times. Chieko had indeed become the good friend she wished to be, attending our open houses as well as the Christmas party we held just before we left for Okayama. Quite unlike the traditional Japanese young woman, she mixed easily with the young men who visited the house, her English constantly improving, yet she avoided the stigma of a *mo ga*, modern girl. My Japanese had, through little effort on my part, improved to the extent that I could now converse somewhat with gentlemen like Mr. Takehata as long as the conversation was confined to the temperature of the sake and the appearance of the garden.

Back home in Wakayama, I enjoyed reading late at night, writing long letters to Bettie in Puerto Rico, sleeping late, visiting Dot and Louie and staying late at their house, listening to their classical records on an old record player like the one Mullins had acquired in a secondhand shop in Austin. Dot had musical scores for Beethoven's violin concerto and several of the piano concerti. We would sit on the floor before the fire and follow the solo passages while we listened. I visited a record shop in town and bought myself, for Christmas, a recording of the complete *La Traviata* and brought it back to their house and listened to it with Dot. Consisting of more than twelve sides of seventy-eight-rpm discs, it was terribly expensive, but I used some of the Christmas money I got from home. Having no record player of my own,

I eventually gave the album to the music club at the university. The winter vacation lasted almost a month, after which there would be a few more weeks of classes, and then the academic year would end followed by another long break. It was a good arrangement, I felt, particularly since there was no central heat in any of the classrooms at Wa Dai. If snow was rare in Wakayama and freezing temperatures rare the winter months in that part of Japan were quite cold. Many days I taught class bundled from head to toe with a muffler wrapped about my throat, the air so cold I could almost see my words freezing in the air as I spoke them, making it unnecessary for me to write them on the chalkboard. Absenteeism was a constant problem except at the open houses we held; they were always attended in even greater numbers since our house, in Wakayama terms, was always overheated.

I attended the last graduation exercise of the Keisai Semmon Gakku, the Economics Higher School, with Inoue sensei, and though I understood not a word, I was glad I attended. Several of my third-year men stopped by and let me congratulate them, and then the sensei and I sat at the long table of revelers, watching them down warm sake chased by Asahi beer. The famous Tagawa sensei, a Communist Party member and professor of economics, was object of toast after toast, obviously a favorite.

Shortly after the graduation exercise and ceremony, President Itoigawa asked if I would take the train to Osaka Central Station and meet the American professor of psychology and education, Dr. Anne N. Edelman, who had just arrived in Japan with a large group of American professors under the auspices of the American Institute for Foreign Study (AIFS). Kameoka, visiting at the house when Itoigawa san called, asked if he could he could go with me. I told him Itoigawa san was sending the university's car to meet her because she may have considerable luggage. Hearing that, he was even more eager to accompany me.

I had been blowing my nose, coughing all morning, and Kameoka was concerned. "I think you are not well, Joe san," he said. "Perhaps you should not go."

I assured him I was well, that it was only a cold, nothing more. The university car, an old prewar Pontiac, drove up as we were discussing my head cold. The drive was much quicker than I imagined it would be, so quick that we had to wait over half hour on the platform in a cold, drizzly atmosphere. Kame suggested I wait in the warm tearoom while he stood on the platform, but I assured him I was fine as I was wearing my warmest overcoat and with it warm sweaters while his coat was only a light rain slicker over his blue school uniform.

We had the name and number of her sleeping car and were told where it would stop on the platform, so there would be no problem eyeing her as she stepped off the train. I was thankful Kameoka san had asked to come even though he admitted it was mainly because he wanted to be the first Wa Dai student to welcome the *hakasi*, the doctor-professor. He was planning to take her business psychology lecture, he said. The train, on time of course, stopped exactly where we were told it would, and she stepped down almost as soon as the car stopped.

Small, very tired looking, but trying to smile as we welcomed her, she announced she had no other luggage than the small overnight case, the rest following as special freight. When she said she was flattered that the university would send a car and two such "handsome" escorts, I liked her immediately; but by the time we reached the car, I felt a terrible chill and a throbbing sense that told me my temperature was rising.

I told her that she would be staying in our house, that we actually had a guest room with an extra bed, not just a set of futon, but a real bed and mattress the Kyodan had sent us for just such a guest as she. The president told me he would send someone to the house to explain fully what she would need and to have her bed ready. I couldn't believe we were so well prepared. There was even an old armoire as well as the bed, and Oba san was able to set up her room, sans heater to be sure. Because I was semi-delirious with fever and coughing by the time we reached the house, Kame acted as host with Oba san's instructions, and from what I could tell, Dr. Edelman found what she needed most, a hot bath.

I dropped into one of the chairs in the small study, opened my coat, and lit the gas fire, caring not a whit for the gas bill that would ensue. And just then, Marty arrived back from Tokyo in a quandary that Kame solved calmly and expertly as if he were the host himself. I asked Marty to telephone Dot Grier with the news of the American professor and incidentally the news of my most imminent demise. My fever was raging, and I knew the only thing I could do was to pack it in, go to bed, and bundle up under the two army blankets and the family's ancient eider down comforter I had packed before leaving Corpus. From that point, I have no memory of anything but seeing Dot Grier bending over, asking me to take a thermometer. *Anata wa taihen biyooki ni narimashita.* I had become very sick.

I was told Dr. Uehara arrived, listened to my breathing, and prescribed heavy doses of a sulpha compound, Dot recalling that I was allergic to penicillin. Marty brought forth his one great luxury, a small electric heater that heated only that which it was aimed at. From time to time, I woke to swallow a broth of unknown elements and to swallow more aspirin. Two days after delivering the *hakasi* to our *Dai Gakku kansha*, I came around and spoke to our wonderful Nordic Florence Nightingale who had been there hovering, watching, touching, and praying.

"Do you need to use the toilet?" were her first words.

I said I did, and she helped me sit up and produced a regular hospital urinal and then left me to my duties. Later, Dr. Uehara returned, his third or fourth visit they said. Smiling his always sparkling smile, he told me I had passed through a pretty stiff case of pneumonia, but it was over except now I must rest and stay warm. I did rest and recuperate, but not in the refrigerator I called my bedroom. Marty moved my bed into the small study that was easier to heat, and it incidentally had much better light for reading and writing. About the fourth day with Dot's permission, I left my sickbed but continued to take it easy, writing letters, accepting visitors and well-wishers, rarely leaving the small, low-ceilinged study.

Letters became most important, even more important than when I was overseas. I had written Bettie long letters, expressing how much I missed her of course, but telling her in great detail about my students and how important I thought assisting Inoue had become. I was determined that a flood of letters filled with details of life in Wakayama, with pictures I'd taken of scenic areas such as Wakanoura, would help convince her that our brief encounter—six weeks in Hartford was brief—would surely be continued one day, though I still had no concrete plan for the future, *our future.* Her letters, never as frequent as I wished, were also filled with descriptions of Santurce, Puerto Rico, where her school was located, as well as historical places on the island. She also included snapshots of herself and the school, and one day, a large photo portrait of her arrived that quite amazed my students attending our open house, several doubting—jokingly, I assumed—that anyone so beautiful could be that interested in me, and accusing me of copying the portrait from a movie magazine.

It took almost a month for the university to put Anne Edelman's house into shape for her to move to. It too was something of an architectural anomaly, but with her suggestions, the university was able to provide a comfortable and easily heated house. Until then, she stayed with us and added much to our colony of gaijin. I don't believe Marty and I greatly impressed her as instructors at first, but as our students dropped by for visits, she changed her mind, noting that their visits came when school was *not* in session. Like any good psychological counselor, she was interested in our plans post-Wa Dai and was concerned that we make the right choices. When she met students like Tanaka and Kameoka, who introduced her to other members of the English Speaking Societies, men like Kuriyama and Katsube, she was even more impressed, not only because their English was so good, but also because they asked such interesting and relevant questions and knew so much about U.S. politics and business.

The winter lingered well into March, but as April approached and the weather became warmer I began to feel quite well and feel the itch to travel a bit before the new academic year began, perhaps Kyoto or Nara, I thought. Bill Asbury and his friend Sykes, now a major, solved my dilemma when Bill wrote that he had developed a mild case of hepatitis and was in the Seventh Day Adventist Hospital in Tokyo. His visit at Thanksgiving and my visit to Tokyo at Christmas had drawn us closer, even though we did not see each other that often. He also wrote that Clark Sykes wanted me to meet him and two friends at the Miyako Hotel in Kyoto. So, as an act of friendship and brotherhood, I decided I'd make a quick trip to visit the ailing Asbury and probably make visits to some of the important Tokyo sites I had missed before while staying at Bill's place to save on money. I wrote him to tell Sykes and company that I would be glad to meet them and be their guest. Sykes had insisted meals and lodging would be entirely on them, if I would take them around Kyoto and then invite them all three to Wakayama. Sykes had told his friends about the excursion we had taken to Waka-no-ura with Dr. Joe, and they decided it would be ideal, particularly for one of their party to take a true R & R. "East the Beast," Major Clyde East, had just left hospital after a long stay and was in need of serious rehabilitation, they said. I agreed and set out on the *Tokubetsu kyuko*, the special express train, from Osaka.

At the hospital, I found Asbury doing much better and was allowed to stay for a long visit. Giving me the schedule of my Kyoto visit, he told me of the plan again and said Sykes and friends were anxious I get to Kyoto and more anxious for their visit to Wakayama. It sounded quite interesting, more like my own R & R, I said. I left Bill, promising another short visit to the hospital after visiting a few temple sites and a museum of traditional Japanese art. Asbury's house was in a compound of fine old American-style homes far out of the area of the firebombing. The house was the childhood home of Edwin O. Reischauer, the famous historian and later Ambassador under Kennedy. Reischauer's book on Japan had been one of our texts at Hartford. Bill's maid who let me in had been, remarkably, Reischauer's childhood nurse. It was strange; it all looked so familiarly 1920s upper-middle class American. When I returned after my long day in Tokyo, his Oba san was not there to greet me, which was very unusual, as she had been so attentive the night before. I found her in the kitchen sitting at the table, weeping as if someone had died.

"Oba san, *nan demo desuka?*" I asked.

She answered in perfect English, "*Ma san*! President Truman fired *Ma san*."

"What? MacArthur's been fired? Truman fired MacArthur?" I was stunned.

She nodded and wept. "But that isn't bad, Oba san. General MacArthur, Ma san, disobeyed the president. In America, that is very serious, very bad." I tried to explain. But she was inconsolable. Two emperors deposed in one lifetime was just too much. We talked a bit and I tried to soften the blow, explaining that the General was growing old, that retirement would be good for him, but I understood clearly that Ma san was a deity, that gods should not be fired or tampered with. But how historically rich, I thought, to witness her grief. I knew that when I returned to Wakayama, my ESS would be elated, especially Katsube san would rejoice. But I wondered what Clark and friends would say.

Because I had neglected to secure second-class reservations on the special express, I had to settle for third class; the hard straight-back benches were too small for tall foreigners and not a comfortable way to travel. To fortify myself for the long, straight-back ride to Kyoto, I stopped at the tax-free import store on the way to the station and bought a half-dozen small bottles of Haig & Haig. I knew I could spend an hour easily in the dining car having a late lunch and then return and order soda and nuts for a couple of hours with the Messers Haig & Haig. I also knew it was likely I would have company, thus avoiding the hard seats and stiff upright backs of third class. The comforts of the Miyako Hotel would make up for the rest.

My plan worked perfectly: I had a good lunch and later shared my scotch with a young businessman who was sipping Suntory with his *tansan* water. He had entered the dining car and taken the table on the opposite side of the aisle and then joined me when I raised a glass and invited him, in Japanese, to share my table and whiskey. It was a spontaneous gesture; I didn't want to drink alone for several reasons. First, I needed someone who could speak for me in Japanese if a conductor stopped and asked a question; second, I would consume the scotch too rapidly and end up too tipsy for safety. This way, and this was a surmise, I would have a companion who probably wanted to polish his English, and I could share the whisky. The plan worked well indeed. I even had a glass of his Suntory and gave him one of the little bottles of Scotch. And when the loudspeaker announced that we would be arriving at Kyoto in five minutes, I was able to return to my third-class seat, retrieve my bag, and step onto the platform just as Clark and friends arrived. And I was just barely mellow enough not to embarrass them or myself.

The Miyako was grand. I wondered how I would be allowed to use the armed services since I had no occupation script. Since military bases and resorts did not allow Japanese currency, I was in a dither about how I would get past the desk with neither military ID nor uniform. Clark and the others assured me it was in the bag. I was preregistered, and they held my room key in hand. Clark explained I needn't check in, and in case a second person arrived to share the room, I should simply say, if asked, that I was part of G-2 military intelligence. If a second man showed up, it would be male DOA civilian who would never ask a second question after that.

In the cab, we introduced ourselves, though Clyde East and I were the only strangers, the other being Clark's roommate at the Goon-jin Kaikan in Tokyo whom I'd met at Christmas. "East the Beast" was the man of interest. I had never seen anyone who wore both the RAF wings and the wings of the ASAF. He had been in the Eagle Squadron, a pilot at seventeen before the U.S. entered the war and had transferred as an F-51 pilot into the Eighth Air Force after Pearl Harbor. I couldn't say it, but at the time ten years later, he looked much older than twenty-eight or twenty-nine. Clark explained later that East had transferred from a fighter squadron in Korea to a training outfit in Japan, giving new pilots their final check flights, when a young pilot crashed them to earth and was killed while East suffered two compound leg fractures. A rice farmer and his wife had heroically pulled him from the crash before the plane exploded and then doctored skillfully by a rural physician who, according to the air force medics, had saved his legs. Other than the two wings, East's chest bore several air medals, a DFC, and its British equivalent, all of which helped explain why he looked older than he was.

After three days visiting temples, shrines and fine restaurants passed without incident, we took the train to Wakayama at which time they became the guests of Marty and me. I thought it interesting that they would so easily shuffle off their military manner and enjoy the almost-rustic world. When they met me at the station in Kyoto, they seemed wired, excited, or tense, perhaps because of East's recent stay in the hospital and the sudden change to the luxuries of the Miyako Hotel; but as they settled back in Wakayama, they changed, relaxed completely, enjoying the steaming *o-furo* we provided. Obaa san's delicious chicken curry and plenty of beer helped. We spent a day at Wakano-uro, where Clark suggested they spend their last night.

The talk was much about how Marty and I felt being a missionary since neither of us fit the profile. We explained, or tried to explain, that there was no clear, well-limned profile to match, that almost any of our J3 cohorts would also fail. Marty described his Hartford roommate Dave, and by contrast, I described Burt Housman's zeal being more akin to a social worker with a cause than the stereotype films and fiction offered. Marty pointed out how each of us approached our jobs differently, something I barely thought about. I tried to emphasize that I had learned in Japan that there was no missionary type as such, no holier-than-thou shouter of scriptures.

Marty and I dipped deep into the small cash reserves we had in order to furnish our men in the service with a comfortable Wakayama-style R & R. But we had no regrets, nor did we when they left and our house went back to normal. We both thought it strange that Clark and friends would spend their time here in Wakayama. Clyde East enjoyed it, seemed most relaxed of the three, while Sykes, who had been there before, became distracted and the one most eager to get back.

A few days before classes began—in Japan the academic year begins in the spring—I received a telephone call from the Kyodan, asking me if I would be able to accept an invitation from the principal of a small rural Christian school in Nagano, a village to the west of Wakayama not far from Osaka. The caller said the principal wanted a J3 missionary to visit this school once a week to teach English conversation to children in sixth, seventh, and eighth grades and to speak to their teachers—in English.

"You really can't teach much English in only one day, probably only one hour a week, but . . .," I paused.

He came back with a soft laugh. "He knows that, Joe, but what he really wants is for the children to meet an American, and wants them to hear *you* speak *English*. Do you think you can arrange a schedule with your classes? He tells me Nagano is a little more than an hour from Wakayama."

While he spoke, I had been thinking; *this is something I can do, ought to do.* "Can you tell the principal I have Monday and Wednesday mornings clear, no classes at Wa Dai until two in the afternoon. But that doesn't leave me much class time at the school."

"Let me call you back. I'm sure we can make something work. Thank you so much. You *are* interested, then?"

"Yes, of course. It sounds interesting. You know, if I got there the night before . . .."

"I was thinking the same thing. I'm sure we can make it work."

I told Marty it looked as if my teaching career was taking off. I'd been offered a conversational class in a Christian middle school, in a place called Nagano.

"That's in the Japanese Alps, for god's sake," he said, half incredulous.

"No, it's a small village between here and Osaka. It blows my free mornings. They just want me one day a week," I said and told him the call was from the Kyodan and I couldn't very well say no, and besides, it was the answer to—I almost said "my prayer"—my concern about not doing any mission work.

The call came back from Dr. Shacklock's office, a secretary I assumed, thanking me again and saying that the school had arranged for me to stay overnight Tuesday and would make sure I made the train back in time for my classes at the university. I thanked her, and she said a letter would follow with details and the name of the person at whose house I would spend the nights.

A letter arrived a couple of days later, explaining more clearly what I was to do, which was essentially nothing but show up and talk to the sixth-, seventh-, and eighth-grade classes. They simply wanted an American teacher to visit them regularly and to teach the students a few common expressions or phrases and to visit with the faculty, several of whom spoke "some" English. It was a modest request, made no heavy demands but simply asked for an opportunity to meet an American short-term missionary. Another letter arrived from Nagano, a more formal invitation in very stiff and formal English, suggesting I arrive at Nagano late the day before and stay the night at the home of the assistant principal. It was all very reasonable; I would be learning something about a part of Japan I would otherwise miss entirely.

Louis, Dot, and I discussed it over dinner one evening; they seemed pleased that I was interested, actually more than interested. Dot said I seemed excited, and I agreed, repeating to them how my teaching career was taking off. Then I said that it seemed really like a coincidence since I had been wondering why I hadn't been called on to do more. "Who do you think thought I would be available?" I asked.

Louie smiled and said, "I told them. You sounded so guilty, I recall, about not having any mission work to do, so I just mentioned at a meeting that you were looking for more mission employment." He smiled. "I didn't think you would mind?"

I told him of course not, and thanked him. "They offered to pay my train fare, but I have a rail pass. I think Nagano is on the same line, may require a transfer. They are feeding me and giving me a place to flop. But all in all, I think it'll be good."

The trip by local train took less than an hour, including a transfer about halfway to Osaka. And when I stepped out of the station, a young man about my age, maybe older, met me and asked in quite good English if I was "Mr.

Gilliland of Wakayama University," his *l*'s sharp and clear. I said I was, and
he introduced himself and explained that he was the "greeting committee," in
those very words. I resisted complimenting him on the correct pronunciation
of Gilliland, lest he tell me he had missed the first fall home game at Del Mar
College or somewhere. However, when he introduced me to his mother, my
hostess, I found she spoke no English other than "you are welcome."

Supper was excellent, a small veal cutlet, bowl of rice, and steamed
broccoli with tea. Kenji, my greeting committee, joined me at the low table,
and we talked about his art, which hung on the wall. He joined me every time
I visited that spring, and we talked about the art scene in Osaka, where he
was sometimes employed at a small gallery. And next morning, I had a fine
Japanese breakfast of rice and miso soup.

It was a delightful class of the youngest students I'd ever taught, possibly
now I think of it, I *have* ever taught. I taught all three classes the same
greetings and the same farewells and found the young sixth graders quick
to learn my hand gestures, eager to repeat individually when I asked. Later,
classes included naming common objects—book, table, chair, window—the
same objects that appeared in my Japanese language texts. I was finished
by eleven, met the faculty again, said my goodbyes and then headed for
the station and arrived in time for my train. Lessons that followed always
surprised me. I was always pleased how their teachers made sure they practiced
between sessions. But in six weeks, the classes ended, apparently having served
the original purpose, theirs as well as mine. Remarkable changes took place
in just six weeks that would alter my place in the J3 short-term missionary
program and change my life forever.

In March, I got the news I had been expecting and dreading. I had
assumed that more calls for jobs like the one in Nagano Cho would be
coming from other schools in other villages or small towns, but the letters
we received were quite unlike the invitation I had received from Nagano. We
knew that as soon as the original J3s finished their three years, we would be
leaving Wa Dai and taking up positions in schools under the Kyodan. Marty's
new assignment was Aoyama Gakuin in Tokyo; mine was for the Palmore
Institute in Kobe. He had been looking forward to moving to Tokyo, where
his friends from the year of the occupation lived. I was not surprised to hear
that Marty was pleased. He had numerous old acquaintances in Tokyo with
whom he had remained in constant contact. Tokyo also represented the world
he was most interested in, a world where he could pursue his serious studies
as well as make contacts for the future. In Wakayama, he had begun his
journey of culture by first studying the koto, a thirteen-string harp that was

one of the most important musical instruments, along with the samisen and *shako-hachi*, the first a three-stringed plucked instrument unlike any ukulele or guitar anyone in the West had ever seen, but the backbone instrument of kabuki and noh performances. The *shako-hachi* is a Japanese flute. Marty's dedication and later his skill amazed everyone, especially his teacher, when he agreed to perform *"Roko Dan"* on the koto at the teacher's recital. The class of some thirty girls ages six through sixteen were dressed in the colorful kimono of young girls while Marty, the one American, the only male, the giant gaijin, was clad in black formal kimono complete with his newly selected family crest.

Marty was elated, but to me, the news was a genuine disappointment. I should have expected it, however, should have known that Wakayama University could never have been a permanent assignment as long as mission schools needed instructors. Being assigned to a government university was an anomaly, I realized, an anomaly due to the war in Korea. Marty and I had arrived in the middle of the normal academic year for Japanese universities. When we received our assignment, no one mentioned the fact it was temporary and that we were joining the faculty at Wa Dai halfway through the academic year. We were never the genuine articles, always at best only potential faculty. I had deluded myself into thinking I'd found my niche. Now I confronted a second career disappointment that, once again, I had not expected or prepared for. Teaching at a university made me believe I was headed for a career in higher education. Being able to work with Inoue sensei on the O'Neill translations smacked of the real thing. In reality, I was only teaching a seriously nonacademic discipline, conversational English, more often taught in those special setups at a YMCA or YWCA or an institute like Palmore or those big city centers for immigrant education. Nevertheless, I did not want to leave.

Earlier in the term that spring, serious feelings of doubt and discontent arose when Bettie's letter was late. I missed her, and her letters said she was missing me too. I had spoken at length to Anne Edelman about Bettie, talked about her interests and how they overlapped my own. When she first saw Bettie's Christmas photo, she asked, "Who in the world is this lovely person?" I told her about Bettie, about our meeting at Hartford, how we had become attracted to each other mainly because we agreed on so many things. Marty was sitting with us there in the small study after breakfast; it was the morning after I left the sickbed. When I said, trying not to evoke any sense of romantic feeling, trying to sound as matter-of-fact as I could, that she was simply, factually, unlike anyone I had known before, Marty confirmed what

I said and agreed others at Hartford also thought she was a one of a kind. Anne marveled that I had let her slip away so easily, but from the tone of her remark, I felt she was teasing, at least in part. It felt good to talk about Bettie with Anne. She listened, and I felt she fully understood me.

Anne's coming had made a difference for all of us. Dot Grier especially found her to be a good friend and confidant. Her interest in Wakayama, in the school, in each of us was like that of an old friend, and her willingness to share her own rich story gained our respect. She had grown up through the Depression, an active union supporter, a defender of strong liberal causes concerning civil rights, and her doctorate in psychology from the U of Chicago had deepened her commitment to human rights, particularly in the workplace. We trusted her frankness, her honesty, and her directness and lack of formality. For me, mainly, it came through when I learned she could easily admit her ignorance about things around her and about her Japanese students. She asked questions easily, and she was never embarrassed to admit she didn't understand. She learned instantly. There was a generosity of spirit in her that I felt was contagious. At first, she found Marty's devotion to all things Japanese unusual to the point of seeming weird; but gradually, she began to understand how his experience in the occupation had marked him.

I learned a great deal from her because of her generous spirit and her willingness to share and to teach. One day, shortly before Marty and I received our letters telling us of our new assignments, I was in a rare slump. Nowadays we'd call it depression, something I had never or rarely experienced. I'd had good classes that morning, but I was tired, distracted, uninterested in my surroundings. It was a warm, clear day, and the large tatami room where we held open house was flooded with sunlight. I decided I would make a martini. The iceman had delivered a new block of ice that morning, and on my last trip to Osaka, I had bought a bottle of tax-free London dry gin and cheap California vermouth; although we had no olives, I felt I could do without the garnish. I was expecting Anne shortly and knew from past Thursday afternoons she would probably appreciate a very dry martini. We both loved that famous DeVoto essay in the *Harper's* "Easy Chair," his paean to the virtues of a *very* dry martini.

When she arrived, I told her to pull up a *sabuton* and join me in a cocktail. Our large tatami room had only one piece of furniture, the large, low black table that required us to have a number of those large, flat square cushions that offered us gaijin a small measure of comfort—*sabutons*. She sank to the floor as I stirred our martinis, her first and my second. She complimented my mixing.

"Pretty good for a young short-term missionary. What?" I raised my glass.

She smiled and nodded and then, looking straight at me said, "Now what are you so depressed about? It's quite obvious."

She wasn't urging or penetrating, just asking a friend why he was in the dumps. Anne often took me by surprise that way, speaking easily as a friend but also immediately to the point.

"I miss Bettie," I said. "I wish she were here." I don't think I had ever spoken those words aloud to anyone since I'd been in Japan, not to Marty or Asbury, no one. Immediately, I wished I hadn't said what I said. But I had spoken, and I meant what I said. I quickly added, "But that's not why I made the martinis."

She sipped the cocktail. "You should ask her then to come to Wakayama. Don't wish, don't just wish."

I thought, *Here's a lesson Joe, listen to her.* She said that she understood what I was feeling and also understood why I couldn't, but she also said she hated seeing me or anyone unhappy, said she was sure Bettie would love to be here too. I changed the subject, and we talked instead about her classes and how Kuriyama and Tanaka were becoming wonderfully helpful students, her best students, not only because they could translate difficult parts of her presentation, but because they encouraged the recalcitrant ones to take part. All three of us admitted that not all of our students were willing to give up the traditional Japanese classroom.

"Tanaka and Kuriyama," she remarked, "are really very fine young men, bright and eager to help and even more eager to learn." She sipped again and smiled, looking into the glass. "Very dry. We're lucky to know these young men."

I agreed and sipped and muttered, "It's better with an olive or two."

But my thoughts were on Bettie and what I could . . .. Her words had stuck.

Chapter 18

A Beginning

The J3 mission program did not allow short-termers to marry and remain short-term missionaries. Several couples married and became lifetime missionaries, and several took Japanese spouses and left the program but remained as teachers or social workers. As I began thinking about my wish to remain in Wakayama, to remain teaching at Wa Dai, I began listing the reasons: I wished to remain an instructor of English, perhaps even really learn how to teach English, and I wished to continue working with Inoue on his translations. Inoue had agreed to let me teach a class in American cultural history. Mostly, I wished to finish my commitment of three years here at the university, not at Palmore Institute, which was a different world. I had visited Palmore Institute and found it a good place to work, and I liked the people: Reverend and Mrs. Cobb, and Morse and Ruth Saito, one of the couples from the first J3 group who fell in love and married and became lifetime missionaries. But . . . Kobe was *not* Wakayama. It was too much *in* the world. I preferred the relative backwater of old Wakayama, where I had just begun to fit, I thought. My likes and dislikes were, however, not part of the agreement I made with the mission board. I knew I was failing to live up to the full commitment, and I knew in my heart that the real reason was Bettie.

That evening I wrote her describing my dilemma about the transfer, and I mentioned the possibility of resigning from the program if President Itoigawa would hire me and keep me on at the salary I was sending to the Kyodan every month. In my mind, a plan was taking shape; but first, I needed to read her thoughts about my resigning and going on my own with the university. At the end of the letter, I mentioned it would be grand if she would come to Japan and live here in Wakayama with me while I continued teaching.

Her reply was swift, but not what I expected.

"No!" she wrote, "not if it means living with you and not being married." Did I forget to ask her to marry me? How could I?

The note was short and emphatic. How could Anne Edelman have thought she would be so willing? She wrote she had been thinking about leaving Puerto Rico, that she was tired of the school and had seen all she wished to see of the place. I replied immediately and made it clear I wanted her to marry me. This reply was as swift as the other. This time she said, "Yes."

After her first letter, I spoke to Inoue sensei, and he was very agreeable that I stay on if I would get the president's OK. President Itoigawa said without hesitating that the job was mine. He even agreed that I could keep the house. I was almost ready to write Dr. Shacklock.

At first, I kept Bettie's letters to myself and did not speak of my conversations with Inoue sensei and President Itoigawa. Everyone knew I was unhappy about moving to Kobe, but only Anne knew how badly I missed Bettie. A whole day passed before I was unable to hold back any longer and told Anne that I had asked Bettie and she had said yes. I also told her that Itoigawa and Inoue agreed that I should stay on. She was not surprised. But as I expected, she wondered if I had thought ahead, if I had any idea what marrying Bettie actually entailed. She had asked quite calmly, not even suggesting I was being rash or impetuous, and I admitted that I hadn't thought all that far ahead.

"This is serious, my friend," Anne said with emphasis. "You have to be real. Think, for her sake *and* yours," she said calmly. "First, you must talk to Louie."

The next day, when I asked Louie if we could speak alone in his library, he beckoned for me for follow him, Dot watching suspiciously. I laid out my plan, such as it was, and he agreed with Anne though less emphatically, his concern being the more immediate question of how the Kyodan and the Board of Foreign Missions would react. He advised me to inform Dr. Shacklock and the Kyodan immediately, which I did.

I wrote Shacklock as soon as I left his study and mailed it. Mail moved fast in Japan, and two days later, I received a telephone call from Dr. Shacklock expressing surprise, though his voice showed no sign of dismay or any negative feelings. He said that I should meet with Dr. Cobb in Kobe as soon as possible and discuss my decision with him. He said he had called Dr. Cobb as soon as he read my letter.

"You see, this will create a scheduling problem for them at Palmore, though I'm sure it can be handled and is really not your concern."

I replied I had thought about that and assured him I would be willing to help in any way I could, although I honestly had *not* considered how I might be able to help them out.

"Rev. Cobb will call you soon and set up the meeting." He paused, and then in a tone of voice I had most often heard him use came a warm personal note.

"Joe, I've read your letter carefully. We'll be sorry to lose you, but from what you've said, I know we will only be losing you as an active member of our J3 family. I want you to know that Mrs. Shacklock and I are happy you have found a person to share your life with. That is most important." He paused, and then he laughed softly. "You know, we had heard that you and Bettie had become *very close* in Hartford. We don't miss much," he said in a tone of self-satisfaction. "She must be quite exceptional. Give her our best wishes when you write her next."

I thanked him for his call and for all the help he had given me in the past year. I was glad I had explained in my letter that I intended to stay on and fulfill my three-year obligation. The truth is, I was unable to say more, but as I hung up, I promised I would say it all or write it all before this chapter of my life was over. When the call from Rev. Cobb came later that same evening, he asked when was the soonest we could meet. Like Dr. Shacklock, the tone of his voice was cordial and revealed nothing critical or accusatory, only a comment that he was disappointed that I might be leaving. I thanked him for his consideration, told him I was free after eleven, and would take the earliest train from Higashi Wakayama.

Marty, of course, was not surprised that Bettie had said yes, though he was surprised her parents were willing to see her leave again. I told him that as far as I could tell by the swiftness of her reply, she had not consulted either of them.

"I doubt she made a long-distance call from Santurce," I told him. "My feeling is she pretty well does what she pleases and they go along—only child?" He laughed and said something about my taking that as a warning, and I assured him I had considered it seriously.

Predictably, my meeting with Rev. Cobb was cordial, and he evinced no hard feelings, only mentioning the problem with the school's scheduling at the very end and then assuring me that something could be worked out. His first concern, like Anne's, was if I had thought it through. I explained that for most of a year, I had been thinking about it, writing letters and reading her letters, and that I held no doubts we were both honest in our hopes and expectations.

"But have you thought about your future after Wakayama. Do you have a plan? You realize there may be more than just the two of you when you do return to the States. And have you thought about the living costs in Wakayama?"

I answered him as best I could and explained I never doubted we would have our family's support and then added, "I worked my way through college.

Before the war, I had no money from my parents, and after the war, only the GI Bill and my job in the library. I know what work is. I plan to become a college teacher, and Bettie fully supports my decision. We've discussed this in letters. President Itoigawa has offered us the house that Marty and I are living in now, well, offered it at a very reasonable rent."

When I had answered all his questions, he reminded me of a financial obligation I had for the summer at the seminary and for my transportation to Japan; then quickly as if he hadn't planned to mention it, he added, "But that can all be worked out, I'm sure."

Three days later I received the letter, informing me the council had accepted my resignation with the condition that I teach the fall term at Palmore Institute. I quickly informed Inoue sensei of the condition, and he assured me he would work out a schedule of classes that would allow me to fulfill my obligations to Palmore and Wa Dai In fact it had already been arranged.

The letter also noted that after December 31, 1951, the Board of Foreign Missions would not be responsible for my return passage to the U.S., and that I would no longer be under the Board's protection. In my letters to Corpus, I had mentioned Bettie and I no longer had guaranteed passage home, now that I had resigned. Fortuitously, in the winter and spring of 1951, just south of San Antonio on a small parcel of land, I suppose you could call the Gilliland legacy, a wildcat driller brought in a gusher and four wells of light Texas crude. In 1918, my father and his sister Kate, both orphans, inherited that same section of grassland that had been part of the original land Drake Grenade Gilliland had homesteaded in 1842. Until that winter, my mother and Aunt Kate had enjoyed only a small annual stipend from the grazing rights that never came to much more than $700 a year for each of them. It was the Texas myth translated into reality. I could barely recall ever hearing Mama even mention the land. But it was there, apparently waiting for someone who really needed it to produce something other than myths. When Mama first heard that I was no longer under the protection of the Mission Board she immediately wrote and assured me of passage home when the time came.

My resignation from the J3 program and Bettie's letter saying she would join me overshadowed everything else that summer. Dot and Louie Greer and children joined the annual missionary "diaspora" and took off for a two-month vacation to the Japanese Alps, where they had a small cabin along with dozens of other missionary families. Every summer most, if not all foreign missionaries vacated the warm, humid coastal lowlands for the high country. I declined their invitation, though they tried to dissuade me from staying in Wakayama alone, saying that Wakayama got very warm and humid in the summer. I had been raised on the flat coastal plains of South Texas—there was no muggier place on earth—and I really looked forward to the rainy season and a chance to read, perhaps write, and make visits to the USIS Library in Kobe. I explained that I hated to be away in case Bettie tried to contact me during the summer. To be honest, I told Louie I did not look forward to spending two months with that crowd from Hartford, particularly since I had just resigned from the program. Then I told him about the prayer vigil for Marty, Bill, and me the night before we departed the seminary.

"Think what they might do or say now that I've resigned, bugged out, so to speak. They'll have a Protestant rite of exorcism to caste out the Devil of temptation and bring me back to the fold. No, I've got to get things ready here for Bettie."

Louie laughed and agreed their zeal would be hard to deal with. That year of the war "bugging out" had become the most derogatory term for quitting when the going got rough. Louie had supported Bettie's and my venture, as had some of his close friends in the field, all Yale theologs like him. They believed Bettie and I would prove to everyone that it was possible to could live well on half the salary of full-time couples whose salary was regularly adjusted to fit the size of the family. Some, and Louie had been one, complained that they lived too comfortably for people doing the Lord's work.

Dr. Anne would be staying also. In the short time she had been in Wakayama, she and I had become friends. We talked books frequently and enjoyed each other's company. She was expecting a visit from a cousin who was now a citizen of Israel and was making her first visit home, via Japan, to Philadelphia since the establishment of the State of Israel. Also, before Bettie had written and agreed to marry me, Anne and I had talked about taking a trip with several students to see the shrine of Amaterasu O mi Kami, the Sun Goddess herself, at Ise Shima. Located on the northern side of Wakayama peninsula, it was the holiest of all Shinto shrines.

My decision to stay in Wakayama was easy. I had much reading to do and many letters to write. And I was looking forward to the rainy season and having an occasional lunch or supper with Anne, whose talk was always interesting. Most of the time, she spoke to me more as a colleague than as a professor addressing a beginning teacher. She would somtimes lecture me on the rudiments of educational psychology and classroom dynamics, or she would make me talk to her about a book I was reading, reminding me she had taught English for a number of years before working on her doctorate in psychology. Anne had brought with her several paperbacks that she passed on to me: *The*

Naked and the Dead, *The Young Lions*, and *Other Voices*, *Other Rooms*, among others. I was not allowed to proclaim one good, the other less, or the other too weird. I had to explain, even explicate the passages I considered key. She urged me to grow out of Scott Fitzgerald and encouraged me to explore Faulkner, though she admitted he was not her cup of *cha*. I would not be idle.

"Fitzgerald is all self-indulgence," she would announce and wait for me to demonstrate why I thought she was wrong.

Swimming at Wakanoura, catching an occasional movie, making trips into Osaka or Kobe, and, if I were lucky, catching up on my Japanese lessons more than filled my time. Finally, I knew I could depend on Miki or Saigo come by for lunch or a chat, and I knew that Yamagami san would also drop around. I would not be alone. So much had happened in the nine months since September that I welcomed the chance to savor it alone. It felt like home now: Wakayama, the strange house in Sekido, and Hara san's little bar not far down the street all felt like home. I would be there and would take care of the house as *ruso ban* so that Tonai san could take off for her visit to her family in Tanabe down the coast.

Bettie wrote she would not arrive before October, maybe even later, red tape and bureaucratic maneuvering being what they were in both the State Department and MacArthur's headquarters. I recalled how my getting a passport and military permit had been a series of Gordian knots. Since Japan was still technically at war with the U.S., all civilians wishing to enter the country had to be approved not by Japanese immigration authorities, but by MacArthur's headquarters. She would first need a military permit as well as a U.S. passport, and only then would she be able to secure passage. When school let out for the summer recess in Wakayama, Bettie would just be arriving at her home in Wichita Falls, and I felt I needed to be on hand in case a letter from her arrived, asking for my help in securing the military permit or in persuading Harold and Edna, her father and mother, of the rightness of her coming to marry me. For nine months, I had written two or three times a week, sometimes more; and while her letters were less frequent, they came often enough and were rich enough to satisfy my hunger. In the days before leaving Puerto Rico, she had written of her plans to sail from San Juan for Galveston on a Lykes Lines freighter. And more recently, she had written that she wanted to cross the Pacific aboard a freighter from a port on the Gulf Coast, presumably Galveston. At a time when flying was becoming the only right way to go, for her—and I agreed—a sea voyage made much better sense.

The day after everyone left town, a delegation of Marty's liberal arts, English Speaking Society led by Jisaka san and Chieko Takehata dropped by the house and invited me to accompany them on a camping and hiking trip into the wilds of southern Wakayama Prefecture. Marty had mentioned that they were coming to see me with a request, but he had not said what kind of request. I knew Chieko and Jisaka san quite well and recognized the others as students in Marty's second-year class. Jisaka san began by apologizing for disturbing my nap. I had been sitting at the low table in the large room, reading my new *Saturday Review*, and had dozed off. Tonai san had shown them in, scolding them, as was her wont, for disturbing *sensei's hiruné*. They began with the usual apologies for disturbing me, but by this time, we were all well enough acquainted that their bows were as much in jest as they were serious. I assured them I was not disturbed and welcomed them and asked Oba san to bring tea, thinking to myself, *now, this is why I stayed home.*

I had really begun to appreciate the large tatami room and especially now with no plans, no one to meet especially, just Jisaka and Chieko. Jisaka began by asking if I were not lonesome or homesick now that all the others had left town. I explained that I was enjoying the time, but that I was hardly alone. The house was full of friends. He said the ESS would like me to go with them on a camping trip to Doro Hacho National Park at the southern tip of the prefecture. He described the river gorge, the waterfall, and the temples they were planning to visit and said they believed I would enjoy seeing that remote part of Japan.

"Doro Hacho is like old Japan," he said, "only small villages in rough country." He described the route and the train and a boat ride up through the deep gorge and explained the club had already bought the tickets. I would have nothing to do but go. I was deeply flattered that they had thought to ask me, particularly since only Jisaka and Chieko could be accused of wanting me along to practice their English.

Chieko san said, "We want you to come with us. We think you will like to see the falls and see Doro Hacho." She paused and then continued, "Tonai san says you are all alone this summer. That you are waiting for your," she paused and said with a smile, "*koibito*, your sweetheart?"

It pleased me to hear her speak about Bettie without embarrassment, without covering her mouth or giggling, and to hear her call me Joe san instead of the awkward *Giriran sensei*. A few students, those I'd known the longest, had begun to use the less cumbersome form of address, but most still considered *Joe san* too informal. I was touched that they had spoken to Tonai san first and found out that I would be home and presumably would be lonely. Looking back now as I write this, I can see the purely Japanese nature of the request, something I had not noticed then. Even more enriching for me is the idea that I had become so closely a part of it all that there was *nothing* to notice. Jisaka and the others nodded.

"Oh, I see," I said. "Then you must want me to go along so you can practice your English."

They laughed and Jisaka said, "I think not, Joe san. Perhaps so you can practice Japanese."

"Joe san" did not come trippingly off his tongue as it had Chieko's. It would take some getting used to for him. Familiarity was, for people like Jisaka, a major step; and in a way, it marked a major step in my relationship with students. I thanked them for asking me and said I would be glad to go. I asked what I would need to take. I had no sleeping bag or hiking boots or even a rucksack. They said I needed only a blanket and told me where I could buy a rucksack if I felt I really needed one. According to Chieko's young brother, who was also going along, all I needed to do was roll my things in an army blanket and secure it at both ends. His father had shown him how, he said. He said we would not be hiking far, that my old white bucks would be comfortable since the trails were neither rocky nor steep like mountain trails. It was the first time anyone had mentioned my dirty white buckskin shoes, the badge of the American undergraduate, that I had been so proud of and had worn so often. It turned out the bucks were a source of humor like my inappropriate red plaid jacket that I wore everywhere during the winter— bright red plaid being for small children and *oji san,* old men.

When Oba san brought the tea, she sat and joined us as they began describing the trip. Jisaka, obviously the leader of the expedition, explained the outing would last five or six days; and as he described our itinerary in detail, Oba san listened as if to make sure they were not going to endanger or inconvenience the sensei. She was in a jovial mood, laughing and smiling as they explained about the rigors of the trip. From time to time, she would exclaim how beautiful it was in the gorge and how she had gone there as a young girl before they had motor-driven boats. All year, Marty and I had grown closer and closer to our group of regular visitors to the open houses and to our ESS students, but I had not felt so fortunate as I did at this moment. When they left, Tonai san lingered beside the table and said she was glad I was going with them and then thoughtfully added that they were all *taihen ii hito sama,* very good people. With her honorific *sama* I knew the sentiment was genuine. Then with a tear in her eye, she told me she was glad because it would make the time pass more quickly for me while I waited for Bettie *chan.* Her endearing *"chan"* pleased me immensely. Language, often a barrier, can also become a rich bridge, I felt, thankful that I was catching on to some of the subtleties.

Chieko's remark about my *koibito* and now Oba san's seemed to connect me to a circle of friends as I had never been. Their invitation was the highest compliment I had received since coming to Wakayama, and it marked an end I felt to my initiation, coming as it did at the end of my first academic year. First, I was no longer *sensei*, an honorific neither Marty nor I felt we were qualified to receive. Second, they had spoken to me in both English and Japanese, albeit simple Japanese enunciated with great care. And finally, offering me no special considerations was a larger step than I realized. Though Marty and I were closer in age to our students than we were to any of the faculty, the barrier of traditional formality, far more rigid than any such division in the States, was always a gap separating teachers and students, more like an abyss in Japan. Until this invitation, I had often felt that the gap would never close.

Two days later, when we arrived at Higashi Wakayama station, there was already a large crowd waiting to board the train for the south. The electric line from Osaka stopped at Higashi Wakayama, and an old coal-burning steam train took over from that point south to the tip of Wakayama Prefecture. It couldn't have been seventy kilometers to the last stop, but it would take us several hours through the mountains and along a winding coastal track to reach our destination. Growing anxious as the crowd increased, Jisaka urged each of us to run for the cars as soon as the train arrived. He was sure we would probably have to stand most of the way, he said. There was only one train a day to the south, so everyone going south had to take the steam train unless he took the bus, which was more expensive. When the train finally backed into the little station, the mob surged forward and consumed the cars as so many army ants. I pushed my way forward and pulled Chieko up to the step, forcing her into the car ahead of me just as the train began to roll. It was a scene out of British India or an old movie of revolutionary China: *The Last Train from Hung Chow.* People clung to the steps and side handles, swaying as the train moved away from the platform at the speed of a fast walker. I leaned back, gripping the railing, hoping someone would squeeze farther into the car so I could stand erect. Had I fallen I would have suffered only light injuries since the cars were moving so slowly, and then I felt a hand on my shoulder and heard Jisaka. "Joe san, come with me."

It was ludicrous. He was walking back alongside the moving train, telling me he had found a place for me to sit back toward the end of the train. I stepped off and jogged along beside the moving car a few steps and then let the cars crawl by until Jisaka directed me into the doorway of the last car where there were no hangers on. A conductor was sitting in a small room at the end of the car and was beckoning me to a small padded bench. Jisaka explained that the conductor had invited sensei to ride with him, and then he moved on through the car to the other members of our party. Before he left, I asked if he made sure everyone was on, and he assured me they were.

Gradually, the train picked up speed and moved inland among the hills, stopping to drop off passengers, rarely adding new ones. It was obviously a normal pattern; no one seemed perturbed by the crowding or the precarious positions of people hanging on the sides. In less than half an hour, no one was hanging from the doorways; and in less than another half hour, all the passengers were seated. The conductor worked over some records or schedules, nodding and smiling at me from time to time. I pulled out a paperback novel I had saved for the trip and tried to read, but the shaking and bouncing made it difficult, so I sat back and watched the wonderful wooded country slip by on one side and occasional seaside views on the other. I thought of the *san sui* (mountain and water) scroll paintings, kakemono, you see so often in the little alcoves of most Japanese homes. From time to time, a light rain fell, alternately cooling and humidifying the compartment and emphasizing the beauty of it all.

It was a little past eleven when we pulled into the small station at the end of the line. Fewer than two dozen passengers in addition to our contingent stepped down onto the platform, sooty and happy to be alive. Jisaka led us to the bus stop where we took an old bus to the temples and the high falls at Nachi. A few minutes later, we bought sushi bento, box lunches of sushi and rice rolled in seaweed, and picnicked below the falls. Until that trip, I had not loved sushi nor it me; but now sitting below the long ribbon of spray and water with my friends, I, for the first time, actually enjoyed the cold rice and seaweed, the raw fish and pickled radish. It was lovely, and were it all to suddenly end here, it would have been worth the trip. Lush green ferns and trees framed the wispy ribbon of falling water against dark gray rock. A cool spray fell on us as we sat looking up. I had never seen such falls, had never hiked anywhere except with full field pack in the army. *How dumb it would have been for me to refuse their invitation*, I thought. From there, we hiked with packs several kilometers along the river's edge and boarded a long, narrow, flat-bottomed boat that would take us up through the deep gorge of Doro Hacho. The boat resembled the long narrow fishing boats in the Hiroshige prints, except instead of the oars or long poles, it was driven by a radial airplane engine and propeller. The boats held twenty-five passengers seated beneath a long canopy in two long aisles. We sat directly on the wooden floorboards with only thin straw matting between the floor and us. The engine and airscrew pushed the craft up the river over rocks often so near the surface we could feel them pressing through the bottom against our butts. A holiday fever hovered over it all, though many of the passengers were regular commuters who took the boats daily on their way home from jobs down river or on their way to work in the forests lining the cliffs high above us. Laughter and exclamations of *oohs* and *aahs* filled the boat when we scraped the rocks or turned a sharp corner in the gorge or entered a wide, still, glassy pool. Though only a handful of us were tourists, a festive mood prevailed all the way through the gorge. In our small group, only Jisaka had visited the gorge before, and he was enjoying our excited responses to the sheer cliffs, the beetling crests, and hanging trees.

In a little over an hour, we reached our destination, a landing and a switch back trail that lead to a small inn perched high above the river on a sheer cliff. I hefted my pack and followed my companions up the trail, where steps had been carved in the rock in some places; also, there were well-crafted handrails and small wooden plank bridges spanning small mountain streams along the way. At the top of the trail less than a kilometer from our landing was the lovely inn built in the style of a Shinto shrine or the traditional Japanese farmhouse with a heavily thatched roof and long, narrow timbers making giant Xs at each end of the roof. The raw-weathered beams seemed as old as the primeval forest surrounding us. We walked past a long veranda and made our way to the clearing near the lip of the gorge, and there we sat up the tents, one a large pyramid tent supported by a stout pole that broke down into sections and stowed away in one of the packs. The other tent resembled a large pup tent, like the ones I had used in the army except it was large enough to hold four instead of the regulation two. The surface where we set up the tents was so rocky that I heard much good-humored harping and complaining to Jisaka, who had planned the trip and picked the spot. Sleeping might be difficult here, someone said, but Jisaka just laughed and said we would be so tired we could sleep on nails. Although I had not camped out or backpacked since basic training, it felt good, even the hike up the long trail from the river. The air was cooler and crisper here than it had been when we left Wakayama, and I was glad I had brought two of my old OD army blankets instead of one as I had planned originally.

Someone asked where I would like to make my bed; since I was the sensei, I had first choice. I laughed because the ground was equally hard and rocky no matter where I chose to spread my blankets. I chose a corner of the big tent where the rocks appeared to be fairly small and level and spread a blanket and my other gear. Everyone began pooling the food and the cooking gear we had brought. As soon as we settled down and had everything organized, everyone agreed it was time to cook supper. I backed off and watched as they all pitched in, some gathering firewood, others hauling water from the spring near the inn, and others pouring rice into the strange-looking Japanese Army mess gear, deep oval-shaped pots with close fitting lids. Our cook, without bothering to measure, poured rice and water into the pots, covered them tightly, set them in the coals, and backed off. There were two pots prepared but nothing else. Chieko brought out two large cans of herring in tomato sauce, a can of pickled *daikon*, a large, white, very spicy radish, and two large cans of pears. I saw they had spared me most of the weight. Canned fish and fruit and bags of rice were all arranged in a neat pile in one corner of the tent, enough food for several days. They had hauled, I noted, a huge quantity of canned goods up with them. When I complained that my pack had been too light, they laughed and said I was the sensei and shouldn't carry heavy loads; someone even referred to me as *ojii san*, or "honorable old man." I was all of four years older than Jisaka, and only three years older than Chieko, but they were right, in a way. I had brought up the rear and was puffing the loudest.

No one timed the rice, but when the time came, the cook fished the two pots off the coals with sticks and gingerly worked the lids off. Then, *voila!* The rice was done. The meal was quite delicious. Apologizing for not bringing my portion of the rice, I spooned out my rice in the tin plate I'd brought. Chieko laughed and said I had indeed brought it; she had gotten my rice ration from Oba san before we left. She also pointed to several cans of fruit she said Oba san had contributed from my larder. It was the first time I had seen them so relaxed and informal. They even felt comfortable correcting my Japanese and made bold as to scold me for not learning to speak better Japanese, suggesting we start a Japanese Speaking Society so Joe san could learn Japanese. That was all spoken in slow and simple Japanese to make sure I understood; it made me feel part of rather than apart from this special group.

One of the older members, a clerk in the dean's office, asked very politely in Japanese if I had understood what they were saying; and when I said I had understood most of it, he made the familiar *saa* sound and then applauded. Someone remarked that he had never teased or jested with a sensei before, to which I responded, "*Omedeto*," congratulation*s*. It was mostly Chieko and Jisaka who first ventured into this no-man's-land of familiarity, but the others, except Mariko, the other young woman, gradually joined in. I was *Joe san*, never sensei, and I was not deferred to or placed first after the initial offer to have first choice in a place to lay my bed, nor was anyone else, with the possible exception of Jisaka, who was our acknowledged leader. When they changed *Joe san* to *O-joo-chan*, I called a halt, pretending I was angry and told them I was not a "pretty girl," the literal translation of *O-joo-chan*. I was, I said, in fact, a "pretty boy." The two young clerks from the dean's office looked shocked at the student's teasing and jesting with a teacher. In truth it was, I felt, the highest compliment I had been paid since arriving in Japan: they were teasing a friend who happened to be a sensei.

We spent the next two days hiking the trails and swimming in the river, more like bathing and washing away the soot of train travel. It was idyllic. The country was beautiful, the deep gorge and lush, jungle-like forests were unlike anything I had ever seen. Our food was simple but tasty, and the company exceptional. When Jisaka announced that the inn had agreed to sell us another day's food supply if we wished to stay, I offered to pay for the extra day, though I would, I said, be leaving. At first, they insisted they pay their share but finally accepted my offer when I had argued it was only fair I pay my share because they had carried the heaviest loads. When I announced I needed to get back, they seemed genuinely disappointed, but I explained I was anxious to begin working on my notes for a history class I wanted to teach in the fall and that I had been looking forward to a couple of weeks alone at the house. Also, I explained that I had promised Oba san that she could have some time with her family at Tanabe on the coast.

Finally, I said I had been away too long and was hoping to have letters from Bettie san waiting for me. By now they knew my plans to marry in the fall and were consumed with curiosity about Bettie, whose picture they had seen on my desk in the study. When I mentioned Bettie, they said they understood and then boldly asked me to tell them about her and how we met, which I did to their rapt attention. One of them, in the most sentimental tones possible, remarked the story was like a motion picture story; and when I replied I also believed it was more like a movie than real life, they grew silent. At breakfast the next morning, I said my farewells and told them how much I had enjoyed being with them all, that they had paid me *o-seji*, a great compliment, by asking me along. Suddenly, they once more became gakku sei and knelt and bowed their respects. Then we all hiked down to the landing where I said farewell again, and then for the second time on the trip, they all bowed solemnly and called me sensei, calling as I got aboard, "*Sayonara, sensei. Kiotsukete!*" The Japanese, I had to admit, do farewells better than anybody.

As I climbed in to find a place, the other passenger and the boatman and crew regarded me, the only gaijin, solemnly and made way offering me the most comfortable spot. And when I disembarked at the end of the gorge, the boat crew bowed and called me sensei. It was a marvelous feeling making my way to the bus stop, sensing the eyes staring at the lone gaijin far off in that remote corner of Japan. I wasn't sure when I left if I should have stayed with them two more days, but I had the feeling that they were both happy and sorry I was leaving early, happy because it meant they could relax and be themselves, sorry because having me along gave their outing a difference. It had been a rare time for me, a perfect way to end my first year's teaching at Wakayama University.

On the train back to Wakayama, I found a seat next to an open window, reached into my pack, and pulled out my new copy of *The Portable Faulkner* and settled back to read. There had been so much to do and so much to see that I hadn't read a word since leaving the house four days ago, and I had been looking forward to reading more Faulkner since buying the volume at the English bookstore in Osaka. Ever since Miki had asked me about Faulkner shortly after we arrived, I had wanted to read more. Now as I opened and read the table of contents, wondering where to begin, I decided to read Malcolm Cowley's introduction. I had read *Sanctuary* and "That Evening Sun" and *Wild Palms* with its oddly arranged tale, *The Old Man.* I regarded "That Evening Sun" as one of the best short stories I'd read at the time, judging it as second only to Fitzgerald's "Babylon Revisited." I was only fifteen when I read both stories and still had much before me. Indeed, there was a whole world of literature that would occupy a lifetime, I thought. At the time, I was undecided what I would teach: history, English, government, or anthropology, though the latter, I believed, was well beyond my powers at that time. I preferred short works then, believing I should sample more authors in less time, than reading larger works like the novels of Wolfe, Tolstoy, Melville, and Dostoevsky, works that required too much time. I felt an urgency to get on with it. I was making up for lost time, trying to read all those works mentioned in Wilson and Trilling.

When I arrived at the house, Oba san greeted me with a handful of letters from home, letters from Jane and Mama, several from Bettie, even a letter from Bill Asbury in Tokyo. Jane's had French stamps, and Bettie's were still postmarked San Juan, though I knew she was by that time on her way home or already there. She had not spoken to her parents, had only written to them about her plans, and I was anxious to read what her parents would say of her plan to join me in Japan. Her two letters were short one-page letters, one reporting she had gotten passage from San Juan to Galveston on a Lykes freighter, the other that she was boarding and that she had written her parents of her plans to come to Japan. The brief letters were filled with hope and joy at the prospect of joining me. I floated as I read them, and I told Oba san, who laughed and cried with joy and said I must be the happiest man in the world.

A few days after I got back from the camping trip, Oba san left for her home down the coast, though she was reluctant to leave me alone in the house without a *ruso-ban* to guard the premises in case I wanted to see a movie or go shopping. I told her I could manage easily, that I could cook my meals and would go to the public bath and spend my time studying. Miki and Saigo came by from time to time when they were in town, usually around lunchtime, which was always simple: a bowl of rice, boiled vegetables, usually kidney beans and onions, with a bottle of Nippon Beer. Inoue sensei and I worked on O'Neill, finished *The Hairy Ape*, *Emperor Jones*, and began working on *Iceman Cometh*.

Shortly before the spring semester ended, a young man had come to the house and introduced himself as Takehara san, a student in literature at Tokyo University. He was finishing his bachelor's degree in English and had come to ask if I could read his bachelor's thesis before he submitted it for final approval by the English department at Tokyo University. It was a study of Virginia Woolf's use of stream of consciousness in four novels. He was fairly certain there were no gross errors in English style, he said, but he would appreciate it if I could just give him my opinion of how it read. I told him I had read only one novel of Woolf's, *Mrs. Dalloway*, and insisted I certainly was not qualified to evaluate anything he might have concluded about her work, particularly regarding stream of consciousness, about which I had only a vague idea. I confessed my degree had not been in English, but psychology, though I had skimming knowledge of what they meant by stream of consciousness. He said he understood and offered me copies of *Jacob's Room* and *To the Lighthouse* in case I wanted to read more Virginia Woolf. I could see how I was being drawn, not by choice, though willingly, more and more into literature, first with Inoue and now with Takehara san.

So with nothing more pressing, I read the two novels. Before I began reading his thesis, I made a point of visiting Anne Edelman to hear her explain about stream of consciousness and to tell me what she thought of Woolf. When Don and I shared rooms with Dick Glover in New York, I read Joyce's *Portrait of the Artist as a Young Man* and found it fascinating, especially the opening passages spoken from the mind of a child, but I'd not known at the time that Joyce was writing in the stream of consciousness mode. Joyce seemed natural now after reading the thesis. I understood clearly what it was all about and even recalled a passage in *Sanctuary* where Benbow becomes obsessed with Little Belle and the odors of flowers and the dripping shrimp and the sound of corn husks all added a deeper sense of reality to the narrative. In reading his thesis, I had come across William James's reference to stream of consciousness, which I mentioned to Anne, and she agreed James's use that grew out of his attempt to describe how mind and memory work—like a stream--defined the method as well as any. Now even the long, convoluted speeches in O'Neill's *Strange Interlude* began to make sense in a way they had not earlier.

Takehara and his brother became regular callers that summer, the older brother a linguist and teacher of English at the Catholic girl's school in Wakayama. The Woolf scholar was an easygoing, much-westernized young man who spoke almost impeccable American English. He had worked off and on for the occupation troops just after the war and had picked up quite a bit more than his strong American accent, which his older brother derided in his own impeccable Oxbridge accents.

After I returned from Doro Hacho, Yamagami also began to come around, usually in the evening after he had gotten off work and after I had eaten. Surprised that I had not left town with the others, he asked me why. I pretended I was immersed in my studies, that I was deeply involved in preparing lectures for a course in cultural history of the U.S. I hoped to teach one day. Then I confessed that the real reason was to save my money because I had asked Bettie to come to Japan to marry me, and that I was resigning from the missionary program. To my chagrin, he seemed not the least surprised and remarked that he was very happy I had found someone who would travel so far. He asked if I had known her for a long time. I pointed to her photo sitting on the desk and told him how we had met in Hartford, how she had flown off to Puerto Rico, and how we had continued to stay in touch by writing letters. I told him that because of the letters, I felt I knew her better than I had known anyone. He laughed and said it was like a story or a movie. He had never known anyone who would do such a thing, or anyone like Bettie for agreeing to, and he hoped that she would like Japan. I admitted it was unusual; no one I knew, I said, would do such a thing.

When I explained that I had to resign from the mission program and apply for a permanent job with the university and would have to be more careful about money, he agreed it would be difficult living on a Japanese teacher's salary. Yamagami understood that without the umbrella of the Kyodan or some other institution, we would be entirely on our own unlike most Americans living in Japan at the time. I agreed it might not be easy, but explained I was an innate optimist, always judging a glass half full rather than half empty, and that she had said it wouldn't matter since she had never been rich anyway. He concluded on the spot that Bettie was exceptional, and I agreed.

When he asked how long I planned to continue to teach at Wa Dai, I said I wanted to stay three years, my original commitment. I felt I had an obligation even though I would no longer be under the auspices of the Mission Board. I explained that I wanted to return to the University of Texas and get my master's degree so I could teach in an American college.

"You shouldn't think I'm sacrificing anything, Yamagami san," I said. "Wa Dai is giving me far more than I am giving back. The university has already given me a great deal."

We talked for a long time, almost past the time for his last train. I urged him to come again when Tonai san returned, and we made plans to go swimming or sailing at Wakanoura. In the next weeks, I began to depend on his dropping by. Occasionally, when Madenokoji accompanied him, the three of us would rent a sailing dinghy at Wakanoura and try our hands at sailing. I regretted not insisting that Luther allow me more time at the tiller of his *Wench* back in Corpus. When Made complained about our lack of skill at the tiller, we willingly let him act as captain.

Yamagami and I often walked along the beach at Suiken or through the shops and inns of Wakanoura, hardly speaking, and other times we would sit and drink tea at a low table in a large room of one of the inns with the best view of the bay and distant hills, and then we would talk about books or movies we liked. I told him how an American sensei, Dr. Joe Yamagiwa, had come here last fall and had recited waka for us in a singsong Japanese style.

Once, he and I walked the entire distance from Wakanoura to my house, taking the road over the low pass down to Suikenguchi and on to the university. He remarked about the legendary importance of Suiken beach and how Jimmu Tenno, the son of Amaterasu O Mi Kami, the Sun Goddess, had come ashore on the beach where we walked thus discovering Japan and becoming the first Emperor of Japan. I said I'd heard the legend that many Japanese took to be authentic history, and he nodded, neither affirming nor disputing the story. We had reached a point in our friendship when we felt comfortable talking about the war, and there on the beach that day he asked what had I done during the war. I told him I missed the combat in Germany by days, but I served there in the occupation and later in the occupation of Korea. Then I asked him what he did.

"I was an officer, an ensign, and commanded a three-man submarine." He smiled, silently amused at my shock. "It was a very small submarine, Joe san. Only a crew of three."

I stammered, "B-b-but . . .."

He nodded. "Yes, it was a suicide submarine. But it never left port. Twice the B-29s blew my submarine out of the water. And then"—he paused—"the Hiroshima bomb ended it. It saved my life."

After a moment of thought, I replied, "You know, Yamagami san, we have more in common than you might think. We are almost the same age, and we both volunteered for service. In June of 1945, after I joined my division in Germany, I volunteered for an active theater. The battle for Okinawa was in full scale. I thought I shouldn't miss out. The day before I was to leave for a port of embarkation, they dropped the bomb on Hiroshima and all troop movements in Germany were frozen. I was an infantryman, a replacement, and would surely have been in the invasion."

"Yes, the bomb saved our lives. It also saved my mother's life and my younger brother's and sister's, I am sure of it. I don't think the emperor or the generals would have ever surrendered."

We were silent for a long moment, and then he said in Japanese, "*Taihen omoshiroi, des né,*" which translates as "It's very interesting, isn't it?" A simple truth lies at the heart of every cliché. We rarely talked about the war, and I don't recall that we ever mentioned it again after that. I have, in fact, forgotten most of what we talked of those days, though I recall he visited the house quite frequently. We never talked about religion as such, but when I told him I had spent some time on Koya San, the seat of Shingon Buddhism, he asked what I thought, and I told him I liked it a great deal, felt very comfortable staying a night in a small temple. I told him that a student, my friend Saigo, whom he had met at the house, invited me along with three or four other students, and we had spent a night in a temple that his family helped support.

I told him how beautiful and peaceful it was and especially impressive when the monks rose early and passed our sleeping room chanting. He spoke of Nara and its great temples and how one day he would like to show me the Todaiji and the Dai Butsu, a great bronze Buddha. I spoke of seeing the great bronze Buddha at Kamakura and how much it had affected me the first time I saw it. The moment it came into view, I felt a great peace come over me. Even from a distance, its graceful posture conveyed a sense of serenity and absolute calm. He nodded, said that he understood but was sure that I would feel the same sense of peace if I were to see the Dai Butsu of Nara.

"I will take you and Bettie to see the Dai Butsu in Nara next spring when the cherry trees are in bloom," he said.

Of all the visitors I had that summer, the visits of Yamagami were the most important. Sometimes when I would come back to the house after a trip to Osaka or Kobe, I would find him there talking to Tonai san, and *I* would join *them*. I understood he had come to visit with her as much as with me, and once she told me that of all my friends who came to the house, Yamagami san was her favorite. Making a gentle sweep of her own face with her fingers as if she were holding a paper fan, she would describe his face and how he made her feel whenever she saw him. I could not follow the exact meaning of her words—my Japanese was still too rudimentary to follow someone's subtle thought—but there was no mistaking the feelings she conveyed.

In his introduction to *Sacred Journey*, Frederick Beuchner says: "all theology, like all fiction, is autobiography, and . . . what a theologian is doing essentially is examining as honestly as he can the rough-and-tumble of his own experience with all its ups and downs, its mysteries and loose ends, and expressing . . . the truths about God that he believes he has found implicit there." He doesn't suggest, however, that the corollary is true, that all autobiography is necessarily theology; logic grants only that it *may* be so. However, a philosophy was evolving out of the experiences of life that was less about God than about the connections in and of all things: mind, experience, history, feelings, friendships, time, and in the words of Norman McLean: *A River Runs Through It*. That summer, I know now, I learned truths that lay outside earlier knowing, everything I had known before in the "rough-and-tumble" of prior experience reaching back even to the abandoned child on the parallel in Korea. Wordsworth's words said it first for me in the "Immortality Ode" when he wrote about thoughts or truths that often "lie too deep for tears." Maclean's river metaphor that serves as title to his great book will stand for Beuchner's God, at least it will in my case, and the line from Wordsworth's ode tells explicitly, to me at least what that epiphany meant in Wakayama, at Suiken Beach, and at Wakanoura when I had tea with Yamagami. Perhaps it was no coincidence, no accident that my resigning from the mission program virtually coincided with these moments. I experienced no visible sign, no bright moment of awakening, no revelation in a dream or a burning bush or vision of a young girl up to her thighs in a river, although my trip up the river in Doro Hacho possessed moments of *knowing* or *understanding* that I had never felt before. And that first night on the rim at supper with the students spoke more than words and in a way assured me I was right. That summer, things began to change, and Yamagami, Jisaka, Takehata san were all instruments or agents the change.

By the end of August, Marty had returned from his trip around Honshu and had packed up and moved on to Tokyo. A short time later, Louie, Dot, and the children returned from Nojiri. Bettie had written that she needed a letter from President Itoigawa stating that I had a contract to teach and a letter from me confirming that I was able to support her. Because I would be teaching the fall term at Wa Dai and at Palmore, I continued to draw my pay from the Board of Missions and was, therefore, still under the protective umbrella of the Mission Board. Possibilities for bureaucratic snafus were enormous. In her original application for a military permit, she stated that I was employed by Wakayama University, which was under the Japanese Ministry of Education, the *Mumbushoo*, and the letter from Itoigawa san would confirm that, but I was also technically under the umbrella of the Board of Missions of the Methodist Church because I would be teaching the fall term at Palmore. Of course, nowhere was there a mention of my impending separation. It was confusing enough for someone in Washington or Tokyo, either in the State Department or the Pentagon, to get it all balled up. I was sure that both the military government under MacArthur or the Japanese Immigration or both would need proof that Bettie and I had guaranteed passages back to the States. By resigning from the mission program, I had given up that guarantee, but I was never afraid that we would be stranded. We would need tickets or a written guarantee that our passage home was secure. When President Itoigawa produced the letter, I sent it off with mine for Bettie to mail to the State Department. By the time classes resumed, word came that her permit had been approved. All she was waiting for was space on a Lykes freighter leaving from Galveston or Houston. It was all quite unbelievable.

Inoue sensei worked out a schedule that allowed me to commute back and forth between Wakayama and Kobe and meet all of my classes at both locations. At first, it looked impossible; but in the end, it worked. I would leave Wakayama every Monday at noon and arrive in Kobe with time to prepare for classes Monday night. On Tuesday, I could sleep late and meet Tuesday night classes at the institute and then take a late train back to Wakayama and meet Wednesday morning classes, returning to Kobe in time for my evening classes. Inoue had scheduled classes Thursday afternoon, allowing me to take a morning train from Kobe. Friday morning classes at Wa Dai would end my week. Saturdays I would die. If I made connections on time, the trip between Wakayama and Kobe took just under two hours, allowing me time to read and go over lesson plans or check composition assignments. Today, the pace would be killing, but that fall of 1951, nothing seemed impossible, no task too daunting, if the end result was to have Bettie with me.

About a week into the semester, a letter from Bettie arrived saying that she had secured a berth on the SS *Charles Lykes* and was sailing from Galveston around the first of October. She planned to take the train from Wichita Falls to Corpus Christi, stay with Mama and Albert for several days, after which they would drive her to Galveston where she would board the SS. *Charles Lykes*. Back in the spring, when I wrote Mama of my plans to leave the program and to get married, I had been surprised that she was pleased that Bettie had accepted my proposal and even more surprised when she assured me that the new oil wells on the old Gilliland homestead outside Floresville would guarantee our return passage when the time came. I had not asked her for the money, but I had mentioned that the only problem I could foresee was the problem of our passage home when the time came. Bettie had written how lucky she had been to have leaped weeks and months of prenuptial teas and showers, along with the well-chosen words of caution and unsolicited advice from well-meaning parents, relatives, and friends of the family. It began to sound as if I were really going to happen.

The trip from the Gulf Coast would take about a month, she said. She would pass through the Panama Canal, stop at San Pedro outside Los Angeles, and then sail straight across the Pacific to Japan. She wrote of her excitement at the prospect of a long sea voyage aboard a freighter, happy that there would be only two other passengers, a middle-aged missionary couple heading to their station in the Philippines..

When she wrote that she had told her parents of her plans to meet me in Japan and get married and that they had consented, or assented, I wrote them expressing my thanks and telling why I had asked her to join me rather than coming back to the States. Having never met Bettie's parents, I could not tell what ordeal she might have endured, what anxieties her parents might have voiced, though from what I knew of her and from what I had read in her letters, I needn't have worried. Harold and Edna had never refused her anything they felt she honestly wanted. When I met Harold and Edna almost two years later, I realized she had never suffered at all. Harold had been mostly silent, she said, and I could believe it. He was never one to argue with the women in the family. Though he had strong reservations about her leaving, he refrained from criticizing anything she did or said. Edna had approved wholeheartedly her daughter's decision. Bettie, an only child, was their life's focus and their pride. Harold told me that Bettie had always been able to get her way no matter how eccentric or lunatic her plans, chiefly because he could never withstand the onslaught of her determination and because Edna always took her side. He was always outnumbered from the start, he said. But he said that with pride in both Bettie and her mother, her going off to Laredo to teach in a church school on the border, traveling into Mexico alone, first on a crowded Mexican bus and then hitching a ride with total strangers, teaching a year in Puerto Rico, and then sailing home from there on a freighter, were not the things young women in Wichita Falls would ordinarily choose to do; but for Bettie, who was anything but an ordinary young woman, they were perfectly normal.

As soon as I learned that the *Charles Lykes* was scheduled to dock at Yokohama about the first of November, I spoke to Inoue sensei and to Reverend Cobb, asking for time off to meet her when the ship docked, and they agreed. There would be no problem finding a substitute for my classes. In the weeks that followed, I was thankful for my heavy schedule of classes in Kobe and Wa Dai and for the hectic commute between cities. Class preparations on two campuses, grading and correcting composition papers at Palmore, made time pass swiftly. Just days before she was due to land, a day after my birthday, a radiogram arrived, saying that the SS *Charles Lykes* would put in at Osaka and not Yokohama. It was better than perfect. All occasions seemed to inform in favor of us, I thought. I would require no time off at all, and there would be no long train trip from Yokohama. The next day, a telephone call from the Lykes agent in Osaka reported that Bettie Jane Crumpton would be disembarking on a Wednesday morning, and telling me that I should be at their Osaka office by eight so they could drive me to the pier where she would come ashore. The night before the ship docked, classes seemed chaotic; the conversation class flew by in a haze, the reading class droned on interminably, and the composition class seemed mired in trivialities. I couldn't sleep, couldn't read, but sat up listening to inanities on the Armed Forces Radio. On my way to the Osaka agency, I wondered how it all could have happened so smoothly. It had seemed impossible back then on that warm spring day when Anne Edelman had shocked me with her point-blank question: "Why don't you ask her?" What we were doing was sheer folly, I knew, everyone knew, but perhaps that was the reason I felt such great joy and satisfaction. Marrying with no more surety for the future than a promise of a job that paid barely enough to support a single person, no secured passage home,* no plans for the future after Japan other than a vague idea of earning a master's degree in *some* subject that *migh*t lead to a college teaching position: surely, this was madness.

If I were able to cite a single explanation of how it all really came about and why, it would be Bettie's persistence, her single-minded vision that travel

---

* At the time, it was not clear that my mother would offer me a portion of the proceeds from the gushers in Texas. That too was part of the incredible and miraculous series of events that worked so smoothly to bring about this marriage of true minds, but when I asked Bettie and she agreed, I did not have a guaranteed return passage.

is an end in itself, like a Kantian imperative that requires no teleological argument. It was not the normal thing for a young woman to do in those days, though there have always been women driven by a desire to take that road less traveled. From our first meeting in Hartford, I sensed the strength that lay behind her refusal to follow conventional paths; I was fortunate to be there at the right time and to point to the road. She had two invitations to travel that summer, she wrote, one was to Wyoming, the other Japan. The trip to Japan having less certitude than the one to Wyoming won out. I liked to believe that my letters made the difference and weighed the argument in favor of Japan. I was under no illusions that Bettie's passion for travel may have tilted the scales, that neither personal charm nor my skill as a letter writer was the deciding factor. Today after more than sixty years, she is still the chief planner of all our treks and trips, whether they be to Trebizond or Moscow, Luxor or Petra, the top of Mount Rainier, the Little Big Horn of Montana, or the Big Bend of Texas.

Louie, who had driven to Osaka in his old Jeep, was waiting at the pier when I arrived, and the SS *Charles Lykes* was anchored out in the bay, off-loading its cargo onto lighters. The Lykes agent who drove me to the pier hustled me onto a motor launch and out to the ship where Bettie was awaiting my arrival. Our meeting at last seemed another part of the miracle. We wasted little time loading her things into Louie's trailer and heading off to Wakayama, a trip that ordinarily took just an hour by train but required almost twice as long on the decaying highway. But it turned out to be far better a way for Bettie to discover the real Japan than taking the speeding train. She was enthralled by it all, even more excited by the sights and sounds than I had been, remarking that she understood immediately why I had been so effusive in my early letters to her, expressing only one disappointment when I told her we would not be able to be married until Monday unless we turned around immediately and drove to Kobe. The Japanese government required all foreigners be married first in a civil ceremony at their consulates. I had classes Wednesday afternoon at Wa Dai and Thursday night in Kobe; the soonest we could get away would be Monday morning. I told her that Reverend Cobb had agreed to officiate at a church ceremony Monday afternoon, when we were finished at the consulate. She agreed, saying we had waited for more than a year. A few more days would make no difference.

When we arrived at Wakayama, we drove directly to Anne's house, where Dot and Tonai san waited to greet her. Bettie moved temporarily in with Anne, and Louie took her trunk on to my house. I was just in time for my early afternoon classes, which passed in a haze and a plethora of questions about the bride-to-be. Anne had jokingly told me not to linger after class as I normally did but to hurry back. She planned a dinner for us the first evening with liberal arts dean Iwasaki. When I got back to Anne's place, a short walk from the liberal arts campus, I found the two of them seated comfortably in Anne's living room, having a cup of tea; it seemed as if she had been there always.

That night at dinner, Iwasaki asked when we planned to be married, and I explained the slight problem of the consulate and was about to ask for some time off. He simplified everything when he announced that he was allowing me a week's leave beginning the Monday we planned to get married at the consulate in Kobe. Then to my surprise, he asked Bettie if she would like to teach classes in conversational English. She replied that she had not planned to and would prefer to be a stay-at-home for the time being. I could see that he, as was everyone, was taken with her. The next morning, I met my classes and then rushed over to Anne's to say goodbye and head off to my Palmore classes. Rather than staying over and taking the early train, I dismissed the composition class a few minutes early and caught the last train for Wakayama; but when I stopped at Anne's, I was told that Bettie had moved out and was awaiting me at home. Anne said she had agreed with Bettie and had helped her move her things. Tonai san was elated and greeted me with the news that Bettie san had moved in.

That weekend, we visited the office of the JTB (Japan Travel Bureau) and made plans for the trip we would take after the ceremony in Kobe. Bettie had stipulated one requirement: that we would visit or see Mount Fuji, which by now would have its first coating of snow. The rest would be up to me. Though transportation was swift and convenient in Japan in 1951, a week was not much time for an extensive trip; so I planned a few days in Kyoto, an hour or so from Kobe, and then a few days at Hakone, a hot spring spa not far from Fuji san. The JTB office made it easy to arrange all tickets and reservations, and being in the center of the city, it gave me a chance to show Bettie the shopping district and the movie theaters. Wakayama's restoration was in full swing, and in a year's time, most of the damage from the war had been cleared and new buildings had gone up in the worst places.

Following the official civil ceremony at the American Consulate in downtown Kobe, Reverend Cobb performed the church ceremony in the chapel of Eiwa Girl's School across the street from Palmore. At first, I had been reluctant to ask Reverend Cobb for any more favors, but Mrs. Cobb had removed all confusion by generously proposing that the ceremony be held in the little chapel. To our surprise, she even arranged a small reception afterward. So on November 4, we traveled to Kobe, met our witnesses, Morse and Ruth Saito, at the consulate, and signed the proper documents that made us husband and wife. The four of us returned to the consulate after lunch, picked up the marriage certificates all stamped and registered at the Kobe City Hall, and then returned to Palmore Institute. Dot Grier, Anne Edelman, Miki, Saigo, and Kame were all there waiting along with Ruth and Morse and a J3 teacher. Anne had thoughtfully invited Dot and my three friends to attend the ceremony—it had completely slipped my mind. After the ceremony, Mrs. Cobb and the ladies at the girl's school, one of whom had been with us at Hartford, gave us a short reception in the school's reception hall. Later, after we had returned from our *shoken ryokan*, Kameoka san told me how interesting the ceremony had seemed to the three of them.

Joe and Bettie, just married, Kobe, Japan

"I have never seen people kiss before, only in the cinema. It was very exciting," he said. I told him he was right; it *was* very exciting, it was *always very exciting!*

Kyoto was a perfect choice to begin Bettie's introduction to Japan. Our agent at the JTB put us into one of the most traditional of Kyoto's *ryokan*. For three days, we were transported to the court of Genji, enjoying the steaming *o-furo*, the most graceful service, and even views of the river and mountains that admitted none of the sights of the modern city. Then two days later, when we headed toward Hakone, the trip across the Lake Ashi on the ferry presented views of Fuji San with an early coat of white that rivaled a Hiroshige woodblock print.

But on the trip back to Osaka, things fell apart, the first time the plan showed signs of failure. First, we missed the special express that would have delivered us in second-class comfort to Osaka in plenty of time to make the connection at Tennoji for Wakayama. Then we found the local bank at Odawara was not allowed to cash American Express dollar checks for yen, leaving me a little more than pocket change for the trip home. The special express would have gotten us back so much sooner it would not matter. Instead, I cashed the second-class tickets, and we took a third-class local sans dining car that took thirteen hours. Just as we stepped onto the platform at Oosaka Tennoji, we saw the last train for Wakayama pull out.

Arriving after the last train would have not been a problem; there were dozens of inns within walking distance of the busy suburban station, but I had no money. I assured Bettie I would find a place for her to sleep or rest until the trains began running in the morning and asked her to wait by the bags while I spoke to the stationmaster. She seemed quite calm, totally undisturbed. Marty and I had spoken to the stationmaster many times as we passed through, and I was hoping now he would be on duty and remember me. But such was not the case. When I asked for the manager, I found him to be a total stranger. I had a fleeting moment of panic, but the gods smiled and my Japanese began to work perfectly as I asked, in all innocence, when the next train for Wakayama would be leaving. He apologized profusely and explained it would not leave until six. I introduced myself, careful *not* to refer to myself as a Wakayama Dai Gakku sensei, but only as a *kiyoshi*. He said he knew who I was and called me sensei. Then I explained: I had just come on the local from Odawara. I had no money and needed a place for my wife— and I used *kanai* instead if the honorific *oku san* when I said wife—and finally, I said that we were just returning from our *shinkon ryoko*, honeymoon. We had been married just a week ago, I said.

All the while I had been carefully explaining in my best Japanese, the others in his little office had been listening, their ears bent in our direction; and when I said, "*Watakushi wa kekkon o shimashita*," they roared with laughter and nudged one another with knowing elbows, nodding their heads, and then bowing deeply and offering Bettie and me profuse congratulations. I asked if my wife could use his warm office to wait for the morning train, perhaps on the bench inside the office. He immediately waved his hand across his face in refusal, insisting his office was too dirty and ugly, and then went out and ushered Bettie in, directing a young man to carry our bags and insisting I wait just a moment. He poured two cups of green tea from the ever-present pot and asked us to sit and then went to the phone at his desk and made a call. I could hear "Wakayama Dai Gakku" and "sensei" and "wedding trip." Then when he hung up, he and the young man took our bags and asked us to please follow. Outside the station, he flagged a taxi, gave the driver direction, and pushed us in, insisting everything was *dai jobu*, OK. In two blocks, we were at a small *yadoya*, well-lit with a garish Chinese lantern and a flashing neon sign, in front of which were two young maids and the tall, elegantly kimonoed proprietress awaiting our arrival. Bettie was escorted in as though she were a movie star, helped off with her shoes, and then led to a large banquet room. Two more maids were spreading a pair of futon on the tatami and setting a low lacquered table and cushions nearby. When the proprietress showed us in and asked if sensei and oku san would like to have supper, we were overwhelmed. She apologized that it was too late for a bath. Shortly after we sat down, laughing in astonishment, two maids brought a pair of hibachi to warm us and, in a short time, a tray of *hamu eigsu* and coffee with a stack of toast. As we finished, the hostess returned and apologized again that the bath was not ready, that it was too late. We assured her it made no difference and thanked her for the meal and all the help. I uttered to myself a prayer of thanksgiving, not so much for the marvelous hospitality but for the gift of language that had come to me from whatever gods of lost travelers hovered there in this part of Japan. Bettie's thoughts must have been priceless. First, I had impressed her with my language if not my planning, and second the stationmaster, the cab driver—who departed without pay—and finally the people at the inn had impressed her. This was hospitality that went beyond all bounds. I was also impressed by her willingness to weather an excruciating day of travel on the most uncomfortable third-class seats. After several hours on the train, we had been able to leave our seats from time to time and stand in the windy vestibule for a smoke—we both smoked in those days—but that respite from the hard benches hardly made up for the long hours of discomfort. When I tried to praise her for her stoical forbearance, she remarked she too was impressed with herself. I had planned a trip that I thought would avoid the typical tourist spots visited by gaijin, and indeed I had. From the time we left the platform in Kyoto, we had been the only Americans in sight.

When we undressed and crawled into the futon, surprised that they had furnished us with oversized ones, we heard sounds from down the passageway that hinted at the hotel's usual function. Close to the station, garishly lit, it was an inn intended primarily for short timers, couples in need of a trysting place. Our suspicions were confirmed when a tall, kimono-clad GI—the first American since leaving Kyoto—burst into our room and then muttered, "Shit! Wrong room," and called out for "Reiko" to come get him. He apologized, muttered, "Goddam gaijin!" and left.

The next morning, they brought us breakfast and then called a cab and delivered us in time for the second train at six thirty where we had a second-class compartment to ourselves. When we arrived at Wakayama, I explained at the wicket that I would bring the money for our tickets in an hour or two. The young man bowed and said that he understood, and it was OK. Someone had called ahead to make sure we would not be stopped at the gate. As we drove up in the cab, Oba san greeted us and paid the driver and then listened as we told the story of the Odawara misfortune.

I never had any serious reservations about Bettie's liking Wakayama or Japan, even though while we were in Hartford, she had admitted never having developed an interest in Asia except India, and only Darjeeling. Like most Americans at that time, many of her thoughts about the Japanese were conditioned by old wartime propaganda and stories of the Bataan death march. But Tonai san, Miki Tanaka, Saigo Nishikawa, Yamagami, and Chieko Takehata soon washed away lingering wartime thoughts. Our treks along the beach at Suiken and through the village at Wakanoura removed from her mind, she said, all earlier misgivings as to whether or not she might have made a mistake in coming to Japan. The wedding trip to Kyoto and Hakone wiped from my mind any misgivings I may have had about her ability to acculturate and certainly erased any doubts I may have harbored regarding her motives.

From the first, Bettie insisted she make the commute with me to Kobe, saying that she had not come all the way to Japan just to be left behind, "a moth of peace," every time I had to be out of town. I was happy not to be making the trip or to be staying over alone in Kobe. During the day, we roamed the shopping streets of Kobe and browsed the stacks of the American Library at the United States Information Service. I had found the USIS Library soon after my classes began at Palmore and had begun selecting books for my cultural history class, which Inoue had allowed me to develop for advanced English students like Jisaka and Chieko. Those visits offered her the resources she needed for current American novels. It was a happy time; her willingness to endure the trips back and forth, rather her insistence, helped the semester pass more quickly. With Palmore's end of term came the end of my connection with the J3s and the Board of Missions, and I felt I had indeed entered into a new existence, but no longer an *isolato*.

Chapter 19

Bettie

To celebrate the holiday and the end of classes at Palmore, we took a week long trip through the Inland Sea, sailing from Osaka to Beppu on the north coast of Kyushu, the southernmost isle. Our trip would take us across the southern island of Kyushu, stopping at an inn smack in the middle of the giant caldera of Mt. Aso, an active volcano. From there an old steam train would take us to Kumamoto; there we'd change back to the fast electric train to Hiroshima, our main reason for taking the trip.

It was about as much off-season as you could get, but we enjoyed the lack of crowds. For instance, we had the small village and the inn inside Mt. Aso's caldera all to ourselves. The view was awesome, and the idea we were in alive volcano was overwhelming. There was only one problem: the train connection at Kumamoto on the southern coast of Kyushu. We had no time for lunch and the train to Hiroshima had no dining car so we had to do with very small ham sandwiches. Though we slept off and on much of the way, we were bone tired and were quite starved when the train pulled into Hiroshima at midnight.

When we stepped onto the platform from the comfortably warm car, a blast of icy air greeted us. It was Christmas morning. As I reached for my schedule with the name of our inn, I discovered I had lost it along with the reservation slip. I couldn't remember whether the name of the inn was the Torimitsu, Torimatsu, Matsutori, or the Mitsutori and had a moment of panic. The friendly cab driver looked puzzled, but then suddenly he nodded and said, "*Dai jobu,*" and pulled away.

I heaved a sigh of relief and settled back and told Bettie, "He said it was OK. Relax."

The ancient prewar Ford coughed and bounced its way to what appeared to be the outskirts of town. As we left the lights of Hiroshima behind and entered a section lacking all electricity, I began to worry—in silence, telling myself it was *dai jobu*. When the cab stopped by the gate of the small inn with an illuminated lantern reading "*Torimatsu ryokan,*" everything seemed *dai jobu*, indeed. As our driver pressed the horn, a light came on in the entrance, and a maid in kimono clopped forth, holding a lantern. There followed a rapid exchange, which I was barely able to translate, the gist being that there was no room at the inn. I interrupted and told her I had a reservation, though I had lost the receipt, and before I could explain further, the driver said I was a *dai gakku* sensei. Her voice then rose, "*Ah, so desuka? Wakayama Dai gakku no sensei desuka?*"

I replied, "*Hai, honto desu.*" It's true!

Immediately, we heard voices of welcome as a very distinguished older lady emerged with another lantern, speaking impeccable (meaning I could understand her perectly) Japanese, bowing politely but not obsequiously and speaking entirely to Bettie, addressing her as *Oku-sama* or honorable wife. Bette bowed and smiled in returned, then we followed our hostess to the door. Two more maids grabbed our bags and ushered us to a lovely room with an electric heater and futon all laid out beside a low table with thick *zabuton*. Our hostess bowed low and asked if we would like something to eat. We nodded and said please. "*Hamu-egus, tostu, kohii wa do desuka?*" she asked, which translated was: "How are ham and eggs, toast, and coffee?" Again, Japan Travel Bureau had selected the most traditional ryokan they could, the difference between this one and the Kyoto inn was that it was brand new, though every detail, except the electric heater, spoke seventeenth century or earlier. Inside our cozy room, there was no way to know we were in the world's most famous city.

The next morning, we awoke to a bright clear day and the muffled sounds of maids carrying breakfast trays to other guests. As if someone in the hotel had been listening, waiting for us to stir, a maid appeared at our door with cups of green tea, apologizing that a hot bath had not been ready the night before and saying that it was ready now if we wished to bathe before breakfast. Eager to check out of the hotel and get back into the city, we took only a quick wash, deciding to forgo the luxury of a long soak in the hot tub, afraid that it would be so soporific we would go back to sleep. As we sat sipping the miso soup, gazing at the fresh-washed stones of our garden, it was hard to believe we were in Hiroshima. It had been pitch dark when we arrived, and few streetlights lighted our way to the inn, so we had no idea what to expect.

All the time I was in Japan, people rarely spoke of Hiroshima. My students hardly ever mentioned it, and only once had I met anyone who had been there when the bomb hit, a young Wakayama high school teacher with a group of high school Marty and I invited to an open house. He had burn scars on his cheek and spots above one ear where hair refused to grow. I wanted to ask him what he had been doing at the time, but I didn't and he did not volunteer to speak of it. What was there to say to two young gaijin instructors? Everyone I knew had read John Hersey's famous "Hiroshima" in the *New*

Yorker along with numerous stories in American magazines about Hiroshima's being named Peace City. The kanji for *heiwa*, or peace, appeared everywhere on billboards and posters. *Pika don* [flash-bang, Japanese for A-bomb] had transformed the Japanese government and people from the most bellicose of nations to the most pacifist: "Knowledge of good bought dear by knowing ill" some would say. Perhaps. Surely, this had been the greatest ill ever visited on mankind. MacArthur's censors suppressed early writings about the bomb, we were told, and lines never appeared in the press describing contemporary attitudes. Hersey's piece that appeared first in the *New Yorker* in 1946 and later in hardback was not translated into Japanese until 1949. When we were planning the trip, we agreed we had to stop and spend the day, to see what Robert Oppenheimer meant when he quoted Vishnu at the time of the first test. More than five years had elapsed; still, I wanted to be able tell any future students or my children what it was like on Christmas Day to stand at the epicenter of the first atomic attack. So far we had no inkling how the people in Hiroshima felt, so strict is the tradition of hospitality toward guests. At the inn, we had been greeted with such ceremony you would have thought they were trying to show their *appreciation* for what had happened that August morning in 1945. Neither of us felt comfortable as tourists. The signs of destruction were still everywhere, though new construction was taking over and beginning to transform it.

At the station, we checked our bags and the schedule and then walked back to the city center through the devastated area. The rubble had been cleared from the streets and walks, but skeletons of one- and two-storied concrete and steel buildings still rose here and there. In the center of the city, new construction was beginning to cover vast spaces emptied by the bomb, and quite a lot of brand new, well-designed four- and five-story buildings seemed ready for occupancy. Trying not to look like the typical tourists, I kept my camera cased. However, no one paid us the slightest attention. Hiroshima was now a city now like any other in Japan, struggling to rebuild and return to at least a modicum of normality. Already several office buildings of five or six stories had gone up along with a large, well-stocked department store.

The rest of the day before time for our train, we walked among the ruins, stood beneath the famous skeletal dome of the Trade Center, the city's trademark that was believed to have been the epicenter of the explosion. The Peace Park nearby was still in the early stages of development, but important sites were clearly labeled—in English as well as Japanese. I had read how the shadows of people incinerated by the explosion had been etched into the concrete along the bridge at the center of town, and we saw them still there.

We walked out to the edge of town where a castle had once stood, where now stood only a graceless plaster and wattle reproduction all in black. From a distance it looked real and curiously out of place, though in a romantic, medieval way. We ended with too much time on our hands and nowhere to go. A stroll through a large, restored department store was interesting only in that it had no interest for us whatever, so similar was it to any department store in Corpus Christi or Wichita Falls.

Joe and Bettie, at home

After the New Year, Yamagami and my regular steadfast friends visited us often. Bettie, as I predicted she would, found Yamagami san and the others to be fine friends. She complimented me for having made friends with people like Tanaka, Kameoka, Nishikawa and Chieko Takehata who seemed to always be asking what they could do for us.

Yamagami usually came alone now, Madenokoji having been transferred. Then one day, shortly after we returned from our trip and before classes resumed, he asked if I would teach a special English class one day a week at the steel plant. The students would be chief engineers and plant managers, along with men in the business offices and in the mills. Shin Fuso Steel Company was working at almost full capacity, Yamagami said, and the company was planning to send several of the managers or engineers abroad. The Wakayama works had hardly been touched by B-29 raids and had gone back into production soon after the war. Shin Fuso, or Sumitomo, in Wakayama was on the verge of a radical modernization, he explained. Yamagami san said that as far back as a year ago his boss had asked him to speak to Pray san or me about teaching an English conversation class, but had noticed that Marty and I were always too busy.

He recalled that a year earlier, Marty and I had toured the plant at the invitation of the plant's superintendent, who at the time was planning a trip to America and Germany. He was hoping to practice his English or discover whether or not he spoke English well enough to make the trip without an interpreter. Our day with him had encouraged him to travel without an interpreter, but when he returned and was promoted to the main office of the company in Tokyo, he ordered all his supervisors and engineers to learn English well enough to travel without an aide. As young men, before the war, Yamagami said, they had all studied English, but most had forgotten much of what they had learned, and none had either spoken English or heard it spoken since before the war. The superintendent's English was fluent enough to guide Marty and me through the plant for a day, but was not adequate to meet the task of speaking to businessmen in America and Europe who were unaccustomed to speaking to Japanese; so when he returned to Wakayama, he directed all of his managers and mid-managers to become fluent in English conversation. Japan's recovery depended on trade with all the major markets of the world, and that meant that everyone must learn English, now the world's lingua franca. I agreed to take it.

I told him I was glad he asked and that I looked forward to meeting the men and was also glad I would be getting an extra salary. Most were in their late forties or early fifties. They could all read English well and could speak it a little, though, not having spoken the language since before the war they were unsure of themselves.

"We will be sending a car for you and will bring you back because the steel mill is a long way from your house," he said. "Do you have free time when it would be convenient?"

"I have a lot more free time now since my job in Kobe is finished. Wednesday afternoon would be perfect," I said.

Then he asked how much my fee would be. I told him how much the university charged the night school students, and he laughed, saying it was not enough, adding the company was expecting to pay about twice that much. So I told him I surely would not argue with company logic.

"You tell your boss to set the rate," I said and told him I was free after four every Wednesday.

For two hours once a week, every four weeks, Shin Fuso would pay me roughly a fifth of my monthly university pay; together with the night classes, it raised my take-home pay to almost twice what I was making a year before from the Kyodan, much more than I had expected to be making when I wrote Bettie and asked her to marry me, and a good deal more than my pay at the Bowery Savings Bank. I forgot to mention that the university treasurer told me because I now had a wife, my pay would go up twenty-five percent when the new academic year began in April. We had so far managed quite well and had even afforded a Christmas trip. The Shin Fuso money would help considerably, though it would stop as would the night classes during the summer break. All the Christmas money we received from our parents in lieu of Christmas presents we deposited in my Bowery Savings Bank account. Inoue and Itoigawa had suggested I offer evening classes in the spring at the same level of conversational English Marty and I had taught. I had no idea how much that would raise, and at first, I thought I would forgo those classes, but the possibility of accumulating a small buffer was too tempting to pass up. The two nights a week for eight weeks would gross almost ¥63,000 ($175), a princely sum and more than enough to pay for a summer trip to the Japanese Alps, I thought.

From the beginning, the classes at Shin Fuso were a delight and turned into one of the most important aspects of our lives in Wakayama. Our sessions, far from my regular classes at the university, were more like long, engrossing conversations between the men and me. Having no texts, no chalkboards or formal exercises, I began by asking each to explain his position and duties. In many ways, the sessions at the plant were much like open houses that Bettie and I were continuing. Whatever teaching I did was limited mostly to correcting errors in usage and pronunciation, and explaining American customs and habits and to describe the kind of life Bettie and I had lived growing up in Texas, understanding American lifestyles and habits being the key to understanding common conversational exchanges. They encouraged me to digress, tell anecdotes about how professional people lived and about the things they might talk about in social contexts. I recall laughing when they explained what they wanted me to teach and told them they wanted sounded to me like a course called "applied cultural anthropology." When I explained what I meant by cultural anthropology, they understood immediately. They rarely resorted to their pocket dictionaries.

Everything that I had learned from reading and discussing Hayakawa's *Language in Action* in freshman English began to make sense all over again in the real world context at Shin Fuso. The most important classes I took as an undergraduate, the ones I would rely on most since graduating, had been the freshman composition and anthropology classes. Kitchens' classes at Hartford had little direct bearing on the classes I was teaching at Shin Fuso and only slightly more bearing on my university or night classes. At UT I had found Helen James's and McAllister's classes the most interesting, the ones that had most stirred my imagination and curiosity, but I had not seriously thought they would ever have any practical uses. Teaching English as a foreign language, I learned, almost from my first night class, required more than pronunciation drills, vocabulary, and sentence patterns.

One afternoon while we were working with O'Neill, Inoue and I discussed a class for advanced English students that would concentrate on American culture and society, and we agreed I should call it American Cultural History. It would be conducted as an informal discussion group in which I offered selected readings focusing on cultural issues, arts, literature, education, family life, all subjects of which I had only the most general understanding. Finding articles and books at my students' level, even as advanced as they appeared, would be difficult. I relied heavily on Ann Edelman's sharp criticism in the early stages, and with her help, I was able to glean from magazines like *Life*, *Newsweek*, and *Time* articles that lent themselves to our discussion. The USIS library in Kobe provided the rest of what I needed.

From my first encounter with the men of Shin Fuso I saw how our conversational sessions would provide subjects that I could use when the Cultural History class began the fall of 1952. Their curiosity provided me the questions I would later incorporate into the class. The class enrolled only a half-dozen well-spoken students, most of whom would be in the Modern American Novel class that I would teach in the spring of 1953, my last term.

The Shin Fuso "students" were mostly from the engineering section plant and came to class straight from the rolling mills, tube mills, or the giant ovens or converters. Some had managed mills or works during the war in remote regions of the Japan's Greater East Asia Co-Prosperity Sphere, places like Manchukuo or Korea. They were all men of culture, highly sophisticated in the arts and ideas of Japan and Asia. Several wrote traditional Japanese *haiku* and *waka*, the most traditional poetry, and several painted in oils and watercolors. English was a third or fourth language for several. One, Tsuyama san, told how he rose early every morning to write in his diary, one morning in English, the next morning Chinese, the next German, and the next in French. He rose early, he said, because he had four boys who were so noisy he could not concentrate and would never be able to write. While he could read and write in all four languages, he admitted his ability to speak the languages was poor. It was true: though he had an extensive English technical vocabulary, his pronunciation bore little resemblance to any English I had ever heard. However, that did not deter him from joining in the dialogue, and as the months passed, his pronunciation improved remarkably.

It was refreshing to meet men who felt no obligation to treat me with the deference I didn't deserve but too often received. They knew I was not a real *sensei*, although they might use the epithet from time to time in jest, and they insisted I answer them without the usual honorifics that their station would have demanded from a Japanese employee my age. They did exhibit a sense of awe in my leaving home so young and coming to Japan and then asking Bettie to join me. My resigning from the mission program and remaining on my own puzzled them more. One complimented me by saying that no Japanese young man my age would be so bold, especially when it came to marrying. I doubted that, I said. Japanese are notoriously adventurous when it comes to business, I said. They agreed, rubbing thumb and forefinger, letting me know it was for money and nothing else; my boldness, they explained, came from an idea.

I decided then that each of them would have a personal assignment to make a ten or fifteen-minute talk about his job or about a favorite pastime or hobby or a favorite site in Japan or some subject of his own choosing. The object would be for others in the class to question him, and my job would be to help each find the most appropriate conversational way of expressing their ideas. In that way, I said, they would be teaching me about Japan and would be developing ways of answering questions about their work and about today's Japan if and when they might take a trip abroad for Shin Fuso. I asked each to imagine himself being asked by a friend, or a person he was visiting at home.

The class met in a large conference room with a large table around which we all sat. At the first meeting, I asked each man to describe his position at the plant and to explain what he did, asking each one to define any technical terms dealing with his specialty since this would most likely be the subjects of conversations when they traveled. They laughed and said maybe not. Most likely subjects would probably be about drinking and girls. We went around the table, and as each one described his job, Yamagami would supply whatever technical terms they might need if they were stumped. Halfway through the session, individuals began interrupting the speaker with questions, trying to stump or confuse him and turning the exercise into a game, thus making my corrections easier. No one appeared to be embarrassed or ashamed of his errors unlike my Wa Dai students or those in night classes. I would jot down the words or phrases or the sentence pattern that seemed to stump them and would offer suggestions, and then I would critique their presentation. Sometimes the speaker would repeat my suggestions, sometimes not, but it was always relaxed and appeared to be more an entertainment for them than a class.

As we began to wind up the first session, someone asked me to tell them about myself. I said I would tell them my story next time. All through that first session, Yamagami sat back from the table, clearly not part of the class. He was there only to assist me. But in the classes that followed, he was invited to sit at the table. When he spoke either in Japanese or in English, everyone paid attention. It was interesting to listen to his Japanese that was so much clearer than the other speakers. Once when I remarked, while he was pit of the room, that I had understood most of what Yamagami had said in Japanese, Mr. Nakata nodded and said it was because Yamagami san spoke the Kyoto *bin*, or dialect, that in that part of Japan was often considered to be the Japanese equivalent to a Florentine dialect in Italy. They all agreed and teased each other for their regional dialects and warned me that because I was learning Japanese in Wakayama, I would speak Japanese with the rough rural Wakayama *bin*. Nakata then asked if the U.S. had a variety of English like Kyoto *bin*. I told him I thought not, but that each American believes his English is standard American English.

"Each person has a favorite American dialect, and each has one he dislikes the most. When I was young my mother thought that Franklin Roosevelt spoke the most beautiful English and believed the Yankee accents of the north were the worst. I probably agreed with her," I said, then explained why I meant by "Yankee."

On the way back to the house, all alone in the old Packard that first evening, I thought of the class and the varied backgrounds of these interesting men, and the thought struck me that in the summer of 1946, there on the Thirty-Eighth Parallel, we could have processed some of the wives and children of these same men. That had all happened many years ago it seemed then. But hen I recalled Ishihara, our Nisei interpreter complimenting our platoon by the way we handled the repatriates, and I was glad we had, now happier than I had been at the time he made his remarks.

One afternoon, when I returned to the house from the liberal arts campus, exhausted from an intense conversational class—all good classes left me gasping for breath and dreaming of a glass of Asahi beer—I noticed as I stepped into the genkan a pair of lacquered zori with rich velvet thongs, not at all the usual footwear I found in our entrance. These were the zori of a well-dressed woman, not a girl, certainly not Chieko Takehata's, who was becoming one of Bettie's most frequent visitors. I could hear women's voices and laughter coming from the large tatami room where we met our students. Bettie was sitting on the tatami at the low table along with Tonai and Suzuko, a geisha Marty and I had met when we gave the party for Dr. Yamagiwa. I hadn't seen Suzuko since early summer. Several times she had visited Marty and me, mostly to visit Tonai we learned, and had once taken Anne Edelman, Marty, and me to view the *sakura*, cherry blossoms, in the country. Suzuko, crowding middle age, had, like most geisha, a style that transcended the ordinary Western definitions of beauty. Today, she was wearing a startling purple-and-white-striped kimono and an obi brocaded with gold threads and a dragon pattern that flashed in the sunlight. It outdid anything I had seen her wear before. Much taller than the other two, Bettie sat there, rocking with laughter as Suzuko held our cat, Yuki chan, and made strange feline noises. Mrs. Uehara had given us Yuki to help keep mice under control. I was amazed that Bettie was able to communicate as well as she apparently was. Suzuko's English was not much better than Tonai san's, probably limited to those words used to serve sake or beer to army officers back during the time when the army was stationed outside Wakayama. She told Marty and me once that it wasn't good for a Wakayama geisha to speak English well, her regular customers—Japanese—preferring her to remain traditional. But Suzuko san was different, and visiting Bettie was a sign of that difference. Partly from curiosity, partly because we had been friends, mostly I believe because she admired and respected Tonai, she would make the long and conspicuous trip from the teahouses and the gay quarters to Horidome, the section of Wakayama where we lived. There was no denying the fact that a visit from Suzuko would raise eyebrows in the neighborhood and at the same time raise Bettie and me in the eyes of our neighbors.

Cherry blossom season is a special time in Japan. Parks and riverbanks where the trees are thickest become infested with picnickers and viewers of the delicate pink blossoms. The crowds are sometimes so thick that it becomes impossible to find a place to spread a mat and gaze at the spectacle of the trees hung with thick white and pink blossoms. It's a time of celebration. Women wear their loveliest spring kimonos and obis, if they have them, and even small children, especially young girls, are dressed in brightly colored kimono. The countryside suddenly bursts into color, and the gatherings begin to resemble the first act of *Madame Butterfly*, when Cio-Cio san enters with her chorus of maidens. Twanging of samisen and windy *shakohati*, however, expel any thoughts of Puccini. Sake and whisky flow in prodigious quantities and most viewing occasions turn into drunken orgies with men and women, faces flushed and clothes askew, staggering and falling, but no one notices or disapproves. Suzuko had come to arrange an outing with Anne Edelman and us. We would be her guests, she insisted, which meant she would arrange the time, reserve a space along a riverbank, and provide refreshments. It seemed extravagant.

At the height of the season, the men at Shin Fuso also arranged a viewing party, inviting Bettie and me to a small inn far into the country where we could view "the loveliest of trees" and then after sunset go in and eat and drink sake and beer, tell stories and perhaps dance the *Tanko Bushi*, the coal miners' folk dance. Yamagami san escorted us from the house to an old inn on the coast, first by commuter train from Nishi Wakayama station and then by narrow gauge cars to the coast along the Inland Sea. The cherry trees, the "loveliest of trees," were incredible. As Yamagami walked with Bettie and me up the path to the old-fashioned inn, Housman's lovely lines about cherry blossoms echoed in my brain, and I began to recite the lines I had memorized long ago in Dr. Fletcher's Introduction to Poetry:

> *Now of my three score years and ten,*
> *Twenty will not come again,*
> *And take from seventy springs a score*
> *It only leaves me fifty more*
> *And since to look at things in bloom*
> *Fifty springs is little room,*
> *About the woodlands I will go*
> *To see the cherry hung with snow.*

Yamagami said it sounded almost like a Japanese poet had written the lines. I told him the poem was by A. E. Housman, a famous English poet of the early part of the century.

"I was only twenty when I first read the poem, and I had never seen cherry trees in bloom before. It's about the poet's country in England, but it fits here too," I said, and he agreed.

The old inn where we were meeting, Yamagami said, was used only for banquets and entertaining dignitaries. It was set in a woodland right on the coast. Thick, white blossoms with just a tinge of pink weighed heavily on the branches, creating a mass of color almost impenetrable to the eye. My class of engineers, metallurgists, and business execs welcomed us as we arrived, each bowing as Bettie entered, each pronouncing his name and nickname—if he had one—and then motioning for us to move on to a long veranda running the length of the building overlooking the thickest, most luxuriously blossoming cherry trees in the little park. We sat on the high veranda and looked out at the scene while several maids, middle-aged women in kimono, poured sake or beer. It was the first time for Bettie to meet my class and for them to meet her. They were all visibly impressed, bowing politely and muttering compliments. Nakata san remarked how exciting it was to meet such a lovely American woman; he thought it was like going to a movie because she reminded him of a movie star. They all confessed they had never spoken to an American woman before and were surprised that they were able to understand her every word, one saying he could understand Bettie's English far more easily than he could mine. I told him that I wasn't surprised, that Bettie had studied speech in college and spoke by far the best English of any one I knew. I confessed that her speech was what first made me notice her. If Suzuko had raised us in the eyes of our neighbors, I could see that Bettie now elevated me in the eyes of my students.

When the sun went down, we passed into a large tatami banqueting room with two long, low tables where we sat facing each other, and the real party began. Sake, beer, and incredibly smooth Suntory whisky flowed along with streams of conversation. And then the dancing and singing, only this time it was the guests who danced. Some recited poetry, some sang folk songs, the Japanese equivalent of Country Western that brought howls of protest and laughter, and one performed a more-or-less kabuki-style dance. Bettie explained that while she had studied dance as a young girl—"tap, toe, and ballet"—she preferred to introduce the mambo and the cha-cha-cha, dances still unknown in Japan, dances she had learned during her months in Puerto Rico. They were all amazed and watched her, trying to imitate her steps accompanied only by her humming and her clapping hands. One Suzuki san, who fancied himself an expert in *barumu dansu*, followed every step she made and was raucously cheered by the others. But the rest is all now just a cloud of falling blossoms.

Content with our own company and enjoying the amazing luxury of semi-isolation, Bettie and I made no effort to cultivate a social life outside the university and the small group of Americans, consisting of Ann Edelman, Louie and Dot Grier, and Dr. and Mrs. Uehara. Our only acquaintances outside that small group and the university were the men from Shin Fuso and their wives, most of whom spoke no English. The wives who were bold enough to join in conversation invited us to their homes in the company's housing development, but because we were so much younger than they, we developed no close friendships except with Yamagami and his small circle of young bachelors.

Only two of the university faculty visited us, Taniguchi sensei, professor of religion and philosophy, and Inoue sensei, who dropped in frequently, partly to work on the O'Neill translations, partly to visit and talk about the students. Taniguchi sensei took lunch with us occasionally. He enjoyed dropping by, he said, just to see how we were managing. People were naturally curious, he said, because they knew of no Americans who were living in Japan without support from the church, the army, or some large corporation. Never having visited with Marty and me, he was drawn to the house, I believe, chiefly by Bettie, whom he said spoke the most beautiful English he had ever heard. Bettie never conformed to what our visitors expected a proper American housewife to be; she was never shy about speaking out and expressing her opinions on things Japanese or foreign. Taniguchi sensei found her comments refreshing and surprising in their frankness.

Our days were full that spring. We took two short trips to Kyoto and one to Himeji, the home of Shirasake-jo, the Castle of the White Crane, probably Japan's most beautifully preserved castle from the era of the shoguns. Shortly before the end of the cherry blossom season, Yamagami and his friend Saito invited Bettie and me to take an all-day trip to Nara to visit Todai-ji, the hall of the Great Buddha, and other art treasures of the Tempyo era, eighth century. I previously told Yamagami of my first impressions of the Dai Butsu (Great Buddha) of Kamakura, and he remarked that he believed the Nara Buddha was even more impressive. For one thing it was larger, made of bronze, and housed in a great wooden temple, one of the largest wooden structures of its kind in the world; but more than size, it was its grace and serenity that most impressed one, Yamagami said. At the time, he promised he would take me there and be my guide one day. Now that Bettie had joined me, he said it was even more important we visit the site.

It was a lovely weekend, and though the cherry blossom season was nearing an end, there were still blossoms enough to create a spectacle. The late season crowds had thinned down, and we were able to pass through the great hall of Todai-ji without hurrying. He was right. Nara's Buddha was even more sublime than the great figure at Kamakura. The Buddha sits with one hand raised palm out, the other resting flat along the folds of his garment, its fingers curved downward toward the earth symbolizing the unity and continuity of life and earth. We had time to gaze and wonder at an object so large and yet so sublimely delicate. But today as I think back, the figure that most often comes to mind when I think on the Buddha is that lone Kamakura figure in bronze, sitting huge and silent in the brilliant sun, unsheltered and serene, or rather sheltered only by the bronze snails that cover his head like a crown. In the early days, it too was sheltered until a typhoon took it away.

After our visit to Todai-ji Bettie, Saito, Yamagami, and I passed quietly and leisurely through the ancient city, feeding the small deer in the park and taking a light sushi bento in the shade of pine and yew trees, watching the small deer walk among the visitors. Avoiding the crowds of tourists, Yamagami directed us to a small, temple-like structure, the Kaidan-in, housing a collection of seventh-century carvings of fierce countenanced temple guards. Back off the main thoroughfare behind a high wall, the square building sat in the middle of a large open space surrounded by carefully raked, tiny white stones. We were, that day, the only visitors. It was as if Yamagami had planned it or sensed we would be alone. Inside the building at each corner of a raised platform surrounded by a low railing and approached on all four sides by staircases stood a fiercely threatening guard, suggesting anything but the peaceful and serene Buddha we had visited earlier. Yamagami explained that these figures represented a phase of popular Buddhism that challenged the quietism most people think of when they think of the Buddha. These guards actually challenge the quietism that the Buddha himself preaches to his followers. But then Yamagami san suggested all the world's religions contain anomalies that contradict the fundamental tenets of the religion.

"These are very old carvings, dating back to the time when Buddhism first came to Japan," Yamagami said. "They came from the mainland of Asia, perhaps seventh century."

Bettie and I passed from one to the other, listening as our friend explained that their purpose was to protect the four corners of the world from evil spirits. I was struck by the fact that all over Japan, I had often come across this same tranquility in the midst of turmoil. There were temples and shrines in the middle of the busiest sections of cities and towns, but it was especially true here. When I mentioned this to Yamagami, he nodded and said he agreed that it was different here, which was why he tried to visit this place whenever he could. As we started to leave, a young monk passed us as we were leaving; but on recognizing Yamagami, he stopped and bowed a greeting.

As they moved aside and began talking softly to each other, Saito whispered, "This happens every time I visit Kaidan-in with Yamagami san. Someone always stops and speaks to him. I think he knows more about this place than anyone living here knows."

In no hurry to leave the calm precincts, we waited while the two continued to talk. I understood now why he had thought it so important for us to visit Nara with him. It had been a wonderful day, in the most literal sense of that word, a day filled with wonder, and it was as it had been with Nishikawa on Koya san. I began to sense a deeper change in myself, inexplicable and ineffable, two word I rarely wrote and almost never spoke. Once long ago, I had been moved in almost the exact same way on reading aloud to myself Wordsworth's *Lines* written above Tintern Abbey. They were not the same, of course, but they touched inexplicably a core of knowing. Nothing I had felt at Hartford during vespers or morning watch had come as close to the sense of unity and harmony I felt there in Nara and also felt when I read the *Lines* from Tintern Abbey.

Other than these short excursions, we stayed close to home, for I'd set for myself a course of study in literature, mostly from several books I ordered from home and from the USIS Library in Kobe. There was so much I had to learn just to stay even with the game. I found Mencken's work on the American language I'd heard of long ago, and I'd read a number of his shorter works, revues, and prejudices, and I found him entertaining but also really informative and most convincing. Anne Edelman passed along to Bettie and me her copies of *New Republic*, *New Yorker*, and *Nation*, the same magazines I had begun to read in earnest when I was in New York, magazines I'd been commended for in my interview with the Mission Board. Now I saw them, more clearly than ever before, as magazines not only dedicated to a high level of written English but also to serious critical thought about the state of culture in America. We continued to subscribe to *The Saturday Review of Literature*, and I began reading regularly the *Times Literary Supplement* that arrived weekly in the liberal arts campus faculty commons.

My hours of reading and studying never presented a problem to Bettie. She was an obsessive reader herself. Whenever I could, I browsed the well-stocked English language section in the Wa Dai library to find books for her. As a result, I supplied myself with reading in the major writers as well: Dickens, James, Hardy, Conrad, Butler, Austen, and others, most in old Everyman and Modern Library editions, but also in the Armed Services Editions left behind when the army moved out. My guides were always Wilson, Trilling, and critical writings of men like Van Wick Brooks, Malcolm Cowley, Morton Duawen Zabel, writers I had not heard of but had come across in the USIS library in Kobe. I was never clear what I was reading *for*, where I was headed, but I knew I was catching up.

Classes at the university now went even more smoothly than they had the year before, and preparations for a history course went ahead. I decided to call it the Short Course in American Culture, concentrating on arts and ideas that I could glean from readings I checked out from the USIS Library in Kobe. Inoue sensei finished his translation of *Desire Under the Elms* and sent it to the publisher, and we began working on another O'Neill play. Two afternoons a week, we explored the world of Hickey's pipe dreams in *The Iceman Cometh*. I read the play slowly, taking notes, jotting down slang or special idiomatic expressions I thought he might find difficult, and I discovered how close reading led me to understand and appreciate O'Neill's language in a way I would not have been able to otherwise.

Everything I had learned from Fletcher and Steffans came into play and increased my appreciation for whatever I was reading. Earlier, we had worked briefly on *Emperor Jones* and *Hairy Ape*, both of which I had read at home before I sailed for Japan, never thinking I'd be reading them again. From that first reading, O'Neill's slang in those plays had sounded stilted, stagy, or dated, and I took it that he was not attempting to convey language realistically at all but was writing a kind of poetry for the theater. Now Inoue was searching for the best Japanese equivalents that would convey the artistic impression O'Neill was attempting to achieve; how he would do that I had no idea.

The *Ice Man* was different from the O'Neill I'd read earlier. Its setting in Harry Hope's run-down Bowery bar with its down and out barflies and bums seemed more naturalistic than the other plays, but still its language was more the language of a poet than a literary naturalist. Our discussions about the slang did not begin until Inoue had discussed the play quite thoroughly, examining the culture of Bowery bars at the time the play was set, along with the psychological profiles of each of the characters. His insight into that aspect of American life was impressive. He urged me to break in and correct him where he might be wrong, but I was afraid he placed too much faith in my understanding of the period and my interpretation of the characters' psyche and the meaning of the language. I reminded him that I just might be in over my head, but he argued I had been of great help with the other plays. My understanding of the Bowery's ethos was limited to what I'd gleaned from popular sociological writings, conversations with New Yorkers working at the Bowery Savings Bank, and the rare instances when I took a stroll into the area.

I wrote what I believed to be the closest Standard English equivalents of all the passages I noted so we could move more rapidly. Inoue liked to talk about the story in play, asking me what I thought of certain passages and what I thought about O'Neill's ideas and asked if I thought that O'Neill reflected a true American life. None of the literature courses I had taken in college had asked me to examine language so carefully or to look so closely at character and speech. I often wondered how much more Inoue would have benefited had he been able to discuss the plays with a more experienced student or an O'Neill scholar. Though I had read more widely and deeply than most of the people I knew, I knew that I needed to read much more before I could truly understand O'Neill's meanings. But I also began to realize that my years in Austin had not been wasted in the idle pleasures of my *un*-required readings. I told Inoue sensei of the similarities I saw in *Ice Man* and Miller's *Death of a Salesman*, probably the most respected dramatic work on the boards at the time. I had seen it in New York, I said, and I thought Miller's play owed something to *Iceman*, especially the theme of "pipe dreams" and their relationship to the lives of the salesmen, Hickey and Willy Loman. I said I thought he should look into it, particularly because pipe dreams seemed so important to the survival of Hickey and Willy and because they expressed, I thought, both playwrights' indictments of false values running through American ideals. I gave Inoue a copy of Miller's play and asked him to read it, but he begged off, saying he was too focused on O'Neill. He said he wanted to finish *Iceman* so he could get on to the other plays. I understood; he could not risk distraction. Inoue had been corresponding with O'Neill and had gained much insight earlier from the letters, but as he explained, O'Neill was ill and could not write as often as he wished. For me the experience of reading O'Neill with a man like Inoue was one of my greatest experiences in Japan and contributed immensely to my education and the direction I would follow when I returned to Austin.

Spring term went well, better than I thought possible. Having started with a firm resolution never to enter class unprepared, I had found a little handbook of conversational English, one with examples of good colloquial English speech in the context of lifelike conversations. When the bookseller near campus assured me he could supply my students, I required it of all my classes. With it I was able to prepare lessons for each class using the set conversations as models for introducing new vocabulary. However, in spite of the success these exercises yielded, I was convinced that I could not make a life of teaching English as a second language. The most rewarding experiences were those working with Inoue on Eugene O'Neill or preparing notes for the cultural history class I was planning to teach in the fall term.

The course I was working on was turning into a course in American culture with more emphasis on arts and ideas than history. My main sources at the time were writers like Louis Mumford, Merle Curti, Vernon Parrington and Robert Spiller. I found literature the most reliable guide into the culture of a people and a time, and I was learning that close examination of a playwright's work could explain many of the social enigmas that surrounded all life in a culture. These ideas were, of course, new only to me. I had begun reading these writers mainly out of curiosity, all the time wondering why I had not been reading them earlier, but such was the situation in college. I didn't realize it at the time, but what I was putting together was a course in humanities, a subject about which I had only the vaguest idea. My unguided personal reading in the years since high school had been, simply put, an accidental course in contemporary American culture.

By the sheerest of accidents one day a year earlier, I learned the real importance of understanding words in context. I was on the express train, the Tsubame, traveling to Tokyo to visit Bill Asbury. Someone had told me to be sure to order the beefsteak in the dining car, and I took his advice. Shortly before the luncheon crowd, I made my way to the dining car, took a seat alone, only to be joined almost immediately by a tipsy, non-Japanese dinner companion. Careful to impress my new arrival and eager to use my Japanese—not simply point to an item on the menu—I had ordered in Japanese: "*Hitotsu beefu suteki o-kudasai.*"

I saw he was impressed, but when the waitress asked, "How do you like it?" in perfectly good American English, I was taken aback a little and replied in English, "Medium rare." As she returned to the galley, I asked, "Did she really understand what I meant?"

He smiled, answered, "She understands it, *but she doesn't know what it's about*" (my emphasis). He didn't have to explain. She had probably never eaten a beefsteak, red meat not being a staple of Japanese diet in those days.

Speaking a language well means more than pronouncing, intoning, and accenting correctly. Knowing definitions of words does *not* mean knowing what it's *about*. I had told Inoue sensei that the American Cultural class would be aimed at teaching the English in the cultural context of the experiential. It was the same as understanding nuances of usage, finding the most effective Japanese equivalents to express the meaning of O'Neill's stage slang. I explained it would benefit students majoring in English and for those who were thinking of teaching it someday. It was so obvious! And for me, the roots of meaning lay in freshman comp with Helen James (along with Hayakawa and Dr. Mac's anthropology).

McAllister had emphasized understanding through experiences in a culture; Hayakawa's little book had made clear that connotations, the *intensional* meanings, carried as much, or more weight, in the process of communicating as the operational meanings of words. If my students were to use English well, I felt I must, if possible, convey to them what the words were *about* in a cultural context and that had to be through my illustrating and demonstrating contexts through narratives. I was unaware that I was moving in the direction of teaching literature and humanities, teaching ideas in contexts of concrete experiences.

In the beginning, literature, drama, and the arts had been, for me, a means of escape and diversion, a means of enriching my own life through the vicarious experience literature offered; but through Wilson, Trilling, and others, it was becoming much more. It was not at all as unrelated to what I was doing in the classrooms of Wa Dai as I imagined. The variety of experiences we had through literature and the arts helped us to understand and to know what it was about. What the "it" was, was always shifting, but it was no longer a shifting abstraction. Trilling and writers like him were not giving me answers so much as understandings of the world of the ambiguities, and in these I felt an overpowering need to share. Teaching from its beginning for me has always meant mission, calling, vocation and never simply work.

I credit the success of that semester and the success of the semesters that followed largely to Bettie. Though she will today happily accept credit for any influence she was able to offer, I doubt that she will accept any responsibility for the part she played. Her penchant for reading widely, directly and indirectly, helped me broaden my own perspectives. We talked books constantly, discussing our understandings and interpretations, and thus our talk inevitably impacted much of what I was trying to achieve in my classes as well as in discussions in the open houses.

When the summer vacation came and Bettie announced that she was pregnant, it came as no surprise. While we hadn't planned it, we had not planned to prevent it. After talking with Dot Grier, a registered nurse and the mother of three children born in Japan, the latest born that spring, Bettie decided she had no reason to doubt that she was pregnant. Early in August, she made an appointment with Dr. Schwerzens, the Swiss missionary doctor in Kyoto. He found her healthy and in the beginning of her second month, advised her what to eat and what vitamins to begin, and told her not to avoid doing anything she would normally do. He didn't think it necessary for her to see him again until late September or October. We were both quite happy, even though we felt it might have been safer to wait until we returned home. I didn't think at the time she really wanted to wait, perhaps didn't want to be constantly concerned one way or another. Planning anything in any great detail was not her style. When she first believed she was pregnant, she was ready, she said. Dot Grier's presence, her understanding and knowledge from experience allayed any anxiety about the future.

We stayed in Wakayama all during the rainy season, taking occasional trips to Osaka and the USIS Library in Kobe. Most mornings I spent in the study taking notes or reading one book in particular, one that would eventually have as profound an influence as Trilling's *Liberal Imagination* and Wilson's *Classic's and Commercials:* Alfred Kazin's *On Native Grounds.* It would be my reading guide in American literature from then on and would convince me where my future in teaching lay. Before finding one day browsing the USIS in Kobe, I had never heard of Kazin or *On Native Grounds*, published in 1942. Anne Edelman, who had read more extensively in American literature than anyone I knew, was happy to talk about my readings in Trilling and Edmund Wilson, but she was unfamiliar with Kazin. However, she was a good sounding board and would listen to what I had to say and question all my assumptions. Anne encouraged me to read on, laughing. "Read everything," she would say; and when I told her I had asked Inoue to let me teach a course in the modern American novel to the same students who would be taking the culture class, she encouraged me even more, though she warned me that I would have to do a lot more reading in primary sources.

Wakayama was a city of almost two hundred thousand people at the time we were there, but the parts of the city we visited, our small neighborhood around the university, the narrow shopping area where the movie theaters were located—the Burakuri-cho—and Wakanoura, were like small towns, compact enclaves within the larger metropolis. Since we were the only gaijin who regularly visited these districts, we became well known to the merchants and coffee houses. In the early days, Marty and I had shopped in the secondhand stores in Burakuri-cho, buying scroll paintings, lacquer ware, tea sets, and vases to send home as Christmas presents and to decorate our house. After Bettie arrived, the keepers of the shops came forth in a whirlwind of service; and each time we passed, people bowed and smiled as if we were old and steady customers.

In Komatsubara-dori, the neighborhood of the university kansha, we were able to do all our shopping for meat, vegetables, fish, and flowers. Just around the corner, within a short walk of our house, there was a barbershop, an icehouse, a family bar, dry cleaners, a camera store and photo shop, even a tailor and a cabinet shop. In a short time, Bettie's Japanese was good enough for her to take over the grocery shopping from Oba san. We rarely shopped at the foreign import stores in Osaka, depending almost entirely on our Wakayama markets. Our only Western indulgence was American coffee that cost about fifty cents a pound in the States sold for two dollars a pound on the open market in Wakayama. We rationed it carefully and drank it only at breakfast and when we had guests, but other than that, we hardly noticed that our lifestyle had changed significantly. We ate less meat and more vegetables, particularly beans of all kinds, and we disappointed Oba san by usually eating our entire rice ration every month. A "legal" black market in rice, usually imported from Southeast Asia or Texas, made up the shortage at the end of the month with only a slight increase in price. Though costlier than it was in the States, fruit was plentiful, apples, pears, oranges, or *mikan* and imported bananas, which we looked on as luxuries.

In spite of the cost, we ate well, we thought, though neither of us gained weight on the diet we followed. When Bettie announced she was pregnant, we were sure there would have to be an adjustment in our diet, particularly since Japan was at the time short of nearly all dairy products. Butter was expensive and often tasted fishy for some reason. The nearest commercial dairy, owned and operated by the Swiss Nestle Company, was on the island of Shikoku and offered only canned condensed milk. For the first time, I was concerned that we might have made a mistake. Fortunately, Japan supported a huge vitamin industry.

One day, early in the summer, Aoki san, one of the senior engineers in my English class at Shin Fuso, came by the house with a special request. He had rarely attended the sessions, and when he did, he rarely spoke. When Marty and I met him a year before, he was superintendent of the rolling mill. A soft-spoken, thoughtful man, somewhat scholarly, he hardly a typical organization man. The first time Marty and I met him, he invited us to visit his one-man show of oil paintings and photographs hanging in the gallery at the Wakayama City Hall. We were both deeply impressed. It was not unusual for Japanese engineers, doctors, and bankers, men of all walks of life, to have serious interests and talents far outside their work. The day we visited the show, Aoki san was there; and when I asked him how he could possibly have found the time to produce such a vast amount of work, he only smiled and said he simply *had* to find time. Painting was as important to him as his work in the rolling mill. But the oils did not appear the work of an amateur or one who paints when he "finds the time." The same was rue of his photography.

When he arrived that afternoon, we took seats in the small study, and right off, he explained that he was soon to go abroad on a business trip for the company, first to America and then to Europe, and he said he had a favor to ask. It was unusual, I felt, for him to come right out and make the request. The usual approach was more circuitous, but obviously, it was too important to follow traditional protocols. I assumed he had come for private English lessons to prepare him for the important trip. While I had earlier said I did not have time to give individual lessons, I was prepared to agree in his case because the men at Shin Fuso had been extremely generous with their time and their friendship. It would give me an opportunity to repay their kindnesses, a form of *giri* and *on*? Perhaps. Before he could finish asking his favor, I offered to coach him privately if that was what he wished. He thanked me but said he was interested in something more than conversational English. He wanted Bettie and me to instruct him in proper American table manners and rules of etiquette. Bettie, who was in the room, agreed that *we* would be happy to help in any way we could. He apologized again, recalling that I had said earlier I did not give private instruction; and because of that, he had a plan. He wished to take us on a vacation trip for a week or ten days to the Japanese Alps and to one of the high mountain resort lakes. Along the way, we would speak only English, and Bettie and I would advise him of Western table manners and social customs in America. The company would pay for the trip, the train tickets, the bus connections, the hotel accommodations, and all meals. Would I agree to accept the expenses as my compensation, he asked. Before I could answer, Bettie said we would be happy to, so I also agreed. I knew the moment he said *Japanese Alps*, Bettie would insist. I told him we had been saving for a trip to the Alps, but we were not sure just what part to visit. Neither of us, I told him, was particularly interested in Nojiri, where all the missionaries went for the summer.

He sat back with a sigh of relief and explained the plan in detail. He said the idea had come to him during the cherry blossoms viewing party. All of the men had been so impressed by Bettie, her easy manner, her clear speech, her charm and friendliness that they had wondered why she had not decided to teach. Bettie laughed and said we had one teacher in the family, and one was enough.

The trip took us through some of the most dramatic mountain country either Bettie or I had ever seen. But then neither of us had seen real mountains. For the first three days, we stayed at Matsumoto in the famous Kamikochi Hotel. Built in the early 1930s in the style of a Swiss mountain hotel, it sat in the shadow of Japan's highest peak, Yaregatake. The food was excellent French cuisine served in a formal Continental style, the menus in French and Japanese—no English. At first, the array of spoons, forks, and knives set at each place baffled Aoki, but when we told him that he was unlikely to face so formidable an arrangement in the U.S., much less often in the States than in Europe, he seemed relieved. He was further reassured when we explained that the rule was to select the spoon or fork on the outside and work in toward the plate as the courses were served. Bettie suggested that there was nothing wrong with simply asking someone. After we ordered from the menu, as if to illustrate our first lesson, the waiter removed all the utensils we were not going to need, leaving only a fork, a knife, and a spoon. That evening after dinner, we sat on the veranda outside our rooms and watched the sun drop behind the snow-covered peaks.

Early the first morning, Bettie and I took a walk in the mist and fog that shrouded the stream near the hotel and the village. Along the way, we had met a dozen or so climbers, young men and women heading up into the hills above the hotel, their packs, ice axes, ropes, and heavily cleated boots setting them apart from the other morning hikers. Bettie declared she wished more than anything that she were hiking with them. After a half mile we returned to the hotel and met Aoki for breakfast. He was concerned, he said, knowing that Bettie was expecting a child, but she assured him she was quite healthy and needed the exercise.

Leaving Kamikochi, we took a narrow gauge mountain train up over a high ridge, switching back and forth up to the ridge and then down into a broad valley. We were still very high but gradually descended back among rice paddies, stopping later in the afternoon at a large inland lake resort. All during the trip, we encountered almost no foreigners and no members of the occupation. The war in Korea was raging to a standstill, yet here far inland—though in Japan there is nowhere in that narrow island that can be truly called far inland—there was no sign that a conflict existed in Asia or anywhere in the world. Aoki had taken us far from the world of reality. Swiss hotels, nineteenth-century railcars, quaint lakeside inns, cormorant fishing on a high mountain lake, and lanterns on the water: it was all a Never, Never land. All through it, Aoki san explained in remarkably improving English all the geological, historical, and social facts we were encountering, and he seemed to grow more sure of himself as time passed.

We had arrived late just as the sun set and moved into a large, semi-Japanese style hotel where we saw for the first time on the trip signs of the military, all officers and wives. Aoki san explained the hotel was very popular with the occupation troops. We took our evening meal in the room avoiding the large, busy dining room and then sat on our private balcony and watched the lamps of the fishing boats. When we awoke the next morning, the spell was broken. Unfortunately, the hotel was also an R & R hotel and was flooded with khaki uniforms with only a scattering of civilians, Japanese and foreign. After breakfast Bettie chose to say in the room and read, while Aoki and I decided to walk through the gardens. Just as we left the lobby he was called to answer a telephone call from shin Fuso. It was turning into a very delightful excursion, I thought, something we would never have done without Aoki san. In the garden I spoke to several of the officers. One, a captain, said he thought the hotel was reserved for the military and DACs, department of the army civilians and couldn't understand why here were so many Japanese. When he asked if I was a DAC, I told him I was a civilian and was quite unconnected and was a teacher at a Japanese university. He looked surprised.

"That was your wife I saw you with last night then?" he asked.

"Yes, we'd been up in the Alps, Nagano," I said. "The Japanese gentleman who came in with us is an engineer with Shin Fuso Metal Industries."

He smiled and turned to join his wife, when a lieutenant about my age approached, said he had overheard me and asked the name of the university where I taught. After I explained where Wakayama was he asked the usual question: how had I avoided the draft? I repeated the old saw about my arrangement with the draft board, but before I had a chance to finish the story of my record, Aoki san joined me and told me he would have to be leaving, that something urgent had come up.

"Is Bettie san still in the room?" he asked.

"Yes. How son must you leave?"

"You and Bettie san can stay," he said as headed back to the lobby. "I have checked out and I paid for the room for tonight for you."

He apologized for cutting the trip short, and asked if we thought he had "made progress with his English. I assured him he had been improving all along the way. In the room he explained that the company had "summoned" him back—his word.

I could see that Bettie was not too displeased though she expressed some disappointment. When I asked her if she thought Aoki was "ready to visit America," she gave him very high marks.

"Please do not apologize Mr. Aoki," she said. "We've enjoyed the trip very much and we thank you for this chance to visit this beautiful part of Japan."

I told him we would be leaving with him because Bettie and I, in any case, had planned to leave him in Odawara when we reconnected with the main line to Osaka. I explained that we had planned to visit a friend on the coast south of Tokyo and would be continuing on to Tokyo for a few days before taking the train back to Wakayama. He seemed to hesitate then nodded and said it was a good plan then. Checking out was easy, and before we knew it we were back on the train. I didn't ask why he was being "summoned" back, assuming he would tell me if he thought it important I should know, but on the return to the main line he spoke little and seemed in deep thought.

We had written Bill Asbury and Marty and told them about our plans to visit Nagano and about the possibility of a side tip to Tokyo. Bill wrote that he had moved out of Tokyo and into a lovely *besso*, or villa, on the coast only two train stops from Odawara. He said that his part of the coast resembled the California coast around Carmel, perhaps not as dramatic a seascape as Carmel, but then Carmel did not have a view of Fuji San. A wealthy Japanese family forced upon hard times after the war was renting out the place, including gardener and maid, to Bill for the yen equivalent of fifty dollars a month. Marty had also moved out of the mission compound at Aoyama Gakuin into his own house in a Japanese neighborhood. Bill offered us a place to stay for as long as we wished, and Marty insisted we spend some time with him in Tokyo. When we arrived at Kozu, we were a day early. Bill was not there, but his maid said he would be there soon and showed us to our room that was up the hill and had a wide veranda and a view of Mount Fiji. There was a hot bath for us and for each of us a summer *yukata*, or a lightweight cotton kimono. The *besso* was indeed quite large, built up the side of a hill in separate units, each level offering its own view of the Pacific, and at the highest point was our room; just on the crest of the hill, was a small teahouse, more like a glassed-in gazebo than a formal teahouse, three walls encased in sliding glass panels looking off to the ocean to the east and to the south. To the west in the distance was the cone of Fuji San. Bettie had hoped to have such a view of the mountain on our wedding trip. Now, finally, there it was.

We had soaked in the o-furo, donned our light kimonos, and were waiting for Bill in the large room next to the entrance when he arrived. Unknown to us his maid had called and told him we had arrived a day early, and he had arranged s surprise party. Just after sundown, Marty joined us along with two air force pilots, friends of Bill's brother, a fighter pilot in Korea. It was the first time I had seen Marty since he moved to Tokyo, the first time for Bettie since we had all gathered in New York City before going our ways. The wine flowed and the talk lasted far into the night. The conversation figured around the subject of our residence in Japan and what we were planning for the future. Both Marty and Bill voiced a strong desire to remain connected in some way to the Far East, neither knowing what it would require or what exactly they wanted to do, Bill's only requirement being a wish to make a life as a writer of some kind. When they looked at me and Bettie, I replied it was pretty certain that in less than a year we were to become parents; but as for a life, I said I hoped to teach college, hoped to have a life in education. That puzzled them, but hearing myself make the commitment felt most satisfying.

When we woke the next morning, everyone had left, but the maid immediately began to fry bacon and scramble eggs. We had the day to ourselves, reading and relaxing all morning in the teahouse high on the hillside, and that afternoon, we walked the pebble beach, watching surf fishers. A warm and muggy wind off the Pacific forced us back up the hill where a light breeze cooled us as we lounged half-naked in the teahouse, gazing off at the shadowy cone of Fuji. That evening, when Bill returned from Tokyo, he took us down the line to the village of Oiso, where a Japanese friend had set up in her family's estate a large orphanage for children of mixed parentage. In Japan as in Korea, racially mixed offspring are often abandoned and severely abused. Bill's friend, a countess in prewar days and a descendant of the Mitsubishi family, had been running the orphanage for several years. Bill was helping her to raise money to keep it running. I was unaware at the time, but Bill had already begun to separate from the J3 program as I had and had begun to work for the Christian Children's Fund raising hundreds of thousands of dollars to support similar homes for orphaned children all over the world. His friend Sykes, who was related to the Palmolive Soap family, had sent crates and crates of soap to the orphanages.

Bill and I laughed when we recalled how the three of us, he, Marty, and me, had been the beneficiaries of a prayer service the night before leaving Hartford, and now I had separated from the J3s and married Bettie. Bill was soon to separate and become the full-time secretary for the Christian Children's Fund, and Marty had won approval of the board to move out of the mission compound and to take on a part-time job with Tokyo Marine and Fire Insurance Company. Marty justified his request for the extra job was based on his ability to make contact with a population not often found in missionary circles, and he was allowed to use his pay from the insurance company to rent and furnish his own house. We agreed that the prayers that night had worked wonders for us and for the mission program in ways no one could have conceived. We also agreed that we had been extremely successful in all our endeavors both for ourselves and for those we had wanted to serve.

We took the train to Tokyo and Marty's house the next day, but it was too hot and muggy to do much sightseeing while we were there. Getting on and off elevated trains and crowding into the subway cars was more fatiguing than Bettie expected, but we did take the train out of town to Kamakura and spent the day visiting the Great Buddha and the Hachiman Shinto shrines. When we left we had a comfortable *ni-to* (second-class) express train from Tokyo to Osaka, even a delicious *bifu-steki*. When we arrived home we were both very tired. Bettie, who had been so full of energy all through the trip, now was clearly exhausted. Aoki and Shin Fuso had lifted the burden of expenses for the trip, thus allowing us to take the second-class car and enjoy a Kobe beefsteak in the dining car. Our last big splurge was taking a taxi from the station instead of the streetcar. It was good to be home.

When Oba san met us at the door, we detected a sadness in her greeting, totally out of character with previous greetings that were always smiles and happy bows. This was different. My Japanese was still so crude that I was unable to express my concern without sounding impolite, but she anticipated me and explained carefully as she handed me an envelope from Saito san, the friend who had accompanied us on the Nara trip with Yamagami san. Very briefly, her eyes filling with tears, she told me that Yamagami was *shinimashita*. I understood immediately: Yamagami was dead. She broke down. Bettie understood immediately, without any explanation. Tonai san pointed to the envelope, and told me Saito had left a letter explaining what had happened and asked that I call him immediately. The three of us moved into the large room and sat at our low table. I opened the envelope and read the letter from Saito san. Then Tonai made the call for me. I understood from what Tonai had said that Yamagami san had been in an accident, and Saito's letter told how Yamagami, Madenokoji, and he had been sailing off Tomogashima, just at the entrance to the Inland Sea, when their small snipe-type sailing boat caught a sudden crosswind and capsized. The currents are strong and treacherous in those straits; it is the closest point between Honshu and Shikoku, where the Inland Sea spills into the Pacific. Yamagami and I had sailed there once the summer before Bettie arrived and had joked about being careful since neither of us was a particularly good sailor. While they clung to the capsized boat, the tide began pulling the small craft out to the ocean; inexplicably, Yamagami, the strongest swimmer of the three broke the basic rule of souls at sea—never leave the boat—and set out to swim to shore for help. He never made it. I could hear the words Luther and Tot repeated again and again: "If you ever capsize, always stick with the boat." Or the words of Stubs to Pip, "Stick to the boat is your true motto . . .." And I wondered what had possessed him to try for the distant shore.

We sat there stunned. I knew then that Aoki call at hotel had been news of the accident, and he had not told us, because he had not wanted to spoil our trip. Saito got to the house within the hour, taking off from his job at Shin Fuso. He was still deeply aggrieved. It had happened almost five days ago, he said, just as I thought, while we were by the lake. As he sat with us he retold the story of how Yamagami, a strong swimmer, a school champion, left the boat to get help but was never seen alive again.

"Next morning fisherman found his body washed ashore on Suiken, Wakayama side," he said, "his body naked but with no mark or injury."

A fishing boat in the straits had picked up Saito san and Madenokoji less than an hour after Yamagami had swum away.

"When we found him, we saw on his face a smile of peace," he said softly and then added with a smile, "He was Buddha, you know."

I knew that Yamagami was a devout Buddhist, recalling our visit to Nara and our many conversations about philosophies and religion. Typically, I corrected his English, "You mean he was a *Buddhist*." Which I thought would account for the peaceful smile in Saito's mind.

"No, Joe san, " he paused here and smiled softly, "Yamagami *was* Buddha." He said it so softly but emphatically with the same soft smile. He lowered his head for a moment and all was silent. I *thought* I understood what he meant, but I really didn't at the time. It would take me years of recalling what I knew about Yamagami and what I had learned just being with him, walking with him at Suiken, that same beach where he was found, years of reading the philosophy of Gautama, before I would even *begin* to understand. Today I know as surely as Saito knew then that Yamagami had achieved Buddhahood. It would come to me years later after I had finally begun to comprehend the meaning of Yamagami's life to me. Yamagami had become, before I even met him, a Bodhisattva, a person who, having reached perfect understanding, what we call nirvana, returns to the life of the world, reenters the common fray to help others to understanding, or, if you prefer, *enlightenment*. It is a Christ-like gesture of total compassion for fellow beings.

Yamagami san

Before he left, Saito handed me an envelope with a small studio portrait of Yamagami along with a snapshot of himself and Yamagami, a candid shot of two young men sitting on a rocky promontory gazing off to the right of the frame. Yamagami is slightly behind, one arm lightly draped over his friend's shoulder, a picture of perfect friendship. The portrait of Yamagami san is a perfect likeness, yet it is more an idealized picture, perfectly calm, serene even, the face of the Bodhisattva we see in so many paintings and sculptures. In life, he was always smiling, almost never as grave as he is in the picture; but today as I look at the photograph, it reveals the Yamagami I knew at the time and conveys a knowledge of infinite peace. That moment when Saito revealed to me Yamagami's Buddhahood was the moment I believe a new path opened for me, the same path I have tried to travel ever since.

We talked for a long time after that, recalling our Nara trip, recalling picnics he and I and Yamagami san had taken into the country and strolls Yamagami and I had taken along Suiken beach and the long and happy conversations. We had laughed but never joked, never told jokes. Later, when he left, Bettie and I sat for a long time in the study, recalling how we had regarded him. After the first tears, there were no others. It did not come to me clearly at the time. It came only years later when I began to study the philosophies of the East in order to teach a course at Cochise College. Reading D. T. Suzuki and hearing the talks by Alan Watts, I began to understand the impact Yamagami made on my life and on the lives of others. By then I discovered something about teaching I have never been able to explain. Sometimes in class, as I am trying to develop a thought—some call it "winging it"—I discover what I want to say by accident. Words, whole thoughts come spontaneously from some part of my brain. I can hear myself almost as though I am one of the students out there in the class. One day in my Philosophies of the East class, trying to describe the nature of the living Buddha, I began, without having planned beforehand, by describing Yamagami, recalling how Tonai san first responded when he came to the house, how his friends would speak to him, and how the men at Shin Fuso spoke of him, and how they would even defer to him automatically as if it were the natural thing to do. In Japan, I explained, the young as a strict rule always defer to their elders. It is a custom so ingrained in the Japanese character that it is almost a genetic factor, but it was not so in the case of Yamagami. The men in my Shin Fuso class would often defer, not ostentatiously or with any suggestion of ceremony, but with little half gestures and quiet attention when he spoke. They had, on occasion stood aside for him or on occasion held a door for him—unheard of ordinarily. In class, when I recalled my attempt to correct Saito's mistake, I would feel a chill or a prickly feeling about my neck. He was, for Saito, indeed the Buddha and had lived the life of a Bodhisattva. And I told the class that he would become the same for me in time as I reached a greater understanding. It was not a planned part of the class, but it would be after that, a segment of every Eastern philosophies class and often in other philosophy classes if the context fit. It would also be a story students would recall and describe clearly just as they heard it, recalling his name always as "Yamagami san." And today when I think of Yamagami, I feel a great sense of peace. But at the time it was inexplicable, a fact that I would learn was also in the nature of Buddhism.

Nothing was fully comprehendible except that a horrible accident had robbed us of a dear friend. His death was more than a cause for grief, for to be honest, it was not grief I felt so much as simply an uncomprehending sense of loss. I ceased all work on the course in cultural history, the course I had looked forward to with such excitement and hope. All the time I was pulling together ideas and sources, I was thinking I was laying the foundation for some larger future study; but now after the news, it all stopped. We did not talk about it much. Bettie would ask why, but of course no answer came. I had never lost a close friend before. None of my friends had died during the war, and I had never known anyone close to me who had ever been ill or in a fatal accident. My father's passing had come at a time when I was too young to understand the meaning of death. Yamagami, whom I had known for only a short time, had come to mean more than I could comprehend.

Then suddenly, as the summer heat and humidity broke and the first signs of autumn began to appear, the urge to get on with my preparations for class returned. Returning to the books, taking notes, even writing practice conversations, I found, was a kind of solace. The important thing now was to get back to what I had come to love "most best." I had learned so much, studying and reading, that my problem now was not whether I had found enough material to cover but how to select and limit the materials. I knew that what I had been doing was not true scholarship; it did not involve digging into primary sources but just knowing what to borrow. I borrowed most heavily from writers like Merle Curti, Vernon Parrington, Trilling, Van Wyck Brooks, Bernard DeVoto, H. L. Mencken, Henry Nash Smith, and, of course, Edmund Wilson. More than once, I felt I was being presumptuous to even attempt to teach a class in American culture, and I knew whatever I taught would lack the focus it needed. It was indeed an act of utmost hubris. Why did I think that a few months reading—regardless how intensive—would prepare me to present the major cultural ideas of America? Bettie raised the same question, and both Dot Grier and Anne had raised eyebrows, though neither voiced her doubts. I admitted that I would be only a few steps ahead of the class and that the major justification was giving advanced English student experiences in using and improving English as much as learning about our cultural history. The impetus to forge ahead, to "damn the torpedoes," came as much from my personal pleasure in discovery as from an overpowering desire to teach to share all this most interesting stuff. Learning was, at that moment, more important than teaching, but it followed that learning by itself was never enough, was only half the journey. I became obsessed with the impulse to impart, to make others see what I had seen, in other words, to *teach*. This was the seminal moment in my evolution as a teacher. Discovering that the joys of learning new ideas must always precede the desire to teach, I understood that teaching must follow. It was, I felt strongly, also something I had to know *if* I could do. More and more, I looked forward to the class, confident I was able to present ideas, able to make them real.

I learned a lot from Anne about how I should conduct the class. All of my students were advanced English majors, third- and fourth-year students who planned to become English teachers; so unlike Anne's class, they were expected to know the language already. When Anne first arrived at Wakayama University, she had boldly undertaken to teach industrial and educational psychology without a textbook, using only a handful of readings in English; and on top of that, she had refused to give formal lectures with a standby translator/interpreter, and it had worked. Already she had acquired a faithful following of students in Miki's and Kameoka's class who had done far more than simply go along. I believed I could do the same, and she encouraged me to try and to avoid formal lectures. Never having taken a class in teaching theories or methods aside from the class with Dr. Kitchen at the Hartford Seminary, I did not have to unlearn a method.

The class, Inoue said, would be smaller than Anne's educational psych and industrial psych classes. Wa Dai had only a handful of advanced English majors, students whom I had known for two years, regular visitors to the open houses with proven language skills. Although not all were as conversationally fluent as Jisaka, they were all volunteers and had expressed a strong desire to take a class where only English would be used as the means of instruction. My preparations had gone so well, I thought, that I asked Inoue if I might conduct a similar class in the spring term for the same students, this one to be a study of the modern American novel, and he agreed. I told him I could select novels having editions in Japanese and that I would be able to secure enough gift copies of the English editions, novels by Fitzgerald, Hemingway, Steinbeck, Lewis, Cather, and Faulkner—all major twentieth-century writers—so that each student would have his or her own copy. When I offered to teach the class in addition to my regularly scheduled conversation classes, he demurred at first, protesting that it would be too heavy a load. But when the university hired Edward Brown as Marty's replacement, Inoue said that he could absorb the load. The American culture and novel courses he felt were important enough to justify, reducing my conversational class load, he said, urging me to go ahead with the plans for the class. It was wonderful news.

Chapter 20

Sayonara

When Bettie learned that Dr. Schwerzen, the Swiss missionary in Kyoto whom she'd visited to confirm she was expecting, was not licensed to deliver babies but only to consult, she settled on Kobe International Hospital and Dr. Tsubaki. Dot Grier said it was as up to date in obstetrics as any hospital in America, and English was the hospital's second language. Nuns of the Franciscan Sisters of Mary ran the hospital, the mother superior herself an MD, who, so we heard, spoke six languages and was licensed to deliver. The only drawback was the two-hour commute to and from Kobe, but that problem was solved when Ruth and Morse Saito invited Bettie to stay with them for the month before the baby was due. Their new house behind the institute had a guest room with its own half bath. Ruth insisted she and Morse would love the company. The baby was not due until March, conveniently right in the middle of the long spring recess. I would move in with Bettie as soon as my classes were over for the term, and until then, I could commute as I had when I was teaching at Palmore Institute. So it appeared as if we had planned it after all.

Altogether, Bettie made four trips to Kobe for regular monthly check-ups with Dr. Tsubaki, and each time he found her strong and healthy with no sign of complications, but each four-hour round-trip from Wakayama was more uncomfortable than the one before. The commuter trains, not designed for comfort, only speed and high capacity, had no first- or second-class cars and varied from uncomfortable to extremely uncomfortable. So near the end of January, when classes resumed after the winter break, Bettie moved to the Saito's in the Palmore Institute compound; and I once more began the commute, taking the train to Kobe every Monday afternoon and then the train back to Wakayama early Tuesday morning in time for classes. On Wednesday evenings after my class at the plant, the company car would deliver me to Higashi Wakayama station, and I would commute to Kobe returning to Wakayama Thursday morning, in time for classes, and then I would leave on Friday for a weekend with Bettie at the Saito's. Ruth always had a tray for me when I arrived late Wednesday evenings. Every Friday, I was back in Kobe with Bettie, staying until Sunday night.

The weekends were special, often including a movie and a supper out alone. Once to show our appreciation for their kindness, I invited Morse and Ruth, but they declined, saying that we should have the time together. I suspected that Morse and Ruth were more concerned about our financial situation than our having time alone together. When Marty Pray came down to visit us from Tokyo at Christmas, he told us that the Tokyo J3s wondered how we could make it on the Wa Dai salary. He had wondered himself, but he said he enjoyed their concern.

We took long walks in the city, visited the USIS Library, attended lectures given at the library, went to the movies, ate at a fancy French restaurant, and even saw Cary Grant and his new wife one day while we were walking in Motomachi, Kobe's main shopping street. To make sure Bettie would get to the hospital in time, we found a taxi service just one street over from Palmore that could rush us to the International Hospital in the suburb of Rokko-Machi when the time came; and just a week after finding the taxi service, at 2:00 a.m. March 4th, Bettie woke me and said it was time. I was up in flash and brought the cab to the Saito house in just minutes. But alas, there was no need to rush. A son, Drake Clay Moore Gilliland did not announce his arrival until 1:30 p.m. It was a long protracted delivery, as were most first deliveries according to the nurses and Dr. Tsubaki, and later confirmed by Dot Grier, but Bettie everyone assured me complained very little.

Though the hospital had the most modern obstetric equipment, Clay's birth took place in Bettie's room, and I was present throughout his delivery. In the months before Bettie read carefully Dr. Grantly Dick Reed's, *Modern Child Birth and* followed closely the anesthetic free natural birth method Reed preached, and to her great relief the method worked as it was supposed to. Also to her great delight, the hospital provided her and Clay a private nurse, Rose Sakamoto who had her own bed in Bettie's room. Clay also remained with her in the large, well-heated room rather than in a nursery.

We were both amazed at the service and the comfort and the simple but tasty meals the hospital served. However, I silently trembled at the cost that I assumed would strip is of all our savings, but all of that, including the nurse's salary, came to ¥2,000 a day, or less than six dollars a day in the U.S. coin of 1953. Dr. Tsubaki's fee was ¥15,000 or about forty-two dollars and covered Bettie's prenatal visits, delivery, and postpartum examination. My gift to the doctor, a carton of Lucky Strike cigarettes, cost us at the black market price of ¥5,000 a third of his fee. When the mother superior learned Bettie and Clay would have to travel in the university car all the way to Wakayama over some fairly bad roads, she insisted Bettie stay at least ten days, raising the total hospital bill to fifty-five dollars. Clay's coming changed our lives considerably though he in no way altered our fundamental goals and purposes.

Baby Clay

The fall term seemed to pass quickly, my culture class going so well that I gave serious thought to changing my major to history when I returned to the university in Austin. I dispensed with formal lectures entirely as Anne recommended and relied entirely on discussions which I began by asking a big question, that later gave way to questions from the students. The USIS librarian allowed me to check out and keep books beyond the deadlines. I passed them on to students after assigning specific passages for individual students. Had the Kobe library not been there I would not have been able to offer the class.

It had become obvious as the semester progressed that I needed to think seriously about what I would do when we returned to the States the following summer, for, as soon as Bettie knew that she was pregnant, we had determined that we would leave Japan in the summer after the baby arrived, the end of my three year obligation. The University of Texas had recently established a graduate program in American Studies leading to an interdisciplinary master's and doctoral degrees that involved history, government, literature, and other cognate areas, such as sociology, anthropology, or philosophy the student and his advisors might consider necessary to fill out his or her area of emphasis. The combination interested me because it was interdisciplinary. All through my undergraduate years I had crossed lines. I knew I would have to begin working toward a master's degree soon if I planned to teach in college. Anne had made it quite clear that I should stay away from psychology. Bettie and I agreed. Even before the fateful afternoon of the martini Anne and I had discussed my plans.

I had never spoken to an academic advisor from the time I enrolled as a freshman but had allowed my whims to guide me. Anne, shifting from the role of friend to that of counselor, firmly advised I decide exactly what I *wanted* to teach, not what I *thought* I wanted or what I thought I *should* teach, and she insisted I talk to Bettie before making any decision. When I told her that Bettie and I agreed that I should teach in college, she said the next step was to decide what it was I wanted to teach or what I believed I could teach best. I knew that I did not want to teach ESL. Admitting frankly that the idea of a graduate degree was daunting, especially because my undergraduate grades clearly defined mediocrity. Most daunting of all, I told her, was the thought of pursuing a PhD. But Anne insisted I should not be concerned about my undergraduate grades. Graduate profs generally ignored what had gone before, she said.

"If you are serious and really want the degree, if *both* of you really want it, you'll get it," she said and added that she had been quite impressed by the work I had done in planning the culture class, particularly by the manner in which I had gone about collecting the readingings, and my making notes on my own.

"Louie Grier and I," she said, "talked about how much you seemed to enjoy it. I could tell then that you could do the work if you wanted to. It was obvious you were enjoying it all, and that is most important," she said, smiling, and then added, "We watched you, were even worried at first, you know."

But the most encouraging thing she said, probably the first evaluation I ever received as a teacher, was that, after watching me during the open houses and after visiting a class and hearing my students' reports, she was convinced I was a born teacher. I believed from the first night class that teaching was my true calling, even as far back as the lessons in letter writing with Gaston and Perkins and my instruction in C Company about the Koreans and their culture and on those occasions when individual GIs would quietly approach me and ask me to explain things they didn't understand.

For months, Bettie and I talked about little else but our future after Wakayama. I relied more and more on her opinions and was still undecided whether I should major in history, government, or English, all these being subject I loved to study and discuss. I had made my best grades as an undergraduate in government, but planning the cultural history class had given me great pleasure and a clear sense of purpose. Now as I began to plan a class in the modern American novel for the same advanced students, I began to see where my interests really lay. I had learned so much about reading critically for ideas and meanings by reading Wilson's *Classics and Commercials*, Alfred Kazin's *On Native Grounds* and others—all of which I had read originally for the sheer pleasure of discovery—and I knew I would be happiest teaching others the way to understanding.

In an effort to nail down a choice of major, to know before I registered for classes in September, I wrote and applied for admission to all three MA programs. Anne was correct when she told me she the graduate departments were less interested in my grades than I thought they were. The English department, the first to reply, accepted me only on the condition that I complete, with a minimum grade of B, twelve hours of senior and graduate-level work in English. This condition, he letter said was based on my not having majored or minored in English. The other departments followed with the same condition. My grade point average was never mentioned. When I completed the application for admission and mailed it in to the department of English, my mind was settled.

Although Texas had a half dozen or so state colleges, former teachers colleges, that also offered graduate degrees I had never considered enrolling in any other graduate school but the university in Austin. In those days, holding a bachelor's degree from the university granted automatic acceptance into the Graduate School—with conditions—and Texas veterans had the added benefit of free tuition for life. I could not afford to look elsewhere. No other graduate school in the state had the stature or the challenge that the University of Texas had. So by the time the new semester began in the spring, our plans were settled for the fall of 1953. I would be beginning again; ten years after first enrolling as a freshman premed student, I would be starting anew as a graduate student in English.

I gave notice to Inoue and Itoigawa that I had been accepted for graduate study at The University of Texas and that we would be leaving Wa Dai in the summer in order to arrive in time for the fall term at the University of Texas. Inoue said he was expecting to hear about our decision when Clay was born. He congratulated me on my decision to major in English, emphasizing his belief that I should specialize in literature, not ESL. We laughed, and I admitted that conversational English was not my calling, and then I added that his O'Neill translation had convinced me I could do graduate-level work in literature. I told him he was my first graduate professor; I would never forget how much he had taught me about reading for meanings, not just *the* meaning. He thanked me, and I believed he knew how important our sessions with O'Neill had been. Everything had happened more smoothly than I thought possible; no roadblocks, not a single tank trap or minefield had blocked our path. The "Purblind Doomsters" had indeed "strewn blisses" about my pilgrimage—at least so far.

We knew we would not be able to afford passage on either the *President Wilson* or *President Cleveland* unless we went tourist or steerage class, and I was sure that steerage class would not be feasible with a four-month-old baby and with diapers, formula, all in a crowded dorm-like cabin. Bettie said she preferred sailing on a freighter, but neither American nor British companies would book passage for infants below the age of one year. It was a dilemma. We could not wait for Clay's first birthday.

Fortuitously, our solution came from Corpus Christi. The *Osaka Maru*, Japan's most modern passenger cargo ship in the OSK Lines, had stopped at Corpus Christi on its maiden voyage and received visitors as part of the promotion of Japan's modern merchant fleet. Mama and Albert, reading about the ship and knowing we were searching for a solution, had gone aboard and met the captain and officers and mentioned Clay. They sent us the clippings along with an OSK brochure and recommended it highly. The line accepted infants who could travel free of charge, and the combined cost for Bettie and me was roughly half the fare we would have had to pay on the *Wilson*. When I contacted OSK in Osaka, I got an immediate reply and an assurance of space on the *Osaka Maru*'s sister ship the *Hawaii Maru*, sailing in late July or early August. Oh, Doomsters, where art thou?

Meanwhile, my classes continued at the university and the steel plant. The American novel course enrolled only six students, all of whom had been in my culture class and regulars at the open house. I assigned each student a different novel, which I supplied from the books I received from Mama's friends at The First Methodist church. I asked each to write a short paper discussing the novel's major theme or idea. The final exam would be an oral presentation—which they could read if they wished—telling the class what most impressed them about the novel. They could emphasize plot, character, theme, setting, or prose style, whatever they considered the dominant feature of the novel and they could use whatever sources they were able to consult.

Each student would meet with me in conference to discuss ideas or problems. Criticism, I emphasized—from my reading of Wilson and other critics and reviewers—was not confined to finding fault but was most concerned with understanding how an author could attempt to express his thoughts. To give them an idea of what I expected I gave them copies of book reviews from *Saturday Review, The Nation, Time,* and *The New Republic,* along with any other periodical. The course I was well aware would not stand scrutiny at an American university, and I'm not sure how much credit my students would receive at Wa Dai. Inoue seemed satisfied that the course achieved the goals I'd set, i.e., giving advanced students a chance to read and discuss in English major American novels.

Never a regular churchgoer, Mama made sure we went to Sunday school. But after I left for Japan, she joined the First Methodist Church in Corpus Christi and became an active member of the Women's Society of Christian Service. One of the members of the group was Mrs. Taylor, the owner of the Six Points Book Store, where I had bought many of my used science books. Naturally I told Mama about the novel course and my students' need for books. I attached a list of authors and titles, eight or ten in all, that I wrote would be the major focus of the class: Wolfe, Cather, Lewis, Fitzgerald, Hemingway, Steinbeck, Faulkner, Katherine Anne Porter (who had not written a novel at the time), and several others. I explained that my students were advanced English majors who had finished a course in cultural history. She answered immediately, explaining how each member of the group had decided to purchase and donate a book by one author from the list. She also wrote how happy and how enthusiastic they were about my request, with one reservation: the language and subjects of some of the novels were somewhat "racy."

While they were reading their novels and were preparing their papers, I discussed the backgrounds to American fiction in the twentieth century and connected these backgrounds to major ideas discussed in the cultural history course. I had been gleaning material from Spiller, Kazin, Granville Hicks, Cowley, Maxwell Geismar, Edmund Wilson, Irving Howe, and sources I found at the library in Kobe. Most of the material was as new to me as it was to the class. If my readings in Wilson had broken the ice and opened to me a whole range of critical scholarship, I was aware I still had far to go before I was ready for a serious college class in the American novel. I'd also begun reading Cooper, Hawthorne, Melville, Twain, James, and Crane in an attempt to make up for my background in American literature and to be better prepared for graduate school. My instincts served me well, for my choice of authors and works for the Wa Dai class would a year later closely parallel Dr. Graham's seminar in American Novel after 1920. I admitted at the first class that I was studying the novels along with the class, explaining that I hoped that by their knowing this, they would feel free to challenge me with their own opinions or interpretations. I told them, half-seriously they should be getting credit for preparing me for graduate study. It worked. Attendance in the class was high, and everyone performed assigned tasks far better than I expected, which suggested to me that they were seriously dedicated to learning English as well as they could. Sharing with the class my own level of scholarship and explaining that I was teaching while learning and that I was using them and this class to prepare for my master's and eventually a doctor's degree, was quite unheard of Inoue said. I said that as far as I knew, it was also unheard of at the university level in the U.S. But I would learn much later that advanced seminars at American universities, particularly at the PhD level, were often learning experiences for the professor conducting the seminar. Many years later, one of my doctoral professors conducting a Melville seminar admitted in the seminar that he had to rewrite his conclusions regarding Melville's "The Lightning-Rod Man" because of a student paper on the same story: I was that student. The professor, Martin Fisher became my dissertation supervisor and my dissertation subject was Melville's uses of the artist-narrator.

My conversational classes went better than usual that last term. It seemed—I had no way of knowing for sure--I had finally learned how to teach ESL, how to draw even the shyest and most reluctant student into our class dialogs, and had learned how to construct practice conversations that my students would attack enthusiastically.

One day during the open house after I had announced we were leaving, Tanabe san, one of my regular ESS students, dropped by the house for a chat. He had become quite close to Tonai san, as had many of the young men who attended the open houses. I was studying at the desk in the bay window, and I recall Bettie's coming into the small study, telling me that Tanabe san had something to talk to me about. She left us alone, and he began, explaining in carefully measured phrases as if he had practiced a little speech just how much Oba san was going to miss Bettie and me and especially *Kurei* chan. It was a most affecting moment, and I realized then how much Bettie and I had come to depend on people like Tanabe and Jisaka and Chieko Takehata, especially since Miki and Saigo had graduated and gone on to jobs in the great world. Tanabe, who had always spoken English quite well, almost as clearly as Miki or Saigo, was explaining patiently, making sure I understood him clearly. I could tell he and Tonai san had talked about what he was about to say.

"Tonai san believes she is Kurei chan's real grandmother, and she is very sad that she will not see him grow up."

"I understand that, Tanabe san," I said. "I wish we could take her with us. Bettie loves her very much and so do I. I will write her often. I'm sure she can find someone to read my letters to her."

He nodded. "Yes, I told her I would read your letters, but she said that she wants to read your letters herself—in Japanese."

I said I understood and told him how I had learned to read and write hiragana a little, that when Bettie and I first decided we would have to return home in time for the fall semester at U of Texas, I had studied hard and learned to write Japanese almost as well as a second grader. He laughed and said that he thought it would be good enough. I told him how Tonai san had teased me about my poor Japanese, about my speaking a woman's dialect or the countrified Wakayama *bin*, so inappropriate for a *dai-gakku* sensei. It was true; my Japanese was still an odd agglomeration of street language, classical idiom, and Wakayama dialect. I told him how Oba san had laughed when I told her all I learned was what she had taught me and how she had insisted she was not a teacher, a *kiyoshi*. When she realized we would be leaving in the summer, she had persuaded me to cram just so she could read the news of *Kurei chan*.

That I succeeded in writing her half a dozen short letters was due entirely to her insistence and her belief that I could do it. Her letters to Bettie and me were almost entirely in hiragana, and I, surprisingly, was able to read them with no difficulty, *but* the final letter from Oba san was in English dictated to Tanabe san. It came just after Christmas with Tanabe's letter telling us that she had died of cancer, a cancer that had been in remission all the time she had been working for us. One evening shortly before Bettie arrived, Tonai san told the story about how she had lost her husband and both children in the great Kanto earthquake of 1923 that destroyed most of Tokyo. Tonai san had wept a little as she told of loosing her two children and her husband some thirty yeas ago. Drying her eyes with the sleeve of her kimono, she told how she had been diagnosed with breast cancer and how she had the radical mastectomy, all in a very clear and rather horrifyingly simple and direct Japanese. I understood she had been declared cured, but then that's only what I *understood*, and it may have been what she wanted me to understand, or after seeing Kurosawa's great film *Ikiru*, I could believe it was all she knew as well. I recalled many other moments that might have clued me in had I been paying closer attention. We never attend to those we most need to attend to, it seems.

For the rest of the spring, Tanabe was a regular presence, visiting Bettie and me as regularly as Tanaka san or Yamagami san. He had been in the first

English classes and then a member of the economics school English Speaking Society. Now he was among the closest like Jisaka and Chieko—who had received her wish and had become the closest of friends indeed, if not an "intimate" one. I missed Tanaka's always-welcome visit and Saigo's proud suggestions about our lives in Japan; Tanabe helped immensely just being there for a visit. These would be the most difficult things to leave behind, we both agreed.

Tsuyama san, the Shin Fuso engineer who wrote in his diary in English, French, German, and Chinese, gave Bettie and me a most unique farewell gift when he invited us to a kabuki performance of *Shu Shin Gura*, the story of the Forty-Seven Ronin, perhaps Japan's most famous samurai tale and clearly the tale that the Japanese felt most succinctly represented the real Japan. We three took the train into Osaka, using the Namba line that delivered us to the city center at the Takashimaya Department Store and close to the major shopping street where many good restaurants were found. We had a lovely lunch at a small Japanese restaurant, and then took a taxi to Osaka's Kabuki-za. I had always wanted to take Bettie to her fist kabuki performance as Marty had taken me when he put me o the test. Tsuyama san's "gift" came at a perfect time, getting us out of the house and giving Bettie a brief holiday and her first trip to Osaka since Clay was born, and it gave Tonai san the chance she had wanted, a chance to be Obaa san, *Kurei chan's* real grandmother.

It was terribly dramatic, terribly tragic, and quite beautiful. We were able to follow virtually every nuance despite the language. Tsuyama san's choice of a farewell gift we felt was a high compliment, indeed; Kabuki is one of the most Japanese of all Japanese art forms and thus does not appeal to many *gaiji*, which explains Marty's use of *kabuki* as a proper test. Bettie was quite overwhelmed by the spectacle and the strength of the performances that conveys so clearly the traditional story of betrayal, intrigue, loyalty, and honor. We were deeply impressed by Tsuyama san's gesture.

Bettie and I had said our farewells to Dot and Louie when they departed earlier in the summer on their first furlough. Before returning home to Philadelphia, they would travel first to Switzerland, where Louie would be attending an international ecumenical institute. Their departure was sad and very moving; Bettie and I had come to depend heavily on their friendship in the seemingly short time we had known them. Dot may have saved my life that first winter when I had pneumonia, and Louie had been a constant guide and mentor in ways I still am unable to explain. Ironically, they would be sailing aboard the USS *General Leroy Eltinge*, the same ship I had sailed on when I went to Korea in the winter of 1946. D deck on the *Eltinge* had been the scene of the great seminar of satire, one of my first successful encounters with teaching. As I write this I am struck how easily it could qualify as another Dahlquist moment and how he connected us some how with tragical events in the future, for when the Griers boarded the *Eltinge* was packed with French soldiers headed for French Indo-China, the first of an ill-fated attempt to save the French colonial adventure in Southeast Asia that would in less then a decade involve the US in its fourth war of the century, truly a portend for future misfortunes.

On August 4, we sailed from Yokohama on the *Hawaii Maru*, the newest, most modern freighter of the OSK Line and probably one of the most automated freighters operating on the high seas at the time. In the week before leaving my students, the Wa Dai English Department, and the Shin Fuso class, held farewell parties for us, the most emotional being the party given by Shin Fuso at a Wakanoura hotel overlooking beautiful Wakayama Bay. Months before, I had said farewell to Tanaka, Saigo, Kameoka, Katsube, and Kuriyama, when they had graduated in the first graduating class of Wakayama Dai Gakku.

Our most difficult farewell was the one with Tonai san, who had become much more than our Oba san, a maid. I had never had an aunt or anyone outside the family to whom I felt so close. She had come to Kobe the day after Clay was born and would have taken Rose Sakamoto's place in the room with Bettie had she been permitted, and when Bettie returned with Clay to Wakayama, Tonai insisted she was Clay's "*honto no Obaa san*" his *true* Grandmother. She accepted all the responsibilities that *grandmother* implied, even to washing and boiling his diapers and to heating and preparing his formula. In far more ways than any ordinary *ruso-ban*, she had become our protector and advisor simply through the power of her love and devotion. Bettie, she told me more than once, was for her the daughter she had lost in the great Tokyo earthquake in the twenties; in spite of the language, they never failed to communicate with each other. She rode with us in the old university Pontiac, sitting in the back seat and cradling *Kurei chan* all the way.

When we sailed out of Yokohama aboard the *Hawaii Maru*, it was less than two weeks shy of three years to the day that I had first arrived. Much had changed. The war in Korea was over. The United States and Japan were officially at peace, the peace treaty having been signed in April of 1952. The greatest change had taken place in us. For the first time since I left home as a freshman, I had a clear purpose, and I absolute confident that it was purpose I would accomplish. I had fulfilled my here year obligation, had married the girl I had found and loved "at fist sight," and had sired a son who was bright as the sun in our lives.

However, as we leaned over the railing, watching our ship slip away from the pier, our thoughts were far from those changes. As the serpentines of thin paper flew from the small group of passengers down to families and friends standing on the pier, my mind leaped ahead to the next three years and what lay ahead. Those years seemed as much an enigma and just as hopeful as my thoughts had been three years before. The narrow strips of paper flying in high arches falling to the pier, the strains of "Auld Lang Syne" pouring from loudspeakers, the shouts of *sayonara*, and hands waving were reminders of countless scenes from old movies, but the difference was Bettie and were part actors in the scene, not spectators in a dark theater.

I felt at the moment that I was living a charmed life: to have come this far, with no clear plan, unscathed, was something of a miracle. I, we, had much to hope for. I had completed, with a degree of success and great satisfaction, three years of teaching at a Japanese university. I had a wife and a son and was returning to the country poised on the brink of a booming economy. Before me were prospects of becoming a college teacher just at the time when college enrollment in the United States was on the rise. There was still much to do before I could feel absolutely secure that I had made the right choice, but vague uncertainty was gone. As the *Hawaii Maru* left the pier, the serpentine strips stretched as if straining to keep the travelers' connections firm, but then like an umbilicus, they were severed and we were off again and on our own.

I had my letter of acceptance to the master's program from the English department at the University of Texas, stating the conditions I would have to meet, but I still had only a vague idea what it actually meant. I knew but one thing for sure: I was not the same person I was when I left the university. We had all changed, Bettie and I, Marty Pray and Bill Asbury. Bettie still recalls that she had no reservations or any doubts about my ability to do the work or that we would be able to weather the next two years of graduate school scraping by financially. She had made it through with me on a Japanese teacher's salary, had given birth to a beautiful and healthy son, and she was certain we would have no problems with the years in grad school.

The Board of Missions had generously created a system that not only allowed and encouraged growth of mind and heart but also demanded it. It was not surprising then that some of us would grow in ways the Board, or we, could not have predicted. It was in the nature of those selected and the nature of the mission itself, that some would grow beyond what we were when we arrived. The members of the Board had seen that change occur again and again whenever they sent people into foreign lands and cultures. That men like Shacklock and Cobb did nothing to stop me but in their way encouraged me was testimony of their generous spirit. Aside from what I learned about Japan, its people, and myself, I had learned something about teaching, about how to conduct myself before a class of college students, and how to convey a thought and to encourage others to think. These were lessons that would last forever.

Through friends like Yamagami, Tanaka, and Nishikawa, I had begun to understand an enduring philosophy, a way of life, from which I would continue to learn for the rest of my life. While Bettie and I often went for days without seeing or speaking to other Americans, we never felt isolated or alone. Students, faculty, the men at Shin Fuso were frequent visitors to our house. The three students who first greeted Marty and me at the house at 316 Sekido continued to call and write even after their graduation, and on the last day Bettie and I were in Tokyo, waiting to board our ship in Yokohama, I met Saigo Nishikawa, and we had lunch and a long talk. After almost sixty years, I am still in touch with both Nishikawa and Tanaka via e-mail, that is for more than sixty yeas at his writing.

My reasons for feeling drawn to Asia after that brief time in Korea were never clear. For years I thought it was the exoticism writers like Conrad, Maugham, or Kipling had spun about the attraction of the "mysterious Orient." I learned earlier that Kipling's belief that East was East and West was West was simply wrong. The twain often met. James Hilton's *Lost Horizon*, the novel and the film, and my earliest encounter, *To Lhasa in Disguise*, haunted me, but living ended the mystery while creating a bold new reality. When I returned to Austin after Korea and moved into my room at the Lambda Chi Alpha house with Bill Mullins, I found someone as obsessed as I with the idea of the Orient. Like me, Mullins no longer relied on books or movies to stir the imagination; we had a memory of living there and knowing it through the senses as well as the mind. People often quoted Lafcadio Hearn, who said only a person with a weak olfactory sense could love the East, but we knew it was more. We often talked about his days and nights in Japan and and mine in Korea. Together we manufactured our own magic and mystery about the East. But beyond the fantasy was a reality that we knew we had become a part of. Bettie had never known the East or thought about it except the part of the East that was the Himalayas, but she was just as affected as I by those feelings, and she still is. We are still mystified and charmed by our youthful acquaintance with Lhasa through the writings of Richard Montgomery McGovern. I had seen Marty fly over the barrier of East and West and submerge himself in the music, art, and language. Each day he grew more a part of the country he loved and became more and more like that mad, half-Irish, half-Greek Lafcadio Hearn, a transplant from New Orleans, who had become so Japanese that in the end they claimed him for their own. Such transformations were not the results of rational processes, but they happened, and each of us in some way was transformed and, I believe, made better. Perhaps that fictional mode of Conrad, Maugham, and Kipling is the only means we have of explaining the effects of the East. Not everyone feels it, many hate and despise the differences between the twain. I am constantly reminded of the RAF wife I met in Tokyo who found the American GI's attachment to their Japanese friends to be odd, curious, if not downright wrong.

But there were times when I had a surfeit of Asia, when Marty's plucking the koto strings, twanging away at *Sakura* or *Roko-Dan*, or when one more cup of green tea, one more serene stone garden would drive me to distraction, and then only a dose of big band jazz or a Cole Porter lyric—"We'll see Manhattan from Staten Island too . . ."—on the Armed Forces Radio would calm my jitters. Then I would immerse myself in Faulkner, Steinbeck, T. S. Eliot, and Carl Sandburg as antidotes to the effects of Nipponization. In the end, I would sink back into the quietude of art, into the serenity of a *kake-jiku* hanging in the alcove, or the cursive strokes of calligraphy on a scroll before which rested a simple vase and a sprig of a blossoming plant, or hear Basho's croaking frog—*furuike ya.* It was Yamagami at Nara, taking Bettie and me first to the great temple of the Dai-Butsu and then to the Kaidan-in with the Buddhist guardians arranged on the small pavilion and then to the walled garden, just walking, speaking not in hushed or reverential whispers, but in the subtle softness of his normal speech. It was then and other times, such as the long weekend with Nishikawa and a group of Wa-Dai students staying in the Shingon Temple on the holy mountain of Koya, walking in the cemetery of the Tokugawa family, absorbing without explanations, without a *ko-an* even, a direct knowing. It was our arriving at midnight Christmas Eve at Hiroshima and being welcomed into the small inn and the next day walking into the ruined epicenter and standing beneath the naked ribs of the commerce building, or it was on a bright spring day gazing at the cherry blossoms of Himeji's *Shirosaki-jo*, the Castle of the White Crane or sitting after our hot bath in the little pavilion at Ozu, gazing at Fuji san on our right or the vast open Pacific on our left. Then maybe it was walking into a class of sixth graders in the school at Nagano cho and hearing them greet me: "Good morning, Mistah Giriran. How are you today?"

I did not return to Asia in order to become an authority on the Far East, but to learn and teach. Those things I learned at Wa Dai would help me through a lifetime of teaching, and some would form the basis of my classes in Eastern philosophies years later. Unlike Marty, I did not immerse myself in the language and culture, nor did I have the talent for winning people as Bill Asbury had. Both of them spoke Japanese so well they encountered few barriers. Yet the people whom we knew refused to let language barriers impede friendships. I continue to correspond with Mikio Tanaka, my best student, and Saigo has stayed in touch as well. Inoue sensei, Anne, Marty, Tanaka, Nishikawa, Kuriyama, Jisaka, Chieko, Tanabe and, of course, Louis and Dot Grier all taught me more than I could have learned in any classroom or by browsing through the best library. And there was Bettie. Had she not been there in Wakayama, or had I gone on to Palmore in Kobe and finished my time in Japan as a J3, I doubt seriously I would have found the path I have traveled so happily for more than half a century. Our reading together and our discovering a world of literature and our learning to know a culture in a living context made a difference. The years of reading uninstructed and unguided except by the mentors I'd met only on the printed page—Trilling, Wilson, Kazin, and others—focused and strengthened my determination to do the MA in English that would one day lead to a PhD.

The *Hawaii Maru*'s passenger list included several Japanese businessmen, a young Nisei woman returning from a visit with grandparents, and two members of the Fujiwara Opera Company, a husband and wife on their way to join the cast of *Madame Butterfly* scheduled to perform in New York and other cities on the East Coast. The husband, a silent, dour figure of unquestioned dignity, sang the bass role of the Bonze in act 1, a small but important role, while his wife sang the role of Suzuki, Cio-Cio san's maid. Bettie and I and the singers shared the captain's table.

Though the *Hawaii Maru* was a freighter and carried only twelve passengers plus Clay, the captain followed all the formalities of a great liner's captain. At meals, he was always in full uniform with braided shoulder boards, never entering the salon until all passengers were seated, and he was always the first to lift his fork. Several said during the war he held the rank of admiral in the Japanese Navy. He spoke excellent English when he spoke, which was infrequently. Why Bettie and I were chosen to sit at the captain's table was a puzzlement at first, but I recalled the exalted position of college professors in Japanese society and realized that the seating arrangements had been made by a company bureaucrat and based only on that information.

The voyage to San Francisco took ten days, the *Hawaii Maru* following the bleak, gray northern circle route via the Aleutians. Except for Bettie's sweater, we had packed all our heavy clothing in hold trunks. Fortunately, the cabins and all the interior areas were well heated. Clay was just four months old to the day when we sailed out of Tokyo Bay. It was a comfortable crossing by any standard.

When we arrived in San Francisco, Marty was waiting for us at the pier. He had been home a month, had a job with the American branch of the Tokyo Marine and Fire Insurance Company, and found a comfortable apartment in the city. He seemed already as acculturated to San Francisco as he had been in Tokyo.

We cleared customs rapidly and drove to Marty's apartment, unable to get to our winter clothing since we had arranged for our hold luggage to be shipped to Bettie's parents in Wichita Falls. Along with Bettie's sweater, I had packed in the cabin luggage a light seersucker suit I'd bought in Kobe, but that was all we had in the way of warmer clothing. I firmly believe that San Francisco has never had a seersucker season. Never had I been so eager to bask in the August heat of Texas as I was those two days we waited for a flight out to Dallas-Fort Worth.

In the next few weeks, Bettie, Clay, and I completed our own re-acculturation, visiting first Bettie's parents in Wichita Falls and then Mama and Albert in Corpus Christi. Meeting Harold and Edna for the first time proved to be much easier than I expected. Bettie had told me much about her family, her grandparents, Aunt Gladys and Uncle Cecil, all of whom lived in a small ranching and oil community southwest of Wichita Falls. Harold and Edna gave me the warmest possible welcome and made me feel as if we had always known one another. At first, understandably nervous, I suppose—I had no job and no clear proof that I could keep their daughter and precious new grandson from poverty—I was afraid I would overcompensate in some way and play the fool. But they never allowed it. While the Crumptons were not wealthy or even "well to do" by the standards of the time, they were more than comfortable. Harold told me he considered himself "land poor," meaning they had much land, probably more than ten thousand acres of West Texas grazing land, but no other wealth. He was a postal mail carrier just three years from retirement, and he and Edna had, like Aunt Gladys and Uncle Cecil, recently been recipients of Granddaddy Moore's largesse, thousands of acres of grazing land along with several hundred head of cattle, all of which turned Harold and Cecil into *ranchers*. In 1953, Texas was in the middle of a long drought cycle, but Mr. Moore's acres had been husbanded with care, never overgrazed; and while many of the ranches in Palo Pinto, Young, and Jack Counties were burned dry by drought and had little water in their tanks, Henry Moore's acres showed healthy pastures and full tanks—that's what

they call the man-made ponds in Texas. Mr. Moore had enjoyed the oil boom
in North Texas but only in the form of continuous leasing of acres by drillers
and oil companies; the wells on his acres never produced anything but salt
water and occasional natural gas that could not be economically marketed at
that time. In other words, he had remained primarily a rancher and farmer but
had benefitted by his own wily awareness of nature's demands and limitations.

I had never, in all my years as a Texan, spent any time in cattle country
or time atop a quarter horse. In those days and weeks before we set out
for Austin, I began to learn why such a life had appeal. Bettie loved the
country around Bryson and Graham, recalling long lazy summer days with
her grandmothers, swimming or fishing in the large stock tanks, walking with
her dog in the brush country, or riding Rusty, her grandfather's quarter horse.
I was impressed by the innate generosity and tolerance of her family and by
their willingness to accept me as I was, as an academic, and useless they say
as tits on a boar. Neither Harold nor Edna ever proposed I give up my wish
to return to Austin and graduate school; they realized it was far too late for
me to learn the ways of a cattleman, though I understood that Harold would
have preferred his daughter to join up with an aggie from Texas A&M rather
than a "tea-sipper" from UT.

Ironically, I was less at home in Corpus Christi than I was in Wichita
Falls or little Bryson. Well, it was far less ironic than it would appear. All of
my friends from my high school days had fled Corpus or were settled into
lives I no longer had any connection with or interest in. My mother placed a
story of our return from Japan in the Corpus Christi *Caller-Times*, assuming
people might call or look us up, but no calls came. Corpus was as foreign
to me as Wakayama had been when I first arrived. To make sure we had a
welcome, Mama invited her friends to the house, mainly to show off Clay.
The neighborhood on Clifford Street where I had grown up had changed
little, but then I had left it only three years before. To say I grew up in Corpus
Christi is really not accurate; I was there only through my high school years,
from ages twelve through sixteen. After that I was never in Corpus for more
than six weeks at a stretch, and that was the summer when I was attending
Del Mar College. The real change was in me, not the neighborhood. The
major alteration I found was my mother's more comfortable outlook on life,
particularly regarding finances. The five producing wells on the Gilliland
land outside Floresville made all the difference in her attitude toward life,
and it benefitted Bettie and me considerably.

Quite soon after we arrived, Mama let me know that she, or rather the
"awl" wells, would take care of half our Austin expenses until I completed

my master's and for longer if I wished to continue beyond the MA—if the wells didn't go dry. I was sure I would be able to find a job to pay the balance needed. Bettie and I had lived well on a Japanese professor's salary and income from classes at Shin Fuso and were certain we could handle the costs in Austin for as long as it might take. If I successfully made it through the master's at UT, I hoped to continue for a PhD, but I had not spoken that thought except to Bettie and only hinted it to others, the PhD seeming far too grand an expectation or hope for one like me. I had less than a month before registration for fall classes, just enough time to find a job, a place to live, and to get moved in. Although Mama was anxious for us to spend a few weeks in Corpus Christi, I had no real desire to return and pick up that existence I had left behind. My connection with Corpus had ended, I felt, when I left home in the fall of 1943 as a freshman. We missed the independence of our lives in Wakayama, and I began to feel the tensions of trying to explain to Mama why I wanted to be a teacher—which paid so little. I had not noticed it markedly before, but now I could not fail to notice my mother's propensity to find fault with her children.

Albert, as usual, said nothing, and I silently thanked him for that. Having never accepted the role or the responsibility of a father or stepfather, he never questioned or advised me on anything, and for that I was grateful. Mama was still unhappy that I had not stayed with medicine or held onto the banking job in New York, had not, in other words, "made more of myself." For some reason I never understood, teaching as a profession was never entirely "respectable," never something to write home about. My choosing teaching as a career was in her mind a sign of failure—a missionary would have been better as far as status was concerned—and now married with child, well, what hope was there? Though I had barely known any of them, there had been teachers galore on the Gilliland side of the family—thirteen teachers, school principals, and superintendents—but they had not, in Mama's eyes, ever amounted to much.

After several days in Corpus, I flew up to Austin to find a job and a place to live. Somehow I had been able to save over five hundred dollars, which lay at that time in the Bowery Savings Bank, enough I figured to move us into an apartment and set up house in Austin. I had written my old roommate Phil Mounger and told him I was coming up to Austin to look for a job, and he called me immediately and offered me a bed and a place to stay while I looked. It was always good to see Phil. We wrote each other while I was in Japan. From the time he was a freshman, Phil, like many of us, had admired and respected McAllister, nay, like most of us had loved that man this side of idolatry. He had worked as his student assistant for the last year, a high honor indeed. The night I arrived in Austin, Phil and I immediately staked out a table at Scholz's Beer Garden and settled down to the serious job of telling stories. Knowing how highly I regarded the man, after the first schooner, he suggested we call McAllister to see if he would mind our coming out for a visit. Classes had just ended for the summer, and Phil was sure Dr. Mac would be at home. I was sure he would not remember me, I said, though I had sent him, along with about fifty friends and relatives, several newsletters written while I was in the mission program, and he was the only person other than relatives and Phil who had answered the letters.

Before we reached his house, Phil warned me that McAllister would probably try to talk him into working on a master's or try to enlist my aid in convincing him he should, and he repeated his decision not to do so. When we arrived, McAllister greeted us and led us into his living room where Mrs. McAllister was waiting. When we were seated, he brought each of us a tall, very icy Tom Collins and admitted right off he didn't recognize me or recall my being in his class, but he did recall the letters and thanked me for putting his name on my mailing list. We talked about Japan, and I told him how helpful Benedict's book *The Chrysanthemum and the Sword* had been and that I had met a young woman, Lily Sowa, who had been at the Poston Relocation Center during the war, recalling also that we had studied Leighton's *Governing of Men* in McAllister's applied anthropology class. He also found it interesting that Morse Saito, an original J3 who had also had been in a relocation center and had served in the navy during the war, was now teaching in Japan. I explained that the applied anthropology class was instrumental in my developing an even deeper interest in Asia and its people, that it had affected all my attitudes toward race and culture and thus my eventually teaching in Japan. He laughed and warned me that he had gotten many a student into deep trouble by influencing them to follow such whims, but he admitted he was flattered. I could also tell that while he was used to this form of testimonial, he enjoyed it immensely. McAllister was never one to put off praise of any kind, excessive or otherwise. When I spoke about visiting Joe Yamagiwa at the Michigan Study Center in Okayama and told him about discussing the applied anthro course, he was even more pleased, especially since the course had continued to attract good students as well as controversy.

Contrary to the image he so loved to project of himself as an angry antagonist, as a sarcastic curmudgeon, he was, that night, a gentle host interested in his two former students. He asked about my plans and congratulated me for choosing to return to graduate school and hoped I would find what I wanted in the English department.

"There are some very good people in that department," he said. Then he turned to Phil. "Why don't you stay and go to graduate school and keep Gilliland company?"

Phil laughed as if he had anticipated McAllister's remark and said, "Dr. Mac, I have a job waiting for me on the Katy. I'm really a railroad engineer,"

The discussion went back and forth for several minutes, and then he looked at me and said, "He's your friend, Gilliland. Can't you talk some sense into him?"

I was about to reply when Phil said, "Dr. McAllister, when you were a boy, did you ever want to be a railroad engineer?"

Dr. Mac said, smiling, "Of course, Phil, we all did."

"Well, I made it, Dr. Mac," replied Phil, smiling.

McAllister looked at me with a sad smile and shook his head slowly, "Well, that's it, Phil. I won't beg." It was sad.

I could see he was sincerely disappointed; he was losing one of his best students. Though I sympathized with Dr. McAllister, I understood Phil's desire to leave the university. He had always been a good student, always made far better grades than I, but he was not in love with academe as I was. I had the warmest feeling of regard for Doctor Mac, for he represented the world that I desired above all things to enter, the world of mentor and student. We stayed about an hour and then left. It was the last time and one of the few times I spoke to him out of class; nothing in all the years since has made me change my belief that he was the greatest teacher I ever had and the single most important influence on my wanting to become a college teacher. I do not believe a semester has gone by that I have not alluded to McAllister's theory of "education by irritation" or that I have not borrowed on his teaching. In that sense, his influence on generations of students has been immeasurable.

The next morning, I visited the student employment service and filled out an application for a job. It was as if they had been waiting for me, holding the job for me. I was prepared to take anything that would pay enough and would allow me to arrange a schedule for classes. As soon as I sat down and explained my needs, the counselor glanced over my application form and then handed me a slip of paper and smiled broadly.

"I see you have experience working in libraries. We got this request about an hour ago," he said. "They must have known you were coming in. All you'll need is a chauffeur's license. Do you think you could drive a bookmobile for the Austin Public Library?"

I said I already had a chauffeur's license from the days when I drove an ambulance, though I hadn't driven a car in three years. When I glanced at the slip of paper with the job description and the pay scale, I could hardly believe my good luck. It was tailor-made for me: three days a week at one hundred dollars a month. The slip even read that there would be time to study on the job. I said I was definitely interested and asked if he could call and set up a meeting for me. I would leave immediately. He seemed as eager for me to take the job as I was and made the call, setting up an appointment within the hour. Half an hour later, I walked out of a meeting with the director of Library Extension for the Austin Public Library, Elizabeth Bagley. She assured me that I had the job as driver and library assistant for the Austin Library Bookmobile. They had designed the job for university students, but when I told her I was a graduate student in English, had worked two years as a page in the university main library, and already had a Texas chauffeur's license, she smiled and said she was convinced they had designed the job just for me.

It was happening again: first Dahlquist, then Hanson and Hollis, now the Bookmobile, and just the day before I had arrived in Austin, hoping I would find a job that would fit my class schedule and pay enough to get us by. Unlike that experience at the VA employment agency in Corpus four years earlier, this job was waiting for me. But then maybe the VA's agent was a disguised Dahl . . . no! Don't go there, Joe.

We would not be rich, would in fact be barely getting by most months, but "barely getting by" was the norm for most grad students with families. And compared to our standard of living in Wakayama, we would be well off; our income of two hundred dollars a month was more than what I made with the Bowery Bank. Compared to the throngs of married graduate students living in the university grad student ghettos, we were wallowing in luxuries. But equally as important as the pay scale and the hours was the idea that I would be working in my natural habitat, a space surrounded by books.

A week later, Bettie, Clay and I moved into a furnished apartment just blocks from the campus; although much larger and more expensive than we needed, it would give us time to search for more economical space. After a month, we moved to a less expensive apartment much closer to the campus and within shorter walking distance of a supermarket and a coin operated laundry. It was all much easier than I expected.

Chapter 21
Back To School

I was back home; our apartment was almost where I had started, only a few blocks from Mrs. Carter's and even closer to the old Lambda Chi house on West Twenty-First Street. This was happiness indeed. As I set out for campus to register I felt like I was home again, and the walk to the campus brought back great memories. However, the truth was that everything had changed; most of all, I had changed. I was no longer the One. It was We.

When I reached Gregory Gym and saw the long lines, I was convinced that all the classes I wanted would be closed. The lines were longer than when I returned in 1947, and the whole place looked jammed with bodies. The enrollment was only seven thousand when I was a freshman, and in the winter of '47 when I returned it had exploded to seventeen thousand. They said the enrollment was over twenty thousand now.

I moved immediately to the sign that read GRADUATE STUDENT REGISTRATION and followed an arrow pointing to a quiet, fenced-off area with no lines or crowds, only tables with names of departments posted. At the sign that read ENGLISH I handed my letter of acceptance and my list of courses to the man who seemed to be in charge. He glanced at the letter, looked at my schedule, and promptly announced that the short story course was closed and asked, "What's your major: British or American?"

Without thinking I answered, "American."

"Good," he said. "Take Dr. Cooke's advanced American lit survey. You won't need the short story course, but you will need the survey."

The other heads at the table nodded agreement, and the elderly gentleman sitting at the far end of the table remarked, "In any case, I wouldn't recommend the short story course for graduate students," and again, all heads nodded.

Wonders of wonders, I thought, *this is the most advising I've ever gotten from anyone at registration.* As it turned out, the advice had come from some of the most distinguished professors in the department, two of whom I would later have in class. While I was writing down the number of the survey course and checking the time it was offered, one of the elders added, as a confidential aside, that intro to short story was an elective intended mainly for non-English majors, a "bread-and-butter course" for the English Department. Again, heads

561

bobbed. The first man added in that he "honestly believed" Cooke's advanced survey should be required of all new grad students in American lit.

The only student at the table, I felt they were speaking to me as if they already knew me. I had never heard anyone at that lofty level divulge so much inside information and wondered, *Is this what it's like as a graduate student?* When everyone at the table had glanced over my courses, the elderly man on the end asked why I was taking only nine hours. I told him I had to work and mentioned I'd been away from the university for four years.

He smiled, "You have a good schedule," and then paused, looked down at my registration card, and added, "Good luck, Gilliland, welcome back." Things had changed, indeed.

Before I left, I thought to ask if the other classes were still open. He took my schedule, scribbled a note, and handed it back: "They are now. All classes are open for graduate students."

A full graduate load of twelve hours would have satisfied my conditions for admission to the graduate program, but because I was working, Bettie and I agreed I should not push it. The MA in English required thirty-six hours or units, three in English language or grammar, three units of Shakespeare, and six of thesis. Twelve of the thirty-six hours could be in minor or even a double minor, if I chose; having a minor was not a requirement. In addition to a thesis and the required courses, the MA candidate had to pass an examination over twenty-five major works to be selected by the candidate and his thesis supervisor. With summer school, Bettie and I figured I could finish the degree in two years, thesis and all.

All in all, it had taken less than fifteen minutes to complete registration. As I walked away, I looked down at my class schedule and was quite pleased at how easy it had been. It was a perfect schedule, I thought: Modern British and American Poetry at nine o'clock, followed by Introduction to Shakespeare at eleven o'clock, then Survey of American Literature at one o'clock. All my classes were on MWF, leaving TTS free for the Bookmobile.

Classes didn't begin for another week, but the Bookmobile job began the day after I registered. My boss, Mrs. Bagley, was pleased that my classes would not conflict with my work schedule and that she wouldn't be forced to juggle my work schedule with Charley Scott's, the other driver. I was glad Mrs. Bagley had asked him to be at the library my first day to make sure I was up to handling the large, moving-van-sized vehicle. I had never driven anything larger than a pickup and hadn't driven anything for three years. Scott, a premed, was finishing his BS and had been driving the Bookmobile for a year After a spin around the block and backing into the loading area a couple of times, Scott announced me "safe."

As head extension librarian, Mrs. Bagley did not usually go out with the Bookmobile; however, she decided to go this time to observe how I handled patrons and the giant vehicle. The usual Bookmobile team consisted of one assistant librarian and a driver, sometimes on the busiest route a second assistant. Today one of the assistants, an attractive older woman named Pansy, also went with us. The route that morning took us far into the hill country west of Austin, stopping at gas stations, country stores, small clusters of homes, a one-room rural school, and the State School for the Deaf that was back in Austin. We left the Main Library at nine o'clock and were back at the loading dock just before five o'clock. It had gone easily, I thought, both the driving and serving customers. It was all quite interesting, a good job, I thought. As I was unloading the books being returned to the main collection, my new boss approached me and said she was pleased with how everything went and she hoped I had enjoyed the day. I told her I enjoyed it and looked forward to driving the routes.

When I got home after my first day on the road, we realized I had not planned well when I chose an apartment so far from a shopping area. Bettie learned she would have to schedule shopping trips and trips to a coin laundry when I was home from work or school so that I could either sit with Clay or push him in his stroller, freeing Bettie to do the shopping, or I could stop off with Clay and do the laundry while she did the groceries. Not having a car required careful planning; we needed Oba san. Although she never voiced concern about the inconvenience, I knew it wasn't easy being alone all day, not being able to shop when she needed or just drive with Clay to one of the parks and just to get out of the cramped apartment. So I began searching for a place closer to a shopping center and laundry.

The first one to arrive for Modern British and American Poetry, I took a desk in the second row and waited; several soon followed and took desks on the back row. A young woman, a studious type, with long black hair and glasses took a desk in front of me, turned and asked if I had ever had Miss Trice before this. I said I hadn't.

"I wonder what she is like," she said, "young, old, hard, easy, interesting, dull, what?"

"Don't worry," a voice from the back shouted, "you'll like her!"

By the time Miss Trice arrived, there were fifteen of us, mostly young women, a couple admitting they were *not* English majors and were taking the class as an elective. All but two said they seniors. I was the only graduate student. Trice, casually dressed, certainly not "dressed-up," appeared to be in her mid-fifties and was rather attractive in a disheveled kind of way.

"Open your books to Thomas Hardy," she said. "Read 'The Darkling Thrush,' while I call the roll. Just raise your hands."

I began to read. Only four stanzas, interesting, I thought, but why "darkling"? I read it twice, got the main idea, and decided "darkling" worked, but nothing more came to mind before she finished calling our names.

"Who would like to start?" she began. "Don't tell me you 'like' it or 'dislike' it. Whether you do or don't is not important to me or anyone else, not yet." She paused, smiled, and said, "But I like it." She laughed, "See, I'm inconsistent."

That's very good, Miss Trice, I thought, *you know how to set a tone.*

She glanced down at the class roster, called a name, and waited. A young woman sitting nearby began commenting about the setting, the sounds, and the thrush's "blast-beruffled plume."

She ended, "That description of the setting was very clear, I thought, and set the tone?" her voice rising as if to question.

"That's quite good. Can anyone describe specifically Hardy's setting?"

"The landscape's appearance of the 'century's corpse out leant,' works well, I think. He wrote the poem at the end of the century," another voice chimed.

"Anyone else?" Miss Trice said. *This is good,* I thought, *no stalling, no coaxing.*

A few more responded; *it's obvious—these people are serious readers,* I thought. One explained why "blast be-ruffled" sounded good to her, and others agreed. Miss Trice, with little effort, had gotten the class off to a good start. I had picked the right class. It felt good.

Then she asked us to turn to A. E. Housman, and we read several, all of which I had read years ago. Then she said turn to Robert Bridges and asked for responses. By the time half the period had passed, everyone in class had spoken, even Gilliland, and her remarks had all been positive. They all seemed to be in the class to read and talk, for after the first remarks, no one had to be called on. At the end of the period, she read off two titles, "London Snow" by Robert Bridges and "Snow in the Suburbs" by Thomas Hardy.

"I know now that you can read poetry and can talk about it. You just showed me. For Friday, I want you to write about the two poems I just asked you to read. Don't ask me what I want. Just write something about what the two poems say to you. Write what *you want*." She paused, continued. "Remember, no one really cares if you like them poems or dislike them. Tell me what you think. Tell me something." That was it.

We scanned several poems by Bridges, made a few brief remarks but nothing particularly profound. It was all comfortably informal and spontaneous.

She said she would expect more comments next period, comments dealing specifically with imagery, language, and added not to concern ourselves yet with *meaning*. It was all very good, I thought, all smart, witty, but no surprises, nothing that I would not have expected. The paper? Well, that would tell me something and tell me early just whether I had chosen the right major.

Before the eleven-o'clock class, I walked to the Chuck Wagon in the Union and had a cup of coffee, (no longer the nickel it was when I was here last) and read the two poems of Hardy and Bridges. When I got to Dr. Cranfill's class and saw that almost every seat was taken, I was thankful I was a graduate student and was ensured a place. Was it the professor or was Shakespeare really that popular? The course was, after all, a requirement for the master's in English, but surely these weren't all English majors. It was Tom Cranfill, of course. Before he arrived, I overheard remarks that explained the overflow, one saying he was the best man in the department, another remarking he was "probably the most popular professor on campus." Only a few in the class were majoring in English, some only minoring. But most were there because they wanted to hear Cranfill read and perform.

When he arrived, he quickly called roll, assigned *Richard III* and all the introductory material that went with it, plus B.B. Harrison's introductory material on the Elizabethan theater, then let us go.

It was easy to see why the room was packed; Cranfill was congenial, easygoing, and nonthreatening. By contrast Dr. Cooke was quiet, spiritless, but clear and distinct, certainly not a spellbinder. Clearly, she was one who demanded much and got much in return. Like Cranfill, she did not keep us the full hour but laid out a list of withering writing assignments for the semester: two short critical papers of seven to ten pages, one long paper of fifteen to twenty-five pages, and a short biweekly report of two pages on critical writings of our own choice. The biweekly reports required us to read scholarly reviews and essays, from journals like *American Literature* and *PMLA,* dealing with the writers and works we were studying in class. In addition, she assigned two novels: Cooper's *Pioneers* and Melville's *Moby-Dick.*

When she announced that we would read Melville's novel, she stopped, smiled. "Do I hear rumblings from below decks?" Silence. "Yes, we're going to read and discuss Melville's great novel, and you'll write a long essay question on the final exam dealing with each novel. If you wish, you may skip the chapters in *Moby-Dick* on *cetology."* She paused. "This is an advanced survey intended for seniors and graduates, so be prepared to work."

By the time I left Dr. Cooke's survey class, I was more confident than ever that I had made the right choices and that my advisors at registration were right. Of the three courses that semester, the most demanding was the survey with Dr. Cooke. As soon as Cooke released us, I went straight back to the apartment and told Bettie that I had selected good classes with excellent professors. She listened, saying they sounded interesting and ask if I thought the assignments would be difficult.

"They probably will, for me. I've already started thinking about the paper for Trice's class," I said. "I know I've made the right choices."

Dr. Tom Cranfill at the time was the undisputed star lecturer and performer of the English Department. His Introduction to Shakespeare class was crammed, not an empty desk in the room; I got in only because of the note my "advisor" had scribbled. Each day he gave a star performance, either concentrating on a single character or entire scenes, in which he performed all parts—young, old, male, or female. He made no effort to carry on deep discussions about the plays; rather, he lectured briefly on the backgrounds and performances and assumed, correctly, that we knew little or nothing about the plays or the world in which they were written. Our G. B. Harrison anthology had rich biographical and historical notes that he expected us to read as closely as we did the assigned plays. We would not discuss the collateral readings in class, but we should be able to discuss the readings in the essay exams. His readings and performances dominated the class time. Students of Shakespeare, he believed, required no detailed explications; dramatic readings and performance was all the illumination required. He was right; his readings forced us to see dramatic poetry as a living and breathing experience, requiring little formal explication beyond Harrison's footnotes. Throwing the class open to discussion would have done little but expose us to the misconstrued notions of classmates.

His reading and his performances gave the plays a depth and coherence that went far beyond the criticisms I had been reading on my own. He insisted we read the text carefully and become acquainted with Harrison's background essays *before coming to class.* When we left his class, we left with an experience backed by understanding; we knew "what it was about." Cranfill filled the fifty minutes with himself, never stopping for questions from the class or asking us to interpret or expand. Pedagogically, he violated all rules of modern teaching method, but in doing so, he held us in thrall and brought the plays to life. His asides referred to standard Shakespearean criticism and warned that the graduate students should, on their own, not neglect such writers as Traversi, Harley Granville–Baker, Theodore Spencer, Wilson Knight, A. C. Bradley, and dozens more he insisted we should "know about." I took it as fair warning and dug them out of the library stack or bought paperback editions when I could find them. I worked on the paper for Miss Trice off and on all week, even while I was driving the Bookmobile. I would read the poems aloud, listen for the effects, reciting first the Hardy lines then the more melodious lines of Bridges. Both described scenes that I had little experience with: a snow in Austin my senior year and snow once or twice in New York and then the only snow in Germany on my nineteenth birthday. I reflected how both poems brought back clear memories that mirrored Hardy's sparrow and the muffled sounds that Bridges described, my emphasis being on the concreteness of the imagery in both, concluding how physical the images were in both poems. I said it all in just over four pages that I typed out the night before, corrected the typos—I thought—and retyped it and turned it in. My first paper as a graduate student filled me with some fear and anxiety. I told Bettie I thought I would rise or fall on this first paper, but she had insisted a first paper would not determine anything, adding it was a good paper. She had read the poems, listened to me talk about them, had made a suggestion here and there, and had read the first draft.

"You're dramatizing it all too much," she said. "I think it's a good paper."

Trice answered my question and erased all doubts about my future as a graduate student in English when she read my paper aloud in class. She gave it an unimagined and un-hoped for A+. I had come a long way from Fletcher's Intro to Poetry, yet there was much of Fletcher in the paper.

A week later, when she asked us to write anything we wanted to about Hardy's 1913 poems, the poems on his first wife's death, I read them over and over and became so depressed, so saddened I couldn't write a word without sounding maudlin or false. My first paper expressed none of my feelings, only my ideas, but for some reason the 1913 poems reached me on an entirely different level. Bettie and I were so happy in our genteel poverty, so pleased with the beautiful boy whom we showed off shamelessly, so proud of our having come through the Japanese experience with our rich and complex memories, that I could not comprehend such a relationship as spoken of in Hardy's poems. When I tried, I could not find the language to express my feelings and reactions with conviction. Hardy had said it perfectly and honestly—too honestly? I told myself again and again these were just words, forms, and sounds, lines on paper, and though I reminded myself of MacLeish's admonition that a poem doesn't mean, that it must simply "be," I found I was incapable of discussing Hardy's expressions of grief, disappointment, anger, and betrayal all mixed with love long passed. They were too honest.

I missed Trice's class that day and sat brooding on my failure in the main reading room, then went to her office after class and told her as honestly and directly as I could why I could not write anything that would make sense. Almost trembling as I explained how I felt, I opened the small volume from the library and went over several of the poems, telling her why I couldn't write. She nodded and said softly, "I understand, Mr. Gilliland. You've explained it." We talked at least an hour right through Cranfill's Shakespeare class. It was the first time I had ever spoken at such length with a professor, and all the time I was there, she said nothing to indicate I was taking too much of her time. Near the end, when I was getting up to leave, in came Cranfill, and she repeated to him what I had said about Hardy's 1913 poems.

He said, "I quite agree, Lois. Why would anyone assign those poems?" He seemed interested in what I had said and complimented me, waving off my apology for missing Shakespeare.

When he sat down comfortably on her old couch, it was obvious he had come to chat. As I turned to leave, I said that I would be happy to write a paper on another poem or topic, but she said we should move on to another poet. Hardy had probably occupied enough of our time. I had just spent the most rewarding hour of my academic life. Although she refused to assign a new topic for me, I wrote a short paper on "Pied Beauty" by Hopkins, which she had read to the class and had briefly talked about the Hopkins rhythms..

As an undergraduate, I had little contact with professors in or out of class other than required conference periods. But that first semester, things changed. If I approached them and raised questions, they always took time to answer and discuss with me any ideas I might have gotten during class or from my reading. Dr. Cooke was never in too much of a hurry to expand on something either she or someone else had mentioned, nor was Cranfill loath to discuss anything as long as it was after class. When I mentioned this one day to Lois Trice, she asked if I ever tried. I said I had tried once or twice, that I had spoken to Dr. Fletcher about *The Ordeal of Richard Feveral,* and he had stopped and talked a bit about the novel, and I had asked Dr. James questions, and she was willing to talk, but no one else was willing.

"You could have persisted," she said.

I came to know Lois Trice quite well before the end of the first term. She was not "Dr." Trice, nor was she a professor or even an assistant professor. A Wellesley BA and MA and a Phi Beta Kappa, she had never taken a PhD. Jane had written that Lois Trice had been Dean Parlin's "administrative assistant," often teaching his classes when administrative business called him away. She said students loved her, less for her brilliant lecturing, which she rarely did, than for her strong personal opinions about the novelists and poets and about anyone else who might come to mind. Rather, she was a conversationalist who knew how to engage the class in wide ranging talks about poetry; it was her method for getting us to think. She rarely mentioned formal or academic poetry criticism, and as far as I could tell, she followed no critical doctrine as such. She could read the poetry of Hardy or Hopkins, Yeats or Thompson, Frost or Eliot in a way that made you feel the poet would have approved; in that way, she was a lot like Fletcher.

I had not expected the semester to be so grand. When it was over, I had my first A as well as my first B in English. The B came in Cooke's class. She praised my long paper on *The Confidence Man*, writing that I had chosen "an interesting and complex novel" and had treated it " extremely well," though she gave it only a B+ because of careless typos and sloppy proofreading. Dr. Cranfill gave me an A+ on my long paper in which I discussed the comic relief in *Hamlet*; he too found fault with my less than perfect proofreading. Apparently, mechanical errors were less important to him than they were for Dr. Cooke. At that point, I believed I could do anything they asked of me. I had never worked as hard or with as much pleasure.

Bettie was great help that first semester, mostly by listening to me talk about the readings and the ideas I was working into the papers, often questioning me about a conclusion and forcing me to "be more specific." I trusted her opinions that I knew they arose from her wide range of readings. In fact, "she's always reading," was the way Mama put it, as if her reading was a flaw in character. It reminded me of how she often criticized Jane or Dorothy for always having their "nose in book." "Put that book down and pick up your room," I would hear her say. One time when I returned to Corpus from Austin, she asked me, "Joe, is all Bettie ever does is read?" I could see it coming and replied that it was all I ever saw her do but tried to make it sound facetious.

"I'm serious, Joe. She's a mother and a wife now, she has responsibilities." Her voice told me she was in mother-in-law mode.

"I know, Mama, but she told me before I left that she was letting you take care of Clay because you would insist on it. Her mother's just like you, a typical grandmother," I replied.

"No, this is different." She was driving and seemed to be concentrating on the road, but I knew she was framing an argument. "She sometimes has two, or even three, books she's reading all the time."

"Mama, I married her *because* she loved books. We both love books. That's why I'm going to be a teacher. Bettie was a teacher who tried to make her kids read books, and they all thought she was a top teacher."

It didn't end there. When she or Albert would drive to Austin on a weekend to see Clay, her looks of disapproval grew more and more serious, though Bettie would cook, wash dishes, do her wifely duties. Mama's letters would still hint at Bettie's "dependence on her books," and more than once, Mama would ask me when we were alone or out of earshot if Bettie ever really helped me, and I did say seriously, without sarcasm, that she was always there to help when she could.

"She reads most of the works I'm assigned to read if she hasn't *already* read them, and we talk about them," I said and tried to explain that most of my fellow students would get together and talk about the works we were studying.

"I can't spend time on campus with other graduate students, but I come home and have Bettie to bounce off my ideas." Then I laid it on. "Mama, Bettie has a mind of her own, a good sharp mind, and that attracted me to her from the first time we met in Hartford. Everyone noticed it, especially the supervisors." I paused. "I don't care if the rooms need 'picking up' or the dishes need washing. We don't have company. Neatness is *not* next to godliness, *not for me, not now.* For me now and for a long time to come, *reading* is next to godliness."

She never spoke of it after that, but later, long after I'd finished the degree, I was speaking to one of Mama's best friends, Ester Pierson, a retired attorney who had worked as an assistant to one of the county judges, and she told me how the subject of my MA thesis disturbed Mama. "Dot's not a reader, you know, and she doesn't understand writers like William Faulkner and Steinbeck." She chuckled. "They are not my cup of tea either as far as that goes. But I know they are great writers, and I know why you'd choose to write about their work."

My spring schedule included three seminars and one regular graduate course. The straight lecture class, Elizabethan and Jacobean Drama, complimented beautifully the Intro to Shakespeare. Dr. Lucetta Teagarden, whom Miss Trice had highly recommended, was teaching in her specialty, she said, but she warned, "Don't expect her to match Tom Cranfill. She'll make you read and write, and she expects a lot of discussion, I understand. She's very good and quite a character."

Two of the seminars, American Thought and Literature of the Nineteenth Century and The American Novel after 1920, would not be too difficult, I thought; I had read heavily in area of American thought for my cultural history class, and I'd read all but three of the novels in Dr. Graham's novel seminar. I decided to take a double minor, philosophy and American history, mainly on the assumption that a second teaching area would make me more employable in a community college. I knew I would not be able continue at UT after finishing my master's.

Another seminar, Philosophies of Democracy, sounded like it would be a perfect fit with Dr Boatright's seminar in nineteenth-century American thought and literature, especially if one day I chose the American Studies route to my doctorate. T. V. Smith, recently retired from Syracuse University, had earned a BA in philosophy at UT in 1907 and his doctorate in philosophy from the University of Chicago. He was returning to his alma mater to wind up a lifetime. According to *Life* magazine, Smith had been a New Deal "Brain Truster" for Roosevelt and was one of the "whiz kids" in Hutchins's years at the Chicago. On the first Wednesday afternoon, he gazed about the class and announced that the rules of the seminar could not hold; he could not assign nor read that many seminar papers; instead, he would require a long essay final covering the main readings he assigned. Smith did not lecture in any formal sense but practiced something resembling Socratic method, aimed chiefly at half a dozen members of the class and ignoring an adoring "gallery" of well-to-do women who, it turned out, were auditors. Since over half the people attending were enrolled as auditors, I doubted he would have had more than ten papers to read had he gone ahead with the seminar.

Dr. Philip Graham's Saturday morning novel seminar was also oversubscribed and could not follow a seminar's format. I was relieved to have my long papers limited to a paper in Jacobean theater and one in Mody Boatright's Nineteenth Century Thought and Literature. At the first meeting, Graham announced he would not be requiring a long critical paper, he would also not be lecturing for three hours, but he would, after his opening remarks regarding leading questions about the assigned novel, expect class discussion to fill the time, and as in a seminar class, he would expect everyone in class to participate. There were low murmurs—some approving, some disapproving. After calling the class roll and making his opening remarks, he handed us a list of critical terms common in all literary criticism. Several PhD candidates in the class groaned, and one remarked that he was treating us like a "bunch of sophomores." He ignored the remark and announced that we would be reading and discussing a novel a week and would have, at the beginning of class, a fifteen-minute "objective" quiz covering the novel for that week, bringing forth more objections .I agreed; it sounded too much like my sophomore world lit class under Guy Steffans.

Graham stared for a long count then replied that he was "damned" if he was going to spend three hours discussing a novel unless he was absolutely sure everyone had read the work carefully, "as carefully as a graduate student should, but often does not." His tone was pretty brittle, cold and clearly aimed at the groaners. He was right, of course. It was a fair warning, though, on the surface, it seemed sophomoric.

Of the twelve novels on the list, the only novels I had *not* read were *American Tragedy*, *Tortilla Flat*, and a novel by the Texas artist Tom Lea, which also drew moans from the same quarter. Graham said he was substituting Lea's potboiler for Ray Bradbury's *Martian Chronicles* because he did not consider science fiction a serious genre "at this time" and would, therefore, not consider a novel about Mars unless he found one written by a "Martian." When he explained that he expected us to know how to use all the critical terms he had passed out, there was another general groan from the same quarter of the room, and he replied that such terms were the basic vocabulary of all literary criticism. In the past he had assumed mistakenly that all English majors were familiar with such terms, only to discover they were not; therefore, for the same reasons, he would be quizzing us on the novels and was expecting everyone in class to be able to use the critical language of literature in discussions and in our written work, adding, in an even more acerbic tone than before, that he was tired of graduate students, "even doctoral students," being unfamiliar with a basic critical vocabulary. At that point, two youngish men on the back row rose and left the class. He smiled and crossed their names off his roster, satisfied that his ploy had produced the desired results. It was true: Graham could be one hard-ass s.o.b.

Dr. Boatwright's seminar was my most serious challenge. In preparation for the culture class at Wakayama, I had relied entirely on secondary sources, works by the likes of Parrington and Curti, while all our readings, as anyone would expect in the seminar, were from primary sources. It was a small class, most of whom were in the latter stages of their doctorates in American Studies, at the time probably the most challenging program being offered at UT. The two of us who were still working on master's degrees felt as if we were being thrown to the lions. Traditionally, students in a seminar expect to challenge and to be challenged as well. The text, a collection of political and social writings by major nineteenth-century figures, was actually only a resource that we were expected to read and use for discussion topics, but the main thrust of the class was our "topic" that we were expected to announce early.

When I was unable, early in the semester, to find a suitable topic for my paper, I felt I might be out of my depth, but Dr. Boatright did not seem concerned when I mentioned I was having difficulty. He said the other MA student was in the same boat and helping me settle on a topic was his job. After a short chat, he suggested I do something on Melville, since I had tackled a difficult subject on Melville for Dr. Cooke. I was quite taken aback that he knew about my paper on *The Confidence Man*. He said he recalled getting my letter applying for admission to the master's program and asked about why and how I had been teaching in Japan. I answered briefly, and then he suggested I read *Clarel*, Melville's long poem based on his travels in the Holy Land. He suggested I see what I could find out if Melville reconciles his struggles with God.

"Find out how Melville's religious thought reflected or conflicted with nineteenth-century religious thought in America. But don't try to turn this into a thesis project," he said smiling. "Come to me if you have an questions."

I had read a good deal of Lawrence Thompson's recent work, *Melville's Quarrel with God*, and I understood the question, but I had not read a line of "Clarel" nor any scholarly critical studies of the poem. But, that was the point wasn't it, I told myself. My paper, the only one dealing with nineteenth-century religious thought, plunged me deeper into Melville's darkness than I was with *The Confidence Man*. Relying heavily on Lawrence Thompson's book and heavy reading in journal articles, plus a dissertation from the early 1930s, I contended that the long poem confirmed the view that Melville was not content with the orthodox Calvinist views of his upbringing and that he had much searching to do before he found peace with God. I ventured beyond "Clarel" and concluded that Melville, not even in his later work, ever found peace. Happily, the paper met Boatright's requirements. After my presentation, I spoke to him and admitted that I had "dived deep" and was indeed over my head. He laughed and said he was afraid everyone who works on Melville has to "dive deep," and carrying the metaphor a step further, he asked if that was not also Melville's problem. Hadn't he himself, like Pip, the Negro cabin boy, leaped from the boat? I recalled the passage in *Moby-Dick* about "leaping from the boat," and when we parted, I felt I was only just beginning to understand how graduate study really worked. Dr. Boatright was one of the most generous men I would meet in my two years as a graduate student at UT.

The novel course under Graham became my most important class that semester because it guided me toward a thesis topic and gave me my supervisor. At first, I was disappointed that the class was too large for him to treat it as a seminar, but as it progressed, I was happy that I had been relieved of another seminar paper and another presentation. Graham was one of my best professors at the university in spite of the hard-ass image he presented. He lectured very little, conducting instead long rambling conversations, stemming from the questions the novels raised. We were always free to interrupt him or whoever it was waxing eloquent, either to ask for clarification or to inject a contrary opinion that he skillfully turned into deeper analysis. Once, I groaned in disagreement, and he insisted I explain my "pain," which I did or tried to do. When I finished he nodded and said "perhaps" but did not disagree outright. When he had finished making his point, he turned to me and asked, "Is that better now?" I agreed in the end, and he continued. It was more like an exchange between equals, though, of course, it wasn't. What seemed like informal rambling, his "conversations" were well organized, deeply critical, and brilliantly insightful, though his style was anything but dazzling. His sardonic wit was off-putting for some, particularly when it was aimed at a comment laden with the clichés or critical jargon, which he openly rejected. Today his acerbic remarks would be called abusive or harassing or a display of professorial power. His "problem" was he did not suffer fools, those who spouted the latest fads in critical thought, though he would allow disagreements, provided they were supported by specific citations and close readings. When challenged once by one who insisted she had a "right" to her opinion, Graham simply replied, "No. Not in this class. Opinions do not have standing unless you have a sound basis for an opinion and providing that basis has some standing." His style may have differed from McAllister's, but his tendency to irritate was the same.

One day during the coffee break midway through the class, several of us walked with him to Hillsberg's across the street. As the others walked on ahead, I asked if he were taking on new thesis students and said I would be signing up for the thesis course in the fall. He asked me if I was majoring in American literature, and I said I was and was thinking about a twentieth-century novelist.

"It better not be Scott Fitzgerald," he said. "I don't think I could read another Fitzgerald thesis."

"Then I'll not do a Fitzgerald thesis," I replied.

He described the flood of Fitzgerald theses that had followed the publication of Mizener's biography that had stimulated a Fitzgerald revival. I admitted I had read *The Far Side of Paradise* and liked it and had, because of it, read all of Fitzgerald's novels, except *This Side of Paradise*. I said that I had even read *The Last Tycoon* and many of the short stories and was looking forward to discussing *Gatsby* in a few weeks. Admittedly, I was trying to impress him in hopes he would find me worthy of his time. He knew it, of course. I had worked hard to impress him with what I knew. It was important I get a supervisor who would make me work. He looked at me thoughtfully for a moment and then said that I should come around to his office and discuss it with him. I had wanted to take that step and had decided early in the semester that Graham would be the best choice.

When I got back to class and took my seat, the young woman behind me leaned over and said she had heard that I was thinking about Graham for my thesis supervisor and added she was also thinking about asking him to supervise her thesis.

"When are you planning to see him?"

"Monday afternoon," I answered and realized I should have kept quiet. The competition for strong professors to chair thesis committees was vicious. I overheard her earlier tell another student the she was working on her second master's and was afraid Graham might turn her down because "I hear he really hates the MEd," which was her first master's. Then she said, "I don't blame him really. It's a rotten degree, but I've made straight As on all my master's classes."

That had been a month ago. I needed to see him as soon as I could, I thought.

The next Monday when I arrived at his office in the Tower, she was just leaving. When she saw me, she said, with a tone of authority, "He's not taking any more thesis students. He told me he was filled up, but I think he's lying." She frowned, "Everybody knows he hates women grad students. The bastard wouldn't even ask me to have a seat!"

I told her, "Not *everyone* knows. *I* didn't *know* he hated women."

"You do now!"

"Well, since I'm here, I might as well speak to him," I said.

She asked if I had a topic, and when I told her I had a couple, she snapped, "Well, good luck!"

Graham's office was a large corner office with metal shelves hanging on steel I-beams, his desk a standard university-issue metal desk with an old, un-upholstered oak chair. A solid wall of books behind his desk softened the cold, hard feeling I had when I entered. All the faculty offices in the Tower had that educational factory-like plainness. A few had carpeting, oak desks, and stuffed easy chairs, but Graham's was plain and functional. As I walked in, first thing, he pointed to another plain oak chair and asked me to sit.

"Tell me your idea," he began. "Don't ask me for suggestions. Any ideas I might have, I'll work on myself."

I told him I had two ideas, but I needed some advice. First, not necessarily my preferred, was Katharine Anne Porter, her fiction and non-fiction. He responded immediately, "Not enough there. What's your other topic?"

"William Faulkner, "I replied. "There hasn't been a lot done here on Faulkner. Only one thesis since he won the Nobel Prize."

"How do you plan to treat him?" he asked.

I really hadn't thought that far, not specifically, but just before my classmate had come out of his office, I'd glanced at the blurb on the back of a Signet Book edition of *Sanctuary/Requiem for a Nun*. On the back was a garishly printed blurb: "Sin and Redemption in the South."

Without thinking, I said, "Sin and redemption in the novels of William Faulkner."

He nodded right away, "Interesting. What novels did you have in mind?"

"To begin with, I thought *Sanctuary* would introduce the idea of sin without redemption. Then I'd discuss *Requiem* and try to point out patterns of redemption *Sanctuary's* sequel and then discuss any other patterns in the middle and late novels. I have not seen any signs of redemption in the early novels, but there is a whole lot of sin. If there is, he disguises it," I said. "It's all pretty much existential despair, a lot of 'sickness unto death.'"

He had listened as if it was really interesting and agreed. Then he asked me what I had read other than the two novels I had mentioned and *The Sound and the Fury* that we had recently discussed in class. I listed four or five other novels, including *Sartoris, Soldier's Pay, Wild Palms,* and a section from *Go Down, Moses* called "The Bear."

We talked some more, and he said I should read *Light in August* and *Absalom, Absalom* and *Go Down, Moses* and anything else as soon as I could. I told him I'd read Irving Howe's and William Van O'Connor's books on Faulkner as well as other criticism, but had not come across any criticism that specifically mentions the sin and redemption theme.

He said, "Stick with the novels and short stories for now. Save critical works until later." Then he said he would be happy to supervise me through the process and would act as my graduate advisor from then on.

"I was afraid you'd be full up," I said and sighed.

He shook his head, smiled and said sourly, "Only for education majors." But there was clearly an uncharacteristic note of humor in his voice.

I left elated, though I understood why some grad students feared him, hated him, and thought him to be a "royal s.o.b." I had a topic, albeit only a title lifted from a blurb, and I had a supervisor, moreover, a good one.

Now nothing short of a major disaster would stand in the way of my finishing the degree. Not even Bettie's news that she was pregnant altered the glory of the moment. Her news had given me only a moment of concern that the cost would do us in, but when she said her ob-gyn would charge us his "student rate" for the whole term and delivery, we settled back into the same happy complacency we had been enjoying all along. It would arrive in December. Mrs. Bagley assured me I would have a job as driver and library assistant on the library's Bookmobile for as long as I wanted it, and insisted she would working out a schedule that fit my summer school classes. Mrs. Bagley was as good and generous a boss as anyone could have been.

A further proof that Hardy's doomsters had chosen to scatter blisses rather than "ills" across my path came when Dr. Tom Cranfill urged me to apply for a Woodrow Wilson Fellowship, a lucrative and prestigious national graduate fellowship. He made the suggestion one late spring day while I was visiting Lois Trice. He was sure, he said, I would make a good candidate. The fellowship would, if I were accepted, pay full tuition to the graduate school of my choice and would ensure my acceptance into any doctoral program in the country, and it included a cost of living stipend. Trice agreed that I should try. But I declined, explaining that there was nothing on my undergraduate record that remotely justified my applying, which would be purely an act of hubris.

He went into deep thought then said, "I think that will make no difference. You write well and have done quite well in all your courses so far. All your professors speak highly of your work."

I was flattered, quite overwhelmed. This had *never* happened. That anyone had even talked about my work came as a total shock.

When he asked what I was planning to take in summer school, I said I was taking the required English language course, Dr. Pratt's Byron seminar and Graham's seminar in Southern literature, mentioning that the Whitman seminar was cancelled.

"I'll complete all the required hours in English, leaving only some history and philosophy on my minor and the six hours of thesis."

When he asked whom I had for my thesis chairman, I told him Dr. Graham had agreed to take it. He whistled softly and smiled. "He'll make you work. You sure you won't apply? You see, I am one of the judges."

"I really am afraid I can't. It would be too crushing for me and for Bettie if I applied and then failed to get it. But I'm applying for a teaching fellowship in the fall," I said. "That's why I stopped in to see Miss Trice. I needed her advice."

"Good. What do you think, Lois?"

"I agree with Gilliland now. I'm sure he could do it, but it's foolish to go through that wringer unless he's sure he'll get it. Besides, Tom, he needs to teach here a year. The fellowship—they call it an assistantship now, I think—will be good for him and for us, Tom."

In all my academic life, I had never received such encouragement as I did that day from two, whom I held in awe. I applied for the assistantship, and before the summer school began, I got my letter of acceptance, announcing that I would be teaching two classes of freshman composition in the fall. The letter quoted a stipend of two hundred twenty-five dollars a month, more than the combined library salary and the gift from the "awl" wells. The letter recommended, although it didn't require, that I limit my class load to twelve hours for the whole academic year. I had planned to take nine hours in the fall, the three remaining classes required in my double minor, two in history and one philosophy. That would leave me only a thesis for the spring, no other course work, but the total for the year would come to fifteen hours. Bettie suggested I not ask for permission, "Just do it."

After the Christmas break we decided that we needed to move away from the old beloved neighborhood on Nueces street, but to do that we needed a car. I loved living in walking distance of class, but the fact was Bettie needed easier access to stores and needed some freedom from the confined space of a campus apartment. Having a car would allow us to find a roomier place with a yard for Clay to play in. When one of the Bookmobile librarians, Ethel, said she was sure her husband, a used car dealer, could find me a reliable used car for less than three hundred dollars, we began to read the want ads for a place we could afford. Before Ethel's husband produced the "reliable used car," I found a 1949 two-door Dodge Fluid-Drive Sedan for three hundred dollars. And the day after I drove it off the lot, we found a duplex apartment in South Austin that rented for less than our place on Nueces.

Bettie could now shop at supermarkets, take clothes to a Laundromat, and get away with Clay to a park to play, giving her some release. Simply driving me to the library or to the campus was liberation she had not known in the noisy apartment. Buying the car for us was an education in the American economy. When I told the salesman at the Dodge agency's used car lot that I planned to pay cash, planned to draw money from our savings in the Bowery Savings Bank, he looked shocked.

"Don't draw it out, give me fifty dollars down and finance the rest, a few dollars a month for a year or two that's all." Thus, I became part of the American dream.

The duplex in South Austin seemed like pure luxury, offering Bettie a lovely neighborhood for pushing Clay in his stroller. The old stone house, its thick walls, and the huge live oaks that shaded the yard provided a much cooler place when summer came to Austin

Summer terms passed quickly. Neither the Byron nor the Lanier seminars required long time-consuming papers. By the end of the summer, I had completed the English course requirements for the degree, lacking only three courses in my minor fields, and of course the thesis, which I had decided I would write in the spring. It was difficult to comprehend at first: my spring grades were all As. Something had change. Bettie pointed out to me, the fact that I had learned how to study, and that She and Clay had been the motivating force. I honestly believed for the first time that I could hold my own even in a doctoral program. Cranfill's offer to support my application for a Wilson, the acceptance letter for the assistantship, Dr. Graham's approval of my oral presentation in the Lanier seminar, and the solid B in Pratt's seminar were all the proofs I needed, although still haunting me was my failure to proofread my papers sufficiently to avoid criticisms of sloppy style.

Just as the summer classes ended we moved by across the river after finding a nicely furnished, two-bedroom house with plenty of room for the growing family and at a rent we could afford. On a quiet street with no traffic, it had a well-shaded yard where Clay could play. The owner, a retiring member of the university custodial staff, was planning an extended trip with his wife and needed someone to live in his house while he was away. The advertisement asked specifically for a graduate student with family. It was quiet, clean, and inexpensive, the same rent as the house on Juliet but almost twice as large.

At the end of the first semester, my mother's hundred dollars a month stopped when the oil wells south of San Antonio stopped pumping. For a brief time, it appeared as if I would have to find a better-paying job and probably cut the number of hours I was taking, but Mama convinced Albert to lend us the same amount she had given us, to be paid off when I finished my degree and found a full-time teaching job. Albert, I learned later, had made such a loan to Jane her last semester at UT, but I suspected he had agreed only because Mama had insisted. Though I was grateful not having to go to the bank, I was deeply annoyed knowing that he too had been a beneficiary of the oil money, which was, in essence, a legacy of my father. It was many years later that I found out Albert was far from the wise, "well-to-do" businessman our mother had figured him to be. Two country club memberships, good clothes, the best shoes, and a Buick car were all "business expenses" made in order to keep up appearances. He did not have "sound investments I the market" although he would spend lunch hours at the small stock exchange watching the "ticker" as if he had real material interest in the market. When I learned that my stipend as a teaching assistant would cover our expenses, some would say "more than cover" the expenses we moved into the new bungalow in high spirits.

Although money was tight, we were "getting by" far better than I hoped. I mention these details because having enough money to pay our living expenses and the coming doctor and hospital bills—we had nothing in the way of health insurance in those days—became a major factor in my success as a student. Ironically, we had fewer financial worries than I had as a single student, certainly fewer than I had as a freshman. While we were only a little surprised to learn of the new baby, Bettie never expressed any doubts or concerns about our economic situation, just as she had never worried about the way we lived in Wakayama. So when we moved to our new place at the end of the summer term, our financial future seemed secure. We were able to adhere to budget and put fifty dollars a month aside to pay the obstetrician. Edna, Bettie's mother, had assured us that the hospital bill itself would be her Christmas present, coming as it would in December.

Joe as a graduate student

Chapter 22

Classroom Teacher

Close contact with fellow students is an integral part of the college experience, especially in grad school, where dialogue should extend collegially beyond the classroom. But in my first year of graduate school, I had not been able to meet and talk to classmates after class; my job off campus gave me little opportunity to develop acquaintances with others like me, people who had the same questions I had, questions that deserved my consideration. With Bettie at home all day, alone with Clay, it seemed unfair that I should spend time on campus with fellow students. Now as a TA, I was forced to maintain office hours that put me in contact with my fellow students who were also colleagues in the classroom. In the first year back at the university, during the summer seminars, it began to change because my Bookmobile schedule allowed me to be on campus for longer periods, and because the seminars were held in the Main Building, it gave me an hour between classes to meet and speak to classmates, something I had not enjoyed before.

As a teaching assistant, I shared a large office on the twenty-third floor of the Tower with a small company of bona fide scholars. McIntyre, Black, and Kinnamon were all on their way to a PhD. Black, the oldest of the lot, was already an "AbD" (all but dissertation). Mac was finishing his required course work and preparing for his comprehensive exams, and Kenneth Kinnamon was just beginning his doctoral course work, having just completed his MA in English at Harvard (on a Woodrow Wilson Fellowship). Of the five in the large cage, Kinnamon was the youngest, only twenty-one, and probably the most gifted. Black, the oldest, was on leave of absence from Stephen F. Austin State College and the most experienced teacher of the five. I was the only one, besides Black, with any full-time teaching experience, though my three years in Japan hardly qualified me as a teacher of freshman composition. Decrying the lack of a creative writing program in the department, the fifth member was a young man who announced he was a novelist, not an "aspiring novelist" but a novelist, albeit an unpublished one; he disdained the title, TA, because he had no intention of ever teaching again after the year was over.

The five of us were of a mind when it came to teaching composition: the basis of all good writing was good and copious reading. Assigning the best essays and stories by the best writers and avoiding tedious exercises in formal rhetoric or grammar texts was the best rout to writing. Kinnamon "professed," and we agreed, the study of formal rhetoric was best left to classical scholars and prep schools run by the Jesuits. No one, except Black, I suppose, had a clear idea of what formal rhetoric actually consisted of. Formal rhetoric was a discipline, at the time, generally shunned by most graduate students and was perhaps better left to colleges of education. There was no stated departmental policy, no course outline or statement of goals and objectives for either instructors or students. The table of contents of Perrin's *Writer's Guide and Index to English* was our course outline, and the *Rinehart Book of Essays* gave us a book full of models for good writing. A generation earlier, people just assumed that all English majors knew intuitively the difference between good writing and bad writing. At least two of us in the office knew what good writing consisted of, but only one probably had any idea what *teaching* good writing entailed. Since we all "knew good writing when we saw it," we forged ahead and made assignments and marked the errors in style and GPU (grammar, punctuation, and usage) according to the *Writer's Guide and Index to English.*

Next to Black, I was the most "experienced" teacher in the office; I had actually taught for three years at a university, with one term in a night school concentrating on only English, but nothing in those three years had prepared me to teach freshman English composition; and the truth was no one, with the exception of Black had any idea what the course consisted of other than what they could recall from their own freshman year. I recalled very well what we did in Helen James' and Dr. Eckfeldt's freshman comp classes. Those recollections *and* the chapters in Perrin's *Writer's Guide and Index to English* would constitute my syllabus. We all took comfort in the knowledge that all we were honestly expected to do was complete requirements for whatever degree we were racing to complete.

Since my leaving New York, the only persons with whom I held anything like serious discussions about literature and ideas were Dr. Anne and Bettie, but neither was interested in critical approaches to the work they were reading for pleasure. They were understandably bored by the jargon and attempts at exegeses. If I asked her to, Bettie might read a piece by Edmund Wilson if it dealt with a writer that interested her. But reading critically did not interest her. She would listen when I ranted on an on about some meaning I thought I had discovered or finally understood, but she was never ever committed to going any deeper. On the other hand the talk in "The Cage"—our name for our TA office in the Tower--was like a running seminar. It might begin with a comment one of our professors may have made in class, or even and argument a student may have raised. Or, I f were lucky, some one would raise a question about a short story in the anthology that he'd assigned, and off they'd go insisting why it was good or bad. It filled the time between grading papers and student conferences. Mac, Ken and I often ate lunch together, browsed the bookstalls at the co-op, and took coffee or a rare beer break at Hillsberg's across from the Law School.

Black never joined us. Older and married with one child and another one on the way (like me), he'd finished with all course work as well as his comps; "all" he had left was his dissertation. Between his family and the dissertation, he had no time for our academic bull sessions. Our fifth member, the novelist, never met with us either, since he was too consumed with creativity, he said, and really had no interest in or comprehension of the topics of our discussions. As for me, I believed these sessions to be an essential part of graduate school.

Until I walked into our TA office that fall, I was convinced that the quantity and depth of my reading had equaled or exceeded that of other graduate students I had met, and through most of the first year I was so convinced, but now I was constantly playing catch up to Kinnamon's and McIntyre's knowledge of literature. I soon discovered, as I began working on my Faulkner thesis, that I had a niche they had not explored, and they had not read widely in Wilson, works like *To the Finland Station, Axel's Castle,* and *The Wound and the Bow,* works that did not conform to the world of university lit departments. As I had with Wilson, I built for me new reading lists from names they dropped and works they mentioned, and as we browsed through the remainder stalls at the campus bookstores, I picked up anthologies of writers at Ken's suggestion and began to read works I had missed by not taking survey courses as an undergraduate. When I noted that I was seriously deficient in the Augustan, Kinnamon stuck a copy of Alexander Pope in my pocket though McIntyre scoffed that no one reads or talks about Pope any more. But if I had the change and if it were a good copy without heavy markings I would buy it and would start reading it when I got home.

Although my meetings my meeting with the seminar in The Cage meant that I had to leave Bettie alone for longer periods, she never complained, and when asked why she didn't, her answer was that I needed the contact more than she needed my company. I could only hope she was teasing. Because babysitters cost money, we almost never went to movies together; rarely ate out, except hamburgers at a drive in; almost never went on picnics; and only occasionally took long walks as we had in Japan. The new neighborhood around East Thirty-Fourth Street, just east of the new freeway that sliced

Austin's eastern section from the city itself, was a lovely tree-shaded area of large sloping lawns and winding streets, excellent for long walks pushing the baby cart with Clay. While it was no idyll, it was quite and a pleasant place to walk.

Our first two years in Japan had insulated us from brushes with in-laws and parents, and these times in Austin were relatively serene because they extended that isolation. But into our demi-paradise, a minor crisis erupted when Mama came to Austin for a visit late in October, a little more than a month before the baby was due. What occurred typified the difference between Bettie's parents and mine. Mama's visits were rare, and this time she dropped in unexpectedly and brought with her my cousin Frances from Beaumont. Frances was closer to Mama's age than mine, her daughter, Evelyn was a freshman at UT. I was very fond of Francis and her family, though I had not seen or spoken to her in years, but I would have like for Bettie to get to know them someday. I was teaching; Bettie, still in bathrobe and pajamas, was alone, reading as usual while Clay was playing on the living room floor. The house was less than neat, breakfast dishes un-cleared, and Clay not yet bathed.

When Bettie answered the door and my mother got one look at the state of the house, the unbathed infant, and Bettie in a bathrobe and quite pregnant, Mama apologized and directed Frances back to the car and left. When I got home from class, Bettie told me how shocked Dot appeared when she answered the door. I laughed, knowing Mama to be pathological about neatness and godliness but told her not to worry, though I agreed that Mama should have called ahead. A few days later, the expected letter of reprimand arrived, and Bettie hit the ceiling, along with me. It accused Bettie of not caring about "appearances," implying that Bettie was lazy and irresponsible, barely avoiding that good Southern word, "shiftless." My mother had never adopted diplomacy as a virtue, except with her well-to-do friends whose money was clearly proof of high moral standing. It was indeed too much, and so—I hoped--was my reply.

We had been forewarned that such times were coming. Once before, Mama had asked about Bettie and her constant reading. What really surprised me at the time was not the question about Bettie's reading, but how easily Mama had adopted the role of "mother-in-law." She never approved of the way Bettie "kept house," though she never said she disapproved. Like many mothers-in-law, she had honed the skills of silent displeasure down to a precision unmatched in the annals of disdain. When we visited Corpus Christi shortly after returning from Japan, Bettie made it clear, to me at least, that in almost every way Mama and she were opposites. She said she liked my mother very much, but she had sensed the difference quickly that time she stopped in Corpus on her way to Galveston. I had taken her comparison as a subtle compliment to me, since I had *not* married "a girl just like the girl that married dear old Dad" but had chosen my own ideal. I pooh-poohed the idea until Mama later confirmed it, more by accident than by intention. She asked me once when we were alone, "Joe, is it true that *all* Bettie ever does is read? She is always carrying a book around."

As usual, I answered flippantly, agreeing it was pretty much all she *ever* did, intentionally implying by my tone that I did *not* disapprove of her habits. Then I said sarcastically in her defense, "Oh, she has babies, and nowadays, she changes diapers, bathes Clay, and feeds him unless, of course, she can get me to do those things, which by the way I enjoy."

"I'm serious, Joe," she said just teetering on the edge of anger. "She's a young mother now and should be concerned about her duties as a mother. You're going to be studying and working now, you know. It's not your job to do her chores." I seriously doubted at the time she understood even the fundamental rules of feminism.

"Of course, I know it, Mama. I knew about her reading and her habits before I married her, and I didn't expect, or even want, her to change. She's really very good at taking care of her duties, as you call them," I said. "I expect her to read. I wouldn't marry an illiterate woman or a stupid one. As far as I'm concerned, that is as much her *duty* as the other things." I perhaps emphasized duty the wrong way. My mother and I were too much alike in that we would not hold our peace or bite our tongues but would sally forth with new arguments at the slightest provocation.

"Well! If that's all you two are thinking about. I just don't understand it. I mean she's reading two or three books at a time, and she's reading *novels*. I didn't read novels until I was past thirty," she said with emphasis. The pain in her voice when she said "novels" was so palpable it almost made me laugh out loud.

I gasped and clutched my heart, "OH MY GOD! Not *novels!* What kinds of novels? You mean Steinbeck, Faulkner, or Jane Austen and that trash?"

She glared at me now.

"Mama! Novels and literature are my *business!* No! *Our* business! That's what I hope I'll be teaching someday. She reads and talks about what she reads, and everything she does, I like. If she neglects Clay, which I doubt, while we are here in Corpus, it's so she won't interfere with *your* pleasures in 'doing' for him. Edna and you are so eager to take care of a baby, like most grandmothers. She just backed off and let you do it without interfering.

Look!" I paused. "We were on a boat cooped up in a cabin for almost two weeks then confined in and airplane for hours, and she never got a break and didn't ask for one. And she *never* whined or complained. When you grew up and you had babies, you had maids to help until we left Beaumont. Bettie and I aren't ever going to have hired help. She takes her breaks whenever she finds them. And I encourage her to. Of course, I bathe and feed and change diapers, but it's not because she's lazy. It's because he's my son. I want to."

"Well, I certainly *hope* you don't hire anyone. It's costing enough as it is. And don't talk to me that way or raise your voice. Remember who's paying the bills."

"How could I forget?" I said, *and then finally*, I bit my tongue.

In reality, our second year in Austin was rich. I was busy, taking philosophy of religion, the Great Plains with the great Walter P. Webb and a social history of the United States *and* teaching two sections of freshman composition as well as attending those "seminars" in The Cage. I was learning there was more about teaching and the art of learning than education classes could ever teach.

It might have all been part of a grand design, placing as many TAs together as possible so that they could share experiences, good and bad, and thereby learn what methods were most effective. Actually, sharing experiences and ideas does not generally continue as one grows into the profession according to Parker J. Palmer, who writes that we teachers traditionally "walk into our workplace [and] close the door on our colleagues. When we emerge we rarely talk about what happened or what needs to happen next."[9] But in The Cage we did share and learn together. We learned even when we were unaware. It was impossible not to overhear the exchanges between teacher and student during conferences inside the cage. Whether a discussion centered on a student's writing or the answers he or she had given on a quiz or the meaning in a passage from a short story, it made no difference. One could not help but learn something about the art of teaching by eavesdropping on those dialogues.

One day, as I was leaving the class in social history, Professor Cotner asked me to come by his office and talk over my "program of study." I enjoyed his class. It complemented nicely the seminar I had taken with Boatright and supplied social and cultural backgrounds that would be useful in case I decided to do my doctorate in American Studies. On top of it, he was a lively lecturer, never dull.

When I arrived, he asked me to take a seat then said, "You're doing quite well in this class, Mr. Gilliland. Are you a history major?"

---

9   Palmer, Parker J. *The Courage to Teach* (San Francisco: Jossey–Bass Publishers, 1998).

I told him that I had taught a similar course to Japanese students at Wakayama University but that my required reading list was not nearly as extensive as his and that we only skimmed the surface where he dug deep. He raised his eyebrows and asked me to explain how I came to teach history in Japan, and I explained briefly, emphasizing that Inoue had really "let me get away with" teaching a history class since I was hardly qualified. Then he asked if I would like to be his graduate assistant. He was surprised that I was majoring in English but said it made no difference until I told him I was already a TA in English. Since that was the case, he said he doubted he could get approval to hire me. He laughed and added something about it probably being against university policy to allow graduate students to make enough to actually live on.

I took his offer as a compliment, though, and began to think seriously about the American Studies option. Interdepartmental programs were often controversial and, therefore, more demanding than other programs, each department wanting to outdo the other or be so strict that no one would question their standards.

In philosophies of religion, Dr. Ginascol spent the major part of the course discussing Hinduism and Buddhism, hardly touching on the early Christian philosophies and saying nothing about Islam. Later, Ginascol's class would help shape my own Eastern philosophy class at Cochise College.

By the end of the fall term I had taken two more important steps: I had learned that what I was doing in freshman composition was working, and I had finished the required number of class hours for a master's in English. Today, as then, I can discern no apparent coherence in my choice of courses, no clear focus or pattern of interest, but they did prepare me in an odd way for teaching in a junior college and, as it would turn out, fit perfectly the teaching I would be doing for the rest of my life, even preparing me for humanities that would become my major teaching field in the end. I had always heard that the purpose of a degree was not so much to guarantee a graduate has acquired the knowledge to perform a given task but that he, or she, has learned how to learn. My MA was shaping into a perfect example of just such a degree.

Teaching freshman composition went far more easily than I expected. I tried to recall everything that Helen James had tried to teach about good writing. I spent what seemed an eternity marking the forty or so papers every ten days. Like the papers I wrote in my freshman year, most of these papers lacked a clear thesis idea or any sense of development, but in the last few weeks of the term, I sensed that something had begun to happen. The themes began to read as if the writers had noticed the comments and suggestions I had scribbled. Since the assigned topics usually resembled the bland leading the blander, I tried to assign papers that allowed the students to choose their own topic. For the last two papers, I assigned no specific topics, asking them to write on a topic they believed important to them personally or on something related to another class they were taking. Our final paper would be a practice theme for their final exam essay.

"Bring a blue book for the in-class theme," I said, "and write your theme as though you were expecting total strangers would be reading it, because that's the way it will be on the final. I won't be reading your essays on the final."

They all did much better than thy had all semester: the previous D became C and so on up the scale; there were even two A papers, one in each class. As Black had predicted, we all had the same experience.

None of my students in either class that first semester made below a C on the final departmental essay graded not by me but by a team of graders, and they all passed the standardized exam over grammar, style, and usage. All in all, I thought the uniform final, including the final essay, gave a fair accounting of my teaching. Since no instructor graded his own classes, the results seemed as good as we had a right to expect. At our orientation meeting at the beginning of the fall term, the director of freshman English shocked us when he said we might expect to fail half the class. Therefore, when none of the TAs in the cage on the twenty-third floor had a student who failed the departmental final, we congratulated one another. I had lost two students along the way and others had lost one here and there, dropouts who were likely failing at the time they left school.

The main complaint we all had was the blandness of their writing, "studied mediocrity" with quantities of "fine writing," a euphemism for overly modified sentences, pretentious choice of words, a style, I believe, acquired in high school after discovering the thesaurus. Some high school teachers reward students for using a thesaurus, for packing a sentence with unnecessary modifiers, and for using the passive voice. It was as if having an original idea or fresh approach to anything was a sign of weakness or a failure of character. McIntyre insisted it was a reflection of the blandness of the age. Reading aloud in class a paper that showed signs of originality or enthusiasm on any topic embarrassed students, not for their own lack of style but for the unfortunate student who had written the paper. To be singled out of the mass for any reason was a sin. I should not have been surprised after reading papers as the course went on. The first paper, written in class, was a simple diagnostic paper on the topic: "Who I Am and What I'm Here For." I explained that I needed to know something about each of them and something about their ability to communicate.

"But please, no confessions or deep psychological revelation," I added. "I'm neither your confessor nor your shrink."

They all described themselves as "average" or "ordinary" people, all aspiring to become average well-rounded citizens. Before I returned the papers, I made a few remarks about general dos and don'ts, urging them—as Helen James had urged my first composition class--to avoid using the familiar second person.

"Unless what you're writing really does apply to the general population, the best thing," I said, "is to avoid 'you' altogether. It's too colloquial, too familiar. These are formal essays. For example, let me read an example of a student paper to show how inappropriate an overly familiar style can be."

I read, "You do not come to college to learn just from books but to learn to live with other girls." When I reached "to live with other girls," I paused and waited. The pause was pregnant, heavy with meaning. One boy chuckled. A young woman put her hands over her face and shook with laughter, and the author of the paper put her face down on the desk just as I said, "Now when my wife read the paper, she asked me, 'Honestly, is that why *you* came here to college?' Well, I had some explaining to do."

Seeing that several still didn't get the point, I explained how the second person had lost its meaning. I asked them all to rewrite their papers but only after they read two of the autobiographical essays in the text.

Most of us tried to "do no harm." Students who wrote well when they arrived, we tried to leave untarnished; those who wrote acceptable English, we pushed ahead with more challenging tasks; and those who were irretrievable, or who lacked the instinctive ability to write a simple declarative sentence, we counseled into dropping English and transferring to a school where remedial English was taught. A few of us spent time in our offices going over the fundamentals the students had missed in high school, but these were rare. When I asked Ray Black whether those methods courses that attempted to teach composition had actually helped him, he said he didn't recall anything in his early education courses that either helped or harmed. The most important resource for me was my freshman English class with Dr. Helen James. None of the TAs I knew was majoring in rhetoric, which was almost unheard of as a major in the large university departments of English at that time. Composition method taught in colleges of education was aimed at elementary and secondary school teaching, which was where the breakdown had occurred in the first place. We were faced with a pedagogical catch-22, and freshman writing was as much a punishment for the student as for the instructor, a sentence to be endured.

Twice in one year, Dr. Wilson Hudson, director of freshman composition, visited our classes to evaluate our performances as teachers, and twice a year, Lois Trice, my faculty mentor, examined a batch of papers I had marked and graded. Hudson was the closest I believe any of the tenured professors ever came to freshman students. He was congenial, generous, and of no help as an evaluator unless his failure. or refusal, to comment was intended as encouragement to continue doing what I was doing. He seemed embarrassed giving me suggestions, telling me that I should move around the class more or that I should use the chalkboard to write new or difficult words. He apparently found neither strengths nor weaknesses in what he saw. I thanked him, and that was the end of it. Other members of the cage reported similar "evaluations." In a way I found it hard to believe that I was doing anything right, other than failing to use the chalkboard or spending too much tome behind he lectern.

The most important event that winter took place neither in the classroom or The Cage: it was the birth of our daughter Lisè, who was born on December 1 shortly after I dismissed my eight o'clock class. I let them go early, explaining that the next time I called roll, I would be a father. Bettie and her doctor had agreed that he would induce labor—partly for his convenience, partly for mine, mainly for Bettie. I would know when to take her to St. David's Hospital, and he would be able to leave early on a vacation, and Bettie would not wonder or wait as she had in Kobe with Clay's arrival. We could also let Bettie's mother know when to take the bus and arrive on time.

Unlike the rush for the taxi and the hospital when Clay was born, I was able to leave class, pick up Bettie, and arrive at St. David's Hospital sans panic. Mama and Albert had driven up to Austin and taken Clay back with them. When we arrived just after 8:30 a nurse took Bettie off to the obstetric area while I registered her and made a deposit of one hundred dollars. A nurse took me to Betties room allowed to sit with Bettie when the contractions began. It seemed rather odd just sitting there chatting, no one acting as if there was anything to be concerned about. Bettie once more had opted for the natural childbirth method, to which her doctor had agreed. I was there when contractions began. The nurse in attendance insisted I go to lunch and return later in plenty of time for the birth. When I returned a little over an hour later, I found that Lisè had arrived and that Bette had returned to her room. Everything went so well after she was born that her doctor and the nurse advised Bettie to check out the next morning. Edna's bus arrived later that same afternoon, and she was amazed that it was over.

When Edna, Bettie's mother, arrived on the bus that afternoon and learned that Bettie would be coming home the next day, she was amazed and quite happy that everything had gone so well. Somehow, it seemed not quite respectable for babies to arrive with so little fuss, but more startling and even less respectable was the total cost. With a student's discount, the doctor's total cost was only one hundred fifty dollars, and when I checked Bettie and Lisè out at 10:00 o'clock the next morning we received a forty-five dollar refund: the hospital cost was only fifty-five dollars.

Baby Lisè with Bettie and Joe, December 1954

In spite of that, however, for the first time since we returned from Japan, money became a serious factor. Albert announced shortly after Christmas that he could no longer send us a check after January 1. Our situation was not exactly dire. We would not be putting aside money for Lisè, and the TA stipend would continue, but we also knew that at the end of term in the spring we would have nothing coming in. We were, we felt, fortunate when he made the offer to lend the money and not ask for payment until I finished and found a job. At the time, he indicated that he would be able to handle the payments through the spring semester of 1955 when I was sure I would be finished. As licensed public accountant and a fine reputation, Albert had a good private accounting practice, and for a time after he left the AMSCO position he acted as treasurer and accountant treasurer for an independent drilling operation. He never spoke to any of us about his financial situation, but he always gave the impression that he was "well-off." When AMSCO sold out and ended operations he received a handsome severance package which, along with the drilling operation he was able to set up his own accounting practice. When he turned down a partnership in the drilling operation, he took on the small corporation as a client at what seemed a handsome stipend. He and Mama owned their home outright, and she had invested carefully in real estate when the oil was pumping. Therefore, his announcement that he would be unable to afford the hundred dollars a month came as a surprise. Albert's monthly dues at the Corpus Christi Country Club and Oso Golf Club—tax deductible as business expenses--came to considerably more than the hundred dollars a month loan to us. Since I had completed my course work, I considered returning to the Bookmobile, certain that I could arrange a schedule that fit with my class schedule. I knew such an arrangement would get us through but I also knew I would not be able to finish my thesis in time to get a full time teaching post for the fall term, 1955.

Bettie suggested we borrow whatever money we needed from her grandfather who was president of a small bank in Bryson, Texas. Granddaddy Moore may have not been the largest landholder or the wealthiest rancher in Jack and Palo Pinto Counties, but he was quite well off. She suggested I write him directly and not ask her mother and father to intercede so that they would not feel they should make the loan themselves instead of Mr. Moore. They would have without a blink. Edna and Harold had been generous themselves ever since we had returned, and Bettie and I agreed we had taken enough from them. So I wrote the letter and waited.

In the meantime, Hardy's doomsters dropped more gifts into our laps. I had just mailed the letter to Mr. Moore when I got a call from Dr. Graham to drop by his office when it was convenient. I had gotten calls from Graham as well as an urgent call from McIntyre in The Cage telling me that Graham had come to the office himself. It was obviously something urgent. When I arrived, he greeted me cordially and asked if I had completed all my course work.

When I said I had signed up for my thesis and nothing more, he asked, "Would you like a full-time teaching job for the spring? There's a job for you at Tarleton State College in Stephenville, just up the road, if you'd like. It's only for one semester, but there's a good chance they can keep you on when you finish your thesis," he said.

Until 1950, when it was made part of the Texas A&M University system, Tarleton had been an outstanding junior college. Stephenville was about half the distance between Austin and Wichita Falls, Bettie's hometown.

"Well! That's quite a surprise," I said. "And it comes at a very good time."

I told him of the potential financial bind we were facing, but I emphasized it was not a crisis. He explained I would be teaching four classes, freshman composition or possibly a class in introduction to literature. Tarleton, he explained, had been one of the best junior colleges in the state. The pay, he said, was double my TA stipend, around four hundred a month. It sounded almost like another wildcat strike on the Gilliland homestead. It was that good.

He saw me hesitate and added, "Stephenville is only a short drive from Austin. We can work on your thesis and finish it by the end of May, I'm sure." Then he hesitated and said, "Don't make up your mind now. Let me know in a day or two," he paused. "When I got the call, Gilliland, I thought of you the first thing. I think you would do well there in Stephenville. You've had some years teaching experience in Japan, I hear, in addition to the assistantship here."

I thanked him, then explained there was a good chance we would be able to borrow enough money from my wife's grandfather, preferring, I said, to write my thesis in Austin, and he agreed it would be better.

But that wasn't all. My doomsters weren't finished!

When I returned to The Cage, and found them waiting anxiously to hear what news I had. I told Mac of Graham's offer for a full time job, saying I had not made up my mind, and then read the memo from the English office informing me that my two composition classes were confirmed for the spring term. At that moment I got a call from Dr. Boatright's secretary asking me to come to the chairman's office immediately. When I hung up, I turned to McIntyre and said, "I'm wanted in the chairman's office. They probably wanted to offer me a job as full-time instructor."

"You're dreaming," he laughed.

When I reached the English office, Dr. Boatright's secretary blurted out, "Oh, thank you for coming right away, Mr. Gilliland. Would, could you take a class of foreign students *in addition* to your two composition classes? It's an introduction to literature class."

She was actually pleading for me to teach a third section. What a day! I could hardly believe it. It was almost unheard. No TA ever got more than two sections of composition and rarely a literature class. I was flabbergasted, gob-smacked! I had never heard of a TA teaching a introduction to literature; certainly, I had never heard of anyone being offered three sections. Our office was filled with people holding master's degrees, yet they had called me. While Boatright was hovering in the office behind her, she was explaining that it was a special section for foreign students, and since I had taught three years at "Wacky-yammy University," they thought I would be the best qualified.

"Mr. Gilliland, we really appreciate you taking this class. We noticed that you were signed up to take only the thesis course, and well, we have literally scraped the bottom of the ba-a-arr uh, uh …" Her voice trailed off to a whisper as her face turned a bright red.

I finished for her, as gently as I knew how, "You mean, the bottom of the *barrel?* Don't be embarrassed, please. TAs can't afford the luxury of pride, false or otherwise."

While his secretary was pleading, Dr. Boatright turned his back to us, his shoulders shaking with silent laughter. She smiled weakly and thanked me.

Stepping up to the window now, Dr. Boatright handed me the class roster and said, "Mr. Gilliland, our barrels, fortunately, have very rich materials in the bottom." He smiled broadly and thanked me. For three classes, I would be making over three hundred a month, the sophomore class, for some reason, paying at a higher rate. It was consistent with English Department logic, however: it paid more because it required *less* work with *fewer* papers to mark than a freshman composition class. Ironically, the full-time load for instructors and professors that spring was only nine hours, the same number of hours I was teaching at a considerably lower rate, though I also had as much "university experience" as several of the new full-time instructors with doctorates; I did not have the degrees, however.

We would not need the loan from Granddaddy Moore after all; it would become a five hundred dollar nest egg, a luxury few married graduate students with children had. It was almost impossible to absorb it all at once—the offer of a full-time job that might turn into a permanent position, followed by a chance to teach a third section, a class in literature for foreign students. I had to call Bettie. We talked about the Stephenville job being only a short drive from Wichita Falls, about the possibility of buying a better secondhand car, and about having a legitimate salary and a possibility of staying on at Tarleton State College. There was a long pause, silence, and then I told her I was frankly unprepared for such largess.

Then Bettie spoke: "Maybe it is *too* short a drive from Wichita Falls, have you thought of that?"

I said I had, and she asked, "Are you sure you can finish your thesis and teach full time? Or do you really want to?"

I waited and then said, "I'll tell Graham I've taken the lit course for foreign students."

She said, "Good. I'm not ready to leave Austin, and I'm not sure I want to live in Stephenville anyway."

Was there any doubt that I was the most fortunate of men? It was the happiest news I could have hoped for; I did not want to leave Austin either, but something more had happened. Bettie had, without prompting from me, given me the greatest boost I had any right to expect, and I had been given a magnificent vote of confidence from Graham and from Boatright. First, it was Graham's thinking of me, and then it was Boatright's digging to the bottom of his barrel. I went straight back to Graham's office and told him I had just been given an introduction to literature class in addition to my composition sections. He smiled and said I was indeed fortune's child. When I told him Dr. Boatright seemed pretty desperate for someone to take the foreign students and told how his secretary had said they had to "scrape the bottom of the barrel," he laughed.

"Good." He smiled again. "It's better that you stay here and finish your thesis. Now have a seat. Let's talk about Faulkner. I've asked J. G. Varner to be the other man on your committee. Varner's a good name for a Faulkner advisor, don't you think? You've read *The Hamlet?*" he said. I said I had, and then we began to talk about the outline I had suggested earlier.

When I left, we had worked out a good approach that avoided dealing with knotty theological definitions of sin by focusing on the misdeeds of specific characters in the novels and the sins of a flawed society, tracing, for instance, the decline of Temple Drake as a representative of traditional Southern upper class male and female respectability. I could see he was testing me to see how well I had read *Sanctuary* and *Requiem* and how well I had thought through my definitions of sin, not only in Temple Drake but other characters like Horace Benbow. He urged me to read other works, particularly *Light in August* and *Absalom, Absalom*, then warned me not to let the essay get too large, that it was, after all, a master's thesis and not a doctoral dissertation. We talked about secondary sources, mentioning Howe, Kazin, O'Connor, Geismar, and others, but he emphasized again my staying with primary sources and saving the criticism until the last when I would be make summations.

When I returned to The Cage, Kinnamon and McIntyre were in the middle of their long-running debate joined by a third TA, Jim Mason, a doctoral student I had met earlier. As soon as I walked in the door, they asked what was up.

Kinnamon asked if I'd gotten Graham's message. "The great man himself came down here looking for you," he said.

I told them about job offer from Stephenville and how I'd turned it down.

"You turned down four hundred dollars a month?" McIntyre said. "Why?"

"Graham agreed it was better to do my thesis here."

Then in as off-hand a voice as I could manage, I explained why I'd turned down the Tarleton State College offer, telling them about Boatright's offer of the section of literature for foreign students. They were even more aghast.

"Goddamn, Joe," Mac sighed, "you must have an angel watching over you, and I don't even believe in angels." Kinnamon nodded and said that I was assured now of strong backing from Boatright and Graham if ever I applied for a job. I replied that I was thinking of applying as soon as possible for a community college job. Though none in our cage had any experience with two-year colleges, they agreed I should because I was really on the edge of the abyss financially. I was glad Mason was there. He had several years junior college experience at Alvin Junior College near Houston and said he had no regrets for his years at a two-year college. I added that I'd taken my government classes at Del Mar and assured them that they were far better than the sophomore government classes then being taught at UT, adding that my sister Jane had graduated from Del Mar and had no problems transferring all her courses successfully to UT. When I said that I had activated my employment file and was applying for a junior college job and that I expected to be interviewing in the spring, Mason jumped in. "Don't take the first job offer you get, Gilliland. There are some junior colleges out there that pay really good salaries. I know. Shop around. Some pay enough to buy your wife a pair of shoes the first year."

We laughed; still serious, he assured us it was true. The fact was that junior colleges were paying entry-level instructors, on the average, five hundred dollars a year more than the state universities or four-year colleges were paying new instructors. Had I had an MA, the Tarleton State College salary would have been at least four hundred dollars a month.

The new semester went too quickly, and my thesis progressed too slowly. Until midterm, Dr. Graham had been reading about a chapter a week, but then I crashed into the wall on the chapters dealing with Popeye and Judge Drake. Each represented Faulkner's idea of "sin in modernism": Popeye was symbolic of the "rise of Caliban," the sort of social evil that allows the sins of characters like Horace, Temple, and Gowan to go unchecked and often unnoticed because of who they are in the eyes of society; Judge Drake represented the sin of corrupted privilege, the same decadence Faulkner depicted in the character of Jason Compson in *The Sound and the Fury*. The sins committed by these characters represented the social ills Faulkner recognized as a failure of modern society, particularly in the South, in contrast to the purity of the Edenic wilderness in the Mississippi Delta that he clearly explicates in "The

Bear" and "Delta Autumn" and most of *Go Down, Moses.* I had these ideas, I believe, clearly outlined and ready to put down, but the midterm exams and a stack of themes interrupted my writing even a first draft.

When I met with Graham in his office during the first week of April he seemed so distracted that he finally had to beg pardon and ask if I would meet with J. G. Varner to talk over the chapters I had submitted earlier. He was having difficulty with a major university committee that was drafting-- attempting to draft is better--a proposal for the new university core curriculum. The College of Engineering and College of Fine Arts, strange partners, or so it appeared, had united to fight the all-university proposal for a common core; the colleges were in strong agreement about the number of required courses they believed would extend the hours for the degrees offered by their respective colleges. When I explained I was so backed up with midterm essays in the composition classes and a stack of critical papers in the literature class that I was unable to finish the section on Judge Drake and the sins in society, Graham told me, emphatically, not to worry about the papers, that my real concern was the chapters: "You're here to finish your degree. Don't worry about those papers."

I was on the verge of suggesting I could get in a first draft before the end of the semester and finish rewriting in the first six weeks of the summer session, but I was really hoping to finish before June, making myself more attractive for the summer job market. The season for recruiting new faculty was just getting under way. In fact, a few days earlier, I had dropped on his desk a form from the University Placement Service requesting a letter of recommendation from him for my file.

My meeting with Dr. Varner was a disaster. It started well. He was cordial and highly complimentary, but halfway through the morning, I could see he was reshaping my thesis and expanding it far beyond the outline Graham and I had agreed on. Several graduate colleagues had warned me that such things happen in a thesis committee; too often, supervisors either grow too eager to rewrite your thesis or become totally indifferent until it's finished and ready for the final approval, and then they find errors, omissions, or redundancies. When I met with Graham a week later and told him I was afraid Varner wanted me to write an entirely different thesis from the one we outlined and settled on, he quickly apologized and said he would select a new member. When I walked into his office I had not expected him so agree with me so easily.

"This happens, Gilliland, but I'm not surprised," Graham said. "Varner's a very good man, but sometimes . . .," he paused again in thought.

"I hope you won't. . .," "then I didn't know what to say.

"Don't worry. I have very good man who needs a thesis. This is my problem, not yours." He smiled and began to talk about the material I had shown him earlier, and when I left an hour later the anxiety I had felt when I walked in had vanished. He was quite pleased with the direction I was moving.

When I activated my file in the Teacher Placement Office, I honestly felt that I had something to offer, but I had no way of knowing how a college dean or chairman evaluated transcripts or applications; I hoped that Dr. Cranfill was correct and not simply trying to make me feel good when he said undergraduate transcripts do not play a major part in a final decision. But the bare fact was my grades in my teaching areas, English and history, were quite mediocre. In the space where I was asked to state the kind of position I was seeking, I wrote "junior college or four-year college," and I made it clear I was not looking for a high school position.

My sophomore lit survey for foreign students was a joy, not just because it required less preparation and grading time than my comp classes, but literature was the ultimate goal for most of us. I had fewer than twenty in the class, all several years older than my freshmen, two older than I. About half the class was from the Mid-East, the rest from South and Central America. The class was all men except for a single young woman from Israel. All had attended private secondary schools where English was the main language, which meant most were as well read as, if not better than, their America counterparts. Except for two or three, they were all eager to participate in class discussion and were always prepared. At the first class meeting I detected several men who seem to be non-plussed that they had been given a young, inexperienced instructor, and when I asked, point blank if they had some complaint, one boldly be blurted it out and asked what experience I had. I admitted I was a graduate student and a teaching assistant, but I had taught three years at Wakayama University in Japan and had taught literature to advanced English majors.

Several students seemed uneasy that the young Iranian had been so rude, and the young woman said, "You should not concern yourself. They are rude like this in every class." The nodding heads suggested she was correct.

I replied, "I 'm not concerned, and I understand they might be worried because I have often been accused of looking too young. " There were smiles then, and when I added, "I am married and have two children. So I am of age."

My uneasy questioner apologized, "I am sorry, sir."

Both sections of my freshman comp were smaller than my fall sections, and I noticed several new faces in both comp classes. My one A student from the fall term, a chap named Moritz, was no longer with me, having moved into the Plan II honors program. His friend, Mr. Wash, the freshman guard, proudly announced the first day that Moritz had left the freshman football squad and "gone Plan II," reminding me with a big smile that Moritz could have had either a football scholarship or a "real scholarship." I recalled how Moritz took considerable umbrage at Thurber's slur regarding college athletes in his essay "University Days."

While members of the class were chuckling over Thurber's satire, an indignant Moritz spoke up, "I don't think it's funny. I'm here on a football scholarship, but I could have come on an academic scholarship if I'd wanted to." he declared emphatically, adding, "The football paid more."

I suggested his criticism was justified and it might even make a good theme topic if he wished. That gave me an opportunity to expand on satire, agreeing that Thurber's humor could be seen as "unfair," if a person was in the group targeted, and I suggested that while humor or satire often *seemed* unfair, it always trumpeted truth. The result of that brief discussion was an excellent argumentative paper by Mr. Moritz.

The English Department's outline for the second semester of freshman composition recommended several supplemental texts in addition to the required *Writer's Guide*, and I chose a collection of modern American short stories, some of which were included in my text for the class of foreign students. But I believe the book that made a difference that semester was Frederick Lewis Allen's, *Only Yesterday*. Allen's book resonated with ideas that some would have considered dangerously controversial at the time; McCarthyism—even after the Senate's censure—and the feverish anticommunist crusades continued to send out ripples of fear on campuses everywhere. I hadn't realized how much the shock effect of the academic pogroms of the forties still reverberated in the mood on campus, even though the new president of the university, Logan Wilson, had brought with him a vigorous philosophy of liberal education and academic freedom. For instance, one of Wilson's first acts after his inauguration was the executive order elevating Dr. J. Gilbert McAllister from associate professor to full professor, tacitly endorsing his propensity to irritate and to cause controversy. When the young assistant professor had achieved tenure and the title of Associate Professor he had announced that he would never write another article for an academic journal, never bow to the pressure to publish but would concentrate all his efforts at the university toward teaching in the classroom. He froze himself in place rather than contribute to journals that very few or no one read.

The fall out of the regents' firings of the forties had contaminated the atmosphere so effectively that many people in the English Department were still gun-shy. In Graham's novel course, for example, we had used Dos Passos' *Manhattan Transfer* instead of *U.S.A.*, which would have been a far more challenging work considering the novel's technique and literary history. All options for fiction and nonfiction were excellent. Allen's social history was then one of the best descriptions of the country's agony and ecstasy after the First World War; it offered insights into political and social conflicts that echoed through the era of the fifties, and even now, it compares favorably with William Manchester's more ambitious *The Glory and the Dream* (1975). The chapters in Allen's book dealing with the Palmer raids and the anti-Bolshevik movement paralleled McCarthy's attacks and HUAC witch hunts and offered us a controversial topic we could use for argumentative papers. McIntyre, Kinnamon, and I assigned papers dealing with pros and cons of the congressional investigations, the Campus Crusades for Christ, and the arguments surrounding the John Birch Society's anti-communist claims, but Ray Black demurred and argued we were asking for trouble. He avoided the issue entirely in his classes, saying that his experiences at Stephen F. Austin State College warned him away from such subjects. Mac and I, who had been tempered in the smithy of McAllister's classes, insisted that we had an obligation to explore these areas with our students. We argued that students could learn to present arguments clearly only if they had real arguments dealing with real controversy. We argued that too many theme assignments were phony as it was. Besides, Mac argued, who was ever really concerned about what happened in a TA's class? Black disagreed, arguing that we had been hired to teach composition, not political liberalism. He was correct, if that were all we were teaching. I felt that failing to challenge our students to think critically about everything contributed to the complacency that dominated the era. Objectivity, Mac and I argued, was a myth. Argumentative papers based on phony arguments, in which neither side defends or attacks questions of value, teach form without substance. I told Black that all my arguments *for* assigning the controversies stemmed from my own classes at the university, namely freshman composition where we read *The Autobiography of Lincoln Steffens* and S. I. Hayakawa's language in action.

Most of our students challenged the liberalism we brought to bear on the Palmer chapters, and all three of us assigned writing topics in which students had to argue a point of view logically and coherently, eschewing the clichés and shibboleths of right or left. Kinnamon had only heard of McAllister's theory of "education by irritation," McIntyre and I had taken the classes, been brain washed, Black suggested. In the end we received no complaints.

I believed that Allen's chapters on the mores of the period, as well as the chapter on Attorney General Palmer and the "Red scare," would serve to stir thought and make for more interesting assignments. The John Birch Society in Texas was soon to be everywhere a threat, and a movement calling itself the Christian Anticommunist Crusade, led by an Australian fundamentalist Christian, had already won the backing of nearly all fundamentalist churches in Texas, chiefly the Southern Baptists, although the Baptists at the time had not entered precinct or national politics as it would later. Although the campus that spring was eerily silent on political issues right or left, many liberal TAs were intimidated and refused to irritate their students with controversy, though the *Daily Texan,* as before, ran liberal commentaries regularly by young thinkers like Willie Morris. Our job was to teach composition; we were told, though the telling was fervorless, not to indoctrinate or to turn English classes into debating societies.

At first, I steered clear of controversy or assignments that raised passions, but the results were dim and the classes dull; arguments, I felt, must involve a commitment to values and must be supported by substantive evidence, not the nurturing platitudes my students had heard all through public school. In the fall, when one of the assigned essays had made a remark about the controversy over evolution that led to the Scopes trial, I passed it off as being dated and no longer a subject of serious debate. Well, over half the class insisted that Darwinism was still a subject for debate and more than one said they seriously disbelieved "we were descended from monkeys," while the others were about evenly split between indifference and acceptance. When I asked if anyone had read Darwin, no hands rose. When I asked why they believed Darwin said *Homo sapiens* sprang from monkeys, a voice came back. "Well, didn't he?" I told them I wouldn't answer the question but that they should make an effort to find for themselves and use what they discovered in an argumentative theme.

The voice came back, "Why can't you tell us your opinion?"

I replied, "I can, but I won't. The library . . .," here I paused and stole from Dr. Mac, "that's the building with the twenty-seven story tower sticking out the top, very easy to find, has all kinds of answers. You are students and I assume you know how to use a library. Don't take my word for it or against it. Look it up for yourself. Arguments based on 'everyone says,' 'they say,' are not arguments," I added that I would not accept such arguments and would sharply discount any papers using such references.

Allen's book had an excellent chapter on the evolution controversy, particularly the Scopes trial, and I used the chapter as the basis of a "library" assignment requiring supporting materials in both primary and secondary sources, hoping to teach students how to cite their sources and the techniques of incorporating direct and indirect quotations as supporting material. A few rose to the challenge, but none were irritated enough to refute any of the claims by either side. I was a bit dismayed when a student claiming to be a biology major said the Darwin issue was "unrelated to [his] field of study." Only after questioning him further would he admit he really didn't know what "evolution" meant. Thanking him for his confession, I said I believed his not knowing was more a reflection on his high school biology class than his failure.

Complacency went deep in those days; my foray into the intellectual wars, via "education by irritation," fell flat. The class simply "wouldn't provoke." By focusing assignments more on real issues and ideas, I did a much better job in the second semester than the first. The papers, in fact, exhibited more focus than those in the first semester, which Black and the others suggested might have been just as easily a factor of their having had more experience writing at the college level than they had when they entered.

In early April, I got my first job offer, which Mason had warned me not to accept, and which Frederick Lewis Allen may have played a vital part, *may*. One Friday morning, a little past eleven, we were discussing the Palmer anticommunist scare and raids of the twenties and were relating the scare to what we had read earlier about the use and abuse of language discussed in Orwell's "Politics and the English Language." The chapter in *Only Yesterday* worked nicely, illustrating how Attorney General Palmer, during the twenties, and the right wing politicians Senators Nixon, McCarthy, Knowland, and others of the 1950s were using and abusing language in the same ways. I suspected several in the 11:00 a.m. class would pick up on my remarks and disagree, and one did.

That morning. I read a story in an Austin paper telling how a school in Bay City, Texas, was purging itself of teachers accused of holding liberal views or views that supported the Supreme Court's *Brown vs. School Board* decision declaring that separate was not equal and was unconstitutional. I was pointing out the similarities in the false logic in all these cases. Lively discussions were *not* generally the rule in that class, but that morning, several students challenged my comparison, saying I was being unfair, was splitting hairs, or arguing technicalities, when "everybody knew the Communists were a threat to national security."

One young girl giggled and said, "Everyone?"

When the class laughed, I applauded the giggling girl and the class, and they applauded themselves. It felt very good.

When the student who egregiously claimed what "everybody" knew came back with "Heck, both sides use slanted language, not just conservatives," I came back with "You are right, and now *you* go to the head of the class."

More applause. It was going well, so well, I added, "Now for your next theme, here's a topic, optional topic: Write a paper comparing or contrasting the abuse of language by both sides, right or left, Democratic or Republican. Take a week, read some papers or magazines, and cite your sources, informally. Make it an open opinion paper, either pro or anti or just plain reporting."

When someone said it was better to "*get* somebody by mistake" than to let a real "Red" get through, I asked what he meant by "*get*"and added if doing that wasn't the same as Al Capp's Fearless Fosdick, the zealous character who always shot up a room of innocent bystanders just to *get* his man, whom he usually missed.[9] I was defending my position while conceding that I had bent the logic the other way by resorting to "glaring generalities" and "slanted language."

It was a good class, one of the best sessions all semester. Not everyone entered into the dialogue, but of those who did, about half took a conservative and half took a liberal slant. When I asked if anyone had taken notes and jotted down examples of the twisted language, I got good responses from both sides. Then going back to *Only Yesterday,* I asked for comparisons between today and *Yesterday.*

As I moved from behind the podium to write their examples on the chalkboard, I caught sight of a man lingering in the hall, appearing to be listening. The normal psychological state of a typical graduate student ranges from mild to extreme paranoia, and my own psychological state at that moment slipped immediately into high-gear paranoia. We were dealing, I recalled, with issues Black had said were best left alone. For a few seconds, I lost track of the discussion, but when I glanced back at the door, I noticed he had gone or had moved. Since the period was almost over, I stopped the discussion, made a reading assignment, and complimented them on their responses. Several had spoken up who had not spoken all semester and a few had even taken my position, which I told them indicated, contrary to the consensus of freshman comp instructors, that they were actually learning

---

9 In 1955, Al Capp, the creator of the popular *Li'l Abner* cartoon strip was an outspoken liberal and human rights advocate. The Fearless Fosdick character was an implied criticism of all overzealous law enforcement types and J. Edgar Hoover in particular, a criticism that even Capp's most devoted fans considered foolhardy in the red scare of the 1950s. By the end of the next decade, Capp had joined the critics of the flower children and the Vietnam protesters. *Thingsa changea.*

something, which brought forth a few low moans of disapproval from several of my stalwarts. It felt so good I began to believe that "education by irritation" was alive and well after all.

Just as I stuffed my copy of Allen's book into my briefcase, along with my notes, the man in the gray pin-stripe suit and homburg appeared just outside the door. I dismissed the class and waited by the podium while they filed out. As the last student left, the man in the hall walked in and introduced himself as Walter Rundell, Dean of Faculty at Lee College in Baytown, Texas, and asked if I was Joe Gilliland. What I heard, instead of Baytown, was *Bay City*, Texas, and, in full bore paranoia, I thought, *My god! They're searching for pinkos all the way up here in Austin.*

When I said I was Joe Gilliland, he told me he had seen my file in the Teacher Placement Office and cordially asked if I would mind talking about my application and said, "We have a position for an English and history instructor open at Lee College in Baytown."

"Oh, you said Baytown, not Bay City."

He smiled and replied, "That's right. Baytown is east of Houston. I don't believe Bay City has a community college." His tone of voice suggested he too had read the morning paper.

On our way to the Teacher Placement Office in Sutton Hall, he asked when I planned to finish my degree. I told him that I regretted I hadn't gotten as far with my thesis as I had hoped that semester, but I said that I would complete it the first summer term and get my degree at the August commencement. In the placement office, we found an empty conference room and began talking about the job and my background of experience, which he thought was "quite remarkable," particularly my three years in Japan and my two years in the army. It was the usual story: I looked too young to have done all that. *How much longer would I hear that*, I wondered. He asked about my job in Japan, if I was considering rejoining the mission program. I told him I had never intended becoming a career missionary, that the J3 program was a short-term program with limited goals and that all the short-termers were men and women in their mid-twenties. He apologized for not being more familiar with the program. He and Mrs. Rundell were lifelong Methodists.

Then he asked me why I wanted to teach in a junior college and if I thought of a two-year college only as a stepping-stone to a university. I had attended Del Mar College in Corpus Christi, I told him, and had liked it, that the best teaching I had had as an undergraduate had been in Mr. Agee's Government 10 class at Del Mar. I admitted I feared teaching in high school and that I intended to teach the rest of my life, and hoped to get my PhD one day and possibly teach at a four-year college, but I wasn't sure I was cut out for teaching at a university and frankly was unsure I could handle the publish-or-perish system. He smiled, nodded, and said he understood what I meant and believed that one of the advantages of the two-year college was the absence of pressure to do research.

"We consider classroom teaching our main reason for existence. I notice you mentioned history as a secondary teaching field. Would you be willing to teach American history? I see you had Webb's course in the Great Plains. My son wrote his MA thesis under Webb," he said.

I suddenly felt he was on the verge of offering me a job. "I'd enjoy teaching it very much," I said. "I taught a cultural history course in Japan."

He nodded and remarked he'd noticed that in my application. At that point, he made a tentative offer based on my application and said he could give me credit for a full four years teaching experience, counting the three years in Japan and a year's teaching assistantship, the maximum allowed at Lee for new instructors. Overwhelmed at first, I had to struggle to keep my excitement under control. He wasn't fooled. The expression on his face told me a lot. I could see he was happy he had made the offer. Then saving the best for last, he quoted a salary that completely floored me: four thousand four hundred for a nine-month contract, a virtual guarantee of a summer job at the same pay rate—if I wanted it. Most community colleges and universities paid summer salaries at about half the nine-month rate, irrespective of tenure or rank.

I told him I was most interested and thanked him for the offer. He asked me to have my official transcripts sent to him at Lee as soon as possible and noted that I had listed several people as references whose letters were not yet in the file. I assured him I would do everything I could to complete the file. I had given letterforms to Graham and Wilson Hudson and Miss Trice and had mailed a letter to Chuck McCauley, Mama, and Albert's good friend in Corpus who had said he would be happy to vouch for my character. I had also mailed a form to Willis Tate, taking him up on the offer he made the summer I graduated.

A few minutes later, I walked into the TA office and announced I had just received a job offer from Dean Rundell at Lee College in Baytown.

Black swiveled around in his chair and said, "Take it! Rundell is a good man, and Lee is a fine college."

When I mentioned the salary, they were all astonished, Black saying that was more than he was making at Stephen F. Austin as an instructor.

When I reminded them that Mason had warned me not to accept the first offer, Mac said, "Screw Mason!"

In the days and weeks that followed, I learned Dean Walter Rundell was one of the most respected college deans in Texas, easily the most astute college administrator in the state, according to everyone I asked who had heard of him.

In the next three weeks, I had three more offers. The dean of Victoria College in Victoria, Texas, near Corpus Christi, called me at home one afternoon and discussed his offer on the phone. He sounded good and made an attractive offer, all English composition and literature at a fair salary but less than Lee's. If I was at all interested, he said, he would like to meet me. When he asked if I had received any other offers, I told him that Dean Rundell of Lee had tentatively offered me a position.

"Oh, you better take Walter's offer," he said right off. "Lee is a very good school, and Walter's a fine man. I am sorry, but we can't touch his offer, Mr. Gilliland."

He went on to say he'd known Walter for years and that I'd be very lucky indeed to work with such a man. A number of years later, I met the man from Victoria at a Texas Junior College Association meeting in Corpus. When I saw from his nametag that he was president of Victoria Community College, I asked if he had once been dean, and he said he had and mentioned he was dean in 1955. I told him he had offered me a job, and I had always remembered his kind remarks about Lee and about Dean Rundell. We shook hands as I told him how impressed I was by his frankness. He was one of the old-timers, one of the men who had laid the foundations for the junior college system in Texas. By then, I had begun to honor these men and admire their vision for insisting their colleges hold to a higher standard of teaching than many of the universities that got their students in transfer.

A week after the call from Victoria College, I had another interview and an offer that was much less pleasant and far more typical of the arrogance of some administrators. I left that interview feeling triumphant, not for receiving the offer but for turning it down *before* it was offered. The call was from the chairman of English at Lamar Technical State College in Beaumont, Texas a four-year institution that had once been a major junior college in the stat, the same college my cousin Herndon had attended before transferring to of Virginia U. Like Hardin Junior College in Wichita Falls, where Bettie began her college career, it had grown into a four-year school. Texas was developing an extensive state college and university system, providing every major population area in the state with a full-service college or university and was tying the junior colleges into that system, creating as uniformly as possible a system of higher education that would reach everyone in the state.

At first, it sounded attractive. Not falling on the tenure track, new instructors who lacked doctorates taught mostly freshman composition, technical writing, and sophomore literature class, and were freed from the rigors of the up-and-out rules. The interviewer introduced himself as Chairman of English, but began badly when he pompously informed me that Lamar Tech was seriously committed to upgrading its entire English curriculum, and in order to do that, the college had brought him in from Northwestern University, adding with great significance that he was now interviewing for new faculty at *major* universities *only*. I wondered if it was usual for a chairman to boast that he had been brought in to upgrade his institution or if such a comment was unique to his brand of jackass. It seemed odd that he held Lamar Tech—probably all state colleges--in such disdain, and I wondered if that was typical of those from such "prestigious" universities as Northwestern. Clearly impressed with himself, he offered me, right up front, "the best salary in the state for beginning teachers": three thousand seven hundred for nine months. He said, more with pride than apology, that he could only give me credit for the three years at Wakayama University because "no one recognized an assistantship as actual teaching." I had decided when he first spoke of himself as proof of Lamar's "upgrading" its English program that I would be wise to take his comments with a large dose of salt. Unlike Dean Rundell or the dean at Victoria, his every word and his attitude dripped with Pooh Bah-like condescension. I shuddered inwardly thinking about what it would be like to work with such an ass.

I told him, as casually as I was able, that I planned to work toward a PhD but needed to teach full time for a few years to pay off debts and because of that I had to "apologize," but was unable to take his offer, that another school in the state was offering me a full four years' credit and a nine months salary of four thousand four hundred a year plus summer teaching at the full rate.

He said, "I can't believe that, a full year for a teaching assistantship? Over four thousand?"

I assured him I was not making it up, and besides, I was teaching nine hours that semester and that a full load for instructors at UT was also only nine hours.

"I really doubt that," he said.

I got up immediately, said, "I can't continue this interview. If you think I was misrepresenting the facts, you should call the English office." I walked out without looking back.

Later, when I told the story to Dr. Graham, he laughed at the idea of Lamar's bringing in a Northwestern man for the purpose of "upgrading anything." Lamar has since become Lamar Technical University and is placed in the fourth tier of American universities by *U.S. News and World Report*, whatever that really means. Having never been interviewed by anyone with such an attitude I assumed that Lamar's later success did not depend on the recruiting talents of their man from Northwestern.

By the end of the semester, I had finished the first draft of Sin *and Redemption in Faulkner* and was struggling through a final revision, moving it from manuscript to the first typescript, the only problem being my typing, which was never more than primitive hunt-and-peck. I would eventually hire a professional typist, but that was weeks away.

A few days before I turned in my final grade rosters, Bettie, Clay, and Lisè, now just six months old, left for Wichita Falls with Edna and Aunt Gladys, leaving me to finish the final draft of *Sin and Redemption in Faulkner*. I had lost my study carrel with the end of the semester and needed a quiet place to work, so Bettie thought it best she and the children visit her parents while I finish my thesis. When Elizabeth Bagley called offering me a full-time job for the month of June at a handsome two hundred dollars, with the strong possibility that I could drive the Bookmobile through July if I needed the job, I was almost speechless. Granddaddy Moore's loan of five hundred dollars still lay untouched in the Bryson Bank. If I got the job in Baytown, it would pay for our move and tide us over until the first paycheck came in the fall. I had never had such a checking balance in my life. With Bettie and the children living with Harold and Edna and with the Bookmobile job, I knew we wouldn't have to touch the money until we were ready to move. Between driving during the day, proofreading at the idle stops, typing in the evening, everything was falling into place now that I had sent off the transcripts and had gotten replies from all my references.

Two days after Bettie and the bairns left with Edna and Aunt Gladys, Dean Rundell called, saying he had my transcripts and letters, and that the Lee College Board had authorized him to invite me for a visit to the campus, the visit being a requirement for employment.

Then he said, "There is one important condition before we go on." I held my breath. "Could you begin teaching in the second summer term that begins after July 4?"

It was actually happening. I stopped to think and answered, "I will not be getting my degree until August. Will that make a difference?"

He assured me it would not matter as long as I was sure that it would be awarded then. I assured him it was only a matter of having my thesis professionally typed—a slight exaggeration.

When I hung up the receiver, I called for flight reservations then called Bettie and gave her the news. When the plane landed at the Houston International Airport the next morning, Saturday, I was in a quandary, not knowing where Baytown was or how to get there. Flush with feelings of success, I asked a taxi driver how much he would charge to drive me to Baytown, expecting the ride in the cab to cost as much as the flight from Austin. Incredibly, it cost only five dollars, which was probably not at all cheap in those days, since, as I recall, the airline ticket from Austin cost sixteen dollars. Shortly before ten o'clock on a Saturday morning, I arrived at the main building of Lee College and was met at the door by Dean Rundell. We chatted in his office, though I recall nothing of the conversation, and then he took me for a "tour" of the college, which consisted of one large, two-storied building housing the library, a large auditorium, classrooms, and faculty offices, along with the administrative offices. There was also a gymnasium and student union with a small cafeteria and several offices for faculty. The buildings, only five years old, were contemporary educational-factory, architecturally speaking—clean, efficient, and totally lacking in character, but they suited me perfectly. When we finished the tour, Dean Rundell drove me around Baytown, showing me housing developments and neighborhoods where some of the Lee faculty lived. At noon, Mrs. Rundell joined us for lunch. I wondered if she were part of the final approval process, but as we were taking our seats, he explained he wanted her along so she could to hear about my life in Japan.

Walter and Olive Rundell were genuinely charming, highly intelligent people, neither evincing even an iota of condescension or pretension and both quite obviously interested in me and my tenure in Japan. When I later came to know Olive Rundell better, I realized that she had not been there to check on anyone, only to enjoy the company and the talk. Walter and Olive Rundell represented the best there was in academe, socially and intellectually. When I finished telling about Wakayama University and the J3s, explaining how and why I had left the program, he began by talking about himself briefly, explaining that he too had majored in English The University of Texas, failing to finish his PhD only because of the Depression. He had taught for a year in Mississippi and almost starved—he and Olive—and then he had taken the job at the newly opened Lee College in what was then Goose Creek, Texas. He was unapologetic for his pride in the college, he said, for he had joined the faculty in its first year when it was a late afternoon and evening college and when classes met in Robert E. Lee High School. He had become its dean, the chief academic officer, in 1950 when the college moved out of the high school into new buildings and began offering day as well as evening classes.

He explained all this while we waited for our fried fish platters. Much of his conversation also reflected what he had learned about me, about my growing up in Beaumont and Corpus Christi, about my leaving for Austin when I was still only sixteen, and about my service in Germany and Korea. When I said I had suffered doubts about being hired because of my mediocre undergraduate record, he brushed it aside, saying some people come into their own later than others and remarked that what I had done in so short a time was for more remarkable than many who had honors level undergraduate work. I began to believe him.

When the food arrived, the conversation turned back to Bettie and me. He began by saying he'd noticed I was under the Methodist Board of Foreign Missions when I arrived in Japan and mentioned that he and Olive were also Methodists. I told him how I had not made up my mind to become a teacher until I stepped into my first class in Wakayama and that even then, I was not sure I would teach English until the English Department letter arrived just a couple of months before we sailed from Yokohama. I almost offered that I was no longer a Methodist and was very likely closer to being a Shingon Buddhist than anything, but I didn't think it wise to confess my lapse at that time. Too much confession would spoil the meal, I decided, and waited for him to ask questions about the kind of teaching I did. There was a pause while I began eating my dessert, and then he said, "Would you sign a contract then if I offered you one now?"

I looked up into the smiling face of Olive, who seemed to look on me as if I were Walter Junior being offered his first job. I wished that Bettie had been there to meet them. *They would love her immediately,* I thought. I had no idea that my first job offer would arrive this way. It was as overwhelming as hearing I had been accepted by the Board of Missions.

I said I would be glad to.

How strange and how marvelous it was! I had cast the dice and rolled a natural first throw. Hadn't I once lived at 711 West Twenty-First Street? Everything I had done, from the time I signed on as a J3 until that moment, had worked as if according to a script pre-written. Were the "purblind doomsters" not so blind after all?

Olive Rundell drove us back to the campus, and we returned to his office where I signed the contract, and afterwards he drove me again through the strange little city on Galveston Bay, with its pumping oil derricks in people's backyards and its giant refinery, at the time the world's largest and the home of Humble Oil and Refining Company, later EXXON. Baytown, he explained, was, until recently, three towns—Pelly, Goose Greek, with Baytown, the site of the giant refinery, while Goose Creek and Pelly were residential areas. I told him I had heard of Goose Creek as a child in Beaumont, that we had neighbors who often took the old doodlebug diesel through the low swamplands of the coast to visit grandparents. When we drove past the ancient station on the edge of the small business district, there they were, the doodlebugs, single car diesels with the zebra-striped fronts. When he left me at the Greyhound station, we shook hands, and he reminded me that classes would begin the first Monday after the Fourth of July.

Three months short of two years, I had finished all my course work toward a master's, completed a year's teaching at the University of Texas, and signed a teaching contract at a college with the best academic reputation and faculty pay scale in Texas, all of which, I was to learn, was because of Dean Walter Rundell alone had believed me suited to the task.

In the weeks before meeting Walter Rundell in my classroom that April morning, I had begun, for the first time, to have doubts: that I was too hasty in taking a double minor instead of taking a straight twenty-four hours of English plus thesis. I worried that I should have taken a Chaucer course, a nineteenth-century American lit seminar, or an advanced grammar course. I asked myself if I really had enough English on my master's to qualify as a teacher of college English? In taking a double minor, was I indulging my whims again as I had done as an undergraduate? However, these doubts vanished when Dean Rundell said that he had pretty well made up his mind to offer me the job when he saw I could teach history and that I had already taught it at the college level. All the way back to Austin on the bus, I kept hammering my brain, asking, *How the shit could I have thought of asking Inoue sensei to give me the history class and the modern novel class? How could I have known that I would get a job because of those classes?* It was a happy puzzlement.

When Dr. Graham returned the draft of my thesis, he said he had no substantive criticisms. All it needed, he said, was close proofreading, adding quite emphatically that I should consider it completed and should get it typed professionally as soon as possible. When I reminded him of the required departmental exam over the "great books," he dismissed it with a wave of his hand and said, "Never mind that, Gilliland. I've already certified that. It's an optional exam, in any case, and is left to the supervisor's discretion."

So, . . . that was it.

TRUE DIRECTIONS

An affiliate of Tarcher Books

OUR MISSION

Tarcher's mission has always been to publish books
that contain great ideas. Why? Because:

GREAT LIVES BEGIN WITH GREAT IDEAS

At Tarcher, we recognize that many talented authors, speakers,
educators, and thought-leaders share this mission and deserve to be
published – many more than Tarcher can reasonably publish ourselves.
True Directions is ideal for authors and books that increase awareness,
raise consciousness, and inspire others to live their ideals and passions.

Like Tarcher, True Directions books are designed to do three things:
inspire, inform, and motivate.

Thus, True Directions is an ideal way for these important voices to
bring their messages of hope, healing, and help to the world.

Every book published by True Directions– whether it is non-fiction, memoir,
novel, poetry or children's book – continues Tarcher's mission to publish works
that bring positive change in the world. We invite you to join our mission.

For more information, see the True Directions website:
www.iUniverse.com/TrueDirections/SignUp

Be a part of Tarcher's community to bring positive change in this world!
See exclusive author videos, discover new and exciting books, learn about
upcoming events, connect with author blogs and websites, and more!
www.tarcherbooks.com

TRUE DIRECTIONS

AN AFFILIATE OF TARCHER BOOKS